T0191611

IFIP Advances in Information and Communication Technology 439

IFIP – The International Federation for Information Processing

IFIP was founded in 1960 under the auspices of UNESCO, following the First World Computer Congress held in Paris the previous year. An umbrella organization for societies working in information processing, IFIP's aim is two-fold: to support information processing within its member countries and to encourage technology transfer to developing nations. As its mission statement clearly states,

> IFIP's mission is to be the leading, truly international, apolitical organization which encourages and assists in the development, exploitation and application of information technology for the benefit of all people.

IFIP is a non-profitmaking organization, run almost solely by 2500 volunteers. It operates through a number of technical committees, which organize events and publications. IFIP's events range from an international congress to local seminars, but the most important are:

- The IFIP World Computer Congress, held every second year;
- Open conferences;
- Working conferences.

The flagship event is the IFIP World Computer Congress, at which both invited and contributed papers are presented. Contributed papers are rigorously refereed and the rejection rate is high.

As with the Congress, participation in the open conferences is open to all and papers may be invited or submitted. Again, submitted papers are stringently refereed.

The working conferences are structured differently. They are usually run by a working group and attendance is small and by invitation only. Their purpose is to create an atmosphere conducive to innovation and development. Refereeing is also rigorous and papers are subjected to extensive group discussion.

Publications arising from IFIP events vary. The papers presented at the IFIP World Computer Congress and at open conferences are published as conference proceedings, while the results of the working conferences are often published as collections of selected and edited papers.

Any national society whose primary activity is about information processing may apply to become a full member of IFIP, although full membership is restricted to one society per country. Full members are entitled to vote at the annual General Assembly, National societies preferring a less committed involvement may apply for associate or corresponding membership. Associate members enjoy the same benefits as full members, but without voting rights. Corresponding members are not represented in IFIP bodies. Affiliated membership is open to non-national societies, and individual and honorary membership schemes are also offered.

Bernard Grabot   Bruno Vallespir   Samuel Gomes
Abdelaziz Bouras   Dimitris Kiritsis (Eds.)

Advances in Production Management Systems

Innovative and
Knowledge-Based Production Management
in a Global-Local World

IFIP WG 5.7 International Conference, APMS 2014
Ajaccio, France, September 20-24, 2014
Proceedings, Part II

 Springer

Volume Editors

Bernard Grabot
LGP ENIT, Tarbes, France
E-mail: bernard.grabot@enit.fr

Bruno Vallespir
Université de Bordeaux, IMS, Talence, France
E-mail: bruno.vallespir@ims-bordeaux.fr

Samuel Gomes
Université de Technologie de Belfort-Montbéliard, M3M, Belfort, France
E-mail: samuel.gomes@utbm.fr

Abdelaziz Bouras
Qatar University, College of Engineering, ictQatar, Doha, Qatar
E-mail: abdelaziz.bouras@qu.edu.qa

Dimitris Kiritsis
EPFL/STI-IGM-LICP, Lausanne, Switzerland
E-mail: dimitris.kiritsis@epfl.ch

ISSN 1868-4238   e-ISSN 1868-422X
ISBN 978-3-662-52604-0   e-ISBN 978-3-662-44736-9
DOI 10.1007/978-3-662-44736-9
Springer Heidelberg New York Dordrecht London

Typesetting: Camera-ready by author, data conversion by Scientific Publishing Services, Chennai, India

Printed on acid-free paper

Springer is part of Springer Science+Business Media (www.springer.com)

Preface

For the last decades, APMS has been a major event and the official conference of the IFIP Working Group 5.7 on Advances in Production Management Systems, bringing together leading experts from academia, research, and industry. Starting with the first conference in Helsinki in 1990, the conference has become a successful annual event that has been hosted in various parts of the world including Washington (USA, 2005), Wroclaw (Poland, 2006), Linköping (Sweden, 2007), Espoo (Finland, 2008), Bordeaux (France, 2009), Cernobbio (Italy, 2010), Stavanger (Norway, 2011), Rhodos (Greece, 2012), and State College (PA, USA, 2013).

By returning to Europe, APMS 2014 took place in Ajaccio (Corsica, France). This issue was organized in a collaborative way, as its organization was supported by four French universities and engineers schools: ENIT-INPT / University of Toulouse, the University of Bordeaux, the University of Lyon and the University of Technology of Belfort-Montbéliard.

The topics of APMS are similar to those of the IFIP WG 5.7. They concern all the facets of the systems of production of goods and services. For its 2014 issue, APMS selects the "Innovative and knowledge-based production management in a global-local world" theme, focusing on innovation, knowledge, and the apparent opposition between globalization of the economy and local production. 233 papers were accepted, based on blind peer-review. They were written and proposed by more than 600 authors and co-authors coming from 28 countries. The main review criteria were the paper quality and contributions to science and industrial practice. Accepted papers of registered participants are included in this volume. According to the new standard of APMS conference, full papers have been submitted and reviewed from the outset, allowing for the final proceedings to be available at the time of the conference.

Through an open call for special sessions and papers, APMS 2014 sought contributions in cutting-edge research, as well as insightful advances in industrial practice. The intent of the special sessions is to raise visibility on topics of focused interest in a particular scientific or applications area. This year, 21 special sessions were planned. They were consistent with the theme of the conference and focused on key areas of simulation, design, service, process improvement, sustainability, human & organizational aspects, agility and flexibility, maintenance, future and smart manufacturing, ontology, co-evolution of production and society, lean production, factories lifecycle, experience, knowledge & competence, and optimization.

Following the tradition of past APMS conferences, the 7th APMS Doctoral Workshop offered Ph.D. students the opportunity to present, discuss, receive feedback, and exchange comments and views on their doctoral research in an inspiring academic community of fellow Ph.D. students, experienced researchers, and professors from the IFIP WG 5.7 community.

Three awards were distributed during APMS 2014:

- Burbidge Award for best paper,
- Burbidge Award for best presentation,
- Doctoral Workshop Award.

The Scientific Committee, consisting of 78 researchers, most of them being active members of the IFIP WG 5.7, played a key role in reviewing the papers in a timely manner and providing constructive feedback to authors, allowing them to revise their manuscripts for the final draft.

Papers in these three volumes are grouped thematically as follows:

Volume 1:

- **Part I: Knowledge Discovery and Sharing**: Knowledge management, creative enterprise, quality management, design tools, system engineering, PLM, ontology, decision support system, collaboration maturity, Business Intelligence, enterprise 2.0, etc.
- **Part II: Knowledge-Based Planning and Scheduling**: Scheduling, optimization, production planning and control, assembly line balancing, decoupling points, inventory management, supply chain management, multi-echelon supply chain, analytic hierarchy process, enterprise resource planning, decision support systems, problem solving, vehicle routing, physical internet, etc.

Volume 2:

- **Part III: Knowledge-Based Sustainability**: Cleaner production, green IT, energy, energy-efficiency, risk management, disturbance management, resilience, end of life, reverse logistics, creative industry, eco-factory, environmental innovation, solidarity economy, social responsibility, glocalization, etc.
- **Part IV: Knowledge-Based Services**: Service production, service engineering, service governance, healthcare, public transportation, customer satisfaction, after sales, smart manufacturing, etc.

Volume 3:

- **Part V: Knowledge-Based Performance Improvement**: Performance measurement system, evaluation, quality, in-service inspection, inspection programs, lean, visual management, standardization, simulation, analysis techniques, value stream mapping, maturity models, benchmarking, change management, human behavior modeling, community of practice, etc.

- **Part VI: Case Studies**: sectors (petroleum industry, aeronautic industry, agribusiness, automobile, semiconductors), tools (ERP, TQM, six sigma, enterprise modeling, simulation), concepts (supply chain, globalization), etc.

We hope that these volumes will be of interest to a wide range of researchers and practitioners.

August 2014

Bernard Grabot
Bruno Vallespir
Samuel Gomes
Abdelaziz Bouras
Dimitris Kiritsis

Organization

General Chair

Bernard Grabot   ENIT-INPT/University of Toulouse, France

Doctoral Workshop Committee

Chair
Abdelaziz Bouras   University of Lyon, France & Qatar University,
                                  Qatar

Organizing Committee

Chair
Samuel Gomes   University of Technology of
                                  Belfort - Montbéliard, France

Members
Cédrick Béler   University of Toulouse, France
Abdelaziz Bouras   Qatar University, Qatar; Université Lumiere
                                  Lyon 2, France
Laurent Geneste   University of Toulouse, France
Raymond Houé   University of Toulouse, France
Daniel Noyes   University of Toulouse, France
Bruno Vallespir   University of Bordeaux, France

Organization

R-Events

Conference Secretariat

Catherine Eberstein   University of Technology of
                                  Belfort-Montbéliard, France
Cécile De Barros   Marie Robert, ENIT-LGP, INP, University of
                                  Toulouse, France

Sponsors

IFIP WG 5.7 Advances in Production Management Systems
IODE: Research Federation on Distributed Organizations Engineering
GdR MACS: CNRS Research Group on Modelling and Analysis of Complex
Systems
IRTES: Research Institute on Transports, Energy and Society
Mairie d'Ajaccio

Special Sessions

Discrete event simulation for distributed production systems
    Paul-Antoine Bisgambiglia   University of Corsica, France

The practitioner's view on "Innovative and Knowledge-Based Production Management in a Global-Local World"
    Gregor von Cieminski   ZF Friedrichshafen AG, Germany

Integrated design in collaborative engineering
    Claude Baron   LAAS CNRS, France

Service manufacturing systems
    Toshiya Kaihara   Kobe University, Japan

Process improvement programmes for sustainability
    Jose Arturo Garza-Reyes   University of Derby, UK

Sustainable initiatives in developing countries
    Irenilza de Alencar Nääs   Paulista University, Brazil

Human and organizational aspects of planning and scheduling
    Ralph Riedel   TU Chemnitz, Germany

Agility and flexibility in manufacturing operations
    D. Jentsch   TU Chemnitz, Germany

Asset and maintenance management for competitive and sustainable manufacturing
    Marco Garetti   Politecnico di Milano, Italy

Manufacturing of the future
    R.S.Wadhwa   Høgskole i Gjøvik, Norway

Smart manufacturing system architecture
    Hyunbo Cho   Postech University, Republic of Korea

Production capacity pooling vs. traditional inventory pooling in an additive
manufacturing scenario
    Jan Holmström   Aalto University, Finland

Ontology based engineering
    Soumaya El Kadiri   EPFL, Switzerland

Co-evolving production and society in a global-local world
    Paola Fantini   Politecnico di Milano, Italy

Lean in high variety, low volume production
    Erlend Alfnes   Norwegian University of Science and
                                        Technology, Norway
Lean system development
    Elise Vareilles   École des Mines d'Albi, France

Managing factories lifecyle in a global-local world
    Claudio Palasciano   Politecnico di Milano, Italy

Experience, knowledge and competence management for production systems
    Laurent Geneste   INP-ENIT, France

IFIP WG5-7 research workshop
    Hermann Lödding   Hamburg University of Technology,
                                        Germany

Optimization models for global supply chain management
    Ramzi Hammami   ESC Rennes School of Business, France

Product Service System information system
    Thècle Alix   University of Bordeaux, France

International Scientific Committee

Bruno Vallespir (Chair)   University of Bordeaux, France
Erlend Alfnes   NTNU Valgrinda, Norway
Eiji Arai   Osaka University, Japan
Frédérique Biennier   INSA de Lyon, France
Umit S. Bititci   University of Stratchlyde, UK
Abdelaziz Bouras   Qatar University, Qatar; Université Lumière
                                      Lyon 2, France
Luis Manuel Camarinha-Matos Universidade Nova de Lisboa, Portugal
Sergio Cavalieri   University of Bergamo, Italy
Stephen Childe   University of Exeter, UK

Dimitris Mourtzis	University of Patras, Greece
Irenilza de Alencar Nääs	UNIP- Paulista University, Brazil
Masaru Nakano	Keio University, Japan
Gilles Neubert	ESC Saint Etienne, France
David O'Sullivan	National University of Ireland, Ireland
Jinwoo Park	Seoul National University, Republic of Korea
Henk-Jan Pels	Einhoven University of Technology, The Netherlands
Fredrik Persson	Linköping Institute of Technology, Sweden
Alberto Portioli	Politecnico di Milano, Italy
Vittaldas V. Prabhu	The Pennsylvania State University, USA
Mario Rapaccini	Florence University, Italy
Asbjörn Rolstadås	Norwegian University of Science and Technology, Norway
Jacobus E. Rooda	Eindhoven University of Technology, The Netherlands
Krzysztof Santarek	Warsaw University of Technology, Poland
Paul Schoensleben	ETH Zurich, Switzerland
Riitta Smeds	Aalto University, Finland
Kathryn E. Stecke	University of Texas at Dallas, USA
Volker Stich	FIR Forschungsinstitut für Rationalisierung an der RWTH Aachen, Germany
Richard Lee Storch	University of Washington, USA
Jan Ola Strandhagen	NTNU, Norway
Stanislaw Strzelczak	Warsaw University of Technology, Poland
Marco Taisch	Politecnico di Milano, Italy
Kari Tanskanen	Helsinki University of Technology, Finland
Ilias P. Tatsiopoulos	National Technical University of Athens, Greece
Sergio Terzi	University of Bergamo, Italy
Klaus-Dieter Thoben	Universität Bremen und Bremer Institut fur Produktion und Logistik GmbH, Germany
Jacques H. Trienekens	Wageningen University, The Netherlands
Mario Tucci	Università degli Studi di Firence, Italy
Shigeki Umeda	Musashi University, Japan
Agostino Villa	Politecnico di Torino, Italy
Hans Wortmann	Groningen University, The Netherlands
Gert Zülch	University of Karlsruhe, Germany

Table of Contents – Part II

Knowledge-Based Sustainability

Knowledge-Based Services

Knowledge-Based Sustainability

Cleaner Production Evaluation Model: Multiple Case Study in the Plastic Industry

Dalton Oswaldo Buccelli and Pedro Luiz de Oliveira Costa Neto

Paulista University-UNIP, Graduate Program in Production Engineering,
Dr. Bacelar St. 1212, São Paulo, Brazil
{dalton_buccelli,politeleia}@uol.com.br}

Abstract. This paper reports a study on the cleaner production program developed in the plastic industry in São Paulo - Brazil. An evaluation model was developed, using as reference the existing literature on business models and process management, as well as excellence models adopted by national quality awards from different countries. The model was applied for in-depth multiple case study in eight plastic companies to validate the importance of management processes in the implementation of cleaner production programs and to observe the results obtained with the cleaner production initiatives. The research has identified two companies with more than 92% compliance to the model which reached important environmental results in the last three years. The results are supplemented with the use of external performance indicators (material intensity, water and carbon footprint savings) to show that little changes inside the companies can reduce upstream impacts and bring greater benefits to the environment.

Keywords: Cleaner production, Environmental indicators, Management processes, Management quality, Plastic industry.

1   Introduction

Stone [1] explains that the most common types of changes that are demonstrated by cleaner production case studies are technical, but these types of changes is unlikely to be enough by itself to bring about cleaner production in organizations. This is because of the human dimensions of organizational change. Taylor [2] recommends the use of tools for behavior change in the context of removing the identified barriers. These change tools could be: obtaining introductory commitments prior to larger requests; providing reminder prompts in appropriate locations; development of community social norms (peer pressure); credible and appropriate communication; and providing incentives.

Vendrametto et al [3] conclude that it is better to use a combination of strategies, as well as awareness speeches, technical training and presentation of success cases to disseminate new approaches in the industrial sector, but initiatives to implement cleaner production opportunities were more effective in companies that had tried other methods to improve production processes, such as Lean Manufacturing and

B. Grabot et al. (Eds.): APMS 2014, Part II, IFIP AICT 439, pp. 3–13, 2014.
© IFIP International Federation for Information Processing 2014

Total Quality Management. These organizations primarily seek to structure their management process as a way to make the initiatives solid and permanent. This is part of the absorptive capacity created with the former experience.

Taking into account these statements and experiences of experts, it is possible to assume that the presence of principles and concepts of cleaner production embedded in the management processes of the business is essential for effective implementation of projects to improve the products and operational processes (value chain), allowing them to achieve positive and lasting environmental results. This initiative requires an action that complements the technical knowledge and incorporates cleaner production concepts and principles into the management processes of companies to get permanent improvements in efficiency of production processes, minimize environmental impacts and increase performance indicators results.

The plastic industry brought the interest in analyzing the effectiveness of recent cleaner production initiatives implemented in the sector. The study began with the development of a model for evaluating the incorporation of cleaner production principles in the management processes of companies. The model was created using as reference the existing literature on business models and process management, as well as excellence models adopted by national quality awards from different countries. After that it was applied during multiple case study, a qualitative research to bring a deeper knowledge on key management processes to achieve positive and lasting results.

Two of the eight companies participating in the research were identified by the assessment model as having management processes with structured principles of cleaner production. Over the last three years consistent results were observed in internal environmental indicators such as reduction in consumption of fossil materials, water and electricity. These results were supplemented with calculations of external performance indicators (material intensity, water and carbon footprint savings), allowing to understand the consumption decreases from the nature perspective and showing that even small internal changes to the company can bring big benefits to the environment and society that would not be perceived with restricted use of internal indicators.

2   Business Processes and Cleaner Production in Plastic Industry

2.1   Business Processes

Gonçalves [4] defines process as any activity or set of activities that receive an "input", adds value and provides an "output" to a specific customer. He classifies the processes of organizations in three categories: Primary Processes; Support Processes; and Business Processes. The French standard AFNOR FD X 50-176 [5] recommends the classification of business processes in families to facilitate their identification and suggests the following grouping: Realization Processes; Supporting Processes; and Management Processes.

Rummler and Brache [6] subdivide existing activities in any company in three types of business processes: primary (processes that belong to the value chain; create products and services that meet the customer needs), auxiliary (processes that support primary processes) and management (processes that govern the operation of the company). Primary processes are concerned to sell, produce, deliver, provide technical assistance, improve and, where necessary, discontinue the product. Auxiliary processes are related to buy materials, recruit and select staff, maintain the company's equipment in working order, control the resources needed to build the product. However, the management processes are related to corporate governance, strategy formulation and deployment, goal setting, information management, definition of guidelines and organizational procedures, knowledge management and customer relationship. The third type of process acquires a prominent position due to assume important guidance and coordination with the other two types of processes.

2.2 Cleaner Production in Plastic Industry

The concept of cleaner production (CP) as the continuous application of an integrated preventative environmental strategy to processes, products and services to increase efficiency and reduce risks to humans and the environment, was first used in 1989 by the United Nations Environment Programme (UNEP) and in recent years has progressively being incorporated into the agenda of the business world. The basic CP principle is the implementation of advanced processes, technologies and equipment, improvement of management and comprehensive utilization of resources to reduce pollution at source, enhance the rates of resource utilization efficiency, reduce and/or avoid pollution generation and discharge in the course of production, provision of services and product use - so as to decrease the high cost generated by company's waste - and the increasingly scarce inputs like water and energy for society as a whole. According to Giannetti et al [7] this concept was developed as a further challenge of continuous improvement on leading companies, to become an integral part of business. The CP can be applied to processes used in any industry, its products and various services provided. It is a broad term that encompasses other associated terms such as eco-efficiency, pollution prevention (P2), waste minimization and green production.

The plastic industry is a very important sector of the Brazilian economy, containing about twelve thousand companies and contributing significantly to the generation and distribution of wealth in the country, and being the third largest employer in the manufacturing sector with three hundred and forty eight thousand jobs, produced 6.66 thousand tons of plastic materials, generating about R\$ 54 billion in 2012. Most companies in the industry are classified as micro and small enterprises employing less than 100 people and are located in the south and southeast regions of the country, which, together, account for more than 85% of the total. São Paulo State is the largest plastic manufacturer contributing with 45% of plastic industry gross revenues. The publication of the Technical Environmental Guide for Plastic Industry – CETESB [8] responds to unanimous global diagnosis that path to socioeconomic prosperity necessarily involves the sustained growth of industrial activity. This guide is part of the CP series of publications by CETESB which contributes to the precepts of sustainable development. In its pages can be found details on the practical implementation of cleaner production's concept specially designed by a group of industry experts to disseminate information and provide guidelines for employers and employees who work directly or indirectly with the plastic industry, as well as other interested parties in understanding the pathways that can lead to environmental preservation.

3   Methodology

3.1   Literature Review and Model Building

In order to build a model for assessing environmental results and the introduction of CP concepts and principles into structured and standardized management processes, an extensive literature review was performed on organizational processes, as well as requirements and criteria to evaluate excellence in management processes, particularly those adopted in national and international quality awards [9].

It is amazing the coincidence in the various approaches to business processes found in the literature review. While adopting proper terms, the types of processes and their meanings are very similar and, according to the subdivision of the business processes proposed by these references, management processes are those that ensure the coherence and integration of core business and support processes.

Management processes play a key role in the coordination and guidance of the other two types of processes (primary/core and auxiliary/support), and help leaders during decision making activities. Their proper structuring is essential for core business and support processes carrying out according to the guidelines established by the leadership and to measure, monitor and improve the performance of the organization.

The model with four macro-management processes (a-Governance, leadership and planning; b-Market, customer and society relationship; c-People and knowledge management; d-Management of core and support processes) and one group of environmental indicators was applied during the qualitative research with eight plastic companies from São Paulo State Plastic Industry Association (SINDIPLAST) to evaluate companies' environmental performance through the implementation of cleaner production opportunities.

3.2   Multiple Case Study

According to Leonard-Barton [10], a case study is a history of past or current phenomena, drawn from multiple sources of evidence. It can include data from direct observation and systematic interviewing, as well as from public and private archives. Yin [11] adds that a case study is a complete research strategy which allows questions such as 'how' and 'why' to be studied. This strategy is moreover applicable to processes or to phenomena which have not yet been studied in depth. The author shows that the multiplication of cases is comparable with a multiplication of experiments, but the selection of case studies must be based on the principles of literal and theoretical replication. The former involves the selection of cases with apparently similar conditions and results; the latter requires cases which produce different results for more or less explicable reasons. The replication is based on theory and not on the statistical principle of sampling. These measures can help to reduce the degree of bias that the researcher is probably undergoing.

Based on these explanations eight plastic producers accepted to participate in the multiple case study to evaluate their management practices and environmental results. The form containing 20 statements about management processes and their examples of existing management practices, as well as 5 statements about outputs and examples of environmental indicators over the past three years was sent to fill.

In the first stage, all eight firms submitted the answered form and assigned the scores they considered appropriate to each of the statements related to existing management processes and the results achieved. Then these questionnaires were analyzed by the authors, who raised some points to be checked during a field visit.

To confirm the data previously collected a semi-structured interview was used. Managers and supervisors were interviewed to address the questions raised during the analysis of the questionnaires. Direct observation occurred during the field visits conducted by the authors. This technique was useful for providing additional information about good management practices and companies' results. Internal indicators were analyzed like as water consumption (m^3 of water / tone of finished product), electric energy consumption (MWh / tone of finished product), plastic waste during production process (tone of plastic / tone of finished product), and product scrap (tone of product scrap / tone of finished product).

To provide a broader vision of the results presented during the visits, to allow consistent evaluation of the benefits achieved from the savings and to compare results from different companies, producing distinct products and volumes, three methods were employed: Material intensity evaluation, Water footprint and Carbon footprint [12].

4   Results and Discussion

Eight companies were visited to verify if they had structured management processes deployed throughout the organization and other stakeholders. The form containing 20 statements about management processes and examples of existing management practices was grouped in 4 categories: a) Governance, Leadership and Planning; b) Society Relationship, Market and Customers; c) People and Knowledge Management; d) Management of Core Business and Support Processes. It was also possible to verify the environmental results obtained in the last three years. The full research form was completed by the responsible managers in each company and the answers were used as a guide of semi-structured interviews.

Table 1 presents the percentages of the management processes and environmental indicators results in compliance with the requirements of the model. As can be seen, companies D and G obtained 92.0% and 95.2% of the total compliance with the model, demonstrating the existence of structured management processes and sustainable results in environmental performance indicators. Companies A, C and F

Table 1. Percentages of companies' compliance with the model

	% of Companies' Compliance							
	A	B	C	D	E	F	G	H
a) Governance, Leadership and Planning Processes	84.0	76.0	100.0	100.0	48.0	84.0	100.0	100.0
b) Society Relationship, Market and Customers Processes	92.0	56.0	92.0	84.0	84.0	92.0	100.0	92.0
c) People and Knowledge Management Processes	76.0	92.0	84.0	92.0	62.0	92.0	92.0	84.0
d) Management of Core and Support Processes	100.0	92.0	68.0	100.0	62.0	92.0	100.0	92.0
Environmental Results	68.0	60.0	76.0	84.0	24.0	68.0	84.0	54.0
TOTAL COMPLIANCE	**84.0**	**75.2**	**84.0**	**92.0**	**56.0**	**85.6**	**95.2**	**84.4**

presented recent environmental results during the review and still don't demonstrate positive trends. The other three companies could not show historical data to demonstrate indicators evolution and this fact is related with some missing management processes like leadership and strategic planning, customer relationship, people and knowledge management.

During the visit companies D and G presented improvement actions taken based on the 29 cleaner production opportunities proposed in the technical guide [8]. It may be noted that these companies had seriously adopted the recommendations of the guide and could show consumption reduction results. Table 2 presents major actions implemented by these two companies and their positive impact (reductions) on environment.

Table 2. Major cleaner production interventions

Cleaner Production Interventions (Technical Guide)	Reduction			
	H$_2$O	Natural Resources	Energy Consumption	Solid Waste
Opp3 - Use of new technologies for energy saving and productivity increase		X	X	X
Opp4 - Optimize the logistics of raw materials and use of more economical and returnable packaging	X	X		X
Opp5 - Reprocessing of no conforming materials		X		X
Opp6 - Improvement in equipment sizing - Production Planning			X	X
Opp7 – Predictive, preventive and corrective maintenance	X	X	X	X
Opp8 - Continuing education of production workers	X	X	X	X
Opp9 - Efficient Lighting and translucent tiles			X	
Opp 11 - Use of additives in the process water	X			
Opp12 - Adoption of efficient cooling towers	X		X	
Opp14 - Use of cooling towers and closed circuit	X			
Opp16 - Use of water saving devices	X			
Opp19 - Avoid losses due to problems in compressed air piping		X	X	
Opp22 - Energy diagnosis			X	

Internal Indicators. Material and energy savings per tons of finished product (tfp) were verified during the visits. The total reduction in water consumption, electric energy consumption and plastic material consumption after three years of CP interventions are shown in Table 3.

Table 3. Reductions after three years of CP interventions

Total Savings	Company D	Company G
Plastic material reduction (kg)	250	400
Electric energy reduction (kWh)	1,110	2,910
Water consumption (liter)	70	3,000

The absolute quantities shown in Table 3 might be, at a first glance, considered small, but reductions in the consumption of material and energy brought significant advantages to the company. The consumption decrease was due to the implementation of some improvement opportunities presented in the technical guide [8]: efficient lighting, translucent tiles and lighting sensors, dispensers and automatic feeders, compressed air loss control, introduction of energy diagnosis, reuse of in-process material, waste recycling (outside process), etc.

External Indicators (Material Intensity Evaluation and Water Footprint). This method, developed at the Wuppertal Institute by Ritthoff et al [13], is a practical application of the material input per service concept (MIPS) to evaluate the environmental harm associated with the extraction or diversion of resources from their natural flows and cycles. Material intensity factors (g/unit) are multiplied by each saving (material or energy), respectively, accounting for the total amount of abiotic and biotic matter, water and air, that are no longer required in order to provide that material to the company. According to Hoekstra [14], water footprint is the total amount of freshwater used directly and indirectly by a person, business, institution or country to produce the goods and services. The interest in the water footprint increased with the recognition that human impacts on freshwater systems is linked to products consumption, and that issues like water shortages and pollution can be better understood and addressed by considering production and supply chains as a whole. The water footprint concept can be used to quantify and map the water use behind consumption and how it can guide reduction of water use to a sustainable level. Table 4 shows the values of material intensities and water footprint of the selected individual savings achieved by CP interventions.

Table 4. Material intensity and water footprint

	(*) Material intensity		
	Abiotic Matter	Air	Water (***)
Polypropylene (kg/kg)	4.24	3.37	205.48
(**) Electric energy (kg/kWh)	0.36	0.12	15.35
Water (kg/kg)	0.08	0.01	2.20

(*) Material intensity is the material input in relation to a unit of measurement. The factors are used to express material intensity of production inputs (materials or energy), expressed in mass unit of resources per unit of input (e.g. kg/kg or kg/kWh). Source: Ritthoff et al [13]

(**) The electricity data were adapted for the Brazilian energetic matrix multiplying the worldwide average of intensity values (Abiotic = 1.55 kg/kWh; Water = 66.73 kg/kWh; and Air = 0.54 kg/kWh) by the value of 0.23. A fraction of 0.23 was obtained by dividing the percentage of the contribution of the thermoelectric in the power generation in Brazil (18.2 %) by the percentage of the worldwide contribution (79.3 %). Source: ANEEL [15].

(***) The water footprint is an indicator of the total water use measured in terms of water volumes consumed, evapotranspirated and/or polluted, expressed in mass unit.

A considerable environmental benefit is related to the avoidance of environmental impact associated with the extraction or diversion of resources from their natural ecosystem pathways. The water footprint quantifies the water use behind consumption and how it can guide reduction of water use to a sustainable level. Table 5 summarizes the material savings in the three environmental compartments (abiotic matter, air and water) achieved by CP interventions. The water compartment corresponds to the reduction in the water footprint.

Table 5. Material and water savings due to CP interventions

Company	Material savings (kg)		
	Abiotic matter	Air	Water (*)
D	1,465	976	**68,562**
G	2,983	1,757	**133,460**

(*) Total reduction in water footprint, showing the total water saved, expressed in mass unit (kg).

It can be observed that the relatively small quantities of materials saved within the companies led to huge external preservation of materials, in particular water.

External Indicators (Carbon footprint). The carbon footprint is a measure of the total amount of carbon dioxide (CO_2) emissions that is directly and indirectly caused by an activity, or is accumulated over the life stages of a product. This includes activities of individuals, populations, governments, companies, organizations, processes, industry sectors etc. Products include goods and services. According to Wiedmann and Minx [16], in any case, all direct (on-site, internal) and indirect (off-site, external, embodied, upstream, downstream) emissions need to be taken into account. Only CO_2 is included in the analysis, being well aware that there are other substances with greenhouse warming potential. However, many of those are either not based on carbon or are more difficult to quantify because of data availability. Tables 6 and 7 show the values of carbon footprint intensities for plastic and electric energy.

The companies D and G carbon footprints (expressed in mass unit kg CO_2), saved after CP interventions are shown in table 8. It can be observed that the CP interventions on reduction of raw material accounts for practically 90% of CO_2 emission reduction.

Table 6. Carbon footprint intensity for plastic

	(i) Intensity of energy contained in the fuel used in material transportation (MJ/kg)	(ii) Intensity of energy contained in the raw material (MJ/kg)	(i+ii) Total intensity of fossil energy (MJ/kg)	(*) Intensity of indirect CO_2 emissions (kg CO_2/kg)
Plastic material (from crude oil)	39.70	51.20	90.90	**6.99**

(*) Intensity of indirect CO_2 emissions obtained by multiplying the total intensity of fossil energy by the value of 76.92×10^{-3} kgCO_2/MJoe (oe = oil equivalent). Source: Brown and Ulgiati, 2002 [17].

Table 7. Carbon footprint intensity for electric energy

Electricity generated in thermoelectric	(*) Intensity of CO_2 emissions (kg CO_2/kWh)	(**) Contribution according to the Brazilian energy matrix (%)	Intensity of indirect CO_2 emissions (kg CO_2/kWh)
Gas	0.60	10.3	0.062
Oil	0.97	5.6	0.054
Coal	1.08	2.3	0.025
Total			**0.141**

(*) Source: Herendeen, 1998 [18].
(**) Source: ANEEL [15].

Table 8. Carbon footprint intensity reduction due to CP interventions

Companies	CP Interventions	Carbon Footprints
D	*250 kg plastic reduction /t_{fp} x 6.99 kg CO_2/kg = 1,747.5 kg CO_2*	**1,904** kg CO_2
	1,110 kWh electric energy reduction/t_{fp} x 0.141 kg CO_2/kWh =156.5 kg CO_2	
G	*400 kg plastic reduction/t_{fp} x 6.99 kg CO_2/kg = 2,796.0 kg CO_2*	**3,206** kg CO_2
	2,910 kWh electric energy reduction/t_{fp} x 0.141 kg CO_2/kWh = 410.3 kg CO_2	

5   Conclusions

The qualitative research has been performed in eight companies in the plastic manufacturing sector and, due to the results relevance, it can be inferred that the proposed evaluation model allows identifying organizations that are effectively managing their processes through cleaner production principles and therefore possess the necessary requirements to obtain favorable environmental results. The multiple case study helped to select two companies that handled more than 90% of the model requirements, compared with the percentage of compliance of 85, 75 and 56% from the other companies. After being identified by the model as having structured and standardized management processes these companies (D and G) demonstrated the deployment of more than ten opportunities for cleaner production presented in the cleaner production technical guide [8] and showed a reduction in the consumption of water, electrical energy and raw material in the last three years.

The results of external performance indicators allowed to look at the consumption decreases from the perspective of nature and showed that even small internal changes to the company can bring big benefits to the environment and society that would not be perceived with restricted use of internal indicators. With these multiple case study findings it is expected that the leading companies in the sector include concepts of cleaner production into their management processes to assist them in developing improved operational processes and obtaining favorable and sustainable environmental results. This will cause the follower companies adopt similar strategies in their management systems, making the concepts of environmental management to solidify in the producing and recycling of plastic industry.

Acknowledgements. The authors thank SINDIPLAST for data and information supplied and PROSUP / CAPES for the financial support in the form of a PhD scholarship.

References

1. Stone, L.: When case studies are not enough: the influence of corporate culture and employee attitudes on the success of cleaner production initiatives. Journal of Cleaner Production 8, 353–359 (2000)
2. Taylor, B.: Encouraging industry to assess and implement cleaner production measures. Journal of Cleaner Production 14, 601–609 (2006)
3. Vendrametto, O., Palmeri, N., Oliveira Neto, G.C., Perreti, O.D.: Cleaner production: A growing movement in brazilian companies. Produção Online 10(1), 49–70 (2010)
4. Gonçalves, J.E.L.: As empresas são grandes coleções de processos. Revista de Administração de Empresas 40(1), 6–19 (2000) (in Portuguese)
5. AFNOR - Association Française de Normalisation - FD X 50-176, Management des processus. La Plaine St Denis Cedex, France (2005)
6. Rummler, G.A., Brache, A.P.: Improving performance: how to manage the white space on the organizational chart. Jossey-Bass, San Francisco (1991)
7. Giannetti, B.F., Almeida, C.M.V.B.: Industrial Ecology: concepts, tools and applications. Edgard Blucher, São Paulo (2006) (in Portuguese)
8. CETESB - Companhia de Tecnologia de Saneamento Ambiental. Guia ambiental da indústria de transformação e reciclagem de materiais plásticos. Série P+L. São Paulo, Brasil (2011) (in Portuguese)
9. Buccelli, D.O., Costa Neto, P.L.O.: Prêmio nacional da qualidade: Gestão da qualidade ou qualidade da gestão? In: XXXIII Encontro Nacional de Engenharia de Produção, Abepro, Salvador (2013)
10. Leonard-Barton, D.: A dual methodology for case studies: Synergistic use of a longitudinal single site with replicated multiple sites. Organization Science 1(3), 248–266 (1990)
11. Yin, R.K.: Case Study Research: Design and Methods. Sage Publications, Thousand Oaks (1994)

12. Giannetti, B.F., Bonilla, S.H., Silva, I.R., Almeida, C.M.V.B.: Cleaner production practices in a medium size gold-plated jewelry company in Brazil: when little changes make the difference. Journal of Cleaner Production 16, 1106–1117 (2008)
13. Ritthoff, M., Rohn, H., Liedtke, C., Merten, T.: Calculating MIPS: Resources productivity of products and services. Wuppertal Institute for Climate, Environment and Energy, North Rhine-Westphalia. Wuppertal Spezial 27e (2002)
14. Hoekstra, A.Y.: The Water Footprint of Modern Consumer Society. Routledge, London (2013)
15. ANEEL – Agência Nacional de Energia Elétrica, http://www.aneel.gov.br/aplicacoes/capacidadebrasil/OperacaoCapacidadeBrasil.asp (accessed in August 24, 2013)
16. Wiedmann, T., Minx, J.: A Definition of 'Carbon Footprint'. In: Pertsova, C.C. (ed.) Ecological Economics Research Trends. ch. 1, pp. 1–11. Nova Science Publishers, Hauppauge (2008)
17. Brown, M.T., Ulgiati, S.: Emergy evaluations and environmental loading of electricity production systems. Journal of Cleaner Production 10, 321–334 (2002)
18. Herendeen, R.A.: Ecological Numeracy: Quantitative Analysis of Environmental Issues. John Wiley & Sons, New York (1998) (incorporated)

Green IT and Waste Paper in Governmental Institutions: The Proposal of the *Infotercio* Financial Model

Nilo Sylvio Costa Serpa[1], Ivanir Costa[2], and Rodrigo Franco Gonçalves[3]

[1] UNIP - Graduate Program in Production Engineering, Brazil
[2] UNINOVE - Graduate Program in Production Engineering, Brazil
niloserpa@gmail.com, icosta11@live.com, rofranco@osite.com.br
http://www.unip.br

Abstract. This work discusses waste paper generation in IT environments and the need to reduce the output of reports, source codes and forms in Brazilian governmental institutions to carry out a true policy of sustainability. Green IT is tackled from the premise that paper is the most bulky solid waste daily generated by informatics and the most easily controllable by people. The authors explain a green IT management model which combines finance and cleaner production so that it makes possible to rescue ethical values little remembered today at governmental level, thus keeping public treasury. Present work also explains the mathematics of the model including a preliminar simulation to clarify basic ideas.

Keywords: green IT, ecological education, waste paper, *infotercio*, sustainability, cleaner production.

1 Introduction

Researchers, environmentalists and professionals in computer science agree that the practice of green IT is a real need today. Green IT not only minimizes ecological impacts but favors cost containments and reduction of energy consumption [3]. In particular, management of paper is of great importance because the significative waste bulk that characterizes its use. Nevertheless, in countries like Brazil, informatics does not seem to have come to optimize processes in reducing emissions of paper (printed reports, source codes and forms). Paper generally constitutes a large portion, if not the greater, of regular office waste. Several institutions feed their giant databases and use BI (Business Intelligence) tools, but, as not satisfied with on line or batching results and not fully proficient in business intelligence, they print a cornucopia of documents, putting a great part into the drawers. More than half of these outputs end up in the trash having attended no objective requests. Worse yet, they fall into the trash with no use as drafts. Also, there is a large information redundancy in administrative proceedings, since the online reports and dashboards add up to printed replicas without

B. Grabot et al. (Eds.): APMS 2014, Part II, IFIP AICT 439, pp. 14–21, 2014.

any logical reason in a counterproductive and paradoxical process of solid waste generation.

There is a slow but growing understanding – as well as a fast increasing of information technology – that environmental problems are not separated from everyday business activity, this latter having become part of the great discussion about environmental sustainability since the nineties. Although green IT is much focused on environmental certifications and metrics on general waste emissions [6], little was writen specifically about IT's office paper disposal. Many works on general waste paper management are published ([7], [8], [14]), and, as a paticular report, the great work of Villanueva and Eder about an end-of-waste criteria and related technical requirements for waste paper to cease to be waste in the European Union [13].

This article seeks to highlight the importance of establishing institutional programs to reduce emissions of printed paper in IT environments in view of the increasing contribution of informatics to the total volume of waste paper released. In addition, it is well known that making paper from raw materials we consume 60% more energy than recycling paper by modern advanced processes, also creating 74% more air pollution and 35% more water pollution [12], a fact that justifies all efforts toward the optimization of paper consumption.

2   Some Remarks on Present State

One of the factors that contributes to the increased generation of waste paper is the lack of political commitment to the realization of certifying entities for the dissemination of systematic security by digital signature. A huge amount of paper consumed is due to the requirement of manual signatures. This feature adds to a pathetic and obsolete system of register offices which only serves to enrich socially dead loss institutions. Thus, almost all that concerns to green IT is just trick in Brazil, where the bureaucracy is the mainstay of some fortunes.

As the authors highlighted above, the literature deals with the disposal of waste paper as a whole, mainly in household trash, with less attention devoted to the waste paper from IT. The problem is that, acting in this way, institutions aimed at environmental preservation leave aside the issue of environmental education in each work sphere. The environmental and ecological information could only contribute to behavior changes in respect to the environmental preservation if we localy develop a mindset beyond the needs of the productive systems as a basis for our actions on the world, decreasing the uncertainties about the future of the Earth. To do this, communication difficulties in transferring information to other social actors need to be overcome in order to make information circulate from specialized spheres to connecting with the people affected by the environmental problems within participatory processes. Also in this field, priorities and lines of research looking at the real needs have to be defined.

In Brazil, each IT governmental area should establish a real library of recycling associated with its Committee on Information Technology (CIT) with the premise that each worker plays a key role in solid waste management, either by reducing consumption, or by reusing materials, or by prior separation of recyclables materials to be sent for recycling. Available documents would be videos, books, magazines, technical reports and scientific journals plus practical experience workshops of reusing materials, mainly fucusing paper recycling, although we know there are limits for this recycling [7].

3   Environmental Reasons to Reduce Paper Consumption

The challenges of paper recycling concern to the amount of generated pollutants and the cost of production. Indeed, in comparison to manufacturing new paper, conventional recycling technology applied to office paper leads to high costs in cover and energy, releasing more carbon dioxide due to the consumption of less renewable fuel sources. Counsell and colleagues described in details conventional and new technologies of paper recycling [1]; they studied energy demands and climate change impacts from life cycle of generic office paper. Nevertheless, prices were diminishing by economies of scale, and by decreasing the average profit margin [10]. In Europe, recycled paper on an industrial scale can cost even cheaper than virgin due to the efficiency of selective collection and more difficult access to cellulose. In Brazil, the recycled paper used to cost 40% more than virgin paper at 2001 against only 3% to 5% at 2004 [10]. Although modern paper recycling is less pollutant and expensive, the ideal measures are to break off paper use replacing it by un-printing or through the use of electronic-paper [2], cutting back demands on energy, impacts on water and emissions of climate change gases.

The only effective way to inhibit the consumption of IT office paper in governmental areas is establishing policies for release of funds associated with reduction of emissions of typical printed outputs as reports, source codes and forms. This is what the *infotercio* financial model proposes to do.

4   The Technical Proposal and Its Ethical and Environmental Implications

Governmental budgets for IT in Brazil are still modest, leaving managers to practically live with leftovers from other areas. This is due to the failure to recognize the IT strategic role in process optimization. On the other hand, corruption scandals succeed in a way that seems to leave no margin of solution at least in the next two generations, a sad reality that leaves a trail of unnecessary purchases and deviances that led to the scrapping of various items of infrastructure along the last two decades. Moreover, there is the fact that people completely unprepared assume by political reasons positions that require extreme technical competence and solid general education. Given the above, only a governmental system of independent IT financial management could minimize the social damage caused by this situation of ethics bankruptcy. And whenever it configures the absence of ethics it becomes impossible to talk seriously about green IT or sustainability.

5   The *infotercio* Financial Model

The *infotercio* financial model has its origins in the early nineties, when it was discussed in some young IT sectors at Brazil the course of informatics, economics and technology in general. Serpa and Chy Hen Gin hypothesized ways to reduce the direct involvement of governmental institutions with funds annually transferred by the central government, creating mechanisms to protect public resources from the embezzlement of unethical politicians [11]. At that time, on the eve of the Gulf War, the IT certifications were still mirages; Michael Stanton honed the former Rio Network, the structural basis for the corporate web which would be established, while systems analysts and programmers seeking the best way to democratize information after so many years of authoritarian government. Ironically, while discussing the idea of the *infotercio* and its benefits in the boardrooms of Dataprev (Brazilian abbreviation for Data Processing Company of Social Security), President Collor, elected by the people, and his colleagues conceived an act of banditry, one of the most sinister plans that we have news, the banking confiscation in blatant disregard to the constitutional right to property.

Twenty years later, the model reappears associated with the concept of "green IT" and advances in digital technology and telecommunications. The *infotercio* (\$INFO) is now a unit of green financial credit based on the principle that the greater the reduction in the emission of printed paper the higher the available credit to purchase equipment for upgrades in machinery and other IT implements including security devices and accessories as tables and chairs. There is no cash involved, just green credits computed in the organ or agency responsible for IT audits. Unlike carbon credits, *infotercio* credits are not matter of trade; they can not be sold, not even exchanged. The name (info = "informatics" + tercio = "a third part") was coined in the sense that the financial amount allocated to IT should be divided into three global groups of major processes, namely Planning, Development and Production.

The fundamental equations governing the evolution of decreasing paper emissions and growth of credits are

$$w = w_0 e^{-\eta t} \tag{1}$$

and

$$c = k \ln(\eta t), \tag{2}$$

where w is the remaining percentage of waste paper, w_0 is its initial percentage, η is the coefficient of waste decay (depending on the internal green IT policies), t is the time in years, k is the financial constant (defined by government in *infotercios*) and c is the final credit in *infotercios*. It is very simple to show that the relation between equations (1) and (2) is given by

$$c = k \ln\left(-\ln\left(\frac{w}{w_0}\right)\right). \tag{3}$$

Exponential functions are widely used because they cover various everyday situations characterized by very fast growth or decrease, that is, situations where the growth or decrease rate is considered very significant. As everything in IT evolves rapidly, exponential functions are excellent for simulations to implementing strategic plans with regard to updates of technology and methodologies with their spendings. They contribute satisfactorily to obtain results from quantiqualitative analysis. Thus, it seems logical to use the exponential function and its inverse, the logarithmic function, to represent conjugated processes of growth and decrease.

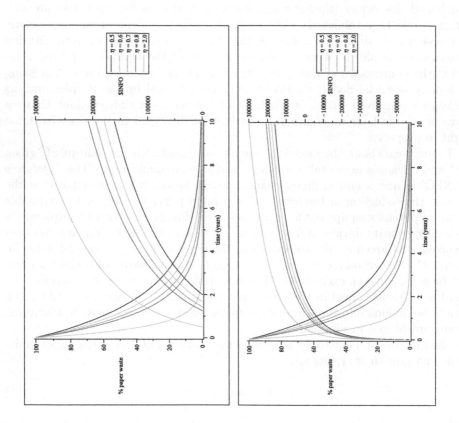

Fig. 1. a (left): the mathematical evolution of the paper waste reduction and the corresponding credits in *infotercios* for distinct values of the coefficient of waste decay; **Fig.1. b** (right): same simulation but since negative values of credits

Fig. 1. a shows how the reduction of waste paper, year after year, from 100% of paper outputs to almost zero output, determines the credit growth in *infotercios*. For the simulation we consider $k = 100,000$. The reader must note that credits start after a period of execution of a waste paper management plan; the more efficient the reduction, the more the bonus in credits. Institutions whose

Fig. 2. First design of the Green IT Card

reduction of paper emission occur more slowly begin to credit *infotercios* later. If equation (2) equals to negative values, this means that institution is still not fully working to credit *infotercios* in face of its coefficient η (Fig. 1. b). So, to credit *infotercios*, the institution must prove that it operates according to a planning for paper outputs reduction.

Each IT manager receives the *infotercio* green IT card as designed in Fig. 2, with which they can monitor the available amount of credits and release the amount required to purchase a given service or equipment when approved by the Federation General Comptroller (FGC). The Sunflower picture is a sponsor trade mark of Gauge-F Enterprises, a company that provides an unpaid program of environmental education for children. The unit value of the *infotercio* is assigned by the government, according to public policies of economy and sustainability. Each governmental institution forwards to the FGC its Term of Reference on the acquisition of some equipment or IT service. Faced with availability in *infotercios*, the term is referred to legal analysis and, once approved, it will be initialized the bidding process based on technology and price. Although each institution manages its bidding processes, only the FGC will approve or not the end result of the bidding and the liberation of funds, making direct payments and auditing the performance of the contracts. No money is transferred to the requesting institutions. Annual credits are available along with the budgets of each ministerial portfolio. Receiving of credits is permanent and works as an independent annual budget for IT, ensuring technological autonomy for each institution and environmental sustainability.

6   Discussion

One immediate advantage of this model is to reduce the risk of malpractice with public resources. Furthermore, we recover the importance of technical criteria in choosing the most advantageous solution for society. Also, the institutional potential to generate *infotercios* is proportional to the ecological enlightenment of workers in IT and to the execution efficiency of the IT strategic planning with regard to environmental issues. Obviously, in practice the reduction process is asymptotic, since it would be difficult to completely abolish IT's office paper. Assuming that the institution shall stabilize at a certain level of containment of paper emissions, it shall remain getting the same value in *infotercios*. Lastly, deadlines must be made less conservatives, something like 4-6 years for the entire cycle of reductions considering internal bureaucracy. Although there is not the case to detail the subject for reasons of strict constraint, it is interesting to consider the future implementation of a study focusing the return on investment associated with the *infotercio* financial model. A promising analysis of return on investment can be found in the explanatory work of Williams and Parker directed mainly to the discussion of the decrease in volumes generated by industrial activities [15]. This work shows how it is possible to calculate in monetary terms the noncash and external costs and benefits coming from a project, converting to dollars the relevant social and environmental impacts of that project. This process of conversion, operating at the intersection of economics and sustainability, is referred to as the Sustainable Return on Investment (SROI).

Another important aspect is that the model gives rise to the need for widespread knowledge about the ways of consuming paper in order to promote a better quality material for recycling, since successful recycling requires paper free from filth, such as grease, food or glue, which make difficult the recycling. Also, wood fibers may be recycled five, six, maximum of seven times before they become too small to be recycled into renewed good paper. But not only this; much of the waste produced in underdeveloped countries is incinerated, releasing in the air a wide range of substances harmful to health. A considerable portion of this waste is constituted by various kinds of paper. Severe health issues like cancer, adverse reproductive development and suppression of the immune system are caused by dioxin, a very toxic chemical release present in smoke from burning waste paper and other trashes ([4], [9]). Thus, the less paper waste is generated by IT, the lower the risk of dioxin emissions, and the more the organization and preparation of waste paper under policies of reuse, the greater the possibility of recycling.

7   Conclusion

Obviously, green IT is not limited to the issue of waste paper generation from unnecessary forms and reports, but, from the point of view of economy and disposal procedures within the reach of technical people in their day-to-day role, waste paper stands out as the most striking solid polluter in terms of spoilage volume. This article presented the so-called *infotercio* financial model to centralize the management of governmental IT resources in Brazil into the scope of cleaner production and sustainability as an alternative for the current administrative patterns still lacking in ecological education. Programs of this type suggest a certification system for both managers and institutions, ensuring quality and environmental responsibility. Such a system will be the subject of another study in the light of the ISO 14000 family and its Brazilian derivatives. Present article also starts a wide debate on green IT, motivating experiments that can show the entire feasibility of the model.

References

1. Counsell, T., Allwood, J.: Desktop Paper Recycling: A Survey of Novel Technologies that Might Recycle Office Paper Within the Office. Journal of Materials Processing Technology 173, 111–123 (2006)
2. Counsell, T., Allwood, J.: Reducing Climate Change Gas Emissions by Cutting out Stages in the Life Cycle of Office Paper. Resources, Conservation and Recycling 49, 340–352 (2007)
3. Cristóvão, A., Costa, I., Neto, A.P.A.: A Case Study on the Benefits that Virtualization Provides the IT and its Positive Impact on the Environment. In: APMS 2012 International Conference Advances in Production Management Systems, The Pennsylvania State University, Pennsylvania (2012)
4. EPA - United States Environmental Protection Agency: Improving Air Quality in Your Community,
   http://www.epa.gov/air/community/details/barrelburn_addl_info.html
5. DEC - Department of Environment and Conservation: Reducing Paper Waste at Work, http://www.livingthing.net.au/rc/guides/05638_Paperwaste.pdf
6. Jenkin, T.A., Webster, J., McShane, L.: An Agenda for 'Green' Information Technology and Systems Research. Information and Organization 21, 17–40 (2011)
7. Levlin, J.: The Limits of Paper Recycling, http://www.cost-e48.net
8. Merrild, H., Damgaard, A., Christensen, T.H.: Life Cycle Assessment of Waste Paper Management: The Importance of Technology Data and System Boundaries in Assessing Recycling and Incineration. Resources, Conservation and Recycling 52, 1391–1398 (2008)
9. MH - Ministry of Health: Technical Guidelines for Preparation of the Program of Health Education and Social Mobilization (HESMP); Implementation, Expansion or Improvement of Systems of Treatment and Final Disposal of Solid Waste for the Control of Diseases. ASCOM/FUNASA, Brasilia, Brazil (2004)
10. Pinto-Coelho, R.: Reciclagem e Desenvolvimento Sustentável no Brasil. Recóleo, Belo Horizonte, Brasil (2009)
11. Serpa, N.: Chy Hen Gin, R.: Talks on the Way You Pay for Nothing. Dataprev, Rio de Janeiro, Brasil (1990)
12. Siegler, K., Gaughan, B.: A Practical Approach to Green IT,
    http://www.itmanagement.com/land/green-it-webinar/?tfso=2058
13. Villanueva, A., Eder, P.: End-of-Waste Criteria for Waste Paper: Technical Proposals. Publications Office of the European Union, Luxembourg (2011)
14. Villanueva, A., Wenzel, H.: Paperwaste-Recycling, Incineration or Landfilling? A Review of Existing Life Cycle Assessments. Waste Management 27, 29–46 (2007)
15. Williams, J., Parker, J.: Measuring the sustainable return on investment (SROI) of waste to energy. In: Proceedings of the 18th Annual North American Waste-to-Energy Conference – NAWTEC, Orlando (2010)

The Green IT Certification Ruled by the *Infotercio* Financial Model

Nilo Sylvio Costa Serpa[1], Ivanir Costa[2], Diego Rodrigues[1], and Rodrigo Franco Gonçalves[1]

[1] UNIP - Graduate Program in Production Engineering, Brazil
[2] UNINOVE - Graduate Program in Production Engineering, Brazil
niloserpa@gmail.com, icosta11@live.com, diego@unip.br,
rofranco@osite.com.br http://www.unip.br

Abstract. Present article gives continuity to the elaboration of the *infotercio* financial model proposed as an alternative to implementing environmental management systems in governmental institutions based on the emission reduction of printed reports, source codes and forms originated from IT activities. It discusses procedures of green IT certification for managers and governmental institutions derived from ISO 14000 family and People CMM, combining both in a new set of requirements. Also it summarizes the reasons for such a certification system, noting that waste paper is now a major global problem, not only in terms of direct environmental impacts but from the point of view of the unreasonable and unnecessary use of paper in governmental business processes, generating high costs, mismanagements and time losses, at the same time causing reduction in the available physical space in corporate environments and increase in fuel consumption for transport.

Keywords: green IT, people CMM, green certification, waste paper, *infotercio*, sustainability, cleaner production.

1 Introduction

From the strong conflicts between public and private interests concerning environmental management during the seventies and the eighties, the growing general awareness about the damage caused to Earth and human health along the evolution of production processes and the huge social inequalities existing around the planet have allowed organizations to manage their ecosystemic impacts with higher responsibility. The concept of sustainable development, created in 1987 by the United Nations, came up with the aim of promoting agreement between contender parties.

In a former work [1], the authors pointed out that paper constitutes a large portion of IT waste in governmental institutions as spurious or unnecessary printed reports, source codes and forms, although the subject is still not treated with the fitting attention but included in a generic approach of sustainable development

---

[1] Entitled "Green IT and Waste Paper in Governmental Institutions: The Proposal of the *Infotercio* Financial Model", also submitted and accepted in APMS 2014.

B. Grabot et al. (Eds.): APMS 2014, Part II, IFIP AICT 439, pp. 22–29, 2014.

([8], [13], [14]). As they note, green IT is now much focused on environmental certifications and metrics on general waste emissions ([5], [12]) and virtualization as a mean for reducing significantly electricity rates [1]. Actions of Green IT supporting businesses have been described with little written specifically about IT office paper use and disposal. To cease to be waste, paper from IT services has to be considered under a set of emissions reduction procedures connected to a certain green certification for organizations and managers.

This article takes as starting point the *infotercio* financial model, explained earlier, proposing a green certification system associated with the model and characterized by maturity levels to both institution and manager. The Standard to be proposed contains only those requirements that can be objectively audited for certification/registration and/or self-declaration refering to waste paper management. Additional guidance on other matters relating to environmental management must be searched in ISO 14000 family. The authors emphasize that it is essential to read the previous article so that we can have a full comprehension of the subject.

2 Background

As we know, more than half of all office waste is constituted by paper. Worldwide paper is one of the biggest sources of trash. The numbers are astronomical; just to give an idea, according to the Department of Environment and Conservation (DEC), Sydney, until 2005 Australians consumed around 3.5 million tonnes of paper each year, in which only 11% of total office paper was recycled [2]. At 2007, Brazil spent 42 kg/inhab.year compared to larger consumers like United States, for example, with a per capita consumption of 288 kg/inhab.year and France with a rate of 144 kg/inhab.year. Founded on these rates, it is expected that consumption shall increase very fast in next decades whether nothing is done ASAP.

The *infotercio* ($INFO), as previously defined, is a unit of green financial credit to promote IT governance in compliance with the green principle that the greater the reduction in the emission of printed paper the higher the available credit to modernize IT areas (see Fig. 1). The value in dollars of that unit depends on the current governmental policies. As no cash is involved, just green credits computed by external IT audits, the model helps to reduce the risk of misappropriation of public funds. It was created specifically for IT governmental management also with the objective of environmental education in public institutions about the use of paper and its disposal after utilization, linking resources availability to corporate performance regarding the reduction of waste paper. Unlike carbon credits, *infotercios* may not be transferred or sold to other institutions. To achieve significant adhesion to green IT under the *infotercio* financial model it is necessary to go through the adoption of a certification ritual that is not limited only to the institution but capable of being extended to the IT manager himself.

Brazilian public institutions are far from achieve consolidated internal processes to reduce waste generation. In particular, with respect to the waste paper

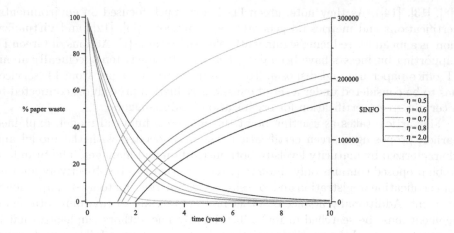

Fig. 1. The mathematical evolution of the paper waste reduction and the corresponding credits in *infotercios* for distinct values of the coefficient of waste decay (η)

there is a complete slouch on the amount of unnecessary or misdefined printed reports, which invariably end up in the trash or in the drawers of managers without even serve as scratch paper. Cardboard boxes accumulated in the corridors of the IT coordinations serve as trash cans for printed papers coming from the bad exercise of environmental sustainability and from the absence of document management frameworks. Although concerned to the issue of resources for IT, the *infotercio* financial model emerges as a solution to the problem of waste paper in governmental institutions, promoting improvements, environmental education and professional qualification.

3   The ISO Environmental State-of-Art and the New NBR-INFO 2014

The ISO 14000 family [4], at first glance regarding only private environmental management, provides an organization with standards and management tools to voluntarily control environmental aspects related to its existence and daily interactions with human beings, urban or rural landscape and others [2]. This set of tools and standards, if well implemented, provides economy associated with environmental benefits. Accordingly ISO, among these benefits we have reduction of waste generation and optimization of waste management, using processes such as recycling to treat solid waste. The only standard series ISO 14000 certifiable with respect to environmental management is ISO 14001:2004.

---

[2] According to NBR-ISO 14004 (1997), the environment is considered the surroundings in which a certain organization conducts its business, including air, water, land, natural resources, flora, fauna and humans, as well as their interrelations.

Although most small and medium enterprises (SME) have little knowledge or interest in environmental issues [3], the number of organizations certified by ISO 14001 has grown worldwide and should remain so in face of the increasing demands for environmental sustainability. In European Union, Marimon et al. point 1,096 IT organizations certified in 2008 compared to only 139 in 2000 [7]. The number does not seem very meaningful in a computerized world partly due to the high costs associated with the implementation of ISO 14000 [15], in particular ISO 14001, a fact that can indeed become a barrier for many institutions. However, for governmental institutions like Ministries not all features of ISO 14000 are necessary, since these organizations do not carry out processes of recycling or incineration but can perform reductions of paper emissions implementing ECM (Enterprise Content Management) and business intelligence dashboards, so that those high costs can no longer be a barrier if institutions start from a basic environmental management systems (EMS). Also, while ISO 14001 specifies only general requirements for operating EMSs with no resolves on how or to what extent to do this [10], organizations can develop their own solutions to be in compliance with the standard's demands. This is what *infotercio* financial model must provide: a green IT certification based only in paper economy. This certification shall be linked to a special Brazilian norm, named NBR-INFO 2014, prescribing scopes, gradual aims and patterns with sudgestions about tools and processes, so that institutions can rationalize the use of renewable and nonrenewable resources.

4   The Green People Capability Maturity Model

The IT manager career has been gaining more and more expression from the beginning of the 21st century at the same time that main focus has shifted to services. It is a sophisticated profile, in a constant process of adaptation and acquisition of diverse knowledge about various subjects. Although not formally recognized, in practice it has, by analogy, the same importance of the old systems analyst during the 80s. As an administrative career on IT processes and technologies, it can be valued through specializations, postgraduate courses and certifications, though none of them replace the accumulated experience. The *infotercio* financial model provides a green certification based on People Capability Maturity Model (P-CMM) as a way to characterize the manager's expertise, offering an important item of professional ascension within a market increasingly competitive in quality.

The P-CMM is a tool that employs a maturity framework of best practices for managing and developing human resources based on the successful Capability Maturity Model for software (SW-CMM), guiding institutions in the improvement of their processes related to the pursuit of the human capital excellence by five maturity levels. P-CMM helps institutions to characterize the maturity of their people practices, establishing a program of continuous amelioration and integrating people development with process improvement. Version 1 of P-CMM was released in 1995. Version 2 has been designed to correct Version 1, since experience has pointed that many organizations start formal development of workgroups while working toward Maturity Level 3, on the contrary of placing team-building activities at Maturity Level 4 as prescribed in Version 1. So, Version 2 starts process-driven workgroup development at Maturity Level 3.

The *infotercio* financial model presumes a green P-CMM solely concerning to management proficiency on environmental issues. Based on the adapted model from Rodrigues [11], we consider a proposal for continuing professional education, inserting the concept of maturity levels targeted to green IT. Rodrigues identifies four levels of maturity in their adapted model: (i) Level 0 - Definition of parameters, (ii) Level 1 - Planning, (iii) Level 2 - Quantification of Performance, (iv) Level 3 - Optimization of Performance, as shown in Fig. 2, considering indicators KMB (Knowledge Monitoring Bias) and KMA (Knwoledge Monitoring Accuracy) [11]. Each of the four maturity levels points to a different stage of organizational capability for managing and developing human resources in the sense of to attain sustainable processes of waste paper control. Maturity levels provide layers for continuous improvement of workforce proficiency in environmental sustainability.

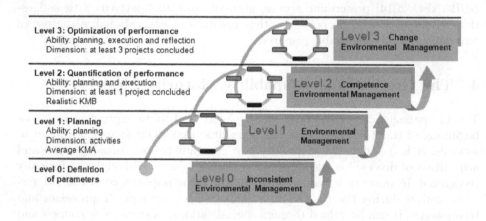

Fig. 2. The four maturity levels of the green P-CMM

On one hand, in the first article the authors established the so-called green IT card to be granted to the IT manager interested in establishing corporate policies to reduce the emission of printed paper. On the oder hand, levels of personal maturity are assessed throughout the career of the manager according to its proficiency to lead the trend of exponential emission reduction of printed paper. Thus, the green IT card shall also have four levels (Fig. 3), each of them offering some additional privileges: i) Level 0 - no stars; ii) Level 1 - one star; c) Level 2 - two stars; d) level 3 - three stars. This card will be activated whenever the manager take public charges and disabled when targeted for natural exoneration.

Fig. 3. The four green cards

4.1   The Perspectives of the NBR-INFO 2014

The NBR INFO-2014 is a standard still under development, now submitted to consideration of many stakeholders, researchers and academics. It applies to those environmental aspects of waste paper that can be controlled by the workforce of a governmental institution like consumption and waste disposal. Since there is already a full standard on environmental management for organizations, the ISO family 14000, it would be redundant to prescribe a new standard with basically the same requirements. Thus, the NBR-INFO 2014 shall specify detailed requirements on environmental management only with regard to the use and disposal of paper generated by the activities of IT and the means to process optimization that can contribute to reduce the emission of reports, source codes and forms according to the *infotercio* financial model and its remuneration policy of continuous improvement of IT in order to achieve sustainable containments on paper consumption. This standard applies to all types and sizes of governmental institutions, adapting to different geographic, cultural and social conditions. Indeed, system's success shall depend on the degree of commitment of all corporate areas, starting with senior management, since there is compliance between corporate governance and IT governance [9]. Thus, the NBR-INFO 2014 adhering institutions shall set their own environmental goals while balancing environmental protection and pollution prevention with social needs.

The reader must pay attention to the fact that this specification shall describe the requirements for certification/registration and/or self-declaration of the EMS of a governmental institution, with guidelines not intending to cover issues with market and competitive implications. It should be noted that this standard does not establish absolute requirements for environmental performance beyond the expressed commitment within the corporate internal policy, in compliance with *infotercio* financial model's prescription of continual improvement.

5   Comments

As an integral part of the overall management system of the organization, the EMS provides order and consistency to addressing ecological concerns through ongoing evaluation of practices, procedures and processes in coordinated action with efforts of other areas such as quality, operations, finance and health [6]. According to proposed approaches in the former article, green IT card allows IT managers to lead the implementation of the EMS sustainability measures, being a symbol of responsability and proficiency since it may only be granted to managers with proven experience and expertise in environmental issues, and ongoing interest in the acquisition and preservation of their certifications.

Unfortunately, in Brazil it is not enough the existence of standards like ISO 14000 to be fulfilled to achieve production improvements. There are serious problems in education and ethical issues that still require additional inspection agencies. Also, institutional maturity remains a barrier to be overcome. The authors have sudgested the Federation General Comptroller (FGC) as the institution responsible for the audits on the results achieved, with their internal automated processes having drastically reduced emissions of reports, keeping working through frameworks for information management and real-time monitoring of their databases related to institutional programs of sustainability. Interacting with this organization, each governmental IT manager detainer of a green IT card, with which he can monitor the amount of available *infotercios*, can also compute professional credits every successful action within the proposed corporate planning, registered and monitored by the FGC, thus composing his portfolio of accomplishments for further analysis of personal maturity level.

6   Conclusion

This article presented the natural extension of the *infotercio* financial model, that is, the green IT certification process for institutions and managers that conduct internal policies to reducing emissions of printed paper from IT services. The proposal is inserted into the scope of cleaner production and sustainability as an option to control current state of paper consumption in governmental institutions still not much concerned to ecological principles in Brazil. Restraining the use of paper in governmental business processes, it shall be possible to reduce costs, mismanagements and time losses, increasing the available physical space in corporate environments and economizing fuel for transport. Our expectation is that the complete model can be presented and tested soon at the ministerial level, demonstrating feasibility and raising discussions that promote improvement of the standard NBR-INFO 2014, now in development.

References

1. Cristóvão, A., Costa, I., Neto, A.P.A., Can, C.J.: A Case Study on the Benefits that Virtualization Provides the IT and its Positive Impact on the Environment. In: APMS 2012 International Conference Advances in Production Management Systems, The Pennsylvania State University, Pennsylvania (2012)
2. DEC - Department of Environment and Conservation: Reducing Paper Waste at Work, http://www.livingthing.net.au/rc/guides/05638_Paperwaste.pdf
3. Halila, F., Tell, J.: Creating Synergies Between SMEs and Universities for ISO 14001 Certification. Journal of Cleaner Production 48, 85–92 (2013)
4. ISO - International Organization for Standardization: Environmental Management: The ISO 14000 Family of International Standards, http://www.iso.ch
5. Jenkin, T.A., Webster, J., McShane, L.: An Agenda for 'Green' Information Technology and Systems Research. Information and Organization 21, 17–40 (2011)
6. Jorgensen, T.H., Remmen, A., Mellado, M.D.: Integrated Management Systems: Three Different Levels of Integration. Journal of Cleaner Production 14, 713–722 (2006)
7. Marimon, F., Llach, J., Bernardo, M.: Comparative Analysis of Diffusion of the ISO 14001 Standard by Sector of Activity. Journal of Cleaner Production 19, 1734–1744 (2011)
8. Merrild, H., Damgaard, A., Christensen, T.H.: Life Cycle Assessment of Waste Paper Management: The Importance of Technology Data and System Boundaries in Assessing Recycling and Incineration. Resources, Conservation and Recycling 52, 1391–1398 (2008)
9. MH - Ministry of Health: Technical Guidelines for Preparation of the Program of Health Education and Social Mobilization (HESMP); Implementation, Expansion or Improvement of Systems of Treatment and Final Disposal of Solid Waste for the Control of Diseases. ASCOM/FUNASA, Brasilia, Brazil (2004)
10. Oliveira, O., Serra, J., Salgado, M.: Does ISO 14001 Work in Brazil? Journal of Cleaner Production 18, 1797–1806 (2010)
11. Rodrigues, D.: Um Modelo de Assistente Reflexivo para Suporte à Educação Continuada em Ambiente Organizacional. Master Thesis, Catholic University of Brasilia, Brasilia, Brazil (2010)
12. Siegler, K., Gaughan, B.: A Practical Approach to Green IT, http://www.itmanagement.com/land/green-it-webinar/?tfso=2058
13. Villanueva, A., Eder, P.: End-of-Waste Criteria for Waste Paper: Technical Proposals. Publications Office of the European Union, Luxembourg (2011)
14. Villanueva, A., Wenzel, H.: Paperwaste-Recycling, Incineration or Landfilling? A Review of Existing Life Cycle Assessments. Waste Management 27, 29–46 (2007)
15. Wiengarten, F., Pagell, M., Fynes, B.: ISO 14000 Certification and Investments in Environmental Supply Chain Management Practices: Identifying Differences in Motivation and Adoption Levels Between Western European and North American Companies. Journal of Cleaner Production 56, 18–28 (2013)

Project and Work Organization in Solidarity Economy: A first Approach According to Production Engineering

Nilo Sylvio Costa Serpa[1], Ivanir Costa[2],
Oduvaldo Vendrametto[1], and Pedro Luiz de Oliveira Costa Neto[1]

[1] UNIP - Universidade Paulista,
Graduate Program in Production Engineering, Brazil
[2] UNINOVE - Universidade Nove de Julho,
Graduate Program in Production Engineering, Brazil
gauge.f.enterprises@gmail.com, icosta11@live.com,
{oduvaldov,politeleia}@uol.com.br
http://www.unip.br

Abstract. This article presents the possible contributions of Production Engineering to solidarity economy as regards projects and organization of work. The authors present logistics as the main channel of introduction to planning and organizing solidarity economy, seeking to show that the participation of Production Engineering leads to a breakage of some strains marked by neoliberalism, making evident the need of serious ecological concerns within the scope of the projects in that sector towards a cleaner production. The authors also point out the impossibility of development of solidarity economy programs without well mapped processes that include environmental impact evaluations and environmental education as pillars of sustainability in any development program.

Keywords: solidarity economy, production engeneering, environmental education, sustainability, cleaner production, organization.

1 Introduction

Solidarity economy is understood as a collaborative style of producing, selling, buying and exchanging goods that are necessary for daily life, including in all transations the sense of a fair trade. Solidarity enterprises are organized mainly in the form of cooperatives, associations, self-managed enterprises, cooperation networks and cooperative complexes. In the current world situation, solidarity economy is considered by many social scientists a global trend of income generation and reinterpretation of the concept of work. Kritikos and collaborators come even to assert that solidarity is "a matter of life or death" [10]. In a certain sense, solidarity economy translates the advent of a new way of production, overcoming the capitalist mode and establishing some kind of post-capitalist relations with peculiar social traits. Contributions to the formation of the idea of solidarity economy were given by thoughts coming from a true melting pot of reflections from socialists, utopian socialists, anarchists and Christians throughout

B. Grabot et al. (Eds.): APMS 2014, Part II, IFIP AICT 439, pp. 30–37, 2014.

the twentieth century. The transformative potential of solidarity economy and the balance of the principal theses about its reasons are pointed out by Gaiger in an elucidating work [5].

The worldwide literature is generous with respect to the solidarity economy. Several papers discussed this subject in all aspects ([4], [7], [8], [10], [12], [13]). In some contexts the term "social economy" is considered a synonym of solidarity economy and the authors also adopt this use. This social economy combines the principle of unity of possession and use of the means of production and distribution with the principle of socialization of these means. In sum, by solidarity economy we understand the whole of economic activities of production, distribution, consumption and credit arranged in the form of self-management. Although solidarity economy has appeared in emerging countries as a possible alternative to scarce and precarious formal jobs, it is now changing to a sign of a new future in larger scale [9].

Despite all the benefits that solidarity economy abridges as an alternative to the current economic system, there are environmental concerns with respect to the sustainability of the production that we need to reinforce in social development programs. It has been observed that social work practices are rarely linked to ecological education and planning. The authors want to discuss the role of Production Engineering in its intrinsic value for solidarity economy, showing how it may aid socio-economic development in Brazil as a Third World country.

2   The Brazilian Solidarity Economy, Its Demands and Challenges

Solidarity movements in Brazil began to be formally taken with seriousness from the creation of the National Secretary for the Solidarity Economy (NSSE) in 2003, the great developer of the program "Solidarity Economy in Development". In collaboration with the FBSES (Brazilian abbreviation for Brazilian Solidarity Economy Forum), the MTE (Brazilian abbreviation for Ministry of Work and Employment) has supported a national mapping project, localizing all the running solidarity enterprises and organizing data in a CD-ROM application (2005) and further in a web application (2008) both named Digital Atlas of Solidarity Economy [14].

The solidarity economy has as principles self-management, democracy, participation, egalitarianism, cooperation in work, human development and social responsibility, none of them matters to the market, whose only concerns are the quality and efficiency of their products and services on competitive terms. Thus, the biggest challenge for the solidarity economy is reconciling its principles with the way of the market without incurring in capitalist vices. Being Production Engineering a technical area focused on the rational management of production, it has methods and tools to give satisfactory answers to the demands of planning and organization in solidarity enterprises, also having as concerns the negative effects of neoliberalism on people such as one forced to working more because partner is unemployed, increased frustration and insecurity, and less health insurance [6].

Among the necessary elements to support competitive strategies of solidarity enterprises, there are technical qualification, productivity, market conquest and expansion capital. Due to the lack of education in Brazil, very few people are able to work with an interdisciplinary view of the overall functioning of the enterprises. Thus, to promote programs and encouraging solidarity economy we need to consider a broad planning of training for the staff already engaged and for newcomers that want to integrate solidarity market. Production Engineering also plays an important role in this planning and the authors consider as a very way for the first trials the logistics approach.

3   The Logistics and Its Immediate Response as Organization Tool

Following the view of Corrêa, some of the areas that Production Engineering can act are [3]:

- Strategies and objectives;
- Network operations;
- Production management;
- Quality of the process;
- Productivity;
- Development of products and processes;
- Project and work organization;
- Ergonomics (physical, cognitive and organizational);
- Strategic planning.

This is a complex universe, of course. One can not expect that the average profile of workers in solidarity economy is able to deal with such complexity. Accordingly, it will be interesting to seek a rational and more compact way to start them on a vision of planning and work organization that will be refining with the accumulation of lessons learned. Thinking in this way, the authors defend the idea that the initiatory path is the intoduction to logistics as a teaching tool.

The logistics – and its more specific embodiment, the business logistics –, as an activity responsible for the movement of materials, services and information through the supply chain, is already well developed. Within the productive organizations, logistics has very specific goals. The success of the operations in the supply chain is defined by the so-called "three rights of the logistics", which means:

- The right product,
- In the right location,
- At the right time.

Certainly the "three rights" point to quality, efficiency and competitiveness. It is easy to implement this conceptual scheme for any situation in which it is possible to identify a chain of events that need to occur in a certain spacetime order to fulfill a goal.

Being part of the logistics, the business logistics has played an important role in several enterprises. It can be set in the context of solidarity economy as "the process of planning, implementing and controlling the flow of goods and services with low costs, from the point of origin to the point of destination, in order to meet not only market demands, but environmental requirements and public policies of sustainability". Within this approach, the main activities are: transportation, inventory maintenance, order processing, purchasing, warehousing, materials handling and maintenance of information.

The logistics vision of the enterprises, in our teaching approach, helps to break some stereotypes inculcated in the worker that areas of the production are forms of exploitation against the employee. Instead, these areas can be developed for the improvement and rationalization of production, the result of employee's labor and resource of its livelihood.

4   Solidarity Economy and Exploitation of Nature: A Dead End?

Another specific challenge arising from the lack of education in dealing with environmental issues is the fighting to the tendency for the replication of capitalist forms of exploitation of nature. Competition between the constituents of the organization itself and the focus of realization in the market create a paradox inside the ideal of solidarity. The reproduction of capitalist behavior obviously leads to a corresponding reproduction of the environmental aggression if ecology and environmental issues do not take part in education of people. The latter is one of the targets of planning, since there is no effective success in organization without knowledge dissemination.

Unfortunately, there is no data to demonstrate in unequivocal manner the environmental impact of agricultural and exploitation activities from solidarity economy. Judging by the correlation between devastated areas and presence of solidary enterprises, and the obvious indifference with which the eco-environmental education has been treated in Brazil, we only may infer the existence of a significant impact. Looking at the relationship between sustainable development and social work practice, Peeters and colaborators start from the assumption that an adequate interpretation of sustainable development for social work should take account of contemporary analyses of the ecological crisis and should recognize synergies between the social/ecological objectives and the critical tradition of social work [12]. It is simple to conclude that, if people are not educated and prepared to deal with the environment to preserve it from wrong production processes, they inevitably replicate what the great devastating enterprises have been doing last decades.

Within the "three rights" logistics vision is relatively simple to introduce environmental concerns in solidarity practices, beginning with the planning of routes for disposal of products, i. e., those routes that cause less environmental damage in the sense of traffic of goods (the planning of deliveries) and choice of means of transport operating in less polluting conditions in accordance with ISO standards. Moreover, when we speak of the right product, we do not talking only about market adequacy, but adequacy of production methods to the environmental sustainability in the long term. For example, the exploitation of rubber – for which the world market demand is increasing – requires a specific technique of cutting the bark of the tree so that it remains productive throughout his long life. Lastly, the "right time" ensures not only the absence of financial loss, but the flow of processes in order to avoid environmental impacts caused by overcrowding or generation of waste by product losses due to long waiting times.

Cultural changes required for the success of the ideas discussed here can take decades, especially in countries whose populations suffer under the weight of corruption. However, it is possible to mitigate the problems caused by lack of environmental education, promoting training programs of distance learning embedded in logistical planning itself for training brigades of environmental supervisors primarily to support the most impactful solidarity initiatives. In this context, teleconferences can constitute a great option. Teleconferencing is a virtual meeting by means of telecommunications, where participants separated by geographical distances can simultaneously interact with each other [15]. Systems of teleconferencing are used with three closely interrelated functionalities: education, formation of virtual communities and knowledge management. All the typical tools of the modern dynamic teaching/learning can be concurrently used, such as PowerPoint presentations, collaborative work in real time using word processor and online whiteboard, file transfer, chat and personal annotations with notepad. Nevertheless, it is essential to convey in those programs, albeit in simplified language, how nature affects in biological and psychosocial levels the individual and collective behavior of human beings in the sense highlighted by Besthorn, who pointed that, ontologically, nature has consequences on both the way we perceive ourselves and the way we interact with others [2]. Only this perception will allow to map and dominate the processes that include environmental impact, leading to minimization of the latter.

It is a colossal (but not impossible) task to prepare people to living in this new world, since it is necessary a reverse engineer from that already exists to that would be close to ideal. There is a long way trip to achieve the effectiveness of this fundamental task. Recent projects conducted primarily by IPEA (Brazilian abbreviation for Institute of Applied Economic Research) are intended to produce as much knowledge as possible about all forms of solidarity enterprises in Brazil with regard to environmental problems that are related to their actions in order to promote improvements in current policies of solidarity economy. One of this projects is now being proposed by Serpa and colleagues about the current situation of human and veterinary medical waste disposal in Brazil, its environmental impacts and effects on individuals that survive from the collection of waste in order to subsidize the PNPD (Brazilian abbreviation for Subprogram of Research for National Development) with information resources to support decision making. Although it is a small portion of the total urban waste, nosocomial waste is highlighted by the high potential of contamination, exposing communities to the risk of dissemination of respiratory illnesses or diseases transmitted by contaminated groundwater. The project is not limited to the presentation of quantitative results, but explains alternative suggestions for the treatment of municipal waste from healthcare unities, such as cottons, glasses, plastics and metals, proposing solidarity enterprises of collectors who are specialized in these wastes, so that the garbage is sent to certain specific destinations physically established by law.

4.1 Some Comments on the Planning and Organization in Solidarity Economy at Third World

Analyzing neo-liberal variants in vigor at Third World, solidarity enterprises are known wanting from the goal of a great integrative and socializing way of development, limited to local needs of survival and livelihood [8]. To enlarge the horizons it is not enough to turn ethnocentric person's mindset into one exhibiting compassion for other people, but attention to introduce environmental concerns and entrepreneurship in major discourses. The reality of solidarity economy often stands in great contrast to both theory and anecdotal practice in part because de lack of planning and organization. Also, the growth of inequality (the income of social distance) may lead to less feelings of solidarity [11], a fact that can bring on less sensibility to perceive the importance of egalitarianism and cooperation in work as fundamental elements of social development in large scale. In practice, Brazil did not decrease that social distance, only masked it with populist policies that in no way contribute to the dignity and the sense of entrepreneurship we need so much to grow socially and economically.

To surpass this contradictory state, an interesting path to follow in planning and organization, as well as in environmental education, would be to establish, like some initiatives in France, the "ecological solidarity" [16], that is, the resulting social state of mind that aims to detect all eco-social interlinks which interfere with biodiversity in order to build a conceptual shell for collective actions to access in a sustainable way a multiplicity of values issuing from the natural world, seeking to lower the social discrepancies by injecting resources in projects of solidarity entrepreneurship motivation aimed at spreading equal profits, inviting more and more partners to expand the solidarity economy as a real way to achieve more equitable distribution of income. Clearly this is a subject in which Production Engineering may contribute building that conceptual shell of actions obeying well mapped and dominated processes. This shell is nothing more than a result of the planning and organization of the work.

Lastly, for the fully success in Brazil of the above mentioned shell, a governmental structural correction would need to be made, locating NSSE in direct connection with the *Casa Civil* (Brazilian equivalent of Department of State), including a sub-secretary for international interchanging about sustainability for social economy in cooperation with other countries, themselves in a true solidarity and permanent dialog.

5   The Role of Cleaner Production

In parallel to the process of ecological-environmental education, it is necessary to establish comprehensive programs for modeling sustainable social exploitation of nature, among which it has a highlight position the so-called "agroforestry systems" based on the consortium of distinct species as alternatives of sustainable solidarity enterprises of low cost and good profitability for small producers. Our considerations culminate in a critical point: the cleaner production (CP), within the scope of Production Engineering, should consider an advisory branch entirely devoted to the solidarity economy, targeting small and medium enterprises along the lines of care described above, since CP has been characterized as a strategy of prevention useful to orient the reduction of loading from production processes of the small-and-medium-sized enterprises [1]. Initiatives have to involve financial support for technical assistance programs to offer correct options and knowledge by consultants prepared to enhance CP especially in high-risk areas. Success of these programs shall depend on the proposed scope reaching out to a large group of enterprises. The offer of alternatives, as well as the orientation of the existing enterprises of extractive activities, must turn to more sustainable patterns of production-in-consortiums in order to ensure the natural capital represented by that environments.

6   Conclusion

Present article presented and discussed the role of Production Engineering in the planning and organization of the work in solidarity economy at Brazil in face of the lack of ecological proficiency in both workers and governors. It showed in what lines Production Engineering may contribute, pointing out logistics as the first way to approach the subject in an educational program for workers in solidarity enterprises. It also emphasizes the prominence of the so-called "agroforestry systems" as alternatives for sustainable solidarity enterprises of exploitation of nature to be considered by local populations. It is hoped that this introdutory discussion will lead to further works to establish the position of Production Engineering as an area of expertise essential for the establishment of public policies aimed at promoting the social economy.

References

1. Baas, L.: To make zero emissions technologies and strategies become a reality, the lessons learned of cleaner production dissemination have to be known. Journal of Cleaner Production 15, 1205–1216 (2007)
2. Besthorn, F.: Radical ecologisms – insights for educating social workers in ecological activism and social justice. Critical Social Work (2003)
3. Corrêa, H.: Administração de produção e operações – manufatura e serviços: uma abordagem estratégica. Atlas, São Paulo (2004)

4. Fonseca, H.: Pronouncement on solidarity economy. In: Seminario internacional - Instrumentos para el Desarrollo Económico y la Protección Social. Asociación Kolping, Uruguay (2008)
5. Gaiger, L.: L'économie solidaire au brésil. Revue du M.A.U.S.S. 21, 80–96 (2003)
6. Garrett-Peltier, H., Scharber, H.: Why we need another world: introduction to neoliberalism. In: Allard, J., Davidson, C., Matthaei, J. (eds.) Solidarity Economy: Building Alternatives for People and Planet. Papers and Reports from the 2007 US Social Forum, pp. 19–27. ChangeMakers Publications, Chicago (2007)
7. Hintze, S. (ed.): Trueque y economía solidaria. Prometeo Libros, Buenos Aires (2003)
8. Jayasooria, D. (ed.): Developments in solidarity economy in Asia. JJ Resources, Malaysia (2013)
9. Kraychete, G., Costa, B., Lara, F. (orgs.): Economia dos setores populares: entre a realidade e a utopia. Vozes, Petrópolis (2000)
10. Kritikos, A., Bolle, F., Tan, J.: The economics of solidarity: a conceptual framework. The Journal of Socio-Economics 36, 73–89 (2007)
11. Paskova, M., Dewilde, C.: Income inequality and solidarity in Europe. Research in Social Stratification and Mobility 30, 415–432 (2012)
12. Peeters, J.: The place of social work in sustainable development: towards ecosocial practice. International Journal of Social Welfare 21 (2012)
13. RELIESS: Public policy for the social and solidarity economy, http://reliess.org/wp-content/uploads/2012/03/bulletinRELIESS-Final-novembre-EN.pdf
14. Serpa, N.: Atlas Digital da Economia Solidária, http://www.mte.gov.br/sistemas/atlas/AtlasES.html
15. Serpa, N.: A short treatise on cyber distance learning and social change in Brazil. International Journal of Data Analysis and Information Systems 5, 1 (2013)
16. Thompson, J., Mathevet, R., Delanoë, O., Gil-Fourrier, C., Bonnin, M., Cheylan, M.: Ecological solidarity as a conceptual tool for rethinking ecological and social interdependence in conservation policy for protected areas and their surrounding landscape. Comptes Rendus Biologies 334, 412–419 (2011)

Agribusiness, Agrienergy and Leadership: The Coaching as a Tool to Guide Talents

Nilo Sylvio Costa Serpa[1], Bruna Brasil Sá[2],
Ivanir Costa[3], and Oduvaldo Vendrametto[1]

[1] UNIP - Graduate Program in Production Engineering, Brazil
[2] FAJESU - Undergraduate Program in Business Administration, Brazil
[3] UNINOVE - Graduate Program in Production Engineering, Brazil
niloserpa@gmail.com, brunabrasil21@hotmail.com,
icosta11@live.com, oduvaldov@uol.com.br
http://www.unip.br

Abstract. This article aims to propose an application of coaching in agrienergy sector. Given the visible growth in demand for renewable energy sources, and the related need to training professionals to deal with the challenges of this branch of agribusiness, the study shows how the coach, the person who pursues coaching, can act to aid those individuals that have potential to exercise leadership in management of agrienergy. The subject is presented and discussed facing the current state of Brazilian agribusiness and treated primarily from an ethical standpoint concerning environmental sustainability.

Keywords: growth, leadership, energy, renewable sources, coaching.

1 Introduction

During the last 10-15 years, the paradigm shift from a simple technical professional or specialist to an interdisciplinary manager, who makes decisions based on diverse knowledge, has led to an intense search for leaders who can drive projects with quality and effectiveness towards the corporate goals. In this sense, it is growing the demand for tools that may assist the search and preparation of leaders with the speed required by modern world. Coaching is presented as an objective option for this task.

The XXI century is being the scenario of profound changes in professional and interpersonal relationships, mainly because of the social effects of globalization, frantic advances in technology, increasing acquisition of knowledge and change of business paradigm from products to services. These changes will continuously affect the modes to using skills and individual talents. The intitutional patrimony in human assets (special abilities, skills, sense of responsibility, etc.) is passing to the status of the main competitive advantage of a corporation. Business world is now widely changeable and uncertain, more than ever demanding resilient leaderships with high degree of adaptability.

Looking through the prism of energy potential and continental geophysical characteristics as a tropical country by excellence, Brazil offers unbeatable conditions to occupy a prominent place in agribusiness. Compared to the rest of the

B. Grabot et al. (Eds.): APMS 2014, Part II, IFIP AICT 439, pp. 38–45, 2014.
© IFIP International Federation for Information Processing 2014

world, it presents a wide availability of fertile lands which allows the cultivation of various species. It also has considerable technological legacy in biofuels, a fact that puts Brazilian nation in unique position in global economy.

Given the above comments, present study was produced to render the conviction that business coaching will be soon an indispensable tool for agile processes of discovery and preparation of leaders for great magnitude sustainable projects, as well as for organization of modern human resources management. Being agribusiness one of the most promising, profitable and important sources of means for human survival against the inexorable fact of the extinction of fossil energy resources, it is essential that efforts are taken to prioritize the retention of the best teams in the field of agrienergy. Specific goals of this study are 1)- the stimulation of interdisciplinary debates (pedagogical, sociological and educational) among professionals and scholars interested in this subject, 2)- the prelusive search of elements that enable a renewal of the dynamics of labor relations in agribusiness faced to the advent of agrienergy as an alternative for human survival, 3)- the delimitation of a green governance structure whose leaders have not only aware of their roles, but sureness about their career choices. Such goals will certainly be guided by ideas brought by coaching.

2 Theoretical Frame

2.1 Breaking Some Myths

It is a very common mistake to consider "non-scientific" a work implemented on a completely new and unexplored area. If this view were taken seriously, it would be impossible to advance knowledge precisely because the latter is accelerated by reflections and conjectures based on more or less general observations on certain trends. It seems that people have forgotten that there is no understanding of what is observed without theory. The collapse of culture from the second half of the twentieth century began precisely with the post-modern delusions with no solid conceptual basis. If we had to wait long years to say something based only on data collected we would be sterile of ideas and ability to drive and create our own destinies.

Liking it or not, it is also obligation of science to open conceptual and theoretical windows so that we can get as fast as possible to the state-of-art where it will be possible to confront, refute and refine our initial models. The lack of foresight and pioneering spirit has led to a poorly creative decade, despite all the technology currently available. Today, novelties are results of collages from existing technologies more than genuinely innovative contributions. Indeed, there are very few papers in all fields of knowledge that are now considered indisputable contributions. Several papers have been published based on insufficient data only to give a more realistic aspect to the matter when it would be more productive and consistent to recognize the lack of sufficient data, working on a theoretical level, organizing conceptual models capable of being thoroughly tested over the years. Barring initiatives of this kind is not loss for the authors, but for an entire youth community waiting for new stimuli of research and creation.

This article is only intended to open rational windows, not to exhaust a topic that is just beginning to awaken interest in corporate environments. Coaching is still a young discipline, opened to many suggestions and investigations. The best results reported in the literature are still partial and inconclusive. International experts acknowledge that many coaching skills programs are introduced and fail [15]. Nevertheless, at the same time they recognize that after several years of trial and error, the application of neuroscience in coaching seems to shed new light on human/business behavior [15]. It will take a long time to earn enough data about coaching's real efficiency in corporate environments. So far, studies have been conducted mainly at the theoretical level with the help of contributions from some fields as pedagogy, psychology and management, and, from now on, neuroscience. Accordingly, papers as the present work should be encouraged to encourage new research teams.

2.2   The Origins of Coaching and Its State in Brazil

As pointed out by Corrêa and Slaughter in a study conducted by the Institute Humanitatis, coaching is a technique that introduces a continuous process of high-level relationships in order to assist the identification of skills and leadership potential [3]. Through meetings, the customers choose the focus of conversation while the coach (professional who performs tasks of coaching) will contribute from listening with questions and suggestions.

Also in accordance with the above study, coaching has origins in tennis and golf. In these sports it was clearly the essence of coaching: releasing the potential of an individual to maximize their performance, helping him to learn about himself and by personal effort, rather than teaching. The English word "coach", most likely from Hungarian "Kocsi", means carriage, vehicle widely used in the eighteenth century. Thus, it is believed to have been used metaphorically to describe the tutor of the eighteenth century, which led the education of children by the various fields of knowledge, just as the carriages carrying the families in the fields of England.

The use expanded until today and it has been established the following words: Coaching - is the process; Coach (coaches in plural) - is the professional qualified to perform the process; Coachee (or client) - is the person who receives coaching. There is, however, as in every area in its infancies, the risk of misinformation and unauthorized appropriation of the title of coach by people without the knowledge and training appropriate to the exercise of coaching in its fullest and utmost responsibility. Asked about the relevance of the topic in Brazil, Andrea Lages, Master Trainer in Coaching, comments that in Brazil coaching gained much strength in recent years and continues to grow. She points that the problem we face is with regard to people who are trying to take advantage of the situation and adopt the title of coach with complete informality, often without knowing what it really means. On the other hand, she says, this reflects the popularity of the profession in the country [11].

From here, we take important lesson for those interested in the career: always seek an institution duly licensed to perform research and provide training in coaching; it is a matter of professional life of people with direct impact on their personal lives, their affections and desires.

2.3 The Coaching and Its Contribution to the Formation of Ethical and Competent Leadership

The literature on coaching is gradually growing. Authors such as Batt [2], Downey [4], Ely et al. [5], Karawejczyk and Cardoso [8], John and West-Leuer [10], Motter Junior [12] and Whitmore [17], show what can be expected from the action of the coach. There is a consensus among these authors that the coaching is based on several areas of knowledge to build your method; they include psychology, education, pedagogy, business management and even aspects related to spirituality and religion, according to the precepts of Motter Junior [12]. Recently, as already noted, new contributions coming from neuroscience have expanded the scientific perspectives of the application of couching [15].

The coaching is focused on leaders, either individuals or team leaders, giving emphasis on action oriented by the more evident skills of the coachee, that is, the human-target of professional coaching. It is not, therefore, therapy, since is distinct the way to provide services, neither mentoring which requires a mentor positioned between the guide that gives support and the driver that dictates rules and paths. The coach is neither one thing nor the other, just a "poker", an instigator whose intervention generates free response of the person in their professional context. In practice, it is true, the intervention of the coach combines elements from other disciplines, but it is his ethical responsibility to bring their actions within the limits of its authority which makes productive such intervention since it does not conflict with the personal characteristics of the coachee.

There are different ways for corporations avail themselves by coaching. Such evaluation needs not necessarily be related to training programs; it can exist as something autonomous. However, Motter Junior points out a fundamental aspect to be considered in the coaching, saying that each coachee is different and the choice of the coach and the methodological approach (non-standard) will be decisive [12]. The latter should be creative, with lots of interactions and self-reflections throughout the process. Reflective practice is proposed to promote learning and change from the action, an awareness process that involves persistent observation and dialogue [12].

In fact, creativity is essential for the activity of the coach, and this is so much clearer the more one gives account of human diversity. In the perspective of Chiavenato, the real difficulty in recruiting and retaining a good work force is not a matter of financial capital, which was once considered essential for business success [9]. This applies to projects of any magnitude. Keeping professionals is not just a question of salary, but a question of motivation and functional suitability to ensure operational sustainability under ever-increasing pressure for results. Agribusiness, and more precisely, the area of agrienergy, is characterized today as one of the spheres of human action under greater pressure for quick results in face of the global expectations about alternative sustainable energy solutions.

3   The Importance of Agrienergy

The authors call "agrienergy" any energy obtained from agricultural sources, and, accordingly this view, the word is a synonym for bioenergy. The term was chosen to maintain a ready lexical and also visceral relationship with "agribusiness", now understood as the set of various business segments, from the production of inputs (seeds, fertilizers, machinery, etc.) until the arrival of final outputs (cheese, crackers, pasta, etc.) to the consumer [16].

Although the word "energy" is freely used in different contexts, the concept of energy is, physically speaking, one of the darkest in science. For practical purposes of common human actions is sufficient to understand that it is a magnitude which turns continuously into work performed by human individuals, machines or animals. This energy is obtained from matter, which is, after all, one of the forms that energy takes. Among the materials more easily convertible by machinary into energy capable of doing work, there are fossil fuels, for example, petroleum and coal, and non-fossil fuels such as vegetable oils and ethanol derived from sugarcane and beet. Beside these, there are indirect sources of the so-called renewable energies, such as hydro, solar, wind and geothermal. The name agrienergy refers to that derived from agricultural matter, that is, organic products such as soya, sugarcane and others.

Energy is absolutely essential to developing the world, as well as steel production. The dynamics of population growth and labor require continuous power to the realization of human activities on the planet. The global reality shows steady growth of energy consumption; so, efforts are needed to increase worldwide production, encouraging the diversification of the energy matrix. In parallel, we need to reduce the impacts on the environment, hence the special attention to more sustainable processes of production. Here is where the promotion of agrienergy becomes imperative. According SEBRAE, in electronic publication on bioenergy, the increase in energy demand will be more significant in countries considered in consolidation of development (China, India, Brazil and Russia), notably in transport, in residential and industrial areas. There is also the need to provide supplies of electricity and coking from modern sources for 2.5 billion people in countries in the early stages of development [14].

Brazil is one of the great suppliers of agricultural products to the world, exporting to many countries. Mainly in terms of domestic consumption, the agrienergy sector is one of the most promising in agribusiness. In 2009, it was estimated that the global demand for biofuel, at that time 3%, would rise to 12% to 15% in the ensuing 15 years [14]. To get an idea, it is expected that 8 million hectares of land occupied at 2009 by the culture of sugarcane in Brazil shall reach 14 million at 2019 [14]. It is not difficult to imagine human demands, logistics and technology required to support such growth. Given this inescapable reality, it becomes cogent to preparing quality human resources in proportion to the dimensions of the challenge. Among the tools that support the task of structuring competent professionals we have the modern executive coaching.

4   Successful Experiences with Coaching

The activity of coaching is still shy. According Karawejczyk and Cardoso, worldwide, there are 16,000 persons empowered in this career, and of those, less than two thousands in Brazil [8]. The growth of Brazilian Society of Coaching is 80-90% per year, according to president Villela da Matta, who also forecasts an expansion of 30,000 registered members by 2020. Looking at human needs for achievement and accomplishments, surveys show that at least 30,000 individuals have passed through the coaching process in Brazil. The president of the International Coach Federation - Brazil, José Augusto Figueiredo, reports that there are 150 registered Brazilian members in that institution [11].

Therefore, empirical studies on the application of coaching are still scarce. We are at the beginning of a new era, with a wide open field for research and new proposals. It is the role of academies welcoming and motivate their students to the innovative work at the moment in which Brazil can take the forefront in the field, having as main target the formation of competent leaders in agribusiness. From the few available data on the experiences of coaching, the authors count up those divulged by the ABC (Brazilian abbreviation for Brazilian Academy of Coaching). According to a survey organized by this institution, one study commissioned by a Fortune 500 company (annual list compiled and published by Fortune magazine that ranks the top 500 U.S. companies) about its own coaching program showed a return on investment of 529% discounted the significant and valuable intangible benefits. Another study, now produced by executives from Fortune 1000, showed that companies which received coaching had an average return of 5.7 times the amount spent on coaching. Yet another study, this time conducted in 2004 on executive coaching at Booz Allen Hamilton, a company of business consulting, showed a return of U.S. $ 7.90 for every dollar spent on the program [1]. One example of success in Brazil has been the Program for Managerial Development of Itaipu Company, which intensified the application of the methodology of coaching in strategic areas and other investments in training [7].

5   A Proposal for Coaching in Agribusiness: Agrienergy in Evidence

Contemporary society has the duty to reduce gas emissions from fossil fuels if it wants to perpetuate on the face of the earth. On the other hand, the depletion of fossil fuels leads inevitably to the search of renewable energy sources. The transition from fossil fuels by the named Green Revolution sets new conceptual paradigms of behavior. The existing and future projects will necessarily be reconstructed according to an ethic of sustainability linked to the idea of generalized wellfare in the world. Given various initiatives, both from governments and society which have been stimulating the production and use of biofuels, how should be the coach's participation in professional organization for the Green Revolution?

According to a recent survey of the Energy Research Company of the Ministry of Mines and Energy [6], renewable sources contribute 87.2 % to the country's energy matrix in the following manner: 81.2 % water, gas 5.8 %, 5.6 % sugarcane biomass, oil 3.1 %, nuclear 2.6 %, coal 1.3% and 0.4 % wind, which demonstrates the potential worldwide use of these sources in face of the increasing demand for energy. It is in this context that the use of sugarcane as an energy source sounds to be the best of the best, since the country has vast arable lands and appropriate environmental conditions to the crop. Nevertheless, although the prospects for continued performance of agrienergy continue promising, there are structural problems that can wither this success. The environmental issue, mainly because of deforestation that has been observed in areas of soybean expansion, creates a serious sustainability problem that the country must face, otherwise while "solving" a problem on one hand (the stubbornness to find that producing commodities we are in the way of the progress) we are creating another for future generations, more dangerous than the problem "solved". Here, the main function of coaching is to motivate leaders in the ethical sense of a parsimonious planning that exceeds the mere question of immediate financial account, looking at the total range of human needs in the short, medium and long term.

That is not all. In 2009 it was aproved the Federal Law 12.187 establishing the National Policy on Climate Change in Brazil with the objective to voluntarily reduce emissions in a rate projected until 2020 between 36.1% and 38.9%. This reduction will occur primarily by reducing deforestation in the Amazonia and Cerrado, adoption of good agricultural practices, renewable energy, biofuels and energy efficiency. Leaders need to understand that willful attitudes are actually coming from the extreme sense of responsibility and obligation to society and to future generations. One of the goals of coaching is to aid leaders to render this aspect a key factor for decision-making. With the establishment of an early coaching program for leaderships in managing agrienergy, adopted and widely disseminated by academies and governmental areas, we can start a solid, innovative and reputable project of bioenergy in Brazil, probably coming to be in near future a worldwide reference on sustainability.

With the formation of ethical managers it will be delivered in good hands the responsibility of strategic plannings for sustainable expansion of agrienergy, taking into account issues of paramount importance as the ecological impact of crops for large production of ethanol and biodiesel, the ethics of producing species that serve as well to feed the starving populations as to supply energy, the standards for responsible exploitation of the soil with mandatory quotas of replacement and, finally, honesty in choosing the best energy source for every situation well analyzed.

6   Conclusion

This work dealt with the application of coaching in agribusiness, specifically in the area of agrienergy. It discussed the contribution of coaching to the preparation of leaderships for the management of agrienergy. It showed the importance of creating new leaders strongly linked to the ethical principles of sustainability with regard to the exploitation of biomass as a renewable energy source. Although this is a research on a discipline considered new in the market, the work met favorable impressions on the coaching and pointed examples of success in other business areas, showing its potential for improving individual performance, personal satisfaction and indicators of productivity and quality. It is expected that the work shall stimulate greater interest in academic and business circles, motivating further research on the topic. To those people preferring to wait long years for data so that one can validate a pioneering model, this paper makes a prospect of intellectual action against the sedentary mindset that has prevailed in emerging countries.

References

1. ABC - Academia Brasileira de Coaching: Pesquisas Sobre os Benefícios do Coaching, http://www.abracoaching.com.br
2. Batt, E.: Cognitive Coaching: A Critical Phase in Professional Development to Implement Sheltered Instruction. Teaching and Teacher Education 26, 997–1005 (2010)
3. Corrêa, M., Abate, P.: O Processo de Coaching em uma Abordagem Transpessoal. Instituto Humanitatis, Campinas, Brasil (2007)
4. Downey, M.: Effective Coaching Lessons from the Coach's Coach. Thomson (2003)
5. Ely, K., Boyce, L., Nelson, J., Zaccaro, S., Hernez-Broome, G., Whymand, W.: Evaluating Leadership Coaching: A Review and Integrated Framework. The Leadership Quarterly 21, 585–599 (2010)
6. EPE - Empresa de Pesquisa Energética, http://www.epe.gov.br/Estudos/Paginas/default.aspx?CategoriaID=345
7. Itaipu Binacional: Relatório de Sustentabilidade (2011), http://www.itaipu.gov.br/responsabilidade/relatoriosdesustentabilidade
8. Karawejczyk, T., Cardoso, A.: Atuação Profissional em Coaching e os Desafios Presentes e Futuros nesta Nova Carreira. In: B. Téc. SENAC: a R. Educ. Prof., Rio de Janeiro (2012)
9. Chiavenato, I.: Gestão de Pessoas: E o Novo Papel dos Recursos Humanos nas Organizações. Elsevier, Rio de Janeiro (2004)
10. John, E.-M., West-Leuer, B.: Coaching in Multinational Companies an Interdisciplinary Analysis of a Management Consultant Case Narrative. Procedia - Social and Behavioral Sciences 82, 628-637 (2013)
11. Lages, A.: O Coaching, Algo que Funciona, http://www.vocevencedor.com.br/artigos/personalidades/o-coaching-algo-que-funciona
12. Motter Junior, M.: A Dimensão do Sucesso em Coaching: Uma Aálise do Contexto Brasileiro. Dissertação de Mestrado. FGV, Rio de Janeiro (2012)
13. Rogers, J.: Coaching Skills: A Handbook. Open University Press, Oxford (2007)
14. SEBRAE: Agroenergia, http://www.sebrae.com.br/setor/agroenergia
15. Sherpa Coaching: The executive coaching survey – evidence and interaction. Sherpa Coaching, Cincinnati (2014)
16. Toledo, M.: Decisões no Agronegócio. In: Costa Neto, P.: Qualidade e Competência nas Decisões. Blücher, S. Paulo (2007)
17. Whitmore, J.: Coaching for performance. Nicholas Brealey, London (2002)

A Multi-objective Mathematical Model Considering Economic and Social Criteria in Dynamic Cell Formation

Farzad Niakan, Armand Baboli, Thierry Moyaux, and Valerie Botta-Genoulaz

Université de Lyon, INSA-Lyon, DISP EA4570, 69621 VILLEURBANNE, France
{Farzad.Niakan,Armand.Baboli,Thierry.Moyaux,
Valerie.Botta}@insa-lyon.fr

Abstract. This paper addresses a Dynamic Cellular Manufacturing Systems (DCMS) problem considering both economic and social criteria, that is, the problem deals with the minimization of the total costs and maximization of social issues. We develop a bi-objective mathematical model of this problem in order to capture the trade-off between these two objectives. The strategic decisions considered in the model define the configuration of cells and part-families in each period. In order to solve our model, we design a new Non-dominated Sorting Genetic Algorithm (NSGA-II) as a meta-heuristic method. Our approach is illustrated on two samples of problems randomly generated.

Keywords: Dynamic cellular manufacturing system, Social responsibility, Multi-objective optimization model.

1 Introduction

Now a day most industries face with dynamic production because of the rapid product changes and reducing the life cycle of products. This observation leads to reorganize the manufacturing cells, from one period to each other, during planning horizons (several periods). On the other hand, in most of cell formation methods, the decision affect the reconfiguration of cells and definition of the part families just for a single-period which might not be optimal in another period. Therefore, this reason motivates researchers and manufacturers to study cellular manufacturing system (CMS) under dynamic condition that is named as Dynamic Cellular Manufacturing System (DCMS). Moreover, pressures from NGOs, social communities and media to respect social issues caused a lot of damages to some of well-known corporations such as McDonalds, Mitsubishi, Monsanto, Nestlé, Nike, Shell and Texaco. Corporate Social Responsibility (CSR) deals with effect of corporate activities on different social entities such as environment preservation, human rights, labor safety, etc. [1]. As the CSR aims to make trade-off between economical aspect and social issues to provide more welfare for the whole society. Despite the importance of CSR, social issues is one of the neglected affaires in the previous study involved in DCMS. This paper presents a new optimization model for DCMS, in which a trade-off between economic and social objectives is made.

B. Grabot et al. (Eds.): APMS 2014, Part II, IFIP AICT 439, pp. 46–53, 2014.

2   Literature Review

Many researches are related to DCMS, hence, we describe more recent studies here. Rheault et al. [2] presented the concept of dynamic environment in cell formation problem for the first time. Schaller et al. [3] developed a new model in DCMS to minimize Configuration and inventory cost of the system. They also proposed a Lagrangian relaxation to obtain the lower bound for their problem. Chen and Cao [4] proposed a new mathematical model in DCMS by considering inventory level. They solve their presented model by Tabu Search (TS) as a well-known algorithm. Tavakkoli-Moghaddam et al. [5] formulated a new nonlinear integer mathematical model in DCMS. The authors minimized constant and variable costs of machine and inter-cell movement costs as objective function. They solved their models by several meta-heuristic methods such as Genetic Algorithm (GA), Tabu Search (TS) and Simulated Annealing (SA) and compared obtained solutions to determine best method. Defersha and Chen [6] proposed a new comprehensive model in DCMS. They considered alternative routings, lot splitting and sequence of operations as well as workload balancing in their model. Safaei et al. [7] presented a fuzzy programming approach in CMS with dynamic and uncertain condition. The authors in this study assumed that demand of parts and availability of each machine have uncertain and fuzzy condition. Safaei and Tavakkoli-Moghaddam [8] formulated a new mathematical model in DCMS by focusing on the operational aspect of the cell formation problem. They made trade-off between production and outsourcing costs on the re-configuration of the system. Javadian et al. [9] proposed a multi-objective mathematical model in order to minimize the variation of cell load and various costs simultaneously. In order to solve model and obtain optimal Pareto frontier, they designed a non-dominated sorting genetic algorithm (NSGA-II). Saxena and Jain [10] proposed a new mixed-integer nonlinear mathematical model in DCMS to integrate important attributes of manufacturing such as the effects of machine breakdowns, production time loss cost effect, inventory holding, lot splitting; alternative process plan and parts sequence of operation. Kia et al. [11] developed a novel mixed-integer non-linear programming model in design of CMS with dynamic condition. The objective function of their model minimize total cost of each period such as costs of intra/inter-cell movement, machine relocation, machine procurement, machine overhead and machine processing. Majazi Dalfard [12] described a new nonlinear integer programming model for DCMS. The contribution of this paper is mentioned in two ways, the first one is related to apply implementation of the idea of more material flow in shorter distance in configuration of the cells and the second one is the proposition of new simulated annealing embedded in branch and cut as solving method. This investigation of literature shows that social issues is a neglected issue in DCMS while only economical aspect have been considered as objective of researches most of the time. Thus, in order to eliminate this deficiency, we develop a new multi-objective mathematical model for DCMS configuration by also considering social aspects.

3   Problem Description

In this section, we present a new bi-objective mathematical model in order to make a trade-off between two important objectives in DCMS. The first objective function is the minimization of relevant costs such as machine fixed and variable costs, inter-cell movement costs, intra-cell movement costs, machine procurement costs, machine relocation costs, salary of labors, etc. The second objective function is the maximization of the social criteria by increasing of job opportunities and decreasing of potential machines hazards for labor during the planning horizon.

Generally, the complex nature and interdependencies of social criteria make it difficult to measure them. In this study, an attempt has been made to select and extract social issues from ISO 26000 and GRI 2011 (credible sustainability reporting framework) [13],[14] that are closely related to DCMS problem and can be simply calculated by the mathematical model. As a result, (i) the number of job opportunities created and (ii) the number of potential hazards of machines were selected as social issues of our model. The first, social issue represents the variation of job opportunities, created due to the hiring and firing of labor and resulting in buying, selling and determining of time capacity of machines. The next one measures the average fraction of potential hazards of each machine, which is how many injuries, illnesses and damages each machine causes for labors according to ergonomic criteria. This value is a continuous number between 0 (the safest) and 1 (most dangerous) and can be defined by the Decision Makers (DM). For this objective, they can use a safety checklist, talking to workers, reviewing the manufacturer's information, and checking the injury and incident reports of each machine. Due to differences in the measuring units of the considered social criteria, the weighting method (normalized weighted) was applied in order to aggregate them as one objective. The main aim of this research work is to study the effects of social criteria on DCMS configuration. Therefore, other social issues may be replaced or involved in the model, based on a normalized weighted method.

3.1   Notations

Sets

p index for part type $(p = 1, ..., P)$

c index for manufacturing cells $(c = 1, ..., C)$

m Index for machine types $(m = 1, ..., M)$

j index for operation of part p $(j = 1, ..., O_p)$

h index for number of period $(h = 1, ..., H)$

Parameters

D_{ph} demand for part p in period h

B_p^{inter} batch size for inter-cell movement of part p

B_p^{intra} batch size for intra-cell movement of part p

γ_p^{inter} inter-cell movement cost per batch

$\gamma_p^{int\,ra}$ intra-cell movement cost per batch. It is assumed that $\forall p\ (\gamma_p^{int\,ra}/B_p^{int\,ra}) \prec (\gamma_p^{inter}/B_p^{inter})$

α_{mh} fixed cost of machine type m in period h

β_{mh} variable cost of machine type m in period h per unit of time

δ_{mh} relocation cost of machine type m in period h

T_{mh} time-capacity of machine type m in period h

UB maximum number of cells

LB minimum number of cells

L_m amount of labor that is required for machine type m

φ_{mh} purchase cost of machine type m in period h

ω_{mh} marginal revenue from selling machine type m in period h

S_m average fraction of potentially hazardous of machine type m

θ_{hd} normalized weighting factor of the total number of potentially hazardous of machine type m

θ_{jo} normalized weighting factor of the total number of job opportunities created

λ_h maximum percentage of variation labor level in period h

sa_{mh}^L salary of labor on machine type m in period h

t_{jpm} time required to process operation j of part p on machine type m

a_{jpm} 1, if operation j of part p can be done on machine type m ; 0 otherwise

Variables

N_{mch} number of machine type m assigned to cell c at the beginning of period h

K_{mch}^+ number of machine type m added to cell c at the beginning of period h

K_{mch}^- number of machine type m removed to cell c at the beginning of period h

I_{mh}^+ number of machine type m purchased at the beginning of period h

I_{mh}^- number of machine type m sold at the beginning of period h

hi_h number of labor hired in period h

fi_h number of labor fired in period h

x_{jpmch} 1, if operation j of part p is performed in cell c in period h by machine type m ; 0 otherwise

3.2   Mathematical Formulation

$$Min \ Z_1 = \sum_{h=1}^{H}\sum_{m=1}^{M}\sum_{c=1}^{C}\alpha_{mh}N_{mch} + \sum_{h=1}^{H}\sum_{m=1}^{M}\sum_{c=1}^{C}\sum_{p=1}^{P}\sum_{j=1}^{O_p}\beta_{mh}D_{ph}t_{jpm}x_{jpmch}$$

$$+\frac{1}{2}\sum_{h=1}^{H}\sum_{p=1}^{P}\gamma_p^{\text{inter}}\left\lceil\frac{D_{ph}}{B_p^{\text{inter}}}\right\rceil\times\sum_{j=1}^{O_p-1}\sum_{c=1}^{C}\left|\sum_{m=1}^{M}x_{(j+1)pmch}-\sum_{m=1}^{M}x_{jpmch}\right|$$

$$+\frac{1}{2}\sum_{h=1}^{H}\sum_{p=1}^{P}\gamma_p^{\text{intra}}\left\lceil\frac{D_{ph}}{B_p^{\text{intra}}}\right\rceil\times\sum_{j=1}^{O_p-1}\sum_{c=1}^{C}\left(\sum_{m=1}^{M}\left|x_{(j+1)pmch}-x_{jpmch}\right|-\left|\sum_{m=1}^{M}x_{(j+1)pmch}-\sum_{m=1}^{M}x_{jpmch}\right|\right) \quad (1)$$

$$+\sum_{h=1}^{H}\sum_{m=1}^{M}\sum_{c=1}^{C}N_{mch}L_m Sa_{mh}^L + \frac{1}{2}\sum_{h=1}^{H}\sum_{m=1}^{M}\sum_{c=1}^{C}\delta_{mh}(K_{mch}^+ + K_{mch}^-)$$

$$+\sum_{h=1}^{H}\sum_{m=1}^{M}I_{mh}^+\varphi_{mh} - \sum_{h=1}^{H}\sum_{m=1}^{M}I_{mh}^-\omega_{mh}$$

$$Max \ Z_2 = \theta_{jo}\left(\sum_{h=1}^{H}hi_h - \sum_{h-1}^{H}fi_h\right) - \theta_{hd}\left(\sum_{h=1}^{H}\sum_{m=1}^{M}\sum_{c=1}^{C}N_{mch}S_m\right) \quad (2)$$

$S.t.$

$$\sum_{c=1}^{C}\sum_{m=1}^{H}a_{jpm}x_{jpmch}=1 \qquad\qquad \forall j,p,h \quad (3)$$

$$x_{jpmch}\leq a_{jpm} \qquad\qquad \forall j,p,c,m,h \quad (4)$$

$$\sum_{p=1}^{P}\sum_{j=1}^{O_p}D_{ph}t_{jpm}x_{jpmch}\leq T_{mh}N_{mch} \qquad\qquad \forall m,c,h \quad (5)$$

$$N_{mc(h-1)}+K_{mch}^+ - K_{mch}^- = N_{mch} \qquad\qquad \forall m,c,h \quad (6)$$

$$\sum_{c=1}^{C}N_{mc(h-1)}+I_{mh}^+ - I_{mh}^- = \sum_{c=1}^{C}N_{mch} \qquad\qquad \forall m,h \quad (7)$$

$$\sum_{m=1}^{M}N_{mch}\leq UB \qquad\qquad \forall c,h \quad (8)$$

$$\sum_{m=1}^{M}N_{mch}\geq LB \qquad\qquad \forall c,h \quad (9)$$

$$\sum_{m=1}^{M}I_{mh}^+ L_m \leq hi_h \qquad\qquad \forall h \quad (10)$$

$$\sum_{m=1}^{M}I_{mh}^- L_m \leq fi_h \qquad\qquad \forall h \quad (11)$$

$$\left| \sum_{m=1}^{M} \left[\left(I_{mh}^{+} - I_{mh}^{-} \right) L_m \right] \right| \leq \left(\sum_{m=1}^{M} \left(\sum_{c=1}^{C} N_{mc(h-1)} \right) L_m \right) \lambda_h \quad \forall h \tag{12}$$

$$x_{jpmch} \in \{0,1\}, N_{mch}, K_{mch}^{+}, K_{mch}^{-} \geq 0 \; and \; int\, eger$$
$$I_{mh}^{+}, I_{mh}^{-}, hi_h, fi_h \geq 0 \; and \; int\, eger \tag{13}$$

Objective function (1) represents the minimization of total costs and includes eight terms: (i) machine fixed costs, (ii) variable machine cost, (iii) costs of the movements of parts between cells (inter-cell), (iv) costs of the movements of parts inside of cells (intra-cell), (v) wages or salaries, (vi) machine relocation cost, (vii) machine procurement cost and (viii) revenue from sales of the machines. Objective function (2) maximizes the social issues of DCMS during the planning horizon, and includes the maximization of job opportunities and minimization of the potentially hazardous of machines. Constraint (3) ensures that each operation of a part is assigned to just one machine and one cell. Constraint (4) guarantees that the process of each part assigned to the machines that can be done it. Constraint (5) ensures that the time capacity of each machine is not exceeded. Constraints (6) and (7) ensure that in each planning period the number of machines is balanced. Constraints (8) and (9) determine the maximum and minimum cell sizes according to the defined upper and lower bound. Constraints (10) and (11) calculate the number of labors that are respectively hired and fired. Constraint (12) guarantees maximum variation of the labor level in each period. Constraint (13) states that decision variables are non-negative, binary and/or integer.

4   Resolution Method

Since such a cell formation problem is defined as an NP-hard optimization problem frequently by researchers. In order to cope with complexity of the proposed model, a Non-Dominated Sorting Genetic Algorithm II (NSGA-II) [15], is designed as a meta-heuristic which is belonged to evolutionary algorithms. This algorithm starts with an initial solution (population) that is randomly generated and in each iteration new solutions (children) are produced from existing solutions with crossover and mutation operators. It should be noted that parents are selected by a binary tournament selection process. In each iteration, the objective value of each solution is compared against two strategies, namely, ranking and crowding distance. In order to improve the efficiency of the proposed NSGA-II algorithm and find best results, a Taguchi design is applied as a statistical technique to find the best combination of the parameters of NSGA-II. Hence, Npop (number of members in each population), MaxIt (number of iterations), CrR (crossover rate) and MuR (mutation rate) are tuned as four vital parameters of algorithm. Table 1 shows the results obtained here.

Table 1. Taguchi result for NSGA-II parameters

Parameters	*Npop*	*MaxIt*	*CrR*	*MuR*
Tuned value	40	50	0.8	0.3

5   Computational Result

In order to verify the performance and applicability of our proposed mathematical model two sets of different test problem in deferent size are generated:

Table 2. The size of samples

	P1	P2
$|O_p| \times |P| \times |M| \times |C| \times |H|$	5×6×6×4×5	9×8×8×7×7

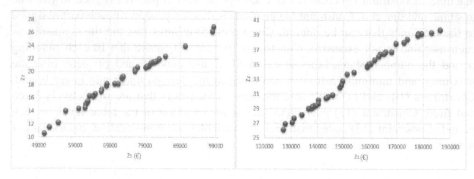

Fig. 1. Optimal Pareto Frontier for P1 (blue) & P2 (Red)

The generated test problems are solved by proposed NSGA-II algorithm which is developed by using MATLAB 2012a on a computer with Intel Core i5, 2.27 GHz and 4 GB RAM (See Figure 1).

Table 3. Computational Times (Sec)

	P1	P2
Computational Time	287.275	417.829

Figure 1 shows the optimal Pareto frontier and a set of solutions can be obtained from trade-off between minimizing total costs (Z_1) and maximizing of social criteria (Z_2). According to the priority of each objective the solution can be selected by DM. For each solution, we can have all information about the total cost of system, social issues, configuration and/or modification in each cell, part families, human resources, processing rout, etc. The analysis of optimal Pareto frontiers shows that the maximum of the social criteria (Z_2) can be obtain by increasing the total cost (Z_1) by about 90% in problem P1 and 60% in P2 with regard to the best economical solution.

6   Conclusion

In this paper, we propose a new bi-objective mathematical model in DCMS by considering social and economic criteria. Optimizing both criteria simultaneously requires making a trade-off between them. Due to the complexity of the problem, a NSGA-II algorithm is developed to solve the model and obtain Pareto frontier for the generated test problems. The proposed DCMS configuration model can be applied in batch production industries, such as part suppliers in automotive industry as well as small household electrical products.

Acknowledgment. The authors gratefully acknowledge the scientific and financial supports of Region Rhône-Alpes, France, ARC8 in developing this paper.

References

1. Carter, C.R., Jennings, M.M.: Social responsibility and supply chain relationships. Transp. Res. Part E Logist. Transp. Rev. 38, 37–52 (2002)
2. Rheault, M., Drolet, J.R., Abdulnour, G.: Physically reconfigurable virtual cells: A dynamic model for a highly dynamic environment. Comput. Ind. Eng. 29, 221–225 (1995)
3. Schaller, J., Selçuk Erengüç, S., Vakharia, A.: A methodology for integrating cell formation and production planning in cellular manufacturing. Ann. Oper. Res. 77, 1–21 (1998)
4. Chen, M., Cao, D.: Coordinating production planning in cellular manufacturing environment using Tabu search. Comput. Ind. Eng. 46, 571–588 (2004)
5. Tavakkoli-Moghaddam, R., Aryanezhad, M.B., Safaei, N., Azaron, A.: Solving a dynamic cell formation problem using metaheuristics. Appl. Math Comput. 170, 761–780 (2005)
6. Defersha, F.M., Chen, M.: A comprehensive mathematical model for the design of cellular manufacturing systems. Int. J. Prod. Econ. 103, 767–783 (2006)
7. Safaei, N., Saidi-Mehrabad, M., Babakhani, M.: Designing cellular manufacturing systems under dynamic and uncertain conditions. J. Intell. Manuf. 18, 383–399 (2007)
8. Safaei, N., Tavakkoli-Moghaddam, R.: Integrated multi-period cell formation and subcontracting production planning in dynamic cellular manufacturing systems. Int. J. Prod. Econ. 120, 301–314 (2009)
9. Javadian, N., Aghajani, A., Rezaeian, J., Ghaneian Sebdani, M.: A multi-objective integrated cellular manufacturing systems design with dynamic system reconfiguration. Int. J. Adv. Manuf. Technol. 56, 307 (2011)
10. Saxena, L., Jain, P.: Dynamic cellular manufacturing systems design—a comprehensive model. Int. J. Adv. Manuf. Technol. 53, 11–34 (2011)
11. Kia, R., Baboli, A., Javadian, N., et al.: Solving a group layout design model of a dynamic cellular manufacturing system with alternative process routings, lot splitting and flexible reconfiguration by simulated annealing. Comput. Oper. Res. 39, 2642–2658 (2012)
12. Majazi Dalfard, V.: New mathematical model for problem of dynamic cell formation based on number and average length of intra and intercellular movements. Appl. Math Model 37, 1884–1896 (2013)
13. ISO, Final Draft International standard ISO/FDIS 26000. Guid. Soc. Responsib (2010)
14. GRI, Sustainability Reporting Guidelines. version 3.1 (2011)
15. Deb, K., Pratap, A., Agarwal, S., Meyarivan, T.: A fast and elitist multiobjective genetic algorithm: NSGA-II. Evol. Comput. IEEE Trans. 6, 182–197 (2002)

Brazilian Consumers' Preference towards Pork

Sivanilza Teixeira Machado*, Irenilza de Alencar Nääs,
João Gilberto Mendes dos Reis, and Oduvaldo Vendrametto

Paulista University, Postgraduate Studies Program in Production Engineering,
Dr. Bacelar 1212, 04026-002 São Paulo, Brazil
sivateixeira@yahoo.com.br

Abstract. Brazilian pork supply chain has various challenges reflected by the consumers' preference perception, which is one of the lowest in the Western world. Several researches have shown that there is a divergence between consumer preferences and actual pork consumption. This study aimed to examine the Brazilian consumers' preference towards pork. An online survey was developed in order to investigate the marketing of pork at the retailer level. Analytic Hierarchy Process (AHP) was applied in order to classify the consumers' alternatives related to the frequency of eating pork, which were weekly, biweekly and monthly consumption. Results showed that the factors that most contribute to the purchase decision of pork are household income, commodity price and the characteristics related to meat quality.

Keywords: Food, Consumers preferences, Market, Brazil.

1 Introduction

Brazilian meat market follows a different pattern of the global market, especially in term of pork consumption [1], [2]. Several surveys related to Brazilian consumers' preference has shown that the most eaten meat are beef, poultry meat, fish, and the last one is pork [2], [3]. However, in the last years this scenario has been changing and due to marketing, and pork has been added more frequently to the table of consumers. It occupies nowadays the third place in the consumers' preference, behind the consumption poultry meat and beef [4].

The ultimate goal of supply chains is to meet the final consumer demands, which, in this specific case, determines the strategies of future business development of the meat market [5]. In order to identify the areas for improvement when analyzing supply chain, the first step is investigating the product attributes which are valued by consumers [6]. Research towards the consumers' demands brings up a new reality, which is a challenge to the supply chains that search for optimization of costs, and to improve the quality during the steps of production. This requires investments in production, marketing and distribution of products.

---

* The authors wish to thank the CAPES.

B. Grabot et al. (Eds.): APMS 2014, Part II, IFIP AICT 439, pp. 54–61, 2014.

It also implies in the involvement and training of stakeholders, in the use of new and efficient techniques [6], [7].

The Analytic Hierarchy Process (AHP) is a mathematical model to support decision making [8]. AHP is a method that is characterized by the ability to analyze a problem and propose a decision-making through the construction of hierarchical levels. The problem is analyzed by pre-established criteria. The criteria are decomposed into sub-criteria up to a determined level. These criteria are organized into a hierarchy descending where the ultimate goals should be at the top, followed by their sub-goals, immediately below, and; finally, the various possible outcomes or alternatives are selected. The scenarios determine the likelihood of achieving the goals [9], [10].

Consumers' surveys are an interesting tool to describe the actual scenario of the retail market, and the results may help the agribusiness to determine the consumers' preferences and expectancies towards the products which are offered in supermarkets shelves. This study aimed to analyze the consumers' preference towards pork. It was also verified the frequency of eating pork in three scenarios once a week, every two weeks, and once a month.

2   Methodology

2.1   Development of the Survey

To develop this work initially literature review was done in order to study the quality parameters and aspects of the consumption of pork in Brazil. This helped to select specific questions for the survey. In a second step, one field survey was conducted using the google docs tool, and it was sent to consumers using the internet resources (emails and social networking) during July-August 2013.

The survey was constituted of 17 closed questions, divided into two parts (1) six questions related to the social and economic status of the participant (gender, degree of education, marital status, age, household income, and the geographic region of residence), and (2) eleven questions related to several aspects of pork production and commercialization. The idea was to identify the relationship between the consumers' perception and the characteristics of the product consumption.

2.2   Calculating Size of Sample

For calculating the size of the sample, we considered the five regions of the country North, Northeast, Midwest, Southeast and South. The sampling error was set in 10% and the size of the population was obtained by [11]. The result reassured for each region was estimated 100 inhabitants. Sample distribution is shown in Table 1.

To perform the data analysis [12] the problem was organized as follows (1) the determination of the goal and definition of alternatives; (2) defining the structure of the decision tree based on the characteristics to be evaluated and

Table 1. Sample distribution by the gender, country' regions, age, degree of education, marital status, and household income

Response Options	North	Northeast	Midwest	Southeast	South	All	p-value
	17(2.8) *	31(5.2)	241(40.2)	200(33.3)	111(18.5)	600(100.0)	
Gender							
Female	9(2.7)	22(6.5)	130(38.9)	112(33.5)	61(18.4)	334(55.6)	0.686
Male	8(3.0)	9(3.4)	111(41.7)	88(33.0)	50(18.9)	266(44.4)	
Age (years)							
13-17	–	–	6(60.0)	2(20.0)	2(20.0)	10(1.6)	0.275
18-21	2(1.4)	4(2.8)	84(60.8)	20(14.5)	28(20.5)	138(23.0)	
22-30	5(2.6)	13(6.8)	74(39.2)	52(27.6)	45(23.8)	189(31.5)	
31-40	2(1.6)	6(4.8)	45(36.3)	55(44.3)	16(13.0)	124(20.6)	
> 40	8(5.7)	8(5.7)	32(23.1)	71(51.1)	20(14.4)	139(23.1)	
Education							
SC	13(4.2)	19(6.2)	78(25.6)	142(46.4)	54(17.6)	306(51.0)	0.020
SI	4(1.9)	6(2.8)	112(53.0)	36(17.2)	53(25.1)	211(35.2)	
M	–	4(8.1)	28(57.1)	14(28.5)	3(6.3)	49(8.2)	
F	–	(4.0)	19(76.0)	4(16.0)	1(4.0)	25(4.1)	
Sc	–	1(1.2)	4(4.4)	4(4.4)	–	9(1.5)	
Marital status							
Single	7(2.0)	17(4.8)	160(45.9)	94(27.0)	70(20.3)	348(58.0)	0.091
Married	8(3.7)	11(5.1)	64(29.8)	95(44.2)	37(17.2)	215(35.8)	
Other	2(5.4)	3(8.2)	17(45.9)	11(29.7)	4(10.8)	37(6.2)	
Household income							
< 1	1(4.5)	2(9.0)	12(54.5)	4(18.2)	3(13.8)	22(3.6)	0.052
1-3	3(1.5)	11(5.7)	93(48.3)	48(24.9)	38(19.6)	193(32.2)	
> 4	13(3.3)	18(4.6)	136(35.4)	148(38.5)	70(18.2)	385(64.2)	

* Consumers number and (%)

the selected alternatives; (3) build up a pairwise matrix for comparison between the attributes in different levels; and (4) using the priorities obtained from the comparisons to determine the weights and priorities of its lower level. The comparison is made as a table of 2 [13].

In order to give proper weight to each attribute ANOVA was applied to the set of data, and the test t-Student was applied to help to select the values for the weights to be applied to each criterion. The measures adopted for attributing the weights were based on the p-value found in the statistical analysis. For p-value < 0.0001 the weight was related to extreme importance, 9; p-value < 0.01 the weight was of demonstrated importance, 7; p-value < 0.05 indicated strong importance, 5; $p-value < 0.1$ indicated moderate importance, 3; and p-value > 0.1 the weight indicated equal importance, 1. This provided an association between the qualitative scales defined by Saaty [12] with the values found with statistical significance.

Table 2. Adopted scale of importance

Importance	Definition
1	Equal importance
2	Moderate importance
5	Strong importance
7	Very strong or demonstrated importance
9	Extreme importance
2, 4, 6, 8	Intermediate values

Model consistency was calculated considering the matrix is consistent if and only if:

$$\lambda max = n \tag{1}$$

However, the inequality $\lambda max > n$ always exists. Therefore, the average of the remaining eigenvalues can be used as a 'consistency index' (CI), which is the difference between λmax and n divided by the normalizing factor $(n-1)$.

The software Expert Choice was applied to the calculations of the Multicriteria Decision Analysis (MCD).

3   Results and Discussion

The results of the pairwise comparisons are summarized in Figure 1.

Results indicated that criteria with higher importance and contribution, in the consumers decision, in relation to the frequency of eating pork were associated to consumers preferences with 49%; while to the market was 45.1%. Brazilian pork consumer has a high preference to eat pork once a month. When focusing on the weekly frequency of eating pork, it was found that market and preferences had similar importance, with the exception of the social criterion (Figure 2).

The criteria followed by the performance bar in Figure 2 show the alternative for consumption of pork, which were once every two weeks and once a month. In this case, they converged to the same value indicating that this is the forecast consumption preference of the market. Studying the consumption of pork in a county within Southeastern Brazil [3], the authors found low consumption rate of pork (63.7%). The participants indicate they ate pork once every two weeks or once a month, agreeing with the results from this present study. Preferences and market are the criteria with higher weights in pork consumption (Figure 3). This suggests that Brazilian pork industry needs to invest in market' strategies in order to increase pork consumption.

Fig. 1. Summary of the criteria and sub-criteria weights

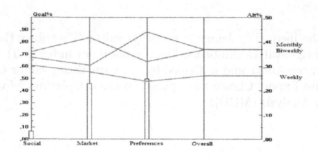

Fig. 2. General results from the criteria and computed weights

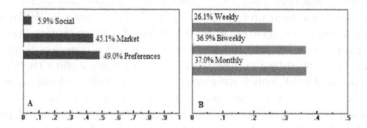

Fig. 3. Weights found for the attributes social status, market and preferences (A) and pork consumption (B)

3.1   Social Criteria

Despite the social criterion shows less value in the frequency of consumption of pork study, in the sub-criteria level household income represented 44.1% of the total weight, followed by the degree of education (28.6%), and marital status (16.3%). In the third level criteria of education, undergraduate was the one that most contributed to the decision of eating pork (68.2%). Marital status in this level was equally important (45.5%), as well as the household income above four minimum wages (48.1%). The criteria gender and age were not important in the decision analysis. Pork consumption changes and social demands affect the whole swine production supply chain [7]. New eating habits may require market alternatives [2], and the consumers search for food which are affordable and easy prepare are a real challenge.

3.2   Market Criteria

Within the sub-criteria involving the market scenario, the price obtained more than half of the weights (54.9%). This should be examined further within the pork supply in order to seek alternatives to keep the meat and its competitive derivatives market. Fixing modest price must be one of the primary goals of the chain [6]. Secondly, the criterion which presented more important was the way the meat is bought (24.8%), and the third level criterion in natura represented 75% in the frequency of consumption of pork. The consumer perception regarding the product was in third place (12.9%) while the product display were the most important (44.4%), the type meat cut (19.7%) and the product brand (13.2%). The understanding of consumers towards meat and its industrial derivatives is complex, and it is a critical issue for the food processing industry [14].

Although the place of purchase was not found to be an important decision, almost 60 of the answers bought pork at a supermarket, showing the relevance of this type of retailer and the trust established with consumers, which is a key factor in the purchase decision [2]. Another important issue is relates to the information in the label of the product, which helps the consumer while selecting food products.

3.3   Preferences Criteria

The criteria related to meat quality which is known as an important factor in the consumers buying decision was 77.8%. Within the sub-criteria the items such as sensorial factors, which are related to tenderness and texture contributed to this results with 59.8%. Sub-criteria associated to health issues an nutritional characteristics of had similar weight (10.4%), while ethnic factors did not impact in the frequency of consumption. This difference in the results occurs due to the notion the consumers perceive regarding tangible attributes at the time of purchasing [6], which reflects the purchasing decision on the product. The pork has good sensory attributes and consumers consider it a tasty meat [3]. Consumers also consider an expensive meat combined with low/average household income, which should influence the frequency of consumption.

With respect to the preferred types of meat by Brazilian consumers and the items which lead them to no consumption of pork, it was noted that beef is the direct competitor of pork (47.0%), agreeing with the demotivation of meat consumption. The sub-criterion 'no preference for pork meat' resulted in 33.6%. The poultry meat and fish are also important in the decision of buying high protein products (17.1%); however, the pork obtained a reasonable good score (13.9%). It is not yet clear which are the items that discourage Brazilian pork consumer, as the sub-criteria health, myths and various other concerns have together 33.6% of the weight in the purchasing decision, showing that there is still a lack of knowledge about the features and benefits of pork [3]. Apparently there are consumers still keeping the idea that pork is harmful to health, due to its fat content, and not appropriate to consumption in the Brazilian diet.

Cultural aspects and price also were found important in not buying pork, and they represented only 14.1% in consumers? preference. Religion was not an issue in the purchase decision.

3.4   Challenges of the Pork Supply Chain in Brazil

The challenges of the supply chain of pork in Brazil is beyond the aspects of meat production and processing, but it involves the factors surrounding the trade and changes in eating habits of Brazilians. Meat and its by products consumption may be affected by the quality characteristics (sensory, safety and convenience), and others as animal welfare, sustainable production process [6], [7], [14]. The analysis of consumer eating behavior and consumption frequency may need an overview on the supply chain in many relevant actions in product improvement, or yet in the development of new strategies to increase demand through consumer incentives. The considerable increase in the consumers and stakeholders demands in late years are impacting Brazilian pig production. Recent research shows that, at low cost (efficiency in the processes of production and processing, logistics) and high quality (food safety, low environmental impact, animal welfare, traceability) are primordial aspects to competitiveness [7].

Results from the present study showed that pork quality parameters were the most important factors with respect to the preference criteria, the criterion market price and household income from the social criterion. It is needed an integration between producers, industries and wholesalers/retailers, and government to develop strategies to facilitate the increase in pork demand.According to other studies, Brazilian pork consumption is related to household income [3]. Therefore, the income increase in the last year generates good opportunities in the meat sector [5].

Both prices of fresh and processed meat are highly valued and consumed by Brazilian. The key factor inhibiting the consumption increase is the price, and the price reduction implies in strategic decisions within the supply chain.

3.5   Conclusion

The results of the study allowed the identification of three key points related to the low consumption of pork by Brazilians, which are the household income, the price, and meat quality. The increase in pork consumption might depend on solutions to address the gap between socioeconomic variables and market.

References

1. Food, of the United Nations, A.O.: FAO statistical yearbook 2013: world food and agriculture (2013)
2. Horta, F., Eckhardt, O.H., Gameiro, A.H., Moretti, A.S.: Strategies of signalization of pork quality to final consumer. Current Agricultural Science and Technology 16(1-4), 15–21 (2010)
3. Santos, E.L., Santos, E.P., Pontes, E.C., Souza, A.P.L., Temoteo, M.C., Cavalcanti, M.C.A.: Consumer market of swine meat and derivatives in rio largo-AL. Acta Veterinaria Brasileira 6(3), 230–238 (2012)
4. Ministry of Agriculture, Lifestock and Food Supply.: Agribusiness projections: Brazil 2012/2013 a 2022/2023. MAPA., Brasilia (2013)
5. Kaimakoudi, E., Polymeros, K., Schinaraki, M., Batzios, C.: Consumers attitudes towards fisheries products. Procedia Technology 8, 90 – 96 (2013), http://www.sciencedirect.com/science/article/pii/S2212017313000753, 6th International Conference on Information and Communication Technologies in Agriculture, Food and Environment (HAICTA 2013)
6. Perez, C., Castro, R., Furnols, M.F.: The pork industry: a supply chain perspective. British Food Journal 111(3), 257–274 (2009)
7. Trienekens, J., Wognum, N.: Requirements of supply chain management in differentiating european pork chains. Meat Science 95(3), 719–726 (2013), http://www.sciencedirect.com/science/article/pii/S0309174013001137
8. Sureshchandar, G., Leisten, R.: A framework for evaluating the criticality of software metrics: an analytic hierarchy process (AHP) approach. Measuring Business Excellence 10(4), 22–33 (2006)
9. Belton, V., Stewart, T.J.: Multiple criteria decision analysis: an integrated approach. Kluwer Academic, Dordrecht (2002)
10. Barros, M.A., Moreira, M.A., Rudorff, B.F.T.: Analytical hierarchical process to identify favorable areas to the coffee crop agroecosystem at municipal scale. Pesquisa Agrop. Brasileira 42(12), 1769–1777 (2007)
11. Brazilian Institute of Geography and Statistics: http://www.ibge.gov.br
12. Saaty, T.: Decision making with the analytic hierarchy process. Int. J. Services Sciences 1(1), 83–98 (2008)
13. Deng, X., Hu, Y., Deng, Y., Mahadevan, S.: Supplier selection using {ahp} methodology extended by d numbers. Expert Systems with Applications 41(1), 156 – 167 (2014), http://www.sciencedirect.com/science/article/pii/S0957417413004958, 21st Century Logistics and Supply Chain Management
14. Troy, D.J., Kerry, J.P.: Consumer perception and the role of science in the meat industry. Meat Science 86(1), 214 – 226 (2010), http://www.sciencedirect.com/science/article/pii/S0309174010001865, special Issue: 56th International Congress of Meat Science and Technology (56th ICoMST), August 15-20, Jeju, Korea, (2010)

The Behavioural Effects of Extreme Events in Global Supply Chains

John Tainton and Masaru Nakano

The Graduate School of System Design and Management, Keio University,
Kyosei Building, 4-1-1, Hiyoshi, Kohoku-ku, Yokohama, Kanagawa, 223-8526, Japan
jrtainton@gmail.com, nakano@sdm.keio.ac.jp

Abstract. Extreme events and disasters have always been part of our lives, however as the world has become increasingly globalized over the past few decades in an attempt to reduce production costs and access new markets, these events are more likely than ever to affect businesses. It is therefore important for business to understand how these events affect their supply chains. This paper identifies behavioural patterns of manufacturing supply chains under the effects of extreme events such as financial crises and big earthquakes. A simulation model is then used to expose the underlying structure of each behavioural pattern.

Keywords: Sustainable supply chain, Extreme events, Supply chain risk management, Disruption behavior, Automotive industry.

1 Introduction

There are many studies in the context of sustainable supply chain including green, competitive and resilient to risk but less in risk management than in green and competitive issues (Nakano [1]). In the past 10 years, the world has experienced many disasters that have directly affected businesses and their ability to deliver goods and services, as well as support their customers. A recent example of this can be seen in the Great East Japan Earthquake and Tsunami of 2011. Toyota Motor Corporation is estimated to have lost production of nearly 700,000 vehicles as a direct result of the earthquake. These events affect not only the direct area but also cause changes in locations distant from the disaster location. Sheffi [2], Norrman & Jansson [3], and Tang [4] provide many alternative case studies for disruptions and risks in supply chains.

Business risks and their classifications have been provided by Nakano [5] and Goshal [6]. Nakano [5], and Manuj & Mentzer [7] transferred these classifications of business risk to supply chains. However the globalization of supply chains has continued to increase and is currently at an all-time high. Due to the distances and complexities of operating in a global environment, the risks in global supply chains are more extreme according to Manuj & Mentzer [8].

B. Grabot et al. (Eds.): APMS 2014, Part II, IFIP AICT 439, pp. 62–70, 2014.

2   Extreme Events

Extreme events have historically been defined in a general sense and have included the terms: rare, severe, unpredictable, large social impact and retrospective predictability Bier [9], Taleb [10], and Casti [11]. In the context of global supply chains the authors define an extreme event as: An event that causes bankruptcy or long term (>1 month) supply or demand disruption to a global supply chain.

Extreme events also have two phases of effects as shown in Fig. 1. "Primary effects" refers to the direct localized impact of a disaster. "Secondary effects" refers to the delayed effects that impact companies after an extreme event occurs.

Fig. 1. Primary and secondary effects of an extreme event

Currently there is a lack of understanding on how and why different extreme events result in different behaviours in supply chains. It is critical for companies and countries to understand the differences in the behaviour of secondary effects of disasters in order to better prepare itself for disaster recovery and business continuity.

This paper aims to identify disruption behaviour types based on how the disaster affects in the supply chain.

3   Behavioural Patterns

Every extreme event is different as each event targets different weaknesses in the overall system to relieve the complexity gap. Therefore it is useful to study a variety of historical events, especially ones in recent history, where supply chains have begun to be more responsive.

The automotive sector of Japan was analysed between 2006 and 2012. Data was collected from JAMA [12]. During this period, two extreme events affected the supply chain significantly. The first event was the financial crisis of 2008 and the resulting global recession. The second event was the Great Tohoku Earthquake of 2011 which significantly affected the production capabilities of Japanese manufacturers with the M9.0 shake followed by big tsunamis and the nuclear reactor meltdown. Fig. 2 below shows the export levels of Japanese passenger vehicles between 2006 and 2012. In the graph above, we can see the 2 distinct supply disruptions and we can recognize that their behaviour patterns are different. A third pattern also emerged during the investigation. Fig. 3 below shows US airline passengers and how the 9/11 attacks affected the airline industry [13].

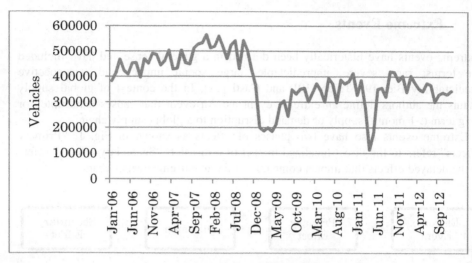

Fig. 2. Japanese Passenger Vehicle Exports

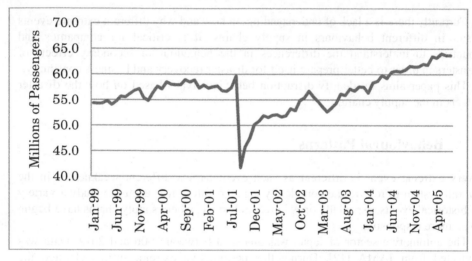

Fig. 3. De-Seasonalised US airline passengers

Three distinct disruptive event patterns have now been identified from the above cases.

- The first event type is based on the Great Tohoku Earthquake behaviour and is a supply disruption event. The disruptive pattern has a short impact period and a short recovery period making it look like a V. This profile is therefore called the V-curve.

- The second event type is based on the Financial Crisis behaviour and is a demand disruption event. The disruptive pattern has a short impact period, but a slow, long recovery period making it look like a mirrored, slanted L. This profile is called the L-curve.

- The third event type is based on the 9/11 passenger behavior and is a mixed disruption event. The disruptive pattern has a short impact period, with two distinctive recovery periods. The initial recovery is sharp, similar to that of a V-curve, but during the recovery, the recovery speed changes to that of a L curve. This behavior pattern looks like a miss-shaped W. This profile is called the W-curve.

Suganuma and Nakano [14] analyzes the dominant effect of the Great Tohoku Earthquake on supply chains in Japanese automotive industry quantitatively by simulating using the inter-industry relations, the Input-Output Table [15]. The study, however, only explains a supply disruption without inventories. Therefore a simulation model is proposed next section to analyze the above three types of behaviors with inventories.

4   A Simulation Model

A simple simulation model of the export of vehicles from Japan to the United States was built to better understand the structure, mechanism and sequence of disruption events. The model follows the structure as shown in Fig. 4 below.

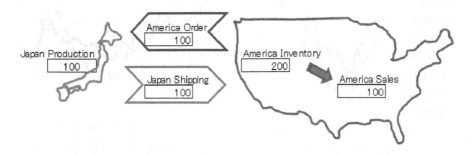

Fig. 4. Simulation Model Structure

The model contains 6 fields that change based on the previous month's data. The elements, descriptions and formulas are described in Table 1 below.

Table 1. Simulation model elements and descriptions

Field name	Description	Formula
America Demand	Demand for vehicles for the month	Input
America Sales	Actual number of vehicles sold	Min(Demand(t), Inventory(t))
America Inventory	Number of vehicle available to be sold	Inventory(t-1) – Demand(t-1) + Shipping(t-1)
America Target Inventory	The desired number of vehicles to keep as inventory	(Average (Demand(t-1, t-2,t-3))) *2
Japan Shipping	Number of vehicles in transit to America	Order(t-1)
America Order	Orders placed by America on Japan.	Target Inventory(t) – Inventory(t) – Shipping(t) + Sales(t-1) + Average (Demand(t-1, t-2, t-3))

The model was calibrated using two variables: the total number of vehicles sold in the US and the number of vehicles imported from Japan using real data for 2008 and 2009. The percentage change in sales was used as the input variable and the output variable was the number of imported vehicles.

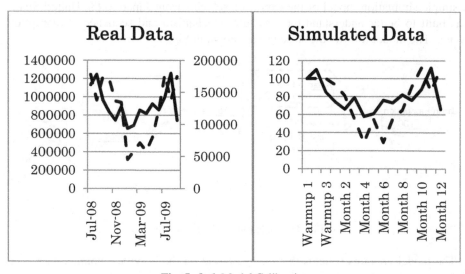

Fig. 5. & 6. Model Calibration

Legend for graphs below

■■■■■■■■■■■■■■■■ The dotted line represents the inventory level.

━ ━ ━ ━ ━ *The hashed line represents the supply level.*

━━━━━━━━━━━ The solid line represents sales.

The figs. 5 and 6 below show the results of the model calibration.

The key behaviour of the two graphs is similar. The difference in behaviour is due to the number of import vehicle only making up roughly 10% of the total sales in the US. For the model, however, it accounts for 100% making the model very sensitive to change. The inventory is not verified due to lack of real data.

The model includes a variable that limits the amount of change in production from one month to another. This variable needed to be calibrated in order to achieve the best fit. The calibration made use of the RMSE (Root Mean Square Error) method to determine the best maximum change in production. The best fit was obtained by minimizing the RMSE. A maximum change of 27% is therefore the best fit for this model. The reason for the large percentage difference is due to the model assumption that total vehicle sales and imported vehicle sales have the same behaviour.

5   Simulation Results

Six case studies were then conducted: two for each of the three behaviour types. For the supply disruption scenario, the supply was changed in Month 1 from 100 to 20 according to the big earthquake in 2011. For the demand disruption scenario, the demand was changed in Month 1 from 100 to 80, 60, 60, 70, 80, 90, and 100 according to the real data in the financial crisis in 2008. The mixed disruption scenario combined the changes in the demand supply disruption scenarios.

The 1st scenario has no limits, whereas the 2nd scenario has a maximum change to production from month to month. The diffusion through the network for supply disruption is: Supply -> Inventory -> Sales. Figs. 7 and 8 show simulation results for supply disruption cases. The figures demonstrate the effect of the change limit.

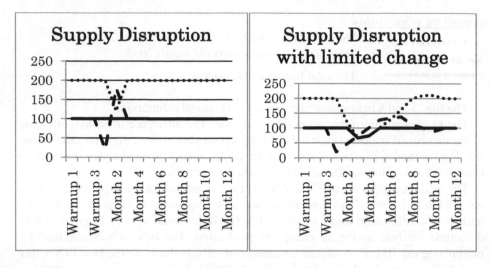

Fig. 7. & 8. Supply disruption cases

For demand disruptions, a drop in demand is shown to cause a big drop in order volume to production due to the increase in inventory levels as shown in Figs. 9 and 10. The diffusion through the network is: Sales -> Inventory -> Supply.

Mixed disruption event behaviour is very similar to that of demand disruption behaviour; however the results are more extreme as shown in Figs. 11 and 12.

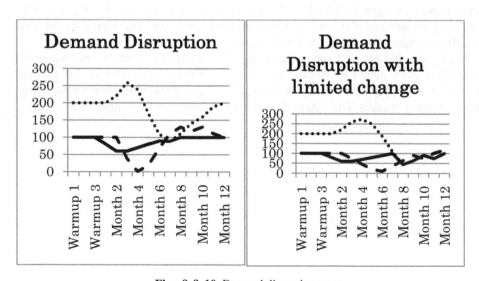

Figs. 9 & 10. Demand disruption cases

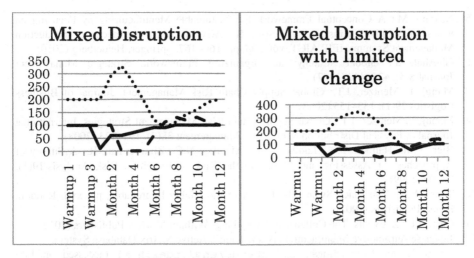

Figs. 11 & 12. Mixed disruption cases

6   Conclusion

This paper analysed the behaviour of automotive supply chains in Japan from January 2006 until December 2012. Three behavioural types were identified: Demand Disruption, Supply Disruption and Mixed Disruption events. A simulation model was then constructed to analyse the underlying structure and behaviour of the supply chain under the disruption events. The limitation of supply change was a key to model the supply chain. Demand disruptions were found to have relatively short impact periods; however the recovery periods are significantly longer. Supply disruptions were found to have short impact periods as well as short recovery periods. A future work is to consider mitigation measures for manufacturers.

Acknowledgments. This work was enabled to the financial support of the Ministry of Education, Culture, Sports and Technology of Japan.

References

1. Nakano, M.: Supply Chain Management for Sustainability. In: Lee, K.M., Kauffman, J. (eds.) Handbook of Sustainable Engineering, pp. 427–450. Springer Science+Business Media, Dordrecht (2013)
2. Sheffi, Y.: The Resilient Enterprise: Overcoming Vulnerability for Competitive Advantage. MIT Press (2005)
3. Norrman, A., Jansson, U.: Ericsson's Proactive Supply Chain Risk Management Approach after a Serious Sub-Supplier Accident. International Journal of Physical Distribution & Logistics Management 34(5), 434–456 (2004)
4. Tang, C.S.: Perspectives in Supply Chain Risk Management. International Journal of Production Economics 103(2), 451–488 (2006)

5. Nakano, M.: A Conceptual Framework for Sustainable Manufacturing by Focusing on Risks in Supply Chains. In: Vallespir, B., Alix, T. (eds.) Advances in Production Management Systems. IFIP AICT, vol. 338, pp. 160–167. Springer, Heidelberg (2010)
6. Ghoshal, S.: Global Strategy: an Organizing Framework. Strategic Management Journal 8(5), 425–440 (1987)
7. Manuj, I., Mentzer, J.T.: Global Supply Chain Risk Management. Journal of Business Logistics 29(1), 133–155 (2008)
8. Manuj, I., Mentzer, J.T.: Global Supply Chain Risk Management Strategies. International Journal of Physical Distribution & Logistics Management 38(3), 192–223 (2008)
9. Bier, V.M., Haimes, Y.Y., Lambert, J.H., Matalas, N.C., Zimmerman, R.: A Survey of Approaches for Assessing and Managing the Risk of Extremes. Risk Analysis 19(1), 83–94 (1999)
10. Taleb, N.N.: The Black Swan: The Impact of the Highly Improbable, pp. xxii. Random House Publishers (2007)
11. Casti, J.L.: X-Events: The Collapse of Everything. William Morrow Publishers (2012)
12. Japanese Automotive Manufacturers Association's Active Matrix Database System, http://jamaserv.jama.or.jp/newdb/eng/index.html (accessed on July 20, 2013) (in Japanese)
13. U.S. Department of Transportation, Research and Innovative Technology Administration, Bureau of Transportation Statistics (November 21, 2005)
14. Suganuma, S., Nakano, M.: Simulating the Dominant Effect of a Few Critical Sites on Supply Chains Using the Inter-industry Relations Table. In: Prabhu, V., Taisch, M., Kiritsis, D. (eds.) APMS 2013, Part I. IFIP AICT, vol. 414, pp. 485–492. Springer, Heidelberg (2013)
15. Ministry of Economy, Trade and Industry of Japan, 2005. Inter-Regional Input-Output Tables (March 26, 2010) (in Japanese)

Lean and Green – Synergies, Differences, Limitations, and the Need for Six Sigma

Jose Arturo Garza-Reyes[1], Gabriela Winck Jacques[2], Ming K. Lim[1], Vikas Kumar[3], and Luis Rocha-Lona[4]

[1] Centre for Supply Chain Improvement, The University of Derby, Derby, UK
{J.Reyes,M.Lim}@derby.ac.uk
[2] Center for Exact and Technological Science, Univates, Lajeado, Brasil
gwjacques@hotmail.com
[3] Bristol Business School, University of the West of England, Bristol, UK
Vikas.Kumar@uwe.ac.uk
[4] Business School, National Polytechnic Institute of Mexico, Mexico City, Mexico
lrocha@ipn.mx

Abstract. Historically, profitability and efficiency objectives have been the prevailing interest for organisations. However, the move towards green operations has forced companies to seek alternatives to combine these with green objectives and initiatives. Green lean is the result of this combination. The purpose of this paper is to critically discuss the green lean approach and the potential benefits of integrating Six Sigma to enhance its effectiveness. The paper is based on a literature review that discusses the synergies and differences of lean and green, and its main limitations. Departing from the limitations identified, the paper then proposes Six Sigma, and specially its problem solving methodology DMAIC, as an approach that may help in overcoming the limitations of green lean. Thus, the paper conceptually proposes Green Lean Six Sigma. It intends to offer academics, researchers and practitioners interested in lean and green with some initial conceptual ideas regarding their possible integration with Six Sigma.

Keywords: DMAIC, Environment, Green, Lean, Six Sigma, Sustainability.

1   Introduction

Recently, with the rise of lean manufacturing and the increasing concerns for the environment, the market dynamic has changed. Historically, productivity has been the dominant concern for manufacturing organisations [1]. However, with the growth of quality management tools and increase in customers' demands for better prices, besides environmental regulations, companies have been forced to rethink how they manage their operations and processes. Since the 1950s lean manufacturing has been gaining fame in a wide range of industries all around the world, disseminating the concept of waste reduction [2]. On the other hand, green initiatives have been adopted as a requirement to comply with environmental regulations and meet market and

B. Grabot et al. (Eds.): APMS 2014, Part II, IFIP AICT 439, pp. 71–81, 2014.
© IFIP International Federation for Information Processing 2014

social demands [3]. The combination of both seems logical, but two main questions arise from this: Can lean and green in fact work together? and Is their integration enough to effectively achieve positive productivity and green results at the same time?

As lean manufacturing aims at the elimination of waste in every area of production, design, supplier network and factory management [2], the combination of lean and green seems natural. Lean is a management approach that has helped companies to improve competitiveness and operational results [4]. Green, on the other hand, is an initiative that emerged from the concern for the environment and the rise of new regulations, norms, and standards on pollution prevention and control [3]. According to Dües et. al. [5], the combination of lean and green to form an integrated approach has only been discussed by a handful of experts and researchers. For example, Dües et. al. [5] carried out a study that aimed at exploring and evaluating, from a conceptual point of view, the existent relations between lean and the green concept. Similarly, Carvalho et al. [6] investigated the synergies and divergences between the lean and green paradigms, and their contribution towards a more sustainable and competitive supply chain. Also, Duarte and Cruz-Machado [7] examined how different business models can contribute to modelling a lean and green approach for an organisation. Mollenkopf et al. [8] investigated the relationship among green, lean, and global supply chain to provide a foundation for future researchers to build upon the company strategies. Hajmohammad et al. [9] tried to help understanding the roles of lean and supply management in relation to improving the firm's environmental performance. For this, Hajmohammad et al. [9] proposed and tested a conceptual model which suggests that the magnitude of environmental practices mediates the relationship between lean and supply management with environmental performance.

In general terms, these studies investigate the relationship between lean and green by highlighting the synergies and divergences between the two, their impact on supply chains' performance, and some of their theoretical implementation aspects when tried to be deployed seamlessly. Although the study presented in this paper also reviews and considers the synergies and divergences of lean and green, its main objective is to identify the possible limitations of the "green lean" paradigm as an integrated approach, and provide some research direction as to how these may be overcome. In light of this objective, the working methodology followed by this paper is based on a systematic review of the existent literature and exploring, analysing, and evaluating the information reviewed.

2   Literature Review – What is Green Lean?

Nowadays lean manufacturing is considered the most influential new paradigm in manufacturing [10] as empirical evidence suggests it improves the competitiveness of organisations [11] by reducing inventories and lead-times, and improving productivity and quality [12]. However, recently other concerns have emerged besides productivity, quality and cost. Today, sustainability has increasingly become important to organisations, as a result of concerns over environmental and social responsibilities [13]. These environmental concerns and the effectiveness of lean manufacturing contributed to the integration of the lean and green paradigms.

2.1   Synergies of Lean and Green

According to Mollenkopf et al. [8], lean companies, which deploy continuous improvement techniques, seem to be more likely to accept environmental innovations. As lean tends to emphasise waste reduction, it provides a better atmosphere to deploy green philosophies, initiatives and tools. In this scenario, the similarity between the two seems logical, waste reduction. However, green goes beyond waste reduction as it is also concerned with process efficiency, reduction of material consumption and recycling, and similarly as all the quality improvement approaches, one of its ultimate objectives is to improve customer's satisfaction. From this view, it is possible to identify several synergies between the lean and green concepts, these being: waste reduction, lead time reduction, and use of different approaches and techniques to manage people, organisations, and supply chain relations [5,8].

According to the literature [5,6,7], waste reduction has different meanings in lean and green. For the lean management philosophy, waste refers to any activity that does not add value to the product while for the green concept waste is related to the wasteful consumption of water, energy or any natural resource [7]. Despite their difference, non-value added activities can also be considered part of wasting energy and natural resources. For example, unnecessary or excessive transportation of products and/or raw materials is not only one of the seven wastes defined by lean but also a waste of non-renewable natural resources. Thus, both practices aim for less transportation in order to save cost (lean) and reduce the consumption of natural resources and CO_2 output (green) [6]. Another example is excessive inventory, which according to lean it is considered waste due to, in most of the cases, it increases lead time, prevents the rapid identification of problems, and discourages communication [14]. Excessive inventory also requires storage space and needs to be lighted, and sometimes heated or chilled, which from the environmental point of view may be considered a waste of energy if the lighting, heating and/or chilling is not done efficiently [15]. In this way, it is possible to relate all the seven lean wastes to those considered and defined by green initiatives. This indicates that lean can serve as a catalyst for green, facilitating companies the deployment of environmental policies and practices. In this way, a new strategy and management form can be defined through the compatibility between these two "cultures". However, there are still some areas in which lean and green cannot be combined as well as there are still some limitations when considering green lean as an integrated approach. The divergences between lean and green are discussed below.

2.2   Divergences of Lean and Green

Green initiatives can no longer be ignored by companies [5]. As it is discussed in the previous section, it is easier to deploy green initiatives in lean oriented companies, and the opposite is also valid. However, there are some objectives of both approaches that may not be possible to combine, for example: their focus, what are considered wastes, the customer, manufacturing strategies, and some practices adopted by organisations [5,8]. For this reason, despite the several synergies identified in the previous section, lean and green cannot perfectly be combined, they are concurrent and thus can effectively work together, but there are still some points that deserve attention when deploying both initiatives simultaneously.

According to Duarte and Cruz-Machado [7] the main difference between lean and green lies in how waste is defined, this divergence is also identified by Dües et al. [5]. As defined in the previous section, in lean, waste is any activity that does not add value to the customer while for green is the inefficient use of natural resources. Despite both meanings take the approach of working to improve processes at an operational level, lean focuses on workforce reduction, space reduction, increase capacity utilisation, higher system flexibility, and the use of standard components [7,16]. Whereas green ranges from practices like reduce, reuse and recycle (3Rs), rework, return, and remanufacture [7]. Another clear difference between lean and green is the type of customer [5]. Lean focus on cost and lead time reduction to satisfy customers [6] while in green, customers are more concerned as to whether the product that they are purchasing is helping them being more environmentally friendly [5,8]. Also, the green customer would not mind paying more for an environmental friendly product, which would not occur with lean customers.

So it is clear that lean and green are not completely compatible, there are still some areas in which they cannot be combined. However, those areas do not undermine or block the utilisation of lean and green simultaneously as an integrated management approach, contrariwise it gives the opportunity to improve both methods in a way that they can perfectly match. However, even as an integrated approach the green lean concept may still find some limitations that require attention, these are discussed in the following section.

3   Limitations of Green Lean as an Integrated Approach

There is little empirical evidence of the extent of adoption and effectiveness of green lean. However, based on the extensively documented success and expansion of lean into other industries different to manufacturing [10], and the fact that it is now accepted as a best practice for many organisations all around the world [17], it may be assumed that green lean will also be able to help organisations in achieving improvements that are not only financial and operational but also environmental oriented.

Nevertheless, despite this assumption, the integrated green lean approach may suffer from the same limitations as the individual lean and green philosophies. In the case of lean, Salah et al. [18] think about it as a toolbox that is comprised of methods and tools that are directed toward the reduction of waste. These methods and tools were not all invented with this methodology, but they have been systematically used in a structured manner to form lean [18]. Limitations of the pure lean approach include the fact that (1) none of its methods or tools control and monitor a process using statistical data, (2) they do not scrutinise variations in processes, which are utilised for making decisions, and (3) there are no practices associated with the use of quality and advanced statistical/mathematical tools to identify further problems still remaining in processes after waste has been eliminated [19,20]. Thus, Assarlind et al. [21] suggest that lean organisations do not extensively utilise data in decision-making and that they should employ methodologies that promote a more scientific approach to quality. In this context, the lack of a data driven approach to process improvement makes lean less accurate and precise [22]. Also, despite lean being an operational approach that focuses on fulfilling customer's needs [2], it does not present a structured approach to control processes, solve problems, and/or systematically conduct improvement projects. The lack of a systematic approach to conduct improvements may also complicate the definition of wastes as previously discussed in Section 2.

On the other hand, in the case of green, although decision support and expert systems as well as design for environment (DfE) methods are available to support this approach, Chan et al. [23] comment that their application to solve green problems is limited. For this reason, unlike lean, green cannot be thought as a toolbox but as an initiative underpinned by the utilisation of a single tool, life cycle assessment. This will result in the green concept not being able to "lend" lean, if integrated with it, methods and tools that could help overcome the lean drawbacks previously discussed. Thus, the limitations of lean will be inherited by the green lean approach.

Following the same reasoning, an integrated green lean approach will not only confront the limitations of lean but also the limitations and challenges of the green approach. From the discussion of Nunes and Bennett [24] on environmental management systems (EMS) and green operations, it is possible to imply that the main limitations of green are not related to operational but strategic aspects. For example, Nunes and Bennett [24] suggest that although there is clear and strong reasons as to why organisations should implement green (i.e. through environmental management practices), it is still unclear to them how to make green decisions when a company faces a challenging strategic decision regarding where to make the investment when there are involved various possibilities (i.e. in facilities, manufacturing, logistics, marketing, process and product design, etc.). Another strategic challenge of green is how to implement its initiatives in a way in which they also meet corporate goals of profitability and other business requirements [24]. This is because in some cases, green activities will not return a profit from individual initiatives or be matched with corporate objectives.

Besides these strategic challenges, green can also present operational limitations. Joseph [25] comments that two of the most common include conversion expense and more expensive products. For example, it can be expensive for an organisation to go green initially as new energy saving equipment (i.e. solar panels) may need to be bought and installed. Unfortunately, cost reductions in energy savings gained by going green are not always enough to offset the initial capital conversion costs [25]. In addition, moving into the use of more environmentally friendly products   can lead to more expensive products for consumers.

Similarly as with the inheritance of the lean limitations by the green lean approach, the limitations and challenges of the green concept will also be passed on to the integrated green lean approach, without lean being able to contribute to overcome some of them. For instance, in terms of prioritising strategic green investment decisions, lean lacks of a prioritisation approach [26] to support a decision of this type. In addition, since lean lacks of a project-based approach to improvement and thus a planning phase, it may not help in aligning the green lean initiatives to corporate goals of profitability as well as to other business requirements. This lack of a project-based approach may also contribute to lean not being able to specifically focus and dedicate a project to identify the most cost effective and environmentally friendly equipment and raw material, which could offset and/or limit the negative impact on operational and product costs that these may have.

The individual limitations and challenges of lean and green, also inherited by the integrated green lean approach, and the lack of methods and/or tools from the "other" concept (i.e. lean or green) to overcome these, calls for the integration of additional methods and tools capable of contributing to the reduction or elimination of these challenges and limitations. These "other" methods and tools can come from Six Sigma.

4   Green Lean Six Sigma?

Initiated by Motorola in the 1980s, Six Sigma is now considered one of the most important developments to process improvement of the last decades [27]. Since then, Six Sigma has gained wide popularity among organisations worldwide, with most Fortune 500 companies using it [27] not only to improve their financial and operational performance but also customer satisfaction through the reduction of defective products and services. Six Sigma is a systematic, data and statistical driven problem solving and improvement methodology that intends to contain defects to 3.4 per every million opportunities, achieving with this lower costs and competitive operations. Garza-Reyes et al. [28] suggest the define, measure, analyse, improve, and control (DMAIC) cycle as one of the Six Sigma's distinctive and essential approaches to problem solving and process improvement. The DMAIC model indicates, step by step, how problems should be addressed, grouping quality and statistical tools, while establishing a standardised routine to solve problems [28].

The systematic, data and statistical driven characteristic of Six Sigma could complement the green lean approach and contribute in overcoming the limitations and challenges of this concept highlighted in Section 3. For example, the use of the DMAIC model could provide green lean with a more specific and holistic project based orientation to the implementation and achievement of green initiatives, which could then be continuously improved through kaizen. Thus, the Six Sigma's DMAIC methodology could be generalised as the umbrella under which green initiatives are implemented, managed, sustained and improved, see illustration in Figure 1. In this context, DMAIC will provide a unique characteristic of sequencing and linking lean and Six Sigma's methods and tools during the five stages of DMAIC when conducting a green project. In this way, lean and Six Sigma will contribute with the provision of methods and tools to help identify, define, prioritise, conduct, manage, achieve, sustain, and improve green initiatives.

In particular, the *Define* phase of DMAIC consists in identifying, prioritising and selecting the right project as well as clarifying the project's scope and defining goals [27,28]. Thus, at a strategic level, the Define phase of DMAIC could help an organisation to objectively prioritise green initiatives and investments in order to determine in which organisational activity/function (i.e. facilities, manufacturing, logistics, marketing, process, and product design) they should be deployed first, and/or in terms of which parameters (i.e. energy consumption, CO_2 emissions, water consumption, etc.) should be targeted. Specific tools promoted by Six Sigma to achieve this may include Pareto analysis, project ranking matrix, project selection matrix, quality function deployment, project assessment matrix, Pareto priority index, cost benefit analysis, analytical hierarchy process (AHP), theory of constraints, etc. This scientific and data driven approach to defining and prioritising green initiatives would also ensure the selection of the right projects and investments, as well as it will aid in clarifying the objectives, scope, and resources of the green initiatives. This will also ensure their alignment with corporate goals.

The *Measure* stage of DMAIC consists in establishing reliable metrics to help monitoring key process characteristics, the scope of the parameters considered, and their performance in order to understand their progress towards the objectives [29]. At an operational level, the Measure phase of DMAIC will "force" an organisation, as an initial step, to identify the similarities, unify, and thus define the lean and green wastes (i.e. excessive CO_2 emissions, water consumption, energy consumption, raw material consumption, inventory, transportation, etc.) into those that will be targeted for reduction/elimination. In addition, specific metrics (i.e. for electricity: KWh, green energy coefficient, energy reuse factor, carbon usage effectiveness, etc.; for CO_2 emission – tonns/week, etc.) for every waste will also need to be determined and agreed. Once that wastes and their metrics have been defined, current lean value stream studies can be conducted to identify the sources of waste and establish the scope of the parameters, as well as their current performance. Based on the DMAIC approach, the latest will be used to help monitoring progress towards the objectives established in the Define phase. This phase of DMAIC will start helping in overcoming the "lack of a data driven approach" limitation of green lean as quantitative data will be collected, analysed, and used as a comparative improvement base.

The *Analyse* phase of DMAIC involves evaluating and identifying key causes and process determinants [29]. If integrated with green lean, this phase of DMAIC will contribute in determining the root causes of wastes in the parameters monitored. Six Sigma methods and tools based on inferential statistics such as scatter plots, analysis of variance (ANOVA), hypothesis testing, regression analysis, design of experiments (DOE), among others, will provide a quantitative-scientific base for the analysis. Other less quantitative, but still effective and systematic, methods that may include cause-and-effect diagrams and "5 whys" could also be used in this stage to uncover wastes and the excessive (i.e. unnecessary) use of energy, water, raw material, CO_2, etc.

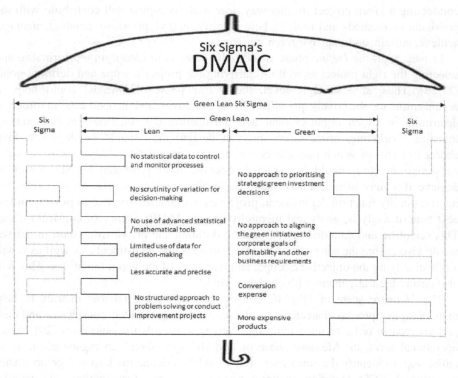

Fig. 1. Overcoming the green lean limitations through the integration of Six Sigma

The *Improve* phase of DMAIC consists of proposing, testing, and implementing creative solutions to eliminate the root causes of problems [27]. Methods and tools such as 5S, brainstorming, corrective action matrix, poka-yoke, among others, can be used to stimulate the development of solutions to reduce/eliminate the wastes identified in the Measure phase. In many cases, the solutions to tackle wastes could be as simple as, for example, installing occupancy sensors to turn lights off in offices when not needed, and reprogramming thermostats to avoid the unnecessary use of heating. Although determining the need to carry out improvements of this type may not require the systematic implementation and conduction of green initiatives, the Six Sigma's DMAIC approach will provide a platform to take decisions and courses of action based on real and scientific facts. Once embedded within the organisation's culture, this fact and scientific driven approach to decision-making will not only be used for green initiatives but also as part of the entire managerial approach of the organisation.

Finally, the *Control* phase involves setting the mechanisms for ongoing monitoring and institutionalising improvements [17]. After the objectives set in the Define stage have been achieved, methods such as Statistical Process Control (SPC) may help to monitor critical environmental parameters such as energy, water and raw material consumption, CO_2 emissions, etc. In this case, SPC control charts will aid in statistically setting specification limits based on the maximum, average, and minimum consumption of the parameters monitored. This will allow differentiating the common and inherent variation in the consumption and use of these parameters from excessive uses due to assignable causes. In this context and based on the SPC methodology, investigations and corrective actions will be taken, specially, if the consumption of energy, water and raw material, or CO_2 emissions exceed the maximum specified limit. SPC will also help to scrutinise and thus understand the degree and causes of variation in the consumption/use of these, which will help organisations in decision-making and assisting in the diagnosis of problems. The formal documentation of all the improvement actions taken and best practices, as suggested by the Control stage of DMAIC, will ensure that all employees perform the processes in a uniform manner, which will contribute to the reduction of variability in the consumptions of the green parameters considered.

5   Conclusions

Environmental sustainability is one of the strategic imperatives that nowadays must be aligned to the traditional organisational priorities of profitability and efficiency as well as customer satisfaction, quality, and responsiveness. The green lean approach has been proposed with the intention of achieving such alignment. However, conceptual and empirical studies regarding green lean are limited, and those conducted have focused on investigating aspects such as the synergies and divergences between the two, their impact on supply chains' performance, and some of their theoretical implementation issues. This paper has mainly focused on discussing the possible limitations of green lean as an integrated approach, which have been determined to be inherited from the individual limitations of every approach, and the fact that the "other" is unable to contribute in overcoming them. For this reason, the paper conceptually proposes and argues the integration of Six Sigma as a possible solution to address these limitations, complement the green lean approach, and enhance its effectiveness.

The paper has provided some initial discussion as to how integrating Six Sigma and creating a green lean Six Sigma unified approach could benefit green lean, but further research can be directed towards the proposal of a conceptual model for their integration, followed by its test and investigation into its empirical relevance to and effectiveness in industry.

References

1. Mohanty, R.P., Deshmukh, S.G.: Work Study Managing Green Productivity: A Case Study. Work Study 48(5), 165–169 (1999)
2. Chauhan, G., Singh, T.P.: Measuring Parameters of Lean Manufacturing Realization. Measuring Business Excellence 16(3), 57–71 (2012)
3. Digalwar, A.K., Tagalpallewar, A.R., Sunnapwar, V.K.: Green Manufacturing Performance Measures: An Empirical Investigation from Indian Manufacturing Industries. Measuring Business Excellence 17(4), 59–75 (2013)

4. Herron, C., Hicks, C.: The Transfer of Selected Lean Manufacturing Techniques from Japanese Automotive Manufacturing into General Manufacturing (UK) through Change Agents. Robotics and Computer-Integrated Manufacturing 24(4), 524–531 (2008)
5. Dües, C.M., Tan, K.H., Lim, M.: Green as the New Lean: How to Use Lean Practices as a Catalyst to Greening your Supply Chain. Journal of Cleaner Production 40, 93–100 (2013)
6. Carvalho, H., Duarte, S., Cruz-Machado, V.: Lean, Agile, Resilient and Green: Divergences and Synergies. International Journal of Lean Six Sigma 2(2), 151–179 (2011)
7. Duarte, S., Cruz-Machado, V.: Modelling Lean and Green: A Review from Business Models. International Journal of Lean Six Sigma 4(3), 228–250 (2013)
8. Mollenkopf, D., Stolze, H., Tate, W., Ueltschy, M.: Green, Lean, and Global Supply Chains. International Journal of Physical Distribution & Logistics Management 40(1/2), 14–41 (2010)
9. Hajmohammad, S., Vachon, S., Klassen, R.D., Gavronski, I.: Lean Management and Supply Management: Their Role in Green Practices and Performance. Journal of Cleaner Production 39, 312–320 (2013)
10. Garza-Reyes, J.A., Parkar, H.S., Oraifige, I., Soriano-Meier, H., Harmanto, D.: An Empirical-Exploratory Study of the Status of Lean Manufacturing in India. International Journal of Business Excellence 5(4), 395–412 (2012)
11. Abdul Wahab, A.N., Mukhtar, M., Sulaiman, R.: A Conceptual Model of Lean Manufacturing Dimensions. Procedia Technology 11, 1292–1298 (2013)
12. Hines, P., Holweg, M., Rich, N.: Learning to Evolve: A Review of Contemporary Lean Thinking. International Journal of Operations and Production Management 24(10), 994–1011 (2004)
13. Sezen, B., Çankaya, S.Y.: Effects of Green Manufacturing and Eco-Innovation on Sustainability Performance. Procedia – Social and Behavioral Sciences 99(6), 154–163 (2013)
14. Hines, P., Rich, N.: The Seven Value Stream Mapping Tools. International Journal of Operations and Production Management 17(1), 46–64 (1997)
15. Franchetti, M., Bedal, K., Ulloa, J., Grodek, S.: Lean and Green: Industrial Engineering Methods are Natural Stepping Stones to Green Engineering. Industrial Engineer 41(9), 24–29 (2009)
16. Pettersen, J.: Defining Lean Production: Some Conceptual and Practical Issues. The TQM Journal 21(2), 127–142 (2009)
17. Forrester, P.L., Shimizu, U.K., Soriano-Meier, H., Garza-Reyes, J.A., Cruz Basso, L.F.: Lean Production, Market Share and Value Creation in the Agricultural Machinery Sector in Brazil. Journal of Manufacturing Technology Management 21(7), 853–871 (2010)
18. Salah, S., Rahim, A., Carretero, J.A.: The Integration of Six Sigma and Lean Management. International Journal of Lean Six Sigma 1(3), 249–274 (2010)
19. Devane, T.: Integrating Lean Six Sigma and High-Performance Organizations: Leading the Charge toward Dramatic, Rapid, and Sustainable Improvement. John Wiley & Sons Inc., N.Y. (2004)
20. Lee, J.H., Garza-Reyes, J.A., Kumar, V., Rocha-Lona, L., Mishra, N.: A Comparative Study of the Implementation Status of Lean Six Sigma in South Korea and the UK. In: Advances in Sustainable and Competitive Manufacturing Systems. Lecture Notes in Mechanical Engineering, pp. 1489–1502 (2013)
21. Assarlind, M., Gremyr, I., Bäckman, K.: Multi-faceted Views on a Lean Six Sigma Application. International Journal of Quality and Reliability Management 29(1), 21–30 (2012)

22. Hilton, R.J., Sohal, A.: A Conceptual Model for the Successful Deployment of Lean Six Sigma. International Journal of Quality and Reliability Management 29(1), 54–70 (2012)
23. Chan, C.C.S., Yu, K.M., Yung, K.L.: Green Manufacturing Using Integrated Decision Tools. In: The IEEE International Conference on Industrial Engineering and Engineering Management, Venetia, Italy, December 7-10 (2010)
24. Nunes, B., Bennett, D.: Green Operations Initiatives in the Automotive Industry: An Environmental Reports Analysis and Benchmarking Study. Benchmarking: An International Journal 17(3), 396–420 (2010)
25. Joseph, C.: The Disadvantages of Going Green for a Corporation. Demand Media (April 14, 2014),
    http://smallbusiness.chron.com/
    disadvantages-going-green-corporation-3318.html
26. Bendell, T.: A Review and Comparison of Six Sigma and the Lean Organisations. The TQM Magazine 18(3), 255–262 (2006)
27. Garza-Reyes, J.A., Oraifige, I., Soriano-Meier, H., Harmanto, D., Rocha-Lona, L.: An Empirical Application of Six Sigma and DMAIC Methodology for Business Process Improvement. In: Proceedings of the 20th International Conference on Flexible Automation and Intelligent Manufacturing (FAIM), San Francisco, CA, US, July 12-14 (2010)
28. Garza-Reyes, J.A., Flint, A., Kumar, V., Antony, J., Soriano-Meier, H.: A DMAIRC Approach to Lead Time Reduction in an Aerospace Engine Assembly Process. Journal of Manufacturing Technology Management 25(1), 27–48 (2014)
29. Basu, R.: Implementing Quality – A Practical Guide to Tools and Techniques. Thomson Learning, London (2004)

Small and Medium Enterprises in Brazil: A Comprehensive Study of the Manager's View of the Business

Fabio Papalardo, L. Claudio Meirelles,
José Benedito Sacomano, and Jayme de Aranha Machado

Paulista University-UNIP, Post-Graduate Program in Production Engineering, Brazil
{Fabio Papalardo,fabio.eng.unip}@gmail.com

Abstract. Small and Medium Enterprises (SME) in Brazil are factors of great economic importance, for they represent employment for more than fifty six million people. When we consider the country's overall population of two hundred million inhabitants we can understand the magnitude of such economic segment, and it means that it is responsible for the sustainability of the employment structure. As in any economic activity, it depends on efficiency and that means specialized management, low costs, low waste, high competitiveness: these factors assure the sustainability of such enterprises in the market. Apart from these factors, which are internal to the management, there are external factors that influence the enterprises' performance, such as policies to foster development, financial cost, qualified work force, the tax burden, value of local currency weighted against foreign currencies, and other factors. Management compliant with this matrix of factors is dependent upon the managers' vision. This comprehension by the managers about the different internal and external factors that influence the enterprise shall define the organizational culture that will prevail in this type of enterprises. For this study, we have researched the vision of SME's managers as far as internal and external factors that influence the management of enterprises.

Keywords: Small ad Medium Sized Enterprises 1, Sustainability Factors 2, Cultural Factors 3.

1 Introduction

Small and Medium Sized Enterprises (SMEs) represent 99% of the Brazilian enterprises [1]. They are responsible for 20% of the Gross National Product (GNP) with 320 billion Dollars and generate 60% of all formal employment posts in Brazil, that is, 56.4 million. These data are by themselves relevant for the Country's economic and social development.

The vision of SMEs managers, the way they see the market, the way they face administration, the importance of these enterprises and above all, the factors necessary to their sustainability, show the possibility of analyzing the segment, as far as its consolidation in the market, according to the time of permanence or survival in the

B. Grabot et al. (Eds.): APMS 2014, Part II, IFIP AICT 439, pp. 82–89, 2014.

market. In Brazil the mortality level is around 25%, after two years of existence [1]. In the worldwide landscape, Brazil is faring well; best levels are: Slovenia 22%, Austria 24%, followed by Spain 31%, Italy 32%, Portugal 49% and Holland 50%. Of course, these countries have different markets, with their characteristics and particularities.

Our analysis takes into account factors that influence the performance of SMEs in two aspects, internal factors, that relate to their operations, divisions and functions; as well as external factors, as public policies, the financial market, among others.

The managers' vision are indicative of how they understand the real aspects of SMEs, but not necessarily how SMEs should be managed, and how they understand the policies for development and sustainability of such an important economic sector, as the SMEs are.

1.1 Theoretic Foundation

Studies about Small and Medium Sized Enterprises are frequently conducted, due to their importance in the development of countries and regions.
Studies report differences of management in large enterprises and SMEs.
The administration of a SME has its particularities; the greatest difference between large enterprises and SMEs is that the SMEs are concerned with day-to-day operational activities, but large enterprises follow strategic planning [1].

Managers do not realize the economic potential of being responsible to the social issues, to the environment and, as particularly it was studied in the research, to the health of the employees. Although the first responsibility of a manager is generating profits, companies can at the same time contribute to social and environmental objectives, through integrating corporate social responsibility as a strategic investment into their core business strategy, their management instruments and their operations [2].
Another particularity of SMEs is the cultural difficulty of cooperation and the establishment of Local Production Consultations, which, a relationship of cooperation among SMEs would ease up access to resources one does not have, as well as would strengthen up one´s own resources and increase the potential of an enterprise's strong aspects. Besides, cooperation between enterprises can represent a manner of developing SMEs competitive advantage and such may become a link to competitiveness [3].

The funds raised are used by small and medium companies in their development, the most innovative, counseling and training staff. In the development of business by SMEs are most helpful database consulting, sample manuals for obtaining financial support and to promote innovation. The current business environment is referred to as hyper-competitive and global. If there are any changes in it, these will be permanent rather of the crisis character than towards certainty and possibility prediction of future development [4].

Informational barriers are the core bottleneck inhibiting energy efficiency improvements in SME sector. Financial and organizational barriers also influence a company's energy saving activities. Data point out three additional barriers to energy saving activities: the role of family ownership structures, lax enforcement of government regulations and the absence of government support as well as a lack of skilled labor [5].

All these factors form a picture that must be studied in all its particularities, so that policies and management systems may be implemented.

2   Methodology

The methodology presented used the comprehensive method, the comprehensive analysis encourages the integration of the largest possible number of elements and connections. This method identifies opinions of managers of small and medium sized enterprises, as far as their sustainability in the Brazilian market [6]. The research, of exploratory character, used the study of a case with data collection through a non structured interview with questions and answers.

Non structured interviews identified the factors the managers considered relevant for the administration of small and medium sizes Brazilian enterprises.

The theme of this proposal represents a contribution to the ways a manager of a small and medium sized Brazilian enterprise evaluates a business.

The research was conducted using the Likert measuring scale for relevant sustainability factors of the enterprise in the market, as well as an evaluation after attributing points 0 to 10 applicable to the enterprise's sectors, depending on each sector importance for administration and performance.

As far as the Likert scale, the number of possible answers is five, keeping in mind that the possibility of answers can be odd or even: an odd answer allows the respondent, for any reason, to keep himself neuter; an even answer does not allow it – the respondent has to take a position.

The format was: 1 – Of no relevance; 2 – Of some relevance; 3 – Relevant; 4 – Of much relevance; 5 – Necessary.

Research was conducted in four areas: Region of Fortaleza and Juazeiro do Norte, in the State of Ceará; the region of Montes Claros and the region of Araxá, in the State of Minas Gerais. The regions of Araxá and Montes Claros, although they both are in the State of Minas Gerais, have different characteristics as far as entrepreneurial culture: Araxá is in the Triângulo Mineiro, an area under the influence of the Southeast Region, and Montes Claros is in the northern part of the State of Minas Gerais, culturally connected to the Region of the Sertão Mineiro and Southern Bahia. The region of Fortaleza and Juazeiro do Norte has cultural aspects typically of the Northeastern Region.

This diversity has the objective of avoiding any regional aspect to the research.

3   Results and Discussion

Fifty seven enterprises were researched in the four regions, and the companies were classified as wholesalers, retailers, industry and services.

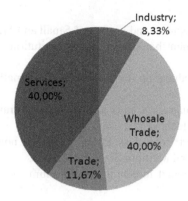

Fig. 1. Profile of the Researched Enterprises

Non structured interviews indicated that the areas of activity considered essential by the managers of small and medium sized enterprises are:

Sales: The volume of sales of products or services is important.

Purchases: Researched enterprises buy products, raw materials and/or labor services.

Production: Transformation of primary products in final products, as well as delivery services to the market.

Planning: Operational and strategic planning.

Product: Product sold or service performed.

Costs: Purchases, and direct and indirect expenses with labor, and taxes.

Administrative: General management of the business, as a sustainability tool of the enterprise in the market.

These are the sectors that matter to the managers' vision, related to the enterprise's Internal Factors.

In this portion of the research what becomes evident is the scale of values perceived by the managers in the different sectors and activities of the enterprises (figure 2).

We can see that, according to the vision of the managers, to have a product of competitive performance is the most important factor, with 7.89 points in a 0 to 10 scale.

The second factor is sales, with 7.75 points, followed by the business administration with 7.52, purchases 7.51, costs 7.32, planning 7.25 and production 6.76.

A detailed vision per region (Table 1).

Enterprise's sectors: products, sales, administration, purchasing, costs, business planning, production, others, none; average.

The second half of the research shows external factors, which, according to the vision of the managers, affect the performance and sustainability of the enterprises.

They are:

Public policies for development and growth of Small and Medium Sized Enterprises.

The financial establishment banks and credit institutions the serve the Small and Medium Sized Enterprise.

Academic or technical education for the workers at Small and Medium Sized Enterprises.

Access to new ideas, congresses, fairs and specialized training, in order to be prepared to face the market's demands.

Contribution and support from class associations and non-governmental agencies for development of Small and Medium Sized Enterprises

Employment posts generated in Small and Medium Sized Enterprises in the national scenario.

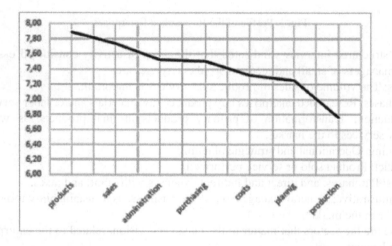

Fig. 2. Internal Factors Importance for the Sustainability of SMEs

Table 1. Values assigned to Internal Factors, per Region

Company sectors	Montes Claros	Fortaleza	Juazeiro do Norte	Araxá	Total
product	8.43	9.00	7.75	6.38	**7.89**
sales	8.13	8.31	7.00	7.54	**7.75**
administration	8.00	7.95	7.00	7.15	**7.52**
purchasing	6.50	8.25	7.67	7.62	**7.51**
costs	7.50	7.75	7.50	6.54	**7.32**
planning	8.14	7.71	6.00	7.15	**7.25**
production	5.50	6.63	7.67	7.23	**6.76**

The Small and Medium Sized Enterprise importance in the national economic development.

The Likert method was used adjusted as follows:

Table 2. Multiple Choice questions concerning External Factors to SMEs

	Of no relevance	Of some relevance	Relevant	Of much relevance	Necessary
The SMEs importance in the economic growth and development is:					
Public policies for the growth and development SMEs are:					
Posts of employment generated by SMEs in the national scenario are:					
Contribution from non governmental agencies, for the growth of SMEs are:					
Academic and technical education at the SMEs is considered:					
To be competitive in the market is:					
Financial System contribution for SMEs is:					

12,69%	Financial system
13,41%	Public policies
13,92%	Technical training
14,42%	Employment posts generated
14,94%	SMEs development
15,11%	Contribution from entities
15,51%	Readiness for the market

Fig. 3. External Factors classified by their importance to the SMEs

The preponderant external factor is to be well prepared to remain in the market, followed by the cooperation and support of class entities, the SMEs importance in the national scenario, employment posts generated by SMEs, capacitating of SMEs' labor, and support by the financial establishment.

Table 3. Values assigned to External Factors according to Regions

	Montes Claros	Fortaleza	Juazeiro do Norte	Araxá	**Average**	
To be prepared for the market	4.58	4.57	4.50	4.33	**4.50**	15.51%
Contributions from entities	4.42	4.43	4.33	4.33	**4.38**	15.11%
SMEs development	3.73	4.43	4.83	4.33	**4.33**	14.49%
Employment posts generated	4.31	4.30	4.17	3.94	**4.18**	14.42%
Technical trainning	3.92	4.22	3.67	4.33	**4.04**	13.92%
Public policies	4.08	9.96	4.00	3.50	**3.89**	13.41%
Financial System	3.25	3.52	3.50	4.44	**3.68**	12.69%

4   Analysis and Discussion

With reference to the internal factors that influence the sustainability of the SMEs, the products to be offered to the market are the main factor, and this leads to a competitive market, as far as the product's performance; however factors like costs and production and delivery times were not mentioned by the participants in the research. This brings up the commercial nature of the SMEs. Quite obviously, the objective of having a competitive product is to make sure it will be sold well, and that appears as second in importance in the research. Even services and industries show this type of focus. The numbers also show that to administration and purchasing is assigned quite well the same importance, and actually the ones interviewed believe that to buy efficiently is synonymous to administer efficiently. Costs are considered a consequence of purchasing, and here it means the buying of materials and labor. The planning factor is viewed as something operational, rather than strategic, and to production the same reasoning is applied.

Commercial activities, as an end in themselves, are important for SMEs' performance and sustainability in the market, but these activities add no value. Considering that the SMEs are responsible for the structural employment in Brazil, activities that add no value have the tendency of forcing the market into imports, and it would focus the economy's sustainability exclusively on the country's internal consumption.

Among external factors, the one of least importance is the expected support from the financial establishment. Due to high financial burdens, enterprises do their best to remain as capitalized as possible. Also, as a low importance factor, is the expectation of help from public policies aimed at SMEs; actually a degree of skepticism is noticed as far as this question is concerned. On the other hand, class associations, support from institutions as SENAI and SESC are recognized as of great usefulness to the

SMEs and a real factor of development, even though the technical training supplied by these institutions many a time is not considered by managers as of relevant importance. This reasoning derives from the fact that managers do not see collaborators as SMEs development agents; they consider that only their own capacitating and expertise are decisive factors for the development of SMEs. These findings open a gap for further research, enabling a better understanding of the characteristics of these factors, pointing the need of the development of public policies towards new strategies of business enterprises in these sizes.

References

1. SEBRAE
   http://www.sebrae.com.br/customizado/
   estudos-e-pesquisas/temasestratégicos/sobrevivência
2. Bakos, L.: Decision-making and Managerial Behaviour Regarding Corporate Social Responsability in the Case of Small and Middle-sized companies. In: Procedia- Social Behavioral Sciences (2014)
3. Gonzáles, G.P.: Asociación Significativa entre los Modos de Conversión de Conocimiento y los Modelos de Decisión en las PYMEs de Cali- Colombia - Estudios Gerenciales Universidad ICESI Colombia (2011)
4. Pellešováa, P.: Position of Small and Medium Companies in Poland and Results of Research in Selected Areas.- Science Direct Contemporary Issues in Business, Management and Education (2013)
5. Kostkaa, G.: Barriers to Increasing Energi Efficiency: Evidence from Small and Medium-sized Enterprizes in China. Journal of Cleaner Production (2013)
6. Alvarado, T.E.G., Granados, M.A.M.: La innovación en Entornos Económicos Poco Favorables: El Sector Auto Partes Mexicano - Estudios Gerenciales Elsevier.es (2013)
7. Mendes Junior, J.N., Ferreira, M.C.: Análise Compreensiva: Conceito e Método, Rio Claro (2010)

The Concept of Sustainability in View of Micro, Small and Medium Brazilian Companies

Claudio L. Meirelles[*], José Benedito Sacomano, and Fabio Papalardo

Paulista University-UNIP, Pos-Graduate Program in Production Engineering, São Paulo, Brazil
Claudio@baumannconsultancy.com

Abstract. The present moment in enterprises scenario show a triple crisis in financial, ecological and social aspects, forcing companies to revise their strategy to make a stand with sustainably in the market. Micro, small and medium organizations (MSMEs) are 99% of companies in the world, main source of employment and are having difficulties to adapt to this moment because of the lack of public policies, knowledge and innovation capacity. The objective is to show what the brazilian MSMEs understand about sustainability, using a descriptive approach, with mixed procedures and survey method in the cross-sectional. The research identified that the factor with more impact in the profitability of the firm, such as cost, is considered the main factor in ensuring the sustainability of the company. And the factors, social and environmental, aren`t considered important to achieve this sustainability, to conclude that these businessman see their business in the short time.

Keywords: Sustainability 1, Micro, Small and Medium Enterprise 2, Social Responsibility 3.

1   Introduction

Present business world is having a triple crisis following to financial, ecological and social areas, forcing companies to show a new approach of governance that allows developing a set of performance indicators to measure the sustainability of these three aspects at the company level [1].

Increasing sustainability enters in the corporative agenda, forcing them to include this theme in their strategies and to create sustainable strategies. However, in practice, the lack of segmented information, discussing issues of sustainability face some difficulties, mainly because this new reality requires a vision in product level, strategic and tactic [2].

At one side, the new legislation is emphasizing social responsibility, corporation image and client awareness and, on the other side, consumers are getting more interested in products and services related to economic viable practices, that are socially just and environmentally correct. This makes the producers worry about producing goods that do not hurt the environment and recycle products after their usage. In this

---

[*] Corresponding author.

B. Grabot et al. (Eds.): APMS 2014, Part II, IFIP AICT 439, pp. 90–97, 2014.

context, sustainable development policies wich benefit companies will be important to local economics dynamics. But it can`t be forgotten that it is necessary for the present policies not to compromise future development [3, 4, 5].

This situation is changing the business models and economic relations that are based in sustainable development as a competitive factor. In this context, it is necessary to adapt micro and small firms according to the importance of job creation, wealth distribution and ability to innovate [5].

The micro and small companies have competitive advantage to be next to the consumer, making it possible to anticipate competition on observation and adjustment of demands on sustainable practices for their stakeholders. It is important to understand that micro and small organizations as being considered the main source of development and employment in most countries, representing approximately 99% of companies in the world, but also stand out as a source of pollution of nature, approximately 30% of the total, due to the difficulty to implement other innovative methods or not to use cleaner technology [6].

SMEs in the European economy are the main sources of employment, entrepreneurship and innovation, representing 66.7% of the jobs in the European Union. In Brazil the micro and small organizations are responsible for 99% of establishments, 51.6% of private formal jobs in the country, no agricultural, and almost 40% of salaries [5, 6, 7].

The commerce is the activity with the greatest number of MSEs, accounts for over 50% of total Brazilian MSEs. The services sector is the second area with the greatest number of MEPs, representing 33.3%, followed by industry with 10.7% and 4.5% of the construction sector. The participation of MEPs in total export companies in 2011 reached 61.5%, and 27.0% in the micro and 34,5% in the small firms. The Industrial sector represents about 60% of total exports made by MPE, against a percentage of 80% corresponding to the larger firms. The commercial sector, in contrast, has more important role among the MPE than among larger firms [8, 9, 10].

Small and medium companies are limited in resources, human capital and technology; they have difficulties in managing new projects. A solution for these firms is business network, as was the case in the autoparts industry in Mexico. Firms that get to improve their capacity to compete are those that reinvent the way to do business, creating a sustainable scenario [7], [11].

The main elements of sustainable business are: a multidimensional concept of sustainability as a central principle of the company, easy comprehension of communication, formulating sustainability concrete goals and detailed strategy for achieving these objectives, the alignment of management incentives intra-organizations and the involvement of stakeholders and, in particular, the employees in the process [1].

Thus, considering the importance of this issue for the competitiveness of companies, one wonders how micro and small businesses understand what sustainability is. To answer this problem, this paper has as main aims to show what the most important concept of sustainability in the MSMEs is.

2   Methodology

With the objective and the research problem chosen, this study used descriptive approach with quantitative and qualitative procedures, methods survey in a cross-sectional. The decision of using descriptive study systems from the claim to identify a population, or subgroups of a population, situations, events, attitudes or opinions arising from certain phenomenon [12]. The procedures were defined from the research objective, which aims to understand the vision of sustainability by a population at a determined moment, using structured techniques for data collection.

2.1   Planning the Research

To operationalize the research, defined data sources, collection method, structure and data processing.

Data Source

The choice of data to be analyzed has as its base in the objective of the research, bearing in mind the constraints and difficulties in collecting. This study in particular, defined as a micro, small and medium size research, and the first decision was to choose which method of classification of the size of the companies was going to be used.

There are two ways to classify the size of the companies. One adopted by BNDES, other banks and governments, which considers the gross income as a form of analysis , and the other adopted by IBGE and SEBRAE, which takes under consideration the number of employees, this classification was chosen for the research. This criterion can be seen in Table 1 [13].

Table 1. Classification criteria for companies (Source: adapted Sebrae, 2012)

INDUSTRY	
Micro	< = 19 Employees
Small	20 – 99 Employees
Medium	100 – 499 Employees
Larger	> 500 employees
COMMERCE AND SERVICE	
Micro	< = 9 Employees
Small	10 – 49 Employees
Medium	50 – 99 Employees
Larger	> 100 employees

Population and Sample

For the research 50 companies were selected; they are associated in the FCDL-CE and FEDERAMINAS, with segments, locations and different sizes. At the request of the companies names will be preserved.

The Interviews were conducted with representatives of the companies that were in the author`s presentation this journal, being mostly socio-directors of organizations.

Companies that participated in the study are located in the state of Ceará, representative of the region Northeast and the state of Minas Gerais, representative of the region Southeast, had sectors of service, commerce and industry.

Data Collection

Data collection in selected companies for research was conducted through a structured questionnaire, composed of closed question about research questions.

According to Martins, the questionnaire "is an important tool for data collection for social research, and it is formed by a set of questions about situations and variables to be measured or described". The same author explains that the interview is required to be a research technique for gathering information, data and evidence to get information from the interviewee that were not collected before [14].

For this article, a part of the collection instrument that is being used for the development of the PHD thesis of the author and presented in Table 2.

Table 2. Instrument for data collection (Source: the author)

In your opinion what concept (or concepts which) is more relevant sustainability of your company?			
Environment		Social development	
Costs		Employee welfare	
Production		Profit	
Productivity		Market stability	

3   Results and Discussion

Results obtained in the study observed the following information.

In the city of Montes Claros, Minas Gerais state, 11 companies that met the classification of companies understood as a source of research, micro, small and medium firms, and with different activities, services, commerce and industry were interviewed.

Business managers were interviewed and after the data charting from the questionnaires, arrived at the following results:

1 - Cost and profit are the most relevant to the organization's sustainability factors, both with 25.81% of the votes;

2 - Social Development is the least relevant to the company's sustainability factor, with 3.23%;

3 - Environment with 6.45% of the indications is the seventh factor less weight to corporate sustainability among eight possible options.

In the city of Araxá, in the state of Minas Gerais, 18 companies that met the classification of companies understood as a source of research, micro, small and medium firms, and with different activities, services, commerce and industry were interviewed.

Business managers were interviewed and after the tabular data from the questionnaires, arrived at the following results:

1 - Social Development is the most relevant factor for the sustainability of the organization with 21.95% of the votes
2 - Stability in the market is less relevant to the company's sustainability factor with no indication;
3 - Environment with 14.63% of the votes is the fourth factor with less weight to corporate sustainability among eight possible options.

In the city of Fortaleza, state of Ceará, 16 companies that met the classification of companies understood as a source of research, micro, small and medium firms, and with different activities, services, commerce and industry were interviewed.

Business managers were interviewed and after the tabular data from the questionnaires, arrived at the following results:
1 - Welfare is the most relevant factor for the sustainability of the organization with 21.74% of the votes;
2 - Production is less relevant to the company's sustainability factor with 1.45% of the votes;
3 - Environment with 10.14% of the votes is the sixth factor less weight to corporate sustainability among eight possible options.

In the town of Juazeiro, in the state of Ceará, five companies that fell into the classification of companies understood as a source of research, micro, small and medium firms, and with different activities, services, commerce and industry were interviewed.

Business managers were interviewed and after the tabular data from the questionnaires, arrived at the following results:
1 - Environment and Social Development are the most relevant to the organization's sustainability factors, both with 21.43% of the votes;
2 - Production and productivity are less relevant to the company's sustainability factors with no indication;

Analysis of consolidated results in Fortaleza and Juazeiro, representing the state of Ceará in the Northeast, the following results are presented in figure 1:

1 - Welfare is the most relevant to the organization's sustainability factor with 20.48% of the votes;
2 - Production is less relevant to the company's sustainability factor of 1.20% of the votes;
3 - Environment with 12.05% of the indications is the fifth factor with less weight to corporate sustainability among eight possible options.

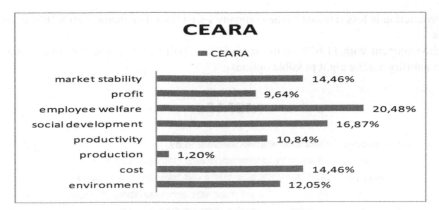

Fig. 1. Search results in the state of Ceará

Analysis of consolidated results of the cities of Montes Claros and Araxá, representing the state of Minas Gerais in the Southeast region, the following results are shown in the Figure 2:

1 - Cost is the most relevant to the organization's sustainability factor with 22.22% of the votes;
2 - Stability of the market is less relevant to the company's sustainability factor with 2.78% of the votes;
3 - Environment with 11.11% of the votes is the fifth factor with less weight to corporate sustainability among eight possible options.

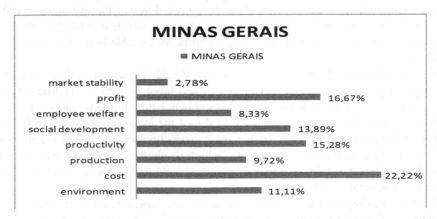

Fig. 2. Search results in the state of Minas Gerais

Analysis of consolidated results of all companies surveyed, representing organizations classified as micro, small and medium sized regions of the Northeast and Southeast, the following results are shown in the figure 3:

1 - Cost is the most relevant to the organization's sustainability factor with 18.06% of the votes;

2 - Production is less relevant to the company's sustainability factor with 5.16% of the votes;
3 - Environment with 11.61% of the votes is the sixth factor less weight to corporate sustainability among eight possible options.

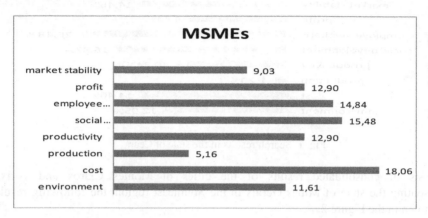

Fig. 3. General search results

4   Conclusions

Sustainability is an important topic in academia and nowadays. Even with the broad debate on what would be a sustainable company, this condition may result from better management practices, adjustments in operating procedures or the use of more efficient technology, the environmental factor stands out , which is related to the demands of the market and society to a company to be sustainable in the long term [1], [2], [5], [6], [15].

Micro, small and medium companies have considerable impact on world economies, mainly by employing a significant number of hand labor with lower qualification is necessary to understand how to position in this segment before this new reality [8].

Whereas only 10.7 % of companies are MSEs of the industrial sector and 89 % of companies have activity as trade , service and construction sector it is an evident characteristic of the non-manufacturing sector , which resulted in the search result as that found factor of greatest relevance to the sustainability of the company "cost " and less relevant , "production " [8].

Different than reported in the media and academic papers, highlighting the "environment " as the main factor for sustainability of companies , the survey found that this factor is not seen as a relevant for achieving sustainability in organizations [1], [2], [4], [5], [6], [15].

Given the results presented, it was identified that the factor in MSMEs that directly impacts the profitability of the company, such as cost, is considered as a major factor in ensuring the sustainability of the enterprise market. The characteristics of being faithful service and commerce sectors as representing most companies in these sizes.

Having the factors, social and environmental, not considered as important factors for achieving sustainability in the market even before new legislation and consumer requirements, leading to the conclusion that these entrepreneurs understand and plan their business in the short term.

These findings open a gap for further research, enabling a better understanding of the characteristics of these factors, pointing the need of the development of public policies towards new strategies of business enterprises in these sizes.

References

1. Ozcure, G., Demirkaya, H., Eryigit, N.: The sustainable company and employee participation as a part of the solution to triple crisis in the European Union and Turkey. In: Procedia Social and Behavioral Sciences, vol. 24, pp. 1274–1287 (2011)
2. Egels-Zanden, N., Rosen, M.: Sustainable strategy formation at a Swedish industrial company:bridging the strategy-as-practice and sustainability gap. Journal of Cleaner Production xxx, 1–9 (2014)
3. Faccio, M., Persona, A., Sgarbossa, F., Zanin, G.: Susteinable SC through the complete reprocessig of end-of-life products by manufacturers: A traditional versus social responsibility company perspective. European Journal of Operational Reserch 233, 359–373 (2014)
4. Musson, A.: The build-up of local sustainable development politics: A case study of company leader in France. Ecological Economics 82, 75–87 (2012)
5. SEBRAE. O que pensam as micro e pequenas empresas sobre sustentabilidade. Estudos-e-pesquisas, Sebrae, Maio (2012)
6. Van Hoof, B., Lyon, T.P.: Cleaner production in small firms taking part in Mexico's sustainable supplier program. Journal of Cleaner Production 41, 270–282 (2013)
7. Sadaba, S.M., Ezcurdia, A.P., Lazcano, A.M.E., Villanueva, P.: Project risk management methodology for small firms. International Journal of Project Management, 32, 327–340 (2014)
8. SEBRAE/DIESSE. Anuario do trabalho na micro e pequena empresa. Sebrae/Dieese, Brasilia-DF, 5ª edição (2012)
9. SEBRAE. As micro e pequenas empresas na exportação brasileira 1998 – 2011. Sebrae, Brasília (2012)
10. SEBRAE. Boletim estudos e pesquisas. Sebrae/UGE, No 6 (January / February 2014)
11. Alvarado, T.E.G., Granados, M.A.M.: La innovcion em entornos econômicos poço favorables: El sector auto partes maxicano. Estudios Gerenciales 29, 167–176 (2013)
12. Yin, R.K.: Estudo de caso: Planejamento e Métodos, 4th edn. Brookman, Porto Alegre (2010)
13. SEBRAE. Critérios de classificação de empresas: EI-ME-EPP. Disponível em
   http://www.sebrae-sc.com.br/leis/default.asp/vcdtexto=4154
   (acesso em March 10, 2012)
14. de Andrade Martins, G.: Metodologia da investigação científica para ciências sociais aplicadas, 2nd edn. Atlas, São Paulo (2009)
15. ESTADAO. Sustentabilidade,
   http://topicos.estadao.com.br/sustentabilidade
   (acessed on: April 2014)

Energy Simulation for the Integration of Virtual Power Plants into Production Planning

Volker Stich, Ulrich Brandenburg, and Julian Krenge

Institute for Industrial Management at RWTH Aachen University,
Campus-Boulevard 55, 52074 Aachen, Germany
{Volker.Stich,Ulrich.Brandenburg,
Julian.Krenge}@fir.rwth-aachen.de

Abstract. Germany pushes its energy industry towards renewable energy sources which results in an increase of distributed energy generation. Therefore, energy supply will fluctuate more and more and companies need to react to higher and volatile prices as well as to a fluctuating supply of energy. One reaction is to reactively consider these changing prices and supply of energy within production planning and control (PPC). PPC therefore acts as a control unit to integrate volatile energy supply into the production process. Within this paper a scenario is considered where a virtual power plant (VPP) combines different types of distributed energy generation. Energy simulation is then used to demonstrate how fluctuating energy prices can be considered within PPC.

Keywords: Energy-Efficiency, Energy Simulation, Production Planning and Scheduling, Virtual Power Plants.

1 Introduction

The results of the climate change and the global warming are becoming more visible every day [1] [2]. Inefficient electricity energy consumption accounts for 80% of all greenhouse gases (GHG) emission in the EU. As a result, the EU has been committed to a new plan (known as 20/20/20) to fight global warming. According to the plan, by 2020 the EU will have cut greenhouse gas emissions by 20% from 1990 levels, increased renewable energy usage by 20%, and cut energy consumption through improved energy efficiency by 20% [3].

As Europe shifts away from fossil fuels, electricity will become an even more important energy sector, and more than 29 European countries have targets for a share of renewables of 5-33% until 2020. Achieving these goals is vital for the EU internal energy market. The implementation of more intelligent and active transmission, distribution and supply systems in the form of Smart Grids is central to the success of such a development. Smart Grids are essential for the integration of distributed energy generation in the power grid, which results in a number of benefits from a sustainability point of view [4].

B. Grabot et al. (Eds.): APMS 2014, Part II, IFIP AICT 439, pp. 98–105, 2014.

On the downside, along with the increasing share of renewable energies in the electricity network, the supply uncertainty and the volatility increase. One possibility to react to this situation is called demand-side-integration which focuses on increasing the demand flexibility of energy consumers. As the manufacturing industry is one of the major consumers of energy there is a need for companies to play a vital role in this transition process. This can be done by proactively integrating fluctuating energy sources such as wind, solar and water into production planning [5].

2   Terminology and Scope of the Study

2.1   Terminology

Production logistics focuses on ensuring a better delivery capability and reliability while minimizing logistics and production costs. Therefore, production logistics improves the productivity in a network by organizing material flow through the producing process. Because production logistics strongly influences the important performance indicators delivery capability and delivery reliability, much effort is taken in industrial application and scientific research on this topic [6].

Production planning and control (PPC) is a key function to every producing company. As a value adding part of the company's organization, the main task is the holistic optimization of the production system. Part of this is the (mathematical) optimization of the production program, the material requirements and the production order [7].

Virtual Power Plants (VPP) unite different types of energy generating units, collectively controlled in order to behave like a conventional power plant. Through the use of various energy generation technologies, a continuous, controllable power generation is enabled as it would not be possible at individual power plants working with renewable energy. Connected are for example photovoltaic, wind and hydro power plants. The usage of Virtual Power Plants is an attempt to use the benefit of the usage of renewable energy but still minimize the fluctuations in the power supply [8].

Simulation is the method of evaluating the performance of an existing or proposed system in order to simulate its behavior under different configurations [9]. Since energy costs will rise continuously, optimizing the energy consumption becomes an interesting opportunity to reduce costs. Simulation can be broadly divided as Mathematical methods and Numerical computer-based simulation. Mathematical models involve the use of various theories for reaching a conclusion. They use a few number of parameters but can reach a very precise result. The draw-back of this system is that it sometimes may prove to be very tedious and almost impossible for complex systems. Therefore for solving complex systems and to provide simple solutions, numerical computer-based simulations are used [9]. More specifically, within **Energy Simulation** the energy flow and consumption is simulated taking into account the material flow process. To optimize the energy efficiency of a production system or parts of the system, the results of these simulations may be used e.g. to determine the optimum batch size and the production sequence. [10]

2.2   Scope of the Study

The study concentrates on discrete manufacturing systems (e.g. Automotive and mechanical engineering). Products to be considered are multi-part products comprising of a simple structure that are being manufactured in small to medium batch-sizes. There is more than one value-added step to the product meaning that each product passes at more than one value-adding element within the production system. The production system is organized as a job shop production therefore machines of the same production technology (e.g. milling, drilling etc.) are set in the same area. The study solely focuses on the area of production excluding interactions with technical building systems (heating, air-conditioning etc.). Additionally, the study focuses on a short-term examination (weeks) therefore factory layout planning etc. is not considered. As type of energy, solely electrical energy is considered as this type of energy is provided by VPPs.

3   State-of-the-Art

In order to include the energy and resource efficiency as a target value into production planning systems, it is necessary to know and understand which factors can influence efficiency and how sophisticated production planning can improve it. Several works have been published in the field of energy consumption of production machines.

The first of these approaches, which has been used by several authors is to analyze the energy consumption of machine tools using high resolution power measurements and assigning specific loads to each operational state of the machine [11], [12], [13].

Weinert et. al. introduced a methodology for planning and operating energy efficient production systems. The key element of this methodology is the knowledge of the power consumption profile of individual machines and the subsequent approximation of the production systems' power consumption using EnergyBlocks. The power consumption profile for the machines used in Weinert's method does not explicitly differentiate the subsystems of a production machine but it represents a machine specific consumption profile. The power consumption profile is approximated by EnergyBlocks and divided in time-variable, production dependent elements and non-variable elements. All elements are analyzed and the dependence on each other is described [13].

Abele et.al. present a simulation-based method for the prediction of the energy consumption of a running machine [14]. A key finding of their approach is that 43% of the specific energy consumption results from the base load of the machine. Therefore, the production process is not very significant for the prediction of the total energy consumption. Once again the machine's base load and dynamic power components are identified as the main drivers behind the energy consumption. Their determination is a key element in assessing the consumption of a machine tool.

Schrems et. al. propose a methodology for designing an energy and resource efficient process chain. A decision-based model was developed in order to identify the preferred production alternative out of several possibilities. The method implements a multi-criteria decision system, weighing ecological, technological and economical parameters to generate the result [15].

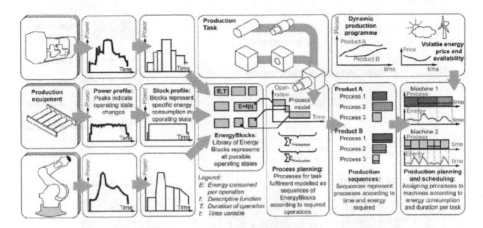

Fig. 1. Energy Blocks method according to [13]

Bruzzone et. al. [16] also propose a mathematical model. This model integrates energy-aware scheduling (EAS) through an advanced planning and scheduling (APS) system. Key to Bruzzone's proposal is an incorporated model that controls the power peaks for a given schedule on the shop floor level. The EAS operates sequentially with the APS. Both share the same optimization criteria and their output is a feasible schedule regarding the main objectives: job-completion-time, cycle time and delay-minimization, additionally the power peak target has been added as a criterion.

Pechman and Schöler [17] present an E-PPC system that is able to create a 24h energy consumption forecast using a similar technique as proposed by Weinert [13]. This technique allows the user to identify upcoming energy peaks in the phase of production planning, therefore allowing him to reschedule accordingly. With a detailed consumption forecast the company has benefits when negotiating the supply [13] contract with the power utility.

4   Energy Simulation

The main objective of the energy simulation is to demonstrate how volatile energy sources represented by a VPP can be integrated into producing company without compromising the productivity of the production system. The software used for this study is called PlantSimulation by Siemens PLM Software which contains an Energy Analyzer module. Therewith, it is possible to model machine profiles according to the EnergyBlocks methodology proposed by Weinert [13], [18]. Fig. 2 illustrates the system under study defined in the scope in 2.2. The modelling of the system is done in accordance to März and Weigert and consists of a model of the production system, actuating variables within PPC, input data and target values [19].

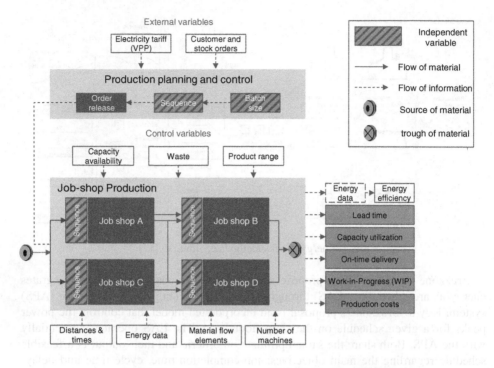

Fig. 2. Energy Simulation model for integrating VPP

The target values have been derived from production logistics such as lead times, capacity utilization and production costs while integrating a target value for energy efficiency. The following target values $Z_{int,dyn}$ are defined:

Table 1. Target values within Energy Simulation

Name	Definition
Energy Efficiency	$\dfrac{\sum Energy\ Costs\ per\ part}{\sum Value - added\ per\ part}$
Capacity Utilization	$\dfrac{\sum Time\ of\ capacity\ usage}{Duration\ of\ simulation}$
Lead time	$T_{output} - T_{input}$ with $T_i = running\ time\ of\ the\ simulation$ at point in time i
On-time delivery	$\dfrac{\sum on - time\ deliveries}{\sum deliveries}$

Table 1. *(continued)*

Production costs	$\sum energy\ costs, machining\ costs$
Work-in-progress (WIP)	$\dfrac{\sum_{i=1}^{n} stock_i}{n}$ with $i = point\ in\ time\ of\ sampling$ $n = simulation\ time\ in\ hours$

According to the efficiency definition energy efficiency is considered as a ratio between input and output. In order to account for fluctuating energy prices the input ration is defined as the energy costs that arise per part. The output can be defined as the value-added per part which can be simplified by production costs.

VPP are represented by a volatile energy price function that accounts for the fluctuating feed in of renewable energy sources. Within production planning orders from different sources (customers etc.) are transformed into production orders. For those production orders lot sizes and production sequences are planned based on energy prices and availability, delivery dates etc. The simulation period is considered to be 4 weeks with a weekly interval of releasing production orders into the job shop. Within the job shop a detailed sequencing for each production capacity (machines or groups of machines) is conducted. Therefore, energy prices are considered to be changing every hour. Additionally, energy prices are considered to be known in advance for the following day of production. Within the simulation model elements of the production system are modelled such as machines, buffers and transportation systems. For each element in the system energy data in different states can be defined in order to obtain the energy consumption profiles. According to the principle of discrete-event simulation the material flow pattern generates different operational states of the model such as producing, waiting, failure, setup, standby, etc. according to the arrival rate of products. After conducting the simulation runs, the output data is analyzed. Based on the parameter settings for lot-sizes, production sequence and order release all of the target values are calculated. Then feasible production plans are selected and communicated towards the operator of the VPP.

5   Conclusion and Outlook

Rising and volatile energy prices due to an increase of renewable energy sources causes producing companies to strive for integrating VPPs into their production. Within this paper an approach for integrating volatile energy sources into production planning and control was presented. First results of the simulation run are promising that integrating volatile energy prices without compromising productivity can be achieved. The next step will be to implement the results within a real system and validate the results from the energy simulation. Consequently, the results will be used to develop a concept for collaborative production planning within a VPP network. Based on the results from the real system the energy simulation can be used to forecast the energy consumption for a given production plan. This information can then be shared with the VPP provider. The first results suggest that rough planning in production (weeks/months) can be used to secure on-time delivery for critical orders due to its high-priority for the customers of producing companies. Once a production plan is validated and the energy consumption is forecasted and communicated to the VPP operator the detailed planning has to ensure that the energy forecast will be realized. Therefore, production sequencing will be very crucial for achieving a high energy-efficiency on the shop-floor level. Once the new concepts for energy-efficient production planning are validated within a real production system consequently Enterprise-Ressource-Planning-systems and Manufacturing Execution Systems (MES) have to be adapted in order to support energy-efficient production planning.

Acknowledgement. The authors wish to thank the Finesce Consortium for their input and their support. The Finesce project is funded by the EU grant FP7-2012-ICT-FI.

References

[1] Kara, S., Li, W.: Unit process energy consumption models for material removal processes. CIRP Annals - Manufacturing Technology 60(1), 37–40 (2011)

[2] Branker, K., Jeswiet, J., Kim, I.Y.: Greenhouse gases emitted in manufacturing a product—A new economic model. CIRP Annals - Manufacturing Technology 60(1), 53–56 (2011)

[3] European Commission: 2020 vision. Saving our energy. Luxembourg (2007)

[4] Diaz-Elsayed, N., Jondral, A., Greinacher, S., Dornfeld, D., Lanza, G.: Assessment of lean and green strategies by simulation of manufacturing systems in discrete production environments. CIRP Annals - Manufacturing Technology 62(1), 475–478 (2013)

[5] Reinhart, G., Reinhardt, S., Graßl, M.: Energieflexible Produktionssysteme. Einführungen zur Bewertung der Energieeffizienz von Produktionssystemen. wt Werkstattstechnik online 102(9), 622–628 (2012)

[6] Nyhuis, P., Wiendahl, H.-P.: Fundamentals of production logistics. Theory, tools and applications; with 6 tables (CD-ROM included), Berlin, Heidelberg (2009)

[7] Schuh, G., Stich, V.(Hrsg.): Grundlagen der PPS. Springer, Berlin (2012)

[8] Fang, X., Misra, S., Xue, G., Yang, D.: Smart Grid — The New and Improved Power Grid: A Survey. IEEE Communications Surveys & Tutorials 14(4), 944–980 (2012)

[9] Banks, J., Carson II, J.S., Nelson, B.L., Nicol, D.M.: Discrete-event system simulation, 5. Auflage, Upper Saddle River (2010)

[10] Bangsow, S.(Hrsg.): Use cases of discrete event simulation. Appliance and research, Berlin, New York (2012)

[11] Duflou, J.R., Kellens, K., Renaldi; Guo, Y., Dewulf, W.: Critical comparison of methods to determine the energy input for discrete manufacturing processes. CIRP Annals - Manufacturing Technology 61(1), 63–66 (2012)

[12] Li, W., Winter, M., Kara, S., Herrmann, C.: Eco-efficiency of manufacturing processes: A grinding case. CIRP Annals - Manufacturing Technology 61(1), 59–62 (2012)

[13] Weinert, N., Chiotellis, S., Seliger, G.: Methodology for planning and operating energy-efficient production systems. CIRP Annals - Manufacturing Technology 60(1), 41–44 (2011)

[14] Abele, E., Schrems, S., Schraml, P.: Energieeffizienz in der Fertigungsplanung. Frühzeitige Abschätzung des Energieverbrauchs von Produktionsmaschinen in der Mittel- und Großserienfertigung. wt Werkstattstechnik online 102(1/2), 38 (2012)

[15] Schrems, S., Eisele, C., Abele, E.: Methodology for an Energy and Resource Efficient Process Chain Design. In: Hesselbach, J., Herrmann, C. (Hrsg.) Glocalized Solutions for Sustainability in Manufacturing, Berlin, Heidelberg (2011)

[16] Bruzzone, A.A.G., Anghinolfi, D., Paolucci, M., Tonelli, F.: Energy-aware scheduling for improving manufacturing process sustainability: A mathematical model for flexible flow shops. CIRP Annals - Manufacturing Technology 61(1), 459–462 (2012)

[17] Pechmann, A., Schöler, I.: Optimizing Energy Costs by Intelligent Production Scheduling. In: Hesselbach, J., Herrmann, C. (Hrsg.) Glocalized Solutions for Sustainability in Manufacturing, Berlin, Heidelberg (2011)

[18] Wolff, D., Kulus, D., Dreher, S.: Simulating Energy Consumption in Automotive Industries. In: Bangsow, S. (Hrsg.) Use cases of discrete event simulation. Appliance and Research, Berlin (2012)

[19] März, L., Weigert, G.: Simulationsgestützte Optimierung. In: März, L., Krug, W., Rose, O., Weigert, G. (Hrsg.) Simulation und Optimierung in Produktion und Logistik, Berlin, Heidelberg (2011)

Sustainability in Manufacturing Operations Scheduling: Stakes, Approaches and Trends

Damien Trentesaux[1] and Vittal Prabhu[2]

[1] Université Lille Nord de France, UVHC, Tempo-Lab., F-59313 Valenciennes, France
Damien.Trentesaux@univ-valenciennes.fr
[2] Marcus Department of Industrial and Manufacturing Engineering,
Pennsylvania State University, University Park, PA 16802, USA.
prabhu@engr.psu.edu

Abstract. In this paper it is explained how manufacturing operations scheduling can contribute to sustainability. For that purpose, the relevant stakes are first presented. Sustainable manufacturing operations are then characterized. Different forms of sustainability in manufacturing operations scheduling are pointed out and some illustrative contributions are positioned.

Keywords: Sustainability, manufacturing operations, scheduling, production control.

1   Introduction

Several recent literature reviews are available in sustainable manufacturing, but most of the time the studies are led at the strategic levels: supply chain design, layout design, cleaner product and production mean design, construction, recycling process, etc., see for example (Garetti and Taisch, 2012), (Gunasekaran and Spalanzani, 2012). One of the main reasons for the strategic level emphasis is that much of the sustainability efforts have been driven by highest levels within organizations. According to (Fang et al., 2011), research on reducing environmental impacts through manufacturing operations control and scheduling has been relatively limited. Early efforts in this direction were applied in the chemical industry (Grau et al., 1995). There has been relatively little effort on energy-aware scheduling of manufacturing operations (Bruzzone et al., 2012).

Despite this, this paper intends to explain how manufacturing operations can contribute to sustainability, and especially to two of the three pillars in sustainable development: the environmental and economical pillars (the social pillar is not addressed in this paper). The present article aims to review these two pillars at the detailed manufacturing operations level with the intent to provide impetus for further research. For that purpose, the relevant stakes are first presented. Sustainable manufacturing operations are then characterized. Different forms of sustainability in manufacturing operations are pointed out and some illustrative contributions are positioned.

B. Grabot et al. (Eds.): APMS 2014, Part II, IFIP AICT 439, pp. 106–113, 2014.

2   Sustainable Manufacturing Operations: Stakes and Trends

Three emerging stakes can be identified in the context of sustainable manufacturing operations.

First, despite the fact that machining represents a small fraction of the whole product life cycle, reducing the energy consumed during this phase was recently identified as one of the most important strategies to improve sustainability in manufacturing (He et al., 2012), (Pusavec et al., 2010). This is driven by the fact that in the 2010's, the industrial sector accounts for about one-half of the world's total energy consumption. More, the consumption of energy by the sector has almost doubled over the last 60 years (Fang et al., 2011). (Garetti and Taisch, 2012) add that manufacturing is responsible of more than 33% of the global final energy consumption and 38% of direct and indirect CO_2 emissions worldwide the remaining are attributed to the transport sector, households and services. Furthermore, energy efficiency of machine tools is generally less than 30% (Hu et al., 2012) combined with dynamic pricing and significant limitations on peak energy will make detailed manufacturing scheduling and control systems will have considerable influence on the energy consumption and associate cost.

Second, manufacturing has a huge impact on the environment and major risk of "unsustainability" comes from the operational levels of the manufacturing phase (pollution, waste, including waste of energy) (Garetti and Taisch, 2012). Some process industry such as chemical, food, refining, paint or metal industries are highly energy consuming and present a high risk to generate important amount of waste or pollution. For example, in (Chen et al., 2013) is pointed the fact that during 2000 about 60% of the $700 million energy expenditures in 37 U.S. automotive assembly plants are spent in painting processes. In such a context, a 5% reduction in energy consumption may result in a saving of more than half million dollars per year for each plant. Given the rapidly increasing energy prices during the past ten years, the saving would be even more remarkable in present days while a significant amount of savings could be achieved without any major equipment investment, focusing efforts on operations. Moreover, low margins in such industries make seeking for efficiency a strategic objective (Akkerman and van Donk, 2008). For these kinds of industry, research is also focused on waste management, leading especially to cleaner production. Manufacturing and industrial processes are also known to produce large amounts of CO_2 but it is difficult for enterprises to consider renewable sources application and emissions reduction when making manufacturing and operation decisions, especially on the production planning and scheduling problem (Wang et al., 2011).

Third, from an industrial point of view, with the successive financial and economic crises, more and more industrial managers face a new kind of problem: their manufacturing systems become oversized compared to the market need and they wonder if they could limit their energy consumption. For example, in (Yildirim and Mouzon, 2012) is related a study of a Wichita, KS, aircraft small-parts supplier, where it was observed that, on average, in an 8-h shift, 16% of the time, machines stand idle. During these idle periods, there is an opportunity to save at least 13% of the total energy consumption by simply turning them OFF when they are not processing any jobs. The problem may be obvious at a first glance, but some unexpected issues arise, such as:

memorization/retrieval of last information before shut-down, re-initialization of robots (programs, parameters and states), re-synchronization of manufacturing processes after restart, etc. (Pach et al., 2014).

Therefore even if the manufacturing operation is not a prime driver of sustainability, it is becoming increasingly important to study various ways in which manufacturing operations can contribute globally to sustainability. Prior work has led to an increasing awareness and interest in integrating sustainability considerations when designing manufacturing operations scheduling and control system as can be evidenced by several recent special issues of international journal, dealing with "automation in green manufacturing" (Li et al., 2013), "sustainable manufacturing" (Garetti et al., 2012) or "Recent cleaner production advances in process monitoring and optimisation" (Klemeš et al., 2012). These special issues addressed some aspects relevant to sustainability applied at detailed manufacturing operations and some of the papers published in these special issues are reviewed in this article. Moreover, previously released literature reviews have been realized on close topics. They focused for example on a specific kind of manufacturing systems, such as: mixed-models manufacturing processes (Neugebauer et al., 2012), specific usable tools, such as simulation software (Thiede et al., 2013), industrial-oriented software, such as manufacturing execution systems (Soplop et al., 2009), energy consumption reduction in manufacturing from a technology (Park et al., 2009) or from a processes and systems (Duflou et al., 2012) point of views. All these reviews contain of course some considerations paid to manufacturing operations scheduling and control, but partially.

3   When Manufacturing Operations Scheduling is Sustainable?

Several notions are often used to describe similar strategy or philosophy in the context of sustainability in manufacturing: lean, clean, green manufacturing to name a few. In this paper, **sustainable manufacturing** refers to the set of technical and organizational solutions contributing to the development and implementation of innovative methods, practices and technologies, in the manufacturing field, for addressing the world-wide resources shortages, for mitigating the excess of environmental load and for enabling an environmentally benign life cycle of products (Garetti et al., 2012).

Manufacturing operations refer in this paper to the low-level short-term or even real time decisions applied to manufacturing systems. Upper levels, such as mid-term production planning, supply chain and business levels are not considered in this paper, as well as lower levels dealing with actuators/sensors and physical behaviour are not considered either. We focus on process monitoring, inventory and tool management, machine control, scheduling and maintenance among the main functions of manufacturing operations (Trentesaux and Prabhu, 2013).

Manufacturing operations management in a broad sense, and especially scheduling in manufacturing, has been one of the most studied problems by the operation research and control communities, and this holds also true considering sustainability issues. **Scheduling** is the allocation of resources (human and technical) to tasks over given time periods and its goal is to optimize one or more (Pinedo, 2008). In this paper, scheduling is taken in a broad sense, encompassing predictive approaches, dynamic/reactive approaches and real-time control techniques.

The question that arises is then: *under which conditions a manufacturing operations scheduling method can be termed as sustainable?* From our point of view, the key point is related to the consideration of means in addition to classical time-based (completion times, flow times, tardiness/earliness…) or mixed time/quantity-based (throughput…) production objectives. In the context of sustainable manufacturing operations, two kinds of means can be identified: the **input means** that enable the realization of a scheduling (energy, machines, inventories, raw materials, tools…) and the **output means** that are consequences of the realization of the scheduling (waste, scrap, pollution). Due to its specificity, money is not present in the input means list in the sense that it is the driver of all the other input means. As a consequence, from our point of view, the answer is: *it is when a method considers in addition to usual production objectives (time-based or time/quantity-based) the optimization of input means and/or output means when computing/constructing these schedules.*

This answer guided us to realize our literature review to determine if contributions are relevant or not to sustainability in manufacturing operations scheduling. Thus, in a sustainable context, input/output means have then to be considered as decision variables when computing schedules in a predictive or reactive manner. For example, energy and resources are such typical means and must be seen as tuning/decision parameters. Other approaches, typically for example the ones that consider energy as a fixed cost, which is not a value to reduce as much as possible, cannot be considered as contribution to sustainability. Typically, in such a context, if the energy consumption for a schedule is assumed to be constant, then it can be ignored (Yildirim and Mouzon, 2012). It is the same for the numerous contributions in the manufacturing scheduling domain that consider the quantity of available machines as a constraint, not a value to be reduced as much as possible. Typically, the literature review proposed by (Hoogeveen, 2005) is out of the scope since the author considered only time-related performance objectives, being mono or multicriteria-based: no attention was paid to input nor output means.

Other numerous works concern the solving a problem known as the resource-constraint scheduling problem (RCPSP) (Brucker et al., 1999). Roughly, a RCPSP problem is a project planning problem considering renewable resources (manpower, machines…) and nonrenewable resources (budget, energy) (Hartmann and Briskorn, 2010). Fundamentally, there exist two ways to optimize a RCPSP problem: either minimizing the project makespan subject to a fixed upper bound on the non-renewable resource (*the budget problem*), or at minimizing the total allocation subject to a given bound on the makespan (*the deadline problem*) (Brucker et al., 1999). A lot of extensions of this problem have been proposed (Hartmann and Briskorn, 2010). These works address high-levels in manufacturing system, which is beyond the scope of this paper. Even if these works are not directly related to sustainability, they have inspired numerous studies related to predictive manufacturing operations scheduling considering sustainability.

More precisely, considering input/output means in scheduling enlarges the debate and leads to the consideration of a new performance indicator, *efficiency*, in addition to the classical *effectiveness* one: seeking for the best use of means refers to efficiency while seeking for the best results, effectiveness (Roghanian et al., 2012). Efficiency and effectiveness are commonly performances indicators used in economy, accounting, business and management. Roughly speaking, efficiency is often assimilated as "doing things right" while effectiveness, "doing the right things" (Roghanian et al., 2012). The ideal sustainable manufacturing scheduling system realizes everything (maximum effectiveness) using nothing (minimum use of means, that is maximum efficiency). In reality, effectiveness and efficiency are conflicting objectives: for example, reducing energy consumption may imply a loss of performances in operations (makespan).

4   Illustrative Works in Sustainable Manufacturing Operations

To illustrate the previous discussion, some contributions from the literature are positioned in this part. This positioning is made according to the addressed means in the sustainable-oriented scheduling models (input, output or mixed). Obviously, the aim is not to provide a complete review.

4.1   Input Oriented Approaches: Energy, Inventory, Machine, Tools

Input-oriented scheduling approaches are the most often developed. For this approach, optimal predictive scheduling are mainly proposed. A first type of predictive approach works is focused on the elaboration of a trade-off between effectiveness and input-means oriented efficiency. It has been widely addressed in the literature. It consists in minimizing input resource consumption while maintaining the quality of the schedule as a compromise, aggregation being made using a mono or a multi-criteria aggregation method, see for example (He et al., 2012), (Zhang et al., 2012), (Vergnano et al., 2010) or (Newman et al., 2012). Most of these approaches are statically handled, but this tradeoff can be realized in real time, in an opportunistic manner, using for example potential fields (Pach et al., 2014). In a second type, less addressed but promising and innovative, the approach consists in optimizing scheduling effectiveness under input means profile as hard constraints (eg., expressed in terms of money or maximum available power for given time windows, typically in the smart grid, or more simply, a maximum peak power value to be respected). This could lead for example to scheduling mechanisms shortening the makespan if more energy is available while increasing the makespan if less energy is available, see for example (Pechmann et al., 2012), (Bruzzone et al., 2012) or (Artigues et al., 2013). In the last type, the scheduling effectiveness is maintained as the main objective, while the input resource use/consumption is minimized, if possible, see for example (Mashaei and Lennartson, 2013) or (Chen et al., 2013).

Approximate predictive approaches are also proposed (Santos and Dourado, 1999), (Yildirim and Mouzon, 2012) as well as simulation/optimization ones (Weinert et al., 2011), (Prabhu and Taisch, 2012).

4.2   Output Oriented Approaches: Waste, Pollution, Scrap, Greenhouse Gases

These approaches are less studied, but some contributions are among the first ones in the field. Especially, chemical plants constitute a classical and historical application field of environment considerations in production operations. For example, (Grau et al., 1995), (Vaklieva-Bancheva and Kirilova, 2010) and (Adonyi et al., 2008) proposed optimal predictive approaches in the context of waste and cleanness management.

4.3   Mixed Approaches

Some mixed approaches, considering simultaneously input and output means have been developed. For example, (Fang et al., 2011), (Wang et al., 2011) considered simultaneously energy and carbon footprint. From our review, mixed approaches are then not well developed as for output oriented approaches.

5   Conclusion and Future Trends

In this article, the role of scheduling manufacturing operations in a sustainable context was addressed. The research activity is growing but still does not fill the gap between research and industrial needs. Input-oriented approaches are the most studied ones but the field is still nascent (most of the references are after 2012). Output-oriented and mixed approaches are clearly unstudied. Given the future evolutions, scheduling under sustainability constraints should be urgently addressed. From our point of view, future trends concern the development of "means-friendly" systems, being manufacturing execution systems or scheduling systems. This concerns typically: the integration of opportunistic behavior in energy savings, the optimization of greenhouse gases emission in scheduling, and more globally the definition of scheduling benchmarks integrating output means considerations. From our review, it is indeed clear that output and mixed approaches should also be urgently addressed. Innovative approaches and concepts such as cyber-physical systems, intelligent products, product-service systems to name a few can bring some insights to contribute to the development of effective and efficient sustainable scheduling systems. This paper did not considered the social pillar which should be studied to complete the view on the addressed issue.

References

Adonyi, R., Biros, G., Holczinger, T., Friedler, F.: Effective scheduling of a large-scale paint production system. J. Clean. Prod. 16, 225–232 (2008)

Akkerman, R., van Donk, D.P.: Development and application of a decision support tool for reduction of product losses in the food-processing industry. J. Clean. Prod. 16, 335–342 (2008)

Artigues, C., Lopez, P., Haït, A.: The energy scheduling problem: Industrial case-study and constraint propagation techniques. Int. J. Prod. Econ. 143, 13–23 (2013)

Brucker, P., Drexl, A., Möhring, R., Neumann, K., Pesch, E.: Resource-constrained project scheduling: Notation, classification, models, and methods. Eur. J. Oper. Res. 112, 3–41 (1999)

Bruzzone, A.A.G., Anghinolfi, D., Paolucci, M., Tonelli, F.: Energy-aware scheduling for improving manufacturing process sustainability: A mathematical model for flexible flow shops. CIRP Ann. - Manuf. Technol. 61, 459–462 (2012)

Chen, G., Zhang, L., Arinez, J., Biller, S.: Energy-Efficient Production Systems through Schedule-Based Operations. IEEE Trans. Autom. Sci. Eng. 10, 27–37 (2013)

Duflou, J.R., Sutherland, J.W., Dornfeld, D., Herrmann, C., Jeswiet, J., Kara, S., Hauschild, M., Kellens, K.: Towards energy and resource efficient manufacturing: A processes and systems approach. CIRP Ann. - Manuf. Technol. 61, 587–609 (2012)

Fang, K., Uhan, N., Zhao, F., Sutherland, J.W.: A new approach to scheduling in manufacturing for power consumption and carbon footprint reduction. J. Manuf. Syst. 30, 234–240 (2011)

Garetti, M., Mummolo, G., Taisch, M.: Editorial: Special issue on "sustainable manufacturing". Prod. Plan. Control 23, 79–82 (2012)

Garetti, M., Taisch, M.: Sustainable manufacturing: trends and research challenges. Prod. Plan. Control 23, 83–104 (2012)

Grau, R., Espuña, A., Puigjaner, L.: Environmental considerations in batch production scheduling. Comput. Chem. Eng. 19(suppl. 1), 651–656 (1995)

Gunasekaran, A., Spalanzani, A.: Sustainability of manufacturing and services: Investigations for research and applications. Int. J. Prod. Econ. 140, 35–47 (2012)

Hartmann, S., Briskorn, D.: A survey of variants and extensions of the resource-constrained project scheduling problem. Eur. J. Oper. Res. 207, 1–14 (2010)

He, Y., Liu, B., Zhang, X., Gao, H., Liu, X.: A modeling method of task-oriented energy consumption for machining manufacturing system. J. Clean. Prod. 23, 167–174 (2012)

Hoogeveen, H.: Multicriteria scheduling. Eur. J. Oper. Res. 167, 592–623 (2005)

Hu, S., Liu, F., He, Y., Hu, T.: An on-line approach for energy efficiency monitoring of machine tools. J. Clean. Prod. 27, 133–140 (2012)

Klemeš, J.J., Varbanov, P.S., Huisingh, D.: Recent cleaner production advances in process monitoring and optimisation. J. Clean. Prod. 34, 1–8 (2012)

Li, J., Morrison, J.R., Zhang, M.T., Nakano, M., Biller, S., Lennartson, B.: Editorial: Automation in green manufacturing. IEEE Trans. Autom. Sci. Eng. 10, 1–4 (2013)

Mashaei, M., Lennartson, B.: Energy Reduction in a Pallet-Constrained Flow Shop Through On/Off Control of Idle Machines. IEEE Trans. Autom. Sci. Eng. 10, 45–56 (2013)

Neugebauer, R., Putz, M., Schlegel, A., Langer, T., Franz, E., Lorenz, S.: Energy-sensitive production control in mixed model manufacturing processes. In: Dornfeld, D.A., Linke, B.S. (eds.) Leveraging Technology for a Sustainable World, vol. 111, pp. 399–404. Springer, Heidelberg (2012)

Newman, S.T., Nassehi, A., Imani-Asrai, R., Dhokia, V.: Energy efficient process plan-ning for CNC machining. CIRP J. Manuf. Sci. Technol. 5, 127–136 (2012)

Pach, C., Berger, T., Sallez, Y., Bonte, T., Adam, E., Trentesaux, D.: Reactive and energy-aware scheduling of flexible manufacturing systems using potential fields. Comput. Ind. 65, 434–448 (2014)

Park, C.-W., Kwon, K.-S., Kim, W.-B., Min, B.-K., Park, S.-J., Sung, I.-H., Yoon, Y., Lee, K.-S., Lee, J.-H., Seok, J.: Energy consumption reduction technology in manufac-turing — A selective review of policies, standards, and research. Int. J. Precis. Eng. Manuf. 10, 151–173 (2009)

Pechmann, A., Schöler, I., Hackmann, R.: Energy efficient and intelligent production scheduling – evaluation of a new production planning and scheduling software. In: Dornfeld, D.A., Linke, B.S. (eds.) Leveraging Technology for a Sustainable World, vol. 111, pp. 491–496. Springer, Heidelberg (2012)

Pinedo, M.: Scheduling: Theory, Algorithms, and Systems. Springer (2008)

Prabhu, V., Taisch, M.: Simulation Modeling of Energy Dynamics in Discrete Manufacturing Systems. In: 14th IFAC INCOM Symposium, pp. 740–745 (2012)

Pusavec, F., Krajnik, P., Kopac, J.: Transitioning to sustainable production – Part I: ap-plication on machining technologies. J. Clean. Prod. 18, 174–184 (2010)

Roghanian, P., Rasli, A., Gheysari, H.: Productivity through Effectiveness and Efficiency in the Banking Industry. Procedia - Soc. Behav. Sci. 40, 550–556 (2012)

Santos, A., Dourado, A.: Global optimization of energy and production in process industries: a genetic algorithm application. Control Eng. Pract. 7, 549–554 (1999)

Soplop, J., Wright, J., Kammer, K., Rivera, R.: Manufacturing execution systems for sustainability: Extending the scope of MES to achieve energy efficiency and sustainability goals. In: 4th IEEE Conference on Ind. Electr. and Appl., pp. 3555–3559 (2009)

Thiede, S., Seow, Y., Andersson, J., Johansson, B.: Environmental aspects in manufacturing system modelling and simulation—State of the art and research perspectives. CIRP J. Manuf. Sci. Technol. 6, 78–87 (2013)

Trentesaux, D., Prabhu, V.V.: Introduction to shop-floor control, in: Wiley Encyclopedia of Operations Research and Management Science. John Wiley & Sons, Inc. (2013)

Vaklieva-Bancheva, N.G., Kirilova, E.G.: Cleaner manufacture of multipurpose batch chemical and biochemical plants. Scheduling and optimal choice of production recipes. J. Clean. Prod. 18, 1300–1310 (2010)

Vergnano, A., Thorstensson, C., Lennartson, B., Falkman, P., Pellicciari, M., Yuan, C., Biller, S., Leali, F.: Embedding detailed robot energy optimization into high-level scheduling. In: IEEE Conf. on Autom. Sci. and Engin., Toronto, Canada, pp. 386–392 (2010)

Wang, X., Ding, H., Qiu, M., Dong, J.: A low-carbon production scheduling system considering renewable energy. In: IEEE Conference on Service Operations, Logistics, and Informatics, pp. 101–106 (2011)

Weinert, N., Chiotellis, S., Seliger, G.: Methodology for planning and operating energy-efficient production systems. CIRP Ann. - Manuf. Technol. 60, 41–44 (2011)

Yildirim, M.B., Mouzon, G.: Single-Machine Sustainable Production Planning to Mini-mize Total Energy Consumption and Total Completion Time Using a Multiple Objective Genetic Algorithm. IEEE Trans. Eng. Manag. 59, 585–597 (2012)

Zhang, L., Li, X., Gao, L., Zhang, G., Wen, X.: Dynamic scheduling model in FMS by considering energy consumption and schedule efficiency. In: IEEE 16th International Conference on Computer Supported Cooperative Work in Design, pp. 719–724 (2012)

Reverse Logistics of Information and Communication Technology Equipment: A Comparative Assessment of Laws and Programs

Marinalva Rodrigues Barboza[1], Rodrigo Franco Gonçalves[1],
Enrico D'Onofrio[1], and Ivanir Costa[2]

[1] Paulista University-UNIP, Graduate Program in Production Engineering,
Dr. Bacelar St. 1212, São Paulo, Brazil
[2] Universidade Nove de Julho - UNINOVE. Avenida Francisco Matarazzo, 612, Água Branca,
São Paulo-SP. Prédio A, 2° andar, sala 203. Brazil
marinalva_barboza@yahoo.com.br,
rofranco@osite.com.br,
enrico.consultor@gmail.com,
icosta11@live.com

Abstract. Considering the environmental issues related to e-waste caused by excessive consumption and early disposal of ICT equipment, this paper aims to analyze policies, programs, regulations and legislation in Brazil and in selected geographies with a higher incidence of e-waste (Europe, USA, China and Japan). A comparison matrix is presented and, within this context, it is clear that the Brazilian law (12.305) relative to international laws is both limited and subjective in regards to producer responsibilities because it is limited to the requirement to structure and implement reverse logistics and defines them as issuer pays. As a contrasting example, the European EPR (Extended Producer Responsibility) system is more efficient in controlling and managing e-waste, since it extends to the end-life of products. As such, it serves as a basis for regulations in many other countries. This paper is theoretical and based on the results of literature reviews.

Keywords: E-waste, ICT Legislation, Reverse Logistics.

1 Introduction

Over the last ten years, Brazil has experienced significant growth, mainly driven by household consumption. According to the IBGE [1], all major regions showed an increase in real average monthly income: North (7.7%), Northeast (10.7%), Southeast (7.9%), South (4.0%) and Midwest (10.6%). Considering also that issues related to globalization have increased competition, the shortening of product life cycles and emergence of new products make the new middle class eager for new products, especially related to Information and Communication Technologies (ICT), increasing consumption and thereby creating higher waste production.

B. Grabot et al. (Eds.): APMS 2014, Part II, IFIP AICT 439, pp. 114–121, 2014.

Also according to the IBGE, between 2009 and 2011, the durable goods that showed higher growth were personal computers with internet access (39.8%), followed by personal computers (29.7%) and mobile telephones (26.6%). More recent data from the IDC [2] [3] confirm growth: in 2012 smartphones and tablets grew by 78% and 171% respectively compared to 2011.

In recent years, economic forces, such as the increasing deregulation of the business world, the proliferation of free trade agreements, increased foreign competition, increased industrial globalization and improved logistics performance were essential to position logistics at a high level. Thus, companies started to think about products and services flowing unhindered from the source of raw materials to end-consumers as well as including the reverse movement of the supply channel [4]. The main drivers of the growth in reverse logistics are general economic growth, increasing purchasing power of lower income consumers and nascent concerns of environmental sustainability.

Among the various factors that drive reverse logistics activity, the legal aspect stands out [5]. The reasons for this importance are related to laws and incentive programs created by global government authorities, whose purpose is to promote and encourage the implementation of reverse logistics processes in organizations, so as to ensure a sustainable return to the production cycle. This way, it is possible to reverse distribution channels or proper disposal, minimizing any environmental impacts and increase the efficiency and sustainability in organizations.

This paper aims to analyze policies, programs, regulations and legislation in Brazil and in countries with a higher incidence of electronic waste production: Europe, USA, China and Japan, for a comparative analysis of initiatives and practices in the countries studied.

This research is theoretical and exploratory, conducted from a literature review of policies, programs, regulations and applicable laws, as well as related work in reverse logistics, particularly related to the disposal of ICT products nationwide and internationally.

2   Literature Review

2.1   Information and Communication Technologies - ICT

The electronics equipment industry is one of the fastest growing in the industrialized world. Waste discarded from the electronics equipment industry is known as Waste Electrical and Electronic Equipment - (WEEE). [6]

The accumulated amount of electronic waste worldwide is approximately 40 million tons, 80% of which ends up in developing or emerging countries like Brazil, which in turn discards about 0.5 kg per capita / year from PCs, more than that discarded by China, which has a per capita volume of only 0.23 kg / year. [7].

Recent data from 2013 show that Brazil produces about one million tons of electronic waste per year [8]. China experienced a significant increase in sales of electrical equipment (computers, air conditioners, refrigerators, washing machines and mobile phones) between 1995 and 2011, which resulted in the disposal of 3.6 million tons of electronic waste in 2011 [9]. The U.S. produced 3.4 million tons of electronic waste in 2011 [10]. The production of electronic waste in Japan is around 4 million tons per year and the annual average in Europe is 9 million tons per year [7] [11].

The volume of ICT equipment sold in the market will result in the generation of large volumes of e-waste as well as human health risks that are inherent in them. Issues related to the production and disposal of electronic waste have been the subject of study by several authors, as well as agencies and organizations like UNEP, StEP [7], EPA [10], who periodically disclose country reports in these respects.

2.2   Reverse Logistics

Direct Logistics is defined as the process of planning, efficiently implementing and controlling at an effective cost, the flow of raw materials, work in process, finished product and related information from point of origin to the end-consumer in order to meet customer needs. [12].The difference between direct logistics as defined by the CSCMP and Reverse Logistics is only the direction in which the process occurs and its objectives. Therefore, Reverse Logistics is defined, however, as the flow going from the consumption point to the point of origin, this time in order to recover the product value or to properly dispose of [5]. This way, Reverse Logistics process adds value of various types: legal, economic, ecological among others.

Among the reasons for performing the reverse logistics process those that stand out are: Competitiveness (65.2%), channel cleaning (33.4%) and legal issues (28.9%) [5].The increasing relevance of legal aspects has led to the emergence of incentive programs and laws that regulate such activity in Brazil and worldwide.

In Reverse Logistics, economic aspects and strategic advantages can be taken into account, and it is not an optional activity for companies that want to be successful, on the contrary, it is mandatory. Three tools can be observed in the reverse logistics process: Innovation, Coordination and Integration. There is a high degree of innovation in terms of creating systems and procedures to find solutions to deal with returns, as the diversity of products and materials requires a high degree of coordination in the management of reverse logistics, thus requiring the participation of several integrated companies in the treatment and final disposal of products and hazardous materials [13] [14]. Business dynamism created in the pursuit of maximum efficiency and waste elimination to cover costs, associate with economic globalization during the last decades, tends to shorten product life cycles, increasing the return rate of unsold items.

2.3   ICT Reverse Logistics

The concern with reverse logistics of electronics waste is driven by a combination of unique features found in this waste stream, a fact that has led governments around the world to develop a system for collecting and processing electronic waste known as the "take-back system" or the "return system" [15]. These factors are:

- The shelf life of the equipment
- Toxic materials found in electronic waste that harm both the environment and human health

- Valuable materials found in e-waste that help reduce mining of virgin materials
- The high cost of the recycling process that often exceeds the value of the recovered material.

The main difficulties in ICT reverse logistics are in the collection and costs of collection involved in this process, which can often derail the process. Industry associations and electronics recycling companies do not have actual data on the quantities of returned materials making it difficult to analyze the percentage of reuse of these materials, their efficiency and their cost. However, there is a business concern with new reverse flow legislation. ICT waste reverse logistics, like that of other products, meets barriers mainly related to the high degree of uncertainty in aspects such as quality, time and especially the place of origin of the goods to be collected, where a fragmented market makes their consolidation difficult [16]. In regulations under the Extended Producer Responsibility (EPR) regime, reverse logistics plays an important role because producers can take back their products for appropriate treatment and disposal [6].

3   Comparison Matrix

Table 1 presents a comparative analysis of Brazilian law 12.305/2010 National Policy on Solid Waste - (PNRS) regulated by Decree No. 7404, December 2010 [17]. In the face of the main laws and international programs, a matrix was created for comparison of countries with the highest incidence of electronic waste production (Europe, USA, China and Japan) to analyze the results generated in their respective countries.

Table 1. Key Laws, Regulations and Programs worldwide in the treatment of waste derived from ICT

COUNTRY	CONSUMPTION VOLUME/ELECTRONIC WASTE	LAWS/REGULATIONS/PROGRAMS/ POLICIES/	RESULTS
Brazil	Generates close to 1 million tons/year. Waste 0.5 kg/per capita/year **Error! Reference source not found.. [Error! Reference source not found.]**	12.305/2010 – Established PNRS (National Policy for Solid Waste) regulated by decree 7.404/2010. State resolution SMA 38 of 08/2011 defines reverse logistics for electronics and others. **[Error! Reference source not found.]**	One of the primary destinations of electronic waste produced in developed countries. **[Error! Reference source not found.]**
Europe	Generates approx. 8.3 to 9.1 million tons/year. **[Error! Reference source not found.]**	WEEE Directive 002/96/EC + RoHS directive - (Restriction of Hazardous Substances) 2002/95 02/2003, into effect 07/2006. EPR Regime **Error! Reference source not found.Error! Reference source not found.. [Error! Reference source not found.]**	The EPR regime was inspired by various other developing and developed countries.**[Error! Reference source not found.]**
USA	Generated 3.4 million tons of electronic waste in 2011. **[Error! Reference source not found.]**	ESAP, a sustainability self-assessment program.**[Error! Reference source not found.]** Federal law H.R. 2284- not approved.**[Error! Reference source not found.]**	No defined responsibility and has different systems. Recycles ~25% of generated electronic waste.**[Error! Reference source not found.]**
China	Disposed of 3.6 million tons of electronic waste in 2011. **[Error! Reference source not found.]**	Law n° 36 of 2000 – prohibition of waste imports I Law n° 115 of 2006 – 3R principle (reutilization, recycling and recuperation) I Ordinance 39 of 2007 – ICT and hazardous material pollution controll Law 40 of 2008 – Adm. measures – prev. EEE waste pollution I Council of State n° 551 – of 2011. Recycling mgmt. and EEE waste disposal and extended producer responsibility– EPR. **[Error!**	Receives ~70% of electronic waste from developed countries such as the USA. **[Error! Reference source not found.].** 35% of EEE imports in 2011. **[Error! Reference source not found.]**

		Reference source not found.]	
Japan	Generates 4 million tons/year. [Error! Reference source not found.]	2001 DHARL Error! Reference source not found., 2004 3R System per G8 summit. [Error! Reference source not found.]	One of the most efficient systems for managing and controlling EEE waste. [Error! Reference source not found.] High incidence of REEE recycling. [Error! Reference source not found.]

Source: The authors.

4   Analysis and Discussion

It is necessary to perform an analysis of the laws, regulations and programs in the countries studied to better discuss the results.

Brazil: Law 12305 [17] in which "polluter pays" is one of the tenets, defines shared responsibility for the product life cycle, individually and linked, covering all participants in the supply chain.   Article 33 speaks of the requirement of manufacturers, importers, distributors and dealers to structure and implement reverse logistics systems, upon return of the product after use by consumers. In this sense, for Leite [17], although the decree does not set goals of any kind, and allows companies to present studies and projects for reverse logistics, the law is pragmatic in placing confidence in supply chain participants for the implementation of reverse logistics. Such a measure may connote subjectivity, as the lack of clear goals will hamper the identification of the obtained results. On the other hand, Ferreira and Vicente [19] believe that the law requires review and a redirection of practices by companies as well as societal awareness, which in turn requires technical knowledge for a proper evaluation of the solid waste destinations. The authors also believe that the law presents complex solutions by engaging political, social, cultural and economic dimensions. Even in a negative aspect, Leite [17] considers the law a bit cautious regarding consumer penalties for breach of product disposal.

Being fairly recent, the Brazilian law establishing the PNRS is still controversial in some aspects, with divergence in the opinions of some researchers. The fact is that possibly due to lack of sufficient time, the PNRS has not generated positive results or sufficient controls to change, for example, the scenario in which Brazil presents itself as one of the main destinations of electronic waste produced in developed countries [7].

Positively speaking, the law provides incentives of various kinds such as financial, accounting and tax, but it will take some time to achieve concrete results for a more effective analysis. In general, the PNRS of 2010 brings hope for an evolution in reverse logistics activities in Brazil, besides the relevant environmental aspects concerning the return process in a sustainable manner, since before PNRS, UNEP studies in Brazil in 2008 pointed to a country that did not have a comprehensive federal waste management law, which could be seen as an obstacle to the development of specific electronic waste regulation in the country. Given this, the study published by UNEP in 2009, concluded that in Brazil electronic waste did not seem to be a priority for the federal associations representing the electronics industry. Currently EEE are covered in Article 33, paragraph IV of PNRS.

European Union - EU: The EU follows the WEEE directive 2002/96/EC [20], the primary objective being the prevention of waste from electric and electronic equipment and also the reuse, recycling and other forms of waste recovery in order to reduce disposal and contribute to the protection of human health, while also improving the environmental performance of economic operators involved in the life cycle of electrical and electronic equipment and its management. The ROHS, beyond the restriction of hazardous substances, establishes the collection, recycling and recovery of electrical goods which is part of a legislative initiative to solve the problem of large amounts of toxic e-waste. The EU designs its regulations under the EPR system, which means that EEE producers have responsibilities beyond the manufacture of their products, including environmentally sound management at the end of their useful life. The WEEE Directive has clear goals to achieve a minimum rate of 45% return by 2016 and 65% by 2019 of the volume of EEE sold in the market in the three preceding years in the member state or alternatively 85% of the EEE waste generated in the territory of the member state. Member states must establish dissuasive and effective penalties for violation of the rules [25].

As a result, in 2010 the majority of European countries achieved a reuse and recycling rate of over 80%, five member states of the EU were between 70% and 80%. In the same year, the return rate was between 30-45% in nine countries and over 45% in four countries [25]. For efficiency the UN recommends that developing countries adopt restrictions found in the EPR system, upon which Europe designed its regulations [21].

USA: In 2011, the U.S. Congress introduced federal law HR 2284 pertaining to the responsible recycling of electronics, but the bill was not approved. The law would have made it illegal to send toxic e-waste to developing countries. Twenty-five American States passed legislation requiring recycling of electronic waste in the U.S., which represents 65%, of the domestic population being covered by a state law for recycling this type of waste [22]. The ESAP is an environmental self-assessment that has the objective of assessing the progress of companies to meet the letter of intent for sustainable development, developed by the Global Environmental Management Initiative - GEMI, together with Deloitte and Touche in the 90s [23]. In the U.S., the lack of a clear definition of responsibilities in the process of returning ICT-derived waste may explain the low rate of recycling in the country, less than 25%, of the total generated [22]. It is also noted that the self-assessment program by itself, does not produce effective results.

China: Over the past decade, China has proven to be concerned about environmental issues by creating important laws and regulations that manage and control the inappropriate disposal of EEE waste [9]. Although this set of laws covers both the EPR system adopted by the member states of the European Union, and the Japanese 3R efficiency principle, (reuse, recycle and recover) it does not connote effectiveness in controlling electronic waste imports, since even with the specific law China is the destination of 70% of e-waste from developed countries such as the USA.[24]. On the other hand, when compared with Brazil, and even with four times the production of electronic waste, China has less than half (0.23 kg) the waste per capita / year than

Brazil (0, 5 kg), which shows greater efficiency in some aspects of its laws. Superficially analyzing the laws and their objectives in Table I, apparently law No. 115 of 2006, which has as a principle the 3R system and EC No. 551 of 2011, which manages the EEE recycling and disposal process and establishes extended producer responsibility (EPR), are responsible for the results, by encouraging reuse, recycling and recovery before disposal.

Japan: One of the most significant laws in Japan is DHARL – the Designated Household Appliance Recycling Law, created in 2001 that regulates the treatment of EEE waste and defines the obligations of the parties involved in collection, transportation and recycling. The country has good EEE waste recycling rates, for example, TVs and air conditioners with a minimum 50% and 70% respectively in 2010, totaling about 26 million recycled units [8]. Japan stands out among developed countries, with the 3R system being the best functioning systems of electronic waste management in terms of scope levels and compliance, despite European countries having developed such practices since the beginning of the 21st century. [9]

5   Conclusions

Brazilian law is relatively new for a conclusive analysis, but compared to the Japanese 3R system and to the European EPR it is possible to perform a preliminary analysis that the polluter-pays and shared responsibility model adopted in Brazil will struggle to deliver effective results, because of its subjectivity and lack of clear goals.

One can see that the volume of produced or disposed ICT waste does not determine the creation of laws or programs to better manage the return of such waste, depending on the awareness of each country in prioritizing this activity for economic, social or environmental reasons. The results show that it is not necessarily the quantity, but rather the efficiency of laws, programs or schemes regarding this question, that determine better rates of return, recycling and reuse of EEE waste.

Continuing the present study, we propose a comparative analysis of the application of the same laws and programs presented in this article, between developed and developing countries

References

1. IBGE – Instituto Brasileiro de Geografia e Estatística: Pesquisa Nacional por Amostra de Domicílio, Síntese de indicadores, 2009/2011, pp. 25–34 (2011)
2. IDC Latin, http://br.idclatin.com/releases/news.aspx?id=1457
3. IDC BR, http://www.idcbrasil.com.br/releases/news.aspx?id=1458
4. Ballou, R.H.: Business Logistics/Supply Chain Management, 5th edn., p. 45. Prentice Hall (2004)
5. Rogers, D., Tibben-lambke, R.: - Going Backwards: Reverse Logistics Trends and Practices, Reverse Logistics Executive Council, pp. 2–33 (1998)
6. Li, R., Tee, C., Tarin, J.C.: A Reverse Logistics Model For Recovery Options of E-waste Considering the Integration of the Formal and Informal Waste Sectors. Elsevier (2012)

7. UNEP - United Nations Environment Programme & United Nations University. Sustainable Innovation and Technology Transfer Industrial Sector Studies. Recycling from E-Waste to resources (2009)
8. ABDI - Associação Brasileira de Desenvolvimento Industrial - Logística Reversa de Equipamentos Eletroeletrônicos - Análise de Viabilidade Técnica e Econômica, p.44 (2013)
9. Wang, F., Kuchr, R., Ahlquist, D., Li, J.: E-waste in China: A country report, STEP - UNU-ISP, United Nations University – Institute for Sustainability and Peace (2013)
10. EPA- Environmental Protection Agency: Municipal Solid Waste in the United States: Facts and Figures (2011)
11. Sthiannopkao, S., Wong, M.: Handling e-waste in developed and developing countries: Initiatives, practices, and consequences. Sci. Total Environ. (2012)
12. CSCMP- Council of Supply Chain Management Professionals, http://cscmp.org/sites/default/files/user_uploads/resources/downloads/glossary-2013.pdfchi
13. Autry, C.: Formalization of reverse logistics programs: A strategy formaging liberalized returns. Industrial Marketing Management 34, 749–757 (2005)
14. Sheu, J.: A coordinated reverse logistics system for regional management of multi- source hazardous wastes. Computers and Operations Research,1442–1462 (2007)
15. Gregory, J., Magalini, F., Kuehr, R., Huisman, J.: E-Waste Take-Back System Design and Policy Approaches. White Paper (2009)
16. Dekker, R., et al. (eds.): Reverse Logistics: Quantitative Models for Closed-Loop Supply Chains, pp. 3–27. Springer, London (2004)
17. BRASIL. Law n. 12305/2010. Brasília/DF, http://www.planalto.gov.br/ccivil_03/_ato2007-2010/2010/lei/l12305.htm
18. Leite, P.R.: Logística Reversa e a Política Nacional de Resíduos Sólidos (PNRS). Revista Mundo logística, pp. 90–92 (2010)
19. Ferreira, G.T., Vicente, S.C.: Logística Reversa de Resíduos Sólidos: Uma análise crítica dos desafios impostos pela lei 12.305/10. SIMPOI (2011)
20. WEEE - Waste Electrical and Electronic equipment: Directive 2012/ EU of the European Parliament and of the Council (2012)
21. UNEP- United Nations Environment Programme, DTIE, Division of Tecnology, Industry and Economics, IETC International Environmental Tecnology, Manual 3: WEEE/E-Waste: Take Back System (2011)
22. EBCT - Electronics Take Back Coalition (2013), http://www.electronicstakeback.com/promote-good-laws/state-legislation/
23. ESAP- Environmental Self-Assessment Program, http://www.gemi.org/toolmatrix/ToolMatrixItem.aspx?i=36
24. BBC Brasil, http://www.bbc.co.uk/portuguese/noticias/2013/01/130118_lixo_eletronico_bg.shtml
25. http://www.eea.europa.eu/data-and-maps/indicators/waste-electrical-and-electronic-equipment/assessment-1

Impacts of Automakers Milk Run Collect System on Suppliers Planning and on Urban City Emissions

Claudia Meucci Andreatini[1], José Benedito Sacomano[1], and Gilberto Gandelman[2]

[1] Paulista University-UNIP, Graduate Program in Production Engineering,
Dr. Bacelar St. 1212,São Paulo, Brazil
[2] Estrateggia – Management Consulting, Roberto Augusto Tavares St.107,
São José dos Campos, Brazil
{Claudia Meucci Andreatini,andreatini}@unip.com.br

Abstract. The milk run system is widely employed on the automotive of industry worldwide. Its usage is derived from an increasing demand of inventory reduction components and finished goods in the whole automotive supply chain. The aim of this paper is to evaluate the benefit perceived by both car manufacturers and suppliers and to analyze the implementation impacts. This evaluation will be based on field research in which the results are based. Another point with great importance nowadays is the energetic efficiency of the milk run in comparison to the conventional routes. As the milk run circuit is not optimized for minimum fuel consumption, we will present, in terms of quantitative calculations for representatives routes, what is the emission penalty of the milk run compared with conventional collect system.

Keywords: Milk Run, CO_2 emission, Load Factor, Supply Chain Integration.

1   Introduction

Optimizing Inventory level has been a challenge during the last 40 years. As long as the market became more competitive, launching new products with a higher mix and shorter lead times. The industries realized that with this more aggressive road map evolution, the uncertainty in sales forecast and the risk of material obsolescence became a real danger to the financial health of the companies.

A breakthrough in the production management system was done by Toyota [1]. It broke the paradigm in the production systems. The commercial demand "pulls" all the production instead of the previous model in which the production "pushes" the sales.

The lean manufacturing concepts then were one of the key factors to achieve operational efficiency and to reduce components, "work-in-process" and finish goods inventories. In the automotive segment, the car manufacturers realized that the achievement of a "lean" concept would not be possible without the participation and implementation of this philosophy also by the suppliers. Some work has been done in simulating the supply chain material flow [2,3,4].

The deliveries of the suppliers became than in lower volumes and higher frequency to minimize stocks at both automaker and supplier side. The milk run logistics [5]

B. Grabot et al. (Eds.): APMS 2014, Part II, IFIP AICT 439, pp. 122–129, 2014.
© IFIP International Federation for Information Processing 2014

arises as a solution to consolidate a group of geographically nearby suppliers in only one vehicle (under responsibility of the car maker) that collect the parts in a predetermined route at a very precise time window.

The concept of milk run was created based on the diary industry delivery method a long time ago. The milk was delivered door to door on a daily base, as the milk could not endure more than one day at the consumer house, which means that the costumer could not store milk. The product was delivered in a pre determined route and time window. This concept applied to the automotive segment means that the car maker can collect from many suppliers at a high frequency rate and in a predefined route small quantities of parts to minimize their stocks.

Therefore the transport vehicle occupation is optimized by introducing more suppliers into the route. The milk run has been in operation in Brazil for a long time with a great acceptance by the automotive community. We will first evaluate and confirm this perception in chapter 2 and will analyze the fuel consumption and consequently the environmental impact of milk run in chapter 3.

2   Impacts on Automakers – Suppliers Relationship and Procedures

The integrated supply chain between car manufacturers and tear 1 suppliers is well established in Brazil. The idea is that the logistics becomes more efficient all over the chain [6]. Many factors contributed to this integration: lean manufacturing concepts (just in time), IT technology with Material Resource Planning (MRP), Electronic Data Interchange (EDI) that enables on-line orders to suppliers. All these factors contributed to fine tune the orders / deliveries in such a way that the automaker places orders in small quantities to avoid stocks and the supplier has to accomplish that with lower production lots and consequently set the PCP and MRP accordingly.

The milk run then appeared as a good transportation solution to the mentioned context in such a way that small lots could be transported from the suppliers to the customers with a highest possible occupation of the transport vehicle.

As a natural evolution of car manufacturers and suppliers relationship , the milk run system demands an integrative (win–win) type of relationship with high degree of interaction between them [7,8]. In the past, the relationships were from a distributive type (zero-sum) focusing more on immediate results.

In order to evaluate the impact and the perception of the milk run at car makers and suppliers operations we made a field research and the results are shown on table 1. The survey was responded by 5 automakers and 8 suppliers.

It can be observed that the milk run is seen by both sides as a very good system for achieving operational efficiency. The profit improvement is sensed more by the automakers side (100% x 62%) as, normally , the smaller tear 1 suppliers cannot apply milk run to their own sub-suppliers. Therefore, although the finished goods stock level is limited, the components stock tends to be high at supplier side

From the overall stock level point of view, the suppliers sense a more positive impact (75% x 50%) as the stock of finished goods is reduced. On the other hand the automakers always applied a policy of receiving small lots from the local suppliers, independent on the milk run system. Therefore, the main advantage for the automakers is the transport cost optimization rather than components stock.

Table 1. Automakers / Suppliers in Brazil Survey

	Automakers		Suppliers	
	Y	N	Y	N
Does your company apply the milk run with the suppliers?	100%	0%	29%	71%
Has Milk run brought an inventory reduction?	33%	67%	71%	29%
Was PCP affected by the introduction of milk run?	33%	67%	100%	0%
Has milk run brought any improvement in terms of loading/unloading?	100%	0%	71%	29%
Has milk run reduced freight costs?	100%	0%	71%	29%

	Automakers			Suppliers		
	+	=	-	+	=	-
How milk run implementation affects the company profit?	100%	0%	0%	57%	43%	0%

	Automakers				Suppliers			
	0-25%	25-50%	50-75%	+ 75%	0-25%	25-50%	50-75%	+ 75%
% of milk run with respect to the Brazilizn suppliers?	33	33	33	0	100	0	0	0

3   Impact on Emissions and Load Factor

The movement of goods in urban areas is quite representative in terms of emissions. It represents from 20% to 30% of the overall kilometers traveled and from 16% to 50% of urban emission due to transportation [9]. As in Brazil the fleet age is higher in comparison to USA, Japan and Europe it is likely that the emission reaches closer to 50% rather than 16%.

As emissions are a crucial issue, it is very important to analyze the impact of the milk run system on the fuel consumption and consequently on the emission of CO_2.

3.1   The "1D" Path

Arvidsson [10] analyzed the fuel consumption and the fuel emission of a milk run system for a distribution center case considering one distribution center and 4 delivery points. The main goal of the article was to show the called load factor paradox for milk run system. The load factor is the ratio between the actual and maximum load of a truck. While in general, higher load factors represent a better utilization of the commercial vehicle, it is shown that in a milk run circuit it occurs in an opposite way: The lower fuel consumption and CO_2 emission occur for the path with the average lower load factor.

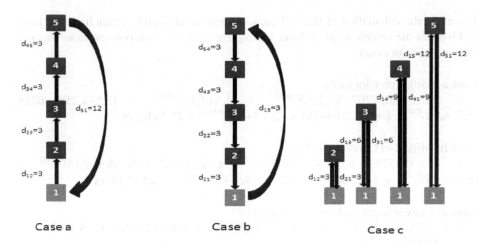

Fig. 1. Path configuration for the "1D" cases

In his example, it was considered an equally spaced delivery points separated by 1,25 kilometers . We will consider here the same geometry (fig. 1), but the analysis will be focused on the milk run collect points instead, where node 1 represents the automaker while nodes 2, 3, 4 and 5 represent the suppliers. The suppliers lie on a straight line starting from the automaker and we will call it a 1D trajectory. The truck starts from point 1 empty, collects the goods on the suppliers and return to the automaker where the parts will be assembled. The distance between the suppliers are 3 Kilometers to be more coherent with great São Paulo automotive industrial area, but the value itself is not important as we perform a comparative analysis. We will simulate 3 cases as follows:

a) Milk run clockwise, where the truck runs most of the path with a high load factor and collect ¼ of the load in each supplier.

b) Milk run counter - clockwise, where the truck runs most of the path with a low load factor and collect ¼ of the load in each supplier

c) Conventional pick up with 1 closed trip per supplier where the vehicle collect the maximum possible load. After the four trips the material collected is 4 times as compared with one single loop of cases a and b.

The fuel consumption depends on the traffic conditions, driver, vehicle type and load. We utilize here a distribution truck [10] with 8,5 tons maximum load and 5,5 kilometers unloaded weight. The urban fuel consumption used is given by the following formula [10,11] where the result is in liters:

$$\text{Urban Fuel Consumption} = \sum_{ii} 0{,}057767 \times d_{ij}(w + I_{ij})^{0{,}6672} \quad (1)$$

Where d_{ij} is the distance in Kilometers between nodes i and j, w is the vehicle weight and I_{ij} is the load carried in each path segment ij.

Therefore the calculation of the fuel consumption in each path, reminding that for a and b cases the vehicle must perform 4 complete cycles to transport the same amount of material as in case c.

Case a: Milk Run Clockwise

$= 4 \times 0,057767 \times 3(5,5^{0,6672} + (5,5+2,13)^{0,6672} + (5,5+4,25)0,6672 + (5,5+6,38)^{0,6672}) + 4 \times 0,057767 \times 12(5,5+8,5)^{0,6672} = \mathbf{27,76\ liters}$

Case b: Milk Run Counter clockwise

$= 4 \times 0,057767 \times 12 \times 5,5^{0,6672} + 4 \times 0,057767 \times 3((5,5+2,13)^{0,6672} + (5,5+4,25)^{0,6672} + + (5,5+6,38)0,6672 + (5,5+8,5)^{0,6672}) = \mathbf{22,15\ liters}$

Case c: Conventional pick up in each supplier

$= 0,057767 \times 3(5,5^{0,6672} + (5,5+8,5)^{0,6672}) + 0,057767 \times 6(5,5^{0,6672} + (5,5+8,5)^{0,6672}) +$
$+ 0,057767 \times 9(5,5^{0,6672} + (5,5+8,5)^{0,6672}) + 0,057767 \times 12(5,5^{0,6672} + (5,5+8,5)^{0,6672}) = \mathbf{16,13\ liters}$

The conventional pick up method by filling the vehicle with only one supplier part per circuit is the most efficient in terms of consumption and consequently CO_2 emission. It should be reminded that in this specific case the inventory level for the automakers will be in average four times greater by compared with the milk run approaches. We summarized the results in table 2 where it is used a conversion rate of 2,66 kg CO_2/l for Diesel [11]. The average load factor (average load/ maximum load) is also calculated as well as the number of kilometers for each case. It can be seen that the best solution (low load factor) of milk run path has a 37,32 % more emission than the conventional pick up as long as the distance traveled is reduced.

Table 2. Results for the "1D" analysis

Case	Fuel Consumption	CO_2 Emission	MilkRun Emission penalty	Average Load Factor	Total Path Lenght
a	27,76 lts	73,84 kg	73,11%	0,69	96 km
b	22,15 lts	58,92 kg	37,32%	0,31	96 km
c	16,13 lts	42,90 kg	0,00%	0,50	60 km

3.2   The "2D" Path

We performed so far all the analysis by choosing a somehow specific geometry where all the OEM – suppliers locations are aligned (1D). An important question which rises is if this alignment does not exist anymore, how the emission penalty for the milk run will vary. In order to model this more generic case, we utilize a path configuration utilizing 1 automaker (node 1) and 2 suppliers (nodes 2 and 3) as it can be seen in figure 2.

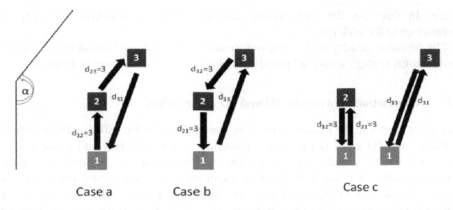

Fig. 2. Path configuration for the "2D" cases

In this case the distance from automaker to supplier 1 (d_{12}) is 3 km, the distance from supplier 1 to supplier 2 (d_{23}) is 3 km and the distance from supplier 2 to OEM (d_{13}) is function of the path angle α, where it can be expressed by using the simple trigonometric triangle relation:

$$d_{13} = d_{31} = (3^2 + 3^2 - 2 \times 3x\ 3 \times \cos(\alpha))^{0,5} = 4,243\ (1\text{-cos }\alpha)^{0,5} \qquad (2)$$

For the particular case where $\alpha = 180°$ we come back to the "1D" path and consequently $d_{13} = d_{31} = 6$ Km.

The calculation of the fuel consumption as a function of the angle α is then straightforward by combining equations (1) and (2). The following relations are then obtained for the fuel consumption, reminding that a complete cycle of case c corresponds to 2 cycles of the milk run cases a and b.

Case a: Milk Run Clockwise
$= 2 \times 0,057767 \times 3.(5,5^{\ 0,6672} + (5,5+4,25)^{0,6672}) +$
$+ 2 \times 0,057767 \times 4,243.(1\text{-cos }\alpha)^{0,5} .(5,5+8,5)^{0,6672}$

Case b: Milk Run Counter Clockwise
$= 2 \times 0,057767 \times 4,243\ (1\text{-cos }\alpha)^{0,5} .5,5^{\ 0,6672}$
$+ 2 \times 0,057767 \times 3.((5,5+4,25)^{0,6672} + (5,5+8,5)^{0,6672})$

Case c: Conventional pick up in each supplier
$= 0,057767 \times 3.(5,5^{\ 0,6672} + (5,5+8,5)^{0,6672}) +$
$+ 0,057767 \times 4,243.(1\text{-cos }\alpha)^{0,5} .(5,5^{\ 0,6672} + (5,5+8,5)^{0,6672})$

We can observe in figure 3, the CO_2 emission for the three cases. The conventional delivery is always better than the 2 milk run cases. Besides, by comparing the milk run clockwise and counter clockwise it can be seen that for $\alpha < 60°$ the clock wise option is better as far as $d_{31} < d_{12}$ and this path represents the minimum average load factor. In this case the conventional delivery introduces a double inventory in comparison to the milk run.

The emission penalty of the milk run strategies (cases a and b) with respect to the conventional strategy among all possible angles ($0°$ to $180°$) is shown in figure 4.

3.3   Correlation between the 1D and 2D Approaches.

As can be shown in the figures 3 and 4 we can realize that the $180°$ condition (which is indeed the 1D case) is the most demanding in terms of fuel and consequently emissions which is quite intuitive as long as the d_{13} & d_{31} segments reach the maximum value of 6 km. But the most important conclusion comes from figure 4 where for the 1D ($180°$) condition, the milk run penalty with respect to the conventional system reaches the minimum value of 24,03%. If we come back to the 1D table 1 we can see that for the case of 4 suppliers the emission penalty is 37,32%. Therefore more suppliers in the path will lead to a higher emission penalty of the milk run. The penalty will increase as the angle becomes smaller then $180°$ which represents a more realistic geometry.

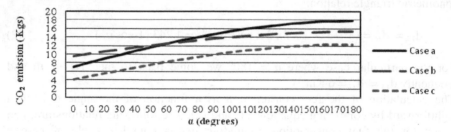

Fig. 3. CO2 emission as function of path angle

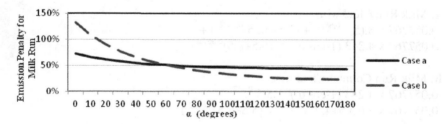

Fig. 4. . CO_2 emission penalty for milk run collect system as function of path angle

It is important to mention that we did not consider in this study some factors which will tend to increase the penalty further. The first is that, as in the milk run due to more pickups at the suppliers, the maneuver of the vehicle represents an extra fuel burden, especially in the great São Paulo area where the maneuver conditions are very tight. Also, as the milk run collect window is narrower in comparison with the conventional window, there is less flexibility for a more efficient route planning to avoid traffic jams and detours due to restricted time zones.

4   Conclusions

We have shown in this article some important points regarding the milk run collect system between the automakers and suppliers. It has been gradually adopted as an important tool for minimizing the inventory level for both automakers and tear1 suppliers. On the other hand, it generates an extra amount of fuel and consequently emission. Depending on the suppliers and automakers location geometry, the emission penalty for the milk run can reach 70% over of the conventional delivery for the case of 2 suppliers, while it can increase further as there are more suppliers. Consequently a detailed route planning accounting for fuel consumption must be performed to minimize the emission penalty.

References

1. Sugimori, Y., Kusunoki, K., Cho, F., Uchikawa, S.: Toyota Production System and Kanban System Materialization of Just-In-Time and Respect-for-Human System. International Journal of Production Research, 553–564 (1977)
2. Kleijnen, P.C.: Supply chain Simulation Tools and Techniques: a Survey. International Journal of Simulation & Process Modeling 1(1/2) (2005)
3. Gandelman, G., Hemerly, E.M.: HS3CM - A New Formulation for Supply Chain Modeling, SAE Technical Paper Series - 2011 -36-0068 E (2011)
4. Shi, W., Shang, J., Liu, Z., Zuo, X.: Optimal Design of the Auto Parts Supply Chain for JIT Operations: Sequential Bifurcation Factor Screening and Multi-Response Surface Methodology. European Journal of Operational Research 236, 664–676 (2014)
5. Moura, D.A., Botter, R.C.: Caracterização do Sistema de Coleta Programada de Peças, Milk Run. RAE-eletrônica 1(1) (Janauary-June 2002)
6. Guarnieri, P., Hatakeyama, K.: Formalização da Logística de Suprimentos: Caso das Montadoras e Fornecedores da Indústria Automotiva Brasileira. Produção 20(2), 186–199 (2010), doi: 10.1590/S0103-65132010005000020
7. Vanalle, R.M., Salles, J.A.: Relationship Between Assemblers and Suppliers: Theoretical Models and Case Studies in the Brazilian Auto Industry. Gest. Prod., São Carlos 18(2), 237–250 (2011)
8. Carvalhal, E., Neto, A.A., Andrade, G.M., Araújo, J.V.: Negociação e Administração de Conflitos, 3rd edn., FGV Management, Serie Gerenciamento de Projetos (2012) ISBN 978-85-225-0969-0
9. Dablanc, L.: Goods Transport in Large European Cities: Difficult to Organize, Difficult to Modernize.Transportation Research Part A: Policy and Practice 41, 280–285 (2007)
10. Arvidsson, N.: The Milk RunR: A Load Factor Paradox with Economic and Environmental Implications for Urban Freight Transport. Transportation Research Part A 51, 56–62 (2013)
11. Liimatainen, H., Pöllänen, M.: Trends of Energy Efficiency in Finnish Road Freight Transport 1995-2009 and Forecast to 2016. Energy Policy 38, 7676–7686 (2010)

A GRASPxELS for Scheduling of Job-Shop Like Manufacturing Systems and CO$_2$ Emission Reduction

Sylverin Kemmoe Tchomte[1] and Nikolay Tchernev[2]

[1] CRCGM EA 3849, Université d'Auvergne, Clermont Ferrand, France
Sylverin.Kemmoe_Tchomte@udamail.fr
[2] LIMOS UMR CNRS 6158, Université d'Auvergne, Aubière, France
Nikolay.Tchernev@udamail.fr

Abstract. The issue of reducing CO$_2$ emission and associated carbon footprint consumption for manufacturing scheduling is addressed. We focus our attention on a job-shop environment where machines can work at different speeds and therefore different energies consumed, i.e. CO$_2$ emissions. It represents an extension of the classical job-shop scheduling problem, where each operation has to be executed by one machine and this machine can work at different speeds, problem which has been introduced by [1]. Energy-efficient scheduling of such type of manufacturing systems demands an optimization approach whose dual objectives are to minimize both the CO$_2$ emissions and the makespan. To solve this new problem, a GRASPxELS is developed. New instances benchmark based on well know Laurence's instances are introduced and numerical experiments are proposed trying to evaluate the method convergence. The performance is evaluated using the optimal solutions found after a strongly time consuming resolution based on a linear formulation of the problem.

Keywords: energy efficiency, job-shop, scheduling, CO$_2$ emissions, GRASP.

1 Introduction

Nowadays, companies are not only facing economics trends with objective to improve profitability and competitiveness, but also reducing their CO$_2$ emissions using the green manufacturing concepts. In this paper, we focus our attention in a job-shop like manufacturing environment where machines can work at different speeds and therefore different energies consumed, i.e. different CO$_2$ emissions generated. When machine speed is high the processing time of the job operation is short and the energy consumption CO$_2$ emission is high. Contrary if the speed is low, the processing time increases and the energy consumption decreases and CO$_2$ emissions are lower. In this type of manufacturing systems there is a close relation between lead times and CO$_2$ emissions. To this end, we analyse the relationship between machine speed, makespan and CO$_2$ emissions in order to obtain a multi-objective solution. Our goal is to find a solution that minimizes hierarchically the makespan and the energy consumption, and therefore CO$_2$ emissions. To model the problem we chose the Job Shop with different Speed Machine theoretical problem (*JSSM*) first formulated by [1] which problem is

B. Grabot et al. (Eds.): APMS 2014, Part II, IFIP AICT 439, pp. 130–137, 2014.
© IFIP International Federation for Information Processing 2014

an extension of the classical *JS* problem, where each job operation should be processed at a determined speed. This paper presents a *GRASPxELS* metaheuristic approach for the *JSSM* problem solving that considers CO_2 emissions and associated carbon footprint in addition to makespan.

This paper calls for the development of more specialized algorithms for this new scheduling problem and examines computationally tractable approaches for finding near-optimal schedules. The rest of the paper is organized as follows. In section 2 the problem is presented. In section 3 a *GRASPxELS* with productivity and environmental objectives is presented. Section 4 is dedicated to the numerical experiments, before some concluding remarks.

2   Job Shop with Different Speed Machine

2.1   Problem Description

Formally the job-shop scheduling problem with different speed machine (*JSSM*) can be defined as follows. The *JSSM* consists of a finite set J of n jobs $\{J_i\}_{i=1}^n$ to be processed on a finite set M of m machines $\{M_k\}_{k=1}^m$. Each job J_i consists of a sequence of m_i operations $O_{i,1}, O_{i,2}, O_{i,3} ..., O_{i,m_i}$. Each operation $O_{i,j}$ is associated with a particular job i and machine j and has an integer duration $p_{O_{i,j}}^{mod}$ and generate CO_2 emissions depending on the speed v. Each machine can work with different speeds, each speed depends on the processing mode and is linked up to a duration and CO_2 emissions. There are $N = \sum_{i=1}^n m_i$ operations in total and therefore, the dimension of the problem is often denoted as $n \times m \times |NbSpeed|$. A feasible solution is a complete definition of operation starting times that satisfies the following constraints: (*i*) delivery times of the products are undefined; (*ii*) no more than one operation of any job can be executed simultaneously; (*iii*) no machine can process more than one operation at the same time; (*iv*) the job operations must be executed in a predefined sequence and mode and once an operation is started, no pre-emption is permitted. The objective is to find a feasible schedule that minimizes the completion time of all the tasks and the energy used, i.e. CO_2 emissions. According to the $\alpha|\beta|\gamma$ notation introduced by [2] the problem can be represented by $J| |C_{max}$ and is known to be NP-hard [2]. In addition an association between duration and energy has been created. For each job operation three different speeds have been defined. Each speed has its own duration and CO_2 emissions generated depending on the energy consumption. When the work speed increases the energy and CO_2 emissions also increase and on the other hand the duration decreases.

2.2   Related Literature

Although the *JS* is well-addressed in the literature (see for survey [3] and some recent papers [4, 5], from best of our knowledge only few articles [1], [6, 7] are concerned with energy consumption. In [6] bi-objective model for energy consumption and makespan optimization for *JS* is formulated and heuristic algorithm is developed to locate the optimal or near optimal solutions of the model based on the Tabu search mechanism. [7] proposed a mixed-integer nonlinear programming model for the hybrid flow shop scheduling problem to minimize energy consumption. An improved genetic algorithm solved this efficiently. Although energy consumption was mainly considered and the makespan was a key constraint, they ignored on-peak times for energy use.

[1] is the first paper which considers the energy in JSSM. In this seminal paper, using constraint programming technology for minimizing makespan and energy consumption, the authors analyzed energy-efficiency, robustness and makespan, and the relationship among them.

In the specialized literature about production scheduling research on minimizing the energy consumption of manufacturing systems has focused on following shop scheduling problems: (*i*) single machine [8]; (*ii*) flow-shop [9]; (*iii*) hybrid and flexible flow-shop [10, 11].

Although many researchers have addressed energy consumption in scheduling, one of them have tried to consider *JSSM* problem. None of this research has proposed a metaheuristic approach for *JSSM* problem.

3   GRASPxELS Based Approach for *JSSM* Solving

In order to find approximate solutions to the *JSSM*, we propose a *GRASPxELS* metaheuristic approach base on Greedy Randomized Adaptive Search Procedure (GRASP) hybridized with an evolutionary local search (*ELS*). Proposed by [12], *GRASPxELS* approach has been used successfully and competitive results have been reported in the literature for the classical *JS* problem [5]. The purpose of this section is to evoke the principles of *GRASP×ELS* where:

- *GRASP* is a multi-start local search metaheuristic in which each initial solution is constructed using a greedy randomized heuristic. The multi-start approach of the *GRASP* provides $np>1$ initial solutions, improved by a local search. It was first presented in [13, 14], by Feo and Resende, and later formalized and given its acronym in [15]. Since then, it has been used to solve a wide range of problems with many and varied applications in the real life such as the design of communication networks, scheduling, collection and delivery operations and computational biology. For recent and comprehensive surveys of *GRASP* we refer the reader to [16, 17, 18].
- The purpose of *ELS* is to better investigate the current local optimum neighborhood during *ni* iterations, before leaving it. Starting from an initial solution, each *ELS* iteration consists in taking a $ns>1$ copies of the incumbent solution *S*, applying a mutation (child solution) and improving the mutated solutions using a local search. The resulting best solution S^* becomes the incumbent solution *S*.

The proposed *GRASPxELS* is based on the following key features which enable scheduling problems solving using evolutionary algorithms and favours efficient global process for solution space investigation:

- Graph representation such as disjunctive/conjunctive graph [19];
- A Quasi-Direct Representation of Solution that is not a whole solution of the problem but a compact representation, such as a sequence of nodes or operations. Bierwirth in 1995 [20] introduces an alternative representation as a sequence of job number. This kind of representation is called: sequence with repetition. Based on his proposal, the solution of Fig. 1 is encoded to: 1 2 3 3 2 3 2 1 1.
- An efficient local search taking advantages of the longest path analysis using, well-known the neighbourhood system of [21] which concern two consecutive operations on the longest path.

Algorithm 1 illustrates the *GRASPxELS* principles and implementation in psedo-code. The *GRASPxELS* iterations are carried out in line 1-18. In line 1, the variable that stores the best solution found is initialized. The block of instructions between lines 2 and 18 is executed iteratively, where each iteration consists of three phases:

- Construction phase (line 3): initial solutions are built, one element at a time, with a greedy randomized heuristic. At each construction iteration the next element to be added is determined by ordering all elements in a candidate list. The probabilistic component of a *GRASPxELS* in this phase is characterized by randomly choosing one of the candidates in the list, not always is the top best.
- Local search phase (lines 4-6): since this solution of the construction phase is not guaranteed to be locally optimal, a local search is performed to minimize the makespan. In line 5, for the last found minimal makespan a local search for minimizing the CO_2 emissions is performed. The quality of the obtained solution is compared to the current best found and, if necessary, the solution is updated (line 6). The use of local search phase based on two search procedures permits to order by strict preference makespan and CO_2 objectives, where the first one is the most preferred. The makespan is the most preferred since it correspond on due dates of customer orders. Using the first level optimization makespan is minimized (see solution Fig2.). The next level minimization the CO_2 emissions are minimized by increasing some operation durations for example J2, J3 and J5 and consequently reduce CO_2 emissions as shown in Fig. 3.
- Evolutionary local search (*ELS*) phase (lines 8-17): to better investigate the current local optimum neighborhood. In line 16, the quality of the obtained solution is compared to the current best found and, if necessary, the solution is updated.

The successive changes of encoding occur between the local search and mutations steps of our *GRASPxELS*. The best overall solution is kept as the result. A *GRASPx-ELS* can be seen as a metaheuristic that captures good features of pure greedy algorithms (intensification), of random construction procedures and of mutation (diversification). In order to avoid premature convergence of iterative search process efficient clone detection is included trying to prevent unprofitable exploration of search space previously investigated. To measure difference between two schedules earliest starting time of operations and CO_2 emissions at each schedule are compared.

Algorithm 1. GRASPxELS metaheuristic principles

```
Procedure name GRASPxELS
Begin
1.   S* ← ∅
2.   for p := 1 to np do
3.        S ← Construction_Phase
4.        S ← Local_Seach_Phase_Makespan
5.        S ← Local_Seach_Phase_CO₂
6.        if( f(S) < f(S*)) then S* ← S end if
9.        for j:= 1 to ni do               // ELS phase
10.            f":=+∞              // initialized best found solution
11.            for k := 1 to ns do           // ELS mutation
12.                 S':= S
13.                 Mutate S'
14.                 S' ← Local_Seach_Phase_Makespan
15.                 S' ← Local_Seach_Phase_CO₂
16.                 if   (f(S') < f") then
17.                      f" := f(S'); S" := S'
18.                 end if
19.            end for
20.            if  (f" < f(S*)) then   S* ← S" end if
21.            S := S"        // update ELS current solution
17.       end for
18.  end for
19.  return S*
end
```

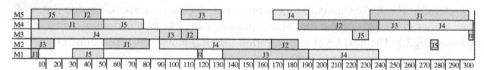

Fig. 1. Gantt chart of schedule when makespan is minimized (C_{max}=299, CO_2=95776)

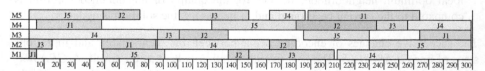

Fig. 2. Gantt chart of schedule when CO_2 emissions are minimized (C_{max}=299, CO_2=95512)

4   Computational Experiment

4.1   Instances

The benchmark is concerned with instances based on the OR-library which instances encompass the well-known Laurence's instances La01-LA10. From these 10 instances of Laurence considered, we have generated 60 instances of *JSSM*. From each original LA instance we built six instances with 5, 6 …10 jobs. Each operation has three modes of treatment, and each operation mode has its own duration. The duration of the first mode is exactly the same of the duration of the classical Job Shop. The durations of the two others modes are randomly generated around the value of the first mode. To generate the CO_2 generated by operations in our model, we considered that the generation of CO_2 is inversely proportional to the processing time of each operation. That's can be explained by the fact that if we have to make a choice between three ways of dealing with different durations, our choice will be the mode of treatment with the shortest processing time, but with this mode treatment, a higher consumption of carbon is observed, due to the high speed imposed on the production line. For example, if the set is composed by three operations with duration 10, 40 and 50 units times, the carbon consumed by these operations are respectively proportional at the values (10+40+50)/10 = 10, (10+40+50)/40 = 5 and (10+40+50)/50 = 2.

4.2   Computational Results

The GRASPxELS is benchmarked over the 60 generated instances and it is compared with solutions obtained by linear programming. All procedures are implemented under Delphi 6.0 package and experiments were carried out on a 2.8 GHz computer under Windows 7 with 12 GO of memory. The results for 13 instances whose optimal solutions are obtained using CPLEX are given in Table 1. As we make ten replications, the average value of the makespan, CO_2 and CPU times are considered in Table 1. For these instances our approach found ten optimal solutions concerning the makespan objective and an average deviation from the optimal solutions of 0.17%. Whit an average deviation of 0.08% from the CO_2 objective optimal solutions we can state that the quality achieved is very good. Solutions are found in rather short computational time (in average of 1.20 s), which proves that GRASPxELS is a powerful method. To estimate the quality of proposed framework we compared the results with the lower bounds (*LB*) calculated by the linear programming with CPLEX 24 hours' time limit. For 33 instances lower bounds are obtained and the average improvement of the lower bounds is 29.53% for makespan and 37.33% for the CO_2. For the rest of the instances (14) no CPLEX solutions are obtained during time limit. Moreover, all 60 solutions (job sequences) obtained by our *GRASPxELS* are compared with those obtained by linear programming as follows: for each best job sequence generated by *GRASPxELS* linear program found the optimal solution concerning the makespan and the CO_2. CPLEX results are compared with these obtained by our metaheuristic. An analysis of comparative results showed that the average deviations are 0.00% and 0.025% respectively from the makespan and CO_2. Therefore, the performance evaluation of the proposed framework clearly shows that it is a particularly efficient method for problem under study.

Table 1. Results of comparative study: optimal solutions

Linear programming optimal solutions						*GRASPxELS* solutions			
Inst.	n	m	C_{max}	CO_2	T (secs)	BFS	C_{max} Dev%	Avg. CO_2	T(s)	CO_2 Dev%
La01	5	5	300	98258	873.25	300.0	0.00	98419.2	0.09	0.16
La01	6	5	333	136929	1504.49	333.0	0.00	136877.1	0.22	0.04
La01	8	5	395	288853	10509.00	401.7	1.67	288970.0	6.16	0.04
La02	5	5	299	95562	1246.08	299.0	0.00	95637.4	0.09	0.08
La02	6	5	342	138536	1121.71	342.9	0.26	138732.0	2.08	0.14
La02	7	5	307	192610	5685.50	307.0	0.00	192702.9	2.46	0.05
La03	5	5	290	96489	1548.49	290.0	0.00	96513.5	0.09	0.03
La03	6	5	283	134679	20460.00	283.0	0.00	134831.1	0.17	0.11
La03	7	5	299	192135	14889.00	301.0	0.76	192163.5	3.41	0.01
La04	5	5	291	82133	1219.41	291.0	0.00	82264.5	0.06	0.16
La04	6	5	322	116491	1487.37	322.0	0.00	116580.0	0.41	0.08
La05	6	5	286	129235	5840.88	286.0	0.00	129369.3	0.17	0.10
La05	7	5	398	179891	19429.00	398.0	0.00	180196.0	0.22	0.17
						Average	0.17%		1,20	0.08%

5   Conclusion

Many real life problems can be modelled as a job-shop scheduling problem where machines can work at different speeds. It represents an extension of the classical job-shop scheduling problem, where each operation has to be executed by one machine and this machine has the possibility to work at different speeds. In this paper, we analyse the relationship among two important objectives that must be taken into account in green manufacturing: Makespan and Energy-efficiency. To solve the problem we propose an efficient GRASPxELS algorithm. The algorithm was evaluated on 60 test problems based on well-known La01, ..., La10 instances and was shown to produce optimal or near-optimal solutions on all instances. The numerical experiment proves that our framework can obtain almost optimal solutions in a rather short computational time. In this paper the makespan is one the objective to minimize, however the structure of the proposed GRASPxELS permits to minimize other criteria like: maximum tardiness or total flowtime, ... This work is a step forward definition of efficient models for job-shops like scheduling problems with multiple speed machines.

References

1. Salido, M.A., Escamilla, J., Barber, F., Giret, A., Tang, D., Dai, M.: Energy-aware Parameters in Job-shop Scheduling Problems. In: GREEN-COPLAS 2013: IJCAI 2013 Workshop on Constraint Reasoning, Planning and Scheduling Problems for a Sustainable Future, Beijing, China, pp. 44–53 (2013)
2. Garey, M.R., Johnson, D.S., Seth, R.: The complexity of flowshop and jobshop scheduling. Math. of Oper. Res. 1, 117–129 (1976)

3. Jain, S., Meeran, S.: Deterministic job-shop scheduling: Past, present and future. E. J. of Oper. Res. 113, 390–434 (1999)
4. Gao, L., Zhang, D., Zhang, L., Li, X.: An efficient memetic algorithm for solving the job shop scheduling problem. C. & Ind. Eng. 60, 699–705 (2011)
5. Chassaing, M., Fontanel, J., Lacomme, P., Ren, L., Tchernev, N., Viullechenon, P.: A GRASP × ELS approach for the job-shop with a web service paradigm packaging. Exp. S. with Appl. 41(2), 544–562 (2014)
6. He, Y., Lui, F., Cao, H.J., Li, C.: A bi-objective model for job-shop scheduling problem to minimize both energy consumption and makespan. J. Cent. South Uni. Techn. 12(2), 167–171 (2005)
7. Liu, Y., Dong, H., Lohse, N., Petrovic, S., Gindy, N.: An investigation into minimizing total energy consumption and total weighted tardiness in job shops. J. Clean. Prod. 65, 87–96 (2014)
8. Yildirim, M.B., Mouzon, G.: Single-machine sustainable production planning to minimize total energy consumption and total completion time using a multiple objective genetic algorithm. IEEE Tr. on Eng. Man. 59(4), 585–597 (2011)
9. Fang, K., Uhan, N., Zhao, F., Sutherland, J.: Flow shop scheduling with peak power consumption constraints. A. of Op. Res. 206(1), 115–145 (2013)
10. Luo, H., Huang, G., Chen, H., Li, X.: Hybrid flow shop scheduling considering machine electricity consumption cost. I. J. Prod. Ec. 146, 423–439 (2013)
11. Bruzzone, A.A.G., Anghinolfi, D., Paolucci, M., Tonelli, F.: Energy-aware scheduling for improving manufacturing process sustainability: a mathematical model for flexible flow-shops. CIRP Ann.–Man. Techn. 61(1), 459–462 (2012)
12. Prins, C.: A GRASP x evolutionary local search hybrid for the vehicle routing problem. In: Pereira, F.B., Tavares, J. (eds.) Bio-Inspired Algorithms for the Vehicle Routing Problem. SCI, vol. 61, pp. 35–53. Springer, Heidelberg (2009)
13. Feo, T.A., Resende, M.G.C.: A probabilistic heuristic for a computationally difficult set covering problem. Op. Res. Let. 8, 67–71 (1989)
14. Feo, T.A., Resende, M.G.C.: Greedy randomized adaptive search procedures. J. of Gl. Opt. 6, 109–133 (2005)
15. Feo, T.A., Resende, M.G.C., Smith, S.H.: A greedy randomized adaptive search procedure for maximum independent set. Op. Res. 42, 860–878 (1994)
16. Resende, M.G.C., Ribeiro, C.: Greedy randomized adaptive search procedures. In: Glover, F., Kochenberger, G. (eds.) ORMS, Handbook of Metaheuristics, pp. 219–249. Kluwer Academic Publishers, Dordrecht (2003)
17. Festa, P., Resende, M.G.C.: An annotated bibliography of GRAS part I: algorithms. Int. Trans. in Op. Res. 16, 1–24 (2009)
18. Festa, P., Resende, M.G.C.: An annotated bibliography of GRASP part II: applications. Int. Trans. in Op. Res. 16, 131–172 (2009)
19. Roy, B., Sussmann, B.: Les problèmes d'ordonnancement avec contraintes disjunctive, In: Note DS N°9 bis, SEMA, Paris (1964)
20. Bierwirth, C.: A Generalized permutation approach to Job Shop scheduling with genetic algorithms. OR Spektrum 17, 87–92 (1995)
21. Van Laarhoven, P.J.M., Aarts, E.H.L., Lenstra, J.K.: Jobshop scheduling by simulated annealing. Op. Res. 40(1), 113–125 (1992)

Management Model for Micro and Small Enterprises Supported by Maslow's Theory: An Option for Graphic Industry in Brazil

Luiz Flávio Suarez Botana and Pedro Luiz de Oliveira Costa Neto

Paulista University-UNIP, Graduate Program in Production Engineering,
Dr. Bacelar St. 1212, São Paulo, Brazil
{flaviobotana,politeleia}@uol.com.br

Abstract. Brazil's graphic industry is mainly composed by Micro and Small Enterprises (MSE), that are undergoing technological and market threats. The proposal of this study is to analyze the feasibility in elaborating a simple and practical management model, based on Maslow's Hierarchy of Needs Theory, for application on MSEs in the graphic branch. The feasibility analysis was performed through the similarities between humans and businesses: a method much used for the development of management tools. It has been revealed, in the analysis of prepositions for the development of a theory of motivation, a high similarity between the original text applied on humans and their interpretation for application in business, which opens doors for the development of the proposed management model.

Keywords: maslow, graphic industry, small enterprises, management.

1 Introduction

The Micro and Small Enterprises have a relevant role in Brazil's economy, but due to its structure, lacks effective business management. Particularly in the graphic industry, whose structure basically consists of micro and small family companies with local operations, it is noticed that the abilities and knowledge of its owners is focused on technical and commercial aspects: lacking proper management. However, the development and implementation of a management model can suit the entrepreneurs needs and provide them with new business tools to enhance their competitiveness in highly competitive markets.

Thus, the objective in the present work is to discuss the feasibility of creating a simple and practical management model, developed in stages and allows the manager of a small or micro graphic industry to conduct their businesses more professionally and with more focus on results.

Micro and Small Enterprises in Brazil
In Brazil the company size is set according to the number of employees. Within the industry branch, micro businesses have up to 19 employees and small businesses are those that have from 20-99 employees [1].

B. Grabot et al. (Eds.): APMS 2014, Part II, IFIP AICT 439, pp. 138–145, 2014.
© IFIP International Federation for Information Processing 2014

Micro and small enterprises (MSEs) have a significant role in Brazil's productive structure. In 2010 there were 6.1 million MSEs, which represents 99% of the total establishments in the country, and they account for 14.7 million jobs, representing 51.6% of the total employment, and 39, 7% of the compensation paid to formal employees in the non-agricultural private enterprises [1].

Another relevant aspect is the growth in numbers of MSEs and the increase of jobs in the 2000s. The number of stores rose from 4.2 million in 2000 to 6.1 million in 2010, with an average growth of 3.7% per year, and the number of jobs increased from 8.6 million to 14.7 million, with an average growth of 5.5% per year [1].

One issue that influences the quality an MSE management, is the scholar history of its owner. PNAD (National Household Sample Survey) 2009 showed that 39.9% of employers, regardless of property size, are illiterate, and have incomplete or complete primary education/ incomplete high school education. If we include those with complete high school education / incomplete higher education, this number rises to 75.9% [1].

The Brazilian Graphic Industry

The graphic industry is an influential segment in Brazil, with gross income of R$ 44 billion annually and employing 225,000 people in 2012. This industry segment has strong participation by the MSEs. A total of 20,631companies in 2012, 90.1% are micro and 8.5% are small. The remaining 296 companies are medium or large companies. Economically the graphic industry represents 0.4% of GDP (Gross Domestic Product) of the country, representing 2.2% of the manufacturing industry [2].

This profile of the Brazilian graphic industry is not peculiar. Compared with the European printing industry, the structure is quite similar. The European printing market consists of 121,000 firms that had income of 88 billion euros in 2010, and 714,000 employees. Among the total number of companies in Brazil, 95% have standards that classify them as micro and small [3].

The Brazilian graphic industry presents indicators that concern the sector managers. Although the physical production of the manufacturing industry had a growth perspective in 2012 of 1,2% for the year of 2013, the graphic industry beckoned with a fall of 5,6% [2].

Furthermore, Brazil's graphic industry's trade balance has decreased in the past recent years. In addition, the commercial income the industry fell from 64.4 millions positive dollars in 2006 to a negative of 269,5 millions of dollars in 2013. This decrease was particularly accentuated since 2010.

Another relevant aspect of Brazilian's graphic industry is a decrease in the level of investment in machines and equipment, which has been dropping since 2008. A descent of 12% in 2012 and 3% in 2013 [2]

The scenario presented is decreasing the confidence for graphic businessman, now standing on the lower level of the last 4 years according to data from the periodic survey conducted by CNI (National Confederation of Industry). Overall, confidence in graphic entrepreneur is lower than average, and has decreased in the last 3 years.

2   Methodology

In applying the similarities between human and business, the feasibility of elaborating a management model with the same structure of the Hierarchy of Needs Theory by Maslow, the results will be analyzed for application in the management of Brazilian MSEs in the graphic area. A SWOT analysis was applied to the Brazilian Graphic Industry in order to sustain the tests, performed through the analysis of 16 "prepositions about motivation that must be incorporated in any realistic motivation theory" proposed by Maslow in the "Preface to the Theory of Motivation" of his work Motivation and Personality [4].

Adopting the similarity between businesses and humans has formed the basis for various applications in the business world. Ichak Adizes presents the Managing Corporate Life Cycle methodology [5], using the behavioral similarities of living organisms and organizations, furthermore, applying a terminology completely related to the human being's life cycle. Jair Moggi also developed the cellular model on business management based on this type of similarities, citing some human characteristics as organizational characteristics that enterprises are seeking to incorporate on their everyday [6]. In this case, the similarities were stated by the authors by reasoning over the existence of a strong, medium or low relation between Maslow's citations and MSEs reality.

The recognition of the Hierarchy of Needs Theory of Maslow and its accessible information , altogether with the fact that it deals with the organization of motivations in steps, reveals an interesting adequacy for use in small companies, object of this study.

3   Theoretical Foundation Applied

Maslow's Hierarchy of Needs Theory
The Hierarchy of Needs Theory was developed by Abraham Maslow (1908-1970) and presented the concepts in his book Motivation and Personality (1954). Although it is a theory challenged many times, it is the most used by the business branch.

Maslow's theory classifies human being's needs in five levels, and the basis of the theory s that each level of need must be fulfilled before the next, following a hierarchy.

Maslow defines the following levels of human's needs:

- Basic/physical needs: items that assure the individual's survival and the preservation of the species. The needs attributed to this level are food, shelter, rest and reproduction.
- Safety needs: stability and maintenance of possessions. It is the search for privacy and protection from threats. This level includes health and well being, physical and financial safety and protection from the unexpected.

- Social needs or association needs: attributed to the need to 'belong'. The aspects included are relationships based on emotion, intimacy, friendship and social interactions, formation and maintenance of family and participation in organizational groups.
- Self esteem or status needs: this level includes self confidence, the need for social approval and acknowledgment, respect, prestige, and the consideration of a group, in addition to the feeling of independence and autonomy.
- Self realization needs: is the highest level of humans' motivations. Consists in enjoying to the fullest the human potential; to do what one wants, what one likes what one knows.

The broad recognition of the Hierarchy of Needs Theory as an instrument for the study of human motivation is attested by the amount of articles that base their conclusions on this Theory. Ferreira et al [7] studies the correlation between the educational level and the perception of motivational factors of Maslow's theory at the workplace. Kotliarov built a mathematical model of Malsow Theory on a basis of special noncontinuous functions[8] and Saeednia et al developed a reliable scale measuring basic-needs-satisfaction for adults[9].

SWOT analysis of Brazil's Graphic Industry
The internet changed the way companies buy, sell and produce. For the graphic industry, in addition to these changes, one more intense was the change in communication, for the core business of the graphic industry is written communication.

Websites, digital documents, emails and ecommerce affected the structure on communication, and consequentially, the traditional structure of the graphic industry. Products that were purchased in print shops can nowadays be printed on personal printers [10]

The graphic industry has also been undergoing technological transformations considered disruptive, such as the digital processing of images and digital printing growing in the graph market, in quantity and value [3], and recently the development of 3D printing.

This new area of business forces the entrepreneurs to rethink the sector's strategies. The SWOT analysis of strengths , weaknesses, threats and opportunities [11] applied to the graphic industry shows the references needed to guide, through new strategies, the Brazilian graphic entrepreneur.

STRONG POINTS

- Installed capacity adequate in quantity and technology, being compatible with the existent technology.
- County's political economical structure is stable and banking system is strong.

WEAK POINTS

- Technical knowledge of employees in the graphic industry is low. In 2009, 86% of   graphic employees had a maximum education of complete High School [12].
- "Cost Brazil" is an additional cost for business owners, much higher than the other countries in emerging markets [13]

- There are few institutions of the area's technical education. In 2014, there is only one college that graduates graphic technicians.

THREATS

- Digital technology, especially on the promotional and editorial markets, that is, the substitution of graphic products by alternatives that dispose the use of paper.
- Increase in the Chinese importation in 2013. One fourth of the product importations in the graphic branch come from China [2].
- Ambient list views on the use of paper

OPPORTUNITIES

- Brazil has a large and expanding domestic market. Its importations represents less than 15% of the GDP, a percentage smaller than most other emerging markets [13].
- The increase in consumption directly affects the packaging market, that tends to be the less affected by technical threats suffered by the graphic industry.
- Digital impressions and technology that allows access to a new market not attained by printed products.
- There are clear signs that the global economic conditions are improving. As a consequence the graphic industry is planning to reinvest in the next few years.[14]
- The graphic industry ceases to focus on products to now focus on services. It is clear that there is a high demand for new solutions and new business models that better attend the clients' needs. [14]

The results verified by SWOT analysis on the Brazilian graphic industry's data and profile, is a strong indicator that the small enterprise that uses traditional resources, do not have the competence and structure to execute modern management strategies to face the threats posed by the current strategic environment.

Turner et al [15] had similar results in the analysis of Product Management Institution (PMI) tool for European micro and small enterprises. It was suggested that the development of a "micro-lite" version of PMI, easier and less bureaucratic for small projects, using informal management techniques. Therefore, the use of tools structured specifically for   small enterprises, facilitating their strategic work, can be useful for the survival and prosperity of this type of business.

4   Discussions and Results

To verify if the use of similarity would be consistent applied on companies, an analysis was performed on Maslow's 16 citations from chapter 3 (Preface to Motivational Theory) of his book "Motivation and personality" [4], where the author presents a series of " prepositions on motivation that should be incorporated in any realistic motivation theory", and searched for a text as coherent as the one presented, having The object of the methodology as an enterprise rather than a human, and characterized the corresponding correlations, as presented on Chart 1.

Chart 1: Similarities between the application of Maslow's Theory for human beings and enterprises

Maslow Citations	Enterprise similarities
"the individual is an integrated, organized whole" ... "It means the whole individual is motivated rather than just parts of him". (INDIVIDUAL AS A WHOLE)	The company is an integrated organized whole. The analysis of the company's motivation should be applied to it as a whole and not in parts. **HIGH SIMILARITY**
"The particular desires that pass through our consciousness dozens of times a day are not in themselves so important as what they stand for, where they lead, what they ultimately mean upon deeper analysis." ... "We may then assert that sound motivation theory cannot possible afford to neglect the unconscious life." (ENDS AND MEANS)	The analysis of the company's activities must become focused on the people involved in the act, rather than on the act itself. The company's motivation analysis will not be consistent if the company's culture is neglected. **MEDIUM SIMILARITY**
"...the primordial and fundamental human desires do not differ as much as their daily conscientious desires" ... "Human beings are more similar that we initially thought." (DESIRE AND CULTURE)	Companies are more alike that they seem, if its primordial and fundamental needs are considered. **HIGH SIMILARITY**
"We will emphasize that is it uncommon and not common, that a conscientious act or desire has only one motivation,". (MULTIPLE MOTIVATIONS)	The company's actions do not occur due to isolated interests, but by a group of them. **MEDIUM SIMILARITY**
"A coherent motivational theory should assume a posture that the motivation is constant, endless and complex, and consider that it is na universal characteristic of practically all particular organisms states". (MOTIVATIONAL STATES)	The motivational aspects of a company can be manifested in various ways, by different people in different situations. It is not the isolated facts that create a general state of motivation for the company. **MEDIUM SIMILARITY**
Two facts: (1)the human being will not be satisfies, except in some moments of his journey; and (2) the desires seem to be organized in a hierarchy of prepotencies. (RELATIONSHIPS OF MOTIVATIONS)	Companies were born to grow and prosper. Independent of the situation, the company will always be trying to improve its performance and results. **HIGH SIMILARITY**
"We must give up once and for all the concern in producing lists in atomistic style, of needs and motivators " (LIST OF MOTIVATORS)	There is no specific formula to attain success in a company. **HIGH SIMILARITY**
"It is only the fundamental targets that remain constant throughout the flow that exerts a dynamic approach on psychological theory". (CLASSIFICATION OF MOTIVATIONAL LIFE)	What is common in companies is the goals to be met in order to obtain success. **MEDIUM SIMILARITY**
"The study of motivation does not nullify or negate the study of situational determinants, but supplements them.	The concept applies literally on the analysis of a company's motivation.

Both have their place in a broader structure" (THE ENVIOROMENT)	**HIGH SIMILARITY**
"Any theory of motivation must take into account not only the fact that the body behaves in the ordinary way, as an integrated whole, but must also consider that sometimes this does not occur, particularly in difficult times" (INTEGRATION)	Strange behaviors towards the company's culture, particularly in difficult times, should be faced as acceptable variations on the management process. **MEDIUM SIMILARITY**
"Not all behaviors and reactions are motivated, at least not in na ordinary sense of search for satisfaction of needs, that is, the search of what one lacks and/or needs.. (UNMOTIVATED BEHAVIOR)	There are isolates actions. Not all that is decided by the company is 100% coherent with its culture and with the fulfillment of its needs. **MEDIUM SIMILARITY**
"In the whole, we search consciously for what is conceivably reachable. The attention given to this reach possibility factor is crucial for understanding the differences in motivation in between classes". (POSSIBILITY OF REACH)	Companies will advance in their management within their possibilities, that vary with time. **HIGH SIMILARITY**
In regards to the ID, the ego controls the path access to mobility, but shifts between desire and action, the procrastinating factor of thought, during which one makes use of experience residues accumulated on the memory. (INFLUENCE OF REALITY)	The company's actions also suffer from external factors, in addition to cultural and motivational internal factors. **MEDIUM SIMILARITY**
"any theory that is worthy of attention should be able to deal with the elevated capacities of the strong and healthy human, as well as defensive maneuvers of handicapped spirits. (KNOWLEDGE OF HEALTHY MOTIVATION)	A management model should be developed to be applied in different companies from different branches and in different situations. **HIGH SIMILARITY**

Out of all 16 prepositions presented by Maslow in this text, only two (absent in chart 1) did not find similarities when applied on companies: "Hunger as a Paradigm" and "Motivation and Animal Info". All other 14 prepositions had similarities, seven being high, which means that the concept presented by Maslow, having as its center study humans and their motivation is perfectly applicable when one thinks on the company and its success as a new central focus.

5   Conclusions

The application of the similarity method showed a high connection between Maslow's Hierarchy of Needs concepts, having as a central object a company rather than a human. It is believed that the use of this theory's concepts as a management model is adequate for small companies, for these concepts are easy to understand and have a high practical application that can be implemented in steps.

Furthermore, with basis on what was exposed, the development of a management model that is simple and practical and can be applied in steps was initialized, focusing on MSEs for testing on the Brazilian graphic industry. We hope to present this model for application in a next publication.

References

1. DIEESE, Work Catalogue on micro and small enterprises: 2010-2011. 4. Ed. /Brazilian Service of Support for Micro and Small Enterprises (Org.); Inter-union Department of Statistics and Social-Economical Studies (responsible for the elaboration of the research, texts charts and graphs.) – Brasília, DF; DIEESE (2011)
2. ABIGRAF – Numbers of the Brazilian Graphic Industry in 2012 – Brazilian Association of Graphic Industry – Social-economic Studies – DECON (2013)
3. INTERGRAF – European Graphic Industry: Facts and Numbers – Laetitia Reynaud – Intergraf (2013)
4. MASLOW, Abraham – Motivation and Personality – 1954,
   http://www.crarj.org.br/site/leitura/textos_class/traduzidos/
   motivation%20and%20personality/publicacao/index.html
   (access in March 24, 2014)
5. ADIZES, Ichak – Life Cycle Corporations: how and why companies grow and die and what to do about it, 2nd edn., São Paulo – Pioneira (1993)
6. MOGGI, Jair – Live Management! The cell as an organization model, 1st. edn., São Paulo – Editora Gente – (2001)
7. Ferreira, A., Demutti, C.M., Gimenez, P.E.O.: Maslow's Theory of Needs: The influence of the educational level over the perception on the work environment. XIII SemeAd – Administration Seminars (September de 2010) ISSN 2177-3866
8. Kotliarov, I.: Mathematical Formalization of Theories of Motivation proposed by Maslow and Herzberg – Fractal: Revista de Psicologia 20(2), 341–346 (2008)
9. Saeednia, Y., Mariani, M.D.: Measuring Hierarchy of Basic Needs Among Adults. In: Procedia Social and Behavioral Sciences – World Conference on Psychology and Sociology (2012)
10. Webb, J.W.: Renewing the Printing Industry: Strategies and Action Items for Success, 2nd edn. Strategies for Mangement, Inc., and WhatTheyThink
11. Porter, M.E.: Competitive Strategy: Techniques for the analysis on industry and competition, 5th edn. Campus, Rio de Janeiro (1991)
12. de Araujo Jr., J.P.: The importance of the strategic view of internal resources of the company. Revista Tecnologia Gráfica – Ed. 77 (2011)
13. Management, H.S.M.: no. 82 – year 14 volume 5, Dossiê BRIC (October 2010)
14. Drupa Global Trends, Messe Düsseldorf (February 2014)
15. Turner, R., Ledwith, A., Kelly, J.: Project management in small to medium-sized enterprises: Matching processes to the nature of the firm. International Journal of Project Management 28, 744–755 (2010)

Decision Making for Sustainability: Review and Research Agenda

Mélanie Despeisse and Doroteya Vladimirova

Institute for Manufacturing, University of Cambridge, United Kingdom
{md621,dkv21}@cam.ac.uk

Abstract. Manufacturers are failing to maximise the benefits from their own sustainability ambitions. Their decision-making methods and tools have not evolved to allow the non-financial dimensions of sustainability to be accounted for. Non-financial information is not systematically used in decision making as manufacturers do not yet know how to value qualitative benefits, opportunities and challenges. This paper reviews current challenges and the literature on decision-making for sustainability in manufacturing. The paper presents the need for a decision-making framework for sustainability and a research agenda for developing such a framework and delivering a supporting tool.

Keywords: Decision making for sustainability, Decision-making framework, Manufacturing strategy, Sustainable manufacturing.

1 Background and Problem Statement

It is argued that manufacturers are missing sustainability improvement opportunities because it is not fully understood how decisions are made outside the traditional value system based on short-term financial value purely [1,2]. Manufacturers find it difficult to consider the medium- and long-term benefits for short-term decision-making for immediate actions, because they seek to monetize all the benefits in developing business cases focused on short-term profit. Additionally, even when there are financial benefits, sustainability activities are not necessarily undertaken [3].

Many manufacturers will already have a sustainability vision and strategy, yet they struggle to bring these into their day-to-day operational decisions [4,5]. Decision-making for sustainability is a growing research area as it has been recognised as a vital ingredient for success in modern businesses [6]. Decisions can be of different scale and frequency, e.g. new factory location vs. cleaning process sequence. Some successes have been achieved when the social and environmental dimensions have been monetized [7]. The traditional view of manufacturing companies' value capture regards the profit which is made when the goods and services are sold in relation to the cost of producing and delivering them, thus decisions are made purely based on financial profit (Fig. 1).

However the value created and potentially captured is not necessarily in the form of financial benefits. Industry is calling for more "useful" information for sustainabil-

B. Grabot et al. (Eds.): APMS 2014, Part II, IFIP AICT 439, pp. 146–153, 2014.

ity decision-making. Useful information can be defined as information that widens and specifies options to enable better results from implementation and to achieve desired objectives. The challenge manufacturers are facing is to monetize the benefits of long-term innovative sustainable solutions, such as organisational learning, knowledge exchange across disciplines and sectors, collaborative business models, closed-loop and resilient industrial systems, or first mover advantage, even when useful information about these solutions are available.

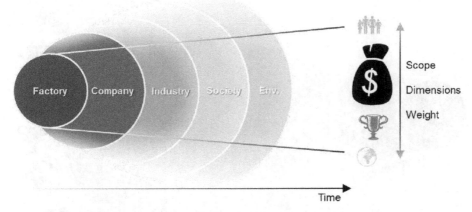

Fig. 1. Decision-making system for short-term financial benefits

In the context of today's increasing interconnectedness, complexity and multidimensionality of business operations and management, it is reasonable to assume that the benefits would become more interdependent and multifaceted as well. To reflect this multidimensionality, organisational decisions around sustainability have been depicted using the triple bottom line of people-planet-profit [8]; each dimension considered separately by experts and later on brought together. The difficulty is to combine these three dimensions for making final decisions [9]. As a result, decision-making is still dominated by a single index based on financial metrics and short-term thinking which do not adequately account for qualitative benefits. In other words, we have under-performing decision-making systems when it comes to industrial sustainability improvements.

There have been many efforts and initiatives to value ecosystem services [10], to link CSR and firm value [11], to develop a three-dimensional framework assessment [12] based on the triple bottom line [8]. There are also numerous tools like SWOT (Strengths-Weaknesses-Opportunities-Threats) [13], Environmental Impact Analysis (EIA), Strategic Environmental Analysis (SEA) and Cost-Benefit Analysis (CBA) [14] which are well-established and widely used for analysis, but the non-financial (yet useful) information is not systematically used in decision-making because we do not know how to value qualitative benefits, opportunities and challenges [15].

There is a gap in knowledge and a need in business practice to make the transition from the traditional decision-making thinking (Fig. 1) to a more holistic approach (Fig. 2) which (1) integrates the multiple dimensions of sustainability into business decision-making in a more balanced manner, (2) considers the benefits and implications of today's actions on the long-term, and (3) expands the scope of decision-making to include the wider society and the natural environment.

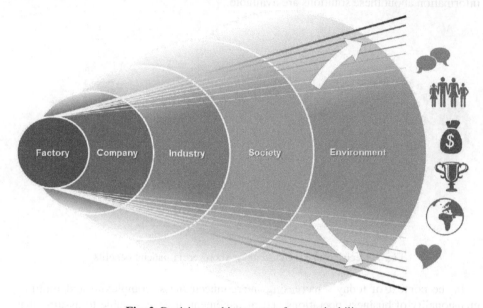

Fig. 2. Decision-making system for sustainability

This paper identifies and scopes the research problem around decision-making for sustainability, presents a set of research questions and proposes a research agenda to address the identified deficiencies.

2   Research Questions and Deliverables

We propose a research project that will help to develop the competencies manufacturers need as they move towards sustainability, for purposes of decision-making as well as value non-financial benefits, building resilience and organisational learning. The research aim is to better integrate sustainability into decision-making. This project will deliver a tool to support top-management in doing so: decision-making tool for sustainability (DMT4S).

We will address the following four research questions (RQ):

RQ1. What are the specific challenges when bringing sustainability into manufacturing decision-making?

RQ2. What dimensions should form part of sustainability decision-making in manufacturing?

RQ3. How to integrate these dimensions into sustainability decision-making tool?

RQ4. What happens when the DMT4S is used?

The principal deliverables of this research are:

- A better understanding of sustainability decision-making in manufacturing.
- A theoretical framework that will identify a set of key themes and dimensions for sustainability decision-making. This will make a contribution to the scholarly literature on industrial sustainability strategy and decision-making.
- A decision-making tool for sustainability, or DMT4S. The tool will support the inclusion of sustainability considerations for better decision-making.
- Evidence of performance from multiple applications.
- A user guide to support companies in using the DMT4S. The tool will be professionally packaged to ensure user-friendliness.
- Workshops throughout the project as well as after its completion.

3   Methodology and Project Plan

The project will deliver a tool to support sustainability decision-making. The objectives are to better understand complex organisational problems in order to address the real-world problem of the integrating sustainability into decision-making, and to access superior opportunities and maximise performance, competitiveness and learning while accounting for the cost and risk involved.

Given the old dichotomy of theory and practice, a wider and deeper form of engagement between researchers and practitioners is needed in the co-production of knowledge [16]. Therefore we will adopt a strategy of engaged scholarship [17,18] as a means of knowledge production and collaborative inquiry between scholars and practitioners. Exploratory expert interviews will be conducted during the first year in phase 1. More intensive engagement will occur at key points such as phases 2 and 4 which will require extensive testing planning and analysis as well as exploitation planning. The core team will also meet bi-annually with the industrial collaborators for phases 2 and 3. This will be done in workshops to be chaired by the principal investigators to gain industry guidance. This participative form of research will obtain the perspectives of key stakeholders (researchers, users and practitioners) to understand a problem of decision-making [18] and make research relevant to practitioners by bridging the gap between theory and practice [19]. Linkages to other relevant teams will be strongly maintained. We will share our findings at an early stage and update them regularly as empirical research proceeds to ensure that any assistance needed by other teams is provided.

The following sub-sections outline the work plan for the three research phases, deliverables and tasks allocation.

3.1 Explore and Plan

This first phase aims at understanding current decision making for sustainability to address RQ1 and RQ2. We will review the literature and existing tools for decision-making in industrial sustainability at three levels to identify the strengths and weaknesses of decision-making at these different levels: best practice (eco-efficiency), technology solution (eco-factory), and business model. A vast body of management literature exists that provides a number of decision support tools but very little in support of sustainable industrial systems. There is a clear gap in knowledge about decision-making for sustainability. We will draw on the well-established stream literature on decision-making in organisations [20,21] to strengthen the theoretical foundation of our work. We will identify concepts and constructs from this established literature and apply them to an emerging body of knowledge on decision-making for sustainability. In addition, we will conduct expert interviews with thought leaders in the area of industrial sustainability. Working closely with industry will allow us to strengthen and validate the theoretical framework and address an industry problem [18].

Tasks:

- Background review: Primarily review industrial sustainability and organisational decision-making literature. Review other relevant fields of research such as organisational learning, risk management, supply chain resilience, and corporate social responsibility.
- Existing tool review: Review existing tool in use by companies as well as tool recently developed for supporting sustainable business practices.
- Translate initial findings into specific questions and guidelines for structured interviews with industrial collaborators to learn from best practice.
- Theory building: Establish a theoretical framework for the decision-making tool.

3.2 Develop and Learn

In this second phase, we will develop a prototype tool for sustainability decision-making, identify and overcome weaknesses of the proposed tool through targeted testing (fast prototyping) to address RQ2 and RQ3. Through the use of fast prototypes, we will test the framework and tool from early stages of development to continuously test and refine the tool. Each fast prototype will focus on specific elements of the tool to insure their validity. We will use lessons learnt from these prototype applications to develop and refine the final DMT4S.

Tasks:

- Define tool specifications based on the theoretical framework and interview results from phase 1.
- Develop the initial tool and use targeted testing (fast prototypes).

- Continuously test and refine the framework and tool using data captured during phases 2 and 3.
- Use lessons learned from the fast prototype applications to inform the DMT4S development.

3.3   Use and Prove

In this third phase, we will test the prototype tool and final DMT4S to deliver results and evidence of performance to address RQ3 and RQ4. We will first test the fast prototypes to validate various elements of the prototype tool before approaching industrial collaborators through our established network. Central to engaged scholarship is building relationships between academics and practitioners through the creation of joint forums, researcher/practitioner gatherings and focus groups that consider issues of concern to both academics and practitioners [22]. We will use workshops to test the usability of the tool and create a user guide. Finally we will package the tool (e.g. website, software development, user guide printing, etc.) to facilitate the dissemination of our findings through the use of the tool.

Tasks:

- Use fast prototype applications to review the validity of the framework.
- Use fast prototype applications to test the performance of the tool.
- Analyse tool use and synthesise users' feedback to refine the tool.
- Finalise the DMT4S and user guide based on lesson learnt from use.
- Assess the overall performance and quality of the tool.
- Package and distribute the DMT4S.

4   Project Outcomes and Implications

Globalisation of manufacturing has resulted in an increasing number of emerging economies competing for a limited pool of resources. In order to remain competitive, manufacturers will need to improve their resource efficiency and improve the resilience of their supply chain against disruptions. Although there is ample knowledge about these issues, manufacturers are still struggling to concretely address them and integrate them into their decision-making. Industry and the environment have long been opposed: industrial improvements for the environment are considered as a cost, although it is not necessarily the case [1].

Manufacturers are often reluctant to take action because they fear it will be at too high a cost in the short-term and result in uncertain generalised benefits in the distant future. To develop more sustainable industrial systems, industrialists and policy makers need to better understand and take decisions on how to respond to environmental, social and economic challenges and transform industrial behaviour accordingly leveraging appropriate investment and implementation of new tools and approaches. Important issues and opportunities around sustainable manufacturing can be addressed by improving decision-making.

We propose a research project that will explore a concrete issue in the manufacturing industry: decision-making for the sustainability transition towards resource efficiency, circular economy, resilience, and organisational learning. The work will provide a better understanding of the multi-dimensionality of corporate decision-making for sustainability and advance the academic fields of industrial sustainability and organisational decision-making. It will also contribute to knowledge in the areas of corporate social responsibility, strategic planning, resilience, uncertainty and risk management. The tool developed will support the sustainability transformation of manufacturing companies in a novel manner and provide a contribution to academic literature, disseminated via journal papers and conference presentations.

This project fits with the need to strengthen the manufacturing sector in a forward-looking and sustainable manner. A greater focus on long-term impact of decision-making will help firms increase resilience and reduce costs. For sustainability improvements to take place, constant efforts are needed in resource efficiency and innovation. Organisations making these efforts will be rewarded with strong performance improvements. This project will involve best practice leaders with high visibility aiming to encourage the rest of the manufacturing industry to follow their lead.

References

1. Porter, M.E., Kramer, M.R.: Creating Shared Value: How to reinvent capitalism—and unleash a wave of innovation and growth. Harvard Bus. Rev. 89(1/2), 62–77 (2011)
2. Lavery, G., Pennell, N., Brown, S., Evans, S.: Next Manufacturing Revolution (2013), http://www.nextmanufacturingrevolution.org/ (accessed July 24, 2013)
3. Tsui, A.: On Compassion in Scholarship: Why Should We Care? Acad. Manage. Rev. 38(2), 167–180 (2013)
4. Epstein, M.J., Roy, M.J.: Sustainability in action: Identifying and measuring the key performance drivers. Long. Range Plann. 34(5), 585–604 (2001)
5. Lueneburger, C., Goleman, D.: The Change Leadership Sustainability Demands. MIT Sloan Manage. Rev. 51(4), 49–55 (2010)
6. Arvai, J., Campbell-Arvai, V., Steel, P.: Decision-Making for Sustainability: A Systematic Review of the Body of Knowledge. Network for Business Sustainability, Ontario (2012)
7. Turner, R.K., Paavola, J., Cooper, P., Farber, S., Jessamy, V., Georgiou, S.: Valuing nature: lessons learned and future research direction. Ecol. Econ. 46(3), 493–510 (2003)
8. Elkington, J.: Cannibals with Forks: The Triple Bottom Line of 21st Century Business. Capstone Publishing, Oxford (1997)
9. Gibson, R.B.: Beyond the Pillars: Sustainability Assessment as a Framework for Effective Integration of Social, Economic, and Ecological Considerations in Significant Decision Making. J. Environ. Asses. Policy Manage. 8(3), 259–280 (2006)
10. de Groot, R.S., Alkemade, R., Braat, L., Hein, L., Willemen, L.: Challenges in integrating the concept of ecosystem services and values in landscape planning, management and decision making. Ecol. Complex. 7(3), 260–272 (2010)
11. Edmans, A.: The Link Between Job Satisfaction and Firm Value, with Implications for Corporate Social Responsibility. Acad. Manage. Perspect. 26(4), 1–19 (2012)
12. Hacking, T., Guthrie, P.: A framework for clarifying the meaning of Triple Bottom-Line, Integrated, and Sustainability Assessment. Environ. Impact. Asses. 28, 73–89 (2008)

13. Rowe, A.J., Mason, R.O., Dickel, K.E., Mann, R.B., Mockler, R.J.: Strategic Management: a methodological approach, 4th edn. Addison-Wesley, Reading (1994)
14. Hundloe, T., McDonald, G.T., Ware, J., Wilks, L.: Cost-benefit analysis and environmental impact assessment. Environ. Imp. Asses. Rev. 10(1-2), 55–68 (1990)
15. McNie, E.C.: Reconciling the supply of scientific information with user demands: an analysis of the problem and review of the literature. Environ. Sci. Policy 10(1), 17–38 (2007)
16. Pettigrew, A.: Management research after modernism. Brit. J. Manage. 12, 61–70 (2001)
17. Van de Ven, A.H., Johnson, P.E.: Knowledge for theory and practice. . Acad. Manage. Rev. 31(4), 802–821 (2006)
18. Van de Ven, A.H.: Engaged Scholarship: A Guide for Organisational and Social Research. Oxford University Press, New York (2007)
19. Barge, J.K., Shockley-Zalabak, P.: Engaged Scholarship and the Creation of Useful Organisational Knowledge. J. Appl. Commun. Res. 36(3), 251–265 (2008)
20. Weber, M.: The Theory of Social and Economic Organization. The Free Press, Glencoe (1947)
21. Miller, S.J., Hickson, D.J., Wilson, D.C.: Decision-Making in Organizations. In: Clegg, S.R., Hardy, C., Nord, W.R. (eds.) Handbook of Organizational Studies. Sage, London (1996)
22. Bartunek, J.M.: Academic-practitioner collaboration need not require joint or relevant research: toward a relational scholarship of integration. Acad. Manage. J. 50(6), 1323–1333 (2007)

Synergizing Lean and Green for Continuous Improvement

Rythm Suren Wadhwa

Høgskole i Gjøvik,
Gjøvik, 2802 Norway

Abstract. For many years small-medium enterprises (SMEs) have attempted to improve their manufacturing and environmental operation performance in a view to achieving competitiveness and operational excellence. This paper looks at the literature in order to investigate the relationship between lean and green management and their relationship to one another while keeping in mind their simultaneous implementation at a foundry SME. Separate literature streams have arisen to address issues in green and lean using systems engineering tools but research has largely neglected the intersection of the two. The presented research synthesizes the literature addressing the intersections of green and lean and suggests a research agenda to address gaps. Suggestions for implementing environmental management systems for sustaining continuous improvement activities have also been provided.

Keywords: Six Sigma, Systems Engineering, SME.

1   Introduction

Today's SMEs (Small-to-Medium sized Enterprises) need to address the increasing global competition, decreasing product life cycles and increasing customer demands. SMEs require more financial and technical assistance when compared to OEMs (Original Equipment Manufacturers) when moving from reactive measures for the end use of products to a more proactive consideration within environmentally benign continuous improvement in plant operation. [1] Improving environmental performance while keeping regulatory costs down is one of the key challenges affecting the future competitiveness of casting foundry SMEs.

Metalcasting produces a number of liquid, gas and solid waste streams, many of which could have an adverse affect on the environment. On the other hand, it also produces some positive impacts on the environment by preventing landfills of large amounts of scrap metal. In the US the foundry industry spends over $1.25 billion/year to comply with federal, state and local government regulations, although this number does not include some smaller foundries, certain categories of environmental compliance costs from captive foundries reported under different industry classifications. [2] About 40% of compliance costs are used for control, treatment, and disposal of air pollutants and related sludge. Solid and hazardous waste disposal-sand bags and

B. Grabot et al. (Eds.): APMS 2014, Part II, IFIP AICT 439, pp. 154–161, 2014.
© IFIP International Federation for Information Processing 2014

slag-account for about 33% of the compliance costs. (Figure 1) Environmental compliance costs are currently estimated to be 2% of the cost of a casting, which is expected to increase to 5% in the near future. Sand casters face major environmental issues related to treatment and disposal of spent sands that may be contaminated with toxic wates.

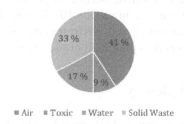

■ Air ■ Toxic ■ Water ■ Solid Waste

Fig. 1. Environmental cost by media

Manufacturing is a dominant sector in the European economy as well. The economic importance of this sector is evident: it provides jobs for approximately 34 million people; and produces an added value in excess of €1 500 billion from 230 000 enterprises with 20 or more employees [3]. However, it is widely perceived to be facing serious challenges. This is particularly true of the manufacturers located in the high-cost regions.

Lean production is often described as both a philosophy and a set of working practices with the goal of achieving high levels of customer satisfaction through increased quality, reduced costs and world-class delivery performance. While there are separate streams of established research on green and lean issues, few authors have addressed the intersection of these in industrial SME scenarios. This is a critical oversight because firms may be missing synergies available through improved concurrent implementation; they may also be failing to address important trade-offs that may arise when there are incompatibilities between strategic initiatives. For example, lean and green strategies are often seen as compatible initiatives because of their joint focus on waste reduction.

The ISO-9000 quality standard has been shown to be highly correlated with the adoption of ISO-14000 environmental standard. There is evidence of this relationship across both lean interfaces, but quality improvement has not been explored at the conjunction of all two strategies. The relationship yet to be explored at the interface of the two strategies. Green initiatives focus on reducing pollution, while this is not a priority driving lean. Managers in companies find it difficult to simultaneously implement these three strategies. For example, buyer-supplier alignment is addressed differently across the three interfaces. Buyers often focus on low costs, whereas suppliers may incur greater costs while attempting to provide more environmentally responsible or higher quality products. Lack of development may be due to the exploratory nature of research regarding the relationships between green and lean.

Environmental management may also represent an untapped avenue for further reduction of manufacturing costs through more efficient use of natural resources [4][5].

The issue, however, of how to address the environmental management practices of vendors may prove to be a costly endeavour if not managed taking into consideration a number of important economic factors. To date there has been only limited anecdotal discussion of the legitimate incentives for SMEs to extend environmental management beyond their immediate boundaries.

The paper is organized as follows. Section II presents the research methodology followed by the industrial use case in section III. Section IV describes the suggested plan for continuous improvement and environmental performance management at SMEs and finally, the summary is presented in section V.

2   Research Methodology

Common drivers and barriers lead to both complementary and conflicting arguments across green and lean strategies. Synthesizing the literature in the areas of green and lean allows the researchers to draw inferences about a combined green and lean strategy. Four major factors motivate firms to adopt some combination of these strategies: cost reductions, customer demands, international standards such as ISO-9000 and ISO-14000, and risk management. Toyota is a good example of a firm that has successfully integrated a green and lean strategy in a global setting. The company's commitment is evident through its ISO certifications and financial investment into quality and environmental research and development. [6][7]

2.1   Lean and Green Manufacturing

Lean manufacturing is based on the principles and working processes of the Toyota Production System, and has been defined as doing more with less [8]. Lean manufacturing's most distinguishing principle is the *relentless pursuit of waste* [9]. It has been most prominent in discrete, repetitive assembly-type operations. Liker [11] suggests that the goals of lean manufacturing are highest quality, lowest cost, and shortest lead time. It can be described as a multi-dimensional approach that encompasses a wide variety of management practices, including Just-in-Time (JIT), quality systems, work teams, cellular manufacturing supplier management, etc. in an integrated system [12]. Distribution and transportation operations networks are important operational characteristics that will affect green manufacturing value stream. [19] With the rapid increase of long-distance trade, supply chains are increasingly covering larger distances, consuming significantly more fossil-fuel energy for transportation and emitting much more carbon dioxide than a few decades ago. [20] Lean manufacturing value streams typically have lower emissions due to reduced inventory being held internally at each company, but the frequent replenishment generally tends to increase emissions. As distances increase, it is quite possible for lean and green to be in conflict. Lean may be green in some cases, but not in others.

The reverse logistics focuses primarily on the return of recyclable or reusable products and materials into the forward supply chain.[21] To reintroduced recycled materials, components and products into the downstream production and distribution systems, it is necessary to integrate reverse material and information flows in the supply chain. Due to the reverse material flow, traditional production planning and inventory management methods have limited applicability in   remanufacturing systems. Therefore, it is necessary to consider the existence of the returned items that are not yet remanufactured, remanufactured items and manufactured items.

2.2   Lean for Better Environmental Management

Some researchers have established links between the occurrence of practices that support manufacturing sustainability and firms adopting lean manufacturing strategies. This work attributes the mutual benefits between lean production and environmental management practice to the reduced waste and continuous improvement philosophies of lean.

The objective of lean is to generate a system that is efficient and well organised and devoted to continuous improvement and the elimination of all forms of waste. The potential for a benefit to manufacturing SMEs environmental management practice is high. The practices that support lean manufacturing are similar to the practices that support environmental performance. Lean production is broadly described as an integrated approach to the management of a manufacturing organisation, that encompasses a wide variety of practices, including JIT, quality systems, work teams, cellular manufacturing and supplier management. The lean production philosophy focuses on avoiding seven forms of waste and on respecting customers, employees and suppliers [7][8][32]. A sizeable body of empirical work supports the capacity of the lean system to remove continuously multiple forms of waste, smooth production flow, improve understanding of human resource management issues, maintain quality and increase customer service, while also yielding a significant competitive advantage.

3   Industrial Use Case

3.1   DMAIC Methodology

There are two major methodology approaches that have been reported in the literature for implementing lean, the DMAIC (Define-Measure-Analysis- Improve-Control) and the DMADV (Define- Measure-Analysis-Develop-Verify) [37][33]. The DMAIC approach is recommended for analyzing and improving the existing product or process, while the DMADV approach is appropriate for designing new product or process.

An exploratory six sigma case study conducted at the parent company based on the five phases of the methodology: Define, Measure, Analyze, Improve and Control (DMAIC) is described shortly. The DMAIC approach is described which was used to dig deeper into the non-conforming components received by the parent company from two tier-one suppliers. This exploratory case study were conducted within the energy industry in order to examine the nature of the complex interactions between the two major constructs lean and environmental sustainability at the parent company and its first tier vendor. Interviews were conducted with key purchasing, production and environment staff within the parent company and case study conducted with one first-tier parts vendor. Interviews with at parent company (government owned, around 15000 employees worldwide) were selected from a sample that represented major groups of responsibility and decision making.

At the first tier vendor (privately owned, around 220 employees, supplies foundry and special sub-assembly components, supplies about 80 per cent of their business to the parent company) two- to three-hour semi-structured interviews were conducted with the operations manager, production supervisor and quality/environment manager. A site tour was conducted to look specifically at shop floor layout, warehouse and receiving inspection areas. The relevant stakeholders completed a self-assessment questionnaire at the completion of the site visit.

DMAIC Process
A. Problem Definition
Defining the problem is the most important step in Six-Sigma project since better understanding of the problem at this stage will help at the later stages of the project. In order to define the objectives of the project, manufacturing company's claims were investigated. The management needed to resolve the problem of *long process lead time*. The relevant KPIs were be identified, linked and then measured.

The critical-to-quality (CTQ) indicator was defined as below:

CTQ= Identified Defects / Shipment Flex Hoses per year
The company claimed that reducing the hose non-conformance issues by 50% would help the company save USD17,629.

B .Measuring the scope of problem
During the measure phase, the various non-conformance issues with the incoming components from the vendor were identified and measured in scope using company proprietary software. The top root causes were identified against the parent company's requirements and standards. The detailed product hierarchy and its relation to the final product assembly is confidential.

The attribute agreement analysis was conducted using data from the company's SAP system which also had the appraisers within the company which were needed to make the assessment. The questionnaire was provided to the appraisers from the company in free-text format.

The operational definitions of *defect* and *opportunity* defined by the company are shown in a flowchart in Figure 2. The measurement system for *defect* and *opportunity* was capable as the Kappa values in the test exceed the allowable value of 0.7.

DEFECTS   OPPORTUNITY

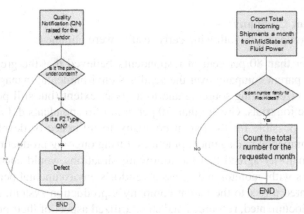

Fig. 2. Operational definitions

C. Analyze the causes

After the first two phases of DMAIC approach, it was decided to focus on the improvement plan to reduce the non-conformances. It was important to further study the potential causes/key input variables (KPIVs) of the non-conformances using 4M (man, machine, material, method) categorization method. Additional cause and effect matrix analysis was conducted in which key output variable (KPOVs), non-conforming product/incoming shipment was selected as the performance measure. A hypothesis test was conducted to compare the capability of the two vendors for the commodity resulted in a P-Value = 0.768 which demonstrated no significant difference in the capability between vendors. One of the vendor related issues uncovered were, for example, missing incorporating the purchase order requirements from the parent as a part of the vendor's internal assembly .

D. Improve the exiting processes

The improve phase consisted of several activities organized to address the non-conformance causing factors. Onsite vendor meetings were organized to discuss engineering drawing requirements, company and industry-wide standards and the importance of compliance to the requested specifications. With the agreement of internal company stakeholders processes were updated to incorporate the suggested improvements.

E.Control

The control phase is the last stage for the DMAIC approach. A control plan was design and introduced to the production line. The plan provides a summary of the control application which aims to minimize the process variation and ensures producing top quality products. In addition, the control plans guarantees that the proposed solution is properly implemented and monitored. It was reported that as a result of the recommendations, the customer claim rate was reduced by 55%.

Results : Parent Company
At the parent company the following early results were obtained:

- Greater than 80 per cent of respondents believed that the greatest influence of the parent company over the vendor's environmental management practices occurred during sourcing and to a lesser extent (but still possible) during production trials. Greater than 70 per cent of respondents did not believe that it was possible for the parent company to influence or develop a vendor's environmental management practices during ongoing production.
- The majority agreed that the following situations would encourage them to discuss with, monitor and assess a vendor's environmental performance: if it presented a risk to the parent company's production system; and if it was a well documented, resourced and standardized aspect of their purchasing.

Tier-One Vendor Company
The vendor had undergone a lean transformation with the direct assistance of the parent company. The vendor had not obtained ISO 14000 certification. The following early observations were gathered at the vendor:

- The commitment to ongoing process improvement an meeting the requirements of the customer at this plant was high. The customer's requirements for environmental performance were a more important driver for change than the regulatory environment.
- The culture for improvement at the vendor was strong, with worker involvement high and worker attitude towards change, highly positive. Resources committed to the environment were very low however, and the SME appeared to be just keeping up with its lean transformation and its significant growth during the year.

When developing the kaizen implementation plan associated with the future state value stream map, it was noticed that continuous improvement events on certain processes may require special attention to EHS issues.

4   Summary

The current literature is abundant with discussion on the individual strategies, but has thus far not addressed how firms can implement these strategies concurrently. A thorough examination of the individual bodies of literature was used as a means to guide future research at the intersection of green and lean strategies. The future research agenda addresses gaps in the current literature, and suggest relevant framework from which to explore this phenomenon. The agenda presented in this paper allows for future research that begins to meet the call for potential work.

In terms of limitations, this research paper makes use of only one case study. Though the case study demonstrate useful insight into working through quality processes and integrating environmental concerns into already in place quality management system; this is simply the start. Research investigating this integration with other manufacturing models outside of the energy business is planned in the near future.

References

[1] Bey, N., Hauschild, M.Z., McAloone, T.C.: Drivers and barriers for implementation of environmental strategies in manufacturing companies. Annals of the CIRP 62, 43–46 (2013)

[2] U.S. Department of Energy (USDOE): Energy and Environmental profile of the US metalcasting industry, Office of Industrial Technologies (1999)

[3] Flegel, H.: MANUFUTURE Strategic Research Agenda. Report of the High-Level Group (2006), http://www.manufuture.org/manufacturing/wpcontent/uploads/Manufuture-SRA-webversion.Pdf

[4] Hart, S.: A natural-resource based view of the firm. Academy of Management Review 20(4), 986–1000 (1995)

[5] Florida, R.: Lean and green: the move to environmentally conscious manufacturing. California Management Review 39(1), 80–105 (1996)

[6] Toyota Motor Corporation, Department of innovation

[7] Åhlström, P.: Sequences in the Implementation of Lean Production. European Management Journal 16, 327–334 (1998)

[8] Liker, J.K.: The Toyota Way: 14 Management Principles From the World's Greatest Manufacturer. McGraw- Hill, New York (2004)

[9] Shah, R., Ward Lean, P.T.: Ward Lean manufacturing: context, practice bundles, and performance. Journal of Operations Management 21, 129–149 (2003)

[10] Srivastava, S.K.: Green supply-chain management: A state-of the- art literature review. I. nternational Journal of Management Reviews 9(1), 53–80 (2007)

[11] Venkat, K., Wakeland, W.: Is Lean Necessarily Green? In: Proceedings of the 50th Annual Meeting of the ISSS(International Society for the Systems Sciences) (2006)

[12] Shah, R., Ward, P.: Lean manufacturing: context, practice bundles and performance. Journal of Operations Management 21(2), 129–149 (2003)

[13] Wadhwa, R.S.: Implementing Manufacturing Process Automation in Metalcasting Facilities, AFS (2014) ISBN 978-0-87433-408-1

Support for Life Cycle Decision-Making in Sustainable Manufacturing – Results of an Industrial Case Study

Teuvo Uusitalo, Jyri Hanski, Markku Reunanen, and Susanna Kunttu

VTT Technical Research Centre of Finland,
Tekniikankatu 1, P.O. Box 1300, FIN-33101 Tampere, Finland
{teuvo.uusitalo,jyri.hanski,markku.reunanen,
susanna.kunttu}@vtt.fi

Abstract. This paper presents results of a case study in which a life cycle cost estimation tool has been developed and tested. Improving sustainability requires holistic information on the life cycle costs of the system. There is a need to increase the transparency of decision-making by informing customers about the costs of the solutions when taking into consideration the whole life cycle. This benefits both the supplier and the customer in forms of showing the total costs of the system and selecting the system with the lowest total costs.

Keywords: sustainability, manufacturing, life cycle cost, case study.

1   Introduction

Sustainability and the analysis of life cycle costs have received considerable attention in the manufacturing industry lately. Procurement and supply chain are in central position in achieving sustainability and are increasingly being demanded to contribute to goals of sustainable development [1,2,3]. Supply chain management studies have emphasised the benefits of sustainability in the form of risk reduction and performance enhancement [4,5]. It is generally believed that assessing the sustainability of the system requires holistic information on the life cycle costs of the system. However, according to the interviews made for this study, the use of life cycle cost as a procurement criterion instead of just the acquisition price is still not a predominant practice among procurers. The main reason for using acquisition price as a main criterion is usually rooted in the preferences of the procurement department.

Miemczyk et al. [1] lists social, environmental and economic measures found in a literature review on sustainable procurement and supply management. The following list includes some of the economic and environmental measures: generic internal processes such as supplier selection and assessment (material, waste, recycling); cost of implementing sustainability practices; inclusion of sustainability criteria in design of products; measurement and control of energy use and greenhouse gas emissions; life cycle analysis principles (LCA); developing activities at procurement strategy level to support sustainability; and developing sustainable products together with suppliers.

B. Grabot et al. (Eds.): APMS 2014, Part II, IFIP AICT 439, pp. 162–169, 2014.
© IFIP International Federation for Information Processing 2014

Procurement decisions are an important application area for life cycle cost related decision-making. A product system's life cycle is characterized by three phases: beginning of life (BOL), including design and production, middle-of-life (MOL), including use, service and maintenance and end-of-life (EOL), characterized by various scenarios such as reuse of the product and components, refurbishing, material reclamation and, finally, disposal [6].

Dowlatshahi argues that most of the total life cycle cost of a product is committed during the design stage [7]. The total costs can be reduced by giving due consideration to life cycle cost issues early in the design. LCC analysis provides the framework for specifying the estimated total incremental costs of the development, production, usage and retirement of a particular item. [8] Tools should be developed to allow a precise estimation of the whole life cycle impact and costs of a product. These tools should be used during the design process to gather information from the real history of existing products. [9]

An important step in LCC analysis is the classification of the analysis objectives and the bounding of the problem so that it can be studied efficiently and in a timely manner. LCC analysis can be used, for instance, in the following decision-making situations [8]:

- decisions on system maintenance concepts and logistics support policies
- decisions on equipment design configuration
- decisions on procurement sources and the selection of a supplier for a given item
- decisions on maintenance plans
- decisions on product disposal and recycling methods

The gap for this study was identified as follows: there is a need to develop a tool for explaining life cycle costs of solutions. Such tools do not currently exist at least according to the interviewees made for this study. Also, there is a need to increase the transparency of decision-making by informing customers about the costs of the solutions when taking into consideration the whole life cycle. This benefits both the supplier and the customer in forms of showing the total costs of the system and selecting the system with the lowest total costs. Typically, purchasing price is only a small fraction of the whole life cycle costs. In addition, reported cases of testing such a tool are scarce. Thereby, the objectives of this study are:

- To describe a decision support tool for a solution provider and the need for such a tool
- To test the tool with customers
- To identify further development needs for the tool

2   Methodology

The research method applied was a qualitative case study. The research data were collected in workshops with the case company and through structured interviews with the case company's customers. The case-specific LCC prototype tool was first developed in close co-operation with the case company. The LCC tool was then tested with key customers of the case company. Testing approach is described in detail in chapter 4.1.

The case company is a small company providing power supply systems to the energy, ICT, transport and process industries. Case company's main focus is on solutions for energy producers and industrial plants. Its battery back-up systems are necessary for guaranteeing the 24/7 operation of critical devices also at any failure situations of the electrical mains network. Case company's products are typically customized solutions for its B-to-B customers, who are project suppliers of larger systems and integrate the solutions delivered by the case company to their own offerings to end-users.

The developed tool is a prototype and its main objective is to demonstrate how LCC calculations can be done and used in practise. The development of the tool has been an iterative process conducted in close co-operation between the case company and researchers. Researchers who were responsible for the development of the tool made the first version of the tool according to the requirement specifications defined at the outset of the development work. Then, during the development process feedback meetings were held on a regular basis between case company personnel and researchers.

3   LCC Tool Description

Figure 1 outlines the development processes of a company as part of the life cycle for B to B products that are typically delivered by establishing a delivery project with the customer. A company that follows this model develops a product portfolio at its own expense and then establishes projects with clients to sell and deliver products that are based on the elements of their product portfolio and are configured and designed to meet needs of the particular customer. LCC tool was originally meant to be utilised in delivery project negotiations with potential customers (External use of LCC calculations in Figure 1) to serve the case company's need to explain higher purchasing price with lower life cycle costs and more sustainable solutions. During the LCC tool development and testing the case company also used the tool to analyse the elements of their product portfolio which elicited new ideas to improve the product from the life cycle perspective (Internal use of LCC calculations in Figure 1).

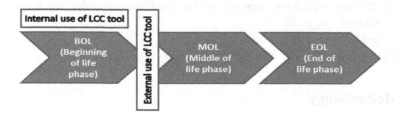

Fig. 1. Life cycle cost calculations can be utilised internally in the company or externally with customers

The use of the LCC tool can be described as a process with following steps:

1. Define the possible solutions that meet the customer's technical requirements and that are options to be analysed.
2. Populate the LCC tool with input data, i.e. give numerical values to the relevant cost parameters for current case. These include preventive maintenance (e.g. cost of person hours/task), corrective maintenance (e.g. MTBF, cost of unavailability), unavailability (e.g. cost/time unit), and disposal (e.g. cost of system disposal)
3. Calculate point estimates of life cycle costs. This is done automatically by the LCC tool.
4. Assess the uncertainty of numerical values of cost parameters given in the step 2. Uncertainty is expressed by statistical distributions defined by a graphical tool implemented in the LCC tool.
5. Calculate expected variation of life cycle costs based on statistical distribution given in the step 4. This is done automatically by the LCC tool.
6. Assess the results and compare the options using result indicators from the LCC calculation.
7. Make the decision for the current case based on economic criteria. For multivariate analysis other criteria can be used to support the decision.

MS Excel was chosen as the technical platform for the LCC tool as MS Excel is widely used in companies. The LCC tool is described in greater detail in [10].

4   Results of LCC Tool Testing

4.1   Testing Approach

The LCC tool testing had two goals. The first goal is to test the tool from a technical point of view to ensure that the created software works correctly. The second, and in this case a more important, goal is to test the usefulness and usability of the LCC tool; i.e. the potential of the LCC tool to support purchase decisions of the customers.

Technical software testing has been done by researchers and case company personnel. The developed tool is a prototype and its main objective is to demonstrate how LCC calculations can be done and used in practise. Thus comprehensive software tests have not been conducted. Technical software tests have been done only to ensure that the tool works properly if user acts as expected. No systematic checks for e.g. wrong input data have been done. In practise technical software testing has been done in conjunction with internal testing at the case company by documenting any identified unexpected behaviour of the tool.

In order to get feedback from the usefulness and usability of the LCC tool in external use, tests were organized with case company's customers. In all, ten persons from seven different companies participated in the test sessions. The first test session was held with three representatives of company 1. General feedback from the conducted test session was positive and the idea of focusing more on life cycle cost than mere acquisition cost was welcomed. The tool was seen a promising way to support life cycle cost based decision-making. The test session, however, failed in the sense that the test persons felt unable to give answers to most of the detailed questions concerning the usefulness and usability of the tool. The tool was demonstrated to the test persons by explaining the basic functionalities of the tool and by showing what kind of results will be received when the tool is populated with input data. The conducted test session revealed the importance of a well-designed test case that would be understood by the test persons.

The subsequent test sessions with test persons from companies 2 - 7 were supported by a test case description of four case company product options each provided with a representative input data set. The selected case system was a 110 kW power supply system which is typically used in power stations. The options to be compared by using the LCC tool were labelled as follows:

1. S1 - Modular solution
2. S2 - Modular solution + solar panels
3. S3 - Modular solution, no-good quality battery type
4. S4 - Conventional solution

Figure 2 presents a summary of the comparison of the test case options. The summary was made available to the test persons by the LCC tool.

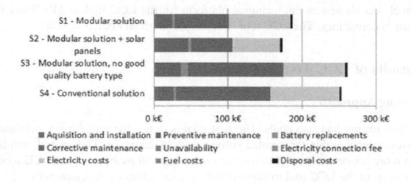

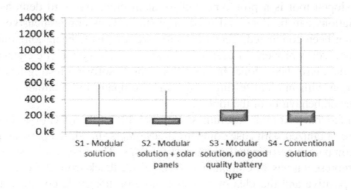

Fig. 2. Summary of the comparison of the test case options (Source: Panarese et al. (2014), p. 73)

In each test session the same improved test case was used to demonstrate the use of the LCC tool to the test persons from companies 2 - 7. After the demonstration the same set of questions that concerned the usefulness and usability of the LCC tool was asked from the test persons to generate deeper understanding on the potential of the LCC tool to support purchase decisions. This improved way of demonstrating the LCC tool to test persons seemed to greatly improve the ability and willingness of the test persons to answer the questions.

4.2   Results of the Testing

Regarding the usefulness of the LCC tool the test persons were asked to give their overall assessment on a scale 1 – 5. The average score was 4 individual points ranging from 3,25 to 5. The test persons seemed to appreciate case company's efforts to develop a tool that would support open discussions on sustainability and life cycle costs between suppliers and customers. None of the test persons had seen a corresponding tool being used by other companies for the same purpose even though life cycle cost often appears as an important aspect in marketing material. The test persons were of the opinion that the ability of a supplier to make life cycle cost information available to the customer can positively influence on who will be chosen as a supplier. The tool was felt especially useful when used in cooperation between supplier and customer.

One of the answers to a question whether the results that can be achieved by using the tool are worthwhile the effort needed was that potential savings from the use of the tool would often justify several days to be used for the LCC studies. Three test persons pointed out that selling and consulting customers always take time and tools that support these efforts are welcomed. One of the test persons pointed out the availability of input data and efforts that would facilitate data retrieval.

Regarding the usability of the LCC tool the test persons were asked to give their overall assessment on a scale 1 – 5. The average score was 4,25 individual points ranging from 3,75 to 5. Answers to the question whether the key performance indicators of the LCC tool are relevant, and whether the results are clearly presented to the user of the tool were positive with one exception. One of the test persons felt that he would need more experience on the use of the tool in order to be able to answer the question. Lack of experience also seemed to hamper the ability of the test persons to answer the questions that concerned the reliability of the results of the tool. Specific questions dealt with the availability of reliable input data and whether all relevant cost factors were included in the cost structure of the tool. One of the test persons was of the opinion that it is easy to find input data that is reliable enough. One of the test persons pointed out that the main purpose of this kind of a tool is to be indicative of major differences between the compared options. One of the test persons in turn pointed out that it is easy to update the comparisons when improved data becomes available. The rest of the test persons felt it hard to express their opinion due to lack of experience.

One of the usability questions concerned the number of options that can be compared by the LCC tool during one session. The current number of options is five and it was considered sufficient by all test persons. One of the test persons, however, noted that he had experience on acquisition projects where the number of options to be compared had been higher. This challenge can be overcome by the current version of the LCC tool by running a new session to compare another 2 - 5 options.

As a final question regarding the usability of the tool the test persons were asked whether the tool is simple enough and easy to use and whether the test persons would be interested in using the tool by themselves. All test persons gave a positive answer to these questions.

5   Conclusions

The test results indicate that the LCC tool is useful especially when used in cooperation between the supplier and a customer. The developed LCC tool provides information to allow estimation of the life cycle impact and costs of a product. This supports decision making related to equipment design configuration, procurement sources, selection of suppliers, maintenance plans and product disposal.

So far the LCC tool has been in test phase and exploited in the preparation of a few offers only. Yet there is no proof of that case company would already have received new orders or new customers by applying the new tool. Case company sees that main benefits of the tool will be achieved in the future when the tool will be fully exploited in the negotiations with customers and in the development of own product portfolio.

The LCC tool still needs development before all benefits from the tool are achievable. Future development possibilities include a web service based on the developed tool combined with a database. With a web service company's customers can make their own calculations and comparisons which can be a competitive advantage for the company because their competitors currently fail to provide corresponding services. Adding a database behind the tool reduces the time needed for data input and enables other than case company experts use the tool. In addition social impacts of the solutions could be included in the tool so that all aspects of sustainability are taken into account.

Acknowledgements. The research leading to these results has received funding from the European Community's Seventh Framework Programme (FP7, 2007–2013) under grant agreement 262931 and Tekes - the Finnish Funding Agency for Innovation. The authors wish to acknowledge the European Commission and Tekes for their support.

References

1. Miemczyk, J., Johnsen, T.E., Macquet, M.: Sustainable purchasing and sup-ply management: a structured literature review of definitions and measures at the dyad, chain and network levels. Supply Chain Management: An International Journal 17(5), 478–496 (2012)
2. Meehan, J., Bryde, D.: Sustainable procurement practice. Business Strategy and the Environment 20(2), 94–106 (2011)
3. Srivastava, S.K.: Green supply-chain management: a state-of-the-art literature review. Int. J. of Management Reviews 9(1), 53–80 (2007)

4. Jayaraman, V., Klassen, R., Linton, J.D.: Supply chain management in a sustainable environment. J. of Operations Management 25(6), 1071–1074 (2007)
5. Zhu, Q., Sarkis, J.: Relationships between operational practices and performance among early adopters of green supply chain management practices in Chinese manufacturing enterprises. J. of Operations Management 22(3), 265–289 (2004)
6. Kiritsis, D., Nguyen, V.K., Stark, J.: How closed-loop PLM can improve knowledge management over the complete product lifecycle? Int. J. of Product Lifecycle Management 3(1), 54–77 (2008)
7. Dowlatshahi, S.: Product design in a concurrent engineering environment: an optimization approach. J. of Production Research 30(8), 1803–1818 (1992)
8. Asiedu, Y., Gu, P.: Product life cycle cost analysis: State of the art review. Int. J. of Production Research 36, 883–908 (1998)
9. Garetti, M., Taisch, M.: Sustainable manufacturing: trends and research challenges. Production Planning & Control 23(2-3), 83–104 (2012)
10. Panarese, D., Schaeperkoetter, C., Raukola, J., Reunanen, M., Macchi, M., Sergent, N.: Demonstration of SustainValue outputs in different environments. Sustain Value deliverable D5.3 (April 9, 2014),
http://www.sustainvalue.eu/publications/D5_3_Final.pdf

Variety Steering Towards Sustainability: A Coupled Evaluation and Optimization Approach

Khaled Medini[1], Catherine Marie Da Cunha[2], and Alain Bernard[2]

[1] Ecole Nationale Supérieure des Mines de Saint Etienne, Saint Etienne, France
khaled.medini@emse.fr
[2] LUNAM Université, Ecole Centrale de Nantes, IRCCyN UMR CNRS 6597, Nantes, France
{catherine.da-cunha,alain.bernard}@irccyn.ec-nantes.fr

Abstract. This paper proposes a coupled evaluation and optimization approach to steer product variety towards environmental and economic sustainability. A predefined set of indicators enriched with weights given by the user ensures the evaluation, while optimization uses linear programming. The paper highlights the impact of variety steering on environmental and economic sustainability indicators. Additionally, the paper underlines the need to translate regulations into concrete company goals through integrating carbon markets into the proposition.

Keywords: Variety, sustainability, evaluation, linear programming, AHP.

1 Introduction

The broadening of customer requirements and emergence of market niches resulted in the proliferation of product variety. ElMaraghy et al. (2013) define variety as a number or collection of different things of a particular class of the same general kind. Producers seek to provide a wider spectrum of choice to gain market share and accommodate as many product variants as possible (ElMaraghy et al., 2013). However, each product variant induces a certain cost and environmental impact and generates a given profit. The challenge is to keep enough variety to meet customer requirements while steering such variety towards sustainability. The scope of current paper is focused on steering variety towards environmental and economic sustainability. It presents a coupled evaluation and optimization approach that helps managers take decisions on product variants' production volumes while considering the economic and environmental criteria. A predefined set of indicators enriched with weights reflecting each indicator's relative importance ensures the evaluation. The optimization uses linear programming to find trade-offs between all indicators while considering carbon markets.

The rest of the paper is organized as follows: section 2 provides a brief review of green supply chain performance evaluation and optimization. Section 3 presents the proposed approach comprised of indicators' weighting and optimization. Section 4 illustrates the proposition with a case study. The paper ends with conclusions and discussion, presented in section 5.

B. Grabot et al. (Eds.): APMS 2014, Part II, IFIP AICT 439, pp. 170–177, 2014.

2   State of the Art

2.1   Sustainability Performance Evaluation

Literature is rich in sustainability evaluation frameworks and indicators' systems. Many of them focus on the external reporting of company performance (Global Reporting Initiative, 2002; UNEP, 2009). Beyond benchmarking purposes, more methodological guidance is required to support decision makers in taking the "right" decisions on product, production process, and supply chain design alternatives. In this vein, life cycle thinking gained a lot of interest as it expanded the focus from production sites to the whole product life cycle. Life Cycle Assessment (LCA) is a method for assessing the environmental impact of product throughout its life cycle phases (ISO 14040, 2006). Dekker et al. (2012) enumerated several metric systems applied to supply chains, which, however, focused only on greenhouse gases emissions.

Recently, a comprehensive assessment model was proposed to assess sustainability performance of mass customized solutions: S-MC-S (Sustainable Mass Customization – Mass Customization for Sustainability) (Bettoni et al., 2013). The S-MC-S assessment model relies on a mixed life cycle and multi-level perspective. The life cycle aspect considers product life cycle phases (i.e. extraction, material processing, manufacturing, logistics, etc.). The multi-level aspect considers the product, production processes and supply chain levels. Indicator formulas are implemented in an assessment engine connected to the Ecoinvent[1] data base which ensures more reliability of the indicator values (Pedrazzoli et al., 2012). However, a critical issue is still the high number of indicators which may compromise the decision making process. One way to address this is by aggregating indicators. The Analytic Hierarchy Process (AHP) (Saaty, 2008) is a common method that can be applied in this context.

2.2   Green Supply Chains Optimization

Dekker et al. (2012) identified a lack of life cycle perspective in green operations optimization through reviewing applications of operations research to green logistics. Most studies that integrate environmental considerations into supply chain optimization focus on transportation, warehousing and inventory management (Bauer et al., 2010; Wang et al., 2011; Abdallah et al., 2012).

Moreover, laws, regulations and government action at large, are often addressed only through empirical studies that analyse their relevance to company strategies (Tan and Rae, 2009). One important achievement in this respect is the EU Emissions Trading System (EU ETS) resulting from the Kyoto Protocol. According to this system, companies receive a certain carbon emission allowance (i.e. threshold). They have to buy or sell a given amount of carbon emissions according to their effective emissions during a given period of time (EP and CEU, 2009). EU ETS motivates companies to engage in sustainable development, since it compels them to jointly optimize both economic and environmental performances.

---

[1] http://www.ecoinvent.org/

3   Proposed Approach

The proposed approach is comprised of two steps: weighting and optimization. First step relies on interviews with company manager, while second one uses these weights for optimizing variants production volumes.

3.1   Weighting

Company managers weight indicators according to their priorities, using the Analytical Hierarchy Process (AHP). AHP is a widely accepted technique used in decision making. In our approach, we assume that a predefined set of m indicators I_j, $j \in \{1..m\}$ is already available at the company, such that I_j is relative to one produced unit of j. Manager performs a pair wise comparison of the indicators during interviews. The result is the matrix P (Eq. 1), where δ_{ij} is the relative importance of indicator i over indicator j. The average value of normalized δ_{ij} (Eq. 2) results in the weight of indicator j (Eq. 3).

$$P = \begin{pmatrix} \delta_{11} & \cdots & \delta_{1m} \\ \vdots & \ddots \; \delta_{ij} \; \ddots & \vdots \\ \delta_{m1} & \cdots & \delta_{mm} \end{pmatrix}, \; \delta_{ij} \in \,]0,9] \tag{1}$$

$$\delta_{ij}^n = \frac{\delta_{ij}}{\sum_{l=1}^m \delta_{lj}}, i,j \in \{1..m, 1..m\} \tag{2}$$

$$\alpha_j = \frac{\sum_{k=1}^m \delta_{jk}^n}{m}, \; j \in \{1..m\} \tag{3}$$

In order to check the consistency of the judgements a consistency ratio (CR) is calculated according to Eq. 4. If CR is lower than 0.2 judgements are said to be consistent (Saaty, 2008).

$$CR = \frac{sum\ product_{k\in\{1..m\}}\ [\alpha_k, \sum_{i=1}^m \delta_{ik}] - m}{RI.(m-1)} \tag{4}$$

3.2   Optimization

Optimization aims to reduce costs and the environmental impact (and thus increase profit) by varying production volumes of product variants, these are represented by x_i. The backbone of the objective functions is indicator values I_j^i such that i refers to product variant and j refers to the indicator, $i \in \{1..n\}$ and n is the number of variants. We define γ_j, such that $\gamma_j = 1$ if an increase of the value of indicator j is desired, -1 otherwise. For each indicator I_j^i, an objective function f_j is calculated as shown in Eq. 5.

$$f_j = \sum_{i=1}^n \gamma_j . I_j^i . x_i \,, \; j \in \{1..m\} \tag{5}$$

We consider the cost/profit that can be induced by Eco taxes as follows: if the amount of greenhouse gases passes a given threshold, T, then company has to pay carbon tax f_T (calculated as shown in Eq. 6). β_j is a Boolean variable such that $\beta_j = 1$ if indicator j contributes to greenhouse gas emissions, 0 otherwise (Eq. 7). CC is the emissions' unitary cost in the company's carbon market. When a company's emissions respect the allowed amount of emissions, it is paid by other companies where emissions exceed such a threshold.

$$f_T = CC \left(\sum_{j=1}^{m} \sum_{i=1}^{n} \beta_j . I_j^i . x^i - T \right) \tag{6}$$

For optimization, we use the weighted sum scalarization technique (Ehrgott, 2013). Accordingly, the function that needs to be optimized is the weighted sum of the objective convex functions f_j. Here, we propose to use the weights $\alpha_j, j \in \{1..m\}$, given by the manager to each of the indicators I_j. The objective function can be written as in Eq. 7, where α_c is the weight of the cost indicator:

$$\max Z = \sum_{j=1}^{m} \alpha_j . f_j - \alpha_c . f_T \tag{7}$$

Eq. 7 can then be written as follows:

$$\max Z = \sum_{j=1}^{m} \sum_{i=1}^{n} (\gamma_j . \alpha_j . I_j^i - \beta_j . \alpha_c . CC . I_j^i) . x^i + \alpha_c . CC . T \tag{8}$$

Let P_{min}^i and P_{max}^i be the minimum and maximum values of possible production volumes of variant i, respectively (Eq. 9). Additionally let P_t be the total production volume (Eq. 10). P_{min}^i, P_{max}^i and P_t can be determined based on expected sales and production capacity.

$$0 \le P_{min}^i \le x^i \le P_{max}^i \tag{9}$$

$$\sum_{i=1}^{n} x^i \le P_t \tag{10}$$

The subsequent optimization model is as follows:

$$\max Z = \sum_{j=1}^{m} \sum_{i=1}^{n} (\gamma_j . \alpha_j . I_j^i - \beta_j . \alpha_c . CC . I_j^i) . x^i + \alpha_c . CC . T$$

s.t.

$$0 \le P_{min}^i \le x^i \le P_{max}^i$$

$$\sum_{i=1}^{n} x^i \le P_t$$

4   Case Study

We applied our proposed approach to a furniture manufacturer providing several variants of customized kitchens to the luxury market. The company has three product lines. Our study involves one product line comprising 6 variants. It aims to balance the production between these variants so as to minimize the environmental impact and costs, for a given demand variation amplitude. Our approach addresses a particular aspect of product diversity by finding optimal production distribution between variants. To do so, the first step is to weight the indicators using pair wise comparisons and AHP. The second step is to solve the linear programming model to come up with a given distribution of the production volumes among variants. In current research we consider only weights that are calculated by AHP. This might be a burden for the optimization because we only consider a single point of the Pareto curve (depicting Pareto optimal solutions). However we base our model on the assumption that the chosen weights are most suitable to the company.

4.1   Indicators Weighting

The predefined list of indicators used in the case study is taken from the S-MC-S assessment model (Medini et al., 2011; Bettoni et al., 2013). It is presented in Table 1. Table 2 summarizes pairwise comparisons of the indicators.

After applying AHP, subsequent weights are represented in the last row of Table 2. Consistency Ratio (CR) calculated according to Eq. 4 is 0.1542. This value is lower than 0.2, and judgements are then said to be acceptable. Afterwards, indicators values are calculated by an assessment engine connected to an environmental data base (Pedrazzoli et al., 2012). Data concerning the 6 variants is entered through a set of product, process and supply chain editors. Each of these variants is characterized with given material type, dimensions, shape, etc. The description of variants, however, is beyond the scope of this paper.

Table 1. Indicators definitions

Indicator	Unit of measure
GWP – Global Warming Potential	kg eq. CO_2
HTP – Human Toxicity Potential	kg eq. 1,4-DCB
ED – Energy Depletion	MJ
NRD - Natural Resources Depletion	Kg antimony eq.
WD – Water Depletion	m^3
WP - Waste Production	kg
UVPC - Unitary Production Cost	€

Table 2. Indicators pair-wise comparisons

	GWP	HTP	ED	NRD	WD	WP	UVPC
GWP	1.00	1.00	1.00	3.00	0.33	5.00	0.20
HTP	1.00	1.00	5.00	3.00	1.00	7.00	3.00
ED	1.00	0.20	1.00	3.00	0.33	3.00	0.33
NRD	0.33	0.33	0.33	1.00	0.33	0.33	0.20
WD	3.00	1.00	3.00	3.00	1.00	3.00	0.33
WP	0.20	0.14	0.33	3.00	0.33	1.00	0.33
UVPC	5.00	0.33	3.00	5.00	3.00	3.00	1.00
Weights	**0.12**	**0.27**	**0.09**	**0.04**	**0.18**	**0.05**	**0.25**

4.2   Optimization

The function that needs to be minimized is represented by Eq. 11 to 13, where i is the variant, with $i \in \{1, 2, 3, 4, 5, 6\}$. We propose the use of another indicator, $Cost$, that includes $UVPC$ and cost incurred by the case company in the carbon market. We introduce an income indicator as depicted by Eq. 15. Let 1500 be the amount of greenhouse gases (T) the case company can emit in a given carbon market, 30 be the emissions unitary cost (CC) and 150 be the total production volume (P_t). GWP is the only indicator that represents greenhouse gases emissions.

$$\max Z = \sum_{i=1}^{6}(\alpha_{HTP}.HTP^i + \alpha_{ED}.ED^i + \alpha_{NRD}.NRD^i + \alpha_{WD}.WD^i + \alpha_{HTP}.WP^i + \alpha_{UVPC}.UVPC^i - \alpha_{GWP}.30.GWP^i).x^i + \alpha_{UVPC}.30.1500 \tag{11}$$

s.t.

$$6 \leq x^i \leq 10 \quad \text{if } i \in \{1,2,3,4\} \tag{12}$$

$$60 \leq x^i \leq 64 \quad \text{if } i \in \{5,6\} \tag{13}$$

$$\sum_{i=1}^{6} x^i \leq 158 \tag{14}$$

Indicators values and production volumes are represented in Table 3. Minimum (P_{min}^i) and maximum (P_{max}^i) production volumes are defined. Their values shown in Table 3 are chosen based on average data from the case company.

Table 3. Variants data

Variants	Indicators							Production	
	GWP	HTP	ED	NRD	WD	WP	UVPC	P_{min}^i	P_{max}^i
1	20.95	11.71	1368.3	0.19	0.17	2.00	11.21	6	10
2	23.56	16.87	1485.2	0.22	0.19	2.27	13.41	6	10
3	22.84	16.69	1444.4	0.21	0.18	2.27	14.35	6	10
4	22.36	12.53	1471.4	0.21	0.18	2.14	13.80	6	10
5	23.07	12.84	1518.2	0.22	0.19	2.18	16.10	60	64
6	22.10	12.57	1466.4	0.21	0.18	2.15	14.86	60	64

The linear programming problem is solved using Microsoft Office Excel solver and by choosing Simplex method. We varied Δ_i in order to check the impact of production volume variance on the indicators. Table 4 shows the results obtained for different values of Δ_i such that $\Delta_i = P_{max}^i - P_{min}^i$. Columns 3 to 10 represent the sum of indicators among all variants. The first row of the table relates to the standard (Sd) situation within the case study, that is: $P_{min}^i = P_{max}^i = 8, i \in \{1,2,3,4\}$ and $P_{min}^i = P_{max}^i = 63, i \in \{5,6\}$. Optimal solution fitting such standard situation is as follows: producing 8 units of each of variants 1 to 5 and 63 units of each of variants 5 and 6. Data relating to this situation are described in detail in Table 3.

Table 4. Production volumes variance impact on indicators ($\sum_{i=1}^6 x^i \leq 158, T = 1500$)

Δ_v	$P_{min}^1,$ $P_{min}^2,$ $P_{min}^3,$ $P_{min}^4,$	P_{min}^5 P_{min}^6	Indicators values							Decision variables					
			GWP	HTP	ED	NRD	WD	WP	Cost	x^1	x^2	x^3	x^4	x^5	x^6
Sd	8	63	3563	2063	234184	33.73	29.07	342	64274	8	8	8	8	63	63
4	6	60	3248	1871	213691	30.78	26.52	312	54628	6	6	6	6	60	60
8	4	58	2979	1705	196184	28.26	24.34	286	46368	4	4	4	4	58	58
12	2	56	2709	1539	178676	25.74	22.16	260	38108	2	2	2	2	56	56

As shown, in Table 3, all indicators values decrease with the increase of the gap between minimum and maximum production volumes of each variant i. Such a decrease is expected, since the model has as many options as the interval of decision variables (production volumes of the variant) increases. It is then more likely to find more optimal solutions. The manager, for instance, can select one of the proposed solutions according to the production system capacity that determines which Δ_i the company can afford. The trend that can be noticed in the solutions offered by the model (i.e. decision variables) values is the minimization of total production volumes of the variants. The lower the variant minimal production volume, the lower is total production volume. Figure 1 shows the variation of the income for different carbon market threshold values, with:

$$Income = -\sum_{i=1}^6 UVPC^i - CC.\left(\sum_{i=1}^6 GWP^i - T\right) \tag{15}$$

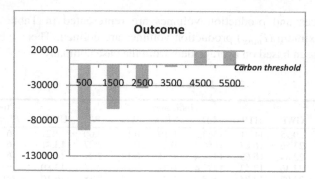

Fig. 1. Carbon threshold impact on income

Company's greenhouse gases emissions amount to approximately $3500\ kg$. Thus, it incurs a carbon cost until the threshold exceeds this value, then revenue is generated by the reimbursement to the company for the non-emitted but allowed amount of greenhouse gases. This highlights the importance of considering the carbon market in the optimization of the economic and environmental performance of the company.

5   Conclusions

In this paper we propose a combined evaluation and optimization approach to mitigate variety impact on sustainability. The evaluation relies on sustainability performance indicators connected to an external environmental data base. Indicators are weighted according to company priorities, thus providing more decision support to managers. Optimization aims to minimize emissions and cost through balancing production volumes between variants and integrating the carbon market. Production capacity and demand are considered at this point. The originality of our approach lies in coupling performance evaluation and optimization. Moreover, the indicators used in the evaluation consider product life cycle phases (i.e. extraction, manufacturing, transportation, etc.).

The paper underlines the impact of variety steering on sustainability indicators. When the variants' production volumes are flexible, the cost and environmental impact are lower. Furthermore, the paper points out the relevance of the carbon market to company environmental and economic performances. From this, it follows that environmental considerations should be considered from a win-win perspective rather than an external constraint. In this sense optimizing company sustainability performance generates economic value (e.g. reimbursement from the carbon market) instead of making companies incur additional costs.

References

1. Abdallah, T., Diabat, A., Simchi-Levi, D.: Sustainable supply chain design: a closed-loop formulation and sensitivity analysis. Production Planning & Control 23(2-3), 120–133 (2012)

2. Bauer, J., Bektas, T., Crainic, T.G.: Minimizing greenhouse gas emissions in intermodal freight transport: an application to rail service design. Journal of the Operational Research Society 61, 530–542 (2010)
3. Bettoni, A., Corti, D., Fontana, A., Zebardast, M., Pedrazzoli, P.: Sustainable Mass Customization Assessment. In: Carneiro, L.M., Jasinski, T., Zolghadri, M., Pedrazzoli, P. (eds.) Intelligent Non-Hierarchical Manufacturing Networks, pp. 249–276. John Wiley & Sons, Inc. (2013)
4. Dekker, R., Bloemhof, J., Mallidis, I.: Operations research for green logistics – an overview of aspects, issues, contributions and challenges. European Journal of Operational Research 219(3), 671–679 (2012)
5. ElMaraghy, H., Schuh, G., ElMaraghy, W., Piller, F., Schönsleben, P., Tseng, M., Bernard, A.: Product Variety Management. CIRP Annals - Manufacturing Technology 62(2), 629–652 (2013)
6. European Parliament (EP) and Council of the European Union (CEU), Directive 2009/29/EC of the European parliament and of the council of Official Journal of the European Union 7:EN:PDF (April 23, 2009),
http://eur-lex.europa.eu/LexUriServ/
LexUriServ.do?uri=OJ:L:2009:140:0063:008
7. Ehrgott, M.A.: A discussion of scalarization techniques for multiple objective integer programming. Annals of Operations Research 147(1), 343–360 (2013)
8. Global Reporting Initiative, Sustainability reporting guidelines, Global Reporting Initiative, Boston, USA (2002)
9. ISO 14040, Environmental Management – Life Cycle Assessment –Principles and Framework. International Organization of Standardization (2006)
10. Jorgensen, A., Le Bocq, A., Nazarkina, L., Hauschild, M.: Methodologies for social life cycle assessment. International Journal of Life Cycle Assessment 13(2), 96–103 (2008)
11. Medini, K., Bettoni, A., Fontana, A., Corti, D., Zebardast, M.: S-MC-S - D3.1 Assessment Model, European Commission, p. 507 (2011)
12. Pedrazzoli, P., Alge, M., Bettoni, A., Canetta, L.: Modeling and Simulation Tool for Sustainable MC Supply Chain Design and Assessment. In: Emmanouilidis, C., Taisch, M., Kiritsis, D. (eds.) Advances in Production Management Systems. IFIP AICT, vol. 397, pp. 342–349. Springer, Heidelberg (2013)
13. Saaty, T.L.: Decision making with the analytic hierarchy process. International Journal Services Sciences 1(1), 83–98 (2008)
14. Tan, K.H., Rae, R.H.: Uncovering the links between regulation and performance measurement. International Journal of Production Economics 122(1), 449–457 (2009)
15. United Nations Environment Programme, UNEP, Life Cycle Management: A Business Guide to Sustainability (2009),
http://www.unep.org/pdf/dtie/DTI0889PA.pdf
16. Wang, F., Lai, X., Shi, N.: A multi-objective optimization for green supply chain network design. Decision Support Systems 51(2), 262–269 (2011)

Product Change in a Small Company: Effects on Eco-price and Global Productivity

Nilson Carvalho, Biagio Fernando Giannetti, Feni Agostinho,
and Cecilia Maria Villas Boas de Almeida[*]

Programa de Pós –Graduação em Engenharia de Produção da Universidade Paulista,
Rua Dr Bacelar 1212, Mirandópolis, 04026-002 - São Paulo, Brazil
cmvbag@unip.br

Abstract. The notion of supply chain thinking working to reduce the environmental and socioeconomic burden associated with a manufactured product or selection of products throughout their value chain was recently recognized. However, there are also several types of small businesses that arise in the sphere of influence of large supply chains in order to fill gaps or serve customers with special needs, which have not been considered or assessed. These small companies, in general, have little or none influence on decisions made along the entire supply chain, and have to adapt their production processes induced by decisions made by the leading companies within the chain. This work assesses the changes in the environmental resource use of a small company operating in the Brazilian automotive aftermarket using emergy synthesis and confirms the idea that the supply chain thinking works to reduce the environmental reducing the burden associated with products manufacturing within the value chain. The simulation performed for the period 2014-2025, within the company's business plan, shows that the sooner the exchange of products is made, the greater the profits of the company with regard to eco-efficiency and environmental responsibility.

Keywords: emergy; automotive aftermarket; resource use, eco-price.

1 Introduction

Manufacturing activities are among the largest contributors for mankind's usage of resources. With the expansion in economic activities, environmental concerns are gaining increasing awareness and environmental actions are developing to preventive approaches. Recently, the adoption of more holistic strategies by authorities and companies, in which all energy and resource use throughout the products' value chain are examined, has been recognized. Thus, the notion of supply chain thinking works to reduce the environmental and socioeconomic burden associated with a manufactured product or selection of products throughout their value chain.

---

[*] Corresponding author.

B. Grabot et al. (Eds.): APMS 2014, Part II, IFIP AICT 439, pp. 178–186, 2014.

In this context, there are also several types of small businesses that arise in the sphere of influence of large supply chains in order to fill gaps or serve customers with special needs. These small companies, in general, have little or none influence on decisions made. Decisions made by the leading companies within the chain end up causing effects, which may or may not be positive, both with regard to the revenue of these small businesses, as the environmental impact they may cause individually.

To provide evaluation external to the economy, and at the same time, adherent to the fundamental laws of thermodynamics, an environmental accounting method for energy invested in environmental and human systems, called emergy synthesis, was developed by [1]. This method of valuation recognizes the relationships between nature's production of raw materials and their consumption by mankind to be quantified in an equivalent physical unit, which can be then translated into monetary terms.

Emergy synthesis has been successfully used to evaluate manufacture processes. [2] analyzed the resource utilization and environmental performance of a multi-product system, which was divided into two categories: inseparable multi-product systems and semi-independent multi-product systems. These authors concluded that if the product belongs to an inseparable multiproduct system, its emergy equals that for the entire system, but if it belongs to a semi-independent multi-product system, inputs must be shared. Announcing a new method, based upon emergy synthesis, [3] highlight the internal relations among the different subsystems and components. The emergy-based method provides insight into the environmental performance and sustainability of an industrial park. Results from Dalian Economic Development Zone case show the potential of emergy synthesis method at the industrial park level for environmental policy making. Emergy advantages and limitations are discussed for future research. The impact of waste emissions on the environment was evaluated by [4],who propose an amplification factor to improved emergy indicator. To illustrate the usefulness and highlight their superiority over standard indices, the improved emergy indicators were used to evaluate the interaction between a commercial polyethylene production process incorporating waste management and its surrounding environment.

In a more comprehensive study, [5] reports the experiences of a medium size gold-plated jewelry company, located in São Paulo, Brazil, in order to reduce waste and pollution. Actions taken, the changes that have been introduced, their cost-effectiveness and the additional benefits accomplished were presented. The results of a waste minimization program and of a Cleaner Production intervention were complemented with the use of global scale performance indicators (Material intensity, MIs, and Emergy accounting), which have shown that little changes within the company reduce upstream impacts and that benefits to the environment are greater than that observed in the company's neighborhood. Human health and environmental concerns were considered at in evaluating the options to reduce or eliminate lead from the manufacturing environment is its replacement with lead-free alloys [6]. Applying emergy synthesis and the DALY indicator (Disability Adjusted Life Years) to assess the impact of manufacturing soft solder showed that more resources are used to produce one ton of lead-free solders than to produce one ton of tin-lead solders, with and without the use of consumer waste recovered through a reverse logistics system. The assessment of air emissions during solder production shows that the benefits of the lead-free solution are limited to the stages of manufacturing and assembling. The tin-lead solder was pointed as the best option in terms of resource use efficiency and with respect to emissions into the atmosphere when the entire supply chain is considered.

The goal of the company is to consolidate its presence in the automotive supply chain in the coming years, totally substituting the production of carburetor gaskets for electronic injection ones till 2025. The objective of this work is to assess and foresee the changes in the environmental resource use of a small company operating in the Brazilian automotive aftermarket during the process of product change induced by the main supply chain.

Company Description
JP JOINTS started its activities for the automotive aftermarket in 1992, with a distribution chain that requires a spread of products and services from suppliers. The company specialty is automotive sealing products, which involve more than 1,500 items this market. The company, which started its activities by providing spare gaskets for carburetor engines, had to adapt to the new demand for gaskets for engines with electronic fuel injection. Today, the leading products of the company are carburetor and electronic injection gaskets, with a production of more than a million units per year.

Figure 1 shows the leading gasket models used for replacement in old engines and the substitute for vehicles with electronic injection.

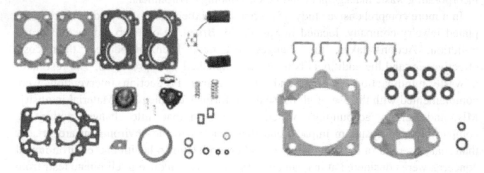

Fig. 1. Carburetor (left) and electronic injection (right) kits produced by the company

2   Methods

Emergy is defined as the available energy previously required, directly and indirectly, through input pathways to make a product or service [1]. The emergy evaluation was performed for the conversion of all contributions received by the production system (metals, energy, oil, and currency) on a single base of measurement (sej). The effect of the product change can thus be compared regarding efficiency in resource use, productivity, environmental burden and global productivity. The evaluation procedure for the system was performed by means of data collection through on the formal documents of purchase, in the year 2013, accordingly to the following steps: (i) study of the context in which the system is inserted; (ii) definition of the system under study including its limits for investigation and description of manufacturing processes; (iii) execution of the mass balance and construction of energy flows diagram; (iv) construction of the emergy tables with data collected; and (v) discussion for future management actions. For each type of gasket, the quantities of electricity consumed, water, paper and cardboard, lubricating oil, labor, were calculated. The quantities of materials used in the implantation of the system were accounted for by considering its useful life. Unit Emergy Values (UEVs) used in this text are mostly taken from the literature, and are relative to the 15.83×10^{24} seJ/year baseline [7].

The Emprice [1] or eco-price [8] have the purpose of more precisely representing the value of environmental resources than the alternative approach of "willingness to pay". The Emprice is the quotient of emergy to dollars of the area where the system is inserted. The emergy to dollar ratio of the State of São Paulo is 1.7×10^{12} sej/U\$ [7]. The Emergy to dollar ratio of the company is also calculated, by the quotient between the total emergy and the company's revenues. The Global Productivity (GP) was calculated similarly to common productivity, which is the ratio of inputs and outputs. Estimated in emergy terms, through the ratio energy to emergy, GP considers resources, energy and services of the biosphere embedded into the UEVs, and consequently is broader than productivity usually calculated.

3   Results

Figure 2 shows the energy diagram of the company.

Table 1 shows the emergy environmental accounting of the company in 2013. This year, equal amounts of both types of joints were produced. However, the emergy spent in the production of carburetor kits was two times greater that used to produce the same amount of electronic injection ones. The emergy costs of the firm, represented by the annual cost of facility building, offices and machinery, account for only 7% of the total annual cost.

The production of the carburetor kit (67,4% of the total emergy) and, as expected, the major contribution for the total emergy comes from the Kevlar gaskets, followed by the cellulose ones.

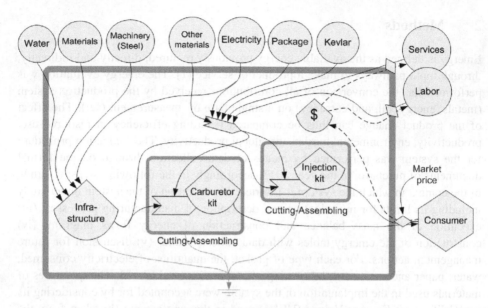

Fig. 2. Energy system diagram of JP juntas

Table 1. Emergy environmental accounting of JP Juntas in 2013

	Item	Quant.	Unit	UEVs/(sej/unit)	Emergy/(sej/year)	%
	Facility building					
1	Concrete	2.62×10^7	g	1.23×10^9	3.22×10^{16}	2.4
2	Steel	7.85×10^5	g	5.31×10^9	4.17×10^{15}	0.3
3	Wood	5.32×10^5	g	4.04×10^8	2.15×10^{14}	<0.1
	Offices					
4	Plastic	1.86×10^4	g	3.80×10^8	7.07×10^{12}	<0.1
5	Copper	4.54×10^3	g	6.80×10^{10}	3.09×10^{14}	<0.1
6	Steel	1.64×10^6	g	5.31×10^9	8.71×10^{15}	0.6
7	Glass	2.00×10^3	g	8.40×10^8	1.68×10^{12}	<0.1
	Production plant					
8	Plastic	3.76×10^5	g	3.80×10^8	1.43×10^{14}	<0.1
9	Steel	8.92×10^6	g	5.31×10^9	4.74×10^{16}	3.5
	subtotal 1				9.30×10^{16}	7
	Carburetor kit					
10	Water	8.48×10^7	g	6.64×10^5	5.63×10^{13}	<0.1
11	Electricity	2.30×10^{11}	J	1.28×10^5	2.94×10^{16}	2.2
12	Labor	6.20×10^9	J	1.15×10^7	7.13×10^{16}	5.2
13	Lubricant	8.65×10^9	J	5.91×10^4	5.11×10^{14}	<0.1
14	Rubber (o'rings)	9.60×10^4	g	2.10×10^4	2.02×10^9	<0.1
15	Copper (diaphragms and coils)	8.64×10^5	g	6.80×10^{10}	5.88×10^{16}	4.3
16	Zinc (diaphragms and coils)	1.30×10^6	g	6.80×10^{10}	8.81×10^{16}	6.5
17	Rubber tubes	1.68×10^6	g	2.10×10^4	3.53×10^{10}	<0.1
18	Cellulose paper	2.78×10^7	g	3.90×10^9	1.09×10^{17}	8.0
19	Red Kevlar	1.34×10^6	g	1.25×10^{10}	1.68×10^{16}	1.2
20	Green Kevlar	3.76×10^7	g	1.25×10^{10}	4.70×10^{17}	34.6
21	Paper	4.80×10^5	g	3.90×10^9	1.87×10^{15}	0.1
22	Cardboard	1.58×10^6	g	3.90×10^9	6.18×10^{15}	0.5
23	Label	2.40×10^5	g	3.90×10^9	9.36×10^{14}	0.1
24	Blister	5.04×10^3	g	3.80×10^8	1.92×10^{12}	<0.1
25	Plastic bag	2.38×10^5	g	3.80×10^8	9.03×10^{13}	<0.1

Table 2. *(continued.)*

	subtotal 2				9.16 x 10^{17}	67.4
	Electronic injection kit					
26	Water	8.48 x 10^7	g	6.64 x 10^5	5.63 x 10^{13}	<0.1
27	Electricity	9.84 x 10^{10}	J	1.28 x 10^5	1.26 x 10^{16}	0.9
28	Labor	6.20 x 10^9	J	1.15 x 10^7	7.13 x 10^{16}	5.2
29	Lubricant	8.65 x 10^9	J	5.91 x 10^4	5.11 x 10^{14}	<0.1
30	Rubber (o'rings)	1.34 x 10^6	g	2.10 x 10^4	2.82 x 10^{10}	<0.1
31	Green Kevlar	2.42 x 10^7	g	1.25 x 10^{10}	3.02 x 10^{17}	22.3
32	Paper	4.80 x 10^5	g	3.90 x 10^9	1.87 x 10^{15}	0.1
33	Cardboard	1.58 x 10^6	g	3.90 x 10^9	6.18 x 10^{15}	0.5
34	Label	2.40 x 10^5	g	3.90 x 10^9	9.36 x 10^{14}	0.1
35	Blister	9.60 x 10^4	g	3.80 x 10^8	3.65 x 10^{13}	<0.1
36	Plastic bag	1.80 x 10^5	g	3.80 x 10^8	6.84 x 10^{13}	<0.1
	subtotal 3				4.43 x 10^{17}	32.6

The total emergy of the company in 2013 accounts for all the resources and energy required to produce 480,000 kits of gaskets for carburetor and electronic injection engines (Tab. 2).

The UEVs, which translate the use of energy and resources in emergy terms per energy unit of product, shows that it takes approximately the double of emergy to produce one carburetor kit. This is unfavorable both to the environment and the company as the carburetor kit is sold by U$2.00 while the electronic injection kit by U$3.50. The kits' EMR also show that less emergy is used to produce electronic injection kits per unit of final product.

Table 2. Summary of emergy environmental accounting of JP Juntas in 2013

	Carbureto r	Electronic injection	Total
Total emergy 2013 (sej/year)	9.63 x 10^{17}	4.89 x 10^{17}	1.45 x 10^{18}
UEV (sej/kit)	4.01 x 10^{12}	2.04 x 10^{12}	2.83 x 10^{12}
Emprice* (Em$/year)	566,198	287,797	799,235
EMR** (sej/U$)	2.01 x 10^{12}	5.82 x 10^{11}	1.10 x 10^{12}
Revenues (U$/year)	480,000	840,000	1,320,000

*The Emprice is the quotient of emergy to dollars (1.7 x 10^{12} sej/U$, [7] of the area where the system is inserted. **The emergy to dollar ratio of the company is also calculated, by the quotient between the total emergy and the company's revenues.

Since the company's plans are to reduce gradually the production of carburetor kits with the end in 2025, a predictive accounting was performed to assess the impact of this managerial decision in the environmental accounting of the company in the next years. The simulation took into account some factors, which were foreseen:

- the reduction in the number of carburetor kits would be compensated with the production of electronic injection ones;
- the reduction of electricity use, due to the reduced number of cutting operations, was calculated and accounted in proportion to the number and kind of kits produced;
- the reduction of labor force, in 2020, was estimated in proportion to the number and kind of kits produced;
- the price of the kits was maintained constant.

Table 3 shows the results of the environmental accounting of the company till 2025. It is clear that as the percentage of electronic injection kits increase, the total emergy of the company decreases along with the use of energy and materials to produce one unit of product (UEVs). The Emprice, which translates the emergy costs into currency values, also decreases by 35%, while the company`s revenues increase by 24%.

Table 3. Summary of emergy environmental accounting of JP Juntas in the period of 2014 to 2025

	2014	2015	2016	2017	2018	2019	2020	2021	2022	2023	2024	2025
% Electronic injection gasket emergy	37	41	45	50	54	60	64	70	77	84	92	100
Total emergy x 10^{18} (sej/year)	1.32	1.28	1.24	1.20	1.16	1.12	1.05	1.01	0.97	0.93	0.89	0.85
UEV x 10^{12} (sej/kit)	2.74	2.66	2.58	2.50	2.42	2.34	2.19	2.11	2.02	1.94	1.86	1.77
EmPrice x 10^{6} (Em$/year)	0.8	0.8	0.7	0.7	0.7	0.7	0.6	0.6	0.6	0.5	0.5	0.5
Revenues x 10^{6} (U$/year)	1.35	1.38	1.41	1.44	1.47	1.5	1.53	1.56	1.59	1.62	1.65	1.68

It is also remarkable that the change of products, despite induced by the larger firms in the supply chain, may bring additional benefits to JP JUNTAS. Figure 2 shows that the emergy embedded into products might decrease by 31% in 2025. This emergy savings will be available to other uses within the biosphere. A decrease of 17% in the emergy costs for maintenance, use of auxiliary materials and labor is foreseen, and the use of packaging materials is expected to significantly diminish by more than 80%, while the company's revenues increase.

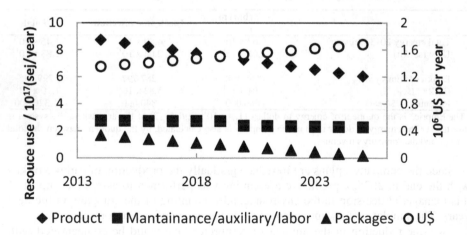

Fig. 3. Emergy into products, maintenance, auxiliary materials, labor and packaging materials from 2014 to 2025

In regard to the emergy costs represented into currency values, results shown in Figure 3 make clear that the product change will benefit not only the company, reducing the environmental costs by 35%, but also that the global productivity will increase by 55%, due to the lesser use of raw, auxiliary and packaging materials and energy savings.

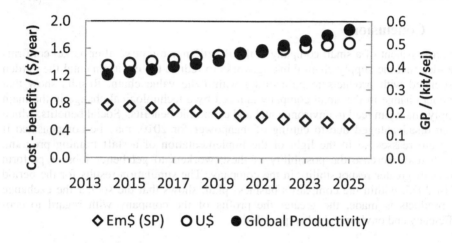

Fig. 4. Cost/Benefit and Global Productivity of JP JUNTAS from 2014 to 2025

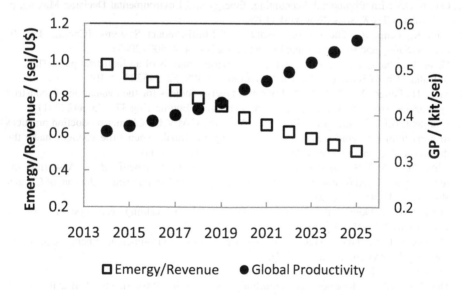

Fig. 5. Emergy/Revenue and Global Productivity of JP JUNTAS from 2014 to 2025

All results show that a technological change that occurred elsewhere in the supply chain can have beneficial effects on small businesses that exist and survive around the main chain. The gains due to increased global productivity benefit not only entrepreneurs and small business owners, but also the environment, since part of saved resources and energy can be used for other purposes (Fig. 4). The Emergy/Revenue relationship, which decreases by 48%, shows that the product change of makes the company more eco-efficient, as it profits more with less use of resources and energy.

4   Conclusions

The assessment of a small company in the Brazilian automotive aftermarket confirms the idea that the supply chain thinking works to reduce the environmental the burden associated with products manufacturing within the value chain. Results show that product change in the small company induced by a technological change in the main supply chain can lead to environmental and economic benefits. Social benefits, which seem disadvantaged due to cutting of manpower for 2010, may be compensated if they are reassessed in the light of the implementation of a staff training program, which may increase the possibility of these workers to get better jobs or perform duties of greater responsibility in the company. The simulation results for the period 2014-2025, within the company's business plan, shows that the sooner the exchange of products is made, the greater the profits of the company with regard to eco-efficiency and environmental responsibility.

References

1. Odum, H.T.: Environmental Accounting: Emergy and Environmental Decision Making, p. 370. John Wiley & Sons, New York (1996)
2. Cao, K., Feng, X.: The Emergy Analysis of Multi-Product Systems. IChemE, Part B, Process Safety and Environmental Protection 85(B5), 494–500 (2007)
3. Geng, Y., Zhang, P., Ulgiati, S., Sarkis, J.: Emergy analysis of an industrial park: The case of Dalian. China Science of the Total Environment 408, 5273–5283 (2010)
4. Mua, H., Fengb, X., Chua, K.H.: Improved emergy indices for the evaluation of industrial systems incorporating waste management. Ecological Engineering 37, 335–342 (2011)
5. Giannetti, B.F., Bonilla, S.H., Silva, I.R., Almeida, C.M.V.B.: Cleaner production practices in a medium size gold-plated jewelry company in Brazil: when little changes make the difference. Journal of Cleaner Production 16, 1106–1117 (2008)
6. Almeida, C.M.V.B., Madureira, M.A., Bonilla, S.H., Giannetti, B.F.: Assessing the replacement of lead in solders: effects on resource use and human health. Journal of Cleaner Production 47, 457–464 (2013)
7. Odum, H.T., Odum, E.P.: The energetic basis for valuing eco system services. Ecosystems 3(1), 21–23 (2000); Demétrio (2007)
8. Campbell, E.T., Tilley, D.R.: The eco-price: How environmental emergy equates to currency. Ecosystem Services (2014),
   http://dx.doi.org/10.1016/j.ecoser.2013.12.002i
9. Demétrio, J.F.C.: Emergy Environmental Sustainability Assessment of Brazil, Ph. D. dissertation. Universidade Paulista,São Paulo, Brazil (2011),
   http://www3.unip.br/ensino/pos_graduacao/strictosensu/
   lab_producao_meioambiente/realizacoes_academicas.aspx#ra4
   (last accessed in July 2013)

Exploring Alternatives of Accounting for Environmental Liabilities in the Company's Balance Sheet

Fernando A. Bortuluzi, Feni Agostinho, Cecília Maria Villas Boats Almeida,
Silvia Bonilla, and Biagio F. Gianetti

Post-graduation Program on Production Engineering, Paulista University (UNIP),
Rua Dr. Bacelar 1212 CEP 04026-002 São Paulo, Brazil
{Feni Agostinho,feniagostinho}@gmail.com

Abstract. Environmental concerns have recently reached the stock market, in which investors want analyze the company's related-risks in causing environmental damages. Usually, the Company's Balance Sheet (CBS) is summarized, disallowing a clear interpretation of environmental issues. Methods used to valuate environmental liabilities are often subjective, which create communication problems. The aims of this work are (i) to explore alternatives for CBS structural presentation to clearly represent environmental liabilities, which allow an efficient communication with society and investors, and (ii) to assess a methodological alternative of valuating environmental liabilities under economical terms. The "Petrobras" S.A. Brazilian Oil Company is taken as a case study by accounting its oil spill related-incidents occurred in 2000 yr. Results show that an improved CBS structure should represent the company's environmental related-issues. Additionally, emergy accounting appears as a powerful alternative to replace/substitute contingent valuation to quantify environmental liabilities under economic terms.

Keywords: environmental liabilities, emergy accounting, integrated report, Petrobras S.A, oil spill.

1   Introduction

History has many examples of companies that passed from successful to failure examples, such as the American Company Enron in the 90's, and, recently, the American Lehman Brothers and the Brazilian EBX group. These examples expose a similar problem: the weakness of the current model to represent the company's balance sheet (CBS). Since 2010, the top-100 worldwide companies are discussing the creation of a new balance sheet structure, considering an integrated thinking and a more holistic perspective. This proposal is being labeled as Integrated Report [1, which main is to clearly represent the company's targets at long term and the strategies to get there. In this sense, several important aspects as human, natural, and intellectual capitals are also being considered instead of exclusively financial results. The Integrated Report, which intends to be in harmony with sustainable development, is severely criticized in some studies [2] due to the difficulties in integrating biophysical accounting with the many existing cores of financial accounting conventions.

B. Grabot et al. (Eds.): APMS 2014, Part II, IFIP AICT 439, pp. 187–196, 2014.

Similarly to Integrated Reports, some studies [3] have already argued that provisioning for environmental damages should be present in the CBS, otherwise, distorted information is obtained in which the liabilities are undervalued and equity overvalued. Not accounting for liabilities at the same year of occurrence – usually due to judicial delay – can also affect the company's future performance and result in economical losses; and investors will not have in traditional CBS enough indicators for the efficient evaluation of the company's economical performance, especially regarding to judge risks on investing in the company.

The traditional financial accounting techniques are unable to measure the resources and services provided by biosphere, as well as all the environmental impacts caused by releasing high concentrated wastes on natural environment. This accounting limitation is due to a lack of market value of environmental goods and services. Some studies [4] have warned about the need for developing and standardizing trustable methodologies to quantify the environmental performance of companies. The valuation of environmental liabilities, for a long time, is realized under subjective approaches, which do not represent real values for repair or substitution [5]. In this sense, the environmental liabilities must be objectively quantified (i.e. under biophysical approaches) to be included into the CBS. Efforts were made to quantify liabilities by using eMergy methodology [6], and to integrate eMergy with bookkeeping techniques [7, 8]. However, none of them have explored the inclusion of the quantified liabilities into the CBS in a the way they can be accessible to interested pubic and clearly represented by scientifically accepted methods.

This work explores alternatives for representing the environmental liabilities into the CBS, focusing on an efficient communication about the company's economical performance for the general society and investors. For this, raw data from [3] is used considering as case study the published 2000's balance sheet of the Brazilian Oil Company "Petrobras" S.A. Emergy accounting [5] is suggested as an alternative scientific methodology in providing a biophysical view (biophysical indicators?) to quantify environmental liabilities.

2   Methodology

2.1   Case Study Description

The main goal of this paper is to explore alternatives to accounting for the environmental liabilities in the company's balance sheet (CBS), through a case study. The case study is considered mandatory to solidify the ideas under discussion and to point out how and where the liabilities could be estimated and included. Negative externalities caused by oil spill incidents are considered due to their high impact on environment and society. It is worth to say that Petrobras S.A. is signatory of the International Integrated Reporting Council. The oil spill incidents that occurred in Brazil 2000 yr were accounted and described in detail by [3]. In short, about 78,740 oil barrels spilled under three different incidents, each one resulting in different damages. For calculation purposes, the kind of environmental damages were considered the same in all incidents, differing only on the impact level. This is valid because this work is a first attempt in assessing alternatives for including damages into the CBS instead of calculating precise value for environmental liabilities.

2.2 Studied Alternatives for Presenting Environmental Liabilities into the Balance Sheet

Two alternatives of presenting environmental liabilities into the company's balance sheet (CBS) are assessed and compared to the traditional CBS labeled as Baseline; considering the current Brazilian law for financial accounting techniques (no. 6,404/1976), as well as recent alterations by laws no. 11,638/2007 and 11,941/2009. It is worth to say that these alterations aimed to get closer and be compared with definitions and structures of international rules. The Baseline and the two alternatives discussed in this paper are the following:

(a) **Baseline:** Traditional accounting approach considered in Brazil according to law no. 6,404/1976. This approach does not foresee any inclusion and/or disclosure of environmental liabilities into the CBS.

(b) **Alternative #1:** Accounting approach suggested by [3] aiming to improve the regulations of law no. 6,404/1976. These authors intended to establish an alternative way to include the environmental liabilities into the CBS by expressing clearly the related economic amount and its influence on the company's "equity" indicator. For this, the company economic investment on environmental issues is included into the "assets" group of the balance sheet, and the economical obligation (i.e. penalties and indemnities) into the "liabilities" group.

(c) **Alternative #2:** The suggested accounting approach in this work according to law no. 6,404/1976 and its alterations by laws no. 11,638/2007 and 11,941/2009. The intention is to establish a clearer structure for CBS compared to that proposed by [3]. Initially, it is emphasized that alterations of law no. 6,404/1976 have created a category "intangible" within the subgroup "noncurrent assets", which represents the value of immaterial assets   (e.g. exploration rights, copyrights, franchise rights, trademarks, licenses, and softwares). Although considering the company's reduction accounts (e.g. mark depreciation and license losses), the creation of "intangibles" could raise the doubt about the need of a counterpart into the "liabilities" and "equity" groups of balance sheet to evidence these impacts, because the existence of "intangibles" allows the company to incur in financial debts. This doubt is valid because there is no regulation about a counterpart from intangible obligations incurred by company, as example, the environmental pollution, social responsibility, among others. This aspect is mainly important in a scenario in which the "liabilities" are higher than "assets", which results in a negative influence on company's "equity". At any case, a clear presentation of this aspect within the CBS is mandatory.

2.3 Studied Alternatives for Environmental Damages Valuation

There are some methods most accepted and used to estimated economic values for environmental attributes, including the contingent valuation. Although the role of using contingent valuation in the assessment of natural resources damage and public-decision making has become a major topic of debate for the economic community [9], this is the most used method to valuate environmental damages [10,11, among several others]. According to [10], contingent valuation is a survey approach designed to create the missing market for public goods by determining what people are willing to pay for specific damage or to accept for compensation for well-specific degradation. Thus, as well as for other valuation approaches, the contingent valuation considers the premise of economic rationality, i.e. it considers exclusively the consumer viewpoint and ignores the production side (e.g. the natural resources and its processes). Additionally, as emphasized by [12], the use of stated preference valuation methods is necessarily sensitive to individual emotional concerns, resulting in high heterogeneity among individual´s samples.

Alternatively to traditional economic approaches, the use of biophysical approaches to quantify environmental damages is increasing in scientific literature, in which eMergy accounting is receiving special emphasis. Emergy (spelled with an "m") is "the available energy of one kind previously used up directly and indirectly to make a service or product" [5; p.7]. In accordance to the second law of thermodynamics, each transformation process degrades the available energy, but the "quality" of the remaining energy is increased. This important concept is considered within the emergy accounting framework under a donor side approach – instead of receiver side used by the economic approaches. A full description of emergy methodology, meanings and rules is beyond the scope of this paper, but deeper information are available at several published scientific works including, among others, the classical book of H.T. Odum [5].

Emergy can be considered as a scientific measure of real wealth in terms of the energy previously required to make something. Due to its ability in showing the real value under a donor side perspective by considering biophysical units rather than economic and subjective ones, emergy is used in this work to estimate the environmental damages caused by the oil spill incidents of Petrobras S.A. Brazilian Oil Company in 2000 yr. For this, the previous emergy evaluation of Exxon Valdez oil spill in 1991 done by [6] is used as reference for the emergy of damage estimation caused Petrobras S.A.; from this work, we have estimated an average value of 8.15E22 seJ representing the impacts on natural biome caused by 258,000 oil barrels spilled in 1991 during Exxon Valdez incident. The emergy per money ratio of Brazil in 2000 yr of 7.80E12 seJ/USD [13] is used to convert the emergy of damage from solar emjoules (seJ) into emdolars (EmUSD) units, which can be later compared to the values of environmental liabilities quantified under economical approach as published by [3]. It is worth to say that USD and EmUSD units should be understand as similar, in which the prefix "Em" expresses that calculation was done under emergy approach.

3   Results and Discussion

3.1   Assessing Alternatives for Presenting the Environmental Liabilities into the Balance Sheet

Table 1 shows the balance sheet as divulgated by Petrobras S.A. related to its performance in 2000 yr. It can be noted the lack of detailed information regarding the economic investment on prevention of environmental incidents in the "assets" group, as well as the absence of a detailed description of economical obligations in the "liabilities" group related to the environmental damages caused. It is worth to say the existence of laws (no. 9,605/1998) regarding the inclusion of these items into the company's balance sheet (CBS) at that time, which foresaw criminal responsibility for environmental impacts. The lacunae in Table 1 represented by symbol "?" indicates items that were not foreseen by the accounting regulation existing in 2000 yr, thus they were not considered in the Baseline structure for the CBS evaluated. The existence of these lacunae highlights the inability of this CBS structure in showing clearly the company's liabilities – when considered! -, which disallow deeper evaluations about the company's economic performance by society and investors. For instance, the "total log-term obligation" item (which indicates the company's debts for long-time period) was 9,122,181 million USD, however no detailed information is provided regarding specificities of this amount, such as penalties, indemnities, funding, etc. The same comment can be done to "equity" of 13,802,668 million USD, in which no information is provided regarding the amount of "shareholder", "earning reserves", and "environmental result".

Table 1. Traditional (Baseline) annual balance sheet of Petrobras S.A. for 2000 yr (values in 1,000 USD)

Asset (A)		Liabilities (B)	
Total current assets	11,670,386	Total current liabilities	12,604,377
Total LG receivables	9,245,301	Total LG obligations	9,122,181
Permanent assets		?	?
Investments	5,300,076	?	?
Properties	9,020,700	?	?
?	?	Equity (C)	13,802,668
?	?	?	?
?	?	?	?
Deferred	292,762	?	?
Total (A)	35,529,227	Total (B) + (C)	35,529,227

LG = long-term

Table 2 shows the structure for CBS as suggested by [3]. This structure highlights several information regarding actions for environmental damages prevention, including investments of 300,546 million USD in environmental protection and damages prevention projects. It is also clear the amount of liabilities occurred by Petrobras S.A. due to the caused environmental damages, reaching a value of 1,602,681 million USD. The suggested CBS structure shows higher values for "total long-term obligations" than Table 1 (from 9,122,181 to 10,724,863 million USD), besides lower values for "equity" (from 13,802,668 to 12,199,987 million USD), which could lead to a negative image of company for investors, at least for short-time period. Under a general view, the suggested CBS structure by [3] as presented at Table 2 can be considered more objective and detailed than the Baseline CBS structure presented at Table 1, allowing better understanding by society and investors about where and how money is circulating within company's boundaries, mainly on the environmental-related aspects.

Table 2. Modified (Alternative #1) annual balance sheet of Petrobras S.A. for 2000 yr (values in 1,000 USD)

Asset (A)		Liabilities (B)	
Total current assets	11,670,386	Total current liabilities	12,604,377
Total LG receivables	9,245,301	Total LG obligations	10,724,863
Permanent assets		Environmental provision	1,602,681
Investments	5,300,076	*Penalties*	122,950
Properties	9,020,700	*Indemnities*	1,479,730
PEE	300,546	Equity (C)	12,199,987
EPP	?	?	?
?	?	?	?
Deferred	292,762	?	?
Total (A)	35,529,227	Total (B) + (C)	35,529,227

LG = long-term; PEE = Program for environmental excellence; EPP = Environmental performance projects

Table 3. Improved (Alternative #2) annual balance sheet of Petrobras SA for 2000 yr (values in 1,000 USD)

Asset (A)		Liabilities (B)	
Current assets	11,670,386	Current liabilities	12,604,377
Noncurrent assets	23,858,840	Noncurrent liabilities	10,724,863
LG receivable assets	9,245,301	Environmental provision	1,602,681
Investments	5,300,076	*Penalties*	122,950
Properties	9,020,700	*Indemnities*	1,479,730
PEE	300,546	Equity (C)	12,199,987
EPP	?	Shareholders	8,251,100
Intangibles	?	Earnings reserve	5,551,568
Deferred	292,762	Environmental result	-1,602,681
Total (A)	35,529,227	Total (B) + (C)	35,529,227

LG = long-term; PEE = Program for environmental excellence; EPP = Environmental performance projects

Table 3 shows the improved structure suggested for financial balance sheet, in which numbers are supplied according to modifications required by laws 11,638/2007 and 11,941/2009. This new structure for CBS includes all essential information for a deeper understand about company's economic performance. Besides highlighting the environmental liabilities as also suggested by Alternative #1 (Table 2), this new structure goes a step forward by detailing other items in the "equity" group to make available and transparent for investors the numbers regarding the reduction of company's goods and services – since this aspect is already regulated by law 11,638/2007. As a result, the item "environmental result" shows the value of - 1,602,681 million USD, which allows an easy-to-understand interpretation about the real impact resulted from the caused environmental liabilities. Moreover, the direct relation between the investments in environmental programs presented in "assets" group (e.g. program for environmental excellence and environmental projects) and the "environmental results" shows a ratio of 1:5, suggesting that low investments in programs for environmental damages reduction could result in higher liabilities.

By comparing Tables 1, 2, and 3, it can be noted that CBS's total numbers are constant (35,529,227 million USD) because this work focuses on the CBS structure presentation. Table 2 shows that "equity" (12,199,987 million USD), which represents the company's economic power, is not detailed in that kind of CBS structure. On the other hand, Table 3 shows the existence of three items for "equity" group: (i) "shareholders", which indicates all money invested by shareholders; (ii) "earnings reserve", indicating the company's activity results; (iii) "environmental result". This last presents clearly the amount of money lost by company due to environmental damages. Inserting the item "environmental result" into the CBS represents, in an easy-to-understand way, the company's expense with environmental damage issues and its commitment in making this information as clear as possible.

Although recognizing that suggested Alternative #2 for CBS could be considered as a better way to present the company's financial annual dynamics, there still are two lacunae containing the symbol "?": "EPP" and "intangibles". The first one was not considered because Petrobras S.A. had no investment value declared in 2000 yr. The second one ("intangibles") was not considered because this item was created by law no. 11,638 in 2007. "Intangibles" can be considered as a key aspect in this new structure for CBS, because it could provide higher capacity for company's indebtedness or even to overestimate its results according to market functioning. The company's indebtedness capacity can be increased as much as higher its "assets" value, thus the item "intangibles" plays important role because it is composed by the value of immaterial goods (i.e. the immaterial goods tends to be higher as much as higher the company's value in the market).

The CBS structure as suggested in this work by Table 3 aims to make available, in a clear way, all the information regarding the company's financial issues, as envisaged by the general principle of accounting. On the other hand, it must be highlighted that the effect of this kind of CBS structure on the investors' perception is not evaluated, for instance, the issues regarding the investor's confidence by investing in the company (low risk) and the consequent cash injection. However, the study of [4] has indicated a strong relation between a clear divulgation of company's liabilities and the investments reduction by shareholders. This is an important aspect because a clear communication about company's environmental liabilities could result, at a first moment, in a negative image of company by society and investors, but later it could push companies for higher investment in prevention programs of environmental damages. In short time periods, a negative image of companies and the increase of expenses with environmental programs could result in lower investments by shareholders and total earnings, but in long term, the consequent reduction of environmental damages allied to company's commitment in preventing them could result in a positive image and higher investments from shareholders. All these aspects are being considered more and more by [1] in the search for a more holistic company's financial report structure, in which using a systemic strategy could lead to the attraction of "faithful investors" for long time periods. In this scenario, the shares volatilization in the stock market would be strongly reduced as well as the risk in the investment.

3.2 Evaluating Alternatives to Quantify Environmental Damages in Economic Terms

Table 4 shows the in-dollar values of environmental liabilities estimated by economic and emergy perspectives for the oil spill incidents of Petrobras SA in 2000. The emergy-based values were estimated using the [6] numbers that have assessed the emergy related to the Exxon Valdez oil spill at Alaska in 1991. Two important aspects should be highlighted in this table: (i) the difference between the economic cost of 1,602 million USD (established by court and other national committees for the environment under a willing-to-pay and other subjective approaches) and emergy-based cost of 55 million EmUSD; (ii) the difference between the emergy-based cost associated exclusively to biota damage of 55 million EmUSD and its equivalent when accounting for all information associated after public pressure (3,170 million EmUSD).

Table 4. Estimative of economic and emergy costs related to oil spill incidents of Petrobras SA.

Description	Value	Unit
Exxon Valdez oil spill in 1991 (258,000 barrels)		
Natural resource loss [a]	8.15 E22	seJ
Petrobras S.A. oil spill in 2000 (78,740 barrels)		
Natural resource loss [b]	2.49 E22	seJ
Economic cost associated [c]	1,602,681,0 00	USD
Emergy cost associated to biota damage [d]	55,619,435	EmU SD
Emergy cost associated to biota after public pressure [e]	3,170,307,7 96	EmU SD

[a] from [6]; it include birds, marine mammals, intertidal producers and invertebrates, phytoplankton, and zooplankton; average value obtained from a Monte Carlo simulation considering a uniform probabilistic distribution function under 10,000 interactions.
[b] assumed as 3.28 times lesser than Exxon Valdez oil spill due to ratio of barrels spilled
[c] from [3]; values set out by court action several years after the Petrobras' oil spill incidents
[d] obtained by dividing the natural resource loss of 2.49E22 seJ by the Brazilian emergy per money ratio in 2000 year of 7.80E12 seJ/USD [13]
[e] according to [5; p.130], the information role related to oil spilled by Exxon Valdez incident resulted in an emergy amplification of 57-fold; this amplification ratio was assumed as the same for Petrobras S.A. case study for calculation purposes

The three different estimated values for the environmental damages caused by Petrobras S.A. in 2000 yr are important as a quantitative reference to be included in the CBS, within the item "environmental provision". Table 3 shows the Petrobras' balance sheet by including the liabilities as estimated under an economical view (1,602,681 million USD), resulting in a company's "equity" of 12,199,987 million USD. Now, considering the liabilities value as estimated under an emergy view (55,619,435 million USD), the "equity" is increased by 12.7% reaching 13,747,049 million USD, resulting in higher credibility of company by investors and economic development. On the other hand, by considering the liability as estimated under emergy perspective after public pressure (3,170,307,796 million USD), the "equity" is reduced by 12.8% reaching (10,632,360 million USD), resulting in disrepute of company by investors and low economic development. As noted, the different approaches used to estimate the environmental liabilities result in different values for "environmental provision" item and different interpretation from investors for CBS.

According to [5], since half of the world´s empower (emergy flow per unit time) comes from the renewable environment, the amplification value obtained for environmental liabilities after public pressure of 3,170,307,796 EmUSD might have been appropriated as a good opportunity to compensate the environmental damage, but mainly to educate companies avoiding future oil spill incidents. This goes in parallel with [11] statement in which, more than educational purposes, there is a need for complementary remediation to compensate for the loss of services during the restoration period. We recognize that there are still some conceptual barriers that must be overcome to reach consensus among the scientific community about the most suitable economic value that should be charged due to oil spill incidents (as well as for any other negative externality caused by different production systems), but emergy methodology suggest to be a powerful alternative which reflects the biophysical donor side perspective.

For those ones currently skeptics or not comfortable yet on using biophysical approaches to estimate monetary values, or even when dealing with practical difficulties regarding environmental liabilities valuation (for example the lack of primary data), [3] suggests that, at least, it must exist a detailed explicative footnote information in the CBS concerning the potential future charges of those liabilities.

4   Conclusions

(a) The suggested structure for company's financial balance sheet could be considered as more appropriated compared to other two assessed ones to show in detail the economical performance of companies, mainly regarding aspects related to environmental issues. Through this improved structure, society and investors can have better-based information about how company is operating or being managed and its concerns related to environmental damages. This structure brings more clarity about company's management and could result in a beneficial image to investors at long time periods.

(b) The quantification of environmental liabilities in economic terms claims for additional efforts among the scientific community. Defining the real objectives in estimating the economical compensation values should be the first criteria, i.e. establishing purposes for repairing the environmental damage or also including educational purposes. To exclusively repair the damage, the emergy-based approach could be applied, and for educational purposes, the amplified emergy values after public pressure seems to be a good alternative. We recognize that this issue still deserves a huge discussion, but we also recognize that using emergy accounting could be a better alternative compared to contingent valuation.

Acknowledgements. We are grateful to Dr. Carlos Alberto Di Agustini for his valuable comments. This work received financial support from the Vice-Reitoria de Pós-Graduação e Pesquisa of Universidade Paulista (UNIP).

References

1. International Integrated Reporting Council, Consultation draft of the international <IR> framework, Integrated Reporting (2013), http://www.theirirc.org/consultationdraft
2. Deegan, C.: The accounting will have a central role in saving the planet...really? A reflection on "green accounting and green eyeshades twenty years later". Critical Perspectives on Accounting 24, 448–458 (2013)
3. Bertoli, A.L.: Passivo ambiental: estudo de caso da Petróleo Brasileiro S.A. Petrobrás. A repercussão ambiental nas demonstrações contábeis em consequência dos acidentes ocorridos. Revista de Administração Contemporânea 10, 117–136 (2006) (in Portuguese)
4. Cormier, D., Magnan, M.: Investors' assessment of implicit environmental liabilities: An empirical investigation. Journal of Accouting and Public Policy 16, 215–241 (1997)
5. Odum, H.T.: Environmental accounting – emergy and environmental decision making. John Wiley & Sons, Inc. (1996)
6. Whoite, R.D.: Emergy analysis of the T/V Exxon Valdez oil spill and alternatives for oil spill prevention. M.Sc. dissertation, University of Florida, USA (1992)
7. Ortega, E., Sarcinelli, O., Souza, P.B.M.: Combining bookkeeping techniques and emergy analysis. In: Brown, et al. (eds.) Proceedings of 3rd Biennial Emergy Research Conference, University of Florida, Gainesville, USA (2005)
8. Campbell, D.E.: Financial accounting methods to further develop and communicate environmental accounting using emergy. In: Brown, et al. (eds.) roceedings of 3rd Biennial Emergy Research Conference, University of Florida, Gainesville, USA (2005)
9. Carson, R.T., Flores, N.E., Meadle, N.F.: Contingent valuation: controversies and evidences. Environmental and Resource Economics 19, 173–210 (2001)
10. Carson, R.T., Mitchell, R.C., Hanemann, M., Kopp, R.J., Presser, S., Ruud, P.A.: Contingent valuation and lost passive use: damages from the Exxon Valdez oil spill. Environmental and Resource Economics 25, 257–286 (2003)
11. Martin-Ortega, J., Brouwer, R., Aiking, H.: Application of a value-based equivalency method to assess environmental damage compensation under the European Environmental Liability Directive. Journal of Environmental Management 92, 1461–1470 (2011)
12. León, C.J., Araña, J.E., Hanemann, W.M., Riera, P.: Heterogeneity and emotions in the valuation of non-use damages caused by oil spills. Ecological Economics 97, 129–139 (2014)
13. Sweeney, S., Cohen, M., King, D.M., Brown, M.T.: Creation of a global emergy database for standardize national emergy synthesis. In: Brown, et al. (eds.) Proceedings of 4th Biennial Emergy Research Conference, University of Florida, Gainesville, USA (2007)

Economic and Environmental Advantage Evaluation of the Reverse Logistic Implementation in the Supermarket Retail

Geraldo Cardoso de Oliveira Neto and Washington Carvalho de Sousa

Nine of July University-UNINOVE, Graduate Program in Production Engineering,
Francisco Matarazzo Avenue, 612, São Paulo, Brazil
{Geraldo Cardoso de Oliveira Neto,geraldo.prod}@ig.com.br

Abstract. In this article it is presented a market study case that allowed a recycling specialized organization with physical space to implement the reverse logistic of the following packing residues: cardboard, Styrofoam, plastic and aluminum into correct residue destination. This study's objective consists in developing a methodology to evaluate economic and environmental advantage of the reverse logistic implementation in the supermarket. The utilized method consists in observing and semi-structure interviewing, allowing it to develop a case study. To analyze the environmental improvement, the Mass Intensity Total was measured, to determine the environmental impact reduction. The research results indicate economic and environmental advantage very representative, which may improve the decision making and access to the reverse logistic, favoring the sustainability in the supermarket retail.

Keywords: Reverse Logistic, Supermarket Retail, Economic and Environmental Advantage.

1 Introduction

The Solid Residue National Plan of Brazil is driving many segments to implement the reverse logistic, to promote the solid residue management by developing procedures to improve the gathering and restitution of solid residues to their producers, so that they are treated and repurposed in new products, by input means, in its cycle or in other productive cycles, seeking the non-producing of tailings [1].

With that, the reverse logistic can reduce costs related to the raw material, storage, finished products and information from the selling point to the origin point with the objective of adding value or the correct use of resources [2] to give the correct direction to material goods [3], ensuring the environmental and economic advantage in the operation by recuperating, reusing and remanufacturing of goods [4].

The reverse logistic use is extending to the retail sector, including supermarkets [3]. The supermarket retail is characterized by the auto-service system with a variety of products, being the edible and non-edible products with, a minimum of, 2 *check-outs* and valid selling space between 300m^2 and 5000m^2 and, still, offers the consumer, shopping carts and baskets to be used while shopping, without a selling-man presence [5].

B. Grabot et al. (Eds.): APMS 2014, Part II, IFIP AICT 439, pp. 197–204, 2014.

Supermarkets could implement the reverse logistic because the commercialized products are the main producers of solid residues of packing, considering edible products and appliances [6, 7].

The reverse logistic implementation could be a differentiation strategy [8], which promotes sustainable marketing [9], as by an example, in the Wal-Mart, that demands the feeders, devolution of damaged products and packing [7], utilizing the same truck that delivers the order to take the residue from the clients, cutting costs with transport [10], generating financial gain [11].

Other researches support the development of a return plan in the solid residue supermarkets and product devolution guaranteed. Especially Wal-Mart, that implemented the reverse logistic to repairing, replacing parts and consumer return, inspection and reuse [12, 13], resulting in a cost reduction and improvement of product recuperation [14, 15], and in Spanish Carrefour that has a specialized recycling infrastructure to manage solid residues [16, 17].

It was noted the need to improve the governmental support to implement the reverse logistic. In Brazil, it is still considered embryonic, due to lack of governmental support, actions by the producing organizations, lack of gathering spaces and environmental conscience from the society [18]. In China, the situation is not different, despite establishing legislation, which pressures the producers [19]. This discovery drives the supermarkets and the recycling organization in the propagation of gathering points and motivating their clients [16], mainly because the majority of the clients don't deposit their solid residues, due to lack of economic support [6].

In the existing researches analysis about the reverse logistic implementation in the supermarket sector it was noted that despite some articles mention in a positive way about the economic and environmental gain they did not evaluate theses gains. With that, the article's objective consists in developing a methodology to evaluate if it has occurred economic and environmental advantage from the reverse logistic implementation in the supermarkets.

2   Methodology

In the research's first phase, it was realized a bibliometric analysis to quantify and select the scientific production [20].

The Databases Proquest, Ebsco, Science Direct, Emerald, Capes and academic Google by using the following keywords: (i) "reverse logistics" AND "supermarket"; (ii) "reverse logistics" AND "grocery"; (iii) "reverse logistics" AND "retail" AND "market"; (iv) "reverse logistics" AND "retail"; (v) "reverse logistics" AND "retailing" (vi) "reverse logistics" AND "retailing" AND "market" in summaries, keywords and scientific publication titles with the objective of analyzing the existence of researches that helps understanding the environmental and/or economic results in reverse logistic implementation process in the supermarkets retail.

In the analysis it was noted 15 articles about the reverse logistic in the supermarket retail, allowing the categorizing of research results about environmental and economic gain [21]. In the analysis it was identified a lack of researches that produced quantity evaluations in economic and environmental terms.

To attend this lack of research, it was realized an exploratory research of qualitative and quantitative nature through the unique-case method, which allowed developing a methodology to evaluate if it has occurred economic and environmental advantage from the reverse logistic implementation in the supermarket.

The case study is a research strategy focused in comprehending the researched scene dynamic, which combine data gathering methods, as data, interviews, questionnaires and observations, resulting in qualitative and/or quantitative evidence [22]. With that, it is possible to create the adequate conditions to comprehend the researched study object [23].

In the case study, it was adopted the observation and interviews as the logistic base, which allowed to gather quantitative data about the recycled goods and the economic results of implementing the reverse logistic. The observation was realized in files and efficiency indicators with recycling data provided by the supermarket, being an adequate technique for case study [24, 25], with support of the semi-structured interview to ask questions and align the comprehension of the observation [26].

With the environmental and economic results obtained it was developed a methodology to evaluate if it has occurred environmental and economic advantage from the reverse logistic implementation in the supermarket.

With the economic results obtained, it was possible to evaluate the economic advantage of reverse logistic implementation by calculating the return of investment (ROI) based on equations 1 and 2 presented [27]:

%ROI = semiannual liquid profit/ reverse logistic investment   Eq. 1
ROI Period= reverse logistic investment / semiannual liquid profit   Eq. 2

After that, with the recycled goods results it was possible to evaluate the environmental gain through the Mass Intensity Factors method (MIF) identified in the file provided by the Wuppertal Institute supported on the abiotic, biotic, water and air compartments.

The ecosystem is composed of biotic and abiotic compartments with interaction between them, the biotic compartment consists of the set of all live organisms as plants and decomposers, while the abiotic compartment is the set of all non-alive factors of an ecosystem, but influences the biotic compartment, consists of temperature, pressure, rain falling in the landscape, among others [28].

With that, the total goods quantity of each compartment that was processed to supply a material data is called Mass Intensity. To determine the Mass Intensity Factors (MIF) in equation 3, the Mass entry flux (M) - express in the corresponding units is multiplied by the Intensity Factors (IF), that corresponds to the quantity of necessary goods to produce an entry flux unity [29]. The IF values used in this research are presented on Table 1.

$$MIF = (M \times IF) \tag{3}$$

Table 1. Goods Intensity Factors used in the Research

	Mass Intensity Factor			
	Abiotic Goods	Biotic Goods	Water	Air
Plastic (g/g)[a]	6.45		294.2	3.723
Cardboard (g/g)[b]	1.86	0.75	93.6	0.325
Styrofoam (g/g)[c]	5.70		146	1650
Aluminum (g/g)[d]	37		1047.7	108.870

Source [a e c] Germany Data
　　　　[b e d] Europe Data

After calculating the IF by recycled residue in relation to compartments, it becomes possible to calculate the Mass Intensity per Compartment (MIC), that measures the environmental impact reduction by abiotic compartment (w), biotic (x), water (y), and air (z), following the Equation 4. And at last, it is realized the calculation of the Mass Intensity Total (MIT) summarizing the total environmental reduction, when applied to MIC's, following the Equation 5.

*MIC = (IF residue A of compartment w + IF residue B of compartment w + IF residue C of compartment w + IF residue n of compartment w)　　　(4)
*MIC example to the w compartment, equal to the others.

MIT = (MICw + MICx + MICy + MICz)　　　(5)

To finish it is compared the economic gain with the environmental gain and vice versa to verify the economic gain index (IGE) and environmental gain index (IGA). To evaluate the IGE, it is considered the Total Saved Goods (MTE) in relation to the GE and to calculate the IGA, is it divided the Mass Intensity Total (MIT) by the GE. The equations are presented:

IGE = (MTE/GE)　　　(6)
IGA = (MIT/GE)　　　(7)

3　Results and Discussion

Economic Advantage
The economic advantage results of the Reverse Logistic implementation were summarized in Table 3. The gathered residues resulted in a semiannual gain of $9.236.77.

In the main project the initial investment was of $20.000.00 for employees training about solid residue management and implementing residue gatherers in the supermarkets so that the clients could deposit its residues and, implemented in the receiving sector the solid residue retention resulting of the delivery process and store assortment. This result shows an practical example of the reverse logistic implementation in the supermarket retail [30], in relation to the adequate destination of the residue to reuse and remanufacture [6, 13, 1] by an specialized organization [16, 17].

To the recycling operation implementation the organization decided outsourcing to a specialized organization. With that, the recycling organization provided infra-structure, as which: press, involved people, load accommodation and transport to the residues destination in a correct way and began to pay the supermarket by Kg of collected residue (Cardboard - $0.17; Plastic - $0.37; Styrofoam - $0.10; Aluminum - $2.30).

Table 2. Economic Gain with the Reverse Logistic Implementation

Period	Cardboard	Plastic	Styrofoam	Aluminum
June	$1.509.00	$552.30	$4.30	$18.98
July	$590.00	$221.00	$4.00	$14.49
August	$1.297.00	$410.40	$0.00	$24.15
September	$1.698.00	$228.40	$1.50	$34.50
October	$598.40	$202.30	$5.00	$26.45
November	$1.068.00	$696.00	$5.00	$27.60
Total	$6.760.40	$2.310.40	$19.80	$146.17

Applying equations 1 and 2 proposed [27], summarized:

%ROI = $9.236.77/ $20.000.00 = 46.18% per semester.
Period ROI = $20.000.00 / $9.236.77 = 1 year and 2 months.

The financial return invested in reverse logistic was of 46, 18% per semester in one year and two months, since this period the monthly liquid gain, considering the reverse logistic increased to $9.236.77, resulting in economic advantage to the market. This result exemplifies the proposition about the possibility of obtaining financial resources with reverse logistic [8].

Environmental Advantage
In the total sum of goods, it is considered all the products that were not disposed in the environment. The organization provided the Mass in goods (M) by Kg of residue that were submitted to the recycling process in the semester, which are: 40.196 kg of Cardboard, 6.327 kg of Plastic, 198 kg of Styrofoam e 63.55 kg of aluminum, con-substantiating 46785 Kg of Total Saved Mass (MTE).

Applying equation 3 it is determined the Mass Intensity Total (MIT) to evaluate the environmental gain, as for an example, 6,327 x 6.45 – abiotic goods, represents MIT of 40.809.15, as it is presented on table 3.

Table 3. Environmental gain with the reverse logistic implementation

	Abiotic Goods	Biotic Goods	Water	Air
Plastic (g/g) [a]	40809.15		1861403.4	23.555
Cardboard (g/g)[b]	74764.56	30147	3762345.6	13063.7
Styrofoam (g/g)[c]	1128.6		28908	326700
Aluminum (g/g)[d]	2351.35		66.581.335	691
Mass Intensity per Compartment (MIC)	119053.7	30147	5719238,3	350946
Mass Intensity Total (MIT)				6100331.5

The recycling total in mass was of 46785 Kg of residue per semester with Mass Intensity Total (MIT) of 6100331.5, representing the environmental impact reduction in compartment (w) abiotic of 119053.5 Kg, contributing with sustainability in global warming matters, the ozone layer waste, the atmospheric pressure, among others; (x) biotic – 30147 Kg, which reduced the vegetation pollution, the soil and the decomposers, (y) water – 5719238.3 Kg and the (z) air with 350946 Kg. The results show that it is possible to measure the environmental gain with the reverse logistic implementation, subject still considered incipient in literature.

Comparison between Economic and Environmental Advantage
To finish it is compared the economic with the environmental gain and vice versa to verify the representation in percentage of the economic gain (GE) and environmental gain (GA).

$$GE = (46785 \text{ Kg of Residue}/\$9236.77) = 5.07 \tag{6}$$
$$GA = (6100331.5//\$9236.77) = 660.44 \tag{7}$$

The results show that in relation to the IGE, that each Brazilian Real saved corresponds to 5.0 Kg of goods. When it is considered the Mass Intensity Total (MIT), by each Brazilian Real, there is a benefit of IGA – 675.42 Kg of goods that are not modified nor taken from the ecosystems. This discovery contributes with the possibility of conquering economic and environmental gain through reverse logistic actions [30, 2], subject that was not explored in quantitative methodology terms to analyze, mainly because it presents just qualitative results.

4   Conclusions

The present research shows that the reverse logistic implementation in the supermarket retail resulted in an economic and environmental gain, which was the research's objective. The action taken to achieve the result was of implementing residue gatherers in the supermarket so that clients could deposit their residues. Also, implemented in the receiving sector the retention of solid residues resulted from the deliver process and the store assortment.

The result in the semester showed the retention and correct destination of 46785Kg, considering just the gathered and weighted residue resulting in an economic gain of \$9.236.77 each semester. When the Mass Intensity Factor was calculated, it was noted that it avoided the pollution of: (i) 119053.7 Kg in the abiotic level, considering as indispensable factors to survival, as temperature, pressure, rain falling in the landscape, among others; (ii) 30147 Kg in the biotic level, represented by the set of all live organisms such as plants and decomposers and (iii) 5719238.3 Kg in the water and 350946 Kg in the air. The results show that despite occurring economic advantage \$9.236.77 to the businessmen the environmental advantage was the most representative when considered the Mass Intensity Total (6100331.5 Kg).

It is important to highlight that the presented and tested methodology may be used in cleaner production processes, environmental projects (DfE), among others. A limitation of the case study consists in the impossibility of generalizing the results, suggesting the realization of new researches to generate comparisons.

References

1. BRASIL. PNRS – Política Nacional de Resíduos Sólidos. Subemenda Substitutiva Global de Plenário ao Projeto de Lei n° 203, de 1991, e seus apensos,
   http://www.revistasustentabilidade.com.br/reciclagem/
   reciclagem/documentosinteressante/
   relatorio-final-da-politica-de-residuos (accessed in: October 09, 2010)
2. Rogers, D.S., Tibben Lembke, R.S.: Going backwards: reverse logistics trends and practices. University of Nevada, Reno (1989)
3. RLEC – Reverse Logistics Executive Council,
   http://www.rlec.org/glossary.html (accessed in: March 2013)
4. Sheriff, K., Gunasekaran, A., Nachiappna, S.: Logistics network design: a review on strategic perspective. International Journal of Logistics Systems and Management 12, 171–194 (2012)
5. Alexander, N., Silva, M.L.: Emerging markets and the internationalization of retailing: the Brazilian experience. International Journal of Retail & Distribution Management 30, 127–141 (2002)
6. Breen, L.: Give me back my empties or else! A preliminary analysis of customer compliance in reverse logistics practices (UK). Management Research News 29, 532–551 (2006)
7. Kumar, S.: A Study of the supermarket industry and its growing logistics capabilities. International Journal of Retail & Distribution Management 36, 192–211 (2008)
8. Fernie, J., Sparks, L., Mckinnon, A.C.: Retail Logistics in the UK: Past, present and future. International Journal of Retail & Distribution Management 38, 894–914 (2010)
9. Sharma, A., Iyer, G.R., Mehrotra, A., Krishnan, R.: Sustainability and Business-to-business: A framework and implications. Industrial Marketing Management 39, 330–341 (2010)
10. Mckinnon, A.C., Ge, Y.: The potential for reducing empty running by trucks: a retrospective analysis. International Journal of Physical Distribution & Logistics Management 36, 395–410 (2006)
11. Junior, S.S.B., Merlo, E.M., Nagan, M.S.: Um estudo comparativo das práticas de logística reversa no varejo de médio porte. Revista da Micro e Pequena Empresa 3, 64–81 (2009)

204   G.C. de Oliveira Neto and W.C. de Sousa

12. Krumwiede, D.W., Sheu, C.: A model for reverse logistics entry by third-party providers. The international Journal of Management Science 30, 325–333 (2002)
13. Reinartz, W., Dellaert, B., Krafft, M., Kumar, V., Varadarajan, R.: Retailing Innovations in a Globalizing Retail Market Environment. Journal of Retailing 87, 53–66 (2011)
14. Jack, E.P., Powers, T.L., Skinner, L.: Reverse Logistics capabilities: antecedents and cost savings. International Journal of Physical Distribution & Logistics Management 40, 228–246 (2010)
15. Stock, J.R., Mulki, J.P.: Product Returns Processing: An examination of practices of manufacturers, wholesalers/distributors, and retailers. Journal of Business Logistics 30, 33–62 (2009)
16. Chaves, A.R.: Estudo das variáveis utilizadas na decisão de compras no comércio varejista de alimentos de autosserviço – Supermercados. Dissertação de Mestrado da Faculdade de Economia, Administração e Contabilidade da Universidade de São Paulo. São Paulo (2002)
17. Combra-Fierro, J., Ruiz-Benítez, R.: Notions for the successful management of the supply chain: Learning with Carrefour in Spain and Carrefour in China. Supply Chain Management: A international Journal 16, 148–154 (2011)
18. Oliveira, C.R., Bernardes, A.M., Gerbase, A.E.: Collection and recycling of electronic scrap: A worldwide overview and comparison with the Brazilian situation 32, 1592-1610 (2012)
19. Ye, F., Zhao, X., Prahinski, C., Li, Y.: The impact of institutional pressures, top manager's posture and reverse logistics on performance – Evidence in China. International Journal of Production Economics 143, 132–143 (2013)
20. Cooper, H.M., Lindsay, J.L.L.: Research synthesis and meta-analysis. Sage Publications (1998)
21. Bardin, L.: El análisis de contenido. Ediciones akal. Madrid (1986)
22. Eisenhardt, K.M.: Building Theories from Case Study Research. Academy of Management Review 14, 522–550 (1989)
23. Yin, R.: Case Study Research. Design and Methods, 4th edn. Sage Publications (2009)
24. Bogdan, R., Biklen, S.: Qualitative Research for education: an introduction to Theory and Methods. 2nd edn. Allyn and Bacon, Boston (1992)
25. Westbrook, R.: Action Research: a new paradigm for research in production and operations management. International Journal of Operations and Production Management 15, 6–20 (1995)
26. Seidman, I.E.: Interviewing as qualitative research. A guide for researchers in Education and the Social Sciences. Teachers College/Columbia University Press. New York (1991)
27. Gitmann, L.J.: Principio de Administração Financeira.7º ed. Harbra, São Paulo (1997)
28. Odum, E.P.: Ecologia. Rio de Janeiro: Guanabara (1998)
29. Wuppertal, Institute, Calculating MIPs, resources productivity of products and services (2008), http://www.wupperinst.org/uploads/tx_wiberitrag/MIT_v2.pdf (accessed in: April 8)
30. Bernoon, M., Rossi, S.: Retail Reverse Logistics: a call and grounding framework for research. International Journal of Physical Distribution & Logistics Management 41, 484–510 (2011)

An Approach to Increase Energy Efficiency Using Shutdown and Standby Machine Modes

Apostolos Fysikopoulos, Georgios Pastras,
Aikaterini Vlachou, and George Chryssolouris[*]

Laboratory for Manufacturing Systems and Automation,
Department of Mechanical Engineering and Aeronautics,
University of Patras, Patras 26500, Greece
xrisol@lms.mech.upatras.gr.

Abstract. Energy efficiency constitutes a very significant factor that requires its inclusion in the manufacturing decision making attributes developing a strategy to produce more with less. The idle state of a machine tool is an inefficient phase. A strategy to increase the energy efficiency of an already balanced production line, using machine tool stand-by or shut-down modes, during the idle phase, is being introduced. This strategy identifies when the application of such modes is gainful from an energy efficiency point of view, based on the available idle time and the consumption of the machine at these modes.

Keywords: Energy Efficiency, Sustainable Manufacturing, Machine Tools, Production Planning, Scheduling.

1 Introduction

The manufacturing industry is one of the greatest energy consumers and carbon emitters in the world [1]. The manufacturing sector is responsible for about 28% of the primary energy use [3] and for 38% of the CO_2 emissions globally [2]. Thus, energy and eco-efficiency has emerged as one of the most significant manufacturing decision attributes [4], especially in countries that are not energy independent [5]. Additionally, energy is an increasingly important cost factor due to its increasing price [6]. Manufacturing enterprises have to reduce energy consumption for both cost saving and environmental friendliness, trying to find new ways to produce "more with less" [7] and furthermore, evolve from the strategy "maximum gain from minimum capital" to "maximum gain from minimum resources" [8].

Several initiatives on energy efficiency are on-going [9-11]. Energy saving management, technologies and policies/regulations [12] are used to deal with the energy efficiency issues [13].

The study of energy efficiency in manufacturing systems can be divided into four main levels (Fig. 1) [4]. The study of each level and their inter-level interactions are important steps towards the effective study of energy and eco-efficiency hence, the need for a holistic approach is necessary [4, 14].

---

[*] Corresponding author.

B. Grabot et al. (Eds.): APMS 2014, Part II, IFIP AICT 439, pp. 205–212, 2014.

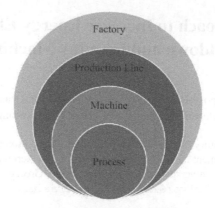

Fig. 1. Energy efficiency analysis division [4]

2   Energy Efficiency at Production Line Level

Decisions on planning and operating production systems are mainly based on traditional metrics such as time, cost, quality and flexibility [15]. In terms of energy cost, a limited number of studies regarding time-dependent industrial planning, under the point of view of electricity cost, have been reported [17-19].

Several reviews on commercially available manufacturing simulation tools reveal that they do not support energy and eco-efficiency indicators yet [20-22]. Fysikopoulos et al. [16] have incorporated simple energy formulas into a "real life" automotive assembly line, with the use of discrete event simulation (DES). DES in combination with the life cycle assessment (LCA) method was presented by Johanson et al. [23]. With the help of this model, the energy aspects of the line along with other performance measures, have been investigated. Wohlgemuth et al. [22] suggested an approach for the integration of DES and the material flow analysis into a component-based framework, based on a single model towards a customized Environmental Management Information System (EMIS). In this framework, production processes and all kinds of energy and material flows can be analysed in terms of both economic measures and their environmental impacts. Herrmann et al. [20] presented an energy oriented simulation model for the planning of manufacturing systems. They reported up to 30% improvement in energy efficiency through simulation-assisted process planning.

Mouzon et al. [24] developed mathematical multi-objective models to investigate the problem of scheduling jobs, on a single CNC machine, towards the reduction of time and energy consumption. An impressive outcome is the finding that when a non-bottlenecked machine is turned-off, the energy consumption savings may reach even 80%. Additionally, by forecasting the inter-arrival time of the orders, significant savings can be achieved with the use of proper dispatching rules. Other studies focus on social and environmental issues and not just on energy consumption [25-28].

It is evident [4, 16, 29, 30, 31] that the reduction of the idle time can significantly assist towards energy and eco-efficiency. Drake et al. [32] have reported significant energy consumption during machine idle time. As presented in [30, 33], in a production machine tool and generally in a mass production environment, the percentage of energy used for functions that are not directly related to the actual production of parts, may be as high as 85% or even more. However, "correct" order distribution (better batch and orders organization) combined with early or periodical "machine shut down" can considerably reduce the idle time, which is the most inefficient state of a system [4]. Additionally, the incorporation of energy consumption measuring, peak power management, monitoring, controlling and scheduling may lead to better prediction of the workflow and thus, to improved energy savings [4, 34, 35]. Thanks to the Information and Communication Technologies (ICT), innovative production management systems can be built to support energy efficient manufacturing [36].

3 Machine Tools and Energy Efficiency

The demand for greener machine tools creates new challenges for the machine tool builders. The state of the art in machine tools is the use of energy-efficient components that can reduce energy consumption during idle times up to 65% [29]. Several studies on the energy efficiency of machine tools exist, regarding both conventional and non-conventional processes [30, 37, 38]. Besides the process variables optimisation, the development of energy and eco-efficient components is a basic task for machine tool builders [34].

The first step towards improving the energy efficiency of machine tools is the identification of the power requirements for different machine tool activities and the categorization of the peripheral devices. Fysikopoulos et al. [4] indicated that the actual consumed energy required for processing is exceeded to a great extent by the energy demand of the related peripheral equipment, especially for the laser based processes. The analysis can become complex, since several peripherals may be shared among different machines in the factory. Furthermore, they concluded that the consumption of machine peripherals per manufactured part depends on process variables through factors such as process time. Moreover, the overall energy consumption can be significantly reduced, if during idle times, the peripherals go to a complete off or stand-by phase (energy-saving mode) by integrating simple technological features. Nowadays, machine tool controls are equipped with the possibilities of switching the machine into energy-saving modes or even to shutting it down completely [39-41]. These new machine tool capabilities can be used for the significant reduction of a production line's energy consumption.

4 A Strategy to Gain Energy Using Shut-down and Stand-by (energy-saving) Modes

In practice, it is not possible to perfectly match the output rates of all the resources in a flow line thus, at least some resources remain idle for some time. The issue is to implement shut-down and stand-by modes in a production line which has already being optimised in terms of idle time. It has to be noted that the incorporation of such modes is not always gainful and actually, it may not even be possible, depending on the idle time available. While a machine is in idle mode, it usually consumes a constant power (P_{idle}). Thus, the energy wasted in the idle mode is equal to $E_{idle}=P_{idle}t$, where t is the idle time available.

Provided that the machine was switched-off, this constant consumption would have been avoided; however, there would be a period of maximum power consumption, necessary to start up the machine for its next task. It is assumed that the duration of the shut-down and start-up procedures is equal to $t_{startup}$ and that the corresponding energy consumption is equal to $E_{startup}$. Then, the energy consumed if the shut-down mode is used equals $E_{shutdown}=E_{startup}$ and it is possible only if the time available is larger than $t_{startup}$. From the above arguments, it is evident that the incorporation of the shut-down mode is profitable only when $E_{shutdown}<E_{idle}$, which is equivalent to the available time being larger than a critical value equal to

$$t_{cr} = \frac{E_{startup}}{P_{idle}}.$$ (1)

Similarly, an intermediate stand-by (energy-saving) mode can be incorporated. In such a mode, some of the machine's peripheral systems are turned off, while the more critical ones remain operative. Such a mode is characterized by some constant power consumption $P_{standby}$, smaller than P_{idle}, while the machine remains in stand-by mode. However, some time and energy is also required in order for the machine to "sleep" and then become operative again, namely t_{wake} and E_{wake}. If both stand-by and shut-down modes are available, it is typically true that $E_{wake}<E_{startup}$ and $t_{wake}<t_{startup}$. The energy consumed if the standby mode is used equals $E_{standby}=E_{wake}+P_{standby}(t-t_{wake})$. The stand-by mode can be used only if the available time is larger than t_{wake}. Similarly to what is stated above for the shut-down mode, the stand-by mode is preferable to the idle mode provided that the available time is larger than

$$t_{cr1} = \frac{E_{wake} - P_{standby}t_{wake}}{P_{idle} - P_{standby}}$$ (2)

and preferable to the shut-down mode if the available time is smaller than

$$t_{cr2} = \frac{E_{startup} - E_{wake}}{P_{standby}} + t_{wake}.$$ (3)

It has to be noted that a standby mode is never profitable if $t_{cr1}>t_{cr2}$.

All the above arguments are summarized in Fig. 2.

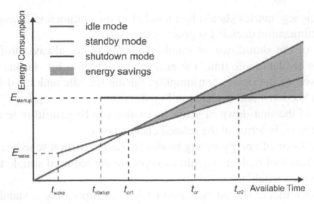

Fig. 2. An indicative diagram for the energy consumption of a machine during non-working time periods under different available modes

According to what was analysed above, a strategy to gain energy using the shutdown and stand-by modes can be specified. For every machine, the idle time durations predicted by suitable simulation method have to be compared with the critical times t_{cr1} and t_{cr2} and then the resource has to:

1. be shut-down, if the idle time is larger than t_{cr2}
2. be switched to stand-by mode, if the idle time lies between t_{cr1} and t_{cr2}
3. remain idle, if the idle time is smaller than t_{cr1}

The procedure has to be repeated for every resource. A logical diagram showing the above for a system consisting of N resources is depicted in Fig. 3. It has to be noted that in the proposed method, the shutting-down or switching to a stand-by mode is not performed manually, but on the contrary, these actions are scheduled during the production planning stage.

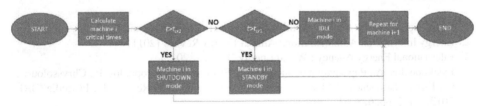

Fig. 3. A basic logic diagram describing the decision process for incorporation of shut-down and stand-by modes

5   Conclusions

In this study, a strategy to increase the energy efficiency of an already balanced production line, using the machine's tool stand-by (energy saving) or shut-down (completely turned-off) modes, during idle time, was introduced. The main outcomes can be summarised as following:

- Energy efficiency metrics should be included in the commercially available multi-objective optimization decision support systems.
- Application of the shut-down or stand-by modes is not always profitable. It depends on the available idle time, the energy consumption for starting up and waking up, as well as the power consumption during the idle and stand-by modes, as described in Section 4 and depicted in Fig. 2.
- Application of the shut-down or stand-by modes can be gainful in terms of energy and consequently, in terms of the related energy costs.
- Since the inclusion of energy saving modes in the production schedule can be gainful, the machine tool builders should incorporate the required simple technological features into their machines.
- Machine tool builders should be careful when incorporating a stand-by function into their machines. Depending on the stand-by power consumption and the necessary wake-up energy, the use of this mode may never be preferable over the idle or shut-down mode (when $t_{cr1} > t_{cr2}$).

Future work will focus on methods to arrange the schedule of a production line so that the duration of the idle states is allowing the use of energy saving modes. Such methods will lead to maximum utilisation of these modes and thus, of the related energy and energy cost gains. Moreover, the method is going to be validated in a real industrial case study.

Acknowledgements. The work reported in this paper was supported by the collaborative program entitled "Energy Efficient Process planning System – ENEPLAN", which is under the seventh framework program - FoF.NMP.2011-1: The Eco-Factory: cleaner and more resource-efficient production in manufacturing Program.

References

1. International Energy Agency.: Worldwide Trends in Energy Use and Efficiency (2008)
2. Energy Information Administration.: Annual Energy Review (2011)
3. International Energy Agency.: World Energy Outlook (2012)
4. Fysikopoulos, A., Papacharalampopoulos, A., Pastras, G., Stavropoulos, P., Chryssolouris, G.: Energy Efficiency of Manufacturing Processes: A Critical Review. In: Procedia CIRP 2013, vol. 7, pp. 628–633 (2013)
5. Seow, Y., Rahimifard, S.: A framework for modelling energy consumption within manufacturing systems. CIRP J. Manuf. Sci. Technol. 4(3), 258–264 (2011)
6. Moreno, B., López, A.J., García-Álvarez, M.T.: The electricity prices in the European Union. The Role of Renewable Energies and Regulatory Electric Market Reforms 48(1), 307–313 (2012)
7. Chryssolouris, G., Papakostas, N., Mavrikios, D.: A perspective on manufacturing strategy: Produce more with less. CIRP J. Manuf. Sci. Tech. 1(1), 45–52 (2008)
8. International Energy Agency, Tracking Industrial Energy Efficiency and CO2 Emissions (2007)

9. Directive 2009/125/EC of the European Parliament and of the Council of 21, establishing a framework for the setting of ecodesign requirements for energy-related products. Off. J. Eur. Union, 10–35((October 2009)
10. Cooperative Effort on Process Emissions in Manufacturing CO2PE!, http://www.mech.kuleuven.be/co2pe/index.php (accessed: April 23, 2014)
11. CIRP Collaborative Working Group.: Energy and Resource Efficiency & Effectiveness, http://www.cirp-eree.iwf.tu-bs.de (accessed: April 23, 2014)
12. Bruzzone, A.A.G., Anghinolfi, D., Paolucci, M., Tonelli, F.: Energy-aware scheduling for improving manufacturing process sustainability: A mathematical model for flexible flow shops. CIRP Ann. - Manuf. Technol. 61(1), 459–462 (2012)
13. Schlosser, R., Klocke, F., Lung, D.: Sustainabilty in Manufacturing: Energy Consumption of Cutting Processes. In: Advances in Sustainable Manufacturing, pp. 85–89 (2001)
14. Herrmann, C., Kara, S., Thiede, S., Luger, T.: Energy Efficiency in Manufacturing: Perspectives from Australia and Europe
15. Chryssolouris, G.: Manufacturing systems: theory and practice, 2nd edn. Springer (2006)
16. Fysikopoulos, A., Anagnostakis, D., Salonitis, D., Chryssolouris, G.: An Empirical Study of the Energy Consumption in Automotive Assembly. In: Procedia CIRP, vol. 3, pp. 477–482 (2012)
17. Nilsson, K., Soderstrom, N.: Industrial Applications of Production Planning with Optimal Electricity Demand. Appl. Energy 46(2), 181–192 (1993)
18. Yusta, J.M., Torres, F., Khodr, H.M.: Optimal methodology for a machining process scheduling in spot electricity markets. Energy Convers. Manag. 51(12), 2647–2654 (2010)
19. Moon, J.Y., Shin, K., Jinwoo, P.: Optimization of production scheduling with time-dependent and machine-dependent electricity cost for industrial energy efficiency. Int. Adv. Manuf. Technol. 68, 523–535 (2013)
20. Herrmann, C., Thiede, S., Kara, S., Hesselbach, J.: Energy oriented simulation of manufacturing systems – Concept and application. In: CIRP Ann. - Manuf. Technol., vol. 60(1), pp. 45–48 (2011)
21. Thiede, S., Seow, Y., Andersson, J., Johansson, B.: Environmental aspects in manufacturing system modelling and simulation: State of the art and research perspectives. In: CIRP J. Manuf. Sci. Technol., vol. 6(1), pp. 78–87 (2013)
22. Wohlgemuth, V., Page, B., Kreutzer, W.: Combining discrete event simulation and material flow analysis in a component-based approach to industrial environmental protection. Environ. Model. Softw. 21, 1607–1617 (2006)
23. Johansson, B., Skoogh, A., Mani, M., Leong, S.: Discrete event simulation to generate requirements specification for sustainable manufacturing systems design. In: Proceedings of the 9th Workshop on Performance Metrics for Intelligent Systems, pp. 38–42 (2009)
24. Mouzon, G., Yildirim, M.V., Twomey, J.: Operational methods for minimization of energy consumption of manufacturing equipment. Int. J. Prod. Res. 45, 37–41 (2007)
25. Yin, R., Cao, H., Li, H., Sutherland, J.W.: A Process Planning Method for Reduced Carbon Emissions. Int. J. Comput. Integr. Manuf., 1–17 (2013)
26. Sheng, P., Srinivasan, M., Kobayashi, S.: Multi-Objective Process Planning in Environmentally Conscious Manufacturing: A Feature-Based Approach. CIRP Ann. - Manuf. Technol. 44(1), 433–437 (1995)
27. Tan, X.C., Liu, F., Liu, D.C., Zheng, L., Wang, H.Y., Zhang, Y.H.: Research on the diagnosis and improvement method of a process route in an enterprise production process in terms of sustainable development III. Int. J. Adv. Manuf. Technol. 33(11-12), 1256–1262 (2006)

28. Srinivasan, M., Sheng, P.: Feature-based process planning for environmentally conscious machining: Part 1: micro planning. Rob. Com. Int. Man. 15, 257–270 (1999)
29. Duflou, J.R., Sutherland, J.W., Dornfeld, D., Herrmann, C., Jeswiet, J., Kara, S., Hauschild, M., Kellens, K.: Towards energy and resource efficient manufacturing: A processes and systems approach. CIRP Ann.-Man. Tech. 61, 587–609 (2012)
30. Fysikopoulos, A., Stavropoulos, P., Salonitis, K., Chryssolouris, G.: Energy Efficiency Assessment of Laser Drilling Process. Phys. Procedia 39, 776–783 (2012)
31. Matta, A., Frigerio, N.: Machine Control Policies for Energy Saving in Manufacturing. In: Proc. of the 2013 IEEE CASE, Madison, Wisconsin, USA, pp. 663–668 (2013)
32. Drake, R., Yildirim, M.B., Twomey, J., Bayram, M., Whitman, L., Ahmad, J., Lodhia, P.: Data Collection Framework on Energy Consumption in Manufacturing, Wichita State Univ. Libr. SOAR Shock. Open Access Repos. (2006)
33. Gutowski, T., Murphy, C., Allen, D., Bauer, D., Bras, B., Piwonka, T., Sheng, P., Sutherland, J., Thurston, D., Wolff, E.: Environmentally benign manufacturing: Observations from Japan, Europe and the United States. J. Clean. Prod. 13, 1–17 (2005)
34. Neugebauer, R., Wabner, M., Rentzsch, H., Ihlenfeldt, S.: Structure principles of energy efficient machine tools. CIRP J. Manuf. Sci. Tech. 4(2), 136–147 (2011)
35. Kara, S., Manmek, S., Herrmann, C.: Global manufacturing and the embodied energy of products. CIRP Ann. - Manuf. Technol. 59(1), 29–32 (2010)
36. ENEPLAN: Energy Efficienct Process pLAnning system. The seventh framework program - FoF.NMP.2011-1: The Eco-Factory: cleaner and more resource-efficient production in manufacturing Program, http://www.eneplan.eu/
37. Li, W., Winter, M., Kara, S., Herrmann, S.: Eco-efficiency of manufacturing processes: A grinding case. CIRP Ann. - Manuf. Technol. 61(1), 59–62 (2012)
38. Mori, M., Fujishima, M., Inamasu, Y., Oda, Y.: A study on energy efficiency improvement for machine tools. CIRP Ann. - Manuf. Technol. 60, 145–148 (2011)
39. SIEMENS AG.: Energieeffiziente Werkzeugmaschinen mit Sinumerik Ctrl-Energy von Siemens sind sparsam und produktiv (2011), http://www.siemens.com/press/de/pressemitteilungen/?press=/de/pre
40. Gildemeister, A.: DMG MORI (2012), http://en.dmgmoriseiki.com/sites/en/
41. Eberspächer, P., Verl, A.: Realizing energy reduction of machine tools through a control-integrated consumption graph-based optimization method. Procedia CIRP (2013)

Environmental and Social Sustainability Practices across Supply Chain Management – A Systematic Review

Handson Claudio Dias Pimenta[1] and Peter David Ball[2]

[1] Federal Institute of Education, Science and Technology,
(IFRN, Brazil) and Cranfield University, UK
handson.pimenta@ifrn.edu.br
[2] Manufacturing and Materials Department,Cranfield University,UK
p.d.ball@cranfield.ac.uk

Abstract. This paper explores the sustainable manufacturing knowledge in the field of supply chain management in order to understand the best practices to diffuse sustainability across supply chain network. A systematic literature review was conducted, covering six databases by combinations of key-words between the periods of 1992 to November of 2013. A total of 92 peer-reviewed papers in English are reviewed. A lack of integration of the core SCM activities (purchasing, performance and collaboration) was found in the diffusion of environmental and social sustainability practices across supply chain. Thus, more studies are needed to cover the adoption of environmental and social practices into supply chain management activities and the process to diffuse them across the supply network. In addition, environmental issues have received more attention than social ones in both upstream and downstream supply chain management activities. Using the outputs of the literature review, a conceptual framework is proposed covered: 1) the interrelationship between the core upstream SCM activities (purchasing, suppliers´ performance assessment and collaboration with suppliers) and 2) the effect of internal cross function in upstream SCM activities.

Keywords: Environmental sustainability practices, social responsibility, supply chain management.

1   Introduction

Sustainable supply chain management (SSCM) is a broad subject itself; hence it covers three dimensions of sustainable development, i.e. economic, environmental and social. In addition, the diversity of activities involved in the cross-organisational functions as well as inter-organisational processes in supply chain management become the subject more complex regarding to promote sustainability. Despite the growth in the body of SSCM knowledge, it is still difficult to understand the effect of sustainability practices involved in supply chain activities to engage suppliers and to promote improvements.

B. Grabot et al. (Eds.): APMS 2014, Part II, IFIP AICT 439, pp. 213–221, 2014.

Seuring and Müller [1] is one the first papers that covered a full view of sustainability (triple bottom line – environmental, social and economic dimension) across supply chain management (SCM). They focused on triggers and barriers for SSCM and presented a framework including strategies for suppliers' management of risks and performance and for sustainable products. However, there was less attention on specific supply chain management activities and on sustainability practices.

A comprehensive view of the purchasing process is presented by Igarashi et al.[2]. This covered a specific activity of the SCM and takes some environmental sustainability practices and focused on one dimension of sustainability (green). Govindan et al. [3] also described some environmental practices, such as Environmental Management System (EMS) and Design for environment (DFE), from papers that involved multi-criteria decision making for supplier evaluation and selection. Zhu et al. [4] conducted a survey in 89 Chinese automotive supply chain companies and assessed one particular company responsible for engines by interviews with key-managers. Even though this study covered plenty of SCM activities (purchasing, cooperation with customers and cross-functional cooperation), environmental practices (e.g. ISO 14001, DFE, audits) were the main focus in this study.

Therefore, there has been no review of SCM activities involved in the adoption and diffusion of environmental and social sustainability practice across supply chain. This paper addresses the gap by examining environmental and social practices adopted in supply chain activities. In this context, sustainable manufacturing knowledge in the field of SCM will be explored in order to understand the practices to diffuse sustainability across supply chain network.

Using the outputs of the literature review, a conceptual framework is proposed. The novelty of this conceptual framework is the inclusion of the interrelationship between the core upstream SCM activities of purchasing, suppliers´ performance assessment and collaboration with suppliers. The effect of internal cross function in upstream SCM activities for diffusion of environmental and social sustainability across supply chain network is also taken into account in the conceptual framework.

2   Method

A Systematic Literature Review (SLR) was conducted based on Tranfield et al. [5] and Denyer and Tranfield [6]. SLR enables the researcher both to map and to assess the existing intellectual territory and to specify a research question to develop the existing body of knowledge further [5]. This systematic review follows a protocol made up of four steps: planning, searching, screening, and content analysis, as described below.

The following research question guided this SLR: how might a focal company diffuse environmental and social sustainability practices across the supply chain and in which context?

In order to encompass a representative number of materials more related to the research question, two groups of key-words in line with social and environmental sustainability issues "sustainab*", "environment*", green, "closed loop", "industrial ecology", "social responsibility", reverse, governance) and SCM ("supply chain", "value chain", network, relationship, "collaborat*", "co*operation", performance, purchasing, procurement) was used to construct search strings with the Boolean connectors "and". The strings were then used to search materials between the periods 1992 to 2013 in electronic databases. Six databases were selected, namely Scopus, Web of Science (Isi), EBSCO (Business Source Complete, Environment complete and GreenFILE) and ABI. The main criterion to choose a database was that it needed to be related to the field of manufacturing, sustainability and supply chain management and index well-rated journals.

Between October and November 10th 2013, papers were searched using the "all fields". This search was based on all possible combinations between those two groups of keywords in order to take into account papers more representative with the research question. 20,059 papers were found. Taking into account the high volume of materials it was considered reasonable to narrow the search due to quality of contribution just to include only peer-reviewed scientific papers in English, resulting in 10,814 papers. Removing duplicates reduced the papers found to 4,131.

The title and abstract were read using explicit inclusion and exclusion criteria in order to select relevant papers. Specifically, the paper needed to provide any insight to the relationship between the focal company and member(s) of the supply chain of the manufacturing base in terms of the diffusion of environmental and social sustainability practices. Papers were excluded when they did not cover this relationship within SCM domain. Other exclusion criteria were: ethical and humanity issues, opinion of stakeholders on sustainability and outsourcing, public purchasing and services supply chain (bank, hotel, supermarket, hospital, education, supply of water, e-market) and supply chain security.

A total of 80 papers were resulted from the screening process. Finally, cited references were used as a secondary source (Citation tracking). A further 12 papers were included. Therefore, these three approaches resulted in a total of 92 studies, which were then coded and analysed.

In order to identify the relevant issues related to sustainability across supply chain network, the content of papers selected was analysed, taking into the following aspects, namely: the dimension of sustainability covered (e.g. TBL, Green or Social), the scope of SCM (e.g. upstream – focus on suppliers, downstream – focus on clients, life cycle view) and SCM activities involved.

3   Results and Discussion

3.1   Environmental and Social Sustainability Practices across Supply Chain Management

The body of the literature covered in this systematic review is still a young field; hence the majority was released in the last 10 years.   According to Seuring and Muller [1] and Srivastava [7], the most research related to SSCM has been published after 1990. In this context, the start year was chosen based on these facts. By 2000, a total of seven papers were published. The first paper identified was done by Roy and Whelan [8]. From 2001 to 2010, 47 papers were released. Finally, more than 40% of the papers identified (38 papers) were published between 2011 and 2013, showing a significant interest in environmental and social sustainability practices across supply chain. Indeed, this subject received great attention mainly in the first 9 months of 2013, when 20 papers were published.

Although it is expected that the three dimensions of sustainability (e.g. economic, environmental and social) integrally work together, it is more common to find research covering just one or two aspects, i.e. just environmental or environmental and economic issues or just social (e.g. [1,9]). This is confirmed in this systematic literature review, with 53 papers (57%) focusing just on environmental dimension of sustainability. Triple bottom line (TBL) and society are covered in 15 and 11 papers, respectively. In addition, there was some overlap between environmental and society (nine papers), environment and economy (three papers) and society and economy (one paper). Papers on pure economic issues across supply chain are not included in this literature review.

To date various authors have investigated different ways to diffuse sustainability across supply chain. These approaches include both direct and indirect activities of SCM. The selection of supplies that achieve minimal requirements and the collaboration with existing or new suppliers in order to reach higher levels of sustainability are identified by several authors as a direct action of SCM activities responsible for diffusing sustainability (e.g. [10,11]). Another study suggests indirect actions [12]. In this approach a focal company can implement measures that are not directly related to its own sourcing or management, such as supporting of NGO´s, philanthropy, or compensation schemes.

Direct actions are wide and cover a plenty of issues. Not only cross-functional aspects (internal function integration) are involved in diffusing environmental and social sustainability across supply chain but also cross-organizational (external integration - direct actions with suppliers and other partners located in downstream). Both integrations are essential for environmental and social collaboration addressed for competitive advantage [13]. In this regard, this systematic literature review found 64 papers that focused on upstream, seven papers focused on downstream and 12 papers both upstream and downstream. In addition, six papers took into account the perspective of lifecycle view though life cycle assessment (LCA) or carbon footprint studies (Figure 1). Considering the papers that covered upstream SCM activities, the majority were related to purchasing (44%) (e.g. [14]), followed by supplier's performance assessment (14%) (e.g. [15]) and collaboration (14%) (e.g. [16]).

To diffuse sustainability across the supply chain it is necessary to adopt the appropriate performance measurement system to identify what actions are needed [17]. In this context, suppliers´ performance management allows focal companies to evaluate a supplier's performance, compare it with the performance of other suppliers, and provide suppliers with direction for improvements [18]. Finally, there is a huge variance of environmental and social KPI's to assess supplier´s performance.

Some environmental and social sustainability practices are adopted in collaboration with suppliers were observed. The focus given was to implement some improvements into process, product and general activities. Pollution prevention and EMS - ISO 14001 were the most common practice reported with focus on process. In terms of collaboration with focus on product, LCA and DFE were substantially reported. Finally, training with purchasing staff of focal company and suppliers staff was a common practice in general activities. Interestingly, social sustainability practices were only briefly mentioned, specifically SA 8000 and code of conducts.

The combination of these activities was also observed, highlighting - purchasing and collaboration (17%) (e.g. [17]). An example of purchasing and collaboration developed by Sony Corporation was reported by Handfield et al. [19]. This company implemented its green procurement policy to ensure the adoption of minimal requirements by suppliers. However, at same time, designers from key suppliers worked together with Sony engineers to find improvements in products and processes in terms of environmental impact control and disposal solutions. Finally, with respect to sustainability dimension in upstream, the majority of papers covered environmental issues with 52%, followed by TBL and social, 14% and 12%, respectively (Figure 1).

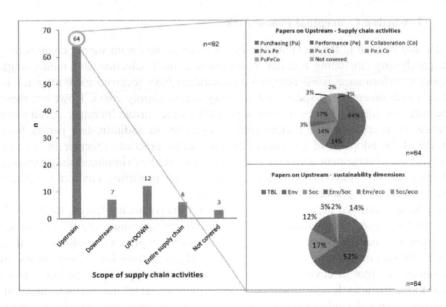

Fig. 1. Scope of sustainable supply chain concepts

The focus of papers that covered downstream activities were related to transportation (two papers) (e.g. [20]), warehousing (1 paper) (e.g. [21]) and the management of product end-of-life (4 papers) (e.g. [8]). Specifically, concerning product end-of-life management, only environmental issues are covered. More attention was given to reverse logistics, product recovery, recycling and remanufacturing. In transportation and warehousing, environmental practices identified aimed to control environmental impacts mainly in terms of energy efficiency (e.g. [22]) and GHG emission control [23]. Specifically, in transportation, two particular practice were covered; the design of vehicles to reduce fuel consumption and routing (e.g. [20]). Finally, with regard to product end-of-life, two main activities are involved: reverse logistics (reuse, dismantled and recycling) (e.g. [24]) and close loop supply chain (remanufacturing) (e.g. [25]). Social practices with focus on safety issues were identified just in transportation and warehouse activities.

A total of 12 papers encompass upstream and downstream supply chain management. In the papers a diversity of SCM activities, such as performance assessment and purchasing were covered. Two papers highlighted the combination of performance and collaboration. For example, Lee and Cheong [26], through a collaboration with 15 key-suppliers, collected in situ details of energy consumption, CO_2 flow and fuel consumption in order to measure the performance and the carbon footprint (raw material, manufacturing and distribution) of a Korean automotive OEM. Finally, the environment was the main sustainability dimension covered by up- and downstream-papers (eight papers), followed by TBL (two papers) and two papers that combined two dimensions of sustainability, one environmental and social and other environmental and economy.

3.2   Towards a Conceptual Framework

As it could be seen in the previous section, in terms of upstream supply chain activities, purchasing (including minimal requirements, final selection and monitoring), supplier´s performance assessment and collaboration have received more attention to diffuse environmental and social sustainability across supply chain. However, these three core activities have been covered separately by the current literature, given more attention on purchasing and performance assessment. In addition, few papers have considered the adoption of environmental and social practices together in specific supply chain management activities. Therefore, few studies simultaneously embrace and integrate these three core SCM activities in order to diffuse environmental and social sustainability practices across supply chain.

In addition, internal departments (e.g operation management, design, R&D, environmental management, quality, etc.) have played an important role to support the definition of specification and select requirements for supplier´s selection as well as metrics for suppliers' performance assessment and alternatives for improvements. In this sense, the rigor of environmental criteria select for suppliers' selection is associated to the maturity level of focal company's environmental management function. However, empirical studies for better understand the relationship between the inclusion of environmental and social practices across supply chain activities and the role of internal functions are poor.

The understanding of the interrelationship between these core upstream SCM activities and the effect of internal cross function might be useful for a better assessment and monitoring of suppliers and identify priority and make sound decisions in terms of spreading environmental and social sustainability.

Therefore, a framework for diffusion of environmental and social sustainability across supply chain network will be presented taking into account these issues. Firstly, upstream supply chain activities, particularly the integration of purchasing, suppliers´ performance assessment and collaboration with suppliers, will be the focus

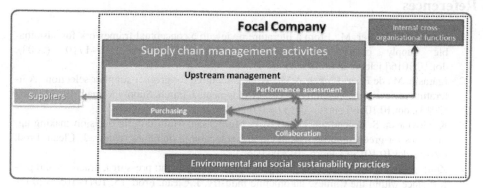

Fig. 2. Conceptual framework for diffusion of environmental and social sustainability practices across supply chain

of the framework. Secondly, the framework will consider the interaction of the internal functions with the upstream SCM activities (Fig. 2).

4   Concluding Remarks

This paper has examined works related to diffusion of environmental and social sustainability practices across the supply chain. It has been observed that the diversity of activities involved in the cross-organisational functions as well as inter-organisational processes in supply chain management become the subject more complex regarding to diffusion of environmental and social sustainability. Despite the growth in the body of SSCM knowledge, it is still difficult to understand the effect of sustainable manufacturing practices involved in supply chain activities to engage suppliers and to promote improvements in terms of sustainability. In addition, the body of the literature analysed on environmental and social sustainability practices across supply chain is still a young field.

The adoption of environmental sustainability practice is more commonly reported both in upstream and downstream SCM activities than social practices. For example, Environmental sustainability practices have received more attention in collaboration activities than social practices, especially prevention pollution, EMS, LCA and DFE.

In order to understand how to strengthen the relationship with suppliers through spreading sustainability practices, future work might focus on empirical studies of upstream SCM particularly the integration of purchasing, suppliers´ performance assessment   and collaboration with suppliers. For example case studies can be conducted to validate the conceptual framework.

Acknowledgments. The research is conducted in collaboration with the EPSRC Centre for Innovative Manufacturing in Industrial Sustainability. This work is sponsored by the Brazilian government (CNPq) through the programme "Science without Borders".

References

1. Seuring, S., Müller, M.: From a literature review to a conceptual framework for sustainable supply chain management. J. Clean. Prod. 16, 1699–1710 (2008), doi:10.1016/j.jclepro.2008.04.020.
2. Igarashi, M., de Boer, L., Fet, A.M.: What is required for greener supplier selection? A literature review and conceptual model development. J. Purch. Supply Manag. 19, 247–263 (2013), doi:10.1016/j.pursup.2013.06.001.
3. K. Govindan, S. Rajendran, J. Sarkis, P. Murugesan, Multi criteria decision making approaches for green supplier evaluation and selection: a literature review. J. Clean. Prod. (2013), doi:10.1016/j.jclepro.2013.06.046
4. Zhu, Q., Sarkis, J., Lai, K.: Green supply chain management: pressures, practices and performance within the Chinese automobile industry. J. Clean. Prod. 15, 1041–1052 (2007), doi:10.1016/j.jclepro.2006.05.021
5. Tranfield, D., Denyer, D., Smart, P.: Towards a Methodology for Developing Evidence-Informed Management Knowledge by Means of Systematic Review. Br. J. Manag. 14, 207–222 (2003), doi:10.1111/1467-8551.00375
6. Denyer, D., Tranfield, D.: Using qualitative research synthesis to build an actionable knowledge base. Manag. Decis. 44, 213–227 (2006), doi:10.1108/00251740610650201
7. Srivastava, S.K.: Green supply-chain management: A state-of-the-art literature review. Int. J. Manag. Rev. 9, 53–80 (2007), doi:10.1111/j.1468-2370.2007.00202.x
8. Roy, R., Whelan, R.C.: Successful recycling through value-chain collaboration. Long Range Plann 25, 62–71 (1992), doi:10.1016/0024-6301(92)90009-Q
9. Ahi, P., Searcy, C.: A comparative literature analysis of definitions for green and sustainable supply chain management. J. Clean. Prod. 52, 329–341 (2013), doi:10.1016/j.jclepro.2013.02.018
10. Vachon, S., Klassen, R.D.: Environmental management and manufacturing performance: The role of collaboration in the supply chain. Int. J. Prod. Econ. 111, 299–315 (2008), doi:10.1016/j.ijpe.2006.11.030
11. Hollos, D., Blome, C., Foerstl, K.: Does sustainable supplier co-operation affect performance? Examining implications for the triple bottom line. Int. J. Prod. Res. 50, 2968–2986 (2012), doi:10.1080/00207543.2011.582184
12. Kogg, B., Mont, O.: Environmental and social responsibility in supply chains: The practise of choice and inter-organisational management. Ecol. Econ. 83, 154–163 (2012), doi:10.1016/j.ecolecon.2011.08.023
13. Gold, S., Seuring, S., Beske, P.: Sustainable Supply Chain Management and Inter-Organizational Resources: A Literature Review 245, 230–245 (2010)
14. Baden, D.A., Harwood, I.A., Woodward, D.G.: The effect of buyer pressure on suppliers in SMEs to demonstrate CSR practices: An added incentive or counter productive? Eur. Manag. J. 27, 429–441 (2009), doi:10.1016/j.emj.2008.10.004
15. Shaw, S., Grant, D.B., Mangan, J.: Developing environmental supply chain performance measures. Benchmarking An Int. J. 17, 320–339 (2010), doi:10.1108/14635771011049326
16. Brockhaus, S., Kersten, W., Knemeyer, A.M.: Where Do We Go From Here? Progressing Sustainability Implementation Efforts Across Supply Chains. J. Bus. Logist. 34, 167–182 (2013), doi:10.1111/jbl.12017
17. Gimenez, C., Tachizawa, E.M.: Extending sustainability to suppliers: a systematic literature review. Supply Chain Manag. An Int. J. 17, 531–543 (2012), doi:10.1108/13598541211258591

18. Simpson, D.F., Power, D.J.: Use the supply relationship to develop lean and green suppliers. Supply Chain Manag. An Int. J. 10, 60–68 (2005), doi:10.1108/13598540510578388
19. Handfield, R., Sroufe, R., Walton, S.: Integrating environmental management and supply chain strategies. Bus. Strateg. Environ. 14, 1–19 (2005), doi:10.1002/bse.422
20. Holt, D., Ghobadian, A.: An empirical study of green supply chain management practices amongst UK manufacturers. J. Manuf. Technol. Manag. 20, 933–956 (2009), doi:10.1108/17410380910984212
21. Chen, C.-C.: Incorporating green purchasing into the frame of ISO 14000. J. Clean. Prod. 13, 927–933 (2005), doi:10.1016/j.jclepro.2004.04.005
22. Holt, D.: Managing the interface between suppliers and organizations for environmental responsibility – an exploration of current practices in the UK 84, 71–84 (2004)
23. Hassini, E., Surti, C., Searcy, C.: A literature review and a case study of sustainable supply chains with a focus on metrics. Int. J. Prod. Econ. 140, 69–82 (2012), doi:10.1016/j.ijpe.2012.01.042
24. Chan, H.K.: A pro-active and collaborative approach to reverse logistics—a case study. Prod. Plan. Control. 18, 350–360 (2007), doi:10.1080/09537280701318736
25. Souza, G.C.: Closed-Loop Supply Chains: A Critical Review, and Future Research*. Decis. Sci. 44, 7–38 (2013), doi:10.1111/j.1540-5915.2012.00394.x
26. Lee, K.-H., Cheong, I.-M.: Measuring a carbon footprint and environmental practice: the case of Hyundai Motors Co (HMC). Ind. Manag. Data Syst. 111, 961–978 (2011), doi:10.1108/02635571111144991

The full list of the papers analysed in this systematic literature review can be accessed on: <https://sites.google.com/site/sustainabilitypractices/>

The Maintenance Function in the Context of Corporate Sustainability: A Theoretical-Analytical Reflexion

José Barrozo de Souza[1], José Benedito Sacomano[1], Sergio Luiz Kyrillos[1],
Francisco José Santos Milreu[1], and Fabio Paparlado[2]

[1] Paulista University-UNIP, Graduate Program in Production Engineering,
Dr. Bacelar St. 1212, São Paulo, Brazil
[1] Espírito Santo Federal Institute - IFES, School Engineering, Vitória St. 1729, Vitória, Brazil
{José Barrozo de Souza,barrozo.pgep.ifes}@gmail.com

Abstract. The paper presents an analytical reflection, based on the context of knowledge management, risk management, quality management, intra-organizational relationships through attributes associated with corporate sustainability. For reasons of theoretical essay, research was supported in mapping the primary references and analysis of different interpretations of sustainability reports from companies associated with the Ethos Institute (Brazil). This paper presents a reflective approach to assess the importance of integration between the maintenance and production, considering some attributes of corporate sustainability.

Keywords: Environmental 1, Operations 2, Production 3.

1 Introduction

1.1 The Background and Purpose of This Study

The term "sustainable development" was popularized by the publication of the report Our Common Future in 1987 [1]. Although sustainable development is a social concept, is increasingly being applied as a corporate concept under the name of "Corporate Sustainability" [2]. Several authors have questioned whether sustainable development actually applies to the corporate level [3].

In particular, firms as actors in society have been pressed to change the way they do business to integrate the principles of sustainability into their everyday business practices and promote their impacts and contributions to sustainable development [4]. Thus arose alternative to the maximization of financial profit captured in phrases like "triple bottom line", where the criteria of economic, social and environmental performance must be integrated [5].

The urgency and magnitude of the threats and risks to global sustainability, together with its opportunities, will transform the disclosure of sustainability and transparency in a key success factor for any company [6]. In his lecture of the day 22/05/2013, titled "From Dilution is the Solution to Pollution to Regional Sustainable Development is the Solution for improved Quality of Life for All: The Long and Challenging Journey", 4rd International Workshop on Advances in Cleaner Production held in São Paulo, Brazil, in 2013, the chief editor of the Journal of

B. Grabot et al. (Eds.): APMS 2014, Part II, IFIP AICT 439, pp. 222–229, 2014.

Cleaner Production, Donald Huisingh urged "global sustainability as the Third Industrial Revolution".

With a growing social demand of corporate sustainability, companies embrace the strategic importance of environmental management practices for competitive advantage. Furthermore, firms tend to increase their market value when they announce that they are adopting environmental management systems such as ISO 14001 [7].

The promotion of sustainable development mission has been shaping the practice of all sectors of activity, for example, including the development of housing for sustainable practice, working to balance the economic, social and environmental performance [8]. Current studies indicate a need to integrate environmental management with the manufacturing strategy, including some themes, such as cross-functional integration, environmental impact and waste reduction [9a].

Reliable information on the operational availability of production systems is of great importance for users of complex production facilities, especially when such facilities operate at capacity. Following the requirements of environmental regulations and the increasing complexity of production systems over the last decades, the maintenance function evolved with the growth of technology [10]. The maintenance function is defined as a set of activities or tasks used to restore an item to a state in which it can perform its designated functions with minimum negative impact on the environment.

Eco-efficiency is a matter of concern at present and is receiving increasing attention in political, academic and business media. In general, this concept refers to the ability to create more goods and services with less impact on the environment and less consumption of natural resources, involving both economic and ecological level issues. Although organizations have embraced the rhetoric of sustainability in their speeches and external reports, little is known about the processes by which systems of management control contributed to greater integration of sustainability into organizational strategy.

Even showing some promise, it was argued that the challenge of accreditation is forcing companies essentially to adopt certifications (hence internalize certifications in daily practice), not just the adoption of certifications symbolic form [11]. For example, emphasize that the quality of maintenance and environmental impact are determined by the use of energy and resources, guided by environmental standards, as well as dependent on the policies adopted by the maintenance function and experience of workers. The adoption of environmental management systems is one of the most important elements of corporate sustainability in recent years. Although theoretically the importance of sustainable business models has become widely accepted in the literature, little is known about how managers deal with practical issues, such as differences in stakeholder interests.

Presented as an introduction to the special volume of the 3rd International Workshop Advances in Cleaner Production, held in Sao Paulo, Brazil, in 2011, the theme of "Cleaner Production Initiatives and Challenges for a sustainable world", the content emphasizes recognition of the urgent and inevitable to make changes from unsustainable patterns of consumption for sustainable production need [12].

Sustainable development depends on more sustainable consumption and production patterns that respond to basic needs and bring a better quality of life while minimizing the use of natural resources so as not to jeopardize the needs of future generations [13].

Research suggests that the preconditions for the ISO 14001 certification motivations can be a good indicator of environmental strategy a company pursues. Moreover, the environmental strategy relates to the environmental performance results and operating company practices [14], i.e., the impact of proactive maintenance policy function in the productive system and hence into the environment are incorporating environmentally benign parameters in the three levels of the model input-processing-output [15a], thus developing the Corporate Sustainability.

Corroborating, [16b] investigated that green teams are often considered in the literature as an essential for companies aiming to implement and improve the approaches and practices of environmental management factor.

The process Maintenance management can be divided into two parts: the definition of the strategy and strategy implementation. The first part, the definition of maintenance strategy, requires the definition of the tasks of maintenance function as an input, which derive directly from the business plan. This initial part of the process for the Management of Maintenance conditions for maintaining the success of an organization determines the effectiveness of subsequently implementing maintenance plans, schedules, controls and improvements.

The second part of the process, the implementation of the chosen strategy - has a different level of significance. Our ability to deal with the problem of deployment Maintenance Management (for example, our ability to secure adequate levels of qualification, preparation of suitable work, proper tools, and performance schedule) will allow us to minimize the cost of maintaining direct (work maintenance and other necessary resources). In that part of the process, we deal with the efficiency of our management, which should be less important. Efficiency is acting and producing with minimum waste, expense or unnecessary effort. Efficiency is then understood as the combination of the Operations and Maintenance Management with providing maintenance function equal to, or better for the same cost.

The third part is to create synergy in the association of operations and maintenance tasks, as it is important for the formulation of tasks, programming strategies and daily operations. However, maintenance should also be integrated throughout the manufacturing industry to better long-term benefits [17], as shown in Figure 1.

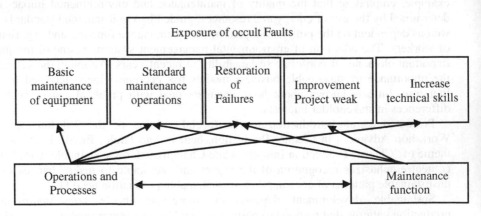

Font: Authors based on mapping the studied literature (2012)

Fig. 1. Relationship between operations and maintenance function

Therefore, for many authors, as [18, 19] the existing research on the prioritization of maintenance tasks have three major limitations: (1) long-term problem is considered as a short-term dynamics is ignored; (2) the relationship between production and maintenance functions, regarding the work order must be clear and (3) decisions are often made by heuristic rules.

Present a proposal for decision support in the short term for the prioritization of maintenance tasks function that can answer two important questions in relation to decision making: (1) On which machines the tasks of maintaining function without affecting the production system will be carried out? (2) Which task of the maintenance function should be performed first so improving obtains the highest throughput? [20]

The growing importance of the maintenance function of the industrial scenario and technological developments, especially the environmental advances of recent years have produced the development of modern maintenance strategies such as condition-based maintenance and predictive maintenance [21].

A major research question guided the construction of this article. "What are the environmental attributes that drive proactive maintenance policy function for a minimal negative impact on the production system to the environment"? In answering this question, this paper contributes by providing objective evidence on how policies influence function of maintaining the potential outcomes of the production system. Furthermore, it provides new evidence on the potential economic, social and environmental benefits of efforts for the development of corporate sustainability.

The other sections of the paper are structured as follows: in section 2, a reflection on the term corporate sustainability, in section 3, a discussion of the methodology used in the study is presented, in section 4, the results of a reflective analysis are reviewed, in section 5, a discussion of the main conclusions is provided. The article ends with conclusions and recommendations for future research in section 5.

2   Methodology

The paper presents an analytical reflection, based on the context of knowledge management, risk management, quality management, intra-organizational relationships through attributes associated with corporate sustainability. For reasons of theoretical essay, research was supported in mapping the primary references and analysis of different interpretations of sustainability reports from companies associated with the Ethos Institute (Brazil). To sort the search and consequently reply the research problem has been taken as the basis for taxonomy, who qualifies on three aspects:

(1)   Regarding purposes - exploratory, because the main objective of the research is to clarify the influence of organizational factors and conceptual integration of the production system maintenance and function in the transfer of the Corporate Sustainability practices, with the understanding that there is little accumulated knowledge and systematized on that strategic integration; (2) As for the means - the

research is classified as documents and literature, and (3) Answer the question: What are the environmental attributes that drive proactive maintenance policy function for a minimal negative impact on the production system to the environment? This research is justified by current and continuing need for theoretical and analytical reflection in the field of management of the production system integration and maintenance function.

3   Results and Discussion

This section presents a discussion of the results obtained in the research. Seeks to systematize and consolidate the literature review and theoretical and analytical reflection contextualized in order to expand the ongoing debate and deepen the nascent field of research. In light of these divergent views, while organizations recognize that environmental sustainability has implications for their competitive positions, companies are not clear about the details of implementation of environmental management practices. Although few environmental attributes that drive proactive maintenance policy function have been suggested in the literature mapping done, the article provides evidence needed for the use of these attributes in practice.

The possibility of benchmarking is particularly relevant for companies and organizations operating in the same sectors in the same country, especially if they are associated with some environmental institution with a mission to mobilize, sensitize and help companies manage their business in a socially responsible manner making them partners in building a sustainable and just society, for example, Institute Ethos (Brazil).

Despite the ongoing debate on the relationship between environmental management and financial performance, the survey allows us to observe inconsistency, making clear between companies, organizations and companies utopia. By identifying possible utopia between the binomial economic developments versus sustainable development are observed needs to work with these underlying conflicts in order to find fair and meaningful solutions to the problems facing us.

The assessment results help not only to choose an alternative design more suitable for a specific set of requirements and maintenance policies with minimal environmental impact, but also to assess the degree to which aspects of proactive maintenance policy can be incorporated into strategic planning. Furthermore, the processes of maintenance and environmentally benign procedures also have a greater role to play in reducing the environmental impact, in particular production systems. Facilitate the interaction of operations with maintenance systems through intuitive interfaces is a competitive advantage in terms of time and costs to industry is shown in Table 1. All the attributes shown in shaded rectangles can be met in the design phase of the product. The other attributes are those that can be maintained during the maintenance operation.

Table 1. Attributes necessary to the practice of consistent policies and environmentally proactive maintenance strategies

Environmental compatibility	Energy Efficiency	Human health and safety risks
Biodegradable Lubricants and Cleaning agents	Synthetic lubricants derived from renewable resources	Rules and regulations
Prevention of leaks	Facility maintenance	Adequate ventilation and lighting
Adaptability during maintenance	Material and energy efficient lubricants	Use of non-toxic solvents and lubricants
Waste treatment policies	Maintenance management system	Maintenance tasks secure and easy
Material with longevity	Reduction of unnecessary travel easy transport	-
Minimal problems with landfill	-	-

Font: Adapted from: [22b].

4   Conclusions and Recommendations

In conclusion, the paper presents a new definition for the Maintenance function: the continuing development of systematic, coordinated, economic and implements through more proactive implementation of intra-organizational relationships in order to develop the optimization tasks in the three levels of the model input-processing-output. As proposed in Figure 3, which shows the connections of continuous improvement with regard to the Maintenance function in the context of corporate sustainability. Finally, it is considered that the points analyzed were able to subsidize the authors of this article with regard to the response of the research question: "What are the environmental attributes that drive proactive maintenance policy function for a minimal negative impact to the production system environment "? In this sense, we believe that the research problem was answered.

Ultimately, we suggest a study on small businesses, because they have not received enough attention and are not represented in our study. Furthermore, the integration of production and maintenance system in the context of organizational culture and corporate sustainability will require further exploration in the context of a small business.

References

1. WCED - World Commission on Environment and Development (WCED). Our Common Future. Oxford University Press, Oxford (1987)
2. Steurer, R., Langer, M.E., Konrad, A., Martinuzzi, A.: Corporations, stakeholders and sustainable development I: a theoretical exploration of business-society relations. Journal of Business Ethics 61, 263–281 (2005)

3. Gray, R.: Is accounting for sustainability actually accounting for sustainability and how would we know? An exploration of narratives of organizations and the planet. Accounting, Organizations and Society 35, 47–62 (2010)
4. Kolk, A., et al.: CSR in China: analysis of domestic and foreign retailers' sustainability dimensions. Business Strategy and the Environment 19, 89–303 (2010)
5. Hopwood, A., Unerman, J., Fries, J.: Accounting for Sustainability: Practical insights. Earthscan (2010) ISBN 978-1-849-71067-1
6. GRI, Sustainability reporting guidelines (2010), http://www.globalreportinginitiative.org (access in: Janeiro 2013)
7. Yang, C.L., Lin, S.P., Chan, Y.H., Sheu, C.: Mediated effect of environmental management on manufacturing competitiveness: an empirical study. International Journal of Production Economics 123(1), 210–220 (2010)
8. Zhang, X., Shen, L., Wu, Y.: Green strategy for gaining competitive advantage in housing development: a China study. Journal of Cleaner Production 19, 157–167 (2011)
9. Jabbour, C.J.C., Da Silva, E.M., Paiva, E.L., Santos, F.C.A.: Environmental management in Brazil: is it a completely competitive priority? Journal of Cleaner Production 5, 1–12 (2011)
10. Ahmad, R., Kamaruddin, S.: An overview of time-based and condition-based maintenance in industrial application. Computers & Industrial Engineering 63, 135–149 (2012)
11. Castka, P., Prajogo, D.: The effect of pressure from secondary stakeholders on the internalization of ISO 14001. Journal of Cleaner Production (2013), doi:10.1016/j.jclepro.2012.12.034
12. Almeida, C.M.V.B., Bonilla, S.H., Giannetti, B.F., Huigingh, D.: Cleaner Production initiatives and challenges for a sustainable world: na introduction to this special volume. Journal of Cleaner Production 47, 1–10 (2013)
13. Delai, I., Takahashi, S.: Corporate sustainability in emerging markets: insights from the practices reported by the Brazilian retailers. Journal of Cleaner Production 47, 211–221 (2013)
14. Gavronski, I., Paiva, E.L., Teixeira, R., De Andrade, M.C.F.: ISO 14001 certified plants in Brazil e taxonomy and practices. Journal of Cleaner Production 39, 32–41 (2013)
15. Ajukumar, V.N., Gandhi, O.P.: Evaluation of green maintenance initiatives in design and development of mechanical systems using an integrated approach. Journal of Cleaner Production (2013), doi:10.1016/j.jclepro.2013.01.010(a)
16. Jabbour, C.J.C., Santos, F.C.A., Fonseca, S.A., Nagano, M.S.: Green teams: understanding their roles in the environmental management of companies located in Brazil. Journal of Cleaner Production 46, 58–66 (2013a)
17. Yamashina, H.: Japanese manufacturing strategy competing with tigers. Business Strategy Review 7(2) (1996)
18. Pintelon, L., Gelders, L., Vanpuyvelde, F.: Maintenance Management, 2nd edn. Acco Belgium, Leuven (2000)
19. Yang, Z., Chang, Q., Djurdjanovic, D., Ni, J., Lee, J.: Maintenance priority assignment utilizing on-line production information. Transaction of ASME, Journal of Manufacturing Science and Engineering 129, 435–446 (2007)

20. Peter, M., Pintelon, L., Ludo, G., Martin, H.: Development of maintenance function performance measurement framework and indicators. International Journal Production Economics 131, 295–302 (2011)
21. Li, L., Ni, J.: Short-term decision support system for maintenance task prioritization. Journal Production Economics 121, 195–202 (2009)
22. Ajukumar, V.N., Gandhi, O.P.: Evaluation of green maintenance initiatives in design and development of mechanical systems using an integrated approach. Journal of Cleaner Production (2013b), doi:10.1016/j.jclepro.2013.01.010

The Effect of Coercive Power on Supply Chain Inventory Replenishment Decisions

Ramesh Roshan Das Guru, Amin Kaboli, and Rémy Glardon

Laboratory for Production Management and Processes
Swiss Federal Institute of Technology at Lausanne (EPFL)
CH-1015 Lausanne, Switzerland
ramesh.dasguru@epfl.ae, amin.kaboli@gmail.com,
remy.glardon@epfl.ch

Abstract. Supply chains often consist of stakeholders with different power levels collaborating with each other in order to meet customer demand. This imbalance of power along the supply chain is a critical factor that affects its short and long-term behavior, as well as its overall stability and efficiency. The role and the impacts of power in distribution channels have been explored quite extensively in Marketing, but far less so with regard to power in the context of supply chains. This paper explores the effect of power on supply chain functioning by focusing on a specific power type i.e. coercive power. More specifically, the impact of power and power awareness on inventory replenishment human decision-making is investigated. An experimental approach with unknown market demand and local information availability is implemented so as to provide a controlled environment for decision-making. Three different treatments are implemented in order to create situations of balanced power, imbalanced power without awareness and imbalanced power with awareness. Results show that power awareness does play a significant role in the way coercive power is exercised. In particular, a significant increase of the size and variability of order quantity and order time interval is observed in the case of imbalanced power with awareness.

Keywords: Coercive power, decentralized supply chain, inventory replenishment, power awareness, human decision-making.

1 Background

Power in supply chain is the ability of one firm (source) to influence the actions and intents of another firm (target) it deals with [Maloni and Benton, 2000]. Power in supply chain can be either balanced or imbalanced. Balanced power exists when stakeholders in the chain possess broadly similar levels of power in influencing each other's decisions, while imbalanced power exists when one or more partners (sources) are capable of manipulating decisions of the other partners (targets) because of their power position [Muthusamy and White, 2006]. The exercising of power in a supply chain can have positive, as well as negative effects on its overall performance. Some of these effects can be visible immediately but most of them emerge out over a longer period of time [Hanf and Belaya, 2009].

B. Grabot et al. (Eds.): APMS 2014, Part II, IFIP AICT 439, pp. 230–237, 2014.

Amongst the various power types defined by French and Raven (1959), coercive power is referred to as the ability of a source to punish a target in case of failures. Based on studies done by Yeung et al. (2009), coercive power tends to improve supplier integrations, with or without the presence of trust, which is again a positive outcome for the overall supply chain. These authors argue that the exercise of power ends up assuring the congruence in goals and activities of different associated partners, particularly in the absence of a well-specified cooperation agreement.

Most of the time, partners in supply chains are not completely aware of the broad scope of their power dimensions and therefore end up not actively managing their own power bases [Cordon and Vollmann, 2005]. Understanding and awareness of power structure is a crucial factor in management of supply chains and selection of the appropriate reactive or proactive strategy, since it can be easily connected to the dominance and interdependence of partners in the chain [Cox et al., 2004]. Thus awareness of power is central since exercising available power is very much dependent on its awareness.

Unlike other attributes of supply chain partnerships, power and its impact cannot be readily measured. Power, as stated earlier, is a mixture of complex social, economic and even psychological factors.

Despite the existence of numerous contributions investigating the role of factors such as trust, commitment and shared meaning, the literature suggests that there is a lack of empirical research examining the effect of power in supply chains. Most of the earlier research works on this topic were done using surveys, interviews and analysis of field data [Cox, 1999; Maloni and Benton, 2000: Yeung et al., 2009]. These empirical studies are generally case based, hence restricting the opportunity to develop general conclusions. This scarcity of empirical research examining the impacts of power exercised by partners in a supply chain is the central motivation for this work. Accordingly, the main goal of this study is to investigate the impact of coercive power on inventory replenishment decision. To this end, a controlled experiment is implemented, using a participatory simulation platform. It allows simulating supply chains with balanced and imbalanced power regimes among different players and analyzing the resulting impact on inventory replenishment decisions. The experiment and further analysis aim at answering the main question of this study: How does imbalanced coercive power and its awareness impact on the replenishment decision-making in supply chains?

The next section provides the methodology and experimental approach. Section 3 provides the results and statistical analysis of the experiment. Finally, a discussion and conclusion are given in Section 4.

2   Methodology

To understand the dynamics and complexity of inventory replenishment decision-making, supply chain simulation has been shown to be an appropriate research tool [Croson and Donohue 2002]. In particular, simulation helps creating a stable and controlled environment that allows reliable observations of the decision maker's behavior over time. In this study, a participatory simulation platform developed at Université Laval, Québec, Canada, called XBG-platform, is used for the experiments with human decision makers [Montreuil et al. 2008]. The XBG-platform mimics the dynamics of inventory replenishment in a decentralized, linear, four echelon supply chain. Order size and order time can be freely chosen; thus any order placement implies a twofold decision about time and quantity.

In Fig. 1, filled rectangles represent echelons with human participants, and empty rectangles represent echelons with computer agents. Human participants, thereafter subjects, played the role of the wholesaler and computer agents played factory, distributor, retailer and market roles. The main reason to use an experimental set-up with one single subject is to avoid interaction of human decision-making between echelons. None of the subjects were made aware of the fact that the computer simulated other echelons.

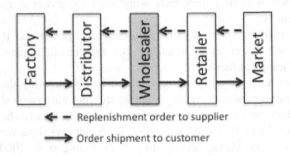

Fig. 1. Structure of the Supply Chain used in XBG simulation

The market demand is stable and follows a normal distribution with a mean of 3000 units/day and a standard deviation of 500 units/day, truncated at zero. This daily demand is randomly split into two orders per day. The demand information is unknown to the subjects.

This experiment is divided into three settings based on the power and awareness levels of the subjects. The imbalance of power between the echelons is achieved by varying the level of backorder costs between them. The awareness of power is incorporated with the introduction of contracts, which the player must sign before starting the game. The contract contains information about the business environment and commercial conditions, which makes the player aware of the power he/she holds over his/her supplier. The objective of the subject is to maximize his/her benefit, which is rewarded with a performance-based payment up to 60 CHF. Three different treatments are used to generate the required levels of power and power awareness.

— **Treatment 1**: Balanced power. Backorder costs are identical for all echelons, therefore leading to power equilibrium between them.
— **Treatment 2:** Imbalanced power without awareness. The backorder cost to be paid by the distributor to the wholesaler (subject) is doubled, but the contract signed by the subject does not mention this fact. All other relations within the supply chain are in power equilibrium.

— *Treatment 3:* Imbalanced power with awareness. The backorder cost to be paid by the distributor to the wholesaler (subject) is doubled and the contract signed by the subject explicitly mentions this fact. All other relations within the supply chain are in power equilibrium.

The supply chain parameters considered in the experiments are defined in Table 1.

Table 1. Summary of the variables

Variable	Symbol	Variable	Symbol
Ordered quantity	OQ	Purchasing cost	PC
Ordering time interval	OT	Backorder cost	BC
On-hand inventory	OI	Inventory carrying cost	IC
Supply line	SL	Operating cost	OC
		Total cost	TC

Twenty-four undergraduate and graduate students representing 15 nationalities from EPFL's engineering and business majors participated in the experiment. The subjects consisted of 21% women and 79% men, with 29% of students in their Bachelor and 71% in their Master. To analyze the evolution of decision-making in the span of four months of game duration, the obtained data are divided bimonthly in 8 rounds. Consequently the database consists of a total of 24 subjects x 8 rounds = 192 results; i.e. 64 observations per treatment.

3   Results and Statistical Analysis

The obtained experimental results are analyzed over the whole game, separately for each treatment T1 (balanced power), T2 (power without awareness) and T3 power with awareness). The values reported for each treatment group (T1 to T3) represent the average of all the subjects in that particular setting throughout the duration of four months of game (64 observations). The statistical significance of all observations is checked using the Mann Whitney test (criterion $p<0.05$). These aggregated experimental results are presented in the next four sub-sections as follows: 3.1 Replenishment decision indicators, 3.2 Inventory indicators and 3.3 Cost components.

3.1   Replenishment Decision Indicators

As described earlier, the replenishment decision in this study involves two indictors, namely ordered quantity (OQ) and order time interval (OT). The results presented in Fig. 2 indicate no significant differences between treatments T1 and T2 but a very significant increase in the magnitude and variability of both OQ and OT in case of treatment T3, i.e. in case of power awareness.

The above observations are statistically confirmed by the Mann Whitney test scores, as indicated in Fig. 2.

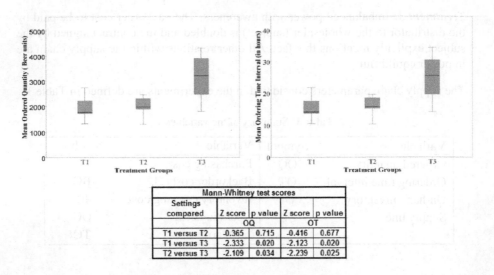

Mann-Whitney test scores				
Settings compared	Z score	p value	Z score	p value
	OQ		OT	
T1 versus T2	-0.365	0.715	-0.416	0.677
T1 versus T3	-2.333	0.020	-2.123	0.020
T2 versus T3	-2.109	0.034	-2.239	0.025

Fig. 2. Mean OQ and OT for treatments T1, T2 and T3

3.2 Inventory Indicators

Two indicators are considered, the on-hand inventory (OI) and the supply line (SL). Fig. 3 shows no significant differences between treatments T1 and T2 but a significant increase in the magnitude and variability of OI in case of treatment T3, i.e. in case of power awareness. With regard to SL, an increase in its variability, but not in its magnitude is noticed for treatment T3.

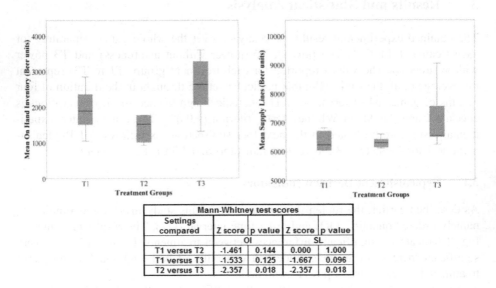

Mann-Whitney test scores				
Settings compared	Z score	p value	Z score	p value
	OI		SL	
T1 versus T2	-1.461	0.144	0.000	1.000
T1 versus T3	-1.533	0.125	-1.667	0.096
T2 versus T3	-2.357	0.018	-2.357	0.018

Fig. 3. Mean OI and SL for treatments T1, T2 and T3

The above observations on OI and SL are confirmed by the Mann Whitney test scores provided in Fig. 3. For OI, a significant difference is confirmed between treatments T2 and T3. For all other comparisons, including T1/T3, no statistical significance is found (criterion $p<0.05$).

With regard to SL, the statistical tests confirm also a significant difference between T2 and T3. Although there is an observable difference between T1 and T3, its significance is not confirmed by the Mann Whitney test for the selected criterion of $p<0.05$.

3.3   Cost Components

As defined above, the considered cost components are:

- The operating cost (OC), defined as the sum of the backorder (BC) and inventory carrying (IC) costs ($OC=BC+IC$),
- The total cost (TC), defined as the sum of the operating (OC) and purchasing (PC) costs ($TC=OC+PC=BC+IC+PC$).

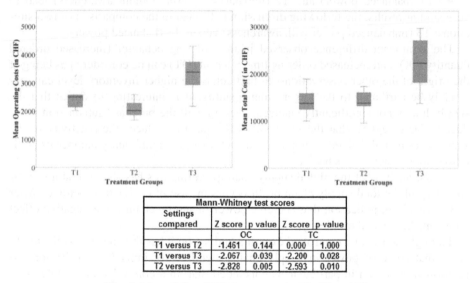

Mann-Whitney test scores				
Settings compared	Z score	p value	Z score	p value
	OC		TC	
T1 versus T2	-1.461	0.144	0.000	1.000
T1 versus T3	-2.067	0.039	-2.200	0.028
T2 versus T3	-2.828	0.005	-2.593	0.010

Fig. 4. Mean OC and TC for treatments T1, T2 and T3

Both OC and TC are considered in the analysis of the experimental results and presented in Fig. 4. They indicate no significant differences between treatments T1 and T2, but a significant increase in the magnitude and variability of both OC and TC in case of treatment T3, i.e. in case of power awareness.

The statistical analysis by Mann Whitney test scores confirms the results described above (see Fig. 4). For both OC and TC, the differences between treatment T3 versus treatments T1 and T2 are shown to be significant.

4   Discussions and Conclusion

It is important to recall that the use of a controlled and reproducible experimental environment assures that all observations are strictly due to changes in the human replenishment decision process. Thus, the statistical analysis of the experimental data in the three different settings T1, T2 and T3, with varying power and awareness levels, leads to the following main observations.

— Observation 1: Holding power without having its complete awareness creates no significant change in ordering behavior, inventory levels and costs compared to a power equilibrium situation (T2 versus T1).
— Observation 2: Holding power and being completely aware about it leads to a significant impact in inventory replenishment decision, inventory levels and costs when compared to a power equilibrium situation (T3 versus T1).

In particular, the following significant impacts are observed: a) Ordered quantity and Ordering time interval are increased, b) Inventory levels are increased c) Cost components are increased.

As T1 (balanced power) and T2 (imbalanced power without awareness) lead to very similar results, the following discussion is limited to the comparison of two situations: T3 (imbalanced power with awareness) versus T1 (balanced power).

The significant difference observed in the ordering behavior (increased ordered quantity (OQ) and increased ordering time interval (OT) can be considered as being at the origin of the other observations. In particular, the higher inventory level can reasonably be attributed to the larger order quantity. It is interesting to notice that the supply line is not significantly changed, even though the purchase satisfaction is reduced. These suggest that the increased order quantity reduces the reactivity of the supplier (as partial delivery is not allowed) but does not significantly hamper its ability to ship; i.e. increase its backlog..

A first analysis of the global supply chain performances has shown that a significant drop of the total supply chain profit occurs in case of exercising coercive power (T3). This is an indication that coercive power in supply chain has a negative effect on its integration and efficiency.

Through the use of a controlled experimental set-up it has thus been possible to observe that coercive power in supply chains significantly impacts its behavior and performances. It can in particular be concluded that, in a controlled and stable environment, exercising coercive power within a supply chain tends to reduce its performance. The Supply Chain costs are increased and the overall profit reduced, but the final customer satisfaction is not so much affected. A first analysis of the intra-supply chain results indicates also that the reduced total Supply Chain profit is shared in a less even way, which is detrimental to the partner under power dependence. This may ultimately lead to additional intra-chain dissatisfactions, and therefore to further degradation of the Supply Chain performances with time.

Real Supply chains are of course significantly more complex and less stable than the well-controlled experimental environment used in this study. Nevertheless, the obtained results being strictly due to human decision-making, it can be expected that similar tendencies would be observed in practice. Consequently, it means that a strong imbalance of power in a decentralized Supply Chain is adverse.

Acknowledgement. The authors wish to thank Prof. Benoit Montreuil and his research team at Université Laval for providing the participatory simulation platform XBG and for efficiently supporting its use and maintenance. Thanks are also due to Mr. Marc Matthey for his technical support and to Mrs. Ioanna Paniara for helping with the preparation of this manuscript.

References

1. Cordón, C., Vollmann, T.E.: Supply Chain Dyads: Developing the Chain Linkages. International Institute for Management Development, IMD (2005)
2. Cox, A.: Power, value and supply chain management. Supply Chain Management: An International Journal 4(4), 167–175 (1999)
3. Cox, A., Watson, G., Lonsdale, C., Sanderson, J.: Managing appropriately in power regimes: relationship and performance management in 12 supply chain cases. Supply Chain Management: An International Journal 9(5), 357–371 (2004)
4. Croson, R., Donohue, K.: Experimental economics and supply-chain management. Interfaces 32(5), 74–82 (2002)
5. French, J.R., Raven, B.H.: The Bases of Social Power. In: Cartwright, D. (red.) The Studies on Social Power. Ann Arbor (1959)
6. Hanf, J., Belaya, V.: The "Dark" and the "Bright" Sides of Power in Supply Chain Networks. Schriften der Gesellschaft für Wirtschafts-und Sozialwissenschaften des Landbaus eV Band 44, 279 (2009)
7. Maloni, M., Benton, W.C.: Power influences in the supply chain. Journal of Business Logistics 21(1), 49–73 (2000)
8. Montreuil, B., Brotherton, E., Glardon, R., Yoo, M.-J., Elamiri, Y., Borter, A.-S., Morneau, A., Naciri, S., Jermann, P.: Experiences in Using XBeerGame Virtual Gaming for Learning Supply Chain Management. In: 2nd European Conference on Games Based Learning, October 16-17. Univesitat Oberta de Catalunya, Spain (2008)
9. Muthusamy, S.K., White, M.A.: Does power sharing matter? The role of power and influence in alliance performance. Journal of Business Research 59(7), 811–819 (2006)
10. Yeung, J.H.Y., Selen, W., Zhang, M., Huo, B.: The effects of trust and coercive power on supplier integration. International Journal of Production Economics 120(1), 66–78 (2009)

Evaluation of Sustainable Mass Customized Habitation: The Case of CAP 44

Alexande Chadeneau, Emilie Dol, Solène Martinez, and Catherine Marie da Cunha

Lunam Universite, Ecole Centrale De Nantes -
IRCCyN UMR CNRS 6597 - 1 Rue de la Noë, Nantes, France

Abstract. Measuring the value of a product before launching its production is a way to assure its good sale. The present study proposes a methodology to evaluate the intrinsic value of an habitation. The value is measured in terms of sustainability and customization.

The methodology is composed of a first step of determination of value drivers, an evaluation step, an aggregation step and finally recommendation. Step.

The methodology is applied on a real case: the CAP 44 housing project in Nantes, France.

Keywords: Satisfaction, Customization, Home, Evaluation.

1   Introduction

Mass customization is a policy than enables the satisfaction of personalized requirements with near mass production efficiency. Among other benefits, it enables to gain competitive advantage on a given market share.

Mass customization can be offered either via product variability or process variability (Daaboul et al., 2011). Numerous researches identify the existence of Mass customization enablers but also of pitfalls (Gilmore and Pine, 1996, da Silveira et al., 2001, Fogliatto et al., 2012).

A raise in customization may lead to a raise in complexity, in the production as well as in management (Blecker et al., 2006). A company should then address several questions before implementing mass customization (Daaboul et al., 2010):

- Can the product be customized?
- Does the customer want a customization?
- Is the company ready for mass customization?

Barlow et al. 2003 reported that Mass customization, which is already functional for Japanese housing industry, could be a new business model for the European one. The challenge is the evaluation of the value of this new type of habitation.

First theories on value go back to ancient Greece (with Plato and Epicurus). Modern research also has interest in this area, promoting transdisciplinary definition and evaluation for this concept (Gallarza et al., 2006) (Ueda et al., 2009). Value is neither a constant in time nor an objective characteristic. Yet this characteristic has a huge

B. Grabot et al. (Eds.): APMS 2014, Part II, IFIP AICT 439, pp. 238–245, 2014.

influence on the customer behavior, particularly on product choice, repeated purchases and product recommendation.

For the particular product which is a "home" the value concept is declined into an elicited valuation named "Housing satisfaction". This indicator measures the proximity of an current and ideal housing of an individual subject to its needs, expectations and achievements (Amérigo & Aragonés, 1997).

The article is structured as follows: section 2 presents the methodology. Section 3 depicts the use case. Conclusion and research directions close the article.

2   Methodology

We followed a generic methodology to evaluate the value of a given product (Daaboul et al, 2011).

1. Identification of the Housing satisfaction drivers
2. Determination of a test population for the drivers' weighting
3. Weighting of the satisfaction drivers

We adapted this methodology to the housing product and add to this 3 first steps a final step of aggregation.

2.1   Housing Satisfaction Drivers Identification

It is mandatory to define the limits of the product. In our case of housing, we limited the product to the private volume belonging to one or several people. The building as a whole, the neighborhood, transportation systems are then exterior elements that should not be considered.

Thanks to a study led by the French housing sector (Century 21, 2010) an exhaustive list of satisfaction drivers has been established. A reduction of this list to the most pertinent ones was done with the architectural staff of the CAP 44 project, see figure 1 for a hierarchical representation.

2.2   Evaluations and Aggregation

For multicriteria evaluation, Analytic Hierarchy Process (AHP) (Saaty, 2008) is often used to weight the different criteria. One of the difficulties in implementing AHP is to limit the number of pairwise comparison the test population has to perform. Therefore a hierarchical partitioning of the criteria can be done, the pairwise comparison will then be limited to criteria belonging to the same subset. The tree representation of those drivers is given in figure 1.

A difficulty occurs when the decomposition levels are not equal for every driver. We choose to address this issue using sparse pairwise-comparison matrices (Tan and Promentilla, 2013).

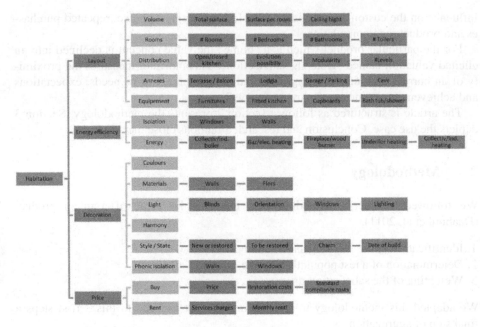

Fig. 1. Satisfaction drivers

The aggregation phase has a significant impact on the obtained results. The choice of aggregation type must answer to two questions:

-    What is the most efficient mean type?
-    When do we have to use it? On the comparisons? On the weight?

We chose to use the geometric mean which is the most congruent with pairwise comparison (Adamcsek, 2008). The order of the operation also has an impact on weighting. The mean can be done either on the comparisons or on the weights (figure 2).

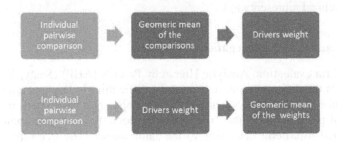

Fig. 2. Aggregation solutions

The choice between the 2 aggregations.

3   Usecase: The CAP 44 Project

3.1   Project Description

CAP 44 is a building that followed Nantes's evolution since its building in 1895. At first was a flourmill, ideally placed along the river Loire, and then it has been transformed into offices.

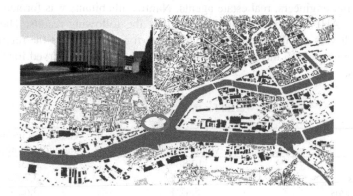

Fig. 3. Localization of CAP 44 building

Today the city wants to transform this building and use it as the center of a new neighborhood based on the "fertile city" concept. The future building should be a meeting point offering housing, offices place, restaurants, services, etc. figure 4 presents the proposed evolution of the building.

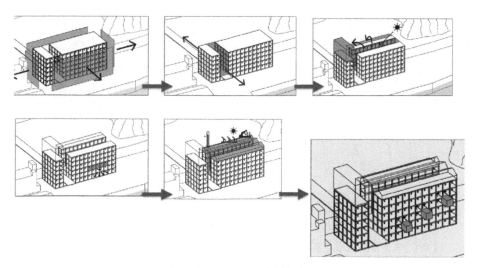

Fig. 4. Evolution of CAP 44

The chosen redevelopment is modular. The architects wish to pre-build the housing and offices and then insert them into the structure, in a Plug & Play approach. This idea of a common plateform for different product is in line with mass customization policies (Martin, 1999).

3.2   Satisfaction Drivers and Housing Evaluation

To weight the satisfaction drivers, a small panel (30 people) of engineer-architect students, civil engineers, real estate agents, Nantes inhabitants was formed and questioned. The AHP method was applied, it gives the following results. The ten most important drivers are the same, see table 1. Yet for some drivers the relative difference can be up to 56% therefore the 2 aggregations will be conserved for the evaluation phases.

Table 1. Weight for the 10 most important Drivers

Drivers	Geometric mean of the individual weights	Geometric mean of the individual comparison
Rent	12,86%	35,38%
# of rooms	5,63%	3,76%
# of bedrooms	5,42%	3,62%
Orientation	4,51%	2,73%
# of widows	4,16%	2,52%
Service charges	4,01%	11,03%
Evolution possibility	3,92%	2,62%
Levels	3,58%	2,39%
Surface per room	3,34%	2,23%
Fitted kitchen	2,81%	1,88%

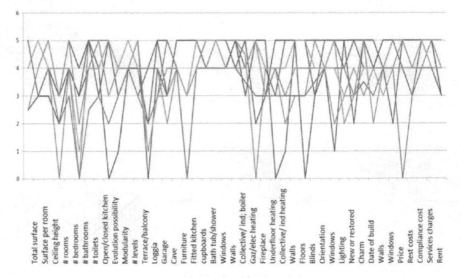

Fig. 5. Evaluation of the drivers

For the evaluation, the housing project was described through: artist's interpretations, 2D-plans and synthesis tables related to satisfaction drivers (surface in m2, description of the heating characteristics,...). Based on this information (which was then unbiased by the interviewer) subjects had to evaluate the housing on a 5-scale basis for each of the 47 drivers. Figure 5 illustrates the variation of the evaluations for 7 of our subjects, the evaluation are given in the y-axis while the drivers are represented in the x-axis.

A special category of drivers can be identified: the ones having an evaluation of 0 resp. 5. These drivers are deal-breakers resp. mandatory for other subjects. These drivers are:

- Fireplace/Wood burner
- Garage/Parking
- Furniture
- Walls material
- Numbers of toilets
- Terrace/balcony

Those drivers are of great interest for a mass customization point of view. They should constitute a set of "modules" that the customers could chose or not.

Figure 6 presents the average weighted evaluation for the different drivers per categories.

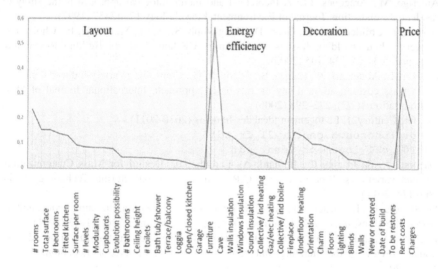

Fig. 6. Average grade of drivers, per category

The drivers having the highest weighted grades are: Total area, Walls isolation, Windows, Services charges.

The average grade of the housing is of 3.92. This evaluation is a reference for further evolution of the project. It should be improved, while the architects take the subjects into account. For instance the initial design proposed a plug-in loggia for each apartment. Thanks to this analysis, they identify that the global preference goes to either a balcony or an extra–room to the housing.

4   Discussion and Conclusion

This study enriches a methodology of Housing satisfaction evaluation. The application to a housing project validates the relevance of the different steps.

The Cap 44 project's architects used the results of the satisfaction drivers' identification and evaluation to better understand the expectation of future users and then to modify the design of the building. Next steps of the projects include in an evaluation of the new design.

Further research should address the genericity of the obtained drivers and the robustness of their weight for the French housing sector. The stabilized Housing satisfaction evaluation grid could then be used for future building development project in Nantes.

References

1. Adamcsek, E.: The Analytic Hierarchy Process and its Generalizations. Master thesis, Eötvös Lorand University (2008)
2. Amérigo, M., Aragonés, J.I.: A theoretical and methodological approach to the study of residential satisfaction. Journal of Environmental Psychology 17, 47–57 (1997)
3. Barlow, J., Childerhouse, P., Gann, D., Hong-Minh, S., Naim, M., Ozaki, R.: Choice and delivery in housebuilding: lessons from Japan for UK housebuilders. Building Research & Information 31(2), 134–145 (2003)
4. Blecker, T., Abdelkafi, N., Kaluza, B., Friedrich, G.: Controlling variety-induced complexity in mass customisation: a key metrics-based approach. International Journal of Mass Customisation 1(2/3), 272–298 (2006)
5. Enquête Century21, Le logement idéal des français (2010-2011),
   http://photosv5.century21.fr/pdf/
   201101_c21_logement_ideal.pdf
6. Daaboul, J., da Cunha, C., Bernard, A., Laroche, F.: Design for Mass Customization: Product variety vs. Process variety. CIRP Annals - Manufacturing Technology 60(1), 169–174 (2011)
7. Da Silveira, G., Borenstein, D., Fogliatto, F.: Mass customization: literature review and research directions. International Journal of Production Economics 72(1), 1–13 (2001)
8. Fogliatto, F.S., da Silveira, G.J.C., Borenstein, D.: The mass customization decade: An updated review of the literature. International Journal of Production Economics 138(1), 14–25 (2012)
9. Gallarza, M.G., Gil Saura, I.: Value dimensions, perceived value, satisfaction and loyalty: an investigation of university students' travel behaviour. Tourism Management 27(3), 437–452 (2006)
10. Gilmore, J., Pine, J.: The four faces of mass customization. Harvard Business Review 75, 91–101 (1997)
11. Martin, M.: Design for variety: a methodology for developing product plateform architectures, Standford university (1999)

12. Saaty, T.L.: Decision making with the analytic hierarchy process. International Journal Services Sciences 1(1), 83–98 (2008)
13. Tan, R.R., Promentilla, M.A.B.: A methodology for augmenting sparse pairwise comparison matrices in AHP: applications to energy systems. Clean Techn. Environ. Policy 15(4), 713–719 (2013)
14. Ueda, K., Takenaka, T., Váncza, J., Monostori, L.: Value creation and decision-making in sustainable societ. CIRP Annals - Manufacturing Technology 58(2), 681–700 (2009)

Sustainability in Manufacturing Facility Location Decisions: Comparison of Existing Approaches

Uwe Dombrowski, Christoph Riechel, and Hannes Döring

Institute for Advanced Industrial Management,
Technische Universität Braunschweig, Braunschweig, Germany
{u.dombrowski,c.riechel,h.doering}@tu-bs.de

Abstract. Facility location decisions concern the positioning of production facilities regarding international, national, regional or local level. Indicator sets and methods for the support of such decisions traditionally focus economic aspects. However, approaches for solving the facility location problem by taking into account the three pillars of sustainability, namely social, ecological and economic aspects, are still rare. This paper complements existing reviews by a structured analysis of established indicator sets and evaluation methods for facility locations in comparison to approaches focusing sustainability aspects.

Keywords: Facility location, manufacturing, sustainability.

1 Introduction

Facility location decisions concern the positioning of production facilities regarding international, national, regional or local level [1], [2]. In a globalized world being characterized by international markets, competitors and supply chains, the importance of decisions on facility locations increases. [3] Indicator sets and methods for the support of facility location decisions traditionally focus economic aspects resulting from distances to customers and suppliers. Moreover, aspects like skills and knowledge have been addressed for several years. [1] Since the Brundtland Commission defined the terminology of sustainable development [4], decisions in companies increasingly consider sustainability aspects [1]. However, specific approaches for solving the facility location problem by focusing the three pillars of sustainability, namely social, ecological and economic aspects, are still rare. Accordingly, to obtain competitiveness, existing methods and indicator sets have to be analyzed and extended by sustainability metrics where necessary. Recently, two related reviews were published. Terouhid et al. reviewed location studies, which concentrate on sustainability [2]. Chen et al. took a broader view. They also reviewed papers focusing sustainability assessment in supply chains and production networks [1].

This paper complements these reviews by a structured analysis of established conventional indicator sets and evaluation methods for facility locations in comparison to new approaches focusing sustainability aspects. Thereby, it aims at the identification of potentials as well as need for improvement in existing concepts.

B. Grabot et al. (Eds.): APMS 2014, Part II, IFIP AICT 439, pp. 246–253, 2014.

2   Methods and Materials

To provide a structured comparison of facility location planning approaches, the review was divided into two parts. Firstly, evaluation criteria were derived from previous reviews in the area of sustainability science and sustainable facility location or factory planning. Secondly, established conventional approaches and sustainability oriented concepts for facility location planning were compared against the criteria. In this chapter, the review process and the developed evaluation criteria are summarized.

2.1   Review Process

Within this paper, two kinds of approaches were reviewed. On the one hand, sustainability oriented approaches, explicitly focusing the facility location problem, were chosen from the review of Chen et al. [1]. The keywords factory location problem and sustainable factory location problem and sustainable factory location assessment were used for an additional search in Scopus and Google Scholar to identify approaches from the last 20 years focusing sustainable factory location. On the other hand, broadly used conventional approaches regarding the facility location problem without focusing sustainability were investigated. Within the conventional methods and indicator sets all approaches that have been published by established German institutes with research focus on facility planning within the past 30 years were analyzed. The conventional approaches with regard to the facility location problem were compared. Thereof, approaches with unique features were recognized further. These approaches were representatively analyzed for similar concepts of other German institutes. The sustainability oriented and conventional Indicator sets and methods were then compared regarding the criteria defined in the following section 2.2. For the assessment, a tripartite scale was used. The approaches were evaluated against the criteria by differentiating full fulfillment, partial fulfillment and non-fulfillment.

2.2   Evaluation Criteria

The evaluation criteria used in this paper were derived from papers found in databases like Scopus, Science Direct, Google Scholar dealing with the comparison or evaluation of sustainability assessment methods or indicators. The research was based on the keywords facility location, facility location meta review and facility location sustainability. Just studies from the last 5 years were used to ensure state of the art. The set of criteria was defined in three steps. Firstly, more than 90 criteria were obtained from related papers. Secondly, criteria with the same content were consolidated. Thirdly, each criterion was checked regarding its relevance for the evaluation of indicator sets and methods in the area of facility location decisions by experts. For instance, criteria focusing the quality of single indicators were excluded as they cannot be used for the evaluation of complete indicator sets. Within this step, aspects which were not named by other authors but show relevance for the facility location problem were added or changes within the scope of criteria were conducted.

The criteria were derived from six recent journal articles with partly different scopes. General demands on sustainability assessment were chosen from a meta-review, which structured reviews on sustainability assessment [5]. Criteria being more specific to the assessment of indicator sets were derived from works, which formulated requirements on indicators [6], [7]. To define criteria that are specific to the evaluation of sustainability assessment for factories and facility location decisions, criteria used in respective reviews were taken into account [2], [8]. In addition, to support a review focusing on specific problems within sustainable facility location, research gaps, which were identified within the review of Chen and colleagues [1] , were taken over into the criteria list. A set of 14 evaluation criteria resulted from the selection. These criteria are shown in Table 1. In the following, their content is summed up.

Completeness of scope: As shown in Table 1, researchers commonly discuss three pillars of sustainability when structuring sustainability assessment methods and indicators. Some authors refer to the Wuppertal sustainable development indicator framework and the (UN) Commission on Sustainable Development. These consider a fourth dimension, namely institutional indicators [6], [9], [10], [11]. Within this work, institutional sustainability is considered as the level at which sustainability aspects from the three pillars are integratively anchored in the legislation of a location.

Strategicity: Sala et al. identified a central relevance of Life Cycle Thinking for sustainability assessment when analyzing comparative studies after 2005 [5]. Terouhid et al. also defined a criterion to evaluate, if methods are life cycle oriented [2]. Within this work, the integration of up- and downstream effects along the product life cycle and supply chain is termed as life cycle orientation. [5] Following Strohm and Ulich, the criteria of a holistic view is used to evaluate, if indicator sets and methods consider people, technology and organization and their interactions [12].

Database: Applicability is used as central criterion for sustainability assessment and is often dependent on data availability [5], [6], [7]. Accordingly, data availability was selected as criterion within this work. In addition, indicator sets and assessment methods are compared regarding the transparency of data sources as well as the transparency of data gathering within the methodological frame.

Indexes and Indicators: Different papers, which were analyzed, support the evaluation of single indicators [6], [7]. Aspects like reliability or relevance are used as criteria. However, within this work, whole indicator sets were compared. Based on the paper of Singh et al. the level of objectivity and quantification were chosen as criteria [6]. They were used to evaluate a general tendency within analyzed indicator sets.

Methodology: The fifth criteria section focuses methodological aspects. Interdisciplinarity was used to evaluate, if perspectives of different functional experts are considered in indicator sets and methods. The grade of generic applicability and flexibility describes if approaches are usable for different sectors. The question, if approaches take a proactive view by including planned improvement into the assessment was addressed as well. The integratedness describes if side effects between the pillars of sustainability are considered. Another criterion, identified by Sala et al., is if alternative scenarios are taken into account [5]. Within this work, this aspect is described as inclusion of external future influences. Finally, the existence of normalization and scaling in indicator sets and the participation of stakeholders were evaluated.

Table 1. Selected criteria for the evaluation of indicator sets and assessment methods

Authors / Source Focus / Topic	Meta-Review Methods / indica-	Studies / Methods	Research Agenda: Methods	Factory assessment tools	Methodologies / indexes	Assessment of quantitative indicators
Completeness of scope						
Dimensions of Sustainability (social, ecological, economic)	X	X	X	X	X	
Strategicity	X					
Holistic view	X					
Life cycle oriented approach	X	X				
Database						
Data availability	X				X	X
Transparency	X					
Indexes/ Indicators						
Quantitative Level					X	
Level of objectivity					X	
Methodology						
Interdisciplinarity		X				
Generic applicability / flexibility				X	X	
Proactive approach			X			
Integratedness	X					
Alternative scenarios / Future	X					
Scaling / Normalization					X	
Participation of stakeholders	X					

3   Results

Based on the derived evaluation criteria, conventional indicator sets and evaluation methods for facility locations were compared to approaches focusing sustainability aspects. The following approaches were selected from a holistic literature review.

Kettner et al. follow a structured approach. It starts with the identification of external and internal factors. These sets define company specific characterizations of the descriptive variables for the location factors. [14] Taking into account the corporate objective, the location problem is then narrowed to a requirement profile for the location to be searched. Using the value benefit analysis (VBA), the indicator set is assessed. The assessment is team based. [14]

The approach of *Aggteleky et al.* is characterized by the recognition of almost all areas of business activity, operational processes and the future possibility for location development. Thus, sustainably aspects with scope on the social and ecological influences are included. The assessment is based on the VBA as well. [15]

Wiendahl et al. focus the location choice by a goal-setting process recognizing technologies, market situation and environment as external factors. As internal factors strategic objectives and vulnerabilities are taken into account. Vulnerabilities are, for example, lack of logistic performance or capacity bottlenecks. The approach proceeds stepwise, following different levels of assessment. [16]

Pawellek et al. differentiate general location factors, function-related factors and global factors. Global factors are, for instance, political, economic and socio-cultural factors. Thereby, they include aspects of sustainability into their indicator set. Similarly to Kettner, Aggteleky, and Wiendahl, they use a variation of the VBA. [17]

Egan and Jones present an assessment tool, which focuses the evaluation of sustainability at company level. This tool can be applied to facility location problems. The main innovation of their approach is the transfer of a fuzzy logic to the sustainable facility location problem. [18]

Corbiere-Nicollier and an aerospace manufacturer developed an approach, which indicates economic, environmental and social aspects. The approach recognizes sustainability and traditional performance indicators of a facility simultaneously. [19]

Reich-Weiser and Dornfeld adopt the location problem by aspects of sustainability. They focus greenhouse gas emission and water consumption. To assess tradeoffs between costs, flexibility and environment they use a quantitative model and life cycle analysis. This model shows direct and indirect effects of transportation and facility location. [20]

The presented approaches with their indicator sets and methods were evaluated in a team of experts, being experienced in factory location problems and sustainable factory approaches. The evaluation was based on the tripartite scale shown in Table 2. The "plus" shows a full fulfillment, the "o" a partially fulfillment and the "minus" a non-fulfillment. In the following the results of the assessment are summarized.

Dimension of Sustainability: None of the indicator sets covers the whole spectrum of sustainability. The indicator sets are mostly specialized on one or two dimensions. The social and institutional dimension of sustainability is not recognized at all.

Strategicity: Strategicity aspects are more or less recognized in all approaches. The scope on life cycle effects by using for example a life cycle assessment method or tool can only be found within the new approaches focusing on sustainability aspects.

Database: The database-criteria are generally fulfilled by all sets and methods. However, the availability of data is a problem in some countries. A similar result is identified for the transparency-criterion. The origin of the database and thus their transparency and integrity is recognized, but does not meet the full extent.

Indexes/ Indicators: Regarding indicators, the levels of objectivity and quantification were evaluated. Conventional approaches of location finding use objective and subjective assessment indicators in their sets. In particular, complex issues are subjectively evaluated by experts. However, the sustainability-oriented approaches based on mathematical models use objective and quantitative criteria.

Methodology: The conventional indicator sets and evaluation methods for facility locations are based on a static environment and do not sufficiently take into account future influences. This applies to the factory itself, but mostly the future development of its environment. Also, the opportunities for a proactive development of locations and their surroundings are not included in methodologies. Another potential of the classical approaches can be identified in the consideration of side effects. In this context, sustainability-oriented approaches based on mathematical models have an advantage. They analyze this interaction by multi-criteria analysis.

Table 2. Results of the evaluation process

Dimension of Sustainability	Social	-	-	-	-	o	+	+	-
	Ecological	o	+	o	-	-	+	+	+
	Economical	o	+	-	o	o	+	+	+
	Institutional	-	+	o	-	-	-	-	-
Strategicity	Holistic View	o	+	o	-	-	+	o	o
	Life Cycle Orientation	-	o	-	-	o	o	o	+
Database	Data availability	o	o	o	o	o	+	+	+
	Transparency	o	o	o	o	o	o	o	o
Indexes/ Indicators	Quantitative level	o	o	o	o	o	+	+	+
	Level ofobjectivity	o	o	o	o	o	-	-	+
Methodology	Interdisciplinary	+	+	+	+	+	-	-	-
	Generic applicability	+	+	+	+	+	+	+	+
	Proactive	-	-	-	-	-	-	-	o
	Side Effects	-	-	-	-	-	+	+	+
	Future influences	-	-	-	-	-	-	-	+
	Scaling / Normalization	+	+	+	+	+	+	+	+
	Participation	o	o	o	o	o	-	-	-

4   Discussion

In the following, the results of the evaluation are discussed and summarized. Conventional indicator sets and evaluation methods for facility locations mainly use qualitative assessment indicators. This creates benefits for the participation and facilitates the evaluation of complex interdependencies. However, the results depend on the composition of the planning team. This includes a risk of incorrect decisions. It was also determined that present assessment indicators are developed under the assumption of a static or slowly changing environment and a low level of complexity. If these assumptions reflect the current conditions of a volatile environment is questionable.

The new approaches with focus on sustainability concentrate on the quantification of location indicators. A major advantage of these approaches is the use of mathematical models with quantitative results for the defined conditions. However, the question is, if mathematical models are applicable to the full complexity of the factory location problem. The life cycle orientation and the consideration of future developments offer potential for future location planning, to sufficiently answering questions in extent.

In conclusion, the reviewed assessment sets and methods need to be combined. The goal of this combination is to minimize the risk and to increase the quality of the factory location finding result. A framework would provide the structural prerequisites to divide the location finding problem into modules that provide a holistic assessment as combination of conventional and new approaches in location finding.

5   Conclusion

This work aimed at the comparison of established conventional indicator sets and assessment methods for facility locations to new approaches focusing sustainability aspects. The comparison showed that conventional approaches support a more qualitative assessment. However, a weakness of conventional approaches is identified in the assumption of a static location environment, not accounting for real complexity. The missing analysis of influences from a volatile factory environment was identified as problematic. The main strength of existing sustainability-oriented approaches was identified in quantification. However, the applicability of quantitative methods in dynamic and complex systems must be examined in future research.

To conclude the results and existing research gaps, the discussion ends up with the recommendation, that existing approaches should be combined aiming at a minimization of future risks and an increase of facility location quality. A possible solution was identified in the development of a framework for combining the approaches and giving a structural concept for the holistic assessment by problem partition.

References

[1]   Chen, L., Olhager, J., Tang, O.: Manufacturing facility location and sustainability: A literature review and research agenda. International Journal of Production Economics, 154–163 (2014)

[2]   Terouhid, S.A., Ries, R., Fard, M.M.: Towards Sustainable Facility Location - A Literature Review. Journal of Sustainable Development, 18–34 (June 2012)

[3]   Dombrowski, U., Ernst, S., Riechel, C.: Methodenframework der Fabrikplanung (MeFa). wt Werkstattstechnik online 104 4(104), 197–201 (2014)

[4]   UN United Nations, Our common future, United Nations (1987)

[5]   Sala, S., Farioli, F., Zamagni, A.: Progress in sustainability science: lessons learnt from current methodologies for sustainability assessment: Part 1. International Journal Life Cycle Assess, 1653–1672 (November 2013)

[6]   Singh, R.K., Murty, H., Gupta, S., Dikshit, A.: An overview of sustainability assessment methodologies. Ecological Indicators, 281–299 (April 2012)

[7]   Cloquell-Ballester, V.-A., Cloquell-Ballester, V.-A.: Monter de-Díaz, R., Santamarina-Siurana, M.-C.: Indicators validation for the improvement of environmental and social impact quantitative assessment. Environmental Impact Assessment Review, 79–105 (January 2006)

[8]   Chen, D., Schudeleit, T., Posselt, G., Thiede, S.: A State-of-the-art Review and Evaluation of Tools for Factory Sustainability Assessment. Procedia CIRP, 85–90 (2013)

[9]   Labuschagne, C., Brent, A.C., van Erck, R.P.G.: Assessing the sustainability performance of industries, pp. 373–385 (2005)

[10] U. U. N. D. f. S. Development, Indicators of sustainable development: Guidelines and Methodologies,
      http://www.un.org/esa/sustdev/publications/indisd-mg2001.pdf

[11] Spangenberg, J.H., Pfahl, S., Deller, K.: Towards indicators for institutional sustainability: lessons from an analysis of Agenda 21. Ecological Indicators 2, 61–77 (2002)

[12] Strohm, O., Ulich, E.: Integral Analysis and Evaluation of Enterprises: A Multilevel Approach in Terms of People, Technology, and Organization. Human Factors and Ergonomics in Manufacturing 8(3), 233–250 (1998)

[13] Kettner, H., Schmidt, J., Greim, H.-R.: Leitfaden der systematischen Fabrikplanung. Carl Hanser Verlag, Hannover (1984)

[14] Aggteleky, B.: Fabrikplanung - Band 1. Carl Hanser Verlag, Wien (1987)

[15] Wiendahl, H.-P., Reichardt, J., Nyhuis, P.: Handbuch Fabrikplanung. Carl Hanser Verlag, Hannover (2009)

[16] Pawellek, G.: Ganzheitliche Fabrikplanung - Grundlagen, Vorgehensweise, EDV-Unterstützung. Springer, Hamburg-Harburg (2008)

[17] Eagan, P.D., Joeres, E.: Development of a facility-based environmental performance indicator related to sustainable development. Journal of Cleaner Production, 269–278 (1997)

[18] Corbière-Nicollier, T., Blanc, I., Erkman, S.: Towards a global criteria based framework for the sustainability assessment of bioethanol supply chains Application to the Swiss dilemma: Is local produced bioethanol more sustainable than bioethanol imported from Brazil? Ecological Indicators, 1447–1458 (September 2011)

[19] Reich-Weiser, C., Dornfeld, D.: A discussion of greenhouse gas emission tradeoffs and water scarcity within the supply chain. Journal of Manufacturing Systems, 23–27 (2009)

[20] Schenk, M., Wirth, S.: Fabrikplanung und Fabrikbetrieb - Methoden für die wandlungsfähige und vernetzte Fabrik. Springer, Chemnitz (2004)

Manufacturing System Design Decomposition
for Sustainability

Marco Taisch, Bojan Stahl, Gokan May, and Matteo Cocco

Politecnico di Milano, Department of Management,
Economics and Industrial Engineering, Milan, Italy
{marco.taisch,bojan.stahl,matteo.cocco}@polimi.it

Abstract. The paper provides insights into the operations strategy definition process. While literature seeks the concept of manufacturing strategy content with competitive priorities, decision categories and manufacturing capabilities to explain strategy definition ambitions, practice shows difficulty in applying this high level concept in practical terms. Sustainability and the wide array of incorporation opportunities and policies make it difficult for companies to leap the gap towards a truly sustainably firm. Based on the methodology of axiomatic design, the study develops in a prescriptive research setting a meta-framework for supporting strategy definition in manufacturing firms.

Keywords: sustainability, manufacturing strategy, axiomatic design.

1   Introduction

How firms can turn sustainable manufacturing into a competitive weapon, so as to alleviate upstream and downstream performance improvements along the triple bottom line, while reducing environmental harm and stimulating social solidarity, is a major area for research [1]. The development and deployment of adequate sustainable manufacturing strategies are still open issues and of utmost interest both for research and practice [2].

Besides a lack of process deployment as well as trade-off understanding, the definition of a sustainable manufacturing strategy coherent with other functional and business strategies is a practical gap [3]. Especially the internal consistency of manufacturing strategy, i.e. the translation of competitive priorities into decision categories in order to form, expand or maintain manufacturing capabilities, and the design of appropriate manufacturing improvement programs to enable strategic choices, is a major obstacle for companies nowadays. The development of competitive edge is not led to by the linear adding of pollution prevention projects or by the adoption of certain environmental or social standards or certifications following the motto one size fits it all. Moreover, taking the XPS (company-specific production system) approach as a model for designing firm-tailored production systems [4], in the same way firms have to be capable to tailor their strategy to their system, structure, culture and product in order to reach beyond low hanging fruits benefits. In this article, we propose a framework based on Axiomatic Design (AD) principles which can guide top management and decision-makers in operationalizing their firm's manufacturing strategy.

B. Grabot et al. (Eds.): APMS 2014, Part II, IFIP AICT 439, pp. 254–261, 2014.

2   Background

Manufacturing strategy as a discipline was initiated ca. 40 years ago as it was recognized by US scholars that linking long-term decisions in manufacturing with business strategy may have a positive impact on business performance and create competitive advantage [5]. Manufacturing strategy is the deployment and adjustment of manufacturing capabilities by patterns of decisions to efficiently and effectively exploit the manufacturing function by means of its resources for the purpose of maximizing the competitive advantage while maintaining consistency with higher corporate goals and strategies. Based on the pioneering work of Wickham Skinner, two different research streams have emerged in the field: manufacturing strategy content and manufacturing strategy process.

The research on content sets the substance of decisions and its junction into the focus and accompanying changes in the structure and infrastructure of a firm's manufacturing system. The research on process on the other hand enlightens the ways in how strategy is formulated and operationalized. Another popular term used by scholars here is also manufacturing strategy formulation or formation. Leong et al. (1990) introduced the predominant theoretical construct in manufacturing strategy content which is composed of competitive priorities, decision categories and manufacturing capabilities [6]. Krajewski and Ritzman define competitive priorities as "the dimensions that a firm's production system must possess to support the demands of the markets that the firm wishes to compete in" [7]. The strategic choices made in manufacturing strategy can be classified into structural and infrastructural decision areas [8]. Decisions in the structural area have influence on the physical resources, while infrastructural decision impact their relationship and activities within operations. Most decisions cannot be ordered along these archetypes, but have a hybrid effect. While competitive priorities are intended capabilities and future models of the strengths of the company, manufacturing capabilities are priorities put in practice or priorities put to work via decision categories [9]. Manufacturing capabilities refer therefore to a firm's operations performance relative to its competitors, and the alignment of priorities and capabilities, i.e. creating good strategic fit, reflects an efficient and effective allocation of resources for capability development [10].

The advancement within the manufacturing strategy process research is rived into macro and micro process views. The macro process view is characterized by a top-down approach, with the aim of emphasizing the link from business strategy to the functional manufacturing strategy, and the focus towards the consistency of hierarchy of strategies. On the other hand, the micro process view is made upon bottom-up or integrative views, emphasizes the link of the manufacturing strategy to the manufacturing function, and the translation function of competitive priorities into strategic manufacturing initiatives [11].

The introduction of sustainability into research on operations management has gained large popularity among scholars. Kleindorfer et.al (2005) define sustainable OM as "the set of skills and concepts that allow a company to structure and manage its business processes to obtain a competitive return on its capital assets without sacrificing the legitimate needs of internal and external stakeholders and with due regard for the impact of its operations on people and the environment" [1].

Sustainability in manufacturing strategy as a research endeavor has gained momentum. In the past years research was mainly empirically investigating the introduction of sustainability as a competitive priority in the corporate agenda. Most researchers have focused on the environmental pillar in their studies, while social pillar has received less attention. Findings are contradictory with no or little explanation for differentiations. While some studies refuse the hypothesis of sustainability as a competitive priority [12], others include it successfully in other manufacturing strategy constructs like the extended sandcone model [13]. While researchers have mainly focused on scientific inquiries on competitive priorities, the areas of decision categories or the entire spectrum within the manufacturing strategy process field are largely neglected. The aim of the paper is to fill this gap and develop a practical framework to incorporate sustainability into manufacturing strategy content.

3   Methodology

Past research in the field was largely empirically driven. Although this is needed and relevant, the theoretical, prescriptive, and modern perspective might be lost and leave innovative ideas and concepts aside.

The research endeavour takes over a pragmatist epistemological point of view in a prescriptive research setting. The research question is: *how can firms translate the sustainability principle into their manufacturing strategy*. Since a pattern or methodological guidance cannot be gathered from its complex environmental situation due to lack of empirical studies and lack of proven approaches, we decided to embed our research in a prescriptive research setting. It enables us to design an approach based on axiomatic instead of empirical reasoning. Through deductive reasoning we can apply and test the approach in a case setting, which in turn can serve later as inductive testing for empirical-based research.

This paper reports research in which axiomatic design methodology is used to model the strategy content of a sustainable manufacturing system which consist of functional requirements, design parameters and process variables. Axiomatic design (AD) as a design framework was created by Professor Suh of the Massachusetts Institute of Technology [14]. Here, design is seen as the interplay between "what we want to achieve" and "how we want to achieve"; thus consistently differentiating between goals and means (or solutions). Typically the design process follows a five step procedure, i.e. identifying customer needs, problem definition (problem to solve for need satisfaction), solution(s) creation, analysis and optimization, solution fit. Using the Axiomatic Design approach by Suh, sustainability goals are purposely translated into functional requirements. The four main concepts around axiomatic design are domains, hierarchies, zigzagging and design axioms.

Typically there are four domains distinguished (see Figure 1). Left domains define what should be achieved while right domains defines how it should be achieved. The customer domain contains customer requirements, needs, expectations, specifications and anticipations. These are then translated into the functional domain as functional requirements (FR). Functional requirements are independent from each other and characterize the minimum solution to a given design problem. The design parameters (DP) are specifications within the solution in the physical domain that are chosen to specify the FRs. In the same way, process variables (PV) characterize the process that satisfies the DPs in the process domain.

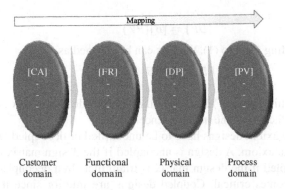

Fig. 1. Domain perspective in Axiomatic Design

Hierarchies are the second main concept in axiomatic design. Hierarchies refer to the design architecture of a model. Decomposition is a terminology often used in this junction and refers to the development of functional requirements and design parameters in the next lower level based upon the next higher level FRs and DPs. This process is iterated until concreteness for implementation is reached. At the end the model is composed of different levels of hierarchies.

The third main concept of axiomatic design is zigzagging that describes the process of decomposing the design into hierarchies by alternating between pairs of domains. Hereby, starting from e.g. of the FR 1 of hierarchical layer a, the designer crosses domains and chooses design parameter 1 for the same hierarchical layer and then crosses again domains and goes back to the functional domain to define sub-level requirements of FR1.

The fourth concept is design axioms. Two axioms provide a basis for the best fit selections among different design scenarios. The Independence Axiom states that the independence of the FRs must be maintained. This means that in an acceptable design, a DP can be adjusted to satisfy its corresponding FR without affecting other FRs. And the Information Axiom states that the information content must be minimized. Of the alternative designs that fulfill the Independence Axiom the best design has the minimum content. It can be translated that simpler designs are more preferable to other designs.

The relationship between FRs and DPs is given as follows:

$$\{FR\} = [A]\{DP\} \tag{1}$$

A is the design matrix from which each element can be expressed as

$$A_{ij} = \partial FR_i / \partial DP_j \tag{2}$$

Each line of the vector stated in (1) can be written as

$$FR_i = \sum A_{ij} DP_j \tag{3}$$

Similarly the relationship between DPs and PVs is described by a design matrix B as

$$\{DP\} = [B]\{PV\} \tag{4}$$

Hence, including (4) into (1), the FRs can be defined as

$$\{FR\} = [A][B]\{PV\} \tag{5}$$

The relationship between FR-DP-PV through the design matrix A and B is important for the satisfaction of the independence axioms.

To satisfy the axiom designs have to be uncoupled or decoupled, while coupled designs infringe the axiom. A design is uncoupled if the design matrix is diagonal; and a design is decoupled if the design matrix is triangular. In a decoupled design the path dependency becomes critical. Coupled designs are inferior since it is impossible to adjust either DP without affecting other FRs. Hence, the construct of the desired FR can only achieved by a iterative trial-and-error procedure. In the following, a glance at sustainable manufacturing system decomposition is presented.

4   Axiomatic Model of Sustainable Production Systems

4.1   Viability as Firm's Objective

In the following we state that the major objective of a sustainable firm is not solely including environmental soundness and social solidarity into their corporate agenda. The major objective is to maximize the viability of the firm. Here, viability is defined according to the systems theory or cybernetics perspective, i.e. maintaining a separate existence. Viability means that a determined configuration of states can be maintained by the organization without time constraints. To emphasize this, from a cybernetic point of view viability is a typical metasystemic measure for the assessment of a system concerning its structural effectiveness. Viability in enterprise context means to maintain a change process due to its environment, its identity, and its primary activities and due to itself [15].

4.2   First Level Decomposition

Based on the concept of viability, all organizations pursue it as their ultimate goal. Viability is the central focus of an organizations purpose and all activities within the organization should be allocated to this target. It is assumed that pursuing sustainability in the broader sense enables an organization to fulfill the viability principle in the best way. Figure 2 shows the top FRs, DPs and PVs as well as the FRs of the first level decomposition based on the viability principle for a manufacturing system pursuing sustainable strategy.

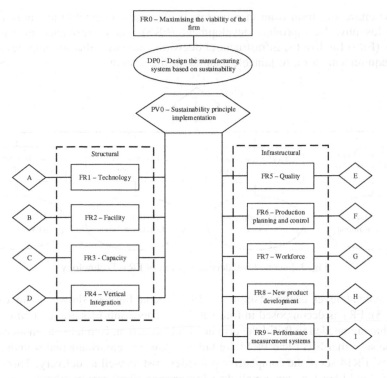

Fig. 2. Organization's top level domain and first decomposition

The technology (FR1) as well as capacity (FR3) asserts emphasis on the product type, i.e. either high volume and undifferentiated or low volume and customer specific. Regarding the vertical integration (FR4) decision-makers ponder developing and producing parts on their own or buying them in. Vertical integration might not only apply to product parts, but to entire departments or product families. The size, capacity and location (FR2, FR3) of facilities are of utmost interest in the manufacturing strategy planning activities. While large factories support economies of scales and high volume production, smaller factories are easier to align to flexibility. The plant location (FR2) may be chosen due to different factors including location of raw material and component suppliers, location of customers, transportation and communication systems, qualification of workforce, legislation and taxes. These structural decisions are added by infrastructural decisions. Production and inventory planning as well as accordant control systems (FR6) are putting two major decisions in place, i.e. centralization and decentralization as well as pull or push systems of the factory. The organizational structure of factories can be based on normality, i.e. hierarchical structure and cost center orientation with clear procedures and low level of decision making, or on autonomy, i.e. viewing the factory as a profit center with enriched degrees of freedom for the middle managers and workforce in making decisions to solve operational problems. Human resource management (FR7) around manufacturing strategy involves areas like payment system, recruitment process, worker-to-job assignment, incentive policies and so on. Quality management (FR5) can be spread from the entire spectrum from merely statistical process control to an entire production philosophy. New product development (FR8) and performance measurement systems (FR9) finalize the infrastructural decision categories that are high level functional requirements for a sustainable manufacturing system.

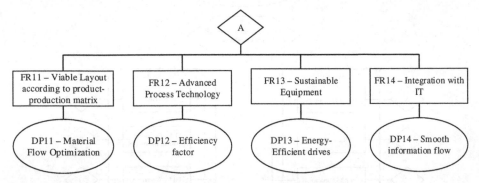

Fig. 3. Second level decomposition of FR1-Technology

The second level decomposition for FR1-Technology is shown as an example (Figure 3). FR1 is decomposed in four sub-FRs. These sub-FRs are the main requirements that are needed to fulfill the primary FR1 objective. Extracted from an example it can be seen that FR11 and FR13 are tailored towards environmental soundness and FR12 and FR14 serve the competitive priorities cost as well as delivery. This decomposition should be done among all decision criteria. Furthermore, the decomposition should be performed in recursions until saturation and clarity of the objectives and the method to reach them is arrived. While in the second recursion the FRs are still quite abstract, following decompositions can define in detail the requirements, parameters and variables for a sustainable manufacturing system.

5   Summary and Outlook

The study presented in the paper developed a framework for the design of a sustainable manufacturing systems and the definition of a sustainable manufacturing strategy. The framework is based on Axiomatic Design principles and builds upon decision categories developed in manufacturing strategy. The research serves two major contributions. First, it presents a scientifically motivated hands-on approach for decision makers to define their firm's manufacturing strategy content. Second, it supports the neglected integration of product and production focus in manufacturing strategy which was largely disregarded in the field of operations management.

The research faces two major limitations. First, an application case is mandatory to manifest the value potential of the approach and should be done in future work. Second, other tools in strategic management like scenario technique or SWOT analysis etc. have not been yet considered, hence predictions how the AD approach can be used in combination with other established techniques is not clear.

Future research shall concentrate on overcoming the above stated limitations. Furthermore, and of utmost importance, is to bridge the gap between strategy definition and strategy implementation. While it is among scholars commonly accepted that manufacturing improvement programs are the way to operationalize manufacturing strategy and build up capabilities, it is theoretically and practically unclear how to translate a defined strategy into concrete actions without lining up certain programs and certifications, but heaving the manufacturing system beyond the low hanging fruits.

Acknowledgements. This work was partly funded by the European Commission through the Linked Design Project (FP7-2011-NMP-ICT-FoF, http://www. linkeddesign.eu/). The authors wish to acknowledge their gratitude and appreciation to the rest of the project partners for their contributions during the development of various ideas and concepts presented in this paper.

References

1. Kleindorfer, P.R., Singhal, K., van Wassenhove, L.N.: Sustainable Operations Management. Prod. Oper. Manag. 14(4), 482–492 (2005)
2. Drake, D.F., Spinler, S.: Sustainable Operations Management: An enduring stream or a passing fancy? Manuf. Serv. Oper. Manag. 15(4), 689–700 (2013)
3. Mirvis, P., Googins, B., Kinnicutt, S.: Vision, mission, values: Guideposts to sustainability. Organ. Dyn. 39(4), 316–324 (2010)
4. Netland, T., Aspelund, A.: Company-specific production systems and competitive advantage: a resource-based view on the Volvo Production System. Int. J. Oper. Prod. Manag. 33(11/12), 1511–1531 (2013)
5. Demeter, K.: Manufacturing strategy and competitiveness. Int. J. Prod. Econ. 81-82(1), 205–213 (2003)
6. Leong, G.K., Snyder, D.L., Ward, P.T.: Research in the process of manufacturing strategy. Omega 18(2), 109–122 (1990)
7. Krajewski, L.J., Ritzmann: Operations Management: Strategy and Analysis, 3rd edn. Addison-Wesley, Wokingham (1993)
8. Hayes, R.H., Wheelwright, S.C.: Restoring our competitive edge: competing through manufacturing. Wiley and Sons, New York (1984)
9. Ward, P.T., Bickford, D.J., Leong, G.K.: Configurations of manufacturing strategy, business strategy, environment and structure. J. Manage. 22(4), 597–626 (1996)
10. Schoenherr, T., Narasimhan, R.: The fit between capabilities and priorities and its impact on performance improvement: revisiting and extending the theory of production competence. Int. J. Prod. Res. 50(14), 3755–3775 (2012)
11. Kim, J.S., Arnold, P.: Operationalizing manufacturing strategy – an exploratory study of constructs and linkage. Int. J. Oper. Prod. Manag., Bol. 16(12), 45–73 (1996)
12. Thuerer, M., Filho, M.G., Stevenson, M., Fredendall, L.D.: Competitive priorities of small manufacturers in Brazil. Ind. Mang. Data Syst. 113(6), 856–874 (2013)
13. Avella, L., Vazquez-Bustelo, D., Fernandez, E.: Cumulative manufacturing capabilities: an extended model and new empirical evidence. Int. J. Prod. Res. 49(3), 707–729 (2011)
14. Suh, N.P.: Axiomatic Design. Oxford University Press, New York (2001)
15. Beer, S.: The Heart of Enterprise. Wiley, Chichester (1979)

Managing Supply Chain Disturbances – Review and Synthesis of Existing Contributions

Michael Schenk and Volker Stich

Institute for Industrial Management at RWTH Aachen University
(FIR an der RWTH Aachen), Germany
{michael.schenk,volker.stich}@fir.rwth-aachen.de

Abstract. Companies suffer the effects of disturbances in supply chains more than ever. Highly dynamical consumer demands and globalized supply chains often lead to unplanned supply chain events through to break-downs causing inability to supply. Consequently, concepts for an efficient supply chain disturbance management are needed, preferably with a real-time reaction to disturbance events. Academic literature comprises many investigations dealing with such approaches. In this paper we examine both a range of methodological contributions to design resilient supply chains and approaches for the flexible coordination of supply chain processes in case of disturbances. After summarizing the major contributions, we point out an approach for a real-time supply chain disturbance management with the target to achieve the required flexibility for coping with supply chain disturbances.

Keywords: Supply Chain Management, Supply Chain Disturbances, Supply Chain Resilience, Supply Chain Event Management, Disturbance Management.

1   Introduction

The rising global cross-linking of production and sales regions increases steadily the complexity of supply chains. This leads to an increasing sensitivity to disturbances while in the meantime the requirements of the availability, the time of delivery and the security of supplies within the supply chain increases. [1, 2, 3]

The complexity of this development affects not only strategic considerations of industrial companies, but is also a constant component of their daily business. The companies have to meet high requirements on all levels, from the supply chain design top-down to the supply chain execution. Especially the security of the infrastructure needs to be ensured and complex supply chain processes need to be feasible, despite the high specialisation within the supply chain partners, the low stock and time buffers and the information shortcoming between supply chain partners. The industrial companies currently show obvious deficiencies in managing disturbances within their supply chains. On the one hand the understanding of disturbances and their impacts on the supply chain as well as a suitable integration of a cross-company disturbance management are not developed. On the other hand the applied ICT systems cannot stand up to the increasing requirements, because their implemented set of actions isn't applicable in most cases to counteract occurring disturbances with the required excellence [4].

B. Grabot et al. (Eds.): APMS 2014, Part II, IFIP AICT 439, pp. 262–269, 2014.

In recent years the research has therefore generated different approaches to deal with the increasing impacts of supply chain disturbances [5, 6, 7]. Also, first ICT based approaches like the supply chain event management are developed to reduce the vulnerability of supply chains by providing real-time information of disturbances.

In the next chapter, we will give an outline both of recent literature on the design of resilient supply chains and operative management approaches for dealing with disturbances in supply chains. In chapter three we will point out the deficits of the existing approaches and finally identify further need for research, including a first example.

2   Literature Review on Supply Chain Disturbances Management

2.1   Designing Resilient Supply Chains

The design of resilient supply chains is one prominent potential to compete with the growing market dynamics and the increasing vulnerability of global supply chains. But due to the recentness of this topic hardly any literature can be found that deals with this subject. According to [4] and [8] resilient supply chains possess the ability to compete with unpredicted disturbances and quickly regain their original state or move over to a new, improved state and to adapt to the new constraints. Therefore, [9] defined four fundamental principles. First of all, the business processes need to be reengineered by taking into account both possible disturbances and the aim to reduce complexity. Further principles are the need for intense cooperation within the supply chain, high supply chain agility as well as the setup of a supply chain risk management culture.

[10] identified based on a literature review different management strategies to mitigate the impact of disturbances with all can be assigned to the above mentioned principles. [11] highlighted in his work that from all assigned strategies, two strategies have the highest potential to achieve resilience. It's the raise of flexibility and the integration of redundancies by provision of additional capacities.

Following the strategy of flexibility [12] described in their approach a design method for a reconfigurable supply chain network by optimizing inventory allocation and transportation routing. [13] also designed a model of a multi-stage global supply chain network including rating a set of risk factors. The model shows, that by an inter-echelon shifting of quantity flows, the overall cost of the supply chain can be minimized in the event of disturbances.

Even though all authors refer in their way to the four principles of [9], some authors indicate that not all of the included strategies are generally adaptive as they have their specific downsides. The strategy of redundant capacities for example is accompanied by high cost and acts opposed to the lean thinking which many companies are following [11]. On the other hand, the strategy to increase flexibility with the effect to react faster to disturbances comes along with significant lower downsides.

[14] developed a method for the evaluation and selection of the preferred strategy to increase the supply chain resilience as preceding to the implementation of any action a cost-benefit analysis is inevitable. [15] also developed a method for evaluation based on a control engineering approach. Counter-intuitively their findings imply that optimum solutions for resilience do not create a system that is robust to disturbances affecting the lead time.

However, many fundamental elements of supply chain resilience, e.g. the links between risks and implications for supply chain management as well as their interconnection, are still unknown and there is still a lot of research that has to be done to close these knowledge gaps.

2.2   Increasing the Flexibility of Supply Chain Planning and Control Processes

As seen in the preceding chapter, based on the design of resilient supply chains, companies need to seek for new management methods to cope with disturbances on the planning and execution levels in existing supply chains with the target to increase their flexibility.

The mayor part of research works on this topic, especially the older ones, is focusing on design models to support the flexibility management in a specific production unit or a particular company and is missing the aspects of cross-company processes between the supply chain partners. [16] gives a comprehensive overview on such approaches.

In the research project PROLOG ([17]) concepts for prospective disturbances in supply chains were developed resulting in a guideline for the implementation of a preventive disturbance management by an early identification of internal and external disturbances. The approach is limited to guidelines for the project management of a individually performed disturbance management.

On the other hand [18] analyzed symptom patterns for disturbances in company networks and allocated adequate action propositions. The work, however, concentrates on the strategic to tactical level of the supply chain planning and control and describes many interdependencies only qualitatively. A coordination concept in the form of processes and information flows for the reaction on disturbances is also not subject of the work. Still, both approaches either don't or only marginally examine enterprise-wide interdependencies in supply chain planning associated to the disturbance management. Therefore the following research approaches explicitly aim to improve the coordination of supply chain planning and control tasks.

[19] developed an agent-based concept for cross-system production planning to increase the responsiveness in the supply chain. The focus of the work is the examination of the information exchange and the design of the various planning agents. However, interdependencies of logistical disturbances are not considered in detail.

The aim of the research project IPRONET [20] was the development of an internet based tool for the cross company support of manufacturing companies in supply chains. However, the disturbance management is reduced to the early identification of capacity constraints by an increased demand or reduced facilities and the simulative calculation of action possibilities.

In the research alliance LINET, the aim of a cooperative requirement and capacity planning was pursued for the supply chains in the automotive industry [21]. Its core functionalities include the monitoring of bottleneck capacity, coordination of production programs, the simulation of capacity allocation plans as well as a workflow supported emergency management. The approach from [22] focused on a collaborative supply chain re-scheduling. It allows cooperative re-scheduling by the selection of the type of transport for sending components from one supply chain partner to another based on the target date and the costs to assemble the final product. Further, [23] designed in his work a case-based reasoning model for the selection of adequate actions to effectively deal with supply chain disturbances.

Another mayor topic to increase the flexibility of supply chain and thus be able to react faster is the enhancement of transparency of information in supply chains [24, 25, 26, 27]. Existing Supply chain event management systems (SCEM systems) are therefore a good leverage point. Based on a target-performance comparison they detect disturbance events and support the monitoring, planning and control of supply chains [27]. Another model for evaluation and control of risks in supply chains regarding both cost and environmental (e.g. traffic, weather) influences can be developed by using available approaches e.g. the complex event processing. Therefore flows of events from the supply chain are aggregated and combined to monitor parameters in real-time [28, 29].

Regarding existing supply chain software [26] underlined the innovation of supply chain event management systems in the functionalities of monitoring and notification as well as in the optimization of supply chain processes using long-term data evaluations. But in general nowadays available SCEM systems are still limited to monitor unplanned events and inform affected business units. To take measures like the replanning of supply chains processes conventional systems as ERP or APS systems are commonly used. SCEM systems still apply as mere pulsing devices which do not give any active decision support [30]. They still lack both in the identification & management and the communication & coordination of disturbances. The limited consideration of logistical interdependences and the insufficient differentiation of disturbances lead to a deficient possibility to derive action propositions and lower the consistency from the identification of disturbances to the adjustment.

[31] stated in his work the importance of incentives and trust among multiple supply chain partners. If supply chain partners lack of trust to each other, then even a basic integration and real-time data flows will be problematic. Also, the whole supply chain will suffer if partners have no incentives to orchestrate their technology with the others.

3   Creating a Real-Time Supply Chain Disturbance Management

The literature review gives an overview, how today's methods and solutions from the supply chain management encounter the challenges of an increasing vulnerability to supply chain disturbances. As the review on the design approaches for resilient supply chains has shown, one mayor potential lies in the strategy of more flexible supply chains including a faster reaction to disturbances and an intense cooperation between the supply chain partners. But as seen, the existing approaches for the operational disturbance management on the supply chain level are still insufficiently designed. In this area, on the one hand the disturbance management is not considered entirely with all its facets, and on the other hand the shown approaches do not focus the real-time reaction to disturbance events and their impacts on the supply chain.This problem is extended by the lack of a comprehensive ICT-based support by supply chain event management systems.

Table 1. Overview of major contributions to the management of supply chain disturbances

Focus of investigation	Supply chain resilience							Operative management approaches										
	Christopher & Peck, [9]	Barroso et al., [10]	Sheffi, [11]	Kristianto et al., [12]	Singh et al., [13]	Ziegenbein, [14]	Spiegler et al., [15]	Meyer, [16]	PROLOG, [17]	Zeller, [18]	Stiefbold, [19]	IPRONET, [20]	LINET, [21]	Lloret et al., [22]	Daohai, [23]	Iijioui et al., [27]	Luckham, [28]	Buchmann & Koldehofe, [29]
Literatur review	●	●					○	●		○							○	○
Methodology and Framework	●		●				●	●	●	●	●	○	○			●	●	○
Analytical Methods				●	●	●	●						○	●	●			
Flexibility strategies	○	●		●	●			○	●	○	●	○	●	●	○			
ICT-support								○				●	●			●	●	●
Simulation study														●	●			

Based on the preceding literature review on existing approaches and the summarization of arisen potentials, different requirements can be derived to achieve the target of a real-time supply chain disturbance management. Besides the basic requirements for a holistic consideration of the supply chain disturbance management, including the cross-company coordination between supply chain partners and an increased transparency by the availability of real-time information on disturbances in the supply chain, also aspects of a sociotechnical integration of human and technics, the recursive design of the system and the sufficient interconnection between the different planning and execution levels need to be ensured. As an example how to lever these potentials, the authors want to highlight the on-going research project SMART LOGISTIC GRIDS. The focus of the research project is the design of an ICT-based system to provide adequate action propositions to encounter disturbance events and consequently increase the efficiency and robustness of the supply chain. This requires a flawless integration of different actors along the supply chain, as well as an increased information transparency and availability of disturbance events. Focal issues are the development of a supply chain monitoring and control unit and the provision of global supply chain events by a cloud service. The information about supply chain events is provided by the cloud service, which gathers and aggregates it to complex events. In the supply chain control unit this information is compiled and visualized. The unit enables an optimized execution and control of the supply chain based on the aggregated real-time information of the supply chain. The system provides different, evaluated action propositions to optimize the supply chain both by economical and resource efficiency considerations. Thus additional transport costs due to problems in the supply chain can be reduced or entirely avoided and an increased deliver capacity of the supply chain can be ensured.

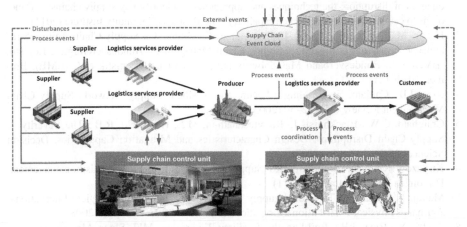

Fig. 1. Target system of the research project Smart Logistic Grids

4   Conclusion

The increasing dynamics in consumer demand patterns and the vulnerability of globalized supply chains leads to an increased requirements for coping with supply chain disturbances. As the literature review shows, different works already approach the topic of designing resilient supply chains and managing disturbances in a supply chain. Further, existing ICT solutions like supply chain event management systems partly support to handle supply chain disturbances. But despite the amount of ongoing research and the flurry of supply chain improvement programs, the competitive advantage and distinguish characteristic of future supply chains will be their flexibility, in particular to react on supply chain disturbances in real-time. Therefore, real-time information, real-time coordination between supply chain partners, and optimized action propositions are needed. The presented research project Smart Logistic Grids focuses such an approach by developing an event cloud and a supply chain control unit. Furthermore, a closer collaboration between industry and research units is need, to develop, implement and evaluate effective actions to supply chain disturbances. Thus, best practices can be gathered and standards be developed.

Acknowledgement. This paper as well as the project SMART LOGISTIC GRIDS are funded by the Federal Ministry for Economic Affairs and Energy (BMWi; funding code: 19 G 13002C).

References

1. Deloitte: Supply Chain Resilience: A Risk Intelligent approach to managing global supply chains, p. 7 (2012)
2. The Business Continuity Institute: Supply Chain Resilience 2011 - An international survey of more than 550 organizations from over 60 countries, which considers the causes and consequences of disruption, the techniques and approaches to identify key supply chains, and methods to gain assurance of resilience capability. The Business Continuity Institute (2011)
3. Henke, M., Lasch, R., Eckstein, D., Neumüller, C., Blome, C.: Supply Chain Agility. Strategische Anpassungsfähigkeit im Supply Chain Management. Bundesvereinigung Logistik (BVL) e.V., Bundesverband Materialwirtschaft, Einkauf und Logistik e.V. (BME), Bremen 10 (2012)
4. Rice, J.B., Caniato, F.: Building a Secure and Resilient Supply Network. Supply Chain Management Review 7(5), 22–30 (2003)
5. Craighaid, C.W., Blackhurst, J., Rungtusanathan, M.J., Handfield, R.B.: The Severity of Supply Chain Disruptions: Design Characteristics and Mitigation Capabilities. Decision Sciences 38(1), 131–156 (2007)
6. Kiryazov, K.: Netzwerkorientiertes Supply Chain Controlling und Risikomanagement. Diplomica Verlag, Hamburg (2011)
7. Manuj, I., Mentzer, J.T.: Global supply chain risk management strategies. International Journal of Physical Distribution& Logistics Management 383, 192–223 (2008)
8. Sheffi, Y., Rice, J.B.: Building the Resilient Enterprise. MIT Sloan Management Review 47(1), 41–48 (2005)
9. Christopher, M., Peck, H.: Building the Resilient Supply Chain. International Journal of Logistics Management 2(15), 1–13 (2004)
10. Barroso, A.P., Machado, V.H., Barros, A.R., Machado, V.C.: Toward a Resilient Supply Chain with Supply Disturbances. In: 2010 IEEE International Conference on Industrial Engineering and Engineering Management (IEEM), pp. 245–249. IEEE Press, New York (2010)
11. Sheffi, T.: Building a resilient Supply Chain. Harvard Business Review 1(8), 1–12 (2005)
12. Kristianto, Y., Gunasekaran, A., Helo, P., Hao, Y.: A model of resilient supply chain network design: A two-stageprogramming with fuzzy shortest path. Expert Systems with Applications 41, 39–49 (2014)
13. Singh, A.R., Mishra, P.K., Jain, R., Khurana, M.K.: Design of global supply chain network with operational risks. Int. J. Adv. Manuf. Technol. 60, 273–290 (2012)
14. Ziegenbein, A.: Supply Chain Risiken: Identifikation, Bewertung und Steuerung, p. 117. vdf Hochschulverlag AG, Zürich (2007)
15. Spiegler, V.L.M., Naim, M.M., Wikner, J.: A control engineering approach to the assessment of supply chain resilience. International Journal of Production Research 50(21), 6162–6187 (2012)
16. Meyer, M.: Logistisches Störungsmanagement inkundenverbrauchsorientierten Wertschöpfungsketten. Shaker Verlag, Aachen (2007)
17. PROLOG (ed.): Handlungsanleitung zur Störungsprävention. Ergebnisdokumentation zum Forschungsprojekt PROLOG: Prospektive Störfallkonzepte in Logistikketten der Zulieferindustrie, p. 4 (2004),
http://www.tu-ehemnitz.de/mb/lnstBF/prologtstart.htm

18. Zeller, A.J.: Möglichkeiten einer maschinellen Verknüpfung von Diagnose undTherapie beim Controlling von Liefernetzen. Teil 11: Diagnose und Therapie. FORWIN-Bericht-Nr.: FWN-2004.005, p. 2. Bayerischer Forschungsverbund Wirtschaftsinformatik, Würzburg (2004)

19. Stiefbold, O.: Konzeption eines reaktionsschnellen Planungssystems für Logistikkettenauf Basis von Software-Agenten. Ansatz zur Planung und Steuerung von verteilten Produktionssystemen mit heterogenen IV-Systemen. Dissertation Universität Karlsruhe. Institut für Werkzeugmaschinen und Betriebstechnik (iwb), Karlsruhe (1998)

20. IPRONET (ed.): Internetbasiertes Werkzeug zur unternehmensübergreifendenkonfigurierbaren Unterstützung von produzierenden Unternehmen in Netzwerken. Abschlussbericht zum Verbundprojekt Karlsruhe (2002),
http://www.3rs.de/ipronetliproneLAB.pdf

21. VDA (ed.): Materialien zur Automobilindustrie. Future Automotive Industry Structure (FAST) 2015. Die neue Arbeitsteilung in der Automobilindustrie. Eine Studie von Mercer Management Consulting in Zusammenarbeit mit dem Fraunhofer Institut für Produktionstechnik und Automatisierung und dem Fraunhofer Institut für Materialfluss und Logistik, Stuttgart, p. 166 (2004)

22. Lloret, J., Garcia-Sabater, J.P., Marin-Garcia, J.A.: Cooperative Supply Chain Rescheduling: The Case of an Engine Supply Chain. In: Luo, Y. (ed.) CDVE 2009. LNCS, vol. 5738, pp. 376–383. Springer, Heidelberg (2009)

23. Daohai, Z.: Study on Supply Disruption Management of Supply Chain Based on Case-Based Reasoning. In: Huang, T., Zeng, Z., Li, C., Leung, C.S. (eds.) ICONIP 2012, Part IV. LNCS, vol. 7666, pp. 668–676. Springer, Heidelberg (2012)

24. Schönsleben, P., Nienhaus, J., Schnetzler, M., Sennheiser, A., Weidemann, M.: Stand und Entwicklungstendenzen in Europa. Supply Chain Management 3(1), 19–27 (2003)

25. Heusler, K.F., Stölzle, W., Bachmann, H.: Supply Chain Event Management – Grundlagen, Funktionen und potentielle Akteure. Wirtschaftswissenschaftliches Studium 35(1), 19–24 (2006)

26. Nissen, V.: Supply Chain Event Management. Wirtschaftinformatik 44(5), 477–480 (2002)

27. Ijioui, R., Emmerich, H., Ceyp, M., Diercks, W.: Supply Chain Event Management als strategisches Unternehmensführungskonzept. In: Ijioui, R., Emmerich, M. (eds.) Supply Chain Event Management – Konzepte, Prozesse, Erfolgsfaktoren, pp. 3–13. Ceyp. Physica Verlag, Heidelberg (2007)

28. Luckham, D.: The Power of Events: An Introduction to Complex Event Processing in Distributed Enterprise Systems. Addison-Wesley Longman Publishing Co., Inc., Boston (2002)

29. Buchmann, A., Koldehofe, B.: Complex Event Processing. IT – Information Technology 51(5), 241–242 (2009)

30. Bretzke, W.-R., Stölzle, W., Karrer, M., Ploenes, P.: Vom Tracking &Tracing zum Supply Chain Event Management – aktueller Stand und Trends. Studie der KPMG Consulting AG, Düsseldorf (2002)

31. O'Leary, D.E.: Supporting decisions in real-time enterprises: autonomic supply chain systems. Inf. Syst. E-Bus. Manage. 6, 239–255 (2008)

A Fuzzy Multi Criteria Approach for Evaluating Sustainability Performance of Third – Party Reverse Logistics Providers

Nadine Kafa, Yasmina Hani, and Abederrahman El Mhamedi

Equipe MGSI/ LISMMA – Université de Paris8,
140, rue de la nouvelle France, 93100 Montreuil, France
{n.kafa,y.hani,a.elmhamedi}@iut.univ-paris8.fr

Abstract. Due to the complexity and specificity of reverse logistics system, some organizations outsource all or part of the reverse logistics process to third –party provider (3PRLP). The selection of the most efficient 3PRLP is a crucial task in which it is important to take into account environmental and social criteria as well as economic criteria owing to economic interests, stakeholder pressures, and environmental legislations. The tie between all three aspects of sustainability in 3PRLP selection problem has been almost ignored. This research work deals with this issue and develops a new integrated approach for selecting the best sustainable 3PRLP. A hybrid multi-criteria making decision model is structured to assign the priority weights of decision criteria using fuzzy analytic hierarchy process (FAHP) and to get the final ranking of providers using fuzzy preference ranking organization method for enrichment evaluation (F-PROMETHEE). A numerical example is also presented to illustrate the proposed approach.

Keywords: Sustainable supply chain, reverse logistics, third-party provider selection, fuzzy AHP, fuzzy PROMETHEE.

1 Introduction

Reverse logistics (RL) is defined as a set of elements (collection, sorting, treatment, information system and distribution system) [1] deals with product returns in order to retrieve sustainable values. In today's competitive environment, different organizations take into consideration the management of reverse flows in their supply chain system. According to Kannan et al. [2] dealing with returns is a complicated issue because of the need of specialized infrastructures, the lack of experience, and considerable uncertainties regarding to delivery, quality and quantity of the returned products. Therefore, many organizations decide to outsource reverse logistics function to third-party providers (3PRLPs). On the other hand, the introduction of corporate social responsibility principles and sustainability issues in RL system is a means of developing a complete sustainable performance model [3].

Several studies have discussed sustainability issues and highlighted the importance of achieving the triple bottom line of economic, social, and environmental goals in

B. Grabot et al. (Eds.): APMS 2014, Part II, IFIP AICT 439, pp. 270–277, 2014.
© IFIP International Federation for Information Processing 2014

conventional supply chain management [4], green supply chain management [5], reverse logistics [3], and supplier selection [6] , while researches consider all three dimensions of sustainable development in 3PRLP selection are rather limited till now. Within supply chain management, the implementation of sustainable initiatives and green practices is difficult without cooperation with all partners in the network. Therefore, selecting right 3PRLPs based on integrated sustainability criteria can assist organizations to improve their sustainability performance. Some of the 3PRLP selection related papers have started paying more attention to this issue. Wang and Zhu [7] proposed a model to solve the problem of selecting an appropriate 3PRLP in environmental viewpoint of low-carbon economy. Tajik et al.[8]developed a hybrid fuzzy AHP-TOPSIS approach for evaluating sustainable 3PRLPs. The framework they proposed is highly stylized. However, there is a real need for research on 3PRLPs selection problem with sustainability concerns because the majority of the present models focuses on economic and slightly on environmental factors. This paper is among the first research works that shed light on this issue. Hence, the main contribution of this paper is to propose a new model for multi-criteria 3PRLP selection problem based on fuzzy AHP-PROMETHEE approach involving sustainability criteria.

The next section presents the hybrid fuzzy AHP-PROMETHEE approach to assess sustainability performance of 3PRLPs. Third section presents an illustrative example and results analysis. Finally, the paper ends with conclusions.

2   Proposed Model for 3PRL Provider Selection

Due to 3PRLP selection problem is a complicated MCDM problem and time consuming assignment, a clear process should be required to resolve it. The proposed model is structured to allocate the priority weights of decision criteria by resolving FAHP algorithm and to rank 3PRL providers by resolving F-PROMETHEE algorithm, as illustrated in Fig. (1).

2.1   Sustainability Decision Criteria

The key criteria for selecting suitable 3PRLP can typically include cost, quality, and financial performance. Furthermore, indexes of low-carbon and social indicators can play a crucial role in selecting 3PRLPs as the need to coordinate and integrate all the business functions with sustainability considerations. Reverse logistics outsourcing should clearly be economically, environmentally and socially applied. The sustainability criteria and sub-criteria have been defined in detail based on specific literature review in the area of 3PRL provider selection by Kafa et al.[9].

2.2   Fuzzy AHP Algorithm

The basic concept of AHP method [10] is to model a general decision problem as a hierarchical structure including sub-problems that can be easily evaluated in order to determine the priorities via pair-wise comparison of the elements at each level of the decision hierarchy. This method has gained popularity observing the amount of

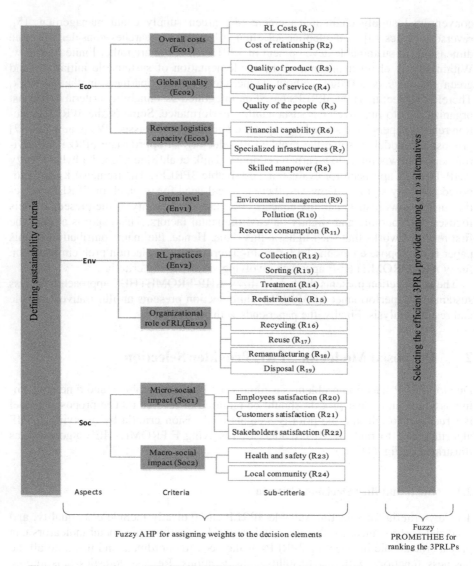

Fig. 1. Proposed fuzzy AHP-PROMETHEE model for selecting the best 3PRL provider

studies that have utilized it including supply chain management. As providers' selection criteria always contain ambiguity and diversity of meaning, the fuzzy AHP algorithm proposed by Kwong and Bai [11] was employed for estimating the weights of selected criteria as follows.

Step 1: Construct the fuzzy judgment matrices (FCMs) for each level. Fuzzy theory set [12] is incorporated with pair-wise comparison in AHP to get more benefit of human reasoning that is approximate rather than precise. The decision maker (DM) preference is represented in form of fuzzy pair-wise comparison matrix (FCM) using the linguistic fuzzy scale represents in terms of triangular fuzzy numbers (TFN) (equally=$\tilde{1}$, moderately=$\tilde{3}$, strongly=$\tilde{5}$, very strongly=$\tilde{7}$, extremely=$\tilde{9}$).

$$\tilde{A} = FCM(\tilde{a}_{ij}) = \begin{bmatrix} 1 & \tilde{a}_{12} & \tilde{a}_{13} & \cdots & \tilde{a}_{1n} \\ \tilde{a}_{21} & 1 & \tilde{a}_{23} & \cdots & \tilde{a}_{2n} \\ \vdots & \vdots & \vdots & \vdots & \vdots \\ \vdots & \vdots & \vdots & \cdots & \vdots \\ \tilde{a}_{n1} & \tilde{a}_{n2} & \tilde{a}_{n3} & \cdots & 1 \end{bmatrix} : \tilde{a}_{ij} = \begin{cases} 1 & i=j \\ \tilde{1},\ \tilde{3},\ \tilde{5},\ \tilde{7},\ \tilde{9} & i>j \\ \tilde{1}^{-1},\ \tilde{3}^{-1},\ \tilde{5}^{-1},\ \tilde{7}^{-1},\ \tilde{9}^{-1} & i<j \end{cases}$$

Step 2: Determine the priorities of different decision elements. The prioritization of the elements of each matrix is done by solving fuzzy eigenvalues and eigenvectors. A fuzzy eigenvalue $\tilde{\lambda}$ is a fuzzy number solution to:

$$\tilde{A}\tilde{x} = \tilde{\lambda}\tilde{x} \tag{1}$$

: $\tilde{x}$ is a non-zero $n \times 1$ fuzzy eigenvector containing fuzzy numbers.
The interval arithmetic and the α-cuts are introduced to perform fuzzy multiplication and addition. By defining the confidence level α in order to integrate the decision maker (DM) confidence over the judgments [13], the TFN can be illustrated as:

$$TFN_{\alpha} = \left[a^{\alpha}, c^{\alpha}\right] = \left[(b-a)\alpha + a, -(c-b)\alpha + c\right] \ \forall \alpha \in \left[0,1\right] \tag{2}$$

For example, with respect to the level α , the lower limit and upper limit of the fuzzy numbers $\tilde{3}$ and $\tilde{3}^{-1}$, can be obtained by applying equation (2).

$$\tilde{3}_{\alpha} = [1 + 2\alpha, 5 - 2\alpha], \ \tilde{3}_{\alpha}^{-1} = [1/(5 - 2\alpha), 1/(1 + 2\alpha)]$$

The degree of satisfaction for the judgment matrix $\tilde{A}$ is estimated from the DM by the index of optimismμ. The larger value of the index μ is the higher degree of optimism that is defined as a linear convex combination [13]:

$$\tilde{a}_{ij}^{\alpha} = \mu \tilde{a}_{iju}^{\alpha} + (1 - \mu)\tilde{a}_{ijl}^{\alpha} \ \forall \mu \in \left[0,1\right] \tag{3}$$

The eigenvector $\tilde{x}$ is calculated by fixing μ and substituting the maximal eigenvalue λ_{max} into the equation (1).

Step 3: Calculate the consistency ratio of a matrix $\tilde{A}$ using the mathematical formula CR= CI/RI as explained by Saaty [10]. A CR of 10% or less is acceptable.

Step 4: Normalize weight vector in order to determine the local and total importance weights (W_i).

Following the above explained steps, the MATLAB package is used to calculate the priority weights of the main aspects, the criteria, and the sub –criteria, (see Table 1.) and then the results are analyzed in the third section.

2.3   Fuzzy PROMETHEE Algorithm

The preference ranking organization method for enrichment evaluation (PROMETHEE) is one of the conventional simple outranking methods to resolve

MCDM problems which is applied in various areas of research. This method was developed by Brans and Vincke [14] based on the exploitation of a valued outranking relation via pair-wise comparisons between the alternatives regarding different criteria. The evaluation table that shows the performance level of each potential alternative for each criterion is required as the first point to apply PROMETHEE method. In this paper, all alternatives (3PRLPs) are evaluated using linguistic scale with corresponding fuzzy numbers (TFN) [very good=(7,7,9), good= (5,7,9), fair =(3,5,7), poor = (1,3,5), very poor=(1,1,3)].The defuzzification of TFNs is done using graded mean integration representation (GMIR) method, proposed by Chen and Hsieh [15].Where TFN= (a, b, c), the GMIR R(TFN) of TFN is:

$$R(TFN) = 1/6 \, (c + 4a + b) \tag{4}$$

Additional information on priority weights of the criteria is also required which is done using FAHP method in this study, as PROMETHEE method cannot distribute weights to the criteria. The various steps of PROMETHEE can be outlined briefly as follows:

Step 1: Calculate preference function of alternative (a) with regard to alternative (b) in the set of "A" alternatives for each sub-criterion:

$$P_i(a, p) = f_i \big[d_i(a,b) \big] \quad \forall P_i(a, p) \in [0,1] \tag{5}$$

Where $d_i(a,b)$ is the difference between the evaluation of "a" and "b" on ith sub-criterion. Several basic preference functions are explained by Brans and Vincke [14] like V-criterion, Gaussian criterion, and U-criterion. In this study, the usual function has been selected which is mostly used with qualitative criteria [16].

Step 2: Calculate outgoing flow and incoming flow for each alternative using equation (6) and equation (7) for ranking the alternatives by a partial preorder "PROMETHEE I" technique that introduces the incomparability between alternatives. Then calculate net flow using equation (8) for ranking the alternatives by a total preorder "PROMETHEE II" technique.

$$\phi^+(a) = 1/(A-1) \sum_{x \in A} \sum_{i=1}^{i} W_i P_i(a, x) \tag{6}$$

$$\phi^-(a) = 1/(A-1) \sum_{x \in A} \sum_{i=1}^{i} W_i P_i(x, a) \tag{7}$$

$$\phi(a) = \phi^+(a) - \phi^-(a) \tag{8}$$

The Visual PROMETHEE software includes the basic of PROMETHEE method is used to calculate outranking flows and rank the alternatives.

3   Application and Discussion of Results

The problem discussed here is related to a manufacturing company wants to implement reverse logistics activities by outsourcing them to 3PRLP. The company desires to consider all the possible key factors which can affect the efficiency of reverse logistics functions. Furthermore, it is important to consider social and environmental as well as economic attributes in 3PRLP selection process in order to achieve sustainable competitive advantage. Currently, the company has four alternatives, namely RLP_1, RLP_2, RLP_3 and RLP_4. To select the right one, the proposed model is applied. The relative importance of each pair of selected criteria is prioritized after asking the global logistics manager as decision maker (DM) in the company concerned to answer a questionnaire including all possible pair-wise comparison.

Table 1. The priority weights of decision criteria

Aspects Weights	Criteria	Local weights	Total weights	Sub-Criteria	Local weights	Total weights	Consistency
ECO (0,64)	Eco_1	0,5076	0,3267	R_1	0,5858	0,1914	$\lambda_{max} = 2,06$
				R_2	0,4142	0,1353	CR= 0.00
	Eco_2	0,4014	0,2583	R_3	0,1159	0,0299	$\lambda_{max} = 3.099$
				R_4	0,5294	0,1368	CR= 0.086
				R_5	0,3547	0,0916	
	Eco_3	0,091	0,0585	R_6	0,2156	0,0126	$\lambda_{max} =3.099$
				R_7	0,6436	0,0377	CR=0,09
				R_8	0,1409	0,0082	
ENV (0,22)	Env_1	0,7387	0,1593	R_9	0,7387	0,1176	$\lambda_{max} =3.061$
				R_{10}	0,7387	0,0244	CR=0.053
				R_{11}	0,1081	0,0172	
	Env_2	0,1532	0,0330	R_{12}	0,5092	0,0168	$\lambda_{max} = 4.21$
				R_{13}	0,0809	0,0027	CR= 0.078
				R_{14}	0,2226	0,0074	
				R_{15}	0,1872	0,0062	
	Env_3	0,1081	0,0233	R_{16}	0,2654	0,0062	$\lambda_{max} =4.21$
				R_{17}	0,5580	0,0130	CR=0.078
				R_{18}	0,1200	0,0028	
				R_{19}	0,0566	0,0013	
SOC (0,14)	Soc_1	0,7388	0,1041	R_{20}	0,0769	0,0080	$\lambda_{max} =3.061$
				R_{21}	0,5400	0,0562	CR=0.053
				R_{22}	0,3831	0,0399	
	Soc_2	0,2612	0,0368	R_{23}	0,8994	0,0331	$\lambda_{max} = 2,006$
				R_{24}	0,1006	0,0037	CR= 0.00

The α-cuts fuzzy comparison matrices for all level were obtained by fixing α=0.5 and μ=0.5. Some revisions of judgment with the DM were necessary as some matrices consistency ratios exceeded 0.1. Based on results shown in Table 1., among of all three key aspects the economic factor is the most significant one in selecting a 3PRL provider for this case company as it has the highest value of priority weights W=0.64.Furthermore, under "Economic" aspect, "Overall costs" was considered the most important criterion with the total weight of 0.3267. Then the 3PRLPs should improve the price besides the other elements. "Green level" was determined as the most important sub-criteria under environmental aspect with the total weight of 0.1593. Consequently, the 3PRL providers would be better to achieve reverse logistics activities with minimum environmental impact to surpass their competitors. Moreover, in the social aspect "Customer satisfaction" is the most significant sub-criterion that has to be considered by 3PRL providers.

Then the 3PRL providers are evaluated regarding each sub-criterion in order to construct the evaluation table. By using the PROMETHEE application software "Visual PROMETHEE 1.4", the outranking flows of 3PRL providers were obtained, as well as a suitable provider selected. The alternative 3PRLP$_1$ and 3PRLP$_4$ are incomparable as per PROMETHEE I but 3PRLP$_1$ is superior to 3PRLP$_4$ according to PROMETHEE II that gives the ranking in the preference order of RLP$_3$> RLP$_2$> RLP$_1$ >RLP$_4$ as shown in Fig.2.

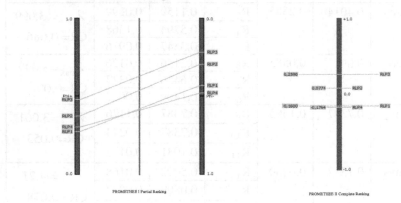

Fig. 2. PROMETHEE Ranking

The proposed approach has an advantage regarding the time and the effort of selection process compared to the existing ones.

4   Conclusions

This paper proposes a new integrated sustainable approach for selecting 3PRLP using AHP and PROMETHEE methods under fuzzy environment. The proposed model provides guidelines to the DM and the results obtained can help not only to select the best sustainable 3PRLP, but also to understand the current state of practice in 3PRLP selection process in the company. In our future research, this will be followed by

GAIA plane which provides a descriptive complement vision. Sensitivity analysis of If-what scenarios will be also carried to analyze the impact of changing the criteria weights on alternatives' ranking. Furthermore, the proposed approach can be illustrated by other case study using other MCDM methods like TOPSIS, VIKOR or hybrid methods and the obtained results can be compared with each other in future research.

References

1. Riopel, D., Chouinard, M., Marcotte, S., Aït-Kadi, D.: Ingénierie et gestion de la logistique inverse vers des réseaux durables. Hermes Science Publications, Lavoisier (2011)
2. Kannan, G., Pokharel, S., Sasi Kumar, P.: A hybrid approach using ISM and fuzzy TOPSIS for the selection of reverse logistics provider. Resour. Conserv. Recycl. 54, 28–36 (2009)
3. Nikolaou, I.E., Evangelinos, K.I., Allan, S.: A reverse logistics social responsibility evaluation framework based on the triple bottom line approach. J. Clean. Prod. 56, 173–184 (2013)
4. Baumann, E.: Modèles d'évaluation des performances économique, environnementale et sociale dans les chaînes logistiques (2011), http://tel.archives-ouvertes.fr/tel-00679706
5. Kafa, N., Hani, Y., El Mhamedi, A.: Sustainability Performance Measurement for Green Supply Chain Management. Presented at the 6th IFAC Conference on Management and Control of Production and Logistics The International Federation of Automatic Control. Center for Information Technology Renato Archer, Fortaleza, Brazil (September 11, 2013)
6. Govindan, K., Khodaverdi, R., Jafarian, A.: A fuzzy multi criteria approach for measuring sustainability performance of a supplier based on triple bottom line approach. J. Clean. Prod. 47, 345–354 (2013)
7. Wang, J., Zhu, Y.: Research on Third-party Reverse Logistics Provider Selection Based on Fuzzy Clustering in Perspective of Low-carbon Economy. Commun. Inf. Sci. Manag. Eng. 2, 63–66 (2011)
8. Tajik, G., Azadnia, A.H., Ma'aram, A.B., Hassan, S.A.H.S.: A Hybrid Fuzzy MCDM Approach for Sustainable Third-Party Reverse Logistics Provider Selection. Adv. Mater. Res. 845, 521–526 (2013)
9. Kafa, N., Hani, Y., El Mhamedi, A.: Sustainable approach for third-party reverse logistics provider selection. Presented at the International Conference on Green Supply Chain, Arras, France (June 25, 2014)
10. Saaty, T.L.: The analytic hierarchy process. McGraw-Hill Book Co., New York (1980)
11. Kwong, C.K., Bai, H.: A fuzzy AHP approach to the determination of importance weights of customer requirements in quality function deployment. J. Intell. Manuf. 13, 367–377 (2002)
12. Zadeh, L.A.: Fuzzy sets. Inf. Control. 8, 338–353 (1965)
13. Lee, A.R.: Application of modified fuzzy ahp method to analyze bolting sequence of structural joints (1995), http://dl.acm.org/citation.cfm?id=922586
14. Brans, J.-P., Vincke, P.: A preference ranking organization method: the PROMETHEE method for MCDM. Manag. Sci. 31, 641–656 (1985)
15. Chen, S.H., Hsieh, C.H.: Representation, ranking, distance, and similarity of L-R type fuzzy number and application. Aust. J. Intell. Process. Syst. 6, 217–229 (2000)
16. Gupta, R., Sachdeva, A., Bhardwaj, A.: Selection of logistic service provider using fuzzy PROMETHEE for a cement industry. J. Manuf. Technol. Manag. 23, 899–921 (2012)

Civil Construction Workers: Technical Training for Complying with a Market Demanding Sustainability

Carla Caprara Parizi, Irenilza de Alencar Nääs,
Sivanilza, Teixeira Machado, and Denise Simões Dupont Bernini

Paulista University. Dr Bacelar St, 1212, São Paulo, Brazil
{Ccapraraparizi,Irenilza,denise.unip}@gmail.com,
sivateixeira@yahoo.com.br

Abstract. Brazilian building construction involves millions of formal and informal workers without technical skills and/or specific training. This study aimed to analyze building workers technical profile and estimate its impact in both their performance and the efficiency of sustainable actions within the companies/contractors. A questionnaire was developed and applied to workers, in order to search their school level, practical experience (basic skills), level of technical qualification (technical skills), level of addiction, wages, construction techniques, program on sustainability, productivity, training programs, level of re-work, amount of waste, overtime performed, difficult in leadership, resistance to the use of equipment for individual safety, the level of accidents, and motivation factors. Results showed that most surveyed companies/contractors do not adopt sustainability programs for worker's education; but those that offer these programs were not successful. Most companies offer more particular training for specific activities, but they are insufficient for the worker, and it only solves a restricted need. However, the lack education that enables learning and reduces the performance also decreases the changes of implementing environmental directed training programs.

Keywords: contractors, housing builders, education, sustainability.

1 Introduction

Brazilian housing construction segment employs 2 million of formal workers, and near 5 million informal workers, with 208,537 thousand formal companies, and from this amount 14 thousand are located in the city of São Paulo [1]. This sector is made of a complex and heterogeneous chain encompassing suppliers, developers, contractors, laboratories using an intensive labor arising from the lower segment of society, and usually low skilled. Much of the construction workers develop their professional activities by observing other more qualified colleagues, and the practical teaching is taught by the most experienced to the others. However, this procedure is not acceptable, and in many cases, the process of repetition is responsible for questionable training, making the employees with wrong practices the teachers.

This scenario generally leads to re-work and construction mistakes which need to be re-done, contributing significantly to generate waste of materials and time. Im-

B. Grabot et al. (Eds.): APMS 2014, Part II, IFIP AICT 439, pp. 278–285, 2014.

provements are needed in order to meet the demand for sustainability through technological innovations, and it is possible to minimize losses and maximize productivity. However, in order to carry on programs on sustainable development on the construction area, more trained workers are needed. Sustainability concepts in this segment bring up discussions focused on topics related to the quantities of waste generated during the construction process, and it is necessary to maintain a balance between the development of the construction environment and the natural environment [2].

This study aims to analyze the profile of the labor technical qualification in housing building and the impact of the workers' skills in improving job performance, as well as their participation in sustainability programs offered by the builders/contractors.

2   Methodology

A field study was carried out applied to specialists and field civil engineers, corresponding to a total of 26 house building companies/contractors, with a focus on the skills of construction teams from Dec. /2013 to Feb./2014. The field study was done using a closed questionnaire with 18 questions developed with the objective of drawing the worker' profile in housing construction. The asked questions were related to the number of years in school, level of basic skills, level of technical training, education degree, if there was addiction issues, wage level, method of construction adopted, sustainable methods adopted, productivity, training programs, amount of re-work made, amount of waste generated, extra-hours worked difficulties in leadership, resistance to the use of safety equipment, and motivation. The level of basic skill was related to knowledge the worker learned by observing others. Technical training was considered as the skills learned by any means of formal teaching related to their tasks. The training offered by the building companies is related to basic best practices.

For data analysis, we used the technique of the frequency distribution, allowing the visualization of the percentage of responses answered to the questionnaire. Descriptive statistics and Pearson correlation were applied adopting a significance level of $p < 0.05$. Data were processed using the computer software SAS® Version 9.0, routines PROC SUMM and PROC CORR, respectively.

3   Results and Discussion

3.1   Overall Scheme of House Building in Brazil

From the questions answered 38.4% adopted the construction in reticular reinforced concrete and 61% used reinforced masonry. Despite the higher percentage is in structural masonry, reticular reinforced concrete is still mostly used in Brazil [3], as it allows bolder structures than others. This construction system is often used as it also allows changes in the original project, and adaptations along the construction, which permits a certain level of tolerance on the labor quality during the construction process. However, waste is very high in this process, and re-work could be avoided.

The structural masonry is usually more rational; it increases the worker productivity and reduces wastes [4]. In the present study the waste from both construction processes was used to analyze labor efficiency. In the construction systems labor performance is assessed in man-hour/m^2 (44%), and in percentage of work finished in relation to the time estimated in the initial project (48%). It also can be assessed using other units such as vol/time, area/time, which in this case represented 8% of the sample. Most work teams do not adopt sustainability programs or program focusing in environmental education during the construction (84.6 %), and there is only 11.4% with some kind of waste management program, such as Environmental Education, and Social Inclusion through Waste Management. The Union of Construction Industry (SINDUSCON) produces booklets for workers, whose intention is to educate them towards sustainability issues. However, tenacious actions in worker education still are needed and must be incorporated by means of rules and a systematic consciousness. Some control mechanisms are also needed to reinforce actions adoption. Over 60 % of the workforce in construction has education below the elementary school, 24.5 % have secondary education, and 12.2 % has some level of training.

Regarding the salary range, nearly 50 % of the teams receive up to 3 minimum wages, which corresponds to approximately US$ 945.00. Thirty percent of the total answers earn up to five salaries, 12 % between 5:07 and 7 % receive wages above 7 minimum wages (the minimum wage ~US$ 315.00). Salary is the key factor on labor productivity, but it does not necessarily imply in high productivity, when the wage is adequate [5]. According to [6] construction companies offer high salaries in exchange for good productivity rate, and this action has not made a good incentive for effective results. These practices are an incentive towards individual actions. The average workers' wages rose at a rate of 7.6 % in 2009, while the rate of worker productivity was 4.2 % [1]. Therefore, the wage growth was beyond productivity. This might be due to the shortage of workforce in São Paulo state. In the case of small companies or contractors, where the rate of productivity is equivalent to one third of the largest companies, this may represent a significant challenge. Other authors [7] assigned weights to the factors leading to worker productivity, which represents the strongest influence on productivity such as 1) the skills and experience of the workforce (0.931), 2) the management (0.916), 3) planning (0.835), 4) the motivation of workers (0.829), and 5) the availability of materials (0.822). These authors suggest that to improve the sector more qualified professionals performing the most difficult, complex tasks are needed; and that managers should make a commitment to productivity in all their actions, including waste reduction training. According to [8] to maximize productivity is necessary to examine the factors affecting this theme which are rarely independent. Low productivity is generally attributed to several factors, including lack of bonding and discontinuity of the worker' technical qualification process.

3.2   Basic Skills and Level of Training Analysis

Analyzing the level of experience and the team' basic skills, a positive correlation of 0.57 (p = 0.002) was found, which indicated that the level of basic knowledge may increase or decrease depending on the level of technical skills (Table 1). This result is consistent with the findings of previous research [4]. In this research after an investment in training (60% within the companies, 58% by Senai-Nat. Ind. Apprent Service- workforce, 52% by especially training companies, and 37% by the Union) the following return were detected, 16 % considered the training enough and satisfactory, 52 % considered it adequate but with unsatisfactory initiatives; and 31 % considered it insufficient. This suggests that although the training is crucial to meet worker' efficiency needs, those lacking formal education cannot acquire new techniques through this technical training. In another study, in the city of Curitiba [9], results indicated that the worker learn their skills from their parents (5%), from another informal jobs (23%), by attending vocational courses (7%), through technical trainings in companies (16%), and other forms including self-learning or watching other professionals, (49%). This scenario indicates that with this workers profile, chances are high that the work execution might be full of uncertain actions leading to further defects or re-work. Workers with low level of education (100%) also presented low level of technical skills. Workers with average and high level of experience are the best qualified for both levels 4 and 5 (75%; Table 1).

Table 1. Level of experience in relation to the worker qualification in construction (%)

	Level*	\multicolumn{5}{c}{Technical training}	Total
		1	2	3	4	5	
Basic skills	1	100	-	-	-	-	100
	2	100	-	-	-	-	100
	3	6.3	6.3	12.5	43.8	31.3	100
	4	-	-	28.6	28.6	42.9	100
	5	-	-	-	-	-	-

*1=very low; 2=low; 3=average; 4=high; 5=very high.

This form of learning is individual; it does not lead to an effective organizational development and a vision of the whole to work. The concept of Learning Organization could be introduced for the benefit of all involved. According to [10] the learning organization's principle modify individual behavior continuously as a result of their socialization, taking into account the culture of the organization, creating new routines and new shares. To [11] the learning organization is a strategy to improve processes in the construction area, but most construction contractors' focus on individualized but continuous learning. This concept gives rise to an important practical benefit as it provides the diagnostic procedures and / or ineffective tasks [12]. In the Brazilian scenario individual learning is insufficient (Table 2 and 3). According to the data from this study, 99% of the companies obtain the labor from other companies; therefore, it does not offer a culture of learning organization. Construction sites are generally mixed companies with varied objectives and philosophies.

3.3   Training and Waste

Brazilian construction industry seeks the difficult in meeting the national laws and resolutions, with a trend to increase levels of legal requirements, including restrictions on financing new projects. Environmental concern is not only a socio-environmental responsibility, but it is a complex and difficult requirement.

Data from Table 1 shows that 100% of workers with low basic skills also presented low learning skills and did not take proper advantage of technical training. Workers with mean to high level of knowledge and learning skills (mean level 3 and high level 4) were those which presented most qualification with practically 41 and 73%, respectively. Approximately 80% of the cost was below 10%, for a level of performance of the trained worker above the average (3, 4 and 5). Some teams presented 100% of re-work cost above 31% for the levels of technical skills mean and high (Table 2). Similar results were found for material wasted along the construction (Table 3). Both tables (Table 2 and Table 3) present similar scenario. No relationship was found between workers technical and the material' wastes; or the amount of re-work during the housing construction process. Labor performed was simply related to the tasks previous contracted, which does not clearly include the need to reduction of material wastes or compliance with the sustainable construction. This result, which leads to large amount of waste and re-work agrees with [9], who found that construction segment in Brazil consumes 40% of natural resources, 40% of energy, and it generates 40% of residues related to human activities. Amongst the programs related to sustainability, the majority responded that there were environmental compensation programs, and re-forestation incentives; however, these programs do not educate the worker in relation to environmental issues. In repetitive activities, trained workers can perform their work, but it does not mean that the work is done in an efficient way. Final results can generate immediate re-work, implicating in greater investment of time, and it generates more waste of materials, and in the medium and long term it may reduce the life' property or yet promote its unsuitability. Workers' competence is, therefore, highly needed in housing construction companies.

Table 2. Percentage of costs with re-work, in relation to the level of level of performance of the technical trained worker (%)

Re-work (%)	Technical Training					Total
	1	**2**	**3**	**4**	**5**	
< 10	22.2	-	22.2	22.2	33.3	100
11<20	16.7	8.3	8.3	33.3	33.3	100
21<30	-	-	-	50.0	50.0	100
31<40	-	-	100.0	-	-	100
> 41	-	-	-	100.0	-	100

1=very low; 2=low; 3=average; 4=high; 5=very high.

Professional competence [13] is defined as the development of information (in conceptual terms or ideas), behavior (actions), and skills (use of learned experience), and its use is desirable in specific actions within the dimensions of education, politics, ethics, culture and environment, when analyzing personal and interpersonal relationships. In general, individuals with low education do not understand issues related to ethics or other concepts within the social and economic context, and the basic citizenship aspect of protecting society from any damage. In this direction, a certain level of education is required to understand sustainability. In the last evaluation of the

Program of International Student Assessment [14], Brazil stayed in the 53rd position amongst 65 countries. According to [15] quality of education influences positively in the economic growth and; therefore, the country has yet much to invest in education in order to change various aspects of its development.

Table 3. Cost percentage of material wasted in relation to the level of achievement acquired by the worker with technical training (%)

Material wasted (%)	Technical Training					Total
	1	2	3	4	5	
< 10	22.2	-	22.2	22.2	33.3	100
11<20	14.3	7.1	14.3	28.6	35.7	100
21<30	-	-	-	-	-	0
31<40	-	-	-	100	-	100
> 41	-	-	-	-	-	0

1=very low; 2=low; 3=average; 4=high; 5=very high.

3.4   Labor Safety and Working Hours

When analyzing labor safety 70% of the surveyed workers do not want to use safety equipment. Positive correlation was found with the lack of safety equipment use and occurrence of accidents (p=0.0001). In general, 65% of accidents were related to workers involved in work between 8 to 9 h daily (Figure 1). This result may be easily justified by the physical exhaustion of the worker, when the recommended time during the work is of 8 hs daily. In addition, many teams work above the permitted hours (due to the time set for the construction), requiring more effort from the teams. However, working overtime interferes negatively on worker productivity [16].

Fig. 1. Accident rate in relation to worked hours

The most interesting comment in the answers in the questionnaire regarding accident rates was that efforts to reduce the number of accidents has only an economic appeal, and there is not a real concern with the physical and psychological integrity of the worker and his family. It has also been seen that there is an occurrence of workers with alcohol addiction in the construction field. In this study, we found that 50% of the surveyed teams have workers with some detected chemical addiction negatively influencing the labor performance. Construction workers do not value their job, they consider their work as "risky", "heavy", "undervalued", and "with no future". While this type of work seems to be the last resort used as a means of survival by untrained workers, they feel socially devalued, without formal education, within a low socioeconomic status [17, 18]. Therefore, they run out of satisfaction and do not perform their assignments properly, and do not have good communication with their immediate supervisors.

4   Conclusions

When workers have the basic skill, they have better performance throughout technical training. However, workers' training has not been fully reached regarding sustainability issues, mainly in issues related to waste of materials and re-work tasks. Job performance is poor due to lack in proper training.

Most companies/contractors surveyed do not adopt sustainability programs within worker' education, but those that offer these programs were not successful. Specific training was proved insufficient, as they supply only a small portion of the education gap, and they do not necessarily enable learning items related to environmental issues.

Organized actions and control mechanisms should be integrated into the construction services to attend a market that demands faster actions, yet not losing sight of the questions facing the sustainability and quality. Everything indicates that use of the learning organization concept would the businesses since adapted to Brazilian scenario, raised in this work. The suggestion is that subcontracts establish strong partnerships with the contractor about to establish the same organizational cultures focused naturally hand-intensive operational.

Acknowledgement. The authors thank CAPES - Coordination of Improvement of Higher Education in Brazil – and Paulista University – UNIP, for the scholarship.

References

1. FIESP/CBIC – Fed. Ind. Est. S. Paulo/ C. Bras. da Ind. da Construção. A produtividade da Construção Civil Brasileira. CBIC (2012),
http://paraconstruir.wordpress.com/2012/07/10/
relatorio-cbic-sobre-produtividade-da-construcao-civil/
(accessed on: March 2014)
2. Al-Hajj, A., Hamani, K.: Material Waste in the UAE Construction Industry: Main Causes and Minimization Practices. School of the Built Environment, Heriot-Watt Univ. Dubai Campus, UAE Pub. (November 16, 2011),
https://pureapps2.hw.ac.uk/portal/files/1954110/
ASCW_IWMM_in_UAE_Journal_AEDM_Sep11_revised_AAH.pdf (accessed on: March 2014)

3. Silva, M.M.A.: Diretrizes para o projeto de alvenaria estrutural: contribuição ao uso. M.Sc. Dissert. Escola Poli. da Univ. de São Paulo (2003), http://www.teses.usp.br/teses/disponiveis/3/3146/.../Dissert acaoMargarete.pdf (accessed on: February 2014)
4. Roman, H.R., Mutti, C.N., Araújo, H.N.: Construindo em alvenaria estrutural, 83 p. Ed.UFSC, Florianópolis (1999) ISBN 8532801668, 9788532801661
5. Kazaz, A.E., Ulubeyli, S.: Drivers of productivity among construction workers: A study in a developing country. Building and Environment 39, 93–100 (2006)
6. Dalcul, A.L.P.C., Mirian, O., Ruas, R.L.: Organização do trabalho: estudo de caso com empresas da construção civil de Santa Maria/RS (July 5, 2002), http://hdl.handle.net/10183/19409 (accessed on: February 2014)
7. Mojahed, S., Aghazadeh, F.: Major factors influencing productivity of water and wastewater treatment plant construction: evidence from the deep south USA. International Journal of Project Management 26, 195–202 (2008)
8. Nasirzadeh, F., Nojedehi, P.: Dynamic modeling of labor productivity in construction projects. International Journal of Project Management 31, 903–911 (2013)
9. Honorio, D.E.: Qualid. de vida do operário da Const. Civil e sua importância na qualidade e produtividade em obras. Masters' Diss, Fed. Univ. St. Cat., Brazil (2002), https://repositorio.ufsc.br/handle/123456789/83250 (accessed on: December 2013)
10. Philip, P.H.: Knowledge creation in strategic alliances: Another look at organizational learning. Asia Pacific Journal of Management 17, 201–222 (2000)
11. Kululanga, G.K., Price, A.D.F., McCaffer, R.: Empirical Investigation of Construction Contractors' Organizational Learning. Journal of Construction Engineering and Management 128, 385–391 (2002)
12. Pentland, B.T.: Information Systems and Organizational Learning: The Social Epistemology of Organizational Knowledge Systems. Accouting, Management & Information Technology 5, 1–21 (1995)
13. ABRAMAT – Assoc. Bras. Ind. Mat. Construção. Capacitação e formação profissional na construção civil e mecanismos de mobilização de demanda. São Paulo USP – Depart. de Eng. de Const. Civil (2007)
14. PISA, Results (2009), http://www.oecd.org/pisa/pisaproducts/46619703.pdf (accessed on: March 2014)
15. Hanushek, E.A., Kimko, D.D.: Scchooling, Labor-Force Quality, and the Growth of Nations? American Economic Review 90, 1184–1208 (2000)
16. Hanna, A.S., Taylor, C.S., Sullivan, K.T.: Impact of extended overtime on construction labor. J. of Construction Engineering and Management 131, 734–739 (2005)
17. Iriart, J.A.B., Oliveira, R.P.: Psicologia em Estudo. Representações do Trabalho entre trabalhadores informais da Construção Civil. Psicologia em Estudo 13, 437–445 (2008)
18. John, V.M., Silva, V.G., Agopyan, V.: Agenda 21: uma proposta de discussão para o constru-business brasileiro. In: II ANTAC/UFRGS, Canela-RS, pp. 91–98 (2001)

The Sustainability and Outreach of Microfinance Institutions

Jaehun Sim and Vittaldas V. Prabhu

The Harold and Inge Marcus Department of Industrial and Manufacturing Engineering,
310 Leonhard Building, University Park, PA 16802, USA
jus238@psu.edu, prabhu@engr.psu.edu

Abstract. Microfinance emerged as an approach with great potential for alleviating poverty and improving access to financial services by offering small loans with no pledged collateral requirement. Due to the growing demand for microfinance, businesses have put more emphasis on the relationship between financial sustainability and outreach. Microfinance Institutions (MFIs) work to increase social sustainability by providing more services to particular clientele, while maintaining the financial and operational sustainability of the institutions.

This study investigates the financial sustainability and outreach of 32 MFIs in India in terms of interest rate and default rate. This study employs a simple methodology for the evaluation of microcredit interest rates proposed by Muhammad Yunus (2007), along with a new methodology for the evaluation of microcredit default rates. As a preliminary stage of using the Black-Scholes (BS) model, this study tests the validation of MFIs' asset values and default rates of geometric Brownian motion (GBM) using data. The Ryan-Joiner test is used to check the independence of data, and the chi-square test on two-way tables is used to check the serial independence of data. The interest rate premium and the default rate from the BS model will facilitate making decisions on the sustainability and outreach of MFIs.

Keywords: Microfinance, Interest Rate Premium, Default Rate Premium.

1   Introduction

After the success of various MFIs over the past decades, microfinance has become a key tool for alleviating poverty and offering financial services to the poor in both developing and underdeveloped countries. MFIs provide the poor with both financial resources such as small loans with no pledged collateral requirement, savings, and insurance, and social services such as health care and education (Sengupta and Aubuchon, 2008).

During the growth of microfinance, MFIs have increased social sustainability by providing additional services to particular clientele in remote and rural areas, while keeping the financial and operational sustainability of the institutions (Hartarska, 2002). As a result, MFIs require more investments to meet the growing demand.

For instance, the World Bank estimates that more than 87% of the vulnerable people still have limited access to financial services in India (The World Bank Group,

B. Grabot et al. (Eds.): APMS 2014, Part II, IFIP AICT 439, pp. 286–293, 2014.

2005). Since there is a limit to the amount of investments from donors, it is critical for MFIs to find a way to maintain financial and operational self-sustainability while expanding the breadth and depth of outreach.

MFIs primarily derive income from the interest earnings of their loan portfolios. Thus they have found it necessary to charge high interest to cover their major costs. The average interest rate MFIs charge is 38%, which is high compared to regular commercial financial institutions. A consequence of such a high interest rate is that MFIs experience difficulty in increasing outreach toward target clientele in remote and rural areas.

Along with high interest rates, another principal issue in microfinance is the high default rate. The default rate issue is a major impediment to MFIs increasing their outreach. MFIs experience difficulty in maintaining financial sustainability because they do not have any mechanism of contract enforcement to collect on their loans.

To analyze MFIs' microcredit interest rates, this study employs a simple methodology for the evaluation of the microcredit interest rates proposed by Muhammad Yunus (2007) based on an interest rate premium. The interest rate premium is calculated by subtracting the cost of funds at the market rate paid by the MFI from the interest rate charged by the MFI. The simple evaluation methodology classifies MFIs into three zones -- green zone, yellow zone, and red zone -- based on the interest rate premium to investigate MFIs' operations. For instance, if an MFI has fallen into the red zone, the MFI's main objective is on profit maximization, not on social missions.

The GBM process has been widely used for describing quantity moves over time with uncertainty, such as in the stock market. As a preliminary stage of using the BS model, this paper first tests whether MFIs' asset values as the value of MFIs follow GBM, based on the study of Marathe and Ryan (2005).

The rest of this paper is organized into four sections. Section Two provides a review of the relevant literature on the sustainability and outreach of microfinance. In Section Three, the geometric Brownian motion validation methodology is presented, along with the methodology for an interest rate premium evaluation. Section Four presents numerical examples through the Indian MFIs case with discussion. Finally, the conclusion is provided in Section Five.

2   Literature Review

Since the debate between the financial sustainability and outreach of MFIs in the 1990s, MFIs have increasingly had to consider both profit maximization and social mission as part of their operations. Increasing outreach to the poor cannot be achieved without solid financial sustainability of MFIs. Despite the growing emphasis towards sustainability and outreach, there has not been much research conducted in this regard.

Cull et al. (2007) conduct empirical tests for 124 MFIs in 49 countries to gain a better understanding of specific aspects of financial performance and the depth of outreach. The study shows that an individual contract-based MFI makes better profits compared with a group contract-based MFI. The study also shows that an individual contract-based MFI increasingly focuses on wealthier clients and dramatically lowers the fraction of both poor and female clients. The study also shows that a high level of fees does not guarantee a high profit.

Hermes et al. (2010) investigate the relationships of the trade-off between sustainability and outreach by analyzing 435 MFIs from 1997 to 2007. The study measures sustainability in terms of cost efficiency and the depth of outreach in terms of the average loan balance, average saving balance, and percentage of women clients. The study indicates that efficient operations in MFIs are helpful for improving financial sustainability.

Cull et al. (2010) investigate how prudential regulation and supervision affect sustainability and outreach of MFIs, using the data of the largest 245 MFIs. The study shows that supervision increases an MFI's average loan balance and decreases the fraction of female clients. Social mission-oriented MFIs significantly reduce their profitability without adjusting loan sizes and fraction of women clients under supervision.

Hudson and Traca (2010) examine how subsidy affects the efficiency of MFIs, based on microfinance rating data of 100 MFIs. The study indicates that the subsidy intensity positively affects the efficiency of MFIs under a certain level. Wydick et al. (2010) employ an elasticity of social imitation to investigate the determinants of outreach of MFIs. The study provides evidence that the magnitude of the social network, such as a church network, plays an important role in the breadth and depth of outreach.

Sim and Prabhu (2013) consider a supply chain microfinance model as a financial sustainability solution in microfinance. Using a game theoretical analysis, the study investigates how investment levels, raw material prices, and manufacture margins are influenced by loan interest rates under three types of decentralized channel policies.

In summary, the literature review shows a relationship between sustainability and outreach of MFIs. It is clear that a marginal increment of financial sustainability in terms of profit creates a marginal reduction of outreach of MFIs. However, it is difficult to determine how a marginal increment of outreach affects a marginal improvement of financial sustainability in microfinance.

3   Methodology

The objective of this study is to investigate the financial sustainability and outreach of MFIs in terms of interest rate and default rate. In the first stage, this study uses a simple evaluation methodology for microcredit interest rates based on the interest rate premium. In the second stage, as a preliminary to using the BS model, this study tests the validation of MFIs' asset values and default rates of GBM.

3.1   Microcredit Interest and Default Rate Evaluation

This section reviews Dr. Yunus's methodology for the evaluation of microcredit interest rates (Yunus, 2007). Based on an interest rate premium, the methodology analyzes MFIs' operations and classifies the MFIs into three zones, as shown in Table 1. The interest rate premium is equal to the difference between the interest rate and the cost of funds. In microfinance, the interest rate premium is calculated by subtracting the financial expense on loan portfolio dividing by gross loan portfolio from the yield on gross loan portfolio.

$$\text{Yield on gross loan portfolio} - \frac{\text{Financial Expense on loan portfolio}}{\text{Gross loan portfolio}} \tag{1}$$

For instance, if a particular MFI's interest rate premium falls into the green zone, it means that the MFI focuses on the poverty reduction mission. On the other hand, if the MFI falls into the red zone, it means that the MFI focuses on the profit maximization mission.

Table 1. The Categorization of an Interest Rate Premium

Zone	Value
Green Zone	$\leq 10\%$
Yellow Zone	$\leq 15\%$
Red Zone	$> 15\%$

In a similar way, this study proposes a new methodology, a default rate premium, for the evaluation of microcredit default rates. In microfinance, the default rate premium is the difference between the loan loss rate and the cost of loan default. The default rate premium is calculated by subtracting the impairment loan loss dividing by gross loan portfolio from loan loss rate. If the value of the default rate premium has a negative value, it implies that the MFI needs to increase its loan loss allowance to keep the financial sustainability of the MFI. In a contrast case, the MFI can still focus on the poverty reduction mission.

$$\text{Loan loss rate} - \frac{\text{Impairment loan loss}}{\text{Gross loan portfolio}} \tag{2}$$

3.2   Geometric Brownian Motion Validation

This section reviews the validation methodology for the GBM proposed by Marathe and Ryan (2005). GBM, defined as the logarithm of randomly varying quantity, follows Brownian motion in a continuous time stochastic process. In order to follow GBM, the data needs to satisfy two assumptions: normality and independence from past data.

This study uses the Ryan-Joiner test, similar to the Shapiro-Wilk test, to check whether the data is normally distributed by detecting all departures from normality. By comparing the correlation between the predicted normal data with actual data, the

Ryan-Joiner test checks normality on a set of data based on what normally distributed data set of a given sample size would be. If the p-value is greater than the level of significance, the null hypothesis of a normal distribution is not rejected. In this case, the data could plausibly be normally distributed. In this test, the hypothesis set is as follows:

Ho: The distribution is normal

Ha: The distribution is not normal

To test the serial independence of data, the study uses the chi-square test on two-way tables. The test investigates the association between the row and column variables in a two-way table by investigating distributions of categorical variables which differ from one another. If the p-value is greater than the level of significance, the null hypothesis is not rejected. This means that the data could plausibly be serially independent. In this test, the hypothesis set is as follows:

Ho: There is no association between the variables

Ha: There is some association between the variable

4   Numerical Examples

In this case study, the financial sustainability and outreach of MFIs in five countries: Afghanistan, China, India, Peru, and Tanzania is investigated in terms of interest rate premiums and default rates. The relevant data is obtained through the MIX Market database in 2011 and 2012. In this study, each MFI is considered as one group. At the first stage, the interest rates in five countries are calculated to investigate whether the MFIs focus on their social mission in terms of outreach using Dr. Yunus's methodology.

The interest rate premium is calculated by subtracting the financial expense per gross loan portfolio from the yield on gross loan portfolio. As shown in Figure 1, MFIs fall into the green zone because their interest rate premiums are less than 10%. MFIs belong to the yellow zone because their interest rate premiums are between 10% and 15%. MFIs fall into the red zone because their interest rate premiums are greater than 15%. Based on this result, it is possible to conclude that some of the analyzed MFIs are attempting to increase their outreach in breadth and depth.

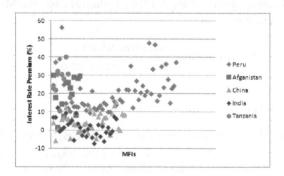

Fig. 1. Interest Rate Premiums

The default rate premium is calculated by subtracting the loan loss impairment expense per gross loan portfolio from the loan loss rate on gross loan portfolio. As shown in Figure 2, some MFIs fall into the zone around zero, which implies that MFIs need to consider the trade-off between the profit maximization mission and the poverty reduction mission. The positive value of the default rate premium of the MFIs can focus on a poverty reduction mission because of the financial sustainability of the institutions, whereas the negative value of the default rate premium of the MFIs can focus on profit maximization mission because the institution needs to increase its financial sustainability.

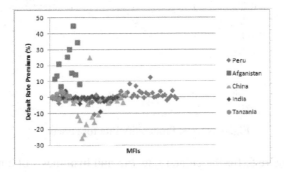

Fig. 2. Default Rate Premiums

Figure 3 illustrates the interest rate premium versus the default rate premium. The MFIs in quadrant one focus on profit maximization mission and the MFIs in quadrant three focus on poverty reduction mission. The MFIs in quadrant three need to attempt to increase profit maximization mission. The MFIs in quadrant two and three need to consider the trade-off between the profit maximization mission and the poverty reduction mission, while considering the institutions' financial sustainability.

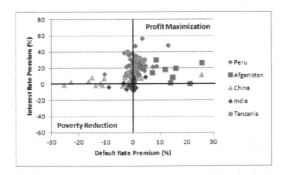

Fig. 3. Interest and Default Rate Premiums Quadrant

In order to use the BS model, the total value of a firm, the value of the underlying assets, needs to follows GBM. Thus, at this stage, the Ryan-Joiner test and the chi-square test on two-way tables are conducted to check the normality and independence of the asset values and the default rates of 32 MFIs in India from 2011 to 2012. In both the Ryan-Joiner test and the chi-square test, the log ratio values of the asset values and the default vales are tested. First, the normality test is conducted. As shown in Figure 4, the null hypothesis of a normal distribution is not rejected because the p-value is greater than 0.1. Thus, it can be concluded that the asset values could be consistent with the lognormal aspect of GBM.

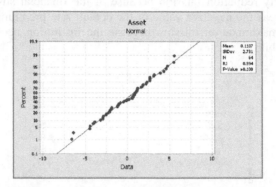

Fig. 4. Normal Probability Plot for Assets

As shown in Figure 5, for the default rate, the null hypothesis of a normal distribution is not rejected because the p-value is greater than 0.1. Thus, it can be concluded that the default rate values could be consistent with the lognormal aspect of GBM. By knowing the default rate following GBM, it is possible to simulate default rate paths. By predicting the future behavior of the default rate, MFIs can prepare for the impending default risk.

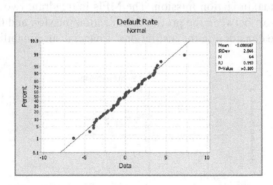

Fig. 5. Normal Probability Plot for Default Rates

Next, the chi-square test on two-way tables is conducted to check the independence of the asset values and the default rates of 32 MFIs in India from 2011 to 2012. The log ratio values of assets are divided into 4 categories. The null hypothesis of no association cannot be rejected because the p-value, 0.861, is greater than 0.05. It can be concluded that the asset values are independent. Similarly, the log ration values of default rates are divided into three categories. Since the p-value is 0.495, which is greater than 0.05, the null hypothesis of no association cannot be rejected. Thus, it can be concluded that the default rates are independent.

5   Conclusion

This study considers the financial sustainability and outreach of MFIs in terms of the interest rate and the default rate. Dr. Yunus's methodology measures interest rate premiums and the proposed methodology measures default rate premiums for MFIs in five countries to analyze whether the MFIs focus on their social mission in terms of outreach. The results show that some of the analyzed MFIs focus on increasing their outreach in breadth and depth.

As a validation of GBM, the Ryan-Joiner test is used to test the normality of the underlying asset and the default rate, along with the chi-square test for the independence. Since the data follow GBM, the BS model is used to calculate default rates of 32 MFIs in India for 2012. The primary assumption of the widespread risk models in bonds and equities is that the data set follows GBM. By validating both asset and default data following GBM, this study demonstrates that it is possible to employ risk models for the microfinance industry. By measuring key risks, the employed models could be used to reveal risk potential as well as implement risk strategies for MFIs. Ultimately, the MFIs can simultaneously achieve both financial sustainability and social mission.

References

1. Charitou, A., Dionysiou, D., et al.: Alternative bankruptcy prediction models using option-pricing theory. Journal of Banking & Finance 37, 2329–2341 (2013)
2. Cull, R., Demirgüç-Kunt, A., et al.: Financial performance and outreach: A global analysis of lending microbanks. The Economic Journal 117(1), 107–133 (2007)
3. Cull, R., Demirgüç-Kunt, A., et al.: The effect of regulation on MFI profitability and outreach. World Development 38 (2010)
4. Hartarska, V.: Three essays on finance for the poor. The Ohio State University (2002)
5. Hermes, N., Lensink, R., et al.: Outreach and efficiency of microfinance institu-tions. World Development 38 (2010)
6. Hudon, M., Traca, D.: Subsidies and sustainability in microfinance. World Development 38 (2010)
7. Marathe, R.R., Ryan, S.M.: On the validity of the geometric Brownian motion assumption. Engineering Economist 50, 159–192 (2005)
8. Sengupta, R., Aubuchon, C.P.: The microfinance revolution: An overview. Federal Reserve Bank of St. Louis Review 90(1), 9–30 (2008)
9. Sim, J., Prabhu, V.V.: Game theoretical approach to supply chain microfinance. In: Prabhu, V., Taisch, M., Kiritsis, D. (eds.) APMS 2013, Part I. IFIP AICT, vol. 414, pp. 48–53. Springer, Heidelberg (2013)
10. The World Bank Group, Microfinance can be the biggest instrument in the fight against poverty. Year of Micro-credit Conference (2005)
11. The World Bank Group, Microfinance can be the biggest instrument in the fight against poverty. Year of Micro-credit Conference (2005)
12. Wydick, B., Karp, H., et al.: Social networks, neighborhood effects and credit ac-cess. World Development 38 (2010)
13. Yunus, M.: Creating a world without poverty: Social business and the future of capitalism. PublicAffairs (2007)

A Lifecycle Data Management System Based on RFID Technology of EPC Class1 Gen2 v2

Young-woo Kim and Jinwoo Park[*]

Department of Industrial Engineering/Automation System Research Institute (ASRI),
Seoul National University, Seoul, Republic of Korea
ywkim@mailab.snu.ac.kr, autofact@snu.ac.kr

Abstract. To cope with pollution, exhaustion of resources and new regulations extending producer responsibility, the original equipment manufacturers are working hard towards an efficient solution that solves those problems. We propose an RFID (Radio Frequency IDentification) based information system which incorporates large user memory banks of EPCC1G2 v2 standard to follow up lifecycle information about the product. We use hierarchical data models to minimize storage requirement while storing all information about the whole product structure including subassembly and end components. Later we can extract the information to utilize maintenance histories and chemical structure of each component. We also consider applicability of our system in XML hierarchical data structure for the possibility of internet usage.

Keywords: Remanufacturing, Data System, Radio Frequency Identification, Closed-loop Supply Chain Management, EPCC1G2 (EPC Class 1 Generation 2).

1   Introduction

As time goes on, environmental problems such as climate change, destruction of ozone layer and depletion of natural resources are getting worse. For the environmental problems, several movements for saving the environments have been taken place both globally and locally. From a standpoint of manufacturing, product recycling is the way to take part in the environmental movements.

Also the development of brand-new materials as a substitute for natural resources could be the solution for preventing the depletion of natural resources, but it couldn't substitute perfectly. So collecting the products in end-of-life (EOL) phase and recovering the returned products as resources could reduce virgin sourcing obviously. Then the product recycling is considered the most active solution.

Product recycling could give an environmental advantage of extending lifespan of natural resources minded before, as well as an economic advantage from reducing the cost caused by virgin sourcing.

But when the manufacturers deal with a problem of product recycling, quality of returned product may vary significantly according to the age or history and environ-

---

[*] Corresponding author.

B. Grabot et al. (Eds.): APMS 2014, Part II, IFIP AICT 439, pp. 294–301, 2014.

ment of usage. Nowadays many products consist of many components and subassemblies. But they may have all different ages and expected lives. For example, a new component whose expected life is 20 years can be used more than once if it was used as a maintenance part for a product whose remaining expected life is, say, 5 years. In that sense if the life history of components and products are not available, recyclable components in good condition may be disposed after being recycled only once.

According to Fleischmann (2001) and Thierry *et al.* (1995), there are uncertainties in terms of timing, quantity and quality of product return flows[1][2]. And Kulkarni *et al.* (2005) describes the importance of information that would be helpful to handle the product disposition decisions on the most appropriate recovery option according to the condition of the returned products – the product can be reused as is, reused after remanufacturing, recycled to recover its material contents or incinerated for thermal energy recovery – and product recovery decisions by inventory visibility [3].

To handle the uncertainty problems, we propose a framework for the lifecycle data management system which gives a unique identifier to as many components and subassemblies as, and tracks historical events such as repair logs and useful data to solve the product disposition decision by tagging in chemical composition information.

To that end, we focus on Electronic Product Code Class1 Gen2 (EPCC1G2) v2 RFID technology because this new standard is shows the way to be adopted by all standard bodies including ISO and if offers a large user bank memory [3].

2   A Framework for the Lifecycle Data Management System

RFID has been considered as an enabler to launch the lifecycle data management system in many researches. Bajic and Chaxel (2002) concerned the use of automatic identification devices (Auto-ID tags) as permanent escort memories associated to the car during its whole life cycle. These memories provide an integration frame for vehicle lifecycle information, which are necessary to support the manufacturing, after-sales services and recycling processes [4]. Jun *et al.* (2009) proposed an overall framework for RFID applications in product lifecycle management with a Product Embedded Information Device (PEID) [5]. And Parlikad and McFarlane (2007) showed qualitatively that the availability of product information has a positive impact on product recovery decisions, and discuss how RFID-based product identification technologies can be employed to provide the necessary information [6].

RFID also could help operating an efficient supply network. It promises to eliminate manual inventory counting, warehouse mis-picking, and order-numbering mistakes by providing precise data on product location, product characteristics, and product inventory levels [7]. Also RFID traceability gives several advantages for enterprises to effectively handle their daily operations with distribution transparency [8]. Networked RFID systems can provide an automated and efficient approach for capturing and delivering complete item level product information in an accurate and timely manner thereby making it possible for high level decisions and process improvements during product recovery stages [3].

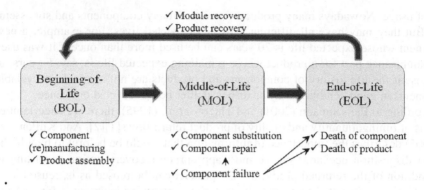

Fig. 1. Events occurred over whole lifecycle

Every data over the lifecycle as shown in Fig. 1 can be stored by combining external databases and the RFID tags attached to a product. The external databases consist of information about every product produced by Original Equipment Manufacturers (OEMs) and every component the OEM produces.

At the beginning-of-life (BOL) phase, products and its components acquire their own identifiers according to the data standard claimed by EPCglobal. EPC is a well-known universal identification system for any physical object and it is considered as the most important data standard for supply chain applications. So it is widely used in informations systems that need to track or otherwise refer to physical objects with RFID tags.

A product could fail during its MOL (middle-of-life) phase. Product failure is caused by single or multiple component failures. At this point, a product user should decide to repair/substitute failed parts or dispose the product. If the user decide to repair the failed component and use the product continuously, the failed product still remains in the MOL phase. Information about the failed component should be written to the history log in the RFID tag attached to the repaired component. Also the product may still enter again into the MOL phase if the user decide to change failed parts to new ones. For this substitution case, only the failed component enter into EOL phase and collected by a 3rd party reprocessing facility or the OEM who is responsible for extended producer responsibility (EPR). EPR is the preventive conceptual strategy to save environment that was quoted first in the report of Swedish government [9] and EPR claims that every OEM takes responsibility to collect, recover, and reuse obsolete products and dispose on their own [10].

For the final option to cope with product failure, the user could decide to dispose the failed product if the repair cost is not worth by repairing or changing the failed component(s).

Failed components itself or components from failed products are collected and they could be recycled as follows.

- Reused after treatment
- Recovered as resources after dismantle, shredding, and additional treatments
- Recovered as thermal energy by incineration

A reprocessing facility should make a recycling decisions among the various options described above by considering visual conditions, expert opinions and history logbooks in the attached tag.

All the returned products and components are came into the remanufacturing shop floor and booked into the inventory database of the OEM. Once the returned products and components are booked in, a preliminary sorting is performed to filter out components that do not apparently have much market value. In this step, automated identification and history logs of returned components about repair logs could be helpful to the experts who filter out the returned components in a bad condition.

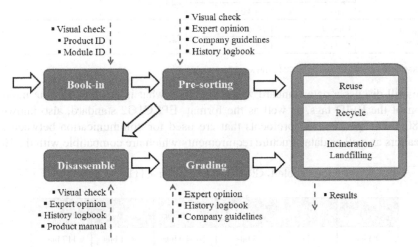

Fig. 2. Reverse process on the remanufacturing shop floor

Also the OEM can calculate environmental and economical effect both caused by different option taken. It is helpful to make more efficient decision while obeying the environmental regulations.

Also after the recovery process ended, results of recovery option actually taken by OEM's decision will be stored in a external database. From an administrative point of view, it could be an obvious clue for penalties incurred to OEMs who don't obey the regulations or for incentives to OEMs showing excellent recycling performance.

3   Proposed System for Applying EPCC1G2 v2

EPCC1G2 is the standard working framework proposed by GS1 in 2006 and is widely used for identification in the ultrahigh frequency (UHF) band. It has been a truly unique international protocol with faster read speed and more powerful security.

And the latest released air interface protocol, EPCC1G2v2, is an answer by GS1 to the requirements of the EPCglobal user community. The most impressive feature is enhanced user memory for alteration electronic article surveillance and supplementary encodings such as maintenance logging [12]. Therefore, EPCC1G2v2 technology seems to be very appropriate for sub-level tagging and launching of the proposed system.

Table 1. Difference between Gen1 and Gen2 [11]

	Gen1		Gen2
Standard	4 UHF standards		Unique international protocol
Reader mode	Single-reader mode		Single/Multi-reader mode
Session	X		O
Tag memory	Class 0	WORM *	WMRM **
	Class 1	WORM	
Data transmission speed	Class 0	80 kb/s	640 kb/s
	Class 1	140 kb/s	
Length of password	Class 0	24 bit	32 bit
	Class 1	8 bit	

* WORM: Write Once Read Many   ** WMRM: Write Many Read Many

We will discuss a data standard which specifies what is contained in the memory portion of the RFID tags, as well as the format. EPCC1G2 standard, also known as ISO18000-6C specifies the protocols that are used for communication between tags and readers as well as data structure requirements which are compatible with the EPC.

Table 1. GRAI-170 EPC scheme [11]

Header	Filter Value	Partition	Company Prefix	Asset Type	Serial Number
8 bits	3 bits	3 bits	20~40 bits	24~4 bits	112 bits

EPCglobal officially announced several data standards for different usage. Using a data standard in existence could pursue interoperability then we could expect enhancing applicability for worldwide usage. We focus on the GRAI (Global Returnable Asset Identifier) standard which is typically used for a specific returnable asset such as reusable shipping containers, pallets because we consider the EOL products and components as resources. Then we select the GRAI-170 EPC tag data standard because memory space of 170 bits seems to be enough space to assign every product and component. Basically we could identify at most 2^{112} individual components with same type by using the GRAI-170 EPC scheme. A company that use GRAI applications could take advantage of identifying the returnable asset ownership for the life of the asset wherever it goes, facilitating cross company asset management tracking, guarding against loss [13]. And also the standard scheme could be adjustable for memory portion by setting different partition value to reflect characteristics of target product's BOM. If the number of companies associated with a target industry is relatively low and the number of components composed in products is relatively high because the products manufactured are somewhat complex, we could assign smaller space to company prefix while assign larger space to asset type.

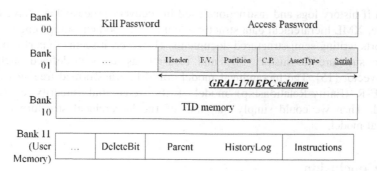

Fig. 3. Conceptual design of EPCC1G2v2 tags

EPCC1G2v2 tags are logically divided into 4 banks with user memory space. So we also analyze an encoding scheme to pack useful data efficiently. In this context, there are two major problems around the encoding issue: We should figure out what kind of data should be contained in the tag, and how to encode data economically.

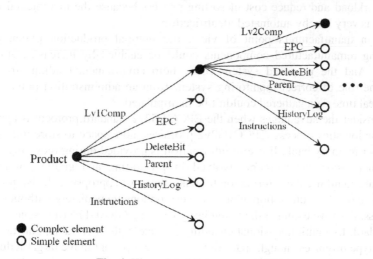

Fig. 4. Hierarchical data representation

We develop a data model taking into account of both the IMS(Information Management System) structure of the old IBM database technology [14] and the XML (eXtensive Markup Language) hierarchical data model for encoding user memory space. XML provides information about the structure and meaning of the data in the Web pages rather than just specifying how the Web pages are formatted for displaying on the screen. So XML has emerged as the standard for structuring and exchanging data over the Web. The XML could represent hierarchical data by possessing relatively smaller space then it could be a solution for tag sizing and reflecting perfectly modular structure because a bill-of-material of any modular product takes the form of hierarchical structure.

Even if history logs and instructions used in recovery process don't have any data structure, XML hierarchical data structure could be a good encoding scheme because it supports writing semi-structured documents. However, it seems to perform better if the data structure for history logs and instructions are well-defined such as the WEEE-vector [15]. The hierarchical model could be transformed tree structure into graph E-R (Entity-Relationship) model if the referential integrity constraint is satisfied. Then we could simply mapping of the hierarchical structure to popular relational model.

4   Conclusion

We propose the RFID-based modular lifecycle data management system with component-level RF tagging to track and manage event log data of products and its components over whole lifecycle. Obtained lifecycle data could handle the quality uncertainty problem then also it could be helpful to take the most appropriate recovery option to maximize resource utilization by multiple recovery. And it could relieve workload and reduce cost of sorting process because the incremental cost of each scan is very low by automated identification.

From an manufacturers point of view, the optimal production planning with considering remanufactured components could be enabled by increasing inventory visibility. And the proposed system could help environmental administrators by playing the role of correct monitoring system from an administration point of view because real time data gathered couldn't be manipulated.

We consider the advantages when the EPCC1G2v2 standard protocol is applied to the reverse logistics process. EPCC1G2v2 promises more space to store user-defined data in user memory bank. If useful information is provided during recycling process on the shop floor, the workers involved in pre-sorting and grading of returned components could use the information to make the most appropriate decision in order to maximize resource utilization about recovery options immediately without external data access. Also we examine the potentiality of using GRAI-170 EPC scheme as the data standard. Its multidimensional encoding scheme with filter value, partition value and asset type promises enough space to tag every component in the target industry.

Also we introduce the XML hierarchical data model as the solution for RF tag data encoding. It would save the memory space by minimizing memory possession that is the main advantage of using hierarchical structure. It also easily transformed into relational data structure widely used.

Obeying current EPC standards promises great interoperability and we hope this work could be the first step to building a centralized monitoring/management system with EPC discovery service.

And structuring of history logs and instructions should be followed up to make perfect structured data-centric XML documents. It would be found out in our following working paper.

References

1. Fleischmann, M.: Quantitative Models for Reverse Logistics. Lecture Notes on Economical and Mathematical Systems, vol. 501. Springer (2001)
2. Thierry, M., Salomon, M., van Nunen, J., van Wassenhove, L.: Strategic Issues in Product Recovery Management. California Management Review 37, 114–135 (1995)
3. Kulkarni, A., Parlikad, A., McFarlane, D., Harrison, M.: Networked RFID Systems in Product Recovery Management. In: Proceedings of the 2005 IEEE International Symposium on Electronics and the Environment, pp. 66–71 (2005)
4. Bajic, E., Chaxel, F.: Auto-ID Mobile Information System for Vehicle Life Cycle Data Management. In: Proceedings of the IEEE Conference on Systems, Man and Cybernetics (2002)
5. Jun, H., Shin, J., Kim, Y., Kiritsis, D., Xirouchakis, P.: A Framework for RFID Applications is Product Lifecycle Management. International Journal of Computer Integrated Manufacturing 22, 595–615 (2009)
6. Parlikad, A., McFarlane, D.: RFID-based Product Information in End-of-Life Decision Making. Control Engineering Practice 15, 1348–1363 (2007)
7. Niederman, F., Mathieu, R., Morley, R., Kwon, I.: Examining RFID Applications in Supply Chain Management. Communications of the ACM 50, 93–101 (2007)
8. Lee, D., Park, J.: RFID-based traceability in the supply chain. Industrial Management and Data Systems 108, 713–725 (2008)
9. Lindhqvist, T., Lidgren, K.: Model for Extended Producer Responsibility: In Ministry of the Environment. From the Cradle to the Grave – six studies of the environmental impacts of products, pp. 7–44. Ministry of Environment, Stockholm (1990)
10. Lindhqvist, T.: Extended Producer Responsibility in Cleaner Production. IIEEE Dissertatons, Lund University (2000)
11. GS1, EPC Radio-Frequency Identity Protocols Generation-2 UHF RFID Version 2.0.0 Ratified (2013)
12. Martin, H., San Millan, E., Peris-Lopez, P., Tapiador, J.: Efficient ASIC Implementation and Analysis of Two EPC-C1G2 RFID Authentication Protocols. IEEE Sensors Journal 13, 3537–3547 (2013)
13. GS1, GS1 Identification Key Series – GRAI (Global Returnable Asset Identifier) Issue 1.1 (2008)
14. Date, C.: An Introduction to Database Systems, 5th edn., vol. I. Addison-Wesley Publishing Company (1990)
15. Luttropp, C., Johansson, J.: Improved Recycling with Lifecycle Information Tagged to the Product. Journal of Cleaner Production 18, 346–354 (2010)

Creative Economy in Solidarity Economy:
A Guide for New Policies

Diego Dias Rodrigues[1], Nilo Costa Serpa[1], Emilly Moura[2],
Luiz Antonio Gouveia[3], and José Benedito Sacomano[1]

[1] UNIP - Universidade Paulista,
Graduate Program in Production Engineering, Brazil
[2] UNIP - Universidade Paulista, Undergraduate Program in Engineering, Brazil
[3] MINC – Ministry of Culture, Secretary of Creative Economy, Brazil
diego@unip.br, {niloserpa,emillymcruz,luizantonio70,jbsacomano}@gmail.com
http://www.unip.br

Abstract. This article was prepared with the purpose of analyzing solidarity economy from the standpoint of its manifestations of creativity, thus fomenting a contribution to the study of the so-called creative economy. This contribution will be investigated in Brazil, Third World country where solidarity initiatives have gained strenght since the early 2000s and where creative talent with regard to survival seems to have no limits. The information compiled and discussed here as an aid to the socio-economic knowledge of the country are intended to provide guidance for new public policies of solidarity that envisage creativity as the main foundation of the success of an economy whatever its market status.

Keywords: creativity, solidarity, economy, creative industry.

1 Introduction

Creativity is the fuel of the evolution of human kind. Culture is the way man burns that fuel to survive, controling nature and giving aesthetic sense to his life. During past decade, many works have been written on the role that criativity plays in economy ([4]; [9]; [10]), but not yet in depth enough to embrace solidarity economy. Even in van der Pol's article, from UNESCO Institute for Statistics, Canada, in which he recognizes that many stakeholders are involved in creative economy process, as cultural public institutions, non-profit sectors which may receive government subsidies and non-governmental organizations [13], nothing was said about solidarity initiatives. Among few authors, Allard and Matthaei referred to the global movement towards the initiatives of solidarity economy as courageous, creative, and diverse [1]; also Wainwright recently emphasized criativity as a determinant labour feature that has to be at the centre of the economy, including solidarity economy [14]. In fact, what we now call "creative industry", and more generally "creative economy", is a new discipline which refers mainly, and almost exclusivly, to the impact of business creativity on the global market, with no great concerns to solidarity and social economy.

B. Grabot et al. (Eds.): APMS 2014, Part II, IFIP AICT 439, pp. 302–309, 2014.

The concept of innovation is intrinsically linked to the concept of creative economy and the latter strongly linked to the solidarity economy in Brazil. Innovation today corresponds to both the improvement of what already exists and the proposal for something new. However, in particular, we commonly draw attention on creative segments such as architectural design and information technology due to the great integration between technological acquisitions and cultural aspects, but solidarity economy as the whole of economic activities of production, distribution, consumption and credit arranged in the form of self-management also encompasses many creative segments, a fact that justifies our researches on creative and solidarity economy together. In order to prevent inappropriate objections, the authors emphasize that this article refers to the study of creative manifestations closely linked to solidarity economy in their forms practiced in Third World, especially in Brazil.

2   Theoretical Frame

In present article, we understand solidarity economy as a collaborative way of producing, selling, buying and exchanging all that is necessary to survival. This collaborative work presumes mainly no exploitation of workers and no wanting to take advantage. Sometimes, we may refer to "social economy" as a synonym of solidarity economy.

This social economy comprises many economic and community practices organized in the form of cooperatives, associations, self-managed enterprises and cooperation networks, which produce goods, provide services, trade and fair trade consumption. Also, solidarity economy appears in emerging countries as an alternative to scarce and precarious formal jobs, but it would be wrong to think solidarity economy only as a form of refuge for the unemployed people, as noted by Kraychete et al. [7]. According to the Digital Atlas of Solidarity Economy (Brazil, 2007-2009), about 30% of solidarity enterprises were due to search for an alternative to unemploymen [11]. Although solidarity economy is, socially speaking, a set of valuable initiatives with great productive potential, little attention has been given to creativity clearly present in several solidarity enterprises.

Creativity is the essence of human evolution. There is nothing new to exalt it. What is new is to consider the creative potential of an enterprise as a collective manifestation of teams to be encouraged and valued by public policies that consider human capital as the only true asset to give materiality for the economic and social development of a nation. Only this will bring technological and scientific independence. There is no obligation to be creative, since innovation is a natural result of brain functions; it is just enough to stimulate the brain to produce innovation. One of the main results of this stimulus is the growth in worker's life quality, once he starts to look at himself as a productive and helpful person. Nevertheless, we must be careful to avoid incurring in the neo-liberal trap of assuming creativity as an intangible individual asset to be galvanized by a covert form of capitalist exploitation obliging workers to be creative, if they want to keep their jobs, as suggested by the Anglo-Saxon culture where the term "creative industry" was coined (it seems to have been born in Australia during the 90s, hence no wonder that the most organized data on creative economy come from the UK). Peuter points out as the European discourse ignores the precarious employment situation [3] in which, one by one, all activities classified within the creative industry are now crumbling beneath the chronic crisis of capitalism, which will end only when governments and companies finally understand that its model of exploitation and profit at any price irretrievably collapsed.

The geographical variety of Brazil offers natural barriers that hinder the access of census groups. Thereby, from the total amount of registered known solidarity enterprises, we can draw those belonging to the segments clearly linked to creativity such as textile and handicraft production, disregarding for the moment the industrial sector for its generality. This corresponds to 28% of the enterprises, a non-ignorable percentage.

3 How Creativity can be Valued in Solidarity Economy

Before presenting the subject of this section, the authors would like to make some observations about modern scientific postures. Hermann Bondi, undoubtedly one of the most eminent physicists of the XX century, noted that the scientist is someone who will never know all the facts, simply because every time something new happens. He concluded that an essential characteristic of science is the ability to describe things so that we can say something without knowing anything [2]. Unfortunately, there was developed, over the last thirty years, a postmodern culture almost completely restricted to the circular reading of articles, leaving aside the critical reading of the great classics that supported and consolidated the knowledge which will build the world of the XXI century. Two results of this abandonment were 1)- the introduction of a generalized inability to realize that to make simple and meaningful things is what is really difficult — indeed, the most universal physical principles are represented by the most simple equations —, and 2)- the incapacity to elaborate conjectures to subject them to tests of refutation. Many modern researchers have difficulty to building models from theoretical conjectures because they have been accustomed to working just about collected data. Only those conjectured models, subsequently subjected to systematic testing, may bring novelty and possibility of observation of hitherto unsuspected aspects. The model which will be presented here, fortunately, belongs to this theoretical category.

From the standpoint of solidarity economy in the third world, what matters are enterprises that aggregate values which are typically derived from creative attitudes; while they may be assigned to individuals, they are shared among the group members and begin to symbolize a joint effort without the capitalist parasitism with all its hate for communities where there is no exploitation of the workforce.

The common classification of creative industries [12] includes:
Advertising, Architecture, Art and Antiques, Crafts, Design, Designer Fashion, Film and Video, Interactive Leisure Software, Music, Performing Arts, Publishing, Software and Computer Services, Television and Radio.

Obviously this is a biased classification in European discourse, since there is no reasonable argument to disregard any human activity as being not likely to assume acts of creation. The creative entrepreneurship itself has become a true philosophy of organizational leadership in the twenty-first century [5]. Even those segments can be said to be the most creative at this moment, since we know that music became a jumble of meaningless banalities and architecture became a barn of futuristic nonsenses, result of an exhibitionism completely distant from the society to which it should serve. Also television, radio and film show complete decay, both in quality of processes and in quality of scripts. What is observed is the great precariousness of work reflected in these sectors in terms of lack of social focus, lack of cultural quality and the almost complete absence of an aesthetic that guides public policies that promote success of economies based on the cultural and biological dimensions, thus building the necessary foundations for promoting real social evolution.

Perhaps, it would be interesting to adopt the following Brazilian definition: the creative industries are those in which productive activities are processes that primarily need a creative act to generating a product, good or service whose symbolic dimension determine its value, resulting in production of cultural, economic and social wealth [8]. Following a global trend, the Ministry of Culture of Brazil launched the Plan of the Secretary of the Creative Economy (2011-2014), the youngest Secretary of this Ministry, following the increased attention that the topic has been gaining in international discussions involving the UNPD (United Nations Program for Development), UNESCO (United Nations Educational, Scientific and Cultural Organization) and UNCTAD (United Nations Conference on Trade and Development).

Since there is creativity in all human productive actions, it will be interesting to compute the "creative impact" of other categories of solidarity enterprises. It would be very difficult to estimate this impact in absolute terms, so let us translate it to a dummy number of creative initiatives that correspond to the above impact. So, we established the formula

$$I = \frac{1 - N_{Sc}}{N_{Sc}} \times n/100,$$

where I is the creative impact, N_{Sc} is the percentage number of typically creative solidarity enterprises, and n is the number of degrees of freedom not typically creative, ie, the number of remaining categories of solidarity enterprises. The result will be added to the percentage of creative solidarity enterprises, thus making the final virtual percentage in creative enterprises.

There are several classifications of creative economic sectors; there is no consensus on the matter. Thus, the degrees of freedom vary according to the interpretations of the structural characteristics of creative production. The creative categories listed above do not correspond to the universe of the solidarity

Fig. 1. Distribution of typically creative enterprises in Brazil

economy, at least not in the Third World. We need a rating closer to the scenarios of social economies in emerging countries. Let us consider the real situation. In accordance with the National Information System of Solidarity Economy, Brazil, the major economic sectors are:

1. Services (Miscellaneous)
2. Agricultural Production, Extraction and Fishing
3. Production of Handcrafted Artifacts *
4. Production of Herbal Medicines, Cleanliness and Hygiene
5. Production and Service of Food and Beverage
6. Production and General Services
7. Industrial Production (Miscellaneous)
8. Mineral Production (Miscellaneous)
9. Textile and Garment Production *
10. Collection Services and Materials Recycling
11. Services Relating to Credit and Finance

Figure 1 maps the distribution of creative segments 3 and 9. The Northern, Northeast and Midwest regions concentrate the most typically creative solidarity enterprises. Except for those marked with an asterisk, which refer to typically creative enterprises, there are nine degrees of freedom to be considered in the above defined equation. Thus,

$$I = \frac{1 - 0.28}{0.28} \times 9/100 = 0.23,$$

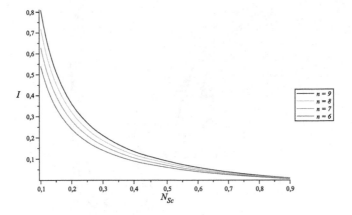

Fig. 2. The theoretical evolution of criative impact of general solidarity enterprises in a society that encourages innovation in all economic segments

from which we obtain the final virtual percentage,

$$F_\% = 0.28 + 0.23 = 0.51,$$

or 51%. Thus, we say that about 51% of the solidarity economy activities manifest considerable degree of creativity. Figure 2 shows how the weight of creative participation of generic productive segments evolves with the relative increase in typically creative enterprises, for different numbers of degrees of freedom. Clearly, the greater the adhesion to policies that encourage innovation projects, the less the creative impact by the simple reason that at the end there will remain no less creative enterprises. What is our intention with this result? Firstly, to show how one should regard creative economy inside the context of solidarity economy in Third World, thus avoiding distortions and concept vices of origin. Second, to estimate the weight of creativity in order to better guide public investment policies in solidarity / creative economy, so that we can establish our own paths of social progress.

4   Discussion

When we seek to mathematically formalize a new hypothesis or set of new hypotheses, we are trying to establish a theoretical model to be further tested and refined through continuous observation and comparison with data from experience. In this study, the proposed formula seeks to establish an evolutionary indicator of the creative economy in the context of the solidarity economy as it stands today in Brazil, so that we can set some initial parameters for the monitoring of the national scenery.

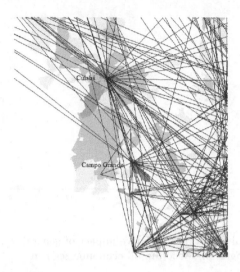

Fig. 3. Airway grid on Midwest region (same legend of Figure 1)

There are very few studies conducted on creative economy in Brazil. These studies need to be directed primarily to the forms of social economy, since in emerging countries there are great deficiencies in public policies that promote the welfare of disadvantaged work forces beneath the defilements of neoliberalism. In Third World, confronting to the present market-driven and neo-liberal economy, the umpteen set of solidarity enterprises are known wanting from the goal of a great integrative and socializing way of development, being more restricted to local challenges of survival and livelihood. For instance, in Asia, the general tendency of social enterprises is to work in isolation [6]. Nevertheless, stimulate and enhance creativity in solidarity enterprises, dividing the merit among the members of the production team and encouraging collaborative behavior as the respect and recognition of individual natural leaders, whether in the field of creation as in the field of ideas in general, can be the way to impart to people the ethical principles of solidarity behaviour as components of a culture of social responsibility and reciprocity in order to constitute a real and solid way of life. Art an criativity are fundamental to transforming ethnocentric person's mindset to one exhibiting compassion for other people, a work absolutely necessary for the success of solidarity culture.

Despite the emphasis on innovation, it is not enough to motivate the solidarity economy without creating a corresponding transport and telecommunication infrastructure to ensure accessibility to products and therefore to people. The Midwest region, for instance, is virtually transparent to the Airway grid with few options of boarding (see Figure 3). Also capillarity by paved roads shows deficient. As we can see, investments for the true creative industry of Brazilian people – linked to social economy enterprises – are heavy and demand long term planning; Zamora was not achieved in a single negotiation.

5 Conclusion

This article discussed how it is possible to analyze the creative economy from the standpoint of solidarity economy, showing the need to build an adequate innovative production model for all Third World countries. It pointed out that debates on creative economy in Brazil can not be conducted in use of the Anglo-Saxon jargon, because this does not fit the reality of the country. It also showed how the emphasis on creativity can motivate the emergence of a culture of solidarity. This paper initiates a collaborative effort between academic researchers and managers of MINC – Ministry of Culture of Brazil – to support decision making in setting parameters for creative economy policies. It is also expected to continue this research in collaboration with other government agencies such as SENAES – National Secretariat of Solidarity Economy.

References

1. Allard, J., Matthaei, J.: Solidarity economy – Building alternatives for people and planet. Papers and Reports from the U.S. Social Forum (2007)
2. Bondi, H.: Assumption and myth in physical theory. Portuguese translation from Paulo César de Morais, pp. 1–53. Editora Universidade de Brasília, Brasil (1997)
3. de Peuter, G.: Creative economy and labor precarity: A contested convergence. Journal of Communication Inquiry 35, 417–425 (2011)
4. Hendrickson, M., Lugay, B., Caldenty, E., Mulder, N., Alvarez, M.: Creative industries in the Caribbean: A new road for diversification and export growth. ECLAC Subregional Headquarters for the Caribbean, Port of Spain (2012)
5. Hagoort, G., Thomassen, A.: On the entrepreneurial principles of the cultural and creative industries (2007)
6. Jayasooria, D. (ed.): Developments in solidarity economy in Asia. JJ Resources, Malaysia (2013)
7. Kraychete, G., Costa, B., Lara, F. (orgs.): Economia dos setores populares: entre a realidade e a utopia. Vozes, Petrópolis (2000)
8. MINC – Ministério da Cultura: Plano da Secretaria da Economia Criativa – políticas, diretrizes e ações, 2011 a 2014. Ministério da Cultura, Brasília (2012)
9. Miles, I., Green, L.: Hidden innovation in the creative industries. NESTA, National Endowment for Science, Technology and the Arts, United Kingdon (2008)
10. Roodhouse, S.: The creative industries: definitions, quantification and practice. In: Eisenberg, C., Gerlach, R., Handke, C. (eds.) Cultural Industries: The British Experience in International Perspective. Humboldt University, Berlin (2006)
11. Serpa, N.: Atlas digital da economia solidária, versão para Internet, http://www.mte.gov.br/sistemas/atlas/AtlasES.html
12. UNCTAD – United Nations Conference on Trade and Development: Creative economy report 2008. UNCTAD/DITC/2008/2, United Nations (2008)
13. van der Pol, H.: Key role of cultural and creative industries in the economy. UNESCO Institute for Statistics, Canada (2011)
14. Wainwright, H.: Notes for a political economy of creativity and solidarity. In: Satga, V. (ed.) Solidarity Economy Alternative – Emerging Theory and Practice. University of KwaZulu Natal Press, Durban (2013)

Simulation for Sustainable Manufacturing System Considering Productivity and Energy Consumption

Hironori Hibino[1], Toru Sakuma[2], and Makoto Yamaguchi[3]

[1] Tokyo University of Science, 2641 Yamazaki, Noda, Chiba, Japan
hibino@rs.tus.ac.jp
[2] MEIJI, Tokyo, Japan
[3] Akita University, Akita, Japan

Abstract. Managing energy consumption of manufacturing systems has become immediately necessary because electricity consumption has become severely restricted in Japan after the Tohoku earthquake on March 11, 2011. Moreover the energy conservation law has been revised in Japan in April, 2010. This law requires management of the energy consumption and reinforces the regulation to reduce more than one percentage of the previous year's energy consumption per unit of production throughput. Manufacturing system simulations to evaluate productivity have often been used when designing and improving sustainable manufacturing systems. However, manufacturing system simulations to evaluate energy consumption per unit of production throughput and the amount of energy consumption have not been proposed. The purpose of our research is to establish a simulation environment for sustainable manufacturing systems considering the productivity and energy consumption. We also propose an implementation for the simulation environment. A case study for a middle-scale semiconductor manufacturing line is carried out to confirm the efficiency of our proposed simulation environment.

Keywords: Sustainable Manufacturing System, Simulation, Productivity, Energy Consumption, Facility State Transition.

1 Introduction

Social interest in environmental evaluation, which originates the awareness of global warming and the finite nature of natural resources, has been rising. In industries, finding and evaluating environmental monitoring items in manufacturing systems has become equally important. For example, after the Tohoku earthquake on March 11, 2011, managing energy consumption of the manufacturing systems has become immediately necessary because electricity consumption has become severely restricted in Japan [1]. Moreover the energy conservation law has been revised in Japan in April, 2010. This law requires management of energy consumption and reinforces the regulation to reduce more than one percentage of the previous year's energy consumption per unit of production throughput [2].

B. Grabot et al. (Eds.): APMS 2014, Part II, IFIP AICT 439, pp. 310–318, 2014.

On the other hand, industries have also paid attention to increase their productivity[3]. Recent manufacturing systems consist of various sub-systems to increase productivity, and each sub-system is complexly related to other sub-systems [3].

To cope with these demands, there are great expectations for designing and improving sustainable manufacturing systems with considering both the environmental and productivity aspects [4]. There are six main requirements to design and improve the environmental aspect of the sustainable manufacturing systems [4]:

1) Establish the prior evaluation of the environmental aspect in a sustainable manufacturing system design and implementation stage.
2) Define the environmental evaluation items.
3) Establish the measuring scale of prior environmental evaluation.
4) Define the data items that information systems must deal with.
5) Establish management methods that take the environmental aspect into account.
6) Enact an international standard.

In this paper, we focuses on requirement 1) of the above list. Especially we deal with the energy consumption as the environmental aspect. Manufacturing system simulation is often used to evaluate productivity when designing and improving manufacturing systems [3]. Methods have been proposed to evaluate energy consumption using simulation concerning a single machining [5] and a single automated guided vehicle [6]. However, concerning sustainable manufacturing systems including a factory and a line, the necessary items and requirements to concurrently evaluate productivity and energy consumption are not clear. It is difficult to evaluate energy consumption using simulation when the sustainable manufacturing systems are designed and improved.

The purpose of our research is to establish a simulation environment for sustainable manufacturing systems considering the productivity and energy consumption. We propose an implementation for the simulation environment. A case study for a middle-scale semiconductor manufacturing line is carried out to confirm the efficiency of our proposed simulation environment.

2   Proposed Simulation Environment for Productivity and Energy Consumption

We define a formula for the energy consumption per unit of production throughput is as follows:

$$A = B / C \qquad (1)$$

where:
  A is energy consumption per unit of production throughput,
  B is the amount of energy consumption and
  C is the production throughput.

To evaluate the throughput using a suitable minimum time unit during the design stage, manufacturing system simulation is often used [3]. Manufacturing system simulations support creation of suitable manufacturing system conditions by means of simulation models. One of the main purposes of the manufacturing system simulation is to evaluate productivity while analyzing material flow and information flow. A simulation is executed paying attention to particular events of interest which are considered to occur instantaneously. The stagnation phenomena for the material flow in manufacturing systems are often evaluated by simulation.

On the other hand, the total energy consumption in a manufacturing system is calculated by summing the amount of energy consumption for each facility. The energy consumption for each facility is calculated by adding the amount of energy consumption in each facility state (e.g. producing state, idle state, stopping state, etc.). For example, in a machining facility that is one of the most fundamental facilities in a manufacturing system, the method of measuring the amount of electricity consumption is defined by the standards organization in Japan [7]. The amount of electricity consumption for the machining facility is measured by a procedure that follows a starting state, idle state, producing state, and stopping state sequence. Therefore, with the machining facility, if the facility states and their state transitions and allotted times are clear, the electricity consumption is estimated by the sum of the electricity consumption in response to the periods for each facility state.

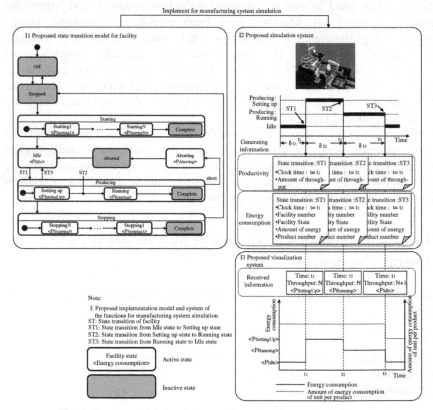

Fig. 1. Our proposed simulation environment for productivity and energy

To evaluate the energy consumption per unit of production throughput and the amount of energy consumption when designing and improving the manufacturing systems, we propose the following requirements:

Requirement 1(R1): Clarifying facility states, their facility state transitions and relationships between each facility state and total energy consumption.
Requirement 2(R2): Simulating the state transitions along a time progression and generating information of the state transitions with a timestamp.
Requirement 3(R3): Generating information of productivity and energy consumption along a time progression.
Requirement 4(R4): Numerically evaluating and visualizing the amount of the energy consumption per unit of production throughput in the minimum time unit.

We propose a simulation environment for productivity and energy consumption. The simulation environment consists of a state transition model for a facility (I1), a simulation system (I2) and a visualization system (I3).

Figure 1 shows an outline of the proposed state transition model for facility (I1), the proposed simulation system (I2) and the proposed visualization system (I3) using the simulation environment for productivity and energy consumption.

2.1   Proposed State Transition Model for Facility

The state transition model for facility (I1) has a necessary function 1 (F1) to realize R1. F1 consists of two sub-functions that define the facility states and their state transition (F1.1), and define relationships between the facility state and energy consumption (F1.2).

First, the definition of the facility states and their state transition (F1.1) is explained. On the basis of our analysis of typical facilities in manufacturing systems, facility states and their state transition are analysed and summarized. Typical facilities are machining facilities, industrial robot facilities and solder reflow facilities. Solder reflow facilities are important facilities in semiconductor manufacturing systems. Using the results of our analysis, we propose the definition of the facility states and their state transition (F1.1). Sub-function F1.1 consists of three characteristics. First, the facility states in our proposed model are divided into five categories: the starting state, the idle state, the producing state, the stopping state and the aborting state. Second, with the starting state, the producing state and the stopping state, there are usually sub-states in each facility state. Each facility state in the proposed model can be divided into sub-states. Third, with the state transition in our proposed model, a facility state usually changes to the next facility state when an activity in the facility state is completed. However, the idle state cannot change to the producing state until an event occurs, such as when production parts arrive. The stopping state and the aborting state also change from the producing state only when a facility stoppage occurs. The proposed state transition model for facility (I1) is expressed using a Unified Modelling Language (UML) model.

Furthermore, the definition of relationships between the facility state and energy consumption (F1.2) is explained. A calculation formula for the energy consumption E_{sn} of the facility state S_n is as follows:

$$E_{Sn} = \int_{t_{n-1}}^{t_n} P_{Sn}(t)dt \qquad (2)$$

where

t_n is the finishing time of facility state S_n

t_{n-1} is a stated time for facility state S_n

$P_{sn}(t)$ is the energy consumption in facility state Sn at time t.

Using $P_{sn}(t)$, it is possible to calculate the energy consumption of the facility state. However, it is difficult to define $P_{sn}(t)$ for all facilities in a manufacturing system. Therefore, in this study, we use an average P_{sn} from t_{n-1} to t_n.

2.2   Proposed Simulation System

The proposed simulation system (I2) has a necessary function 2 (F2) to realize R2 and R3. F2 consists of three sub-functions that simulate the state transition along a time progression (F2.1), generate productivity information including the throughput with a timestamp in the minimum time unit (F2.2) and generate information of the energy consumption with a timestamp in the minimum time unit (F2.3).

First, the simulation of the state transition along a time progression (F2.1) is explained. The simulation supports suitable manufacturing system conditions by means of simulation models. The simulation model consists of facility simulation models that include the proposed state transition model for the facility. The simulation is executed paying attention to particular events of interest which are considered to occur instantaneously. Each event marks a change of the facility state in the simulation. Between consecutive events, the simulation directly jumps in time from one event to the next. Then facility state information with a timestamp and event information for each state transition that occurs are generated by the simulation.

Second, the generation of productivity information including the throughput with a timestamp in the minimum time unit (F2.2) is explained. The production throughput information with a timestamp along a time progression is generated. Then the production throughput information at the place we define, such as a facility level and/or line level, is obtained.

Third, the generation of information of the energy consumption with a timestamp in the minimum time unit (F2.3) is explained. The energy consumption with a timestamp along a time progression is generated. Then, the energy consumption at the place we define, such as a facility level, is obtained.

2.3   Proposed Visualization System

The proposed visualization system (I3) has a necessary function 3 (F3) to realize R4. F3 consists of two sub-functions that are used to receive information for the productivity and the energy consumption, to calculate the energy consumption per unit of the production throughput in the minimum time unit (F3.1) and to visualize the energy consumption per unit of production throughput (F3.2).

First, the receipt of information for the productivity and the energy consumption and the calculation of the energy consumption per unit of the production throughput in the minimum time unit (F3.1) are explained. The generated information is a simulation clock, facility numbers, the amount of production throughput, the amount of energy consumption and so on. The generated information with a time stamp is sorted and stored in ascending order. The energy consumption per unit of production throughput for each facility is calculated using the generated information and the formula while considering the minimum time unit.

Second, the created energy consumption per unit of production throughput for each facility is visualized using the spraying figures feature.

3   Implementation of Proposed Simulation Environment for Productivity and Energy Consumption

In this chapter, the implementation for the proposed simulation system (I2) and the proposed visualization system (I3) is proposed.

First, implementation for the proposed simulation system (I2) is described. The proposed simulation system has three sub-functions used to satisfy requirement 2 (R2). The function to simulate the state transition along a time progression (F2.1) is implemented in Witness that is a commercial discrete event simulator. Witness provides a simulation engine function and a simulation programming support function. The simulation engine function controls the simulation along a time progression while paying attention to particular events of interest that occur instantaneously. The simulation programming support function helps engineers to develop extension functions using the Visual Basic (VB) programming language. The facility simulation models that include the proposed state transition model for facility (I1) are implemented in Visual Basic.

Second, implementation for the proposed visualization system (I3) is described. The receipt of information for production throughput and energy consumption and the calculation of the energy consumption per unit of the production throughput in the minimum time unit (F3.1) are implemented in Excel that is a commercial spread sheet. We developed a macro program in Excel. The generated information with a time stamp from the simulation is saved in a text file using the CSV format. The macro program in Excel makes it possible to read the CSV file. The generated information with a time stamp is sorted and stored in ascending order in Excel. The energy consumption per unit of production throughput for each facility is calculated using the generated information.

4   Case Study

The purpose of this case is to evaluate the application of the simulation environment to a middle-scale semiconductor manufacturing line consisting of three facilities, the solder printing facility, the IC mounting facility (mounter facility), and the solder reflow facility. The three facilities were modelled in Witness using our proposed state transition model. Figure 2 shows a simulation model of the middle-scale semiconductor manufacturing line and simulation input data. There are four types of products. There are three types of lot sizes as 60, 120, 240. The simulation period in this case study is 40 hours over five days.

Using the above conditions, the simulation was performed. The simulation generated facility state information with a timestamp as well as event information for the state transitions with a timestamp including clock time, facility number, amount of electricity consumption, type of product and product number. The simulation also generated the production throughput with a time stamp.

Using the generated information from the simulation, the dynamic changes in the energy consumption per unit of production throughput along the time axis were visualized in the visualization system. The energy consumption per unit of production throughput was numerically expressed along the time line.

Figure 3 shows transitions of the energy consumption per unit of production throughput in the solder reflow facility. The energy consumption per unit of production throughput was getting smaller when the lot size was getting larger in Figure 3.

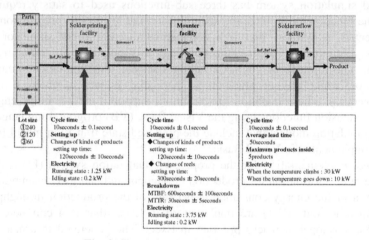

Fig. 2. Simulation model of case study

To analyze their factors, we focused on the amount of no-load running periods in the solder reflow facility. Figure 4 shows histograms of the no-load running periods in the solder reflow facility. S1 in Figure 4 means influence of setting up changes of kinds of products in the mounter facility. S2 in Figure 4 means influence of setting up changes of the reels in the mounter facility. The frequency of S1 was becoming increasing by decreasing the lot size. The more frequency of S1 increased, the longer no-load running periods became because the stagnation phenomena of the material flow occurred. The stagnation phenomena decreased the throughput. Thus the amount of waste energy in the solder reflow facility increased.

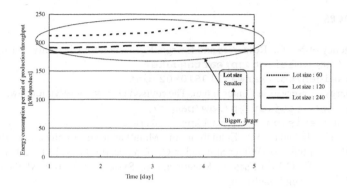

Fig. 3. Energy consumption per unit of production throughput in solder reflow facility

It was confirmed the efficiency of the proposed simulation environment through the case study.

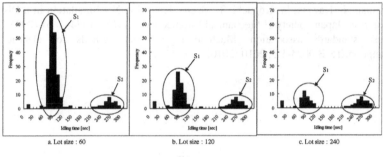

Note :
S₁ : Influence of setting up changes of kinds of products in the mounter facility
S₂ : Influence of setting up changes of the reels in the mounter facility

Fig. 4. Histogram of no-load running periods in solder reflow facility

5   Conclusion

In this paper, we proposed a simulation environment for sustainable manufacturing systems considering the productivity and energy consumption. A state transition model, a simulation system and a visualization system were proposed and implemented considering the necessary items and requirements for the simulation environment. Finally, case studies for a middle-scale semiconductor manufacturing line was conducted to confirm the efficiency of the proposed simulation environment.

References

1. The Agency of Natural Resources and Energy, Restriction for electricity consumption,
   http://www.meti.go.jp/earthquake/
   shiyoseigen/pdf/kanwai110610-02.pdf
2. The Energy Conservation Center Japan, The revised energy conservation law,
   http://www.eccj.or.jp/law/pamph/
   outline_revision/new_outline2010.pdf
3. Hibino, H., Fukuda, Y.: Emulation in Manufacturing Engineering Processes. In: Proceedings of the 2008 Winter Simulation Conference, pp. 1785–1793 (2008)
4. Hibino, H.: MSTC Idea Factory, Manufacturing System Evaluation Method Considering Green Factor Using Simulation,
   http://www.mstc.or.jp/event_report/20120608/
   h24_if_soukai4.pdf (in Japanese)
5. Narita, H., Kawamura, K., Norihisa, T., Chin, L., Fujimoto, H., Hasegawa, T.: Development of Prediction System of Environmental Burden for Machine Tool Operation: 1st Report, Proposal of Calculation Method of Environmental Burden. Japan Society of Mechanical Engineers C 71(704), 1392–1399 (2005)
6. Murayama, N., Kawata, S., Koguchi, T.: Scene Transition Net Simulation in a Distributed Environment. Japan Society of Mechanical Engineers C 71(703), 1054–1061 (2005)
7. Japanese standards association, Machine tools –test methods for electric power consumption, TS B 0024-1-5, 2010 (2010)

Life-Cycles and Sustainable Supply Chain

Nicolas Malhéné and Claude Pourcel

EIGSI – Ecole d'Ingénieurs en Génie des Systèmes Industriels,
26, rue des Vaux de Foletier La Rochelle Cedex 1 17041, France
nicolas.malhene@eigsi.fr, claude-pourcel@orange.fr

Abstract. The former Prime Minister of Norway, Gro Harlem Brundtland defined sustainable development as "forms of progress that meet the needs of the present without compromising the ability of future generations to meet their needs." This definition must become the cornerstone of a renewed economic thinking even though companies simply offer a somewhat altered standard model to incorporate environmental considerations. In this article, we propose a discussion about the life-cycle concept from different points of view in order to consider the design and the implementation of Supply Chain to be more compatible with sustainable development.

Keywords: Sustainable Development, Supply Chain, Logistics, Product Life-Cycle.

1 Introduction

A company is a system, i.e. an organic whole which groups together a limited number of elements organized according attributes and relationships. According to the systemic paradigm [1], the company interacts with its environment to evolve i.e. to modify/adapt its structure and/or its operation. This dynamic evolution results from succession of cycles including classical steps from development until removing. The result of companies interacting together in a Supply Chain intensifies this dynamic and multiplies the number of cycle to be managed.

In this article, we propose a reflection on the use of life-cycle concept as a structuring element in the design of a Sustainable Supply Chain. First of all, we present two points of view about the life-cycle concept; one focusing on industrial point of view and the second integrating upstream and downstream stakeholders in order to fit with circular economy concept. Next we discuss major types of logistics in particular sustainable logistics too often limited to an environmental dimension. In the third part of this article we propose an approach to design a sustainable supply chain based on the use of the life-cycle concept.

2 Life-Cycle Concept

Much research has been done to describe the life-cycle concept. In this article, we discuss two specific points of view about the life-cycle concept:
- From the "Idea" until the "Removing" (Industrial Life-Cycle);
- From the "Extraction" of raw materials to the "Disposal of waste" generated by the product's utilization (Life-Cycle Assessment).

B. Grabot et al. (Eds.): APMS 2014, Part II, IFIP AICT 439, pp. 319–325, 2014.
© IFIP International Federation for Information Processing 2014

Industrial Life-Cycle describes the process from the emergence of a concept to the reality of the product available to consumers. Whether the product is tangible or symbolic [2, 3], it can be defined as "an object transformed by Man through a process which is not natural". Based on the assumption, any product impacts negatively the environment.

Life-Cycle Assessment focuses on "Production" phase of ILC such as presented in Figure 1. LCA takes into account all the activities that are involved in the Supply Chain: raw material extraction, manufacture of the product, its distribution, its use and the disposal or recycling of this product. LCA aims at identifying all environmental negative impact of these steps in order to reduce these impacts.

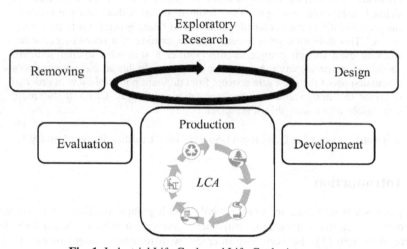

Fig. 1. Industrial Life-Cycle and Life-Cycle Assessment

One considers that negative impacts will be minimal if a closed Supply Chain is implemented. This is the objective of "cradle to cradle" which proposes to create and to recycle in an infinite way [4]. The recovery of waste and the use of recovered materials should be encouraged in order to manufacture products again and again to conserve natural resources. Figure 2 presents such a proposal and insists on the necessity of the transport between all steps. Today's business model now joins the shortening of product life cycle. In fact, although efforts are being made on each step of the cycle, they are offset by the increased weight of transport.

In previous research [5], we insist on circular economy principles. Moving away from the linear model, the circular economy model advocates in favor of long-life goods, reusable products, reconditioning activities and waste prevention. Therefore business models today must break away from 17th century heritage of accounting constraints and focus on how products are used to increase the quality of company decisions about sustainable development needs by lengthening product life-cycle. This implies that LCA back in ICL to be built in the first phase to configure the entire Supply Chain.

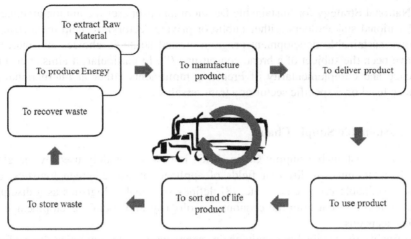

Fig. 2. Closing the loop

3   Sustainable Supply Chain

3.1   Supply Chain and Logistics

Supply Chain Management considers combination and implementation of various logistics operations. Logistics plans, implements and controls the flow and storage of goods, services and related information from raw material extraction until product delivery in order to meet customer needs. Four different categories may be considered:

- *Inbound logistics* considers activities for the production of transformable resources (some call raw materials), the production of consumable resources (such as water, gas, electricity, ...) and the production recycled resources and different means of transport of these resources;
- *Internal logistics* concerns all flow of raw materials, components, subassemblies and products within the production system;
- *Outbound logistics* considers activities associated to product's transportation, product delivery and product use;
- *Reverse logistics* considers operations related to the reuse of products and materials. It includes the management and the sale of surpluses, as well as products being returned to vendors from buyers [6].

A new transversal approach, *Sustainable Logistics*, answers actual and future production problematic. It does not consider a specific operation but aims at achieving all operations in coherence with sustainable development definition. For this reason it fits in the context of national strategies for sustainable production and consumerism. In France, it aims at guiding the economy toward a green and fair economy:

"The National Strategy for Sustainable Development proposes a common architecture for all national stakeholders (either public or private sectors), to help them structure their own sustainable development program around strategic choices and indicators that have been the subject of a broad consensus [7]". In particular, it aims at ensuring coherence and complementarity of French commitments either at international and European level on a specific sector or a transversal way.

3.2   Sustainable Supply Chain

Research on Sustainable Supply Chain (SSC) is new and widely used by the global research community in different fields of application: waste, green logistics, eco-design, sustainable procurement, etc. [8] defines sustainable logistics as a discipline that takes into account both the economic, ecological and social development in the logistics decisions.

The finality of sustainable supply chain management is to maximize the profits of the chain while minimizing environmental impacts and maximizing social issues [9]. Considering this finality, SSC management must prolong product life-cycle while focusing on Sustainable Logistics operations management, resources, information and financial flows.

3.3   Sustainable Supply Chain strategy

Supply Chain or Sustainable Supply Chain SSC can be considered as a system of systems according following definitions:
- Metasystem that are themselves comprised of multiple autonomous embedded complex systems that can be diverse in technology, context, operation, geography and conceptual frame" [10];
- System resulting from the collaborative functioning of independent component systems (which can function independently to meet their own operational mission)" [11];
- System of systems respects five necessary conditions: operational and managerial independence, evolutionary development, emergent behavior and geographic distribution are respected [12].

Supply Chain global strategy must target system collaboration and existing management tools such as SCOR®[1] which aims to achieve this objective. Level 1 is the most conceptual level of SCOR® and is used to describe the scope and high level configuration of a supply chain. SSC must integrate all steps of product life-cycle and in particular the "Exploratory Research" to focus on the use of the product by the customer for prolonging the cycle. This proposal increases the number of stakeholders and the dimension of the system of systems. The strategy must consider four views and projects these views on a 3 dimensional performance referential (Figure 3).

---

[1] Supply Chain Council: https://supply-chain.org/

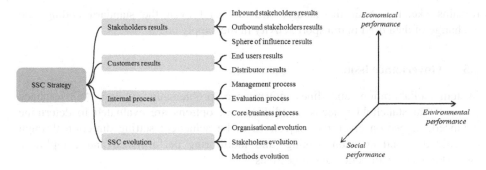

Fig. 3. SSC strategic definition

Decisions associated to this conceptual representation are done in an integrated way considering that they directly impact the performance in LCA, for example:

- to guide sustainable consumer behavior,
- to manage sustainable production,
- to preserve natural resources (minimize raw materials / maximize recycling),
- to save energy and to develop renewable energy,
- to promote sustainable transport,
- to improve the governance of sustainable development.

The first four decisions above fit naturally with circular economy principles that that we have presented. Transport and governance issues need to be developed.

3.4   Transport Issue

It seems obvious to favor short product channels or networks since we have highlighted the great carbon impact of transportation in a "cradle to cradle" close loop (Figure 2). In reality, the reasoning is not so simple. A European example, such as exotic fruits, does not necessarily worsen the ecological carbon footprint of a product. Exotic countries propose ideal climatic conditions for local fruit growth. The same climatic conditions can be artificially imitated in Europe with substantial energy consumption (Greenhouses maintained at 20°C and simulated lighting). The carbon footprint of exotic fruit produced in Europe is 6 times greater (3 grams) than exotic fruit produced in Africa - yet transported by plane! Therefore, if a production process is CO_2 efficient, it is not so obvious that transport increases systematically carbon footprint of consumer products.

Of course, it is healthier and preferable to consume fruit locally according to the seasons of given geographic latitudes especially as it promotes local economies.

The carbon impact of transportation is increasingly important as a product nears its final destination, i.e. a city, since the logic of mutualizing is very difficult to implement. Research has been conducted to optimize such transport mutualizing in cities [13, 14]. Research shows such approaches are very demanding in information and underlines the limits of existing management tools. For example, even SCOR®

remains sketchy about the nature, structure and even the standard coding and exchange of data used in transport activity in the supply chain.

3.5   Governance Issue

System collaboration underlines governance problematic solving. "Governance ensures that stakeholder needs, conditions and options are evaluated to determine balanced, agreed-on enterprise objectives to be achieved; setting direction through prioritization and decision making; and monitoring performance and compliance against agreed-on direction and objectives"[2].

SSC increases the size of the system of systems, the number of stakeholders and thus, the number of needs, objectives to take into account. It is therefore necessary to define in a very precise way the management mode when developing SSC strategy in order to ensure the balance between all these elements. Governance topic has been discussed in AFIS forums and led up to a tutorial entitled "System of Systems Architecture and Engineering." As an example, last kilometer delivery is very important in term of financial and environmental costs in the supply chain. Different ideas emerged to reduce these costs but many experiments have been abandoned due to stakeholder interest incompatibility. Research is actually conduced to solve such problem merging public and private interest implementing global governance.

4   Conclusion

The historical model of industrial development has been in a crisis for a long time. The industry is entering a spiral negatively impacting the environment, the human society and even the world economy. Far from the definition of Gro Harlem Bruntland, this historical development undermines the integrity systems of living and unbalances the sharing of excessive wealth. The result is the development extreme social tensions.

Research on sustainable logistics seeks an escape from this spiral. It cannot ignore research about "Systems Engineering and Sustainable Products". This includes following sub-themes such as: strategy, governance, operational and support functions, life cycle design (or eco-design), modeling, architecture, assessment, etc. This research is carried out within a virtual workshop whose aim is to deepen the impact of Reasonable Sustainable Development. Participants explore different fields of application but in the same philosophical framework for introducing the circular economy. This article is a natural result of these discussions and proposes a more global vision, based on the concept of product life-cycle, when designing SSC to go beyond "cradle to cradle" cycle to include: circular economy principles and prolonging product life-cycle. Our more global vision proposes companies must break with traditional basic economic models, to adopt a more collaborative sustainable development model which allows the sharing of common issues.

---

[2] IT Governance Institute: http://www.itgi.org/

The outlook is promising but is based upon the profound questioning of attitudes, and in particular, the questioning of economic models developed over the past two centuries. Major industrial powers are now asking many questions. For example in China, the "Law for the promotion of circular economy" came into force on the 1st of January 2009. Now local Chinese governments in more than 100 cities are participating in a national government competition to the best circular economy city system. You can be sure that they will become worldwide showcases of circular economy.

References

1. Le Moigne, J.L.: La modélisation des systèmes complexes. Collection AFCET Systèmes. Editions Dunod, Paris (1990)
2. Gourc, D., Jia, A., Pourcel, C., Pourcel, P.: Approche objet à la modélisation d'entreprise. Communication présentée au 4ème Congrès International de Génie Industriel, Marseille, France (1993)
3. Gourc, D.: Contribution à la réingénierie des systèmes de production. Thèse pour l'obtention du titre de Docteur de l'Université François Rabelais de Tours. Génie Industriel, Spécialité (1997)
4. Mc Donough, W., Braungart, M.: Cradle to Cradle: Remaking the Way We Make Things. North Point Press (2002)
5. Pourcel, C., Breuil, D.: Dossier Cycle de vie - Dossier rédigé à l'occasion d'une réflexion collective sur l'apport du Génie Industriel et de l'Ingénierie Système aux projets de développement durable. Dossier de recherche EIGSI (2013)
6. Monnet, M.: - Les stratégies de logistique inversée: une perspective théorique. Logistique & Management 19(1) (2011)
7. MEDDE: Ministère de l'Ecologie, du Développement Durable et de l'Energie, La logistique: tour d'horizon – Rapport de la Direction générale des Infrastructures, des Transports et de la Mer (2013)
8. Pan, S.: Contribution à la définition et à l'évaluation de la mutualisation des chaines logistiques pour réduire les émissions de CO_2 du transport: application au cas de la grande distribution. Thèse de doctorat, Ecole des Mines de Paris (Décembre 2010)
9. Hassini, E., Surit, C., Searcy, C.: A litterature review and case study of sustainable Supply Chain with a focus on metrics. International Journal of Production Economics 140(1) (2012)
10. Keating, C., Rogers, R., Unal, R., Dryer, D., Sousa-Poza, A., Safford, R., Peterson, W., Rabadi, G.: System of Systems Engineering. Engineering Management Journal 15(3), 36–45 (2003)
11. Fiorèse, S., Meinadier, J.P.: Découvrir et comprendre l'ingénierie système. Collection AFIS. Editions Cépaduès, Toulouse (2012)
12. Maier, M.: Architecting Principles for Systems of Systems. In: Proceedings of the Sixth Annual International Symposium, Inter. Council on Systems Engineering, Boston, MA (1996)
13. Masson, R., Trentini, A., Lehuédé, F., Peton, O., Tlahig, H., Malhéné, N.: Optimization of a shared passengers & goods urban transportation network. Odisseus (2012)
14. Malhéné, N., Trentini, A., Marques, G., Burlat, P., Bénaben, F.: Freight Consolidation Centers for urban logistics solutions: the key role of interoperability. In: IEEE DEST-CEE 2012, Campione d'Italia, Italy, June 18-20 (2012)

Sensitivity Analysis of Reverse Supply Chain System Performance by Using Simulation

Shigeki Umeda

Musashi University, 1-26 Toyotama-kami Nerima Tokyo 176-8534, Japan
shigeki@cc.musashi.ac.jp

Abstract. This paper proposes a methodology of performance sensitivity analysis of reverse supply chain systems by using simulation. This paper discusses two types of reverse logistics model: PUSH-type and PULL-type. And, it proposes a generic method to analyze system performance by using discrete-event simulation and factorial experiment design. The characteristics of reverse supply chain systems (PUSH-type and PULL-type) are shown in detail. The result of these analyses would provide useful data for planning reverse supply chain systems.

Keywords: Reverse supply chain, Reverse logistics, Simulation, Performance evaluation, ANOVA.

1   Introduction

Supply chain management (SCM) has received tremendous   attentions both from the business world and from academic   researchers during the last two decades. SCM is a set of approaches utilized to efficiently integrate suppliers, manufacturers, warehouses, and stores, so that merchandise is produced and distributed at the right quantities, to the right locations, and at the right time, in order   to minimize system-wide costs while satisfying service level requirements. Problems for supplier selection [1] and performance evaluation models [2] are, for examples, discussed from various points of view.

In the last decade, due to environmental and ecological responsibility, enterprises are trying to reuse, remanufacture and recycle the used products to reduce the negative impact on environment, especially the manufacturers of the electrical consumer products. Requirements for corporate responsibility and sustainability are getting more urgent. Kara and Onut discussed a two-stage stochastic and robust programming approach to strategic planning of a reverse supply network through a case of paper recycling supply chain [3]. Kenne et al. applied a similar approach to production planning of a hybrid manufacturing–remanufacturing system under uncertainty within a closed-loop supply chain [4]. Kocabasoglu et al. discussed a investment issue on supply chains linking with reverse flows [5]. Kuma and Malegeant discussed a closed-loop supply chain thorough a case of manufacturer and eco-non-profit organization [6]. Nativi and Lee discussed RFID information-sharing strategies on a

B. Grabot et al. (Eds.): APMS 2014, Part II, IFIP AICT 439, pp. 326–333, 2014.

decentralized supply chain with reverse logistics operations [7]. Rahman and Subramanian scoped computer recycling operations in reverse supply chain and analyzed factors for implementing system operations [8].

Performance analysis of supply chain systems is a critical issue in its design stage. Simulation is such a generic approach that gives solutions of performance analysis of supply chain systems. Chan et al. applied simulation to analysis of impact of collaborative transportations in supply chain systems [9]. Chatfield et al. developed a supply chain simulation system by using an object-oriented modeling method [10]. Labarthe et al. proposed an agent-based modeling and simulation of supply chain systems [11]. Umeda and Lee developed a general purpose supply chain simulator [12].

Tannock et al. developed a data-driven simulation of aerospace sector's supply-chain [13]. Yoo et al. proposed a hybrid algorithm for discrete event simulation based supply chain optimization [14]. Zhang et al. used a simulation software for analysis of a demand-driven Leagile supply chain Operations Model [15]. Persson and Olhager applied a performance simulation of supply chain designs. This work is based on discrete-vent simulation technologies [16], meanwhile, Fiala used SD simulation to analyze information sharing in supply chains [17]. Tako and Robinson reviewed journal papers that use these modeling approaches to study supply chains, published between 1996 and 2006 are reviewed. A total of 127 journal articles are analyzed to identify the frequency with which the two simulation approaches are used as modeling tools for DSS in LSCM [18].

Previous researches discussed system concepts of reverse supply chain system, and proposed methodologies of performance evaluation by using simulation methodologies. This paper proposes a methodology of performance evaluation of reverse supply chain systems by using simulation and experiment design. Generic models are introduced and analysis examples of individual features will be provided [19].

2   Scenarios and Models

2.1   Reverse Logistics Scenarios

Reverse logistics systems require taking back products from customers and the repairing, remanufacturing (value-added recovery), or recycling (material recovery) the returned products. The reverse logistics in supply chains is strongly related to all stages of a product development and is also a critical problem to all level of the industry.

There are many types of reverse logistics [20]. We, here, consider a virtual supply chain system, which is composed of the following components: Chain manager, Supplier, Manufacturer, Retailer, Customers, Collector, and Remanufacturer (Fig.1). This model supposes home electric appliances such as PCs, TVs, and refrigerators.

Supplier, Manufacturer, and Retailer are members that form arterial flows (production generation flows) in a chain. Supplier provides parts or materials to Manufacturer according as supply orders from Chain manager. Manufacturer provides products to Retailer according as production orders from Chain manager. Retailer provides products to Customer according as Demand (Purchase) order from Customer. Customer uses products and disposes them (generates the disposed materials).

S. Umeda

Meanwhile, Collector and Remanufacturer are members that form venous flows (reverse logistic flows) in a chain. The Collector reclaims used products from Customer, when he/she disposes the used product. And, it detaches reusable materials from the disposed product, and sends them to Remanufacturer. Remanufacturer regenerates products by using materials provided by Collector. And, it provides them to Manufacturer, such as spare-parts.

Chain Manager is a supervisor of the chain the processes order information in the chain. It receives demand order from Customer. It predicts demand in next ordering duration by using Customer's order. It also gives production orders production orders to Manufacturer and Supplier by using the predicted demands. Deliverer connects these members and carries materials from its upstream to its downstream.

The configuration of these members is shown in Fig.1 and Fig.2. These models are based on an analogy between arterial-venous blood flows in a human body and material-flow in a supply chain. Solid lines are production generation flow (arterial-flow), meanwhile, dashed lines are reverse logistics flow (venous-flow) in Fig.1 and Fig.2. Arterial-flows and venous-flow should be synchronized with each other. The system synchronizes venous flows with arterial flows.

2.2 Reverse Logistics Models

The flow from Customer to Remanufacturer by way of Collector is a reverse logistics flow. Customer sends "used-products" to Collector, when Customer disposes them. The role of Collector is to distinguish reusable materials from the disposed products, and stores them. This paper introduced two types of logistics model that controls this reverse logistics flow: PUSH-type and PULL-type.

The PUSH-type is that Collector and Remanufacturer sends reverse products to Manufacturer in an orderly manner. In PUSH-type, remanufactured products are sequentially pushed into Manufacturer, synchronizing with occurrence of reverse. Remanufactured product would be kept as material inventory in Manufacturer. In PUSH-type, remanufactured products are sequentially pushed into Manufacturer, synchronizing with occurrence of reverse. Remanufactured product would be kept as material inventory in Manufacturer (Fig.1).

Meanwhile, the PULL-type is that Collector and Remanufacturer work according as PULL signals from their downs-streams. In PULL-type, reverse products are stocked at Collector. These products stay at there, during no PULL signal from Remanufacturer. And, Remanufacturer does not work until it receives PULL signal. In Fig. 2, Collector works as "Stock-driven" mode. Collector continuously observes stock volume at Remanufacturer. It starts to produce products when the stock volume is smaller than the stock-replenishment level, and continues to work until the stock volume is equal to or greater than the stock-volume level. This works according to the following operational sequences:

1. Collector periodically observes stock volume data at Remanufacturer.
2. Collector starts producing while stock volume at Remanufacturer goes down below the stock-replenishment level.
3. Collector stops producing when the stock volume reaches the stock-volume level.

This logic is also applied to the case of between Remanufacturer and Manufacturer.

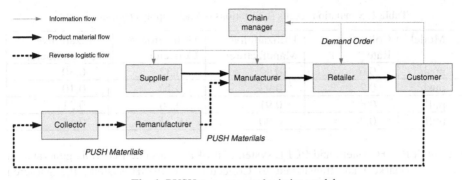

Fig. 1. PUSH-type reverse logistics model

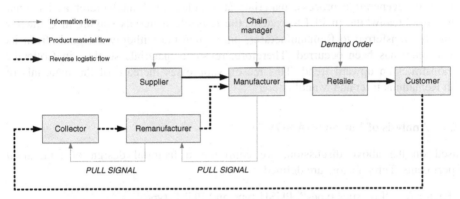

Fig. 2. PULL-type reverse logistics model

3   System sensitivity Analysis by Using Simulations

3.1   Preliminary Experiments and Experiment Design

We, first of all, did preliminary experiments to extract major of this system model. The conditions of this experiment are: simulation duration (100 days), Customer's orders interval (5 days), Distribution function of customers' demands (Uniform distribution between 6 lots to 10 lots (U(6,10)), and Collection rates of Collector (high level (0.6) and low level (0.2)). This experiment result demonstrates that models and collection rates are major factors giving effects on system performance. Table.1 represents the differences between PUSH-type reverse and PULL-type reverse. The PULL system indicates higher utilization of Collector than the PUSH system. In PUSH system, the Collector works only when the materials arrive from its Upstream (Customer). Meanwhile, in PULL system, Collector works to replenish inventories at the downstream (Remanufacturer). This mechanism, accordingly, makes higher resource utilization, when the Collection Rate is at low level.

Table 1. Simulation results (Utilizations of each supply chain member)

Model	Collection Rate	Utilization@ Manufacturer	Utilization@ Collector	Utilization@ Re-manufacturer
push	0.6	0.92	0.32	0.30
push	0.2	0.92	0.12	0.10
pull	0.6	0.91	0.36	0.21
pull	0.2	0.90	0.24	0.15

In both PUSH system and PULL system, all of the reusable materials generated at Customer (market) are transferred to Collector. In PUSH system, the gathered materials in Collector are sent to Remanufacturer, which is a re-production process. After this regeneration process, materials accumulate on Manufacturer as its input materials. Meanwhile, in PULL system, the reusable materials staying at Collector would be transferred to Remanufacturer, only when the withdrawal signals from its downstream has been occurred. Therefore, reusable materials stocked in Collector demonstrates an upward trend. This reason suppresses increase of the materials in both Remanufacturer and Manufacturer.

3.2   Analysis of Variance (ANOVA)

Based on the above discussion, we configure a factorial design of simulation experiments. Three factors are defined;

- Factor A: "Logistics types", PUSH-type and PULL-type
- Factor B: "Range of demand distribution". Three distribution functions are defined U(4,12), U(6,10), and U(7,9), respectively.
- Factor C: "Collection Rate: Three rates are defined, high-level (0.7), middle-level (0.4), and low-level (0.1), respectively.

Therefore, 18 simulation runs are required. Factorial experiments are designed with respect to these three factors. Table 1, 2, and 3 represent inventory means. The factor A (Logistics type) and the factor C(Collection Rate) are significant in the case of Manufacturer (Table.4). The factor A (Logistics type) and the factor B (Demand variance) are significant in the case of Retailer (Table.5). And, the factor A (Logistics type) and the factor C (Collection rate) are significant in the case of Collector (Table.6). The F value of factor A (Logistics type) is large in every case. This result is as a corollary. The effect of Collection rate variance is large in Manufacturer and Collector. This result is considered reasonable and proper judging by chain structure.

In contrast, it is Retailer that the effect of demand variance (factor B) is large. Moreover, it should be noted that mutual factor with factor A (Logistics type) is large. Manufacturer and Collector are sensitive with Factor A and Factor C (Collection Rate).

Table 2. Average of inventory volumes at "Manufacturer"

Factors		C (Collection Rate)		
A(Logistics types)	B(Demand)	0.1	0.4	0.7
PUSH	D(4,12)	27	30	36
	D(6,10)	25	32	37
	D(7,9)	25	30	35
PULL	D(4,12)	33	33	33
	D(6,10)	34	34	34
	D(7,9)	33	33	33

Table 3. Average of inventory volumes at "Retailer"

Factors		C (Collection Rate)		
A(Logistics types)	B(Demand)	0.1	0.4	0.7
PUSH	D(4,12)	8	8	8
	D(6,10)	13	13	13
	D(7,9)	10	10	10
PULL	D(4,12)	11	11	11
	D(6,10)	9	9	9
	D(7,9)	8	8	8

Table 4. Average of inventory volumes at "Collector"

Factors		C (Collection Rate)		
A(Logistics types)	B(Demand)	0.1	0.4	0.7
PUSH	D(4,12)	11	13	17
	D(6,10)	11	14	16
	D(7,9)	11	14	17
PULL	D(4,12)	2	3	9
	D(6,10)	2	3	8
	D(7,9)	2	3	7

Table 5. Analysis of Variance (ANOVA) of "Manufacturer")

Factor	Squared Sum	Freedom	Mean Square	F0
A(Logisics)	29	1	29	38.67**
B(Demand)	5	2	2.5	3.33
C(Collection)	81	2	40.5	54**
AxB	0	2	0	0
AxC	78	2	39	52**
BxC	3	4	0.78	1.04
Error	3	4	0.75	

Table 6. Analysis of Variance (ANOVA) of "Retailer"

Factor	Square Sum	Freedom	Mean Square	F0
A(Logisics)	5	1	5	40**
B(Demand)	14	2	6.8	54.4**
C(Collection)	0	2	0	0
AxB	39	2	19.5	156**
AxC	0	2	0	0
BxC	1	4	0.25	2
Error	1	4	0.125	

Table 7. Analysis of Variance (ANOVA) of "Collector"

Factor	Square Sum	freedom	Mean square	F0
A(Logisics)	401	1	401	1604**
B(Demand)	0	2	0	0
C(Collection)	108	2	54	216**
AxB	0	2	0	0
AxC	2	2	1	4
BxC	3	4	0.78	3.12
Error	1	4	0.25	

4   Conclusion and Future Research

Full factorial design of simulation experiments and analysis of variance (ANOVA) represent that difference of systems factor gives a large influence on system performance of reverse supply chain systems. Manufacturer and Retailer are, especially, affected by interactions of independent factors. In PUSH system, material inventory volume at Manufacturer increases according as time progress. Meanwhile, the inventories at both Collector and Remanufacturer do not fluctuate so much. In PULL system, the material consumption at Collector synchronizes with material inventory volume at Remanufacturer, and the material consumption at Remanufacturer synchronizes with material inventory volume at Manufacturer. When the Manufacturer possesses sufficient volume of input material, Remanufacturer does not need to provide Manufacturer with materials any more.

The next stage of this simulation analysis will need to consider processes cost factors at both reverse supplier (Collector and Remanufacturer). When the regeneration process at both Collector and Remanufacturer is expensive, the PULL system would be better choice.

References

1. Amin, S.H., Zhang, G.: An integrated model for closed-loop supply chain configuration and supplier selection. Expert Systems with Applications 39, 6782–6791 (2012)

2. Estampe, D., Lamouri, S., Paris, J., Brahim-Djelloul, S.: A framework for analyzing supply chain performance evaluation models. International Journal of Production Economics (2010), doi:10.1016/j.ijpe.2010.11.024
3. Kara, S., Onut, S.: A two-stage stochastic and robust programming approach to strategic planning of a reverse supply network: The case of paper recycling. Expert Systems with Applications 37, 6129–6137 (2010)
4. Kenne, J., Dejax, P., Gharbi, A.: Production planning of a hybrid manufacturing–remanufacturing system under uncertainty within a closed-loop supply chain. Int. J. Production Economics 135, 81–93 (2012)
5. Kocabasoglu, C., Prahinski, C., Klassen, R.: Linking forward and reverse supply chain investments: The role of business uncertainty. Journal of Operations Management 25, 1141–1160 (2007)
6. Kumar, S., Malegeant, P.: Strategic alliance in a closed-loop supply chain, a case of manufacturer and eco-non-profit organization. Technovation 26, 1127–1135 (2006)
7. JoseNativi, J., Lee, S.: Impact of RFID information-sharing strategies on a decentralized supply chain with reverse logistics operations. Int. J. Production Economics 136, 366–377 (2012)
8. Rahman, S., Subramanian, N.: Factors for implementing end-of-life computer recycling operations in reverse supply chains. Int. J. Production Economics (2011), doi:10.1016/j.ijpe.2011.07.019
9. Chan, F., Zhang, T.: The impact of Collaborative Transportation Management on supply chain performance: A simulation approach. Expert Systems with Applications 38, 2319–2329 (2011)
10. Chatfield, D., Harrison, T., Hayya, J.: SISCO: An object-oriented supply chain simulation system. Decision Support Systems 42, 422–434 (2006)
11. Labarthe, O., Espinasse, B., Ferrarini, A., Montreuil, B.: Toward a methodological framework for agent-based modelling and simulation of supply chains in a mass customization context. Simulation Modelling Practice and Theory 15(2), 113–136 (2007)
12. Umeda, S., Lee, Y.T.: Integrated Supply Chain Simulation – A Design Specification for a Generic Supply Chain Simulation, NISTIR 7146, National Institute of Standards and Technology, US Dept. of Commerce (2004)
13. Tannock, J., Cao, B., Farr, R., Byrne, M.: Data-driven simulation of the supply-chain-Insights from the aerospace sector. Int. J. Production Economics 110, 70–84 (2007)
14. Yoo, T., Cho, H., Yücesan, E.: Hybrid algorithm for discrete event simulation based supply chain optimization. Expert Systems with Applications 37, 2354–2361 (2010)
15. Zhang, Y., Wang, Y., Wu, L.: Research on Demand-driven Leagile Supply Chain Operation Model: a Simulation Based on AnyLogic in System Engineering. Systems Engineering Procedia 3, 249–258 (2012)
16. Persson, F., Olhager, J.: Performance simulation of supply chain designs. Int. J. Production Economics 77, 231–245 (2002)
17. Fiala, P.: Information sharing in supply chains. Omega 33, 419–423 (2005)
18. Tako, A.: The application of discrete event simulation and system dynamics in the logistics and supply chain context, Stewart Robinson. Decision Support Systems 52, 802–815 (2012)
19. Umeda, S.: Performance Analysis of Reverse Supply Chain Systems by Using Simulation. In: Prabhu, V., Taisch, M., Kiritsis, D. (eds.) APMS 2013, Part II. IFIP AICT, vol. 415, pp. 134–141. Springer, Heidelberg (2013)
20. Gupta, S., Omkar, D., Palsule, D.: Sustainable supply chain management: Review and research opportunities. IIMB Management Review 23, 234–245 (2011)

Comprehensive Improvement of Industrial Energy Efficiency: Pilot Case in a European Rolling Stock Factory

Nils Weinert[1], Rafael Fink[1], Christian Mose[1], Friedrich Lupp[1], Florian Müller[1], Jan Fischer[1], Ingo Bernsdorf[2], and Alessandro Cannata[1]

[1] Siemens AG Corporate Technology, Munich, Germany
{nils.weinert,rafael.fink,christian.mose,friedrich.lupp,
muellerflorian.ext,jan.fischer.ext,alessandro.cannata}@siemens.com
[2] Siemens AG Corporate Technology, Berlin, Germany
ingo.bernsdorf@siemens.com

Abstract. Energy and resource efficiency requires more suitable approaches to be consistently implemented in industry. Factories are more complex systems than residential or commercial buildings; in industrial domain, improvements for energy efficiency require measures that are difficult to be identified and that vary from building to manufacturing processes fields. This paper presents a comprehensive approach to systematically address industrial energy efficiency improvement. The approach has been developed and tested at a European rolling stock manufacturer. Insights from the pilot case presented confirm that this holistic view helps properly address energy efficiency in industrial domain.

Keywords: eco-factory, rolling stock manufacturing, energy efficiency.

1   Introduction

Manufacturing is one of the main consumers of global primary energy consumption and producer of related emissions. Improvement of energy efficiency in factories is a key driver to support the achievement of European 20/20/20 goals. Hence, industry has to rethink current approaches about design and management of manufacturing systems, to take a significant step towards energy efficient factories.

However the task is challenging, since factories are complex systems made of interacting elements such as people, production assets, material handling equipment, building service equipment, etc. A holistic approach which, moving away from local optimization, considers the factory as a whole has been developed within EMC²-Factory, an on-going FP7-European Research project (www.emc2-factory.eu).

To show its industrial applicability, the approach has been tested in a real case, a European rolling stock factory several measures to improve energy efficiency have been identified and developed, of which the most relevant and impactful are presented in this paper.

The approach is briefly introduced in section 2; section 3 and 4 describe the pilot case and the identified measures; section 5 includes final conclusions.

B. Grabot et al. (Eds.): APMS 2014, Part II, IFIP AICT 439, pp. 334–341, 2014.
© IFIP International Federation for Information Processing 2014

2   Approach Adopted

EMC²-Factory project aims at developing new solutions for planning and operating eco-efficient factories, as well as using existing methods and tools combining them in a more effective way. An integrated view has been adopted in the project to prevent problem shifting due to the mentioned complex system interconnections, e.g. from production to technical building services. This integrated view fully considers all the components in a factory and their reciprocal influence on each other. Solutions (both developed within EMC²-Factory and available externally) for this variety of fields are very diverse and end up in a high-number of alternatives that the decision maker can choose. Moreover, since factories are significantly different for every specific case, this complicates the decision making for energy efficiency improvement in the individual industrial case.

Hence, a method to identify the case-specific measures has been developed. This method, of which details are published in [1], helps the user to systematically address the most impactful measures and optimize energy efficiency and lean production for the overall factory system by selection of appropriate solutions for a specific discrete production environment. Solutions, in this context, are for instance technologies, organizational principles and frameworks or software tools developed in the EMC²-Factory project by all partners, in addition to existing and established approaches from academia and industry. The methodology was tested against the pilot described in the following chapter – an existing Siemens AG rail car factory. The methodology is based on two phases with six sequential process steps. A numerically ranked set of applicable solutions is derived by narrowing down possible solutions from a larger set and thus improving the proposed ranking stepwise.

In the first phase, the user specifies preferences for certain types of solutions by specifying criteria values that differentiate between solution elements. Criteria are e.g. the applicable factory level, the life cycle phase or the problem solving phase. Each criterion is then numerically weighted against one another by the user.

In the second phase, a hierarchical, class-based factory model is set up, mainly describing the physical elements of a factory. This model is used in the extended energy value stream analysis (EEVSA) [2] to store the properties of the physical elements required for deriving the values of the EEVSA. The main goal of the EEVSA is to map the total energy consumption of a factory to individual process chains/value-streams, taking all peripheral systems into account. Based on the KPIs coming from the EEVSA, a set of certain Energy Drivers can be ranked in order to differentiate sources for the total energy consumption of processes. In the next step the ranked Energy Drivers are mapped to the so-called Design Parameters, returning a ranked set of these. Design Parameters are levers of a factory that can usually be utilized to improve energy efficiency or lean performance (e.g. factory layout, long-term production schedule, machine control). Since the correlation between Design Parameters and the solutions can be numerically approximated, these solutions can be ranked in a subsequent mapping step by matrix multiplication. The ranked solutions are then selected for application in a final step, using Total Cost of Ownership (TCO) methodology and cross-impact analysis.

3   Pilot Case Description and Motivation

The selected pilot case is a Siemens AG rolling stock manufacturing site located in Vienna. It produces rail vehicles of stainless steel or of aluminium for Metros, Coaches and Light Rail. Several processes are there performed, such as machining, grinding, joining, coating, and final assembly in a shop floor area of 63000 m². Before this research activity started, the site already addressed the topic of energy and resource efficiency with different projects on building renovation (insulation, ventilation systems, etc.), a new surface treatment center, and product design improvement from product life cycle perspective (e.g. lighter materials to consume less energy during the use phase of the trains, use of recyclable material), however the holistic factory perspective adopted in this project was not yet part of the considerations.

In order to show impact of the developed approach on energy efficiency, the pilot has been focused on a single building of the site. In this building, the main train components such as undercarriages, roofs and sides of a train car are manually grinded and manually and/or automatically welded. Moreover in the same building two machining centres are available for pre- and post-welding processes. With an area ca. 4500 m², the building was chosen for three reasons:

- Representative: It includes typical manufacturing processes of train production;
- Relevant: It shows complex material flow and interaction among processes;
- Challenging: It was recently improved from energy perspective such as air heat exchangers, building insulation, and air doors. Hence, further improvement requires going beyond state-of-the-art technologies and approaches.

4   Overview of Measures Analysed

For the investigated building and the affected part of the metro car's value stream, the solution finding process was applied as described in chapter two. First the as-is analysis has been performed gathering both energy and production-related information.

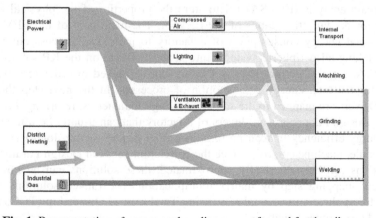

Fig. 1. Representation of energy sankey diagram performed for the pilot case

Based on one-time measurements, several shop floor visits and available production data the required information to set up the hierarchic factory model and to derive the extended energy value stream could be acquired. The total energy consumption of the building (visualized as an Energy Sankey diagram in Fig. 1), indicated high consumption of peripheral hardware like lighting, heating and ventilation among others.

Using the results of the EEVSA, the solution finding process was performed with several iteration loops. Each iteration loop was defined with different user preferences according to the momentary step in the problem solving process and the related focus of application (e.g. analysis vs. solution phase, process vs. process-chain perspective). Fig. 2 depicts the results of an exemplary iteration loop, targeting the analysis phase and the value stream process utilizing the biggest electrical consumer.

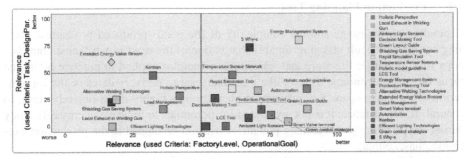

Fig. 2. Results of exemplary iteration cycle of solution finder

After several iterations, the solution finder indicated the biggest potential for energy management, production planning, alternative welding-technologies and layout.

4.1   Energy Transparency and Management System

As one of the common principles in engineering, knowledge gained from transparency is often seen as a prerequisite for improvement. Following this maxim, as a first step certain relevant production entities have been energetically measured using one-time measurements. First insights on energy consumption and distribution were used as input for the solution finder [3].

One-time measurements are sufficient for providing a basic knowledge on the consumption in a steady application, but in a dynamic environment like present in production continuous monitoring is required to detect shortages. Beyond developing transparency, actual management of energy consumption becomes possible, leading to the decision to implement an Energy Management System (EMS) for the investigated building. The system consists of several measuring points for electrical energy and pressurized air. Using an industrial PC, measured consumptions are monitored automatically in real time, generating signals for control measures like machine standby opportunities or air leakage detection. The architecture (Fig. 3) is designed for later enhancements, e.g. automated interventions in those cases, or for being integrated in an overall, factory-wide Energy Management System as required, e.g. by ISO 50001 or by future integration in Smart Grid environment.

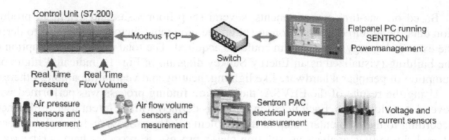

Fig. 3. Energy Management System - concept

4.2   Production Planning Tool

Depending on the range and the complexity of the goods produced production planning can be a difficult task. Presumably that is one of the reasons why most contributions from scientific literature and scheduling principles applied in practice often just focus on single economic aspects like the adherence to delivery dates or the minimization of the make-span. Yet, production planning is a highly multi-objective task, in general. If, for instance, it is not accounted for potentials to improve energy efficiency during the planning process, these potentials will not be tapped in the production execution phase, either.

In the following some examples for levers are provided to include the aspect of energy efficiency into the production planning process:

- A minimization of non-value-adding work (e.g. setup and transportation activities) helps to avoid the wasting of time and energy. Additionally it reduces the logistic complexity of the production process.
- An appropriate choice of the utilized production machines and modes can help to reduce the energy cost without harming other planning objectives (e.g. if alternative machines are available or velocity can be regulated).
- Load balancing and the minimization of peak loads can contribute to significantly lower energy costs, if peak-load is charged and the production process is very energy intensive.
- A smart production organization (e.g. synchronization of individual shift systems) can help to reduce energy costs related to TBS like air conditioning, lighting, heating and exhaustion systems, etc.
- The anticipation of applied control strategies (which e.g. decide if and when machines are switched off during idle periods) can lead to a smoother course of production and therefore contribute to improve energy efficiency.

Based on this list of levers and the circumstances in the industrial pilot case, a multi-criteria production planning software tool was developed and implemented within the EMC²-Factory project. With the help of that tool production planners can now simultaneously optimize the production process with respect to different KPIs like adherence to delivery dates or the energy consumption. Tradeoffs between these KPIs can now be quantified by calculating and evaluating not just one single solution but a set of alternative non-dominated schedules. The algorithmic approach is based on a multi-start priority rule based schedule construction heuristic. For details on the algorithmic concept that has been realized in the software tool see [4].

4.3   Alternative Welding Technologies

In a factory, the total energy consumption is significantly higher than the actual energy required for the main, value adding manufacturing steps. One reason for this is the effectiveness of the processes as well as secondary processes that are required to perform the core process. Furthermore, a complete process chain includes several pre- and post-processes consuming energy themselves, e.g. milling a work piece as preparation for a joining process. Additionally large variety of secondary energy consumers is required, including maintenance and transport operations and technical building services (TBS) [5].

All of these pre-, post- and secondary processes are consuming energy only for enabling the actual value adding manufacturing steps. Consequently, in the design of a process chain, it is not sufficient to focus on the main steps only, but rather to investigate energetic demands more comprehensive to achieve an overall optimum.

For doing so, process designers need to have the possibility to compare alternative process chains by providing an indicator, including the energy demand of all relevant primary and secondary consumers. This key element has been developed as a process-dependent, normative energy indicator. Focussing on welding processes as the prevalent manufacturing process in the rail car industry, the specific energy demand per welded length is used. The indicator was defined as the accumulated energy over all considered process states and the whole production sequence, divided by the total length of weld created in that time [6]. Dominant factors influencing the indicator are found within the areas of:

- A particular process technology (e.g. GMAW or FSW);
- Particular process parameters for the observed work piece;
- Auxiliary systems implemented in the observed manufacturing equipment;
- Amount of non-productive time and associated energy demand on the equipment;
- Organizational influence by equipment's productive - non-productive time ratio;
- Organizational influence through the load of the equipment.

The approach introduced was applied in the Siemens plant to investigate alternative welding processes. Essential results are that within welding processes for aluminium, Friction Stir Welding (FSW) has an advantage over Gas-Metal-Arc Welding (GMAW) regarding its energy demand of the main process and even more for secondary consumptions - mainly caused by the fume emission of GMAW and the required exhaust systems - emphasizing the need to explicitly consider these in process chain design. However, a short term change of process chains for existing products is difficult to realize due to reasons of approved designs and processes, etc. Anyways, now the data is available to consider this advantage for future product designs.

4.4   Layout Reconfiguration

The production system layout is of special interest for an energy efficient design of buildings. A production system is the surface organization and the area where production environment conditions (e.g. illumination, temperature) interact with the equipment. While general planning guidelines (e.g. minimal floor load zones) are state of the art in planning, the planning of elements like layout, TBS and disposal infrastructure across interfaces requires to enforce communication, collaboration and a faster decision making. Additional multidisciplinary experts need to provide knowledge and analytical methods together if the planning activity is properly designed.

A workshop-based green layout planning method was developed to position machines and equipment with environmental aspects in mind (for details see [7]). Concerning the pilot case three alternative layouts were developed that can be beneficial:

- Separation of welding and machining: Welding and machining of metal parts requires filtering and exhaust ventilation of a different kind. If welding and machining operations would be locally separated smaller and better designed TBS for one specific function could be used. A local decentralized exhaust system would be another option to avoid a central TBS system completely. Security and process barriers caused by electrical conductibility of car bodies make this an unrealistic option.
- Isolated preheating zone for car body: Because of quality reasons the car body needs to have a certain temperature to be processed so a preheating time up to 24 hours can be necessary in the facility. Therefore additional heat will be supplied through the radiators. Preheating next to surface treatment to use waste heat from there would make the heating system consume less energy and reuse otherwise wasted thermal sources.
- Discrete milling area: Despite local chip disposal, coolant system and workplace lighting the two milling centers are on the both outsides of the building with machining and welding operations. If the milling would be separated, there would be no exhaust and TBS system required. Additional transport way and handling effort has to be considered for the production planning.

Since cost for a building and TBS change are disproportionately high the implications have to be considered in the future building (re-)planning of the site. Nevertheless they are general principles, whose implications from environmental side can be easily identified through layer evaluation (for details on this approach see [8]).

5   Discussion and Conclusions

The proposed approach started from creating transparency with an energy management system and covered different areas normally assessed only for production-related performance (production planning, substitution of processes and layout reconfiguration). The solutions highlighted from the approach are highly interdisciplinary and they address the challenge of energy efficiency from different perspectives.

Two transversal remarks came out from testing the approach:

1. To address energy efficiency, the complete system made of production machines, processes, TBS, and building shell has to be analysed as entity. For example, the improvement of the direct energy requirement for welding process (local optimization), can have less impact than the reduction of energy for auxiliary systems (fume exhaust) or to the substitution of process technologies to avoid fumes.
2. Although countless measures for energy efficiency improvement are available, each case has specific features and issues that can be almost unique. An approach that helps to structure the problem and focus on the most impactful measures is a promising approach to extend and facilitate decision making when implementing energy efficiency measures in industrial domain.

Since industrial decision-making is driven by cost-benefits analysis, the presented approach should include economical analysis to be smoothly accepted by decision-makers. This aspect is already under consideration and will be integrated in the approach within future developments.

Acknowledgment. This research is partially funded by the European Commission under the 7th Framework Programme - research project EMC²-Factory (www.emc2-factory.eu).

References

1. Fischer, J., Weinert, N., Herrmann, C.: Method for selecting improvement measures for discrete production environments using an extended energy value stream model. Submitted to 12th Global Conference on Sustainable Manufacturing, Johor Bahru, Malaysia (September 2014)
2. Posselt, G., Fischer, J., Heinemann, T., Thiede, S., Alvandi, S., Weinert, N., et al.: Extending Energy Value Stream Models by the TBS Dimension – Applied on a Multi Product Process Chain in the Railway Industry. Accepted for 21st CIRP LCE Trondheim (June 2014)
3. Weinert, N., Fischer, J., Posselt, G., Herrmann, C.: Lean and Green Framework for Energy Efficiency Improvements in Manufacturing. In: Seliger, G. (ed.) Proceedings of the 11th Global Conference on Sustainable Manufacturing, pp. 512–516 (2013)
4. Fink, R.: A priority rule based multi criteria scheduling framework for energy efficiency aware detailed production planning. In: Proceedings of the 39th IEEE IECON, Vienna, pp. 7508–7512 (November 2013)
5. Mose, C., Weinert, N.: Evaluation of Process Chains for an Overall Optimization of Manufacturing Energy Efficiency. In: Advances in Sustainable and Competitive Manufacturing Systems, FAIM 2013, pp. 1639–1651 (2013)
6. Mose, C., Weinert, N.: Process and process chain evaluation for an overall optimization of energy efficiency in manufacturing – The welding case. In: Robotics and Computer Integrated Manufacturing (accepted for publication)
7. Mueller, F., Cannata, A., Stahl, B., Taisch, M., Thiede, S., Herrmann, C.: Green Factory Planning - Framework and modules for a flexible approach. In: Prabhu, V., Taisch, M., Kiritsis, D. (eds.) APMS 2013, Part I. IFIP AICT, vol. 414, pp. 167–174. Springer, Heidelberg (2013)
8. Müller, F., Cannata, A.: Integrierte Bewertung als zentraler Bestandteil einer grünen Fabrikplanung. In: Vernetzt Planen und Produzieren 2013. TU Chemnitz (2013)

Optimal Sizing of Energy Storage Systems for Industrial Production Plants

Simone Zanoni and BeatriceMarchi

Dipartimento di Ingegneria Meccanica e Industriale, Università degli Studi di Brescia,
via Branze, 38, 25123, Brescia, Italy
{simone.zanoni,b.marchi}@unibs.it

Abstract. Most developed countries around the world are seriously concerned about recent global warming, the depletion of fossil fuels and environmental degradation. So as to meet the environmental burden reduction targets set by different international agreements, manufacturing companies are seriously encouraged to invest considerable efforts in the field of energy. Energy storage systems (ESS) have the potential to revolutionize the way in which electrical power grids are designed and operated. Presently, power grids require that the generation of electricity continuously balance the demand. The constant balancing of supply and demand has significant operational and cost implications. Incorporation of storage devices into the grid should reduce this constraint by enabling electrical energy to be withdrawn from the grid when there is excess generation and held in reserve until needed. In this work we consider stationary applications with medium discharge time (minutes to hours), thus batteries have been considered. The object is to find the optimal sizing of the energy storage device (i.e. batteries) with which it is possible to minimize the cost of energy in a production plant.

Keywords: Energy storage systems, renewable energy sources, batteries.

1 Introduction

Most developed countries around the world are seriously concerned about recent global warming, the depletion of fossil fuels and environmental degradation. Accordingly, effective energy use and reduction of greenhouse gas (GHG) emissions are becoming increasingly important goals. The development and use of renewable energy sources (RES) has experienced rapid growth over the past few years and, in the next 20-30 years, all sustainable energy systems will have to be based on the rational use of traditional resources and greater use of renewable energy [1]. One of the main characteristics of most of the RES is the variability in the energy production, generally linked to environmental conditions, often disjointed from real necessity of energy from users. Valuable energy produced by RES can be effectively used by storing surplus energy in a storage device and using it when required; in this way RES can be used to aid the transition for a newer and cleaner energy generation technology [2].

The main characteristics of electricity is that ideally it must be used at the same time and in the same place as it is generated. The proper amount of electricity must

B. Grabot et al. (Eds.): APMS 2014, Part II, IFIP AICT 439, pp. 342–350, 2014.

always be provided to meet the varying demand, and an imbalance will damage the stability and quality (voltage and frequency) of the power supply even when it does not lead to totally unsatisfied demand. The issues caused by these characteristics are:

- High generation cost during peak-demand periods;
- Need for continuous and flexible supply to meet changing power consumption, relying on an accurate forecast of the variations in demand;
- Needs for a more efficient grid: in order to avoid congestions, interruptions in the supply ...

In the last years, the concept of self-consumption has become increasingly relevant thanks to the many benefits that introduces in terms of energy efficiency. The use of ESS leads to a growth of the rate of energy self-consumed and improves the utilization of the PV system. For that reason, in this paper we will analyse the affordability of energy storage for an industrial plant. We consider the scenario in which a PV system is integrated with an ESS. The analysis made leads to relevant considerations on the barriers and opportunities on the use of energy storage devices.

The paper will be structured as follow: in Section 2 is presented a literature review on the ESSs; in Section 3 it is shown the proposed model and the results of the analysis and, finally, in Section 4 the concluding remarks are presented.

2   Energy Storage System

ESS refers to a process of converting electrical energy from a power grid into a form that can be stored for converting back to electrical energy when needed [3]. ESSs have the potential to revolutionize the way in which electrical power grids are designed and operated. Presently, power grids require the constant balancing of supply and demand and it has significant operational and cost implications. Incorporation of storage devices into the grid would relax this constraint by enabling electrical energy to be withdrawn from the grid when there is excess generation and held in reserve until needed [4]. ESS is expected to play an important role thanks to the rapidly accelerating rate of technological development with anticipated unit cost reductions as shown in Figure 1 [3].

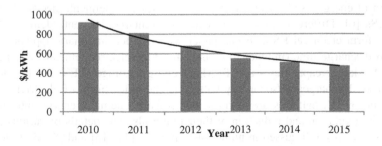

Fig. 1. Lithium Ion Battery Price per kWh

From the viewpoint of consumers, the main roles of ESS are:

- *Time shifting and cost savings* by using ESS to reduce peak power and to purchase electricity at off-peak times;
- *Emergency power supply* to operate during an outage.

There are two major emerging market needs for ESS as a key technology: to utilize more renewable energy and less fossil fuel, and the future Smart Grid. The increased ratio of RES generation may cause several issues in the power grid. First, the fluctuation in the output of RES generation makes system frequency control difficult. Secondly, RES output is undependable since it is affected by weather conditions, and any surplus power may be thrown away when not needed on the demand side (see Figure 2). ESS may intervene against those issues, stabilizing RES output, increasing self-consumption and through time shifting (i.e. matching the supply and demand of energy). Therefore valuable energy can be effectively used by storing surplus electricity in ESS and using it when necessary and it can also be sold when the price is high (i.e. generation shifting scenario). As is said in [5], the generation shifting scenario is expected to be the first widespread application of ESSs as it is the one that may potentially generate additional revenues in a PV project.

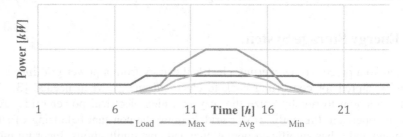

Fig. 2. Energy consumption and PV production

ESSs can be characterized in terms of: energy and power capacity, round trip efficiency, response time, discharge duration, discharge frequency, depth of discharge and self-discharge. A complete definition of those characteristics can be found in [4]. A widely-used approach for classifying ESS systems is the determination according to the form of energy used: mechanical, electrochemical, chemical, electrical and thermal ESSs [6]. Different applications with different requirements demand different features form electrical ESS. In this paper we consider stationary applications with medium discharge time (minutes to hours), in which electrochemical ESS (i.e. batteries) – for larger capacities - and flywheel energy storage (FES) are the dominant technology. Rechargeable/secondary battery is the oldest form of electricity storage. As is said in [7], batteries are devices that convert chemical energy into electrical energy, by oxidation and reduction of their materials. The details of various types of batteries have been discussed in numerously paper - [1] - [3] and [8]. Batteries are in some ways ideally suited for electrical energy storage applications because they provide fuel flexibility and environmental benefits, they can respond very rapidly to load changes and enhance the system stability. Batteries usually have very low stand-by losses and can have high energy efficiency. The construction of a secondary battery is facilitated by the short lead times and the technology's modularity. However, battery storage has some disadvantages too: low energy densities, small power capacity, high maintenance costs, a short cycle life a limited discharge capability and most batteries contain toxic materials. Hence the ecological impact from uncontrolled disposal of batteries must always be considered [3]. Some of the most used technologies are: Lead Acid, Sodium Sulphide (NaS) and Lithium Ion (Li-Ion) Batteries. In Table 1, are shown the main characteristics from literature of the mentioned batteries:

Table 1. Batteries' Characteristics

	Lead Acid	NaS	Li-Ion
Cost [€/kWh]	150	250	1000
Round Trip Efficiency [%]	80	89	98
Life [cycle]	2000	2500	4000
Life [years]	12	15	20
DOD [%]	80	100	80
Self-Discharge [%/month]	5	0	1

3   The Model

The objective of this work is to analyze the situation depicted in Figure 3, in order to find the optimal sizing of the energy storage device (i.e. batteries) with which it is possible to minimize the cost of energy management and purchase in an industrial system.

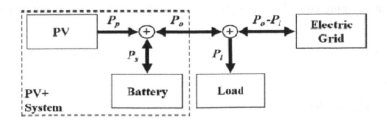

Fig. 3. Reference scheme of the PV+ESS system [9]

The main notation used is given in the following table:

Table 2. Main Notation

$p_{e,t}$	Unit price to sell a kWh to the grid in t [€/kW h]	$E_{stored,t}$	Energy stored at the beginning of t [kW h]
$p_{self,t}$	Unit premium price to self-consume a kWh of renewable energy produced in t [€/kW h]	$E_{losses,t}$	Energy loss in t due to the characteristics of the battery [kW h]
$c_{e,t}$	Unit cost to buy a kWh from the grid in t [€/kW h]	$P_{c,t}$	Charging power from the grid in t [kW]
D_t	Energy demand in t [kW h]	$P_{d,t}$	Discharging power from the device in t [kW]
P_t	Energy production in t [kW h]	E_{max}	Device's energy capacity – i.e. maximum energy the device can store [kW h]
$E_{grid,t}$	Energy taken from the grid in t [kW h]	P_{max}	Device's power capacity – i.e. maximum charge or discharge rate [kW]
$E_{sold,t}$	Energy sold to the grid in t [kW h]	P_{nom}	Device's nominal power capacity [kW]
$E_{self,t}$	Renewable energy self-consumed in t [kW h]	DOD	Depth of discharge [%]
α	Battery's cost reduction	C_{BESS}	Total cost of the energy storage device [€/year]
L_{BESS}	Batteries' lifetime [years]	t	Hourly time interval [h]
ρ	Discount rate [%]	N	Time interval for BESS investment [years]

The model consists in the minimization of the total annual cost of energy (i.e. cost for the energy purchased from the grid and costs due to the investment and use of BESS):

$$\min TC\left(P_{nom}\right) = \sum_{t=1}^{8760}\left(c_{e,t}\cdot E_{grid,t}\left(P_{nom}\right) - p_{e,t}\cdot E_{sold,t}\left(P_{nom}\right) - p_{self,t}\cdot E_{self,t}\left(P_{nom}\right)\right) + C_{BESS}\left(P_{nom}\right) \quad (1)$$

where

$$P_{max} = P_{nom}\cdot DOD \quad (2)$$

$$C_{BESS}\left(P_{nom}\right) = \frac{C_{BESS,0}\left(P_{nom}\right) + \sum_i \dfrac{C_{BESS,i}\left(P_{nom}\right)}{\left(1+\rho\right)^i}}{N} \quad (3)$$

with $i = L_{BESS}, 2\cdot L_{BESS},..., N - L_{BESS}, \quad i > 0$

$$C_{BESS,i}\left(P_{nom}\right) = C_{BESS,0}\left(P_{nom}\right) - \alpha\cdot\ln\left(i\right) \quad (4)$$

The constraints of the model are following reported:

$$D_t + E_{sold,t}\left(P_{nom}\right) = P_t + E_{grid,t}\left(P_{nom}\right) - E_{losses,t}\left(P_{nom}\right) \tag{5}$$

$$0 \le P_{d,t}\left(P_{nom}\right), P_{c,t}\left(P_{nom}\right) \le P_{max}\left(P_{nom}\right) \tag{6}$$

$$0 \le E_{stored,t}\left(P_{nom}\right) \le E_{max}\left(P_{nom}\right) \tag{7}$$

Due to the presence of several key technologies of electrochemical storage, it has been decided to compare different scenario considering the three types of batteries mentioned in the previous section. The proposed model guarantees that the hourly demand of the production plant is met by the joint action of the energy generation of the PV system and the energy stored in the batteries. The connection to the power grid serves as a backup resource, if the production from RES is not sufficient to cope with the demands.

The data used in the implementation of the model are referred to an industrial plant in Italy already equipped with a photovoltaic system (PV), whose profiles of demand and PV production are shown in Figure 4. For the electricity cost and incentives it has been considered the regulatory framework of the country.

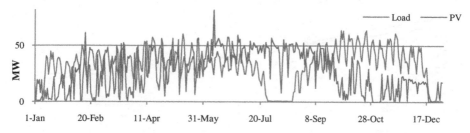

Fig. 4. Demand and PV Production patterns over a year

In addition to the total cost, it is interesting to observe how the values of the following indexes change: self-consumption (share of the energy produced that is self-consumed without being fed into the grid) and self-sufficiency (share of total energy demand that is satisfied with that produced by the PV system).

Table 3 shows the results of the model:

Table 3. Model's Results

		PV	PV+BESS		
			Lead Acid	NaS	Li-Ion
P^*_{nom}	[MW]	0	3,83	4,21	0
TC	[€/year]	1.351.550,12	1.323.523,91	1.306.654,44	1.351.550,12
Self-Consumption	[%]	36%	44%	44%	36%
Self-Sufficiency	[%]	30%	36%	37%	30%

In Figure 5, it is possible to observe the benefits and costs introduced with BESS. As it can be seen, the use of new more performing technologies (Li-Ion) is replaced by mature technologies because of the cost of investment still too high. When the investment in storage technologies is profitable, we attend an increase of both the indices (i.e. self-consumption and self-sufficiency). See Table 3.

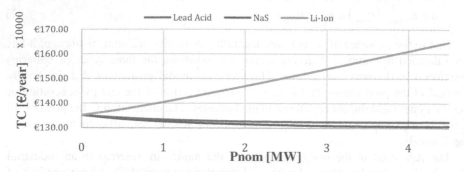

Fig. 5. Total annual energy cost varying the nominal power of the BESS

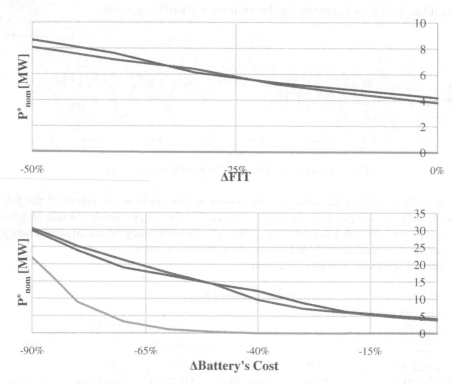

Fig. 6. Sensitivity analysis: (a) reduction of Financial Incentives and (b) the Batteries' Cost

Other interesting observations are:

- Lower financial incentives (or even higher energy cost) leads to an increased installed power (Figure 6a);
- Total costs are very sensible to the cost of the batteries; thus, with a low reduction of the battery's capital cost it is possible to obtain a great increase of the benefits (Figure 6b). Even Li-Ion batteries become affordable, when their cost is at least halved.

4   Conclusions

ESSs is a recent and relevant topic in energy efficiency, as they may help to overcome the intermittency of RES and they may also be used to shift electricity to times when it costs less. Thus, it will be very interesting and useful to consider its impact in a production plant, already equipped with a PV system.

This work is one of the first attempt to depict the problem of affordability of the integrated system PV+ESS. Similar analysis has never been yet considered in the industrial context: actually, does exist only some studies on the domestic storage.

In the present work an analytical model has been developed so as to perform an economic analysis of the problem presented, in order to analyse the economic convenience of an investment in energy storage devices. From this point of view the analysis is strongly affected by the country and year considered (due to the incentive framework). From the analysis carried out, it can be concluded that the economic benefit introduced through the use of BESS and due to the increase of plant's self-consumption is highly dependent on the type of battery used, and most importantly, on its cost of investment. In the specific case considered, it is possible to observe that Lead Acid and Sodium Sulphide batteries results convenient while, on the contrary, the most efficient Lithium-Ion batteries are still too expensive. Given the recent advances in technology, in the next few years, it is expected a trend characterized by a significant reduction in the investment cost that will make the same Lithium-Ion battery affordable: i.e. able to generate economic benefits greater than the costs introduced in the system.

Finally it should be noted that the analysis included here, if properly adjusted, could be applied to any kind of production plants, ESS (e.g. batteries, supercapacitors, ...) and energy system (e.g. wind power, biomass or biogas systems).

References

1. Ibrahim, H., Ilinca, A., Perron, J.: Energy storage systems—Characteristics and comparisons. Renew. Sustain. Energy Rev. 12(5), 1221–1250 (2008)
2. Mahlia, T.M.I., Saktisahdan, T.J., Jannifar, A., Hasan, M.H., Matseelar, H.S.C.: A review of available methods and development on energy storage; technology update. Renew. Sustain. Energy Rev. 33, 532–545 (2014)
3. Chen, H., Cong, T.N., Yang, W., Tan, C., Li, Y., Ding, Y.: Progress in electrical energy storage system: A critical review. Prog. Nat. Sci. 19(3), 291–312 (2009)

4. Bradbury, K., Pratson, L., Patiño-Echeverri, D.: Economic viability of energy storage systems based on price arbitrage potential in real-time U.S. electricity markets. Appl. Energy 114, 512–519 (2014)
5. Rudolf, V., Papastergiou, K.D.: Financial analysis of utility scale photovoltaic plants with battery energy storage. Energy Policy 63, 139–146 (2013)
6. (IEC) International Electrotechnical Commission, Electrical Energy Storage (December 2011)
7. San Martín, J.I., Zamora, I., Aperribay, J., San Martín, J.J., Eguía, P.: Energy Storage Technologies for Electric Applications. In: International Conference on Renewable Energies and Power Quality, no. 2 (2011)
8. Divya, K.C., Østergaard, J.: Battery energy storage technology for power systems—An overview. Electr. Power Syst. Res. 79(4), 511–520 (2009)
9. Hanna, R., Kleissl, J., Nottrott, A., Ferry, M.: Energy dispatch schedule optimization for demand charge reduction using a photovoltaic-battery storage system with solar forecasting. Sol. Energy 103, 269–287 (2014)

Implications for Collaborative Development of Reverse Distribution Network: A System Perspective

Yulia Lapko[1], Paolo Trucco[1], Andrea Trianni[1], and Cali Nuur[2]

[1] Politecnico di Milano, Milan, Italy
{yulia.lapko,paolo.trucco,andrea.trianni}@polimi.it
[2] KTH, Royal Institute of Technology, Stockholm, Sweden
cali.nuur@indek.kth.se

Abstract. One of the recurring challenges that industries and society face is the availability of and access to resources. The scarcity of resources creates instability in the supply chains of firms and in turn affects competitiveness. In recent years, the notion of a reverse distribution network has been put forth as a possible solution to remedy not only the volatility of the supply chains but also as an indispensable approach for sustainable development. This paper examines the current state of the literature on reverse distribution networks from a system perspective. Two major findings were identified. Firstly, there are no clear grounds for decision making regarding supply network development. Secondly, collaborations offers great opportunities to develop reverse distribution networks and build robust supply chains.

Keywords: resource scarcity, collaboration, reverse distribution network.

1 Introduction

Available research indicates increasing constrains on availability and production of resources [1, 2] as well as that resource scarcity is turning to be the major problem for many industries [3]. Economic growth and rapid increase of population impose great pressure on the supply of resources while at the same time, environmental and social cost of mining is increasing [2]. Several studies have discussed the problem of resource scarcity and have criticality assessed the role of raw materials on economic performance, supply risk, vulnerability to supply disruptions and ecological risks [4, 5]. They have highlighted how the scarcity of Critical Raw Materials (CRM) can become a bottleneck for deployment of emerging technologies (e.g., electronics and green energy) due to high geographical concentration of supply, low recycling rates and low (or even impossible) substitutability [6, 7, 8, 9]. Although technology plays important role for mitigation risks related to resource scarcity, there is a need for the supply chains that could ensure both resource efficiency and secure sources of their supply [10].

Reverse Distribution Network (RDN) has been proposed as a possible solution to offset the challenges related to resource scarcity [10]. RDN can be defined as the

B. Grabot et al. (Eds.): APMS 2014, Part II, IFIP AICT 439, pp. 351–357, 2014.

logistics structure for managing the backward flow of materials (from customers back to suppliers). RDN is also important since companies are required to engage into material recovery operations by governmental policies [11], downstream partners and other stakeholders [12]. Nevertheless, RDNs are the subject of a wide range of uncertainties, which create many obstacles for network development and maintenance. As a result, companies keep struggling to set up an efficient system [12, 13].

In order to gain understanding of such a complex phenomenon as RDN, it is important to take into consideration all elements within their interconnections. System perspective allows to meet this requirement. Adopting this perspective highlights two implications for RDN development (based on the systems theory [14, 15, 16]): consistency and complexity. Firstly, it is necessity to ensure consistency of the system through the pursuit of involved parties to the common (system) goal – maximization of the value creation (where value defined as the amount of recovered (recycled) materials). Secondly, complexity of RDN leads to decrease of the network agility. As RDN is a backbone solution for the problem of resource scarcity, it is necessary to ensure its adaptability to the changing environment.

Against this background, this paper aims at identifying the new prospects (new business opportunities, new forms of organization) for RDN development. It examines the existing knowledge base using the lens of the system perspective (enabling consistency and dealing with complexity).

Apart from this introduction, the paper is structured as follows. The subsequent section presents the methodology of the paper. In section 3, the results of the review are presented. The paper ends with conclusions and suggestions for further studies.

2   Methodology

To address the research aim, a literature review was performed. A sample of articles was selected from Scopus database using the following steps. An initial search using the four key words: 'green supply chain', 'closed loop supply chain', 'reverse logistics', 'product recovery network' was conducted on eight subject areas: engineering, business, management and accounting, decision science, environmental science, energy, economics econometrics and finance, material science, chemical engineering. The results were limited to academic articles from peer-reviewed journals. Only articles published after 1999 were considered, as at that time the EU started to shape new regulatory framework for companies' operations through new environmental-related directives, e.g., [11]. Moreover, according to the Scopus, the majority of research was developed after 1999, with a high attention from academia during last ten years. The relevance of the articles was evaluated in terms of their relation to resource scarcity mitigation and operating channel development, and was conducted through review of title and abstract in the first place. Afterwards, the selection was refined by reviewing the full texts of the articles. At the end, an examination of references cited in each relevant literature was performed in order to find additional sources of information.

3   Results

Our results show that the literature, devoted to reverse distribution networks, can be divided in two streams: network design modelling and practical issues related to operating channel implementation. The former issues were discussed by [17], who summarized the addressed questions through number, location, type and capacity of recovery activities. Researches [18] examined networks in relation to a degree of centralization, number of levels, links with other networks, open vs closed loop structures, degree of branch co-operation. This stream of research mainly focuses on examination of structural, configuration issues of reverse distribution networks. It should be noted that existing models suffer several limitations and simplifications (e.g., considering only single-entity flow or only single reprocessing option), what makes developed models very specific. Models tend to use objective function to minimize costs of reverse distribution or maximize profit, what does not meet the necessity to pursue the system objective to maximize the value of returned items.

Another stream of research has more business orientation and deals with implementation of the reverse distribution networks. That stream is mainly represented by the following topics: collection of cores, remanufacturing activities and selection of suppliers and third party service providers. Researchers [19, 20] examine operating channels for collection activities arranged through different options (e.g., though Original Equipment Manufacturer (OEM), existing retailers from forward distribution, third party service providers and a joint venture). [21] proposed different strategies to acquire cores from customers (e.g., buy-back and voluntary based relationships). Great body of research is also dedicated to remanufacturing issues. Although researchers identify benefits of performing remanufacturing activities by (OEM) - e.g., secured spare part supply [22] and balanced production lines [23] - there are still a lot of uncertainties and risks, like cannibalization of the sales for the OEM's new products, which lead to designing products to prevent remanufacturing [24]. Research in selection of suppliers and third party service providers is presented in different sets of criteria and algorithms that should be applied for estimation of a potential supplier/service provider [25].

Thus, it is worth noting that both streams of the literature were developed with focuses on different issues. Among the exceptions, we can mention studies of [26], who applied systems theory to formulate supply resiliency reducers; [27, 28], who developed constructs for successful collaborations in supply chains; [29] who presented a boundaries and flows perspective of green supply chain management; [30], who reviewed reverse logistics through inputs, processes and output; [24], who demonstrated the necessity to involve upstream actors for reverse operating channel development. Furthermore, little attention were paid to generalization of findings and developing guidelines for industries on how responsibilities should be divided in the network and which operating channel is suitable to every process. The latter issue is very important as many companies, that successfully implement forward logistics operations, have difficulties in efficient management of reverse direction of materials flows [12, 13].

There are few examples of OEMs that have integrated reverse logistics operations as a result of proactive planning measures, the majority is pushed by legislation to take responsibility for end-of-life products [11] or by requirements of a downstream partner and a stakeholder [12]. It is common, that OEMs tend to displace the burden-some processes through outsourcing of reverse logistics operations rather than involve them into their business models [12], [31]. This strategy leads to the loss of control of the further materials streams (strategic resources). Furthermore, it causes separation of decision-making and may lead to the conflicts of interests, as the decisions might not comply with the goal of the system in the whole and subsystem in particular. Therefore, problems of managing reverse flows also might be explained by lack of system consistency.

According to the systems theory, efficient operation of RDN depends on its consis-tency and complexity. Through the literature review, it was identified that both of them could be ensured through collaborations. Firstly, collaborations can help enable shared vision on the RDN development (pursuit to the common system goal), and secondly, they can help reduce uncertainties related to reverse flow operations thanks to collective creation and sharing of knowledge between involved parties. For exam-ple, according to the study [24], independent attempts of OEM to develop additional flows of resources through product recovery options can push suppliers to adjust re-source/component prices, and eventually devalue OEM's activities to ensure supply and improve performance efficiency.

Supply chain collaboration means that "two or more independent companies work jointly to plan and execute supply chain operations with greater success then when acting in isolation" [27, p. 19]. Collaborations could be vertical, horizontal and lateral [27], all these types offer new prospects for development of RDN: collaborations between OEMs to perform reprocessing activities (horizontal), between OEM and suppliers to arrange a secondary resource flow (vertical), combination of previous examples would form a lateral collaboration.

Collaborative relationships as an important construct of an efficient supply chain performance has found support in several theories and perspectives [27], [32, 33]. For example, [34] considered supply chain collaborations from a transaction theory and resource based view. In addition, [35] discussed collaborations both from resource dependence theory and information theory, while [36] used the lens of resource-advantage theory. Therefore, through collaboration it is possible to acquire necessary competences, to reach required level of trust and control between actors, to eliminate non-value-adding activities [33, 34], [37]. Moreover, [38] noted that collaborative initiatives help to share significant costs of establishment and maintenance of a recov-ery network as well as obtain required infrastructure and expertise. Collaborative development should help mitigate operations challenges of reverse flows, for exam-ple, by ensuring required capacity of flows from economic perspectives. Therefore, it is possible to consider collaborative development as an enabler and enhancer of build-ing secondary streams of supply, what becomes increasingly important nowadays, when the problem of resource scarcity is raised.

4   Conclusion

The aim of this paper was to identify the new prospects (new business opportunities, new forms of organization) for RDN development based on examination of existing knowledge base through the lens of system perspective (enabling consistency and dealing with complexity). Three major findings were highlighted.

Firstly, there is a gap in terms of providing a system picture of forward and reverse operations. There are different streams that focus on various particular issues without taking into consideration holism of the system and its consistency. Few efforts were put into generalization of findings and prescribing guidelines for industries on how the network should be developed in a stable way (papers have rather conceptual than practical orientation). The influence of the made decisions on performance efficiency of a system in the whole and its parts in particular requires further examination.

Secondly, the system perspective for RDN development highlights two implications: it is suggested to develop RDN to enable efficiency and effectiveness of the whole system rather than with orientation to the benefit of a particular stakeholder; it is necessary to develop RDN in a way to handle its complexity without following drawbacks for network adaptability.

Finally, it was identified that collaborative relationships can address requirements from both implications of the system perspective. They offer great opportunities to develop RDN. It is necessary to gain better understanding of creating new business opportunities, forms of organization and their influence on the system performance.

Acknowledgments. This paper is produced as part of the EMJD Programme European Doctorate in Industrial Management (EDIM) funded by the European Commission, Erasmus Mundus Action 1.

References

1. IEA: Energy technology perspectives 2008: scenarios & strategies to 2050 (2008)
2. Prior, T., Giurco, D., Mudd, G., Mason, L., Behrisch, J.: Resource depletion, peak minerals and the implications for sustainable resource management. Glob. Environ. Chang. 22, 577–587 (2012)
3. PwC: Minerals and metals scarcity in manufacturing: the ticking time bomb (2011)
4. Achzet, B., Helbig, C.: How to evaluate raw material supply risks—an overview. Resour. Policy 38, 435–447 (2013)
5. Erdmann, L., Graedel, T.E.: Criticality of non-fuel minerals: a review of major approaches and analyses. Environ. Sci. Technol. 45, 7620–7630 (2011)
6. Department of Energy: Critical Mineral Strategy (2011)
7. European Commission: Critical raw materials for the EU. Report of the Ad-hoc Working Group on Defining Critical Raw Materials (2010)
8. European Commission: Report on critical raw materials for the EU. Report of the Ad-Hoc Working Group on Defining Critical Raw Materials (2014)
9. Moss, R.L., Tzimas, E., Kara, H., Willis, P., Kooroshy, J.: Critical Metals in Strategic Energy Technologies (2011)

10. Krautkraemer, J.A.: Economics of Natural Resource Scarcity: The State of the Debate. Resour. Futur. (2005)
11. Directive 2000/53/E: Directive 2000/53/EC on End-of-Life Vehicles. Off. J. Eur. Union (2000)
12. Bai, C., Sarkis, J.: Flexibility in reverse logistics: a framework and evaluation approach. J. Clean. Prod. 47, 306–318 (2013)
13. Govindan, K., Palaniappan, M., Zhu, Q., Kannan, D.: Analysis of third party reverse logistics provider using interpretive structural modeling. Int. J. Prod. Econ. 140, 204–211 (2012)
14. Skyttner, L.: General systems theory: origin and hallmarks. Kybernetes 25, 16–22 (1996)
15. Ackoff, R.L.: Creating the corporate future: Plan or be planned for. Wiley (1981)
16. Yourdon, E.: Modern Structured Analysis. Yourdon Press, Prentice-Hall International, Englewood Cliffs, New Jersey (1989)
17. Akçalı, E., Çetinkaya, S., Üste, H.: Network Design for Reverse and Closed-Loop Supply Chains: An Annotated Bibliography of Models and Solution Approaches. Networks, 231–248 (2009)
18. Fleischmann, M., Krikke, H.R., Dekker, R., Flapper, S.D.P.: A characterisation of logistics networks for product recovery. Omega 28, 653–666 (2000)
19. Savaskan, R.C., Bhattacharya, S., Van Wassenhove, L.N.: Closed-Loop Supply Chain Models with Product Remanufacturing. Manage. Sci. 50, 239–252 (2004)
20. Senthil, S., Srirangacharyulu, B., Ramesh: A Decision Making Methodology for the Selection of Reverse Logistics Operating Channels. Procedia Eng. 38, 418–428 (2012)
21. Östlin, J., Sundin, E., Björkman, M.: Importance of closed-loop supply chain relationships for product remanufacturing. Int. J. Prod. Econ. 115, 336–348 (2008)
22. Seitz, M.A., Peattie, K.: Meeting the Closed-Loop Challenge: Calif. Manage. Rev. 46, 74–90 (2004)
23. Bulmuş, S.C., Xhu, S.X., Teunter, R.: Capacity and production decisions under a remanufacturing strategy. Int. J. Prod. Econ. 145, 359–370 (2013)
24. Xiong, Y., Zhou, Y., Li, G., Chan, H.-K., Xiong, Z.: Don't forget your supplier when remanufacturing. Eur. J. Oper. Res. 230, 15–25 (2013)
25. Meade, L., Sarkis, J.: A conceptual model for selecting and evaluating third-party reverse logistics providers. Supply Chain Manag. An Int. J. 7, 283–295 (2002)
26. Blackhurst, J., Dunn, K.S., Craighead, C.W.: An Empirically Derived Framework of Global Supply Resiliency. J. Bus. Logist. 32, 374–391 (2011)
27. Simatupang, T.M., Sridharan, R.: The Collaborative Supply Chain. Int. J. Supply Chain Manag. 13, 15–30 (2002)
28. Simatupang, T.M., Wright, A.C., Sridharan, R.: Applying the theory of constraints to supply chain collaboration. Supply Chain Manag. An Int. J. 9, 57–70 (2004)
29. Sarkis, J.A.: boundaries and flows perspective of green supply chain management. Supply Chain Manag. An Int. J. 17, 202–216 (2012)
30. Pokharel, S., Mutha, A.: Perspectives in reverse logistics: A review. Resour. Conserv. Recycl. 53, 175–182 (2009)
31. Krikke, H., Hofenk, D., Wang, Y.: Revealing an invisible giant: A comprehensive survey into return practices within original (closed-loop) supply chains. Resour. Conserv. Recycl. 73, 239–250 (2013)
32. Whitten, G.D., Green Jr., K.W., Zelbst, P.J.: Triple-A supply chain performance. Int. J. Oper. Prod. Manag. 32, 28–48 (2012)
33. Frohlich, M.T., Westbrook, R.: Arcs of integration: an international study of supply chain strategies. J. Oper. Manag. 19, 185–200 (2001)

34. Cao, M., Zhang, Q.: Supply chain collaboration: Impact on collaborative advantage and firm performance. J. Oper. Manag. 29, 163–180 (2011)
35. Sarkis, J., Zhu, Q., Lai, K.: An organizational theoretic review of green supply chain management literature. Int. J. Prod. Econ. 130, 1–15 (2011)
36. Bell, J.E., Mollenkopf, D., Stolze, H.J.: Natural resource scarcity and the closed-loop supply chain: a resource-advantage view. Int. J. Phys. Distrib. Logist. Manag. 43, 351–379 (2013)
37. Flynn, B.B., Huo, B., Zhao, X.: The impact of supply chain integration on performance: A contingency and configuration approach. J. Oper. Manag. 28, 58–71 (2010)
38. Schultmann, F., Zumkeller, M., Rentz, O.: Modeling reverse logistic tasks within closed-loop supply chains: An example from the automotive industry. Eur. J. Oper. Res. 171, 1033–1050 (2006)

Importance of Risk Process in Management Software Projects in Small Companies

Marcelo Nogueira[1] and Ricardo J. Machado[2]

[1] Software Engineering Research Group, University Paulista, UNIP,
Campus of Tatuapé, São Paulo, Brasil
marcelo@noginfo.com.br
[2] ALGORITMI Centre, School of Engineering, University of Minho,
Campus of Azurém, Guimarães, Portugal
rmac@dsi.uminho.pt

Abstract. Since the attacks of Sept. 11, companies around the world started to value and adopt the process of risk management in their operations. Models and frameworks have been created and enhanced with focus in risk. Successive studies have been published about the failure in software projects where the percentage has remained high. One of the reasons for the failures are directed to cases of non-adoption of systemic processes in their activities. Begin to identify, analyze, assess and treat risks systematically is not an obvious task. Specifically in small companies, where financial and human resources are limited, the difficulty in introducing new processes is even greater. To contribute to these software projects, this work presents the activities of a risk management process, in order to insert the culture and capacity of professionals who work in such projects, can objectively target to the mitigation of risks into which such projects are exposed.

Keywords: software engineering, risk management, software crisis, quality software, information systems.

1 Introduction

In a competitive environment of increasingly complex change, the appropriate management of information is crucial in the process of decision making in organizations (Nogueira, 2009).

Being this subject both comprehensive and specialized, the adoption of the practices of software engineering as a baseline of information management enables the development and consolidation of knowledge in the production of software.

These practices also prepare professionals to confidently face new challenges in the business world, strengthening their skills and abilities and keeping them up to date on the potential of information systems and new technologies in a globally competitive business perspective.

The objective this paper is present applicability of risk management through the roadmap with critical points the process of software production identified in the literary review.

B. Grabot et al. (Eds.): APMS 2014, Part II, IFIP AICT 439, pp. 358–365, 2014.
© IFIP International Federation for Information Processing 2014

This literary review consists of a merger between the classical scientific references in the area production software and the recent consolidation the ISO 31000.

2   Software Quality and Software Crisis

Software engineering has as primary objective the quality improvement of software products and the increase of the productivity of software engineers, in addition to meeting the requirements of efficiency and effectiveness (Maffeo, 1992).

In the study of software engineering, author Roger S. Pressman (2011) mentions the "Software Crisis", where numbers are given that express the problem with non-completion of software projects. The same author points out that one of the main factors that cause such "Software Crisis" is the lack of adoption of methods, procedures and tools in building software.

Software engineering can be defined as a set of methods, procedures and tools aimed at the production of software with quality, in other words, in accordance with customer requirements (Nogueira, 2009).

The term "Software Crisis", which began to be used in the 60s, historically alludes to a set of problems recurrently faced in the process of software development (construction, deployment and maintenance) (Maffeo, 1992).

In general terms, the "Software Crisis" occurs when the software does not meet the customers, users, developers or enterprise needs and exceeds cost and time estimates (Nogueira, 2009).

Despite the enormous variety of problems that characterize the software crisis, in computer systems development field, engineers and project managers tend to focus their concerns on the following point: "There is huge uncertainty of estimates of time-lines and development costs" (Nogueira, 2009).

Many of these errors could be avoided if organizations could have a software engineering process defined, controlled, measured and improved. However, it is clear that for many IT professionals these concepts are not very clear, which certainly hampers the action of managers in the improvement of their production processes (Blaschek, 2003).

There are several techniques, methodologies and quality standards to contribute to the development of software, including risk management. Professionals who do not embrace them find difficulties in performing software projects which are free of maintenance and re-work, so directly condemning the product quality.

Adoption of software engineering leads the individual to perform the activities related to their professional role through systematic methods throughout the software life cycle, allowing the developed product to represent the company actual processes and to meet in fact the company needs.

Achieving a high quality product or service is the goal of most organizations. It is no longer acceptable to deliver products with low quality and fix the problems and deficiencies after the products were delivered to the customer (Sommerville, 2011).

Quality is a result of processes, people and technology. The relationship between product, quality and each of these factors is complex. Therefore, it is much harder to control the degree of product quality than to control the requirements (Paula Filho, 2009).

When producing software with quality, the real possibility of extracting relevant information from a system is created. This may not only contribute to the decision, but to be a factor of business excellence, enabling new business, retention and survival in an active market. Thus, it is of paramount importance to identify and analyze risks that threaten the success of the project and manage them so that the business objectives may be achieved.

Aiming at quality in the process of software production, risk management has the focus to address the uncertainties inherent to software projects, because many factors that involve technology, people and processes are in conflict and can determine whether the development of the software product will be successful or not.

According to Standish Group (2013), through a study called "Chaos Report", for projects in the area of information technology, the following conclusions were drawn (Table 1):

- 39% of projects finish on time and on budget;
- 43% of projects are challenged;
- 18% are canceled before its deployment.

Table 1. Chaos Report (Standish Group, 2013)

Projects/Year	1994	1996	1998	2000	2002	2004	2006	2008	2010	2012
Successful	16	27	26	28	34	29	35	32	37	39
Contested	53	33	46	49	51	53	46	44	42	43
Cancelled	31	40	28	23	15	18	19	24	21	18
Failed	84	73	74	72	66	71	65	68	63	61

As for cost and schedule, the following information was obtained:

- Overruns in original estimated cost in 59% of the projects.
- Overruns in original schedule in 74% of the projects.

Other collected data are:

- 94% of the projects have at least one restart (Standish, 2009);
- 9% of projects in large companies come into operation within initially estimated cost and time.
- In software projects only 67% of originally proposed requirements are delivered in the end.

Despite the "Software Crisis" is not a new problem, even nowadays its impact and its negative effects are faced. The scarce use of methodologies and models of quality in Brazil indicates that this reality has to be modified.

According to the Ministry of Science and Technology (2002), only 11.8% of companies in Brazil have adopted risk management in software projects.

Due to the relevance of the theme and its direct impact on the success in producing software, the number presented by the ministry is alarming because the sample used for the research included both the major software companies and the small and medium enterprises in the country (Nogueira, 2009).

The concerning fact is that small and medium enterprises, which hold 65.1% of the software market in Brazil (MCT, 2002), lack a culture of risk management. Besides contributing to the possibility of failure in current projects, this situation undermines the still promising future opportunities that this sector needs to explore in both domestic and foreign markets.

New research in 2005, 2008 and 2010 were made by the Ministry of Science and Technology, but the item risk management was not added to the survey.

3   Risks in Software Engineering

Risk, such as science, was born in the sixteenth century, during the Renaissance. In an attempt to understand the games of chance, Blaise Pascal, in 1654, discovered the "Theory of Probability" and created the "Pascal Triangle", which determines the likelihood of possible outcomes, given a certain number of attempts (Bernstein, 1997).

Risk in the software area was represented in a systematic manner by Barry Boehm in the 80s through the Spiral Model, which has as its principle be iterative and directed to risks, because for each iteration it is performed an analysis of risk (Boehm, 1988).

Risks in software cannot be mere agenda items. They should be the "heart" of the business, as in other areas (Chadbourne, 1999).

Currently, the area that addresses risks in software engineering has evolved from an analysis within the model of development, as proposed by spiral model, to become a management technique that should permeate all the processes of software life cycle.

Risk management is understood as a general procedure for resolution of risk, ie when it is applied in any instance, the possible consequences are all acceptable, and policies to cope with the worst outcome must be defined in the process.

Risk management, in software design domain, is a defined and systematic process with the purpose of treating risk factors in order to mitigate or minimize its effects, producing a quality software product that meets customer needs, within estimated time and costs (Nogueira, 2009).

According to Robert Charette (1989), the definition of risk is:

First, risk affects future events. Present and past are irrelevant, because what is reaped today was planted by our previous actions. The issue is changing our actions today. Can opportunity be created for a different and possibly better situation tomorrow?

Secondly, this means that risk involves change, such as change of thought, opinion, action or places. Thirdly, risk involves choice and the uncertainty that choice entails itself.

Thus, paradoxically, the risk, like death and taxes, is one of the few certainties of life.

In a simplified way, a risk can be thought as a probability that some adverse circumstance will really occur. The risks may threaten the project, the software being developed or the organization.

Sommerville (2011) has described the types of risks that may affect the project and the organizational environment in which software is being built. However, many risks are considered universal and they include the following areas: Technology, personnel, organizational, tools, requirements and estimation.

The estimation of risks involves the following tasks:

* Identification of possible risks to the project;
* Analysis of these risks, evaluating their probability and likely impact;
* Prediction of corrective or preventive countermeasures;
* Prioritization of risks, organizing them according to likelihood and impact.

Risks do not remain constant during the execution of a project. Some disappear, new ones arise, and others suffer changes of probability and impact, therefore changing the priority. Therefore a monitoring report of the project along with an updated table shall be used for monitoring the risks. The estimation table should be reviewed and updated to reflect the modifications until the risks are realized or completely eliminated (Paula Filho, 2009).

The adoption of risk engineering is part of the critical success factors in software projects. The management of risks throughout the life cycle of development is critical to project success (Nogueira, 2009).

Risk management is particularly important for software projects, due to the inherent uncertainties that most projects face (Sommerville, 2011).

Project managers of information systems should regularly assess the risks during the development process to minimize the chances of failure. In particular, the problems of schedule, budget and functionality of the software can not be totally eliminated but they can be controlled through the implementation of preventive actions (Higuera, 1996).

Risk management has six well-defined activities that are: Risk identification, risk analysis, risk planning, risk monitoring, risk control and risk communication (Higuera, 1996).

The activities of risk identification and risk analysis, critical risk assessment, risk mitigation and contingency plans should be made. The methods of risk assessment should be used to demonstrate and evaluate the risks. Constraint policies of the project must also be determined at the time when discussions with all others involved take place. Aspects inherent to risks of software, such as the tendency of professionals to add features that are difficult to measure or even the risks of intangible nature of software, should influence the risk management of project (SWEBOK, 2004).

The Orange Book (2004), originally developed by the British government, now an international reference handbook, details the guidelines for good risk management, involving the following activities: Identifying risks, assessing risks, risk appetite, addressing risks, reviewing and reporting risks, communication and learning.

The ISO 31000 (2009) standard directs the policy for risk management with the following activities: establishing the context, risk identification, risk analysis, risk assessment, risk treatment, communication and consultation and monitoring and review.

4   Risk Management Process

After the literary review, it was possible to identify critical areas in the process of software development.

However, to support risk management in software projects, it is necessary to use a roadmap with activities where the decision maker can use it as an auxiliary instrument in the process of risk management.

Therefore, the following activities make up this roadmap: Communication and consultation; establishing the context; risk identification; risk analysis; risk evaluation; risk treatment and monitoring and review.

These activities are described below according to the complexity of application in accordance with ISO 31000.

4.1   Communication and Consultation

Communication and consultation with external and internal stakeholders should take place during all stages of the risk management process. It should take place in the beginning, with the first meeting of sensitization, during activities and in the end, with the presentation of results.

4.2   Establishing the Context

By establishing the context, the organization articulates its objectives and defines the external and internal parameters to be taken into account when managing risk, and sets the scope and risk criteria for the remaining process.

4.3   Risk Identification

The organization should identify sources of risk, areas of impacts, events (including changes in circumstances) and their causes and their potential consequences. The aim of this step is to generate a comprehensive list of risks based on those events that might create, enhance, prevent, degrade, accelerate or delay the achievement of objectives.

It is important to identify the risks associated to not pursuing an opportunity. Comprehensive identification is critical, because a risk that is not identified at this stage will not be included in further analysis. It is recommended to use a universal framework with risks common to different designs when it is the first iteration.

4.4   Risk Analysis

Risk analysis involves developing an understanding of the risk. Risk analysis provides an input to risk evaluation and to decisions on whether risks need to be treated, and on the most appropriate risk treatment strategies and methods.

Risk analysis can also provide an input into making decisions where choices must be made and the options involve different types and levels of risk. A framework can be used with the universal risk weights established from expert opinion, especially when you do not have a knowledge base.

4.5   Risk Evaluation

The purpose of risk evaluation is to assist in making decisions, based on the outcomes of risk analysis. It defines which risks need treatment and the priority for treatment implementation.

Risk evaluation involves comparing the level of risk found during the analysis process with risk criteria established when the context was considered. Based on this comparison, the need for treatment can be considered.

4.6   Risk Treatment

Risk treatment involves selecting one or more options for modifying risks, and implementing those options. Once implemented, the provision of treatments or modification of controls must be performed.

Risk treatment involves a cyclical process of: Assessing a risk treatment; deciding whether residual risk levels are tolerable; if not tolerable, generating a new risk treatment; and assessing the effectiveness of that treatment.

4.7   Monitoring and Review

Both monitoring and review should be a planned part of the risk management process and involve regular checking or surveillance. It can be periodic or ad hoc.

Responsibilities for monitoring and review should be clearly defined. The organization's monitoring and review processes should encompass all aspects of the risk management process for the purposes of: Ensuring that controls are effective and efficient in both design and operation; obtaining further information to improve risk assessment; analyzing and learning lessons from events (including near-misses), changes, trends, successes and failures; detecting changes in the external and internal context, including changes to risk criteria and the risk itself which can require revision of risk treatments and priorities; and identifying emerging risks.

5   Conclusion

In this literary review, it was found that the authors recognize the difficulty in the production process of software. It's possible to realize that the scenario of the "software crisis" provides failure to projects. And that the adoption of software engineering and its assumptions are critical to project success. Despite the existence of activities and processes focused on the production of software, its adoption is insufficient, especially in the Brazilian context. However, when teams of software production are guided through a risk process, it becomes easier to understand "what to do". With the defined scope it is possible to sensitize stakeholders to the adoption of risk management as a common organizational practice. The compliance risk process in relation to ISO 31000 is essential. As future work, we intend to present the applicability of the process of risk in projects of small companies that never used the risk management in software production.

Acknowledgements. This work has been supported by FCT – Fundação para a Ciência e Tecnologia in the scope of the project: PEst-OE/EEI/UI0319/2014 by Portugal and University Paulista - Software Engineering Research Group by Brazil.

References

1. ISO 31000, ISO 31000: Risk management – Principles and guidelines: ISO (2009)
2. Bernstein, P.: Desafio aos deuses: a fascinante história do risco. Campus, RJ (1997)
3. Blaschek, J.R.: O principal problema dos projetos de software, Rio de Janeiro (2003)
4. Boehm, B.: A spiral model of software development and enhancement. IEEE (1988)
5. Chadbourne, B.C.: To the heart of risk management: teaching project teams to combat risk, Pennsylvania (1999)
6. Charette, R.N.: Software Engineering risk analysis and management. McG. Hill (1989)
7. Higuera, R.P., Haimes, Y.Y.: Software risk management technical report, CMU (1996)
8. Maffeo, B.: Engenharia de Software e Especificação de Sistemas. Campus, RJ (1992)
9. MCT, Qualidade e Produtividade do Software Brasileiro. MCT - Secretaria de Política de Informática, Brasília (2002)
10. Nogueira, M.: Engenharia de Software. Um Framework para a Gestão de Riscos. Ciência Moderna, Rio de Janeiro (2009)
11. Orange Book, Management of Risk – Principles, HM Treasury. Crown, London (2004)
12. Filho, P.: Engenharia de Software: fundamentos, métodos e padrões. LTC, RJ (2009)
13. Pressman, R.S.: Engenharia de Software, 6th edn. McGraw-Hill, São Paulo (2011)
14. Sommerville, I.: Engenharia de Software. Pearson A.Wesley, São Paulo (2011)
15. Standish. CHAOS Summary 1995...2009. Standish Group, Boston (2009)
16. Standish. THE CHAOS MANIFESTO. Standish Group, Boston (2013)
17. SWEBOK, Guide to the software engineering body of knowledge. IEEE Computer Society, USA (2004)

Production of Sustainable Electricity in Landfills: The Case of the Bandeirantes Landfill

Marise de Barros Miranda Gomes[1,2], José Benedito Sacomano[1],
Fabio Papalardo[1], and Alexandre Erdmann da Silva[2]

[1] Universidade Paulista (UNIP), Post Graduate Program in Production Engineering,
Dr. Bacelar St. 1212,São Paulo,Brazil
[2] Centro Universitário das Faculdades Metropolitanas Unidas – FMU, São Paulo, São Paulo.
marise.gomes@superig.com.br

Abstract. This study shows the potential of biogas in urban solid waste land-fills which, according to estimates and based on the international experience, did not show satisfactory results. The issue of solid waste in Brazil has been discussed by society over the years. Besides dealing with the issues of green-house gases emissions, it comprises the context of sustainability in the use of methane as a source of renewable energy. Waste landfills generate gas emissions that are harmful to people and to the environment. In Brazil, there are few projects on the use of methane energy. They are located in the south and south-east regions and some of them show technical difficulties due to failures in pre-dicting the production of landfill gas. Specifically, the country has three projects for waste management for large-scale production of energy. Among them, there is the object of this case study, the Bandeirantes Biogas Plant in São Paulo, supported in mathematical modeling.

Keywords: Landfill, production optimization, sustainability, energy, renewable energy.

1   Introduction

Currently, megacities worldwide are faced with the generation of solid wastes. The result of the intense urbanization and the search for different solutions aim to mitigate the environmental damage. Many solutions are the best practices in the recovery of such wastes when disposed of in landfills. Recent concepts in modern landfill management, incorporate sustainability strategies in their lifecycle, so since the beginning of the land-fill, different techniques are tested to stabilize the amount of methane gas emissions [1]. Energy recovery is one of the indicators of sustainability for landfills [2].

The methane gas produced at the landfill, depending on the waste deposited there, may have its production confined with the goal of producing electrical energy, by burning in combustion engines.

The concept of sustainability created by the Helmholtz Institute [3], an important center of research and technology from Germany, highlights the use of energy and natural resources in an efficient, safe and sustainable way. Therefore, it defines the

B. Grabot et al. (Eds.): APMS 2014, Part II, IFIP AICT 439, pp. 366–373, 2014.
© IFIP International Federation for Information Processing 2014

minimum requirements that are universally valid for the global sustainable development, unconventionally. It assigns the deficit of sustainability indicator to the forecasts of global energy shortage, to power supply or generation, to the extraction of raw materials and waste disposal without its energy recovery.

In this sense, over the years, Brazil and the world concentrate their efforts and studies on the subject that defies all: solid waste in the context of landfills [4]. In its management, an order of priority should be observed: no generation, reduction, reuse, environmentally appropriate treatment and disposal. The same author also mentions, based on German law, that unavoidable wastes must be recovered, in the form of material recovery or energy recovery.

The United Nations/ONU [5] warns, in its report, that some challenges of sustainable development of the cities up to 2050 are related to renewable energies and urban waste management. In Brazil, despite the implementation of measures of selective collection, much of the waste is not targeted for recycling, going directly to landfills and increasing environmental pollution. Among the common challenges, we must consider the specificity of the disposal practice related to the economic development.

The relation between economic development and waste generation is direct. The increased purchasing power, coupled with the population growth and the increasing consumption of disposable materials contribute to the problem of depletion of landfills and the pollution generated by the improper disposal [6].

The few projects on biogas energy use in Brazil are located in the southern and southeastern regions, but some of them show technical difficulties due to failures in predicting the production of landfill gas [7; 8]. We took Bandeirantes Landfill as a case study in order to contextualize sustainability in relation to waste disposal and energy recovery. Parameterizations were needed, from the data collected, because of the indeterminacy of the waste types and amount of moisture, for example, and of how these two indicators have been distributed over the years of the landfill existence.

1.1   Lifecycle of a Productive Plant of Landfill Gas

The former Bandeirantes landfill, since 2008, started to generate energy and to be named as Bandeirantes Thermal Power Plant because of the stimuli in the production of electricity and carbon credits from the burning of methane. The case study is a dynamic environment that has undergone changes throughout its production cycle, initially just as a place of accumulation of waste, and after many years, it started to generate electricity.

This study indicates that the productive lifecycle of Bandeirantes landfill is divided into 4 stages. These four stages represent the dynamics of the landfill. Over 51 years, it went from trash dump to a controlled landfill for 11 years. With an operating license it has become a landfill. From 2008, the Bandeirantes landfill began to operate as an independent producer and supplier of electricity. The expectation of this last phase is estimated to expire in 2030. The highest peak of sustainable productivity and methane generation was recorded in 2004, when it was still operating as a landfill.

Many research concluded that the design method estimates lower rates of methane generation, since it takes into account the average of disposition of different types of waste, leading to inaccurate results. They suggested that the method of first-order decay is more complete and that it best approximates the reality, since it takes into account the long periods of time in the emission of methane gas and the increase of waste each year, within its lifecycle as a landfill [10; 11]. The reasons given below demonstrate the motivation for using this model in the current study, in addition to the representation of the selection criteria used, which will be explained in the next section.

2   Methodology

2.1   Model for Estimating the Production of Methane gas in Landfills

The parameters of the models cannot represent the actual conditions of the landfill because they are based on experimental studies without effective measures in the field. Also, the dynamics of a landfill in relation to the disposal, the accommodation of waste, the heterogeneous accumulation of material types and the emanation of methane gas are random variables [12; 13].

The first official calculation methodology for reducing emissions of greenhouse gases approved by the Clean Development Mechanism/CDM Executive Board is based on Intergovernmental Panel on Climate Change/IPCC [14], which was an evo-lution of the methodology proposed in 1996, described hereafter as a first-order decay equation.

The purpose of this equation is the functionality in the calculation and a possible implementation in computational tools, and the validation through in situ measure-ment of values is in the audit stage [11]. This result that the mathematical model serves as a support for predicting the generation of methane gas easy to implement in computer systems.

2.2   Modeling Parameters in the Landfill Methane Gas Production

The decay function or exponential increase is a derivation with respect to discrete time, this means that there were differences in the time variable, for example, t1 - t2, t1- t3 and so on, to then integrate these differences and present them in graphical form.

Mathematical models are often used to describe real-life phenomena or the behavior of a system [15]. The construction of a mathematical model of a system begins by iden-tifying the variables responsible for the behavior of the system. The same author also points out that in the initial model the incorporation of all variables is not necessary because, at this stage, the desired specification is for the validation of the model and not on the resolution level required. Some variables in the first-order equation have no data-base, there are difficulty of finding the database in order to estimate accurately the val-ues of Potential of methane generation and Methane generation rate [16].

This emission factor associated with the site of residue destination interferes with the estimated portion of generation of methane gas. Landfills have factor 1 of 100%. It is estimated that these sites have adequate control regarding the handling and compaction of waste.

The controlled landfill has a 20% lower factor, due to the environmental monitoring, but it does not have the same operating and control conditions of the landfills. Lastly, the trash dump, which has no operational, management or environmental monitoring control, has its potential factor reaching only 40% of the methane generation.

In this factor, it is also applied a collection efficiency parameter that is around 60-85%, depending on the impossibility of capturing all the gas generated. The total amount of waste generated is not the same amount collected and destined to landfills. In addition, a percentage of the population does not receive the services of the public waste collection system.

In this case study, the production of landfill gas is supposed to be a set of derivations of various speeds of gas production, which are not known or mastered. The speed is the kinetic involved in the equation, and it is a dependent variable of time, which relation between time and the gas kinetics, at all points of the facility, is very difficult to be determined or measured. This demonstration of the first-order equation was required so the steps to be implemented in the simulation can be followed in this subject matter. The algorithm ode45 of Matlab will be used for the integration of the dynamic system and simulation in Simulink.

By converting methane gas into thermal energy and then into electrical energy, it is possible to estimate the energy potential of Bandeirantes Thermal Power Plant, and also the equivalent carbon credits in these processes, both vital for a sustainable project.

In this context, explainations about in order to calculate the emission of a certain gas, we multiply the mass emitted by this gas by the ECD (Equivalent Carbon Dioxide) or CO^2eq of the aforementioned (destroyed) gas [17].

Finally, due to the price on the Carbon Market, it is possible to calculate the sales values of equivalent Credits of Carbon (CRCeq) that have been mitigated to different opportunities for energy generation and recovery of landfill gas. However, they are only tradable for projects certificated by the CDM board.

Clean Development Mechanism/CDM shows that the Certified Emission Reductions (CERs) are traded as commodities that can be bought by countries that fail to meet emissions reduction targets or that do not want the adhesion within their development plans. Each tonne of CO^2e (tCO^2e) reduced or removed from the atmosphere is a unit issued by the CDM Executive Board or other voluntary markets, called Certified Emission Reductions (CERs).

The market for Carbon Credits is complex. It counts on the participation of several entities worldwide. There are conditions and goals to be achieved and agreed deadlines to be fulfilled by the involved countries, both developed countries interested in purchasing carbon credits and developing countries that want to sell by the best market price.

In summary, all parameters were defined and established to be used in the simulation. We sought, in previous studies, to justify the parameters involved and possible flexibilities that are the setting for the simulation. Carbon credits are processed only for simulation purposes in quantity and sales value in the market, representing only a positive output of the system.

3   Results and Discussion

3.1   Modeling of Sustainable Electricity Production in the Bandeirantes Landfill

In this modeling of the sustainable production of electricity, the Bandeirantes landfill is named as Thermal Power Plant. In its initial design, it aimed to turn methane gas into energy and to recover carbon credits. Figure 1 shows the stages in this process. Each process uses the baselines recommended by the Executive Board of the CDM, established in the ACM0001 methodology, in order to simulate large-scale projects. These practices contribute to the research on the applicability of methodologies in different scenarios, especially for the developing countries to establish sustainable development paths.

Thermal Power Plant Bandeirantes Landfill

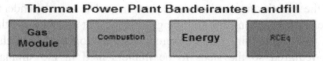

Fig. 1. Stages of the Bandeirantes Thermal Power Plant process

For each stage, there is a mathematical model that represents the estimates. The initial phase, called gas module by the author, is a composition of matrices, and so each stage is composed of a mathematical modeling.

From these arrangements, there are steps which are composed of other equations. For simulation purposes, each step is a process or system, which may have derivative subprocesses or subsystems. The Gas Module stage was modeled in Matlab and Simulink, and the others, since they were only calculations, were aided by Matlab's Toolbox. To accomplish this calculation, the adaptive Simulink module was used with data input of matrices. Three composite inputs were necessary to form the three geometric axes. Next, Figure 2 shows the partial simulation scheme for two input matrices (x, y).

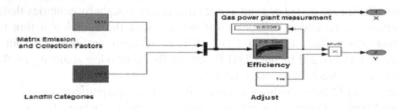

Fig. 2. Gas Module Simulator (partial) – 2 input matrices

The tool limitation prevents the construction of a three-dimensional chart. The volumetric module in Simulink library is a 2–D T(u) module (two-dimensional module). To solve this problem, two other modules were constructed for vector outputs (X, Z) and (Y, Z). At the output of the three matrices, an adaptive module was included to determine L0 throughout the production cycle.

In the simulation shown in chart following, the three categories were divided into 1 for landfill, 2 for controlled landfill and 3 to trash dump. The last one had the lowest result regarding the Potential of methane generation variable. The blue bar was coded for the results of 60% collection percentage and the red bar to 85% performed collection. The potential of methane generation had the following results in the simulation compiled, from the reading of chart 1.

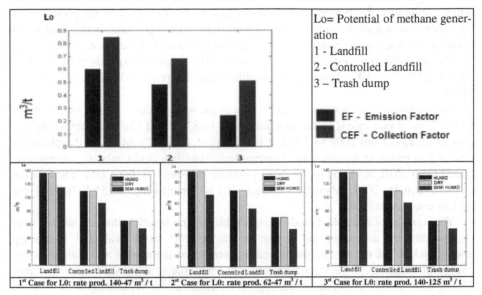

Chart 1. Simulation result for L0 (m³/ton)

The simulation of this scenario shows, in chart 1, that there was an improvement in the performance of methane gas generation in all sites of waste disposal, even more at the dump. The two locations of inappropriate disposal had their emissions increased. The simulation was repeated, by changing the vector order of the matrix elements. The result was exactly the same, proving that the result of the first simulation was correct, thus confirming the increase in methane generation in plants considered inadequate, but with the amount of gas production that is not used.

The performance in humid and dry climates improves gas production and affects it in semi-humid climate according to the result of chart 1. Although it has adopted the worst values for methane production, the performance to landfill improved in the 2nd case when compared with the 1st case.

The humid and dry climates positively affect the production of gas in the controlled landfill, staying above the result influenced by semi-humid climate in the landfill.

In 3nd case, the results show a balanced performance. The semi-humid climate improves gas production in the landfill staying above the gas production in controlled landfill and landfill influenced by the three climates. The current Bandeirantes Thermal Power Plant was initially a trash dump, evolving to a controlled landfill and then to landfill, which was closed in 2006. This three-stage production cycle generated a volume of methane gas with potential for energy recovery.

4   Conclusions

This study shows that the current methods do not simulate optimal conditions or minimum conditions. They work with data directed to the future when the project goes into operation as a plant, and they do not consider methane potential in the production cycle, discarding energy production since the establishment of the plant. In this scenario, the plant did not value 2,095,724,529 m^3 of GHG; this corresponds to the production of 2,356,207 MWh. It would be possible to fuel the plant and still have 2,244,175 MWh.

The simulation shows that by 2030, the plant will produce 1,424,148,778 m3of GHG. This is equivalent to the generation of 1,683,183 MWh, and subtracting the cost of energy, from 2008 to 2030, it could inject 1,552.479 MWh in the electrical grid of São Paulo. In the estimate of carbon reduction they could only be "commercialized" from 2010, referring to the latest contract approved by the CDM. There is the estimate that by 2017, when the contract will be terminating, 1,751,497tCO^2e/year will be commercialized.

The number of controlled landfills, trash dumps and landfills that are not recovering the methane as energy and carbon credits deserves to be evaluated. Producing energy and, on the other hand, trading carbon credits on the market as a commodity of energy production can be a good investment. The issue of controlled landfills, landfills or trash dumps undergoes a recent great transformation. With the goal closing the landfills up to 2014, there should be a huge incentive to the recycling and reuse of materials. However, as well as in Germany, although it is mature regarding waste disposal processes, landfills will continue to exist.

Several readings can be completed in this study. Brazil needs to review its security policies and maintenance of the energy matrix. In the case studied, the former Bandeirantes landfill, São Paulo, did not add the amount of 1.5 Tera Watts/hour to its power grid in little more than 20 years. More than that, it lost more than 1.5 TWh of energy. Somehow, this process of Bandeirantes Thermal Power Plant did not efficiently contribute to the environment. If we consider the period that it did not use GHGs, in this case methane, Bandeirantes Thermal Power Plant could have been better utilized in terms of energy source if it had been rethought in its entire production cycle.

References

1. Hrad, M., Gamperling, M., Huber-Humer, M.: Comparison between lab- all full-scale applications of in situ aeration of an old landfill and assessment of long-term emission development after completion. Waste Management 33, 2061–2073 (2013)
2. Martinez, T.G., et al.: The potential of a sustainable municipal waste management system for Santiago de Chile, including energy production from waste. Energy, Sustainability and Society 2 (2012)

3. Helmholtz Association og German Research Centres. Helmholtz – With Enregy into the Future. Annual Report. Berlim (2010)
4. Jardim, A., Yoshida, C., Machado, F.J.V.: Política Nacional, Gestão e Gerenciamento de Resíduos Sólidos, p. 19, 34–36, 62–63. Editora Manole, Barueri (2012)
5. ONU – United Nations. Sustainable Development Challenges. World Economic and Social Survey. Department of Economic and Social Affairs, UN, New York, 181 p., p. 68 (2013)
6. Dias, S.G.: O desafio da Gestão de Resíduos Sólidos Urbanos. Sociedade e Gestão. Revista RAE, Fundação Getúlio Vargas 11(1) (January/June 2012)
7. Maciel, F.J., Jucá, J.F.T., Neto, A.C.: Avaliação do Projeto Piloto de Recuperação do Biogás no Aterro da Muribeca/PE. In: VI Congresso de Inovação Tecnológica em Energia Elétrica, Anais, Fortaleza, Ce, 8 p., p. 1 (2011)
8. MMA – Ministério do Meio Ambiente. Agenda 21 brasileira: resultado da consulta nacional / Comissão de Políticas de Desenvolvimento Sustentável e da Agenda 21 Nacional, 2nd edn., 158 p. Ministério do Meio Ambiente, Brasília (2004)
9. Mendes, L.G.G., Magalhães, S.P.: Estimate Methods of Biogas Generation in sanitary landfill. Universidade Estadual Paulista – UNESP. Faculdade de Engenharia, Campus Guaratinguetá – FEG. Departamento de Energia – DEN. Rev. Ciênc. Exatas 11(2), 71–76 (2005)
10. Gomes, M.B.: Sustentabilidade Ambiental no Brasil: biodiversidade, economia e bem-estar humano. Comunicados do IPEA (instituto de Pesquisa Aplicada) n° 80. Série Eixos do Desenvolvimento Brasileiro, 27 p., pp. 10–17. Edição de fevereiro (2011)
11. USEPA – Environmental Protection Agency. United States International Best Practices Guide for Landfill Gas energy Projects. Landfill Gas Modeling. Global Methane Iniciative. Capítulo 6, 14 p., pp. 63–67 (2012)
12. Christensen, H.T.: Journal of Solid Waste Technology and Management, vol. 1&2, pp. 61–84. Wiley, Capítulo 2.1. Waste Characterization: Approaches and Methods (2010)
13. Worrell, W.A., Vesilind, P.A.: Solid Waste Engineering, 2nd edn. Cengage Learning, p. 401, pp. 118–119 (2011)
14. IPCC - Intergovernmental Panel on Climate Change. Guidelines for National Greenhouse Gas Inventories (1997), http://www.ipcc-nggip.iges.or.jp/public/gl/invs6.html (acessado em: Maio 29, 2012)
15. Anton, H., et al.: Cálculo, 8th edn., vol. I, Capítulo 9, 1181 p., pp. 582–611. Bookman, Porto Alegre (2005)
16. ABRELPE. Atlas Brasileiro de emissões de GEE e Potencial Energético na Destinação de Resíduos Sólidos. Abrelpe – Associação Brasileira de Empresas de Limpeza Pública e Resíduos Especiais. Diretor Executivo: Carlos R. V. Silva Filho, 172 p. (2012)
17. Taboada, C.: Gestão de Tecnologia e Inovação na Logística. Iesd Brasil SA. Curitiba, 104 p., pp. 80–85 (2009)

Cooperation as a Driver of Development and Diffusion of Environmental Innovation

Peter Gerard Higgins and Mohammad Yarahmadi

Department of Mechanical and Product Design Engineering,
Swinburne University of Technology, Hawthorn 3122, Australia
{phiggins,myarahmadi}@swin.edu.au

Abstract. Environmental management and innovation literature has revealed gaps concerning the influence of business cooperation on environmental innovation and diffusion. Cooperation with external partners in the development of environmental innovation is explored using the Australian Business Longitudinal Database. Complementing this is the exploration of the cooperation of supply chain partners in the adoption of environmental products and processes through three case studies from the manufacturing industry.

Keywords: environmental innovation, business cooperation, green supply chain practices, compliance.

1 Introduction

Despite the many advantages of environmental innovations, they are not easily developed and diffused. Unwillingness of firms to promote their development and adoption are in part due to the characteristics of environmental innovations. Other factors are associated with the internal characteristics of a firm (e.g., the lack of financial resources, skills, knowledge and physical capital) and the external environment (e.g., the lack of pressure from influential stakeholders). Forming partnerships, however, may be a feasible strategy to overcome these barriers. Partners may support each other in managing common problems, such as awareness of and compliance with new environmental regulations. Partners may provide access to resources and capabilities that are not available in-house.

In many aspects, development of environmental innovation represents a separate sub-group of general innovation with the aim of avoiding or reducing environmental harm. Likewise, diffusion of environmental innovation across the supply chain requires firms applies a subset of processes known as green supply chain practices. Both buyers and suppliers are involved in implementing these practices, with the aim to eliminate or reduce environmental impacts.

This paper focuses on the role of cooperation between businesses in development of environmental innovation and diffusion of environmental practices across the supply chain. It explores the extent to which buyer organisations implement such practices and the corresponding ways they interact with their suppliers.

B. Grabot et al. (Eds.): APMS 2014, Part II, IFIP AICT 439, pp. 374–381, 2014.
© IFIP International Federation for Information Processing 2014

2   Nature of Environmental Innovation

Carillo-Hermosilla et al. [1] distinguish three groups of environmental innovation in processes: component, sub-system and system. Component change consists of incremental improvements to extant systems, in which companies opt for less demanding incremental changes to "end-of-pipe" technologies for reactive solutions for polluting emissions [2]. In sub-system changes, the replacement or modification of underlying systems eliminates sources of some emissions. Whereas, system changes are systemic redesigns of open-loop systems—in which polluting emissions breach system boundaries—into closed loops that divert wastes into inputs for new processes.

Trifilova et al. [3] distinguish four types of environmental innovation, from the sterile to the potent. The "weakest" type is the chicanery they labelled passive/cosmetic in which there is "cosmetic" publicity of "green credentials" without any active innovation. Next is improving existing products or processes, followed by opportunity-driven creation of new products or processes that go beyond compliance with the aim to gain competitive advantage. System-level creation of innovation by engaging external organizations in designing new processes and services is the most efficacious. It belongs to the class of systemic improvements that cause radical instrumental changes in place of incremental changes normally associated with technological change [1], [4].

3   Characteristics Beyond Conventional Innovation

The factors associated with environmental innovation are more expansive than conventional innovation, which focuses on the development of a new or improved product or process that is a "game changer" in terms of functionality and/or productivity. It includes changes to social norms, cultural values and institutional structures [5,6,7].

Drivers of conventional innovation are market expectations and consumer preferences (demand pull) and research and development (push factors). Environmental innovation also often has governmental regulation as a key driver [6], [8]. Where an environmental innovation is not aligned with normal drivers of the market, its success depends on transformation of societal behavior through changes to beliefs, knowledge and values [4]. Hellström [6] contends that as eco-innovation needs evolution in social arrangements and institutional support, a radical innovation strategy is required to break out of entrenched social practices that incremental changes do not provoke.

An innovator of a new product or process has to ensure that the competitive advantage gained has to significantly offset the disadvantages accrued in its development. A competitive advantage is dependent in part on legal protection of intellectual property, but critically on the ownership of valuable and rare resources and capabilities that cannot be easily imitated and in which there are no readily available substitutes. To offset financial exposure, companies may pool resources by collaborating with other businesses for mutual gain.

Unlike conventional innovation, dominant drivers may not be located in the market. While wide adoption of an environmental innovation reduces the impact on the environment, this positive externality may not be realized. If it is not valued by the market, then it is likely to fail, with consequential impact on the financial sustainability of the innovating firms. Consequently, the likelihood of them becoming a casualty of the gap between the private and social returns provides little incentive in becoming pioneers of environmental innovation [4].

4   Cooperation and Environmental Innovation

In the literature on environmental innovation a commonly stated proposition is that the inclusion of environmental aspects requires more extensive cooperation with external sources than does conventional innovation of products or process [9,10,11,12,13,14,15]. In testing the proposition that research and development tends to move from an internal activity to collaboration with other organizations, Yarahmadi and Higgins [16] explored the relationship between environmental innovation and cooperation between businesses by reprocessing data from the Business Longitudinal Database, which is the product of a survey of 2,732 Australian businesses by the Australian Bureau of Statistics for the period 2006 to 2007. They deduced that for 28.8% of firms that environmental innovation was a major reason for businesses to cooperate, which they compared to 15.3% claiming cooperation for other types of innovation (see Table 1). However, this increased to 73.3% and 60% for customers and suppliers, respectively. Putting this in context of conventional innovation, 37.7% stated that they had introduced improvements in goods or services, operational processes, organizational/managerial processes or marketing methods. While cooperation may be significant for innovation, by far a major reason for innovation was profit-related (79.4% of respondents), with factors concerning responsiveness to customer needs, maintenance of market share, establishment of new markets and increasing efficiency of delivering goods and services (54.1%, 47.3% and 39.2% of respondents, respectively) were also dominant reasons for innovation. The least important drivers for innovation were responding to government regulations (10.9%) and standards and reducing environmental impacts (12.1%).

The industrial sector that had the largest group of innovators was manufacturing[1]. While 35% of firms within this sector were innovators, only 8.23% of these were environmental innovators. The largest group of environmental innovators was in the construction industry; 21% were innovators of which 20% were environmental innovators.

Performing a logistic regression analysis of the data, Yarahmadi and Higgins [16] found three significant variables associated with innovation: cooperation, research and development, and size of the firm. Thus, partnering and investment on R&D distinguish between firms who do and do not introduce environmental innovation and the distinction is very strong. Size of the firm is significant and its coefficient is positive, indicating that larger organizations are more engaged in introducing environmental innovations than small to medium enterprises. Nevertheless, exports, grants, subsidies and industry were not significantly different from zero at 5% level.

---

[1]   Some reservation most be noted on the representativeness of these results. Most firms in the database were small: 46% had less than 19 employees. Furthermore, manufacturing and construction firms only comprised 16.4% and 5.2% of the dataset, respectively.

Table 1. Major factors for environmental innovation derived from Business Longitudinal Database

Factor	Main reason: environmental-innovation	Main reason: Other
Size 0-4	13.5%	26.4%
5-19	44.2%	36.1%
≥20	42.3%	37.5%
Exports	25%	25.7%
Subsidies	5.8%	3%
Grants	15.4%	9.8%
R&D	30%	15.9%
Cooperation (Yes/No)	28.8%	15.3%
Cooperation with clients, customers	73.3%	39.7%
Cooperation with suppliers	60%	48.3%
Cooperation - other	60%	46.6%

Firms that introduced innovations—20% in the construction, 12.82% in the whole-sale trade, 11.90% in the transport and storage, and 11.76% in the personal and other services industry—reported reduced environmental impacts (environmental innovation) as the prime motivator. Surprisingly, given the size and propensity of the Australian mining industry, it showed no evidence of innovation that aimed to reduce impact on the environment. For firms that identified the environment as a main concern, manufacturing firms scored as the largest environmental innovators with 25%. For the wholesale trade, construction, personal and other services, and transport and storage, environmental innovation were 19%, 12%, 12%, and 10%, respectively.

There are numerous reasons why firms do not develop or adopt environmental innovations [17,18,19]. Nevertheless, it is not easy to come up with a solution, as this is a multi-faceted issue. However, there is ongoing research on the positive role of cooperation with external partners in helping firms to develop environmental innovations. The analysis of the data set of Australian businesses also confirms this hypothesis. The sign and the magnitude of the regression coefficient of cooperation show this strong relationship. According to the resource-based view and institutional theory, the advantages and competitive benefits that result from cooperative arrangements include: access to new markets, acquisition of sources of technical support and expertise, increased market power, risk and investment sharing, economies of scale and scope, reductions in government or trade barriers, and the acquisition of institutional legitimacy [20,21]. Nevertheless, as Carrillo-Hermosilla et al. [1] state, this may be a chicken and egg situation, where the more competency that firms possess, the more they engage in cooperation.

5   Case Studies

Yarahmadi, Clements and Higgins [23] further explored the role of cooperation
through in-depth interviews of three manufacturing firms in Victoria, Australia. The
manufacturing was chosen as it is a major contributor of greenhouse gas emissions
(27.7% total emissions of Australian industry), ranking second to the agriculture industry. Contrastingly, they are among the largest green innovators (25% of all Australian industry [16]). The firms were selected to contrast situations (see Table 2). For
the objective of exploring practices of green supply chains, the firms selected had
already proven to be environmentally aware and had provided evidence of commitment to adopt or develop environmental practices. Also, they were medium or large
size manufacturers with the ability to influence their suppliers.

Table 2. Characteristics of interviewed firms

	Firm B1	Firm B2	Firm B3
Sector	Automotive	Clothing	Machinery and Equipment
Size (number of employees)	139	~3000	180
Presence of an environmental department	Yes: embedded in the quality function	No: but has risk an compliance department that handles environmental issues	Yes: six employees
Environmental management system	Yes: ISO 14001	No	Yes: ISO 14001

Firm B1 is a supplier of automotive parts, for which the supply network quality assurance is mandated to comply with ISO/TS16949:2009. Reducing costs and meeting
delivery times are major concerns. However, although an environmental system is not
mandatory for the suppliers of B1, it prefers that its suppliers are certified to
ISO14001 or have either an environmental policy or engaged in some environmental
activities such as recycling. To control for the conformity of suppliers with desired
criteria, B1 monitors suppliers regularly and checks the expiry date of their certifi-
cates. If a supplier fails to meet the requirements, B1 first considers the extent that the
failure is affecting its business and operations. In one occasion, B1 had to stop dealing
with a supplier because the supplier did not have adequate OH&S, environmental and
quality systems and was not willing to take any action.

Firm B2, a clothes manufacturer, has hundreds of stores worldwide. It has a few
thousand employees in Australia, including employees in the retail sector. The company does not have an environmental department. However, it has a "risk and compliance department" that handles environmental issues. Its major suppliers are Asian,
with the China being the largest. Suppliers must agree not to avoid environmental
harm. Compliance is checked through twice yearly audits that examines suppliers
against ethical, environmental and quality requirements. B2's expectation is in line
with ISO standards ISO9001, ISO14001 and ISO18001 for quality, environmental,
and health and safety issues, respectively. Nevertheless, since certification is difficult

to obtain, B2 evaluates the suppliers only on the critical elements of those standards. The audits are conducted without notice: either by an internal team from B2 or a third party.

Firm B3, a manufacturer of water-related equipment that has 180 employees, is certified to ISO 9001 and ISO14001 and sources its materials and products both locally and abroad. It has worldwide export to many countries. Its environmental policy emphasises continuous improvement of its environmental performance. The company has adopted a proactive approach towards the environment since 2006 and has, as a consequence, won environmental awards. As its policy emphasises waste reduction, it demands that all packaging must consist of recycled materials (paper, wood paper, and cardboard). Other than these demands, it does not incorporate environmental requirements in tenders or contracts. Their audit of suppliers is purely quality driven. Furthermore, it does not dictate suppliers to use environmental management system such as ISO14001.

A comparison of three case studies suggests that there are similarities and differences in the way purchasers implement Green Supply Chain Practices. In all cases, buyers implemented compliance and monitoring practices. For B1 and B2, there were formalised practices for assessing and evaluating suppliers. Although environmental criteria are part of the suppliers' rating, they were not mandatory. All buyers indicated that decisions regarding selecting or maintaining a supplier are more flexible concerning environmental qualifications than price, quality and delivery.

In implementing green compliance and monitoring-oriented practices, the three cases treat all suppliers similarly. Contrastingly, for cooperative-oriented practices, buyers prefer to work with those suppliers who are keen and a major part of their business. One possible justification for such an approach is that compliance practices are less expensive to implement, while safeguarding buyers from the risk of breaching regulatory requirements due to the poor environmental performance of their suppliers. On the other hand, cooperative arrangements would not generate successful outcomes, unless participants dedicated resources and were willing to share their knowledge and capabilities, which in fact is not easy to handle.

When asking buyers about the impact of their practices on suppliers, compliance practices were directed towards avoiding risks of not meeting legal requirements. These practices, at their maximum potential, have enforced suppliers to generate incremental innovations. For instance, B3 enforced suppliers to change their packaging. Whereas, cooperative-oriented practices exhibit more breakthrough and systematic changes as in the case of B1's supplier, the partnership lead to certification to ISO14001. Likewise, the cooperation between B2 and a supplier provided the opportunity to produce a more efficient product.

6   Conclusion

The findings from the study of the Business Longitudinal Database imply that cooperating with external partners increases the likelihood of introducing environmental innovations. Having this knowledge helps corporate managers with intention to develop environmental innovation strategies to reinforce their relationships with existing partners (e.g., supply chain partners) or/and form new partnerships. The implication for policy makers is to set regulations and strategies [8],[22] that facilitate the cooperative activities of businesses.

The conclusion of the case studies is that buyers use both compliance and monitoring-oriented and cooperative-oriented practices to some degree. However, the results suggest that there is more emphasis on compliance practices and firms are in the early stages of incorporating environmental expectations into their supplier selection procedures. Cooperative practices are not yet well established and there were only limited occasional cooperation with suppliers on small environmental improvement projects. Further research could study how buyers and suppliers can move beyond compliance to cooperative practices and become more innovative in their supply chains with benefits to all supply chain members.

Regardless of the industry sector, while all claimed cooperation with suppliers on environmental innovations, examples of such practices were not demonstrable. The main reason for this could be that environmental issues are perceived as new areas for collaboration but are not historical suppliers' measures. Another reason could be that environmental innovations are costly and the payback period of such investments is often longer than other business investments. Therefore, those firms who have access to limited fund prefer to invest it on joint initiatives that result in more immediate returns.

References

1. Carrillo-Hermosilla, J., del Río, P., Könnölä, T.: Diversity of eco-innovations: Reflections from selected case studies. Journal of Cleaner Production 18, 1073–1083 (2010)
2. Klassen, R.D., Vachon, S.: Collaboration and evaluation in the supply chain: the impact on plant-level environmental investment. Production and Operations Management 12, 336–352 (2003)
3. Trifilova, A., Jia, J., Witzel, M., Bessant, J., Gosling, J.: Sustainable Innovation in Action: Experiences from China. In: The XXIII ISPIM Conference – Action for Innovation: Innovating from Experience, Barcelona, Spain (2012)
4. Hellström, T.: Dimensions of environmentally sustainable innovation: the structure of eco-innovation concepts. Sustainable Development 15, 148–159 (2007)
5. OECD: Eco-innovation in industry: Enabling green growth. OECD, Paris (2009)
6. Rennings, K.: Redefining innovation: eco-innovation research and the contribution from ecological economics. Ecological Economics 32, 319–332 (2000)
7. Falk, J., Ryan, C.: Inventing a sustainable future: Australia and the challenge of eco-innovation. Futures 39, 215–229 (2007)
8. Porter, M.E., van der Linde, C.: Toward a new conception of the environment-competitiveness relationship. Journal of Economic Perspectives 9, 97–118 (1995)
9. Peña, N.A., Fernández de Arroyabe, J.C.: Business cooperation from theory to practice. Palgrave Macmillan, London (2002)
10. Chesbrough, H.: The logic of open innovation: managing intellectual property. California Management Review 45, 33–58 (2003)

11. Terziovski, M.: The relationship between networking practices and business excellence: a study of small to medium enterprises (SMEs). Measuring Business Excellence 7, 78–92 (2003)
12. Beyerlein, M.M., Beyerlein, S.T., Kennedy, F.A.: Innovation through collaboration. JAI Press, Amsterdam (2006)
13. Mohannak, K.: Innovation networks and capability building in the Australian high-technology SMEs. European Journal of Innovation Management 10, 236–251 (2007)
14. Soosay, C.A., Hyland, P.W., Ferrer, M.: Supply chain collaboration: Capabilities for continuous innovation. Supply Chain Management 13, 160–169 (2008)
15. Bigliardi, B., Bottani, E., Galati, F.: Open innovation practices and supply chain management: a case study in the food machinery supply chain. International Journal of Engineering, Science and Technology 2, 244–255 (2010)
16. Yarahmadi, M., Higgins, P.G.: Motivations towards environmental innovation: A conceptual framework for multiparty cooperation. European Journal of Innovation Management 15, 400–420 (2012)
17. Biondi, V., Iraldo, F., Meredith, S.: Achieving sustainability through environmental innovation: The role of SMEs. International Journal of Technology Management 24, 612–626
18. Schaper, M.: The challenge of environmental responsibility and sustainable development: Implications for SME and entrepreneurship academics. In: Füglistaller, U., Pleitner, H.J., Volery, T., Weber, W. (eds.) Radical changes in the world: Will SMEs soar or crash?, pp. 525–534. Recontres de St Gallen, St Gallen (2002)
19. Collins, E., Lawrence, S., Pavlovich, K., Ryan, C.: Business networks and the uptake of sustainability practices: the case of New Zealand. Journal of Cleaner Production 15, 729–740 (2007)
20. Dacin, M.T., Oliver, C., Roy, J.P.: The legitimacy of strategic alliances: An institutional perspective. Strategic Management Journal 28, 169–187 (2007)
21. Lin, H., Darnall, N.: Strategic Alliances for Environmental Protection. In: Sarkis, J., Cordeiro, J.J., Brust, D.V. (eds.) Facilitating Sustainable Innovation through Collaboration, pp. 233–246. Springer, London (2010)
22. Horbach, J.: Determinants of environmental innovation: New evidence from German panel data sources. Research Policy 37, 163–173 (2008)
23. Yarahmadi, M., Clements, M., Higgins, P.G.: Greening supply chains: compliance and monitoring-oriented practices vs. cooperative-oriented practices. In: Issa, T., Isaías, P., Issa, T. (eds.) Proceedings of the IADIS International Conference on Sustainability, Technology and Education (STE 2012), November 28-30, pp. 53–60. IADIS Press (2012)

Negotiation Strategy for Economical Reuse in Closed-Loop Supply Chains

Yoshitaka Tanimizu, Kenta Matsui, Yuusuke Shimizu,
Koji Iwamura, and Nobuhiro Sugimura

Graduate School of Engineering, Osaka Prefecture University, Osaka, Japan
tanimizu@osakafu-u.ac.jp

Abstract. Environmental problems are recognized as one of the most serious issues in these last few decades. Green supply chain management and sustainable supply chain management have gained increasing attention within both academia and industry. Previous studies proposed a closed-loop supply chain model and a negotiation protocol for increasing the amount of reused products and reducing waste products. This study improves the negotiation protocol for further increasing the reused products and reducing the waste. A remanufacturer can economically collect a lot of used products by negotiating with a client in consideration of both the required prices from the remanufacture and the possible times to dispose of the used products from the client. A prototype of a simulation system for a closed-loop supply chain is developed in order to evaluate the effectiveness of the new negotiation protocol. Experimental results show that the new protocol can reuse more products than the previous one.

Keywords: Closed-loop supply chain, Reverse supply chain, Reuse, Negotiation, Scheduling, Genetic algorithm, Weibull distribution.

1 Introduction

Environmental problems are recognized as one of the most serious issues in these last few decades. Many manufacturing enterprises focus on incorporating not only economical but also environmental concerns into their strategic decisions [1]. Green supply chain management [2, 3] and sustainable supply chain management [4-7] have gained increasing attention within both academia and industry. The concept of the green supply chain management (GrSCM) covers all the phases of a product's life cycle, from the extraction of raw materials through the design, production and distribution phases, to the use of products by consumers and their disposal at the end of the product's life cycle including reconditioning, reuse, and recycling of products.

Products and materials are returned from customers to suppliers or manufacturers through reverse supply chains in order to be recycled, reused or reconditioned. Gungor and Gupta [8] indicated that the effort must be made for environmentally conscious manufacturing and product recovery systems to be profitable so that the incentive for development and planning of these systems continues. Then, it is required to establish a method for reconditioning, reuse, and recycling of used products

B. Grabot et al. (Eds.): APMS 2014, Part II, IFIP AICT 439, pp. 382–389, 2014.

in consideration of the feasibility of realizing a balance between environmental and economic concerns.

Previous study have proposed a basic model of closed-loop supply chains and a negotiation protocol for reusing products in consideration of economic efficiency [9]. The negotiation protocol provides a method for synchronizing the demand of reusable parts and the supply of used products among the organizations in the closed-loop supply chains. However some used products may become waste products by inconsistency between the demand and the supply of the used products from the viewpoint of product value. This study improves the negotiation protocol for further increasing the reused products and reducing the waste. A customer usually discards a product by stochastic means in consideration of its life cycle. New protocol provides a customer with a method for discarding a product systematically. A remanufacturer can prospectively enter into a contract with a customer through negotiation with the customer in consideration of both the required prices from the remanufacturer and the possible time to dispose of the used product from the customer.

The reminder of this paper is organized as follows. Section 2 shows literature review. Section 3 briefly describes the previous supply chain model. Section 4 explains new negotiation protocol. Finally, Section 5 demonstrates experimental results.

2   Literature Review

A large number of literatures have been published on a closed-loop supply chain which involves studies on network design problems, product acquisition management, marketing-related issues, etc. [10]. Guide et al. [11] takes a contingency approach to explore the factors that impact production planning and control for closed-loop supply chains that incorporate product recovery. Nielsen and Bruno [12] analyzed the possibility to utilize closed loop supply chains in mass customization settings and required certain aspects to be considered regarding product design as well as manufacturing and supply chain design. Hassini et al. [6] indicated that quite few papers addressed the pricing issue in a sustainable supply chain context during the last decade.

The market requires environmentally conscious products, such as electric vehicles and wind turbines. However, most of them include rare earths and other rare materials in main component parts, such as batteries and magnets. The U.S. Department of Energy reports that five rare earth elements, such as dysprosium, terbium, europium, neodymium and yttrium, are found to be critical in the short term (present - 2015) and other elements, such as cerium, indium, lanthanum and tellurium, are found to be near-critical [13]. The approach to proactively address material supply risks and prevent supply chain disruptions while building a robust clean energy economy has three pillars: achieving globally diverse supplies, identifying appropriate substitutes, and improving capacity for recycling, reuse and more efficient use of critical materials. Used products that incorporate rare resources like rare earths can be considered as a valuable resource.

A product is usually discarded in consideration of its life cycle. Takata et al. [14] analyzed the actual life cycle data of copying machine. Based on the analysis of the data, they proposed several models for identifying a collection rate and a discard rate of copying machines. Umeda et al. [15] analyzed product lifecycles of several products, such as a single use camera, a photocopier, and an automatic teller machine (ATM), from the viewpoint of the reusability. They point out that a product can be reused only when a manufacturer manufactures and sells same types of products in the market. In consideration of the reusability of product in the market, the used product should be returned from customers to suppliers or manufacturers as soon as possible, since the product life cycle appears to becoming shorter in recent years.

A lot of used products may become waste products in traditional recovery approaches, since customers discard products without consideration for reuse of the products whenever they want. A strategy for economical reuse of products is required to collect suitable products from customers and to provide manufacturers with reusable parts disassembled from the used products. Our study proposes a negotiation protocol which synchronizes the demand of reusable parts and the supply of used products among the organizations in the closed-loop supply chains. In the case where a lot of usable parts are required for generating new products, customers are stimulated to discard products for reuse. On the other hand, when few parts are required, customers are discouraged from discarding products. As if the remanufacturer deals with customers like virtual warehouses, the remanufacturer can economically collect suitable used products without various kinds of additional cost for warehouse and safety stock.

3   Previous Supply Chain Model

3.1   Modeling of Forward Supply Chains

This section briefly describes a model of forward and reverse supply chains which we have proposed in previous studies [8, 16, 17], in order to help understanding our closed-loop supply chain strategy. The previous studies have represented a framework for dynamically forming and reconfiguring a supply chain as a dynamic supply chain [16, 17]. Each organization in the supply chains can change business partners for every order to find suitable business partners and enter into profitable contracts.

A three-layered supply chain model consisting of a client, a manufacturer, and a supplier has been proposed as a basic model of forward supply chain which involves make-to-order (MTO) companies with no inventories [17]. It is assumed that only the supplier has sufficient raw materials but no inventory of final products. The model has provided with both the negotiation process to determine the suitable prices and delivery times of products among the three-layered organizations and the modification process of the production schedules in the supplier and the manufacturer. A client and a manufacturer sequentially send orders which include the requirements of delivery times and prices of the ordered products. A supplier and a manufacturer modify their existing production schedules by using a genetic algorithm (GA) and send offers for the orders, respectively. The offers include information about possible delivery times and bid prices of the ordered products. The actual delivery times and prices are determined by the negotiation processes among the organizations.

3.2   Modeling of Closed-Loop Supply Chains

The forward supply chain model extended to a closed-loop supply chain model consisting of both MTO companies in forward supply chains and remanufacturing-to-order companies in reverse supply chains [8]. Figure 1 shows a basic model of a closed-loop supply chain. A model component in the reverse supply chain receives a used product from a client and provides assembly manufacturers with usable parts. The component is referred to as a remanufacturer in the study.

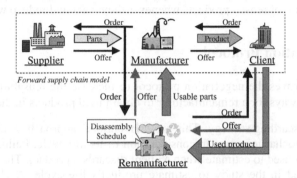

Fig. 1. Closed-loop supply chain model

A remanufacturer has neither stock of usable parts nor used products. A remanufacturer generates an order for used product and sends it to clients when the remanufacturer receives an order for a usable part from a manufacturer. After receiving an offer for a used product from a client, a remanufacturer generates an offer for a usable part and sends it to a manufacturer. A remanufacturer modifies its disassembly schedule and estimates the possible delivery time $dtr^F_{s,h,n}$ and the bid price $pcr^F_{s,h,n}$ of the usable part by using the following equations.

$$dtr^F_{s,h,n} = ctr_{s,h,n} \tag{1}$$

$$pcr^F_{s,h,n} = tcr_{s,h,n} + rwr_{s,h,n} - pnr_{s,h,n} + \sum_{g=1}^{G} \Delta pnr^{Rv(s,n,r)}_{s,h,g} \tag{2}$$

where
$ctr_{s,h,n}$ Completion time of a usable part recovered by remanufacturer R_s
$tcr_{s,h,n}$ Total cost for buying, disassembling and repairing of a used product
$rwr_{s,h,n}$ Reward for a usable part required by remanufacturer R_s
$pnr_{s,h,n}$ Penalty charge due to delay in delivery time of a usable part

The estimated profit $epf_{s,h,n}$ is calculated by the following equation.

$$epf_{s,h,n} = rwr_{s,h,n} - pnr_{s,h,n} + \sum_{g=1}^{G} \Delta pnr^{Rv(s,n,r)}_{s,h,g} \tag{3}$$

A remanufacturer considers a balance between supply and demand of reusable parts in the negotiation protocol. When a lot of usable parts are required by manufacturers, a remanufacturer stimulates clients to discard products for reuse by indicating high required prices for the used products to the clients. The clients discard products even if the products don't satisfy the condition of their life cycles estimated based on the Weibull distribution which is commonly used to model life data [18]. On the other hand, when few usable parts are required, remanufacturers indicate low required prices to discourage clients from discarding products. Then, the remanufacturer can increase the amount of reused products whenever they want and reduce waste products.

4   Negotiation Protocol

This study improves the negotiation protocol to increase the reusability of products. There are three ways for a remanufacturer to obtain used products in the following:

1. Push type discarding strategy: This is a conventional approach. A client discards a product by stochastic means in consideration of its life cycle. Failure rate of product is usually used to estimate when a client discards a product. The Weibull distribution is used in the study to estimate product's life cycle. A client discards a product, when it has been used beyond its life cycle. The discarded products should be stored temporarily, since a client does not consider the condition of reuse of the product. A remanufacture can obtain only the stored product for reuse. In the case where no remanufacturers need the stored product for a certain period, it must be disposed as a waste product.
2. Pull type discarding strategy: This is proposed in the previous research. A remanufacturer stimulates the intention of a client to discard a product, when a used product is required for reuse. A remanufacturer indicates high required prices for a used product to a client. The product's value is estimated based on the Weibull distribution in the study. It decreases with the time of usage of the product. The client evaluates a motivation for discarding a product by using the following equations and determines which product is discarded. If a much lower price is indicated for a used product, it is stochastically discarded and may become a waste product.

$$mv_{p',n'} \geq rn \qquad (4)$$

$$mv_{p',n'} = \frac{pcr_{s,n}^{O} - \left(PV(t) - dcc_{p',n'}\right)}{pcr_{s,n}^{O}} \qquad (5)$$

$$PV(t) = PV(0) \times \exp\left\{-\left(\frac{t}{\eta}\right)^{\beta}\right\} \qquad (6)$$

where
$mv_{p',n'}$ Motivation for providing a remanufacturers with a product for reuse
rn Random numbers

$pcr^{O}_{s,n}$	Required price for a product. It is determined by a remanufacturer
$PV(t)$	Product's value. It is estimated based on the Weibull distribution.
$dcc_{p',n'}$	Cost for discarding a product by client C_p'
$PV(0)$	Initial value of product. It equals to the purchase price of product.
β	Shape parameter which determines the mode of failure.
η	Scale parameter which defines the life of product.
t	Time of usage of product.

3. Negotiation type discarding strategy: In the case where a client does not accept an order from a remanufacturer for discarding a product from the viewpoint of the required price, the client provides the remanufacturer with a possible time to dispose of the product as an offer. The product's value decreases with the time of usage of product according to the Weibull distribution, as shown in Fig. 2. The client estimates the time when the product's value equals to the required price sent from the remanufacturer by using the following equation.

$$\ln t = \ln \eta - \frac{1}{\beta} \ln \left\{ \ln \left(\frac{PV(t)}{PV(0)} \right) \right\} \tag{7}$$

The remanufacturer evaluates the offer from the client by modifying a disassembly schedule and estimates a profit by using Eq. (3). The remanufacturer prospectively enters into a contract with the client by accepting the offer from the client. Then, the remanufacturer can obtain a lot of used products by negotiating with the client in consideration of both the required prices from the remanufacturer and the possible time to dispose of the used products from the client.

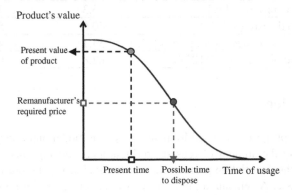

Fig. 2. Estimation of time to dispose of product based on the Weibull distribution

5   Computational Experiments

A prototype of a simulation system for closed-loop supply chains has been developed using Windows-based networked computers (Intel Core 2 Duo E8500 3.16 GHz CPU with 1.99 GB of RAM). Two suppliers, two manufacturers, a remanufacturer, and a client were implemented as agents on different six computers, respectively.

In the initial conditions, the suppliers and the manufacturers had same job-shop type production schedules consisting of 5 resources and 20 contracted parts, and 10 resources and 20 contracted products, respectively. The client continuously generated 100 new orders and negotiated with two manufacturers during the experiments for about 6 hours. The manufacturers generated orders and negotiated among the two suppliers and one remanufacturer every 30 seconds of bidding time in order to generate offers for the client. Population size, crossover rate, and mutation rate of the GA were 30, 0.8, and 0.2, respectively.

Experimental results of the model with new negotiation protocol including negotiation type discarding strategy were compared with ones of the model with the previous protocol including only push and pull type discarding strategies. Ten experiments were carried out for the new model and the previous model, respectively. The experimental results are summarized in Table 1. The remanufacturer in the new model can increase the amount of reused products more than the one in the previous model. The new model can reuse about 10 % more products than the previous one. According to the rate of reused parts in new products, there are more chances to assemble the reusable parts into new products in the new model than the one with the previous model. However the remanufacturer doesn't obtain a very large profit, since it should pay the penalty charge in the case of delay in the required delivery time of usable part.

Table 1. Comparison between experimental results of the two models

	Previous model	New model
Number of reused products [av]	24.8	31.7
Number of waste products [av]	36.3	31.6
Rate of reuse to discard [av] (%)	40.6	50.0
Rate of reused parts in new products [av] (%)	33.1	42.1
Profit of remanufacturer [av] ($*10^3$ $)	62.8	64.8

6   Conclusion

Previous studies proposed a closed-loop supply chain model and a negotiation protocol for increasing the amount of reused products and reducing waste products. This study improves the negotiation protocol for further increasing the reused products and reducing the waste. A remanufacturer can prospectively enter into a contract with a client by accepting the offer for possible time to dispose of product. Then, a lot of used products are economically collected by a remanufacturer through negotiation with a client in consideration of both the required prices from the remanufacture and the possible times to dispose of the used products from the client. Some experiments were carried out by using the developed simulation system for a closed-loop supply chain. Experimental results of the model with new negotiation protocol were compared with the one of previous protocol. The results show that the new protocol can reuse about 10 % more products than the previous one.

References

1. BearingPoint: 2008 Supply Chain Monitor "How Mature is the Green Supply Chain?", Survey report, online (2008), http://www.supplychainstandard.com
2. Srivastava, S.K.: Green Supply-Chain Management: a State-of-the-Art Literature Review. International Journal of Management Reviews 9(1), 53–80 (2007)
3. Sarkis, J., Zhu, Q., Lai, K.: An Organizational Theoretic Review of Green Supply Chain. International Journal of Production Economics 130, 1–15 (2011)
4. Seuring, S., Muller, M.: From a Literature Review to a Conceptual Framework for Sustainable Supply Chain Management. Journal of Cleaner Production 16, 1699–1710 (2008)
5. Gupta, S., Palsule-Desai, O.D.: Sustainable Supply Chain Management: Review and Research Opportunities. IIMB Management Review 23, 234–245 (2011)
6. Hassini, E., Surti., C., Searcy, C.: A Literature Review and a Case Study of Sustainable Supply Chains with a Focus on Metrics. International Journal of Production Economics 140, 69–82 (2012)
7. Seuring, S.: A Review of Modeling Approaches for Sustainable Supply Chain Management. Decision Support Systems 54, 1513–1520 (2013)
8. Gungor, A., Gupta, S.M.: Issues in Environmentally Conscious Manufacturing and Product Recovery: a Survey. Computers and Industrial Engineering 36, 811–853 (1999)
9. Tanimizu, Y., Shimizu, Y., Iwamura, K., Sugimura, N.: Modeling and Simulation of Closed-Loop Supply Chains Considering Economic Efficiency. In: Prabhu, V., Taisch, M., Kiritsis, D. (eds.) APMS 2013, Part I. IFIP AICT, vol. 414, pp. 461–468. Springer, Heidelberg (2013)
10. Llgin, M.A., Gupta, S.M.: Environmentally Conscious Manufacturing and Product Recovery (ECMPRO): A Review of the State of the Art. Journal of Environmental Management 91, 563–591 (2010)
11. Guide, V.D.R., Jayaraman, V., Linton, J.D.: Building Contingency Planning for Closed-Loop Supply Chains with Product Recovery. Journal of Operations Management 21, 259–279 (2003)
12. Nielsen, K., Brunø, T.D.: Closed Loop Supply Chains for Sustainable Mass Customization. In: Prabhu, V., Taisch, M., Kiritsis, D. (eds.) APMS 2013, Part I. IFIP AICT, vol. 414, pp. 425–432. Springer, Heidelberg (2013)
13. The U.S. Department of Energy: Critical Materials Strategy (2011)
14. Takata, S., Watanabe, M., Ohbayashi, Y.: Collection Rate Estimation Model in Closed-Loop Manufacturing. In: Proc. of CIRP International Conference on Life Cycle Engineering, pp. 601–606 (2006)
15. Umeda, Y., Kondoh, S., Sugino, T., Yoshikawa, H.: Analysis of Reusability using 'Marginal Reuse Rate'. CIRP Annals -Manufacturing Technology 55(1), 41–44 (2006)
16. Tanimizu, Y., Yamanaka, M., Iwamura, K., Sugimura, N.: Multi-Agent Based Dynamic Supply Chain Configuration Considering Production Schedules. In: Proc. of International Symposium on Flexible Automation, pp. 572–578 (2006)
17. Tanimizu, Y., Ozawa, C., Shimizu, Y., Orita, B., Iwamura, K., Sugimura, N.: Flexible Multi-Layered Dynamic Supply Chain Models with Cooperative Negotiation. International Journal of Automation Technology 7(1), 128–135 (2013)
18. Mazhar, M.I., Kara, S., Kaebernick, H.: Remaining Life Estimation of Used Components in Consumer Products: Life Cycle Data Analysis by Weibull and Artificial Neural Networks. Journal of Operations Management 25, 1184–1193 (2007)

Energy-Aware Models for Warehousing Operations

Vidyuth Anand, Seokgi Lee, and Vittaldas V. Prabhu

The Pennsylvania State University, University Park, U.S.A.
{vua109,sul201}@psu.edu,
prabhu@engr.psu.edu

Abstract. There is a growing need in industries worldwide to become more sustainable and energy efficient. Due to rapid increase in demand of goods, there has been a rise in demand of logistics and operational services. This necessitates needs for a large number of warehouses and distribution centers to satisfy demand. It is imperative that warehouses follow the same sustainable development model practiced in other industries. This paper extends energy efficiency techniques suggested for manufacturing to warehousing. Specifically, warehouses are modeled as M/M/c queues where forklifts are servers and this model is used to evaluate performance of energy control policies. The model is then extended to general distribution queues. Experiments based on real-world data yield results that indicate that for system utilization values between 40% and 100%, as the number of servers in the system increases by a factor of 4, energy consumption increases by a factor of 3.78.

Keywords: Energy control, Queueing, Warehousing, Forklifts.

1   Introduction

The world today has incorporated a more ecological approach in the utilization of energy resources, targeted toward the exploration of "green" options and renewable sources of energy. Various efforts have been taken to understand and reduce the consumption of energy in the manufacturing sector [1]. From a logistics standpoint, research has been undertaken to find more sustainable choices due to increase in demand of various products. To put this into perspective, the amount of money invested in business logistics in the U.S. in 2012 was $1.33 trillion, which is 8.5% of the GDP [2]. Warehousing, a critical element in the logistics sector, accounts for 8% of the total energy consumption of all commercial buildings in the country [3]. According to an analysis of the energy consumed in warehouses/distribution centers (DCs) [4], HVAC and lighting are critical components for both non-refrigerated and refrigerated warehouses, accounting for a significant portion of energy utilization.

Discounting the smaller consumers of energy such as office equipment, it is safe to assume that other than heating, ventilation and air conditioning (HVAC), a predominant contributor to energy usage is the movement of material from place to place within the DC. Material movement contributes to a significant portion of the final product's cost, and warehouses contain specific "Warehouse Management Systems" (WMS) to aid in handling the material, including non-automated and automated sys-

B. Grabot et al. (Eds.): APMS 2014, Part II, IFIP AICT 439, pp. 390–397, 2014.

tems [5]. Automated Storage/Retrieval Systems (AS/RS) are an important tool used in material handling in warehouses and most modern factories for work-in-process storage [6]. However, manually operated forklifts continue to play a major role in the efficient functioning of a warehouse. In 2012 alone, the top twenty manufacturers of lift trucks worldwide shipped $30.4 billion worth of forklifts, and the forklift domain is increasingly becoming a platform to enable better technology for more productivity. Forklifts, in performing the functions of order picking and put-away in warehouses, contribute to most of the energy consumption among all other material handling systems in terms of fuel cells and electric charge required [7]. Warehouses may be roughly modeled as a queueing system in which stock-keeping units (SKU's) are customers that arrive at the receiving dock, where they join a queue usually serviced by forklifts for storage, until they are shipped out [8]. The primary concern of this paper is to establish a queueing system considering forklifts as servers and relate the same to an energy model with the inclusion of energy waste reduction controls during forklift idling, similar to idling of machines in a manufacturing unit [9].

A majority of existing literature is devoted to research in the modeling of energy aware manufacturing systems, useful in the shop floor. Reduction of wastage of energy by using heuristics for various dispatch rules has also been proposed [9]. In terms of warehousing, literature is focused on the development of energy efficient material handling applications by finding an optimized travel path sequence, considering the Traveling Salesman Problem (TSP) to address the problem of order picking [10]. Algorithms have been designed for effective performance end-of-aisle order picking systems, and travel times have been analyzed considering queueing models for item location in warehouses [11]. Queueing models for centralized inventory information in warehouses and warehouses with autonomous vehicles have been developed to evaluate congestion effects in storage and retrieval transactions [12], and there has been recent research dedicated to the development of queueing models for warehouse AS/RS [6], [13]. There is a requirement to develop computationally intuitive energy-aware warehousing models as it relates to queueing theory, which effectively captures the consumption of energy on a large scale, to facilitate more productive insights during warehouse planning and design stages.

2   Warehouse Layout

The design of work-in-process warehouse layouts are heavily influenced by response times of the material handling system. Pandit and Palekar (1993) propose a warehouse layout for a multi-vehicle handling system. The warehouse is considered to be rectangular in shape to facilitate ease of storage of rectangular units in the form of pallets, stored within the warehouse on racks [14]. The racks are arranged back-to-back in the form of blocks, and space between blocks form aisle, creating a guide-way network which expedites forklift movement and reduces congestion. The layout suggested is a probable aisle arrangement in large warehouses, in which the rack accessibility of forklifts is maximized. Fig. 1 details the warehouse layout considered for the purpose of this paper.

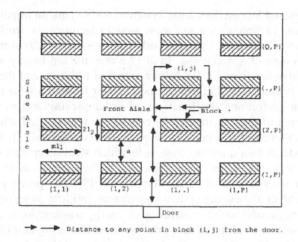

Fig. 1. Layout details (Source: Pandit & Palekar, 1993)

The warehouse operates under the following assumptions: storage and retrieval requests arrive at a door whenever a truck moves into the loading/unloading dock. Immediate fulfillment of the request is done if a forklift is free. If the order is waiting on a forklift, it enters itself into a queue which empties on a first-come, first-serve (FCFS) basis rather than a priority based emptying of the queue, for ease of calculation. The system is modeled as M/M/c queue, in which c indicates total number of forklifts operated in the warehouse.

3   Warehousing Energy Control Model

The recently proposed machine-level EC1 energy control policy is considered to be the basis for the model proposed in this paper. The main objective of the policy is the reduction of energy consumption during machine idling, thus reducing wasted energy. The policy states that this can be achieved if the machine is switched to a lower power consumption state if its idle time exceeds a minimum threshold value τ [1], [9]. Determining an optimal value of τ could involve a trade-off between energy savings and loss of production [1]. The concept of utilization of a minimum threshold value of time to conserve energy has been explored in terms of manufacturing systems where production schedules are fixed at least τ ahead of time [9]. The understanding of interplay between energy control (EC) policies and production control (PC) policies as it relates to key performance indicators (KPIs) becomes necessary. It is safe to assume that the same model can be applied to a distribution center as well, seeing as the loading or unloading of trucks in loading docks to pick material for packing and shipping or to put-away material in storage respectively takes place on a fixed schedule, with planned shipments [15].

In the context of this paper, we consider τ to represent the average idle time threshold of the forklift system in the warehouse. The EC1 energy control policy serves to link warehousing decisions which would influence KPIs of the system with EC and

PC policies. Major warehousing decisions include configuration issues viz., how material flow should be organized, design of the order picking and shipping process, sizing of the warehouse, allocation of storage capacity, determining lighting and electricity requirements, batch sizing and scheduling, and level of automation required [5]. The KPIs of interest include energy consumption per forklift, total system energy consumption over the long term, cycle time for each forklift, throughput of the facility, and utilization and availability of the forklift system.

4   Multi-server Queueing Model with Energy Control

A key characteristic of discrete manufacturing is that the energy consumed by a machine tool while it is idling or busy is quite similar [10]. For any system, energy can be expressed as the product of power and time. Power consumed by any machine in the system, in this case c forklifts, changes according to the state of the system. For practical purposes, systems tend to consist of two states on average: *busy* and *idle*. We define an intermediate third state for the system which occurs when forklifts perform non-value added activities. We consider this to be the *apparent idling* condition of the forklift system. Average power values for the 3 system states are defined as W_0 for idle condition, W_1 for apparent idling and W_p for busy state. The idle time of the system is composed of time taken by the forklifts to perform non-value added activities (considered as *apparent idle time* of the system) and time in which the forklift is idle (*real idle time* of the system). An average idle time threshold τ is specified for the system. We define power consumption during real idle time (W_0) to be zero, i.e., the forklift is switched off when not performing any activity.

Probabilistic models will be constructed in this section to find out the state of the system at any given time, enabling us to estimate consumption of energy in the system. Consider a multi-server machine system. Orders arrive at the loading dock at a rate λ according to a Poisson process with exponential inter-arrival times and get serviced at a rate μ according to an exponential distribution, with c forklifts being the servers. The queue is processed on a FCFS basis, with jobs departing the system after they have been processed by any of the servers. This is the M/M/c model under consideration.

For M/M/1 queue, utilization of the machine is given by the following relation [16]:

$$\text{Utilization } \rho = \text{Arrival rate/Service rate} = \lambda/\mu \tag{1}$$

For the M/M/c queue, average utilization of the system is expressed as:

$$\rho = \lambda/c\mu \tag{2}$$

For stability and to provide bounds to the system, the utilization value should be lower than 1. Utilization parameter ρ represents the average fraction of time during which each of the c servers is occupied with a task. The fraction of time that the system will be idle is expressed as [17]:

$$\delta = \left[\frac{(c\rho)^c}{c!\,(1-\rho)} + \sum_{n=0}^{c-1} \frac{(c\rho)^n}{n!}\right]^{-1} \tag{3}$$

Prabhu et al. (2012) calculated the probability that inter-arrival time is more than the average threshold idle time τ by the following equation:

$$P(x > \tau) = \int_{\tau}^{\infty} f(x)dx = e^{-\lambda\tau} \tag{4}$$

where $f(x)$ for an exponential distribution $= \lambda e^{-\lambda x}$. By logic, $(1 - e^{-\lambda\tau})$ will be the probability of forklifts doing non-value added activities. Consequently, the probability that the system is in the idle state and time between arrivals is greater than τ is calculated as:

$$\left[\frac{(c\rho)^c}{c!\,(1-\rho)} + \sum_{n=0}^{c-1} \frac{(c\rho)^n}{n!}\right]^{-1} P(x > \tau) = \left[\frac{(c\rho)^c}{c!\,(1-\rho)} + \sum_{n=0}^{c-1} \frac{(c\rho)^n}{n!}\right]^{-1} e^{-\lambda\tau} \tag{5}$$

Under steady state condition, arrivals are independent of the state of the system. Thus the long term energy consumption equation for the system over time T is:

$$E = \left\{cW_p\rho + W_0 \left[\frac{(c\rho)^c}{c!\,(1-\rho)} + \sum_{n=0}^{c-1} \frac{(c\rho)^n}{n!}\right]^{-1} e^{-\lambda\tau}\right.$$
$$\left. + W_1 \left[\frac{(c\rho)^c}{c!\,(1-\rho)} + \sum_{n=0}^{c-1} \frac{(c\rho)^n}{n!}\right]^{-1} (1 - e^{-\lambda\tau})\right\} T \tag{6}$$

Substituting the value of W_0 as 0 in Equation (6),

$$E = \left\{cW_p\rho + W_1 \left[\frac{(c\rho)^c}{c!\,(1-\rho)} + \sum_{n=0}^{c-1} \frac{(c\rho)^n}{n!}\right]^{-1} (1 - e^{-\lambda\tau})\right\} T \tag{7}$$

The ratio of energy wasted during idle time (E_w) to the energy that is actively used when the forklifts are accomplishing value-added activities (E_p) is given by the following relationship:

$$\frac{E_w}{E_p} = \frac{W_1 \left[\frac{(c\rho)^c}{c!\,(1-\rho)} + \sum_{n=0}^{c-1} \frac{(c\rho)^n}{n!}\right]^{-1} (1 - e^{-\lambda\tau})}{cW_p\rho} \tag{8}$$

The model presented has assumed a Poisson input process. However, this assumption would be violated if arrivals definitely do not occur randomly for the warehousing system. This necessitates the use of an arbitrary distribution queueing model [18]. The queue is classified as a G/G/c model, where arrival and service distributions usually follow different processes but can be the same as well. Using Equation (7) as a basis, different energy relations based on various inter-arrival distributions can be calculated using the following general equation:

$$E = \left\{cW_p\rho + W_1 \left[\frac{(c\rho)^c}{c!\,(1-\rho)} + \sum_{n=0}^{c-1} \frac{(c\rho)^n}{n!}\right]^{-1} F(\tau)\right\} T \tag{9}$$

where $\int_{\tau}^{\infty} f(x)dx = 1 - F(\tau)$ for any distribution.

When the utilization of the forklift is high, $W_1 \to 0$ and the only term that will affect the equation is $W_p\rho$. Similarly under low utilization condition, only the W_1 term would affect the equation. It is to be noted that when utilization is high, i.e., $W_p \to 1$, the EC1 energy control policy will not influence energy consumption. For a 100% utilization of the system, i.e., when all forklifts are in operation,

$$E = cW_p \rho T \qquad (10)$$

Depending upon the type of warehouse system considered, certain constraints are introduced to the equation which is then differentiated with respect to c to find the optimal value yielding minimum energy consumption. Constraints could be the maximum amount of throughput a warehouse is capable of handling, layout of warehouse, capacity, response time, storage density and inventory availability.

5   Experimentation and Results

The analysis of the real time operations of one of the DCs of a personal care manufacturer located in Brazil was done for experimentation purposes. The layout of the DC in consideration is similar to the one suggested in Fig. 1 of this paper. Analysis of arrival rates of products over a three-day period showed that the products arrived with a beta distribution on day 1 with shape parameters $\alpha = 1.87$ and $\beta = 2.05$; a triangular distribution on day 2 with parameters $a = 0.58$, $b = 4.9$ and $c = 0.62$; a beta distribution on day 3 with shape parameters $\alpha = 2.17$ and $\beta = 2.26$.

Assuming average forklift speed of travel is 5 mph for all operations, the worst case scenario assumes that on average, each forklift travels to all rack positions in the DC to drop off orders and picks up orders to drop them off at the loading dock every day. Since average demand per day is a constant number, it is safe to assume that service rates follow the same arrival distribution over the three days observed.

Consider that $W_1 = W_p$, a fair assumption to make as forklifts would usually spend the same amount of power doing non-value added activities as they do for value-added work. By logic, average idle time threshold τ decreases with an increasing number of forklifts in the system. The number of forklifts in the system would be dependent on the size of the warehouse. Let us consider 5 forklifts for a smaller warehouse and 20 forklifts for a larger one. Consider that for 5 forklifts, τ value is 60 minutes, and for 20 forklifts, it is 10 minutes. Varying utilization, using Equation (9), surface plots of the daily energy values for the three distributions are illustrated in Fig. 2. For different utilization values, the energy consumption increases by an average of 278.8% as number of forklifts in the system increase from 5 to 20. Thus it can be seen that larger warehouses with n times the number of forklifts as smaller ones consume nearly n times more energy for any arrival distribution.

It is observed that the values obtained for the general distribution model do not vary significantly between distributions, because of the scaling down of the W_1 term due to minute values of idle probability of the system. This is because the chance of the entire forklift system being idle at the same time is almost zero. In such situations, only the W_p term of the equation would affect the energy value. Energy varies proportionally with utilization for a constant c value and number of forklifts for a constant ρ.

Fig. 3(a) details the variation of daily energy with respect to change in utilization with 5 forklifts in the system. Fig. 3(b) illustrates energy variation with respect to number of forklifts at 70% utilization. It is observed that variation of energy is almost linear in both cases.

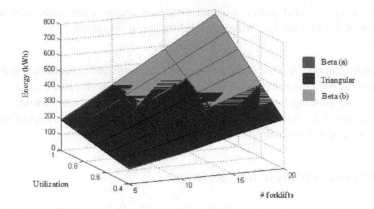

Fig. 2. Energy surface plot of different distributions

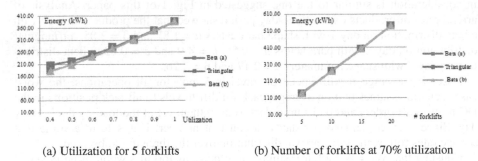

(a) Utilization for 5 forklifts   (b) Number of forklifts at 70% utilization

Fig. 3. Variation of daily energy

6   Conclusions

The motivation for this work was the need for an energy-aware warehousing model which leveraged the principles proposed by the EC1 energy control policy to forklift queues in warehouses and DCs. The paper suggests a model for which the recently proposed M/M/1 manufacturing model with energy control is the basis, and extends it to an M/M/c queue in a warehouse. Experimentation on the model yielded results which are largely dependent on the number of servers considered in the system. For a larger number of servers, the apparent idling energy of the system would tend to be on the lower side. The analytical model developed can be used to determine availability of forklifts to accomplish tasks and assignment of forklifts for the same, determination of energy spent by forklifts, and calculation of optimal number of forklifts to reduce energy in the system based on certain constraints. Future work can be extended to the determination of the energy consumption in other avenues in warehouses, especially newer ones with higher capital investment where automation will come into play, and implementation of other energy control policies for the same. Validation of the suggested model can be carried out by simulating the queueing of forklifts in Arena and employing the suggested equation to calculate energy.

References

1. Prabhu, V.V., Jeon, H.W., Taisch, M.: Simulation Modelling of Energy Dynamics in Discrete Manufacturing Systems. Service Orientation in Holonic and Multi Agent Manufacturing and Robotics 472, 293–311 (2013)
2. Penske Logistics: State of Logistics Report. Council of Supply Chain Management Professionals (2013)
3. Williams, K.: A No-Brainer: Retrofitting Warehouse Heating Systems. Retrofit Magazine (2010)
4. U.S. Energy Information Administration: Commercial Buildings Energy Consumption Survey (2003)
5. Rouwenhorst, B., Reuterb, B., Stockrahmb, V., van Houtumc, G.J., Mantela, R.J., Zijmc, W.H.M.: Warehouse design and control: Framework and literature review. European Journal of Operational Research 122(3), 515–533 (2000)
6. Hur, S., Lee, Y.H., Lim, S.Y., Lee, M.H.: A performance estimation model for AS/RS by M/G/1 queuing system. Computers & Industrial Engineering 46, 233–241 (2004)
7. Greenway, S.: Fuel Cell Lift Trucks: Key Considerations for Fleet Conversion. SC Hydrogen & Fuel Cell Alliance (2012)
8. Bartholdi, J.J., Hackman, S.T.: Warehouse & Distribution Science. Atlanta (2011)
9. Prabhu, V.V., Jeon, H.W., Taisch, M.: Modeling Green Factory Physics - An Analytical Approach. In: 8th IEEE International Conference on Automation Science and Engineering, Korea, pp. 46–51 (2012)
10. Makris, P.A., Makri, A.P., Provatidis, C.G.: Energy-saving methodology for material handling applications. Applied Energy 8(3), 1116–1124 (2006)
11. Chew, E.P., Tang, L.C.: Travel time analysis for general item location assignment in a rectangular warehouse. European Journal of Operational Research 112, 582–597 (1997)
12. Roy, D., Krishnamurthy, A.: Queuing Model for Unit-Load Warehouse Systems using Autonomous Vehicles, Stochastic Models for Manufacturing and Service Operations (2011)
13. Lee, H.F.: Performance analysis for automated storage and retrieval systems. IIE Transactions 29(1), 15–28 (2007)
14. Berry, J.R.: Elements of Warehouse Layout. International Journal of Production Research 7(2) (1968)
15. Frazelle, E.: Supply Chain Strategy. McGraw-Hill (2002)
16. Hopp, W.J., Spearman, M.L.: Factory Physics. McGraw-Hill (2000)
17. Askin, R.G., Standridge, C.R.: Modeling and Analysis of Manufacturing Systems. Wiley (1993)
18. Hillier, F.S., Lieberman, G.J.: Operations Research. Holden-Day, Inc. (1967)
19. Pandit, R., Palekar, U.S.: Response Time Considerations for Optimal Warehouse Layout Design. Journal of Manufacturing Science and Engineering 115(3), 322–328 (1993)

Anthropocentric Workplaces of the Future Approached through a New Holistic Vision

Andrea Bettoni[1], Marco Cinus[1], Marzio Sorlini[1], Gókan May[2],
Marco Taisch[2], and Paolo Pedrazzoli[1]

[1] University of Applied Sciences and Arts of Southern Switzerland, ISTePS, Galleria
2 Via Cantonale 2c, CH-6928 Manno, Switzerland
{andrea.bettoni,marco.cinus,marzio.sorlini,
paolo.pedrazzoli}@supsi.ch
[2] Politecnico di Milano, Piazza Leonardo da Vinci 32, I-20131 Milano, Italy
{gokan.may,marco.taisch}@polimi.it

Abstract. The human dimension is growing in importance in the cul- tural and scientific debate surrounding the arising of workplace and fac- tory of the future visions. Having people at the centre of the factory is already recognized as a main enabler for making the most out of their skills and capacities while at the same time achieving an environment that can both motivate employed workers and attract new skilled ones. The present paper proposes a novel concept aimed at defining new so- cially sustainable workplaces that adapt to workers' anthropometric di- mensions within worker-aware production systems that are designed and operated to capitalize on workers' skills and experience while at the same time promoting their development. Moreover it envisions the integration of the factory in the social and environmental context by promoting the creation and provision of worker-centric services that turn the factory from a society-affecting entity into an integration-promotion body.

Keywords: socially sustainable workplaces, anthropocentric workplace, context-aware factory.

1 Introduction

Companies today are declaring in their Corporate Social Responsibility (CSR) reports that they consider as primary the attention towards all the company stakeholders' and especially employees' behaviour, where the workers are referred as the company's greatest asset. However, few organizations actually treat their employees this way. In his book [28], Walker discusses on the methodologies and approaches that an organization can implement in order to put the employee at the centre of the working environment, postulating that "only when man- agement recognizes that the firm exists to provide an ethical environment in which employees can fully develop and apply their business skills, will the firm be positioned for true success". Royer et al. [21] points out that in a strategic perspective the employees' voice is an important business component where

B. Grabot et al. (Eds.): APMS 2014, Part II, IFIP AICT 439, pp. 398–405, 2014.

or- ganizations can rely on for pursuing success. Recognizing the worker as a critical resource for the enterprise success, as detailed in [18], has been the starting point for the development of structured employee-centred Human Resource Manage- ment (HRM) strategies. This vision produced the notion of employees as human capital: they collectively represent the sum of all their knowledge, skills, and abilities, as well as additional characteristics such as energy, drive and moti- vation they bring with them to the factory [3]. "Knowing" the worker is thus fundamental in order to be able to foresee the value generation capabilities of the company.

According to Sinha et al. [22], the "organizations of tomorrow will be employee- centric". The positive correlation between organizations' performances and em- ployee recognition as a critical resource in strategic management has been demon- strated by case studies and investigations on real production environments' per- formances [16,26].

But, what does it mean putting the employee "at the centre" of the orga- nization? Which are the tools supporting this shift? Which are the levers and the knowledge areas employee-centric organizations may rely on to pursue their objective?

Guided by the above mentioned research questions, this study aims at defin- ing the new anthropocentric workplaces of the future. In this sense, Chapter 2 investigates the interaction between employee and working context, and Chapter 3 highlights the main cornerstones of these anthropocentric workplaces. Finally, Chapter 4 tries to summarize the key developments of the next years.

2   Employee and the Working Context Interaction

Achieving the transition to an industry where the human dimension is a key cor- nerstone requires, in the first place, to know each single person involved in the production processes. A reliable, holistic and accessible characterization of work- ers is thus called for. According to surveys of the European Commission [6, 17] quality of work and employment has four complementary dimensions: ensur- ing career and employment security, maintaining and promoting the health and wellbeing of workers, developing skills and competences, and reconciling working and non-working life. Accordingly four elements through which the employee - working environment / context interaction are here identified and examined: (1) Ergonomics and Anthropometry, (2) Functional Capacities, (3) Knowledge and (4) Personal needs and private life - work balance.

2.1   Ergonomics and Anthropometry

Ergonomics encompasses the relationship between humans, machine systems, job design and the work environment. Various studies [5, 8, 10–12, 15] argue that the goal of ergonomics is to enable workers to be more effective by matching the requirements and demands of the job to the abilities and limitations of the workers rather than trying to force the workers to fit the job.

The social impacts of ergonomics are obvious and empirical studies reported in [20] have proven that ergonomics in the workplace has also an impact on effectiveness and profitability, making this discipline important even from a pure economic point of view. The most obvious cause of the increasing interest in this field is the rising costs related with injuries on the workplace. In order to foster the adoption of ergonomics in manufacturing strategies it is also important to raise the perception that proper prevention measures can have positive impact on productivity and quality. The introduction of advanced technologies and automation in production has not yet been accompanied by parallel advances in ergonomics, resulting into workers' pathology that are not necessarily major accidents, but injuries deriving from repeated micro-traumas at muscoloskeletal and nervous system level [5, 19].

2.2 Functional Capacities

Modern ergonomics evaluation practices also consider functional capacities of the workers. In order to put a strong emphasis on the relationship between the workers' abilities and the assigned task, the analysis of ergonomics and functional capacities are kept separated.

Tasks assignment strategies and methodologies can be traced back to 1911 in Taylor's "Scientific Management" [25]. Taylor's principles for manual workers productivity emphasized efficient and effective object motion to ensure the best possible outcome. The object, its necessary and sufficient motion in space and time, and the manual worker's movements are integrated to achieve control over the manufacturing variables and meet the requirements for a quality product.

Approaches deriving from traditional scientific management theories require a careful and in-depth analysis of the operations and working tasks, on one side, and of worker physical capacities and characteristics on the other. In fact, physical characteristics of the worker have a meaningful impact on its perfor- mances [24].

The analysis of the matching between the worker functional characteristics and capabilities and the assigned tasks is elicited in a proper workplace design. This simultaneous consideration of worker/workplace and worker/job binomials is often at the basis of Total Quality Management [7], or Business Process Re-engineering methodologies, with the goal to improve working conditions and promote a sustainable working life where work environment improvement efforts are a resource for both the workplace and the individual.

2.3 Knowledge

As stated by Waitley [27] "Today, the source of power has shifted from capital resources to human resources, from natural resources to knowledge resources, from position status to relationship process, and from shareowner power to cus- tomer power". Knowledge is one of the most important resource employees bring to the company, and those who want to succeed have the challenge to identify, create, share, store, and internally disseminate the employee's knowledge [14].

Adopting Knowledge Management tools in industrial contexts has become a ne- cessity, and organizations need to manage these intellectual assets effectively. This is true for both big competitors and for SMEs.

Investing in KM systems is a way to facilitate the experience and knowledge flow between the employees of a firm [13]. Bhattacharya et al. [1] shows that knowledge and skills are strongly related with company performances. Proper Knowledge Management Systems have been thus adopted in various industrial contexts in order to both collect and reuse workers knowledge for the benefit of the company, using direct and indirect techniques [23].

2.4   Personal Needs

Finally, workers' behaviour and personal needs are rarely gathered and included in workers' profiles. These data are usually collected using traditional (e.g. questionnaire-based) means and included in ad-hoc "workers-care" initiatives or campaigns. Many social studies can be mentioned reporting results of these investigations and several tools and methodologies [2] are adopted especially in big companies in order to ensure workers personal wishes collection and re-use for organizational improvement.

Nowadays, many companies are trying to respond to the worker require- ments enhancing the working conditions on one hand, and a sustainable work participation on the other hand. Some of these initiatives are suggested by CSR implementation strategies, where the employee is one of the (most important) stakeholders the company has to take care of. The characteristics related to the production processes, such as scheduled time, machine productivity, etc. may im- pose a constraint when addressing the worker personal requirements during the setting phase of the working conditions. These conditions, in fact, include sched- ule and workplace flexibility, autonomy and accountability, teamwork, manage- ment by objectives, strict deadlines, etc. that are all elements constrained both to processes and workers characteristics [9].

3   Anthropocentric Workplaces of the Future

This chapter provides a novel concept that aims at defining new socially sus- tainable workplaces where the human dimension is a key cornerstone. Workers are foreseen at the centre of the factory, on the one hand, in terms of workplace adaptation and production planning, to skills, expertise and characteristics of each single worker and, on the other hand, in terms of capability to make the most out of workers' knowledge and potentials across all age groups and different roles, simultaneously fostering enhanced workers safety. Moreover, this concept promotes the vision of an effective integration of this anthropocentric factory within the social environment toward the implementation of context-aware fac- tories that encourage and take advantage of extended services to the workers in terms of accessibility, inclusiveness, work-life balance and work satisfaction.

The main human-centric factors governing production taken into considerations are: (1) Efficiency, (2) Occupational Health and Safety with related Risk Management and (3) Effective use of workers knowledge. In this sense, evolving characteristics of each single worker in terms of age, expertise, attitudes and health conditions, imply an ever changing profile of skills and tasks, that needs to be taken into consideration in terms of work organization and workplace adaptation and in terms of capability to make the most out of workers' knowledge and potentials.

The Anthropocentric Workplace of the Future concept will lays its foundation on four cornerstone, which are:

1. KNOW the worker / factory / context
2. Design & Deploy the workplace
3. Plan the Production and Organize the Work
4. Produce with context-aware factories integrated in their social environment

In the following subsections, a brief description of these cornerstones are pro- vided.

3.1 KNOW

Know the Worker. Knowing the worker means to track in real time the evolving profile of the worker, through his characterization in the following four dimensions: (1) Anthropometry, a detailed picture of the worker with the most significant dimensions of the human body, (2) Functional Capacities intended as the sensorial, physical and cognitive capacities considering also age and gender related issues, (3) Knowledge resident in each worker which could be of any benefit for the factory or colleagues, (4) Personal needs of the worker, paying particular attention to aspects more related to the personal and private life of the worker such as territorial origin, nationality, family composition, physical activity, mobility, religion, leisure, etc. [4].

The collection of all these elements will be combined in order to create a worker profile, which is complete and changing over time.

Know the Factory. Unlike the traditional characterization of a factory which is based on production capacity, productivity, lead times and other economic and financial driven KPIs, the proposed concept aims at characterizing the factory from a worker point of view. This is done to identify and track potential interac- tions between workers and the elements of the working environment interacting with them. The main factory elements represented will include production KPIs, jobs/task with required skills, working shifts, organizational structure, processes, workplaces shapes and placing, intra-worker interactions and corporate services. These elements will form the basis to create a formalized representation of the factory also complemented with all the key risk factors, essential to assess the adequacy of workers' evolving conditions to the assigned jobs.

The combination of these elements will allow to create a reliable, evolving worker-centric view of the factory.

Know the Context. The environmental and social context in which factories are placed will be analyzed through stakeholder-specific relationship manage- ment approaches, deployed on the three dimensions of sustainability (economic, social and environmental). This will allow to create a comprehensive awareness and understanding of the territory and trends in which the factory is located, pro- viding valuable inputs to a dynamic decision making process, promoting context-aware strategies and objectives.

3.2 Design and Deploy the Workplace

Data and information gathered thanks to the KNOW cornerstone represent a comprehensive, consistent and evolving knowledge base enabling the design of worker-centric, factory-conscious and context-aware workplaces. This will result into designs of effective workplaces based on: (1) worker characteristics, (2) factory requirements and (3) context/environment needs and constraints. Concrete outputs will be thus the designs of anthropocentric model workplaces addressing the needs of the specific target group "plant and machine operator" working in manufacturing production environments.

3.3 Plan the Production and Organize the Work

The KNOW knowledge base and the worker-centric workplaces designs deriv- ing from the previous two cornerstones are taken as structured inputs for the worker- and context- aware organization and planning of production-related jobs, tasks and human resources. Methodologies and tools of this third cornerstone are enabling the valuable and dynamic integration of workers, workplaces and production requirements taking into account constraints and opportunities de- riving from the factory and the contexts. The solutions and approaches allow the identification and characterization of the better performing allocation of re- sources to changing and evolving jobs and tasks, also including comprehensive plans for human resources management and effective training of the workforce.

3.4 Produce with Context-Aware Factories Integrated in Their Social Environment

The last cornerstone is meant to favour and ease the integration of the work- ers into the social and environmental context where the factory is placed. The collected personal needs of the workers, and constraints/requirements and op- portunities of the social context where the factory is placed, are both matter of this cornerstone in order to (1) minimize the environmental impact of the fac- tory activities (identifying sustainability-enhancing strategies), (2) transforming the factory from a society-affecting entity into an integration-promotion body proactively favouring workers valuable inclusion into the social environment.

4   Conclusion

The paper presented a novel concept that places the worker at the centre of the factory by defining the next generation of socially sustainable workplaces. An analysis of the key elements for achieving these workplaces has been carried out identifying the main areas of development and the related gaps and needed improvements.

The four cornerstones at the basis of the proposed concept, also currently investigated within the European FP7 project Man-Made, have been then presented. Starting from the formalization of the knowledge concerning the worker, the factory seen from a worker's perspective and the context where the factory operates, methods and tools for anthropocentric design of the workplace and of the factory operation management at large have been identified. Finally, means for a valuable integration of the factory in the social environment through the provision of personalized services aimed at improving the balance between working and non-working life are discussed.

The piece of research described in this paper represents the starting building block for the development of specific methodologies and tools aimed at supporting the implementation of the discussed vision in real production environments. This will promote a leap towards the next level of human-factory-context balance for the factory of the future.

Acknowledgement. This work has been partly funded by the European Commission through Man- Made (MANufacturing through ergonoMic and safe Anthropocentric aDaptive workplacEs for context aware factories in EUROPE) project (Grant Agreement No: FoF.NMP.2013-3 6090730). The authors wish to acknowledge the Commis- sion for its support. The authors also wish to acknowledge their gratitude and appreciation to all the Man-Made partners for their contribution during the development of various ideas and concepts presented in this work.

References

1. Bhattacharya, M., Gibson, D.E., Doty, D.H.: The effects of flexibility in employee skills, employee behaviors, and human resource practices on firm performance. Journal of Management 31(4), 622–640 (2005)
2. Burchell, M., Robin, J.: The Great Workplace: How to Build It, How to Keep It, and Why It Matters. Wiley (2010)
3. Cardy, R.L., Miller, J.S., Ellis, A.D.: Employee equity: Toward a person-based approach to hrm. Human Resource Management Review 17(2), 140–151 (2007)
4. Corti, D.: Human resource management. In: Errasti, A. (ed.) Global Production Networks: Operations Design and Management. Taylor & Francis (2013)
5. Eby, R., Mahone, D.: How to use ergonomics as a loss control tool. Risk Management 38(3), 42–47 (1991)

6. European Commission: Europe 2020: a strategy for smart, sustainable and inclusive growth. Brussels: European Commission (2010)
7. Evans, J., Lindsay, W.: The Management and Control of Quality. Thomson/South-Western (2005)
8. Fernberg, P.: Tayloringthe workstation to the worker. Modern Office Technology 37(6), 26–30 (1992)
9. Frenkel, A., Bendit, E., Kaplan, S.: The linkage between the life style of knowledge-workers and their intra-metropolitan residential choice: A clustering approach based on self-organizing maps. Computers, Environment and Urban Systems 39, 151–161 (2013)
10. Griffin, G.: Understanding ergonomics. Rural Relecomunciations 11(5), 58–61 (1992)
11. Hoffer, W.: Errors on the job can be reduced. Nation's Business 76(4), 62 (1988)
12. Knill, B.: Human factors engineering: An on going quest at AT&T. Material Handling Engineering 44(2), 37–38 (1989)
13. Lee, L.T.S., Sukoco, B.M.: The effects of entrepreneurial orientation and knowledge management capability on organizational effectiveness in taiwan: The moderating role of social capital. International Journal of Management 24(3) (2007)
14. Liker, J., Meier, D.: Toyota Talent: Developing Your People the Toyota Way. Mc-Graw Hill Professional, McGraw-Hill Education (2007)
15. Lindo, D.: It's time to emphasize ergonomics. Supervision 52(5), 14–16 (1991)
16. Nayar, V.: Employees First, Customers Second: Turning Conventional Management Upside Down. Harvard Business Review Press (2013)
17. Parent-Thirion, A., Vermeylen, G., VanHouten, G., Lyly-Yrjanainen, M., Biletta, I., Cabrita, J., Niedhammer, I.: Fifth European working conditions survey. Eurofound, Publications Office of the European Union, Luxembourg (2012)
18. Pfeffer, J.: Producing sustainable competitive advantage through the effective management of people. The Academy of Management Executive 9(1), 55–69 (1995)
19. Rickert, K.: Ergonomics in the office. Risk Management-NewYork 39, 18 (1992)
20. Rowan, M.P., Wright, P.C.: Ergonomics is good for business. Work Study 43(8), 7–12 (1994)
21. Royer, S., Waterhouse, J.M., Brown, K.A., Festing, M.: Employee voice and strategic competitive advantage in international modern public corporations: an economic perspective. European Management Journal 26(4), 234–246 (2008)
22. Sinha, N., Kakkar, N.K., Gupta, V.: Uncovering the secrets of the twenty-first- century organization. Global Business and Organizational Excellence 31(2), 49–56 (2012), http://dx.doi.org/10.1002/joe.21414
23. Small, C.T., Sage, A.P.: Knowledge management and knowledge sharing: A review. Information, Knowledge, Systems Management 5(3), 153–169 (2006)
24. Smith, E.A.: The role of tacit and explicit knowledge in the workplace. Journal of Knowledge Management 5(4), 311–321 (2001)
25. Taylor, F.W.: The principles of scientific management. Harper (1914)
26. Ulrich, D., Ulrich, W., Goldsmith, M.: The Why of Work: How Great Leaders Build Abundant Organizations That Win. McGraw-Hill Education (2010)
27. Waitley, D.: Empires of the Mind: Lessons to Lead and Succeed in a Knowledge-Based World. Positive paper backs. Nicholas Brealey Publishing Limited (1996)
28. Walker, J.: Ethics and the Employee-Centric Firm. Itasca Books (2011)

A Proposal of Consumer Driven Framework for Enabling Sustainable Production and Consumption

Jing Shao[1,2], Marco Taisch[1], and Miguel Ortega Mier[2]

[1] Politecnico di Milano, Milan, Italy
{jing.shao,marco.taisch}@polimi.it
[2] Universidad Politécnica de Madrid, Madrid, Spain
miguel.ortega.mier@upm.es

Abstract. Sustainability becomes the key towards success of manufacturing industries now. Besides increasing efficiency of sustainable industrial processes, sustainable consumption becomes an important complementary strategy for making economies more sustainable gradually. Hence, the research in sustainable production and consumption (SPaC) keeps emerging and the approach of information transition became noticed as the key to promote SPaC. Therefore, there is a notable need for generating proper approach in order to achieve the goal of providing sustainable information of a product for consumers has been discussed.

This paper is looking forward to support the implementation of SPaC by developing a framework aimed at providing sustainable information of a product for consumers. Aspects and attributes have been elicited, and a novel metrics of attributes integrate with life cycle has been developed. Furthermore, a conceptualized framework aimed at evaluating social and environmental performances of a product in its production phase has been developed.

Keywords: Facilitator, SPaC, indicator, framework, consumer driven.

1 Introduction

Consumers are key to drive sustainable production and they play a central role in sustainable development [1]. Presently, consumers, even green consumers could not get sufficient information that enable them making greener buying decisions. Facilitator which indicates "Laws, policies and administrative procedures" has been defined in AFI framework, and it used to enable information transition from sustainable production to sustainable consumption[2]. Facilitator is the key element in the whole system and could properly reflect consumers and other stakeholders' attitudes, and it is assured to be function well with the help of infrastructures. From literatures, many kinds of approaches have potential to play the role of facilitator and provide sustainability information for consumers. However, from a systematic review on available approaches, it is showed that in both industrial engineering and marketing science, available approaches or instruments could hardly be directly applied for consumers

B. Grabot et al. (Eds.): APMS 2014, Part II, IFIP AICT 439, pp. 406–414, 2014.
© IFIP International Federation for Information Processing 2014

[3,4]. There is a notable need for generating proper approach or strengthening available approaches in order to get the goal of providing sustainable information of a product for consumers[5].

One of the most possible ways of generating facilitator to achieve the goal is to measure sustainability of a product. The instrument could be generated by applying industrial engineering approach and face to stakeholders through appropriate presenting method. Indeed, in last several decades, indices are commonly used approaches for attracting attention and often simplify the problem in order to make the impact of energy consumption and environmental impacts visible in industrial engineering [6]. And they are beneficial for policy making and public communication in sending information of countries' performances about environment, energy, society and economy [7] . Although it is challenging for researchers to cover all topics at the same time, it is still possible to launch by squeezing objective scope to consumers who direct relevant to buying decisions.

This paper will propose a consumer driven framework for enabling sustainable production and consumption by providing sustainability performance information of a product for consumers. This framework is designed to select possible attributes which used to evaluate social and environment performance, from which companies can choose to assess sustainability for their products associated with manufacturing. We used methodology of seven steps of "Sustainability evaluation process" [8] to assess sustainability and employed "Stepwise approach to development of environmental indicators" [9] to select proper indicators. After reviewing on attributes in available sustainability assessments, and considering the objective of this research, a conceptualized framework of facilitator focusing on social and environmental impact in the production phase has been generated.

2   Methodology

2.1   Steps of Sustainability Assessment

Indices for assessing sustainability adopt different constructing steps [8][10][11] . In this research, the methodology adopted is the seven-step "Sustainability evaluation process" [8] (Shown in Table 1). The choice was made based on its property of general applicability of generating single indicator in sustainability assessment.

Table 1. 7 Steps of Sustainability evaluation process (Source: [8])

Step 1. Set sustainability objective	Step 2. Select indicators
Step3. Specify measurement procedures	Step4. Analyze data
Step 5.Report	Step 6. Make managerial decision
Step 7. Evaluate impact	

From previous study[4], the sustainability objective has been fully discussed and well defined as: provide sustainability performance information of a product for consumers in order to make collaborative buying behavior become an incentive for greener manufacturing possible. In Step 2, even though set of indicators are chosen and decided by experts, it is a subjective process since selection of the right set of indicators depends on many factors, such as the type of product, type of processes, final reporting format, budget, approvals required, market, and time availability. Therefore, in this paper, we focused on step 2 "selecting indicators" and the methodology of choosing appropriate indicators will be discussed in the following section.

2.2   Top-Down Approach for Selecting Indicators

A stepwise protocol to develop appropriate sustainable indicators was proposed by Olsthoorn, X., as shown in figure 1 [9]. It is a general protocol for generating environmental indicator that starts from available data collection and then proceeding with normalization, aggregation, together with standardization. An indicator will be presented for its data users at the end.

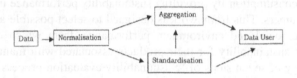

Fig. 1. Stepwise approach to development of environmental indicators (Source: [9])

Compared to above commonly applied stepwise protocol for developing general sustainable indicator, this study focused on providing meaningful, accurate, relevant and cost-effective information for consumers. Therefore, a high emphasis has been put on research on the information needed of consumers.

The selection of key attributes is a crucial task in this study. The very first time the four basic rights which includes safety, information, choice and legal representation of consumer were declared by US President John Kennedy in 1962. Later, the rights to the satisfaction of basic needs, redress, consumer education and a healthy environment were added and adopted by The United Nations in 1985 [12]. Harrison et al. (2005) have proposed some external factors that influence the growth of ethical consumer consumption- a variant of sustainable consumption [13]. And "social and environmental effects of technological advance" was the first dimension of all the perspectives. Therefore, in order to promote sustainable consumption, only sustainability assessment information should be included in this framework, and furthermore, only the information on social and environmental impact of a product should be included.

3   Development of Life Cycle Integrated Metrics

In the field of sustainability assessment, numerous indicators were developed by researchers and practitioners. Past research on reviews of sustainability indicators from the perspective of industrial engineering are common to see [10][14][15]. Various weighting methods of composite indexes have been summarized in [16]. A full list of sub-categories of sustainable performance assessment of a country and involved indicators, plus their related information such as definitions, calculation methods and references were reviewed in the literature [17]. Literatures on achievements and challenges regarding measuring sustainable development were proposed by Organization for Economic Cooperation and Development [18] .

3.1 Dimension and Aspects Comparison of Indices

From systematic review of available indicators, six publicly available indicators which associate with social and environmental performance assessment have been selected to have a detail study and analysis on [4]. Table 2 shows the list of dimensions of the index. Two main streams of indicator generation could be found in the list of dimensions of indices. One stream is generated in line with the three pillars of sustainability [19]. Impact of social, environmental, and economic performances have been assessed by sub-indicators. Some of them added extra dimensions, such as "well-being" (e.g., CS), or "technical aspects" (e.g., CSPI), or "cost house" (e.g., LInX), to have a complementary list of assessment measures (Reference see Appendix).

Table 2. Comparison of dimensions of index

	CS	CSPI	F-PSI	EPI	G score	E99
Environmental Health	x	x	x	x		
Societal	x	x	x			
Economics	x	x	x			
Organizational Governance		x				
Well-being	x					
Technique		x				
Production Phase			x		x	x
Use Phase			x		x	x
End of life			x		x	x

Another stream of indicators considered life cycle assessment as an important approach when measuring the sustainability of product, so production, using and disposal phases of a product have been regarded as dimensions in this indicator, e.g., E99. In addition, G Score focuses on the production phase of a product, combine with environmental impact. F-PSI has considered both two streams of generation approach and combine sustainability dimensions with life cycle dimensions. This study adapts with definitions of themes and sub-themes in the literature [17].

3.2 Life Cycle Integrated Metrics

In order to carry out the novel metrics integrated life cycle process, a hierarchical diagram is defined using a top-down approach. It includes Dimensions, Aspects and Attributes.

Aspects and attributes are clusted in line with five phases of life cycle of a product. Besides Production, Using and Disposal phases, Transportations between manufacturing and using, and between using and disposal phase should be included. It is suggested that, as a comprehensive framwork for faciliating sustainable consumption, above aspects and attributes should be considered. In the table 3, aspect of Nature has been listed as a feature which should be assessed through entire life cycle. It is because long term consideration is required in these attributes. In currtent state of research, focus of Consumer Driven Framework was consentrated on aspects and attributes in Production phase and attibutes impact caused in manufacturing phase (as shown in grey area).

Table 3. Metrics of attributes in Consumer Driven Framework with life cycle

	Social Impact	Environmental Impact	
Production	**Human :** Employee Training Employee participation (human right) Child labor Working safety	**Material:** Reuse/recycling of resource (energy, material, product) Raw Material Extraction Specific Raw material consumption	
	Company image: Law suit Local community	**Energy Using:** Energy Efficiency Renewable Energy Specific energy consumption	**Nature:** Life cycle Air Quality Water Consumption
Transportation			
Using	Customer health & safety	Fuel Production and Consumption Maintenance Material Production Noise-in-use	Regional Ozone Urban Particulates Biodiversity and Habitat Average noise level in the periphery of plant dB(A)
Transportation			
Disposal		Waste Management Energy Process Supplementary Materials Residual value Shredding Dismantling	

4   Development of Consumer Driven Framework

4.1   Goal of Consumer Driven Framework

This framework is designed to integrate all the possible attributes which used to evaluate social and environment performance, from which companies can choose to assess the sustainability for their products associated with manufacturing. Further developed instrument could function well in the mechanism of sustainable consumption as a facilitator. It well connects stakeholders and infrastructure and promotes entire system moving forward.

4.2   Criteria of Developing Consumer Driven Framework

The development of consumer driven framework is decided by following five criteria that suggested for developing a tool for promoting sustainable consumption [5]. First of all, the framework should be capable for meeting consumers' preferences regarding its focusing scope. From the perspective of consumers, the product is the interface they are facing and should make buying decision upon. So it will be much clear if the information is measured and provided based on unit of a product. Beyond considering the content and assessment unit, requirements from consumers are more critical on their presenting format of information. The goal of making information transparency could not be achieved without appropriate format. Therefore, the last three criteria are concerning information transparency ability of the approach. Unless the framework is designed and implemented from consumers' origination, it could hardly be properly applied for consumers. Besides, weather the information is recognizable and weather it has appropriate presenting format are key features. Furthermore, consumers need comparable information regarding their green preferences in order to make greener buying decision.

Therefore, the criteria of consumer driven framework consist of:

(a) Focus on consumers' preferences;
(b) Product based assessment;
(c) Consumers originated;
(d) Degree of recognition by consumers;
(e) Degree of comparability among same type of products.

Additionally, it considered applicability of attributes in the process of developing Consumer Driven Framework.

4.3   Structure of Consumer Driven Framework

The selection of the dimensions of interest to be included in the final model has been based on the literature analysis that led into a preliminary list of associated attributes.

This preliminary consumer driven framework has two dimensions which indicate environmental impact and social impact. Aspects of Nature, Energy Using and Material Using are included in the dimension of environmental impact. Dimension of social impact has aspects of Human and Company Image. Detail attributes are listed in table 4.

Table 4. The proposed list of key aspects and attributes of Consumer Driven Framework

Dimension	Aspect	Attribute	
Environmental Impact	Material Using	Reuse/recycling of resource (energy, material, product)	
		Raw Material Extraction	
		Specific Raw material consumption	
	Energy Using	Energy Efficiency	
		Renewable Energy	
		Specific energy consumption	
	Nature	Air	Life cycle global warming
			Greenhouse gas emissions
			Indoor Air pollution
			Regional Ozone
			Nitrogen Loading
			Life cycle Air Quality
		Reducing water stress	Water quality/Drinking Water
			Water Consumption
		Noise level	Average noise level in plant
		Biodiversity	Wilderness Protection (Eco region Protection)
			Timber Harvest Rate
			Agricultural Subsidies
			Overfishing
			Land
Social Impact	Human	Employee	Training
			participation (human right)
			Child labor
			Working safety
		Customer	Satisfaction
			Safety & health
	Company Image	Law suit	
		Local community	

5   Conclusion

This research proposed a framework that aimed at evaluating social and environmental performances of a product in its production phase to help consumers to access the sustainability performance information of a product, and then enhance greener buying decision. The research piece presented in this paper is going to be developed further by introducing detailed formulas for indicators and validating through case studies. Therefore, the proposed framework contributes to the literature in the field development of facilitator in SPaC. The final proposal is a supporting tool for practitioners who can choose to assess sustainability for their products associated with manufacturing based on this framework. A fine-tuned version is thus expected to be released in the near future.

Acknowledgement. This research is partly conducted within the framework of the European Doctorate in Industrial Management (EDIM) which is funded by The Education, Audiovisual and Culture Executive Agency (EACEA) of European

Commission under Erasmus Mundus Action 1 programmes. Furthermore, this research is partly funded by the European Commission through the PREMANUS Project (FoF-ICT-2011.7.3: Virtual Factories and Enterprises, www.premanus.eu).

References

1. OECD, Promoting Sustainable Consumption-Good Practices in OECD Countries (2008)
2. Akenji, L.: Consumer scapegoatism and limits to green consumerism. J. Clean Prod. 63, 13–23 (2014), doi:10.1016/j.jclepro.2013.05.022
3. Taisch, M., Shao, J.: Critical Mapping of Sustainable Index Methodologies. In: IEEE Int. Conf. Ind. Eng. Eng. Manag. (2013)
4. Shao, J., Taisch, M., Ortega Mier, M.: Sustainability Assessment Instruments for Consumers. In: 20th ICE Conf. - IEEE TMC Eur. Conf. (2014)
5. Shao, J., Taisch, M., Ortega, M.: A Systematic Review on Information Transition Approaches of Sustainable Production and Consumption (SPaC) (submitted, 2014)
6. Bell, S., Morse, S.: Sustainability Indicators-Measuring the immeasurable?, 2nd edn. Earthscan, London (2008)
7. Amacher, G.S., Koskela, E., Ollikainen, M.: Environmental quality competition and eco-labeling. J. Environ. Econ. Manage. 47, 284–306 (2004), doi:10.1016/S0095-0696(03)00078-0
8. Joung, C.B., Carrell, J., Sarkar, P., Feng, S.C.: Categorization of indicators for sustainable manufacturing. Ecol. Indic. 24, 148–157 (2012), doi:10.1016/j.ecolind.2012.05.030
9. Olsthoorn, X., Tyteca, D., Wehrmeyer, W., Wagner, M.: Environmental indicators for business: a review of the literature and standardisation methods. J. Clean Prod. 9, 453–463 (2001), doi:10.1016/S0959-6526(01)00005-1
10. Singh, R.K., Murty, H.R., Gupta, S.K., Dikshit, A.K.: An overview of sustainability assessment methodologies. Ecol. Indic. 9, 189–212 (2009), doi:10.1016/j.ecolind.2008.05.011
11. Lehni, M.: Ecoefficiencia World Business Council for Sustainable Development Presentation at WBCSD: Progress toward Sustainability (1999)
12. Ha, H., Coghill, K., Maharaj, E.A.: Current Measures to Protect E-Consumers' Privacy in Australia (2009), doi:10.4018/978-1-60566-012-7.ch006
13. Harrison, R., Newholm, T., Shaw, D.: The Ethical Consumer. SAGE Publication (2005)
14. Arena, M., Ciceri, N.D., Terzi, S., et al.: A state-of-the-art of industrial sustainability: definitions, tools and metrics. Int. J. Prod. Lifecycle Manag. 4 (2009)
15. Dahl, A.L.: Achievements and gaps in indicators for sustainability. Ecol. Indic. 17, 14–19 (2012), doi:10.1016/j.ecolind.2011.04.032
16. Freudenberg, M.: Composite Indicators of Country Performance: A Critical Assessment. OECD Sci. (2003)
17. CSD, Indicators of Sustainable Development: Guidelines and Methodologies (2001)
18. OECD, Policy Brief: Sustainable Manufacturing and Eco-innovation: Towards a Green Economy (2009)
19. Brundtland, H.: Our common future (1987)

Appendix: List of Indicators and References

Compass of Sustainability	CS	Atkisson, B. A., & Hatcher, R. L. "The compass index of sustainability: A five-year review", write for conference "Visualising and Presenting Indicator Systems", Switzerland, 2005.
Composite Sustainability Performance Index	CSPI	Singh, R.K., Murty, H.R., Gupta, S.K., Dikshit, A.K., "Development of composite sustainability performance Index for steel industry", in Ecological Indicators, 7, 565–588, 2007.
Eco-Indicator 99	E99	Pré Consultants, "The Eco-indicator 99 – a damage oriented method for life cycle impact assessment", in Methodology Report. Available at: http://www.pre.nl/, 2001.
Environment Performance Index	EPI	http://epi.yale.edu/
Ford of Europe's Product Sustainability Index	F-PSI	Fleming, J., Ford of Europe's Product Sustainability Index Cost, 2007.
G Score	G	Jung, E., Kim, J., & Rhee, S., "The measurement of corporate environmental performance and its application to the analysis of efficiency in oil industry", in Journal of Cleaner Production, 9(6), 551–563, 2001.

Environmental Impact and Cost Evaluation in Remanufacturing Business Decision Support

Rossella Luglietti[1], Federico Magalini[1], Marco Taisch[1], and Jacopo Cassina[2]

[1] Politecnico di Milano via Lambruschini 4b, 20156 Milano, Italy
{rossella.luglietti,federico.magalini,marco.taisch}@polimi.it
[2] Holonix Corso Italia 8, 20821 Meda, Italy
jacopo.cassina@holonix.it

Abstract. The research implements a business decision support system to evaluate environmental and economic implications for different end of life alternatives strategies. The case study described in the paper is the evaluation of end of life automotive engine. In detail, the analysis consists of the evaluation of environmental impacts and economic costs of engine remanufacturing process. In particular, will be compared three different alternatives: remanufacturing, reuse and recycling (material recovery). Thanks to remanufacturing, it is possible anyway to increase end-of-life benefits, compared with recycling, avoiding, from a life cycle perspective, the manufacturing process of new products through refurbishing or reuse, preventing at the same time certain generation of waste. Results will be shown in a bi-dimensional graph displaying the three alternatives with their economic revenue and environmental gain.

Keywords: LCA, Remanufacturing, End of Life, Recycling, ICT.

1 Introduction

Waste is a key environmental and economic issue and a growing problem. The amount of waste generated in Europe continues to rise each year; approximately 3 billion tons of waste are thrown away in the European Union annually. This amounts to about 6 tons of solid waste for every European [1].

On this scenario, waste management is going more and more an important part of European business. Good practices will increase the benefits from waste collection. In fact, the improvement of separated collection will increment the secondary raw materials sold, and the benefit in terms of profits and environmental gain.

The connection between economic growth and environmental impacts associated with waste generation is a key objective of the EU's revised Waste Framework Directive (Directive2008/98/EC). The policy of European Commission is to reverse the waste growth. The European legislation introduced the waste hierarchy within the EU's Sixth Environmental Action Programme [2], developing the waste overturned pyramid, which identifies waste management priorities. The pyramid base represents the best option, identified by prevention, and the vertex expresses the worst choice in terms of environmental gain [3]. The European Commission promotes waste recovery

B. Grabot et al. (Eds.): APMS 2014, Part II, IFIP AICT 439, pp. 415–422, 2014.
© IFIP International Federation for Information Processing 2014

as key strategy to reduce the quantity of waste for disposal and saving natural resources, in particular by reuse, recycling, composting and recovering energy from
waste. From the European perspective, remanufacturing includes the activities to
prepare for reuse of products.

It was recognized that the identification and selection of the best end-of-life options should regard to environmental and economic effects, taking into account scientific and technological progress and life cycle analyses to be further developed. Reuse
and material recovery should be considered preferable where and in so far as, they are
the best environmental options [4].

Remanufacturing is a standardized industrial process of bringing used products,
worn or non-functional, to "like-new" functional state with equivalent condition and
function than the new original one. Remanufactured parts have the same as the warranty required for new products equivalent. Remanufacturing is going to be a common practice, especially for complex products with high value to implement the waste
prevention. At the moment, the major sectors where remanufacturing is developed
are: automotive, ICT equipment, ink and toner, medical, precision and optical equipment, pumps and compressors and tires [5].

The research presented is being developed in the context of the PREMANUS
project, a co-funded project by the European Union under the ICT theme of the 7th
framework program for R&D. Part of the project is focusing on development of a
business decision support system to take the best selection, considering both the economic aspects and environmental implications, for different end of life alternatives of
complex products. In detail, this research is focused on remanufacturing of automotive light engine, one of the three case applications developed under the PREMANUS
project.

The eco-efficiency diagram is introduced (Fig. 1), allowing the interaction between
economic and environmental dimensions into the decision making process. On the Y-
axis of the diagram it can plot an economic indicator (in this case €) for the total costs
occurring during the remanufacturing process. The X-axis represents the environmental indicator (it has been chosen the equivalent CO_2 emission).

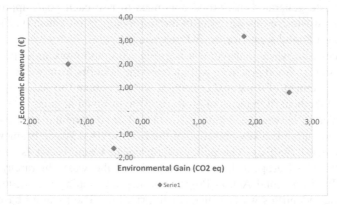

Fig. 1. Example of Eco-efficiency diagram

2   Literature Review

The aim of this research is to evaluate the environmental impacts of end of life alternatives. The innovative approach developed in many studies during the last years, is the integration of economic dimension to the environmental one. The meaning of Sustainability includes the three dimensions: environmental, social and economic. The social sustainability has been excluded because is a qualitative dimension, and it does not have a bearing into the remanufacturing scenario. Might be interested, in the future, analyzing this aspect in waste management strategy. For the environmental evaluation, the methodology utilized is the Life Cycle Assessment, in a streamlined form. Life Cycle Assessment (LCA) is a structured, comprehensive and internationally standardized method. It quantifies all relevant emissions and resources consumed and the related environmental and health impacts and resource depletion issues that are associated with the entire life cycle of any products or services [6]. It has been implemented a simplified approach to include streamlining into the whole LCA framework. The methodology is compliant with the Society of Environmental Toxicology and Chemistry (SETAC) guidelines that, on July 1999 [7], established a list of streamlined part of a full LCA. Their investigation starts identifying a level of efforts required for each study, with two different approaches. In the first case, they introduce streamlining within the existing LCA framework, and in the second alternative streamlining approaches based on life cycle concepts. The purpose of these guidelines is to:

- redefine streamlining as an inherent part of any LCA approach;

- describe various ways that streamlining LCA has been attempted and investigated and the possible implications in different decision making contexts.

A small and simple Life Cycle Inventory has been developed, embracing the potential impacts for the inputs and the processes included into the analysis; Manmek S. and Kara S. [8] have chosen a similar approach. They presented a Simplified Life Cycle Assessment (SLCA) methodology to assess the environmental impacts, which are incurred during the life cycle stages of a product. The life cycle stages included into the work are materials, production processes, usage, transportation and end of life stages. The LCI has been applied with the case study of photocopier machine, and they have verified with a full LCA.

About the costs evaluation, the literature review shows the many differences between system boundaries and user goal. Richard Wood and Edgar G. Hertwich introduce the LCC as possible indicator in economic evaluation [9]. They have related the potential contradictions in system boundary to an environmental LCA. Further, it has an inherent contradiction between user goals (minimization of cost) and social goals (maximization of value adding), and has no clear application in a consequential setting.

In the context of PREMANUS project, a literature review about product remanufacturing research has been done. It has been investigated potentials interesting studies about environmental benefits of remanufacturing, to compare the methodology used in this research and the one used by others authors. In details, some studies about environmental evaluation have been analyzed; Some authors introduced a comparison between different alternatives of dismantling (e.g. recycling, reuse) and new products.

In particular, it has been analyzed the study of Amaya J. et al. about the remanufacturing of truck injector [10]. The study shows how to established environmental assessments for remanufactured products life cycles and how to compare them to environmental assessments for new products life cycles.

This work tried to include the consideration of multiple cycles of remanufactured and reused products, to evaluate the comparison within new products. A similar approach has been used by Sutherland J. et al. that has been analyzed a comparison of manufacturing and remanufacturing energy intensities with application to diesel engine production [11]. They developed a procedure to standardize the benefits of remanufacturing. Their research determines the energy intensity and benefits of remanufacturing as compared to new manufacturing.In extensive literature research carried out on the broader remanufacturing field, only few papers have been found with a focus on LCA and remanufacturing of automotive engines comparing different end of life strategies. In none of those papers a specific link between environmental and economic implications was described. At the end, the innovation of this work is to exploit the results and the methodology in a software platform, using the life cycle data specific for a physical product. In this way, the results might be more accurate.

3   Research Application

The research defines the total benefit of end of life alternatives in term of environmental gain and economic profit. Within the PREMANUS project three industrial cases have been analyzed: the automotive engine and wind turbine gearbox remanufacturing strategy, and WEEE (Waste of Electric and Electronic Equipment) management. At this stage, the automotive engine case study has been fully implemented. As described in the Introduction the results will be expressed in a bi-dimensional graph to discover the best solution in terms of Environmental gain and economic profits.

3.1   Methodology

The methodology is different considering the environmental measurement and economic aspect.

About environmental dimension, the Life Cycle Assessment methodology has been applied in a streamlined form [7]. As mentioned in ISO 14044 the Life Cycle Assessment has been divided in 4 phases [12]:

1. Goal and Scope definition;
2. Life Cycle Inventory;
3. Life Cycle Impact Assessment;
4. Life Cycle Interpretation.

During the goal and scope definition the functional unit and system boundaries has defined. The research outlines the environmental implication about one engine sent to remanufacturing plant.

The Fig. 2 shows the system boundaries analyzed during the evaluation. The section investigated in this research is the product End of Life, and in particular, the re-manufacturing process and the material recovery. In detail, a complex product can be undergone the remanufacturing process or reused as such; in addition, the components can be sent to material recovery, in some case only one of this option is acceptable, and the practitioner can follow only one direction. Each of those alternatives makes benefits (except the dispose). The phases not included into the analysis are in grey, and the area focus on the research is in bold.

As it can see in Fig. 2 remanufacturing and reuse allow to avoid the impacts related to "beginning of life", like the extraction of raw materials and manufacturing phase. In the reduction of environmental impacts point of view, this situation is very important, because one of the most impacts is caused by the engine production and in particular by the raw materials extraction and procurement. An important difference between reused products and remanufactured ones is the life expectancy. As introduced before, the remanufacturing process bring a used or non-functional good to a "like new" functional one. In this case, a core may have a new complete residual life (around 20 years, or a certain mileage). Instead, a used engine, put back on the market, has a lower life expectancy depending on its previous life (e.g. mileage).

The material recovery allows to save raw materials, and in this way to reduce the impacts caused by extraction.

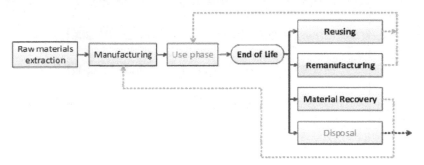

Fig. 2. Product life cycle flow

3.2 Results

Fiat operates a remanufacturing plant, which manages all types of FIAT Group engines every year. As analyzed during the case study, around 45% are light engine, the type under discussion. Some simplifications, particularly in terms of engine components, have been considered in the research. In specific, only the major following components have been considered: cylinder block, cylinder head, pistons, connecting rods (conrods), crankshaft, flywheel, camshaft, turbo.

A core, after disassembly and washing process, is inspected and each component undergo a specific treatment. In some cases it may be necessary add new components, for example if the engine is incomplete, or if some components are useless. During the process the input considered for each step are electricity, compressed air, water consumption, oil consumption.

In Fig. 3, energy consumption and other resources used for each option, expressed in percentage, and the distribution of energy consumption during each phase for the three options are displayed. In the graph on the left, some activities have the same energy consumption for the three options. At this stage of life cycle, the remanufactured engine cause higher energy consumption than the others options. In detail, only the remanufacturing process use resources in addition to electricity and water. The figure on the right shows the results in percentage to highlight the absorption of energy during the process.

Only for remanufacturing process accurate information has been used, about data to evaluate the processes avoided (e.g. manufacturing phase and raw material extraction) qualitative and statistical information have been extract from database Ecoinvent. Once listed the input interested to the remanufacturing process impact assessment can be evaluated. As explained in the previous section, the environmental performance indicator chosen for the analysis is equivalent CO_2 emission, with the carbon footprint methodology [13], with Simapro 7.3. This indicator expresses the life cycle assessment limited to emissions that have an effect on climate change [14].

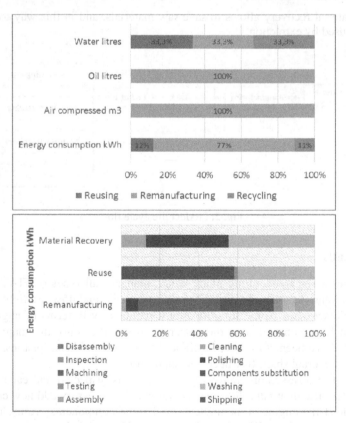

Fig. 3. Resources consumption reported in percentage for each activity and energy consumprtion for each options during the process phases

Table 1 shows the results of analysis displayed as kilograms of equivalent CO_2 emissions (Carbon footprint) and Euros (€). Results include the impacts of the entire process conducted into the remanufacturing plant. As can be seen from the results, the remanufacturing causes more impacts during the process; the main reason is the resource consumption during the process. From life-cycle perspective, anyway remanufacturing leads to more environmental benefits compared to the other end-of-life alternatives. Indeed, the recycling processes have an important impact that reduce the benefits linked to avoided impacts about raw materials extraction. The difference between reuse and remanufacturing is mainly linked to the avoided manufacturing phase of new product. For reused goods, those benefits are anyway lower than remanufactured ones. From the economic perspective, materials recovery scenario revenues generated selling raw materials have been calculated. The final value shows that remanufacturing is the best solution, and a reused engine has more benefits compared to material recovery scenario.

Table 1. Impact assessment of three end of life options expressed in kilograms of equivalent CO_2 emission

Results	Reuse	Remanufacturing	Material recovery
kg CO_2 eq. treatment process	561	10.920	502
kg CO_2 eq. for recycling process			337.154
kg CO_2 eq. avoided manufacturing [10]	28.978	72.446	
kg CO_2 eq. avoided raw materials extraction	640.719	640.719	640.410
Benefits	**-669.137**	**-702.245**	**-302.754**
Revenue selling materials			€ 108,46
Steel			€ 5,17
Cast iron			€ 34,85
Aluminum			€ 68,44
Revenue selling engine	€ 612,00	€ 2.562,00	
Operations costs	€ 43,47	€ 263,46	€ 158,20
Energy consumption	€ 3,91	€ 24,85	€ 3,50
Workforce costs	€ 39,56	€ 238,60	€ 154,71
Total revenues	**€ 568,53**	**€ 2.298,54**	**-€ 49,75**

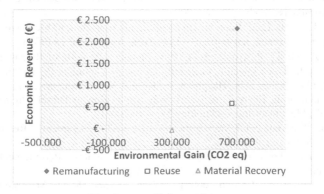

Fig. 4. Eco-efficiency diagram

As described in the previous sections results are shown in a bi-dimensional graph (Fig. 4); in this way, it is possible see the difference of each option in term of environmental impacts and costs. This visualization allows decision makers to combine the two dimensions (environmental and economic) setting their own priorities.

Results may be different for different products. Indeed, this model will be used in a business decision support system to evaluate the three options into the remanufacturing plant of FIAT Group. As described in the previous sections the algorithm works with defined input, which will change with the life cycle data of the engine. Each core and its components will follows these three paths and the results will change on the graph.

Acknowledgment. Thanks to CRF (Centro Ricerche Fiat), which has supplied the data about remanufacturing process. The research leading to these results has received funding from the European Community's Seventh Framework Programme (FP7/2007-2013) under grant agreement n° 285541.

References

1. EUROSTAT and European Environment Agency statistics (2013),
   http://epp.eurostat.ec.europa.eu/statistics_explained/
   index.php/Waste_statistics
2. Directive 2008/98/EC European Commission, of the European Parliament and of the Council, on Waste and Repealing Certain Directives (2008)
3. European Commission, "Being wise with waste: the EU's approach to waste management", Luxembourg, Publications Office of the European Commission (2010)
4. The European Parliament, the council: "Directive of the European Parliament and of the Council on Waste from Electrical and Electronic Equipment (WEEE)". Brussels (2002)
5. Walsh, B.: Remanufacturing in Europe – the Business Case, Sustainable Industry Forum, Brussels (2013)
6. European Commission, Istitute for Environment and Sustainability, "ILCD Handbook. Analysis of Exixting Environmnetal Impact Assessment Methodology for Use in Life Cycle Assessment", 1st edn. (2010)
7. Weitz, K., Sharma, A., Vigon, B., Price, E., Norris, G., Eagan, P., Owens, W., Veroutis, A.: Streamlined Life-Cycle Assessment: a Final Report from the SETAC North America, Streamlined LCA Workgroup, SETAC (1999)
8. Manmek, S., Kara, S.: Application of the Simplified Life Cycle Inventory for a Product Life Cycle. In: Proceedings of the 7th Australian Life Cycle Assessment Conference, Melbourne, Australia, November 22-24 (2009)
9. Wood, R., Hertwich, E.G.: Economic modelling and indicators in life cycle sustainability assessment. The International Journal of Life Cycle Assessment 18 (2013)
10. Amaya, J., Zwolinski, P., Brissaud, D.: Environmental Benefits of Remanufacturing: the Case Study of the Truck Injector., G-SCOP Laboratory, Grenoble, France (2010)
11. Sutherland, J.W., Adler, D.P., Haapla, K.R., Kumar, V.: A Comparison of Manufacturing and Remanufacturing Energy Intensities with Application to Diesel Engine Production. CIRP Annals, Manufacturing Technology 57, 5–8 (2008)
12. ISO 14044, "Environmental Management - Life cycle assessment - Requirements and guidelines" (2006)
13. ISO 14067, "Greenhouse gases – Carbon footprint of Products – Requirements and Guidelines for Quantification and Communication" (2013)
14. European Commission, "Carbon Footprint - What it is and How to Measure it", European Platform of Life Cycle Assessment (2007)

Sustainability Assessment and Advisory in Mould&Die: Implementation Challenges and Solutions

Marzio Sorlini[1], Alessandro Fontana[1], Marino Alge[1], Luca Diviani[1], Luca Canetta[1], and Ingo Specht[2]

[1] University of Applied Sciences and Arts of Southern Switzerland, Manno, Switzerland
{marzio.sorlini,alessandro.fontana,
marino.alge,luca.diviani,luca.canetta}@supsi.ch
[2] INTERROLL SA, S.Antonino, Switzerland
i.specht@interroll.com

Abstract. The paper describes a possible but concrete implementation pattern that is currently used to introduce and apply a sustainability-centered strategy in a mould&die company (INTERROLL SA). Focus of the analysis, implementation requirements, designed procedures and a draft software architecture are here outlined, forming the conceptual basis for a value-adding and easily adoptable approach intended to promote the implementation of a so widely-speculated strategic theory. The described path could be easily adapted to other mould&die companies and further extended to different industrial sectors.

Keywords: Sustainability assessment, mould and die, injection moulding.

1 Introduction

Most innovative manufacturing companies are today exploring **sustainability-related strategies** as a guide to re-design their business processes, either motivated by end customers' increased pressure towards environmentally- and socially- compliant products and processes [7] or, less virtuously, interested in catching the latest marketing wave. In both cases, such prospective adopters are looking for actual implementation examples and practical procedures to follow in order to become "sustainable" or "more sustainable" (than before or than the competitors). Unfortunately, a **formalized approach** supporting sustainability strategy implementation is still missing (some examples are available but focusing on mere environmental parameters or with limited applicability [8]): which are the steps a potential sustainable entrepreneur has to follow? Which are the available tools he can adopt? Which product/company lifecycle phases are more appropriate for starting such a path? A practical, experimented and industrial-oriented sustainability implementation procedure has been never described in literature (apart from [2], where authors propose an *exercise* addressing a wooden furniture): lack of descriptive capabilities or lack of actual examples?

According to literature [10, 12], one of the major problems with sustainability-centred business models relates to the simultaneous pursuit of private (companies'

B. Grabot et al. (Eds.): APMS 2014, Part II, IFIP AICT 439, pp. 423–430, 2014.

and customers') and public (society and environment) benefits. As long as public benefits don't result into countable private advantages, more sustainable production systems and products may be competitively disadvantaged. From here it comes the first pre-requisite for sustainability strategies implementation: the availability of **metrics**. Metrics enable the *measurement* of sustainability and, specifically, of private (and, incidentally, public) benefits. Measuring allows comparison, thus enables decision-making. Many international initiatives have developed indicator sets, formulae and recommendations for this purpose, even if rarely addressing specific requirements of manufacturing environments. Authors coordinated and successfully completed an FP7 research project[1] addressing this specific purpose: now a set of manufacturing-focused metrics has been consolidated and validated in real production contexts [1].

Being metrics an (almost) achieved pre-requisite, target identification is the second required step. The selection of a proper business case is fundamental to provide a value-adding, extensible and comprehensive analysis for future adopters. Manufacturing environments more likely adopting sustainability-enhancing practices are those where private and public benefits are (both) virtually significant. This happens in industries: (i) with a relevant impact on at least one of the sustainability spheres, (ii) with large room for improvements, (iii) witnessing relevant pressure from important stakeholders on sustainability-related themes, (iv) facing cost-based competition from low environmentally- and socially- sensitive countries.

Injection moulding is the most important commercial method of plastics processing. It is used to mass-produce components fast and with little or no finishing operations. Nearly all markets use injection moulded plastics (from packaging to building). The interaction with final customers is thus continuous and, sooner rather than later, there will be standards for carbon footprints or social friendliness in injection-moulded products manufacturing (point (iii)).

AMI [6] estimates that there are approximately 16,500 injection-moulding sites in West and Central Europe operating over 220,000 machines. This makes mould&die numerically relevant. The environmental profile of injection moulding has demonstrated its great impact: the overall injection moulding energy consumption in the U.S. in a yearly basis amounts to 2.06×10^8 GJ [11], similar to the energy consumption of some developed countries (see points (i) and (ii) above).

In a 2010 report entitled *The Future of the European Injection Moulding Industry*, AMI observes that the European injection moulding industry faces weakness in demand across a range of end use sectors, with customers looking to reduce the price of components, while raw material and energy costs rise. This favours producers willing and able to relocate to lower-cost manufacturing sites out of Europe. As a result, the number of moulders operating in Europe have fallen by 9% over the past six years. European injection moulders are asked to identify a radically different competitive framework, and sustainability-focussed strategies are a really attractive chance to proactively reposition their business and capitalize on the environmental gaps of their operations, also considering the available options of performances improvements

---

[1] FoF.NMP.2010-2 – Sustainable Mass Customization, Mass Customization for Sustainability.

enabled by appropriate mould design [4], careful material selection [9] or adopted manufacturing technology.

Exploiting preliminary results of the Swiss research project SAM (see § 6), promoted by SUPSI and INTERROLL SA, in this paper, authors are not meant to present and revise the state of the art of sustainability evaluation, but would like to describe their current experience in implementing sustainability assessment and advisory in a mould&die company. Preliminary decisions concerning the target of the analysis are discussed in § 2, while § 3 presents the specific requirements for sustainability adoption in the mould&die context. The designed solutions are conceptually presented in § 4, where the SAM platform architecture is formally described. Considerations on the achieved results and planned next steps are finally presented in § 5.

2   The Focus of the Sustainability Assessment

In conformity with the methodology of Life Cycle Assessment (LCA) [5], the focus of the analysis has to be identified before a sustainability assessment is performed.

In mould&die industry, both the mould and the moulded product can be considered as the subject of the sustainability assessment, depending on the focus companies are more interested in. Within this industrial sector, companies activities and products are highly diversified ranging from (i) companies that directly design and produce the moulds and (sometimes) sell the moulded product as components for other final products, to (ii) enterprises that directly produce and commercialize the moulded plastic parts as final product, so moulds are not necessarily designed and realized by the company itself. The first group of companies seems to be more focused on the mould sustainability analysis, whereas the second group is more interested in calculating the sustainability level of the moulded products. In this perspective INTERROLL could be classified into the first group, but in order to confirm the common sense suggestion, the INTERROLL mould and moulded product lifecycles have been analysed.

2.1   The INTERROLL Mould and the Moulded Product Lifecycles

Lifecycle perspective is considered a *must* in the evaluation of the environmental, economic and social performances of a product [1]. Considering the mould and moulded product lifecycle, the following steps can be described. The *Extraction* takes into account the extraction of metal ore for the mould production, while the extraction of petrol for moulded part realization. *Material processing* considers the millwork of mould metals components and the transformation of the polymer in granules for the moulded product. In *Part manufacturing* metal milling is considered in mould production, while injection moulding for moulded parts. In *Assembly* the junction of mould components (e.g. plates) are considered for the mould. Starting form *Assembly*, the lifecycle of the moulded product is intimately related to those of the final product the plastic component belongs to. In the case of INTERROLL, *Assembly* includes the insertion of the plastic parts within the conveyor roller. The *Use* phase of the mould, injection moulding, corresponds to the manufacturing of the moulded product.

Whereas, the use phase of moulded products coincide to the conveyor roller functioning. Mould *Maintenance* includes the substitution of some mould parts. In the case of the moulded part, *Maintenance* has to be evaluated within the conveyor roller repairing. The *End of life* of the mould is well known by INTERROLL, while it has many uncertainties for the moulded product since the conveyor roller could face different end of life scenarios in different countries. Eventually, the *Transportation* phase concerns the transportation of the mould components and the distribution of the moulded products. The description of the mould and the moulded product lifecycles of INTERROLL ease the definition of the focus of the sustainability assessment.

2.2   Analysis Focus

The lifecycles description allows to identify all the lifecycle activities directly managed by INTERROLL and that are affected by the decision taken by the company.

Focusing on the mould, all the processes performed during lifecycle are either carried out or influenced by INTERROLL and decisions performed in mould design directly affect the sustainability performances of the mould. Extraction and material processing are influenced by mould design since the materials constituting the mould are here selected. Manufacturing and assembly processes are the results of design decisions. The use of the mould is the injection process, so it is the meeting point between the mould and the moulded product. In this phase, some elements as the energy consumed or the plastic wasted are actually affected by mould design; others are related to moulded product design as the quantity of the material injected. Eventually, also maintenance, End of Life and transportations are directly influenced by decisions performed during the supply chain configuration.

Analysing the moulded product lifecycle, it is possible to note that INTERROLL design decisions address the extraction, the material processing, the manufacturing phase and the upstream transportation. On the contrary, the company has a scarce control on the assembly, use, maintenance, end of life and downstream transportation phases since the moulded product is a part of a more complex product, i.e. the roller conveyor. In this perspective, choosing the mould as the focus of the sustainability analysis, INTERROLL is able to directly influence the environmental, economic and social impacts of the mould. Moreover, this approach allows to model and include into the analysis the impacts of the moulded product.

3   The Mould&Die Requirements in Sustainability Assessment

As mentioned in § 1, marketing and labelling is neither the only, nor the main goal of SAM, since the conceptualized tool/procedure is meant to promote awareness creation of both designers and managers, and guide them towards a more sustainable way to handle their products. In this chapter, requirements gathered and worked out in the preliminary steps of the project are presented and discussed.

What's the object to assess?
As discussed in § 2, the mould is the focus of the sustainability assessment, both targeting already existing and new moulds that have to be designed.

Which are the assessment dimensions?
The sustainability assessment has to be performed through the calculation of appropriate indicators. The process of identifying and selecting these indicators constitute a background for this work [1]. The use of numbers enables assessors to objectively evaluate the sustainability level of mould allowing to determine a benchmark and compare alternatives. Moreover, the chosen assessing dimensions have to be holistic from three complementary points of view, considering: (i) all the three sustainability areas (environment, economy and society); (ii) the product, the process and the supply chain; (iii) the lifecycle approach. This entails the need to get information of phases carried out by other actors and integrating them into a unique system.

Which are the needed data?
Data required for sustainability assessment can be grouped into three sets: (i) product-specific data, that need to be filled from time to time by the designer or the technician. These are morphological, technical and operational data strictly related to the given product and production process; (ii) company-specific data, related to the company and to its supply chain, and that can be updated on a longer time basis (e.g. when a new supplier joins the supply chain); (iii) general-knowledge data, usually coming from third-party databases (e.g.: Ecoinvent – www.ecoinvent.ch).

Who's the assessor? When are they performing the assessment?
Assessors are all the decision makers having some sort of power over the sustainability performances of the assessed object. Here two are the most relevant *users*: technical profiles (i.e.: mould designers) and managerial profiles. The first group is usually well alphabetized on the use of design software, but has no expertise on sustainability issues. Managerial profiles are usually not keen to handle shop-floor data and complex design software: they need a high-level management platform enabling comparison and storage of data intended for tactical to strategic decision support.

Two requirements are connected with the "timing". According to [3], assessors are expected to act both ex-ante, during the design phase and ex-post, for *pure* assessment purposes. The analysed object is respectively the design of future moulds or existing moulds. The sustainability level of new moulds has to be measured in real time during the design phase in order to drive designers' choices. The sustainability level of already used moulds have to be measured for benchmarking and product labelling.

What's the envisaged response?
In general it is not possible to define "the sustainable product", but a "more sustainable product" compared to a benchmark. The array of indicators values concerning different mould configurations calculated by the platform is a valuable information for designers that are thus aware of the design decision effects on sustainability impact, and are driven in identifying an improvement path. The platform has to enable decision makers to identify a benchmark or select product concepts already assessed. In this perspective, this diagnostic feature would enable an iterative design path aim-

ing to enhance the mould sustainability performances while designing. Finally, the analysis of sustainability impacts has to be carried out at <u>different levels of detail</u>. The final values of indicators provide an aggregate picture of how well the designed mould performs. This could be analysed through the above-mentioned comparison between two or more product configurations or "zooming" on a single indicator value or to given steps of the lifecycle or of the solution space.

4   The Solution Concept

In order to properly satisfy the requirements for the sustainability assessment of a mould, and considering the focus of the evaluation, a possible solution to implement the analysis of the environmental, economic and social performances is here drafted.

This solution is thought to be implemented via a software tool since a huge amount of data has to be gathered and managed and many calculations are required. In this perspective the design of the solution is presented through the Component diagram depicted in Fig. 1 obtained using the UML 2.0 notation. Two main macro-blocks could be identified, such as the front-end block and the back-end block.

The front-end block handles the interaction with the user and it is practically constituted by the Company Editor, the Mould Editor and the Diagnosis tool. The Company Editor encapsulates all GUI and logics that interact with the company-level data representation. Therefore, it's used to edit the information characterizing the company and its suppliers (e.g. the number of injuries, the sales turnover...), information that are needed for the sustainability assessment but that have not to be edited or added for each new SAM project. The *Mould Editor* contains GUI and logics used for the description of the mould in analysis. The *Mould Editor* component is indeed supported by the Diagrams Module that provides tree diagrams edit functionalities used for bill of material representation. It provides a specific live data model representing tree diagrams and their editing modelling, and undo/redo functionalities implemented as memento pattern. It also delivers graphical representation of the editing process. Answering to the management requirements, the *Diagnosis Tool* encloses GUI and mechanics used for browsing, analyse and compare sustainability assessment of various moulds and mould families.

The back-end block is meant to expose a series of services that are crucial for the calculation of the indicators values such as the *Core*, the *Engine Block* and the *Importer*. The *Core* module is thought to be the repository of the main live data model of the SAM platform and is responsible for its management, ensuring the continuous consistency of data. It also provides listening capabilities for other modules, enabling them to have a targeted reaction to every update of the model state. Moreover the core module provides generic GUI functionality to directly interact with the underlying data representation. The *Engine Block* is indeed constituted by the *Assessment Service*, the *Simulation Service* and the *Maintenance Classifier*. The *Assessment Service* module enables the sustainability assessment impacts computation. It will rely on specific live data model and a computational engine that is meant to calculate a defined set of sustainability indicators. The *Simulation Service* and the *Maintenance*

Classifier modules have an important role for the indicators calculation performed during the design phase of the mould since they are meant to provide designer with forecasted data concerning the use and the maintenance phases.

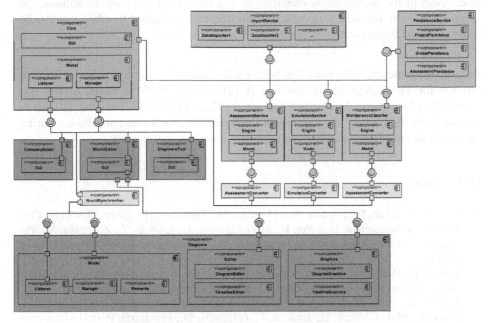

Fig. 1. Component diagram of the solution concept

The *Simulation Service* provides simulation capabilities in order to predict energy consumption and other critical parameters for the detailed characterization of the injection moulding process. The *Maintenance Classifier* provides expert system functionalities to predict the required maintenance effort for different moulds. The *Importer* module contains data import functionalities that are registered in the application in order to allow the user to import various types of external data to facilitate the data entry process. This component thus represents the connection with the IT system already existing in INTERROLL (e.g. CAD, ERP…). The sustainability assessment in fact requires a certain variety of data concerning the product, the manufacturing system and the supply chain [3] thus many data sources are needed.

5   Conclusions

Preliminary results achieved in implementing sustainability assessment and advisory in a mould&die company are here presented with the goal to provide prospective sustainability-conscious entrepreneurs with a practical path to follow when moving their business towards a more sustainable profile. Achieved results contemplate the focus of the sustainability analysis definition, requirements gathering and identification of a possible solution that could be easily translated into software platform conceptual architecture. Further steps are mandatory (and planned) addressing the final development and validation of the software platform, data collection and sustainability benefits measurement of the project, for both private and public audience. Since most of the requirements identified in § 3 have a general-purpose attitude, the approach and the solution here outlined could be easily adapted to other mould&die companies and further extended to different industrial sectors.

Acknowledgements. This work has been partly funded by the Swiss Federal Commission for Technology and Innovation (CTI), through SAM – Sustainability Assessment in Mould and die (project number: 13522.1 PFES-ES). The authors wish to acknowledge the CTI for its support and INTERROLL SA for its contribution during the development of various ideas and concepts presented in this work.

References

1. Bettoni, A., Corti, D., Fontana, A., Zebardast, M., Pedrazzoli, P.: Sustainable Mass Customization Assessment. In: Poler, R., Maia Carniero, L., Jasinski, T., Zolghadri, M., Pedrazzoli, P. (eds.) Intelligent Non-hierarchical Manufacturing Networks. Wiley, Hoboken (2012)
2. Boër, C.R., Pedrazzoli, P., Bettoni, A., Sorlini, M.: Mass customization and sustainability. An assessment framework and industrial implementation. Springer, London (2013)
3. Canetta, L., Corti, D., Boër, C.R., Taisch, M.: Sustainable Product-Process-Network. In: Poler, R., Maia Carniero, L., Jasinski, T., Zolghadri, M., Pedrazzoli, P. (eds.) Intelligent Non-hierarchical Manufacturing Networks. Wiley, Hoboken (2012)
4. Gantar, G., Glojek, A., Mori, M., Nardin, B., Sekavčnik, M.: Resource Efficient Injection Moulding with Low Environmental Impacts. Strojniški vestnik-Journal of Mechanical Engineering 59(3), 193–200 (2013)
5. Guinée, J.B., Heijungs, R., Huppes, G., Zamagni, A., Masoni, P., Buonamici, R., Ekvall, T., Rydberg, T.: Life cycle assessment: past, present, and future. Environmental Science & Technology 45(1), 90–96 (2010)
6. https://www.amiplastics.com/pubs/cat.aspx?catalog=Publishing&category=Injection
7. Jounga, C.B., Carrell, J., Sarkara, P., Fenga, S.C.: Categorization of indicators for sustainable manufacturing. Ecological Indicators 24, 148–157 (2012)
8. OECD Sustainable manufacturing toolkit: seven steps to environmental excellence, http://www.oecd.org/innovation/green/toolkit/48661768.pdf (accessed on May 14, 2014)
9. Recchioni, M., Mandorli, F., Germani, M.: LCA as eco-design tool to support the development of injection moulded products. In: 13th CIRP International Conference on Life Cycle Engineering, Proceedings LCE 2006 (2006)
10. Schaltegger, S., Wagner, M.: Managing the Business Case of Sustainability. Greenleaf, Sheffield (2006)
11. Thiriez, A., Gutowski, T.: An environmental analysis of injection molding. In: Proceedings of the 2006 IEEE International Symposium on Electronics and the Environment. IEEE (2006)
12. Wüstenhagen, R., Boehnke, J.: Business models for sustainable energy. In: Tukker, A., et al. (eds.) System Innovation for Sustainability: Perspectives on Radical Changes to Sustainable Consumption and Production, pp. 85–94. Greenleaf, Sheffield (2008)

Green Virtual Enterprise Broker: Enabling Build-to-Order Supply Chains for Sustainable Customer-Driven Small Series Production

David Romero[1,2], Sergio Cavalieri[3], and Barbara Resta[3]

[1] Tecnológico de Monterrey, Mexico
[2] Griffith University, Australia
david.romero.diaz@gmail.com
[3] University of Bergamo, Department of Engineering,
CELS – Research Group on Industrial Engineering, Logistics and Service Operations, Italy
{sergio.cavalieri,barbara.resta}@unibg.it

Abstract. Global businesses are moving towards 'glocalization' and 'mass-customization' strategies to serve in a more personal and sustainable way their customers. Advances in ICT and green manufacturing technologies are enablers of this phenomenon. This paper explores a new business model, and its related supply chain model, the Green Virtual Enterprise Broker, which is fully customer-driven and aware of the environmental footprint of products and services to serve customized and small series production demands.

Keywords: Glocalization, Mass-Customization, Sustainability, Build-to-Order Supply Chains, Small Series Productions, Green Virtual Enterprise, Brokerage.

1 Introduction

To satisfy the consumers' desire for personalized products, many manufacturing enterprises have nowadays diversified their product lines to appease every consumer taste. Nevertheless, this approach to product diversification has backfired, resulting in failed product launches, huge overstock and significant upfront costs, since a greater variety of product options usually leads to more dissatisfied consumers, due to raised expectations and unattainable perfection [1]. This reality has left many manufacturing enterprises with negative economic, social and environmental footprints that can be translated into capital losses on new product development investments, unsatisfied consumers in target customer segments, and wasted resources related to unsold products [2]. As a result, new business models, and their related supply chains, are required to support in a sustainable way the emerging consumer trends of mass-customization (small series production) and personalization (single product) to individual customers or communities [3], relying on novel production paradigms characterized by flexible open manufacturing networks of small production units. Furthermore, Internet sales, both B2C & B2B, have made any product globally accessible for purchase, but its delivery and provisioning of life cycle services is a

B. Grabot et al. (Eds.): APMS 2014, Part II, IFIP AICT 439, pp. 431–441, 2014.

different challenge for traditional business solutions. In this sense, the notion of a *Glocal Networked Enterprise* presents a promising hybrid agile and lean supply chain and business model that can effectively and efficiently support highly customized and service-enhanced products along their lifecycle by involving manufacturers, customers, communities, third-party logistics providers and local service suppliers in a business ecosystem.

This paper explores a new business model, and its related supply chain model, the *Green Virtual Enterprise Broker*, which is fully customer-driven and aware of the environmental footprint of products and services along their lifecycle.

2   Sustainable Customer-Driven Business Models

New sustainable and customer-driven business models will continue emerging in the coming years due to the rapid advances in information and communication technologies, as well as in green manufacturing technologies, that have the potential to support a new generation of supply chain models. Such models will be characterized by the customer involvement in the supply chain as co-inventors (e.g. Quirky), co-designers (e.g. mi Adidas), or even as part of the assembly and delivery activities (e.g. IKEA); retailers as virtual business brokers; independent manufacturers as product development networks; and independent suppliers as logistics and product servicing networks. As a result, future business scenarios are based on collaborative and participatory business models and networked enterprises [2].

2.1   Sustainable Business Models

Sustainable business models seek to go beyond delivering economic value - in accordance with a triple bottom line approach. According to Lüdeke-Freund [4] a *sustainable business model* seeks to create balanced social, environmental and economic value through integrating sustainability more fully into its business model and value proposition(s). Furthermore, Short et al. [5], define a *sustainable value proposition* as a long-term shareholder value created as a scalable source of competitive advantage by embracing opportunities and managing the risks/benefits associated with their economic, environmental and social developments.

Moreover, Stubbs and Cocklin [6] state that *sustainable business models* use both a system and firm-level perspective, built on the triple bottom line approach, to define a supply chain model with a wider range of stakeholders. *Sustainable business models* require collaboration between companies, governments, communities and households; people and their communities play a critical role to bring such a change if provided with the smart thinking to increase efficiency and improve the usage of environmental resources, waste reduction and communal use of products or services (where possible) [7]. As a result, next generation supply chain models will be based on *sustainable business models* capturing economic value, while protecting the environmental and generating social value for the customer by improving his/her quality of life through highly customized value propositions.

2.2   Customer-Driven and Community-Driven Business Models

Customer preferences are an important element in any business model and supply chain, since economic value is captured from customers [8]. *Customer value* refers to what the customer wants with certain limitations related to his/her purchasing power [9]. Therefore, in this context a *customer-driven business model* can be defined as a business model that echoes the voice of the customer and aims to meet or exceed his/her personal preferences based on main basic judging elements, such as: product functional features, service mix and quality, total cost of ownership, social and environmental impact.

Such customer-driven viewpoint, which can be seen as an on-demand manufacturing approach, can offer customers the opportunity for customizing or personalizing their products and manufacturing enterprises to increase their manufacturing resources productivity by avoiding unsold products.

In addition, to create new sources of value, several industrial sectors are striving to provide integrated product-service solutions, breaking down the traditional barriers between products and services. *Product-Service Systems (PSS)* prevail as a systemic approach for enabling a strategic and managerial transition from selling the pure artefacts to deliver a customized and result-oriented solution providing a unique and positive experience to the user throughout his/her journey with the adopted solution [10].

With result-oriented solutions customers get the ownership benefits with less personal burden, cost savings and lower impact on environment, hence showing more captivating alternative to standard and traditional buying and ownership styles. The focus is not limited to the communal use of products and services, but the primary objective is to promote and encourage the active role of consumers towards sustainable communities. Collaborative lifestyles are ideas based on people with similar interests coming together to share and exchange less tangible assets such as time, space, skills and money. As a result, customer-driven models are escalating towards *community-driven models*, considering that the choices of the single customers are not taken on an individual base but rather with their explicit awareness of the benefits or the rebound effects that their decisions could exert on the community they belong to. *Collaborative business models* like: sharing, lending, exchange, swapping, and bartering are now able to operate again on a large scale, across geographic boundaries, thanks to the advent of modern technology [11].

3   Production Challenges in Small Series Productions

Capturing *sustainable value* in small series productions and/or personalized products in a global marketplace requires the interplay of various collaborative networks (e.g. a business ecosystem), such as product development and servicing networks, including customers and local stakeholders, co-creating highly customized and service-enhanced products [12] [13].

In the following sections, different production approaches will be explored to offer highly customized products to single customers or community of customers in a sustainable way.

3.1   Small Series Production (Special Edition Items)

A *Small Series Production (SSP)* is characterized by a small run (small lot size) and a low number of repetitions (frequency a product run is repeated) [14]. From a marketing perspective, a small series production is known as a *special edition,* and represents a restricted number of products being produced every once in a while (e.g. season) with some extra materials of some kind included and/or certain level of customization. For example: textiles, clothing and footwear seasons collections.

Small series productions, or special editions, call for a *Configure-to-Order (CTO)* production approach offering customers a standard customization based on a pre-defined number of customization alternatives (e.g. a solution space[1]) aiming to satisfy their demand. Special editions are customized based on standard product designs, have a slightly higher cost, a limit variety, and are produced only when an order is placed.

Table 1 presents some of the production and supply chain management (SCM) characteristics and challenges of a *CTO operational model* to support global small series productions.

Table 1. Production & Supply Chain Management Challenges in SSPs

Process	Characteristics	Challenges
Design & Engineering	• Standard customization. • Medium customer-driven design.	• Designs based on common parts and modular subassemblies.
Production	• Pull order system. • Medium volume. • Medium flexibility. • Medium to Short cycle time. • Medium inventory costs. • Medium total costs.	• Inventory management across the supply chain.
Logistics & Distribution	• Medium to Short cycle time.	• High supply chain management and integration.

3.2   One-Time Production (Limited Edition Items)

A *One-Time Production (OTP)* is characterized by a small run; i.e. only one small lot is produced and the product is not manufactured again (repetitions = zero) [14]. From a marketing perspective a one-time production is known as a *limited edition,* and represents a restricted number of products being produced for a unique time with a particular design. For example: exclusive sport and luxury cars production.

On-time productions, or limited editions, call for a *Make-to-Order (MTO)* production approach offering a high level of customization (one of a kind) and high quality. Limited editions are tailored (an exclusive design), have a high cost, a limit number of units, and are produced only when an order is placed.

Table 2 presents some of the production and SCM characteristics and challenges of a *MTO operational model* to support global on-time productions.

---

[1] A *solution space* encompasses all the possible designs a toolkit can produce.

Table 2. Production & Supply Chain Management Challenges in OTPs

Process	Advantages	Challenges
Design & Engineering	• One of a kind customization. • Tailored customization. • None customer-driven design.	• Low standard parts ratio. • Customization extent is high.
Production	• Pull order system. • Medium to low volume. • Medium flexibility. • Medium cycle time. • Low inventory costs. • Medium total costs.	• Demand quantity is small. • Production planning based on order. • Manufacturing is trigger by customer orders. • Medium delivery time.
Logistics & Distribution	• Medium cycle time.	• None supply chain integration.

3.3   Personalized Production (Deluxe Item)

A *Personalized Production (PP)* is characterized by a one item production according to single customer requirements [14]. From a marketing perspective, a personalized production is known as a *deluxe item,* and represents a unique engineering design or significant customization according to be produced according to specific customer's requirements. For example: a personalized competition sportswear or equipment for a professional athlete.

Personalized productions, or deluxe items, call for an *Engineer-to-Order (ETO)* production approach offering a complete involvement of the customer in the item (product) design and engineering (e.g. unique design, set of part numbers, bill of materials, routing, etc.). Deluxe items are developed from scratch for each single customer, and therefore have a high cost and are produced only when an order is placed.

Table 3 presents some of the production and SCM advantages and challenges of an *ETO operational model* to support global personalized productions.

Table 3. Production & Supply Chain Management Challenges in PPs

Process	Advantages	Challenges
Design & Engineering	• High customization (personalization). • High customer-driven design (full involvement).	• High product complexity.
Production	• Pull order system. • Low volume. • High flexibility. • Large cycle time. • None inventory costs. • High total costs.	• Long delivery time.
Logistics & Distribution	• Large cycle time.	• Long delivery time.

3.4   Collective Production (Shared Item)

A *Collective Production (CP)* is characterized by the production of a bundle of products and services according to the requirements of a close community of customers. From a marketing perspective, a collective production could be termed as shared item,

since design, engineering and delivery requires a significant customization according
to the specific local and cultural needs of the community sharing the common solution.
For example: energy management systems, local mobility systems, healthcare systems.

This kind of solutions call for a novel *Participatory-Engineering-to-Order (P-ETO)*
production approach, since the whole community, through a participatory mechanism,
needs to be involved in the definition of the requirements and the engineering of
the shared solution. A top-down approach (without the involvement of the community
since the beginning) would inhibit its widespread adoption.

Some of the related challenges that can be foreseen are: (a) engineering and
delivering community-driven solutions requires a variety of professional skills,
including among others sociologists and urban planners; and (b) given the complexity
and the local features of the solution, deriving from an integration of more products
and services, the configuration of the supply chain would be *one-of-a-kind*,
specifically designed and scarcely repetitive.

Table 4 presents some of the production and SCM advantages and challenges of
a *P-ETO operational model* to support global personalized productions.

Table 4. Production & Supply Chain Management Challenges in CPs

Process	Advantages	Challenges
Design & Engineering	• High customization (personalization). • High customer-driven design (full involvement).	• Long design and engineering time. • Contradictory requirements.
Production	• Pull order system. • Very low volume. • High flexibility. • Large cycle time. • None inventory costs. • High total costs.	• One-of-a-kind supply chain.
Logistics & Distribution	• High service costs.	• Long delivery time.

4   Green Virtual Enterprise Broker/Brokerage and Their Glocal Networked Enterprises

Global businesses are moving towards *glocalization* (globalized but localized) [15]
and *mass-customization* strategies to serve in a more personal and sustainable way
their customers [16]. Authors define a *Green Virtual Enterprise Broker (GVE-Broker)*
as a new business model where a focal enterprise[2] creates sustainable value by
mobilizing and managing processes and resources rather than owning them. A *GVE-
Broker business model* relies on a *Glocal Networked Enterprise (GNE)* composed by
a network of enterprises, with *global* presence as network, but with *locally* available

---

[2] A *focal enterprise* "is the initiator of an international business transaction, including
multinational and small/medium size enterprises, that conceives, designs, and produce
the offerings (goods and services) intended for consumption by customers worldwide" [17].

skills or core-competences and resources at the localities of their member enterprises to better serve customers worldwide.

A *GNE* is a breeding environment[3] for the dynamic creation of *Build-to-Order (BTO) supply chains* [3], named: virtual manufacturing and/or service enterprises [2], to meet the specific requirements of customers, and at the same time adopt, under case by case bases (the business opportunity characterization) the proper supply chain strategy/model (e.g. agile, lean, flexible) to cope with the uncertainties faced by the demand and sustainable and competitive supply of small series productions and personalized products, and their related services [18]. By associating the right business partners in a *Green Virtual Enterprise (VE), BTO supply chains* [3] [16] can face the challenges of a customer- or community-driven and sustainable supply chain with global added value product-service systems as customized 'value propositions'; at the same time they would achieve a sustainable competitive advantage through the efficient use of locally available resources and competences in *glocal networked member enterprises* to reduce costs, lead time, environmental footprint and social negative impacts.

GVE-Brokers activities will be performed by means of a *web-based collaborative solution platform* (e.g. an e-marketplace) for the realization of sustainable business ecosystems for the co-creation, manufacturing and delivery of customized product-services in distributed markets.

This *web-based collaboration solution platform* (see Table 5) will have a threefold service support offer for: (a) services for *customers* based on *user toolkits*[4] for mass-customization, personalization and participatory engineering of value propositions, where customers can access to a solution space for co-innovating, co-creating and/or co-developing his/her own products and services [19] [20] [21] [22], (b) services for *GVE-brokers* based on *GVE creation tools* named: opportunity identification and characterization, GVE rough planning, GVE partners search and suggestion, GVE composition, GVE partners negotiation, detailed GVE planning, GVE partners contracting, and GVE set-up [23] [24] [25], and (c) services for *GVE coordinators* based on *GVE management tools* such as: project planning and decision support, project execution and monitoring, and customer follow-up [23] [26].

User toolkits as virtual tools build an interface between manufacturers and service providers and their customers. *User toolkits* can be employed by manufacturers and service providers to get an exact purchase order and therefore produce customized products just when the customers need them and only in the quantity they are needed. Hence, *user toolkits* offer two advantages: (a) allow users to exactly specify their design preferences reducing the possibility of unsold products and increasing customer satisfaction, and (b) improve customer relationship [19] [20] [21] [22].

---

[3] A *virtual enterprise breeding environment* is a long-term strategic alliance of enterprises aimed at offering the necessary conditions to support the rapid and fluid configuration of virtual manufacturing and/or service enterprises [2].

[4] A *user toolkit* is a technology that allows users to design a novel product via trial-and-error experimentation and deliver them an immediate (simulated) feedback on the potential outcome of their design ideas [19].

Table 5. The Green Virtual Enterprise Broker and its Solution Platform Overview

Building Blocks	Types		
Value Proposition(s)	• Mass-customized • Personalized • Shared		
Customer Segments	• Individual customers • Customer niche • Customer community		
Customer Relationships	• Customer-driven (co-innovation, co-creation, co-development)		
Channels	• e-Marketplace		
Key Partners (stakeholders)	Glocal Networked Enterprise: • Manufacturers • Service Providers • Customers & Communities • Brokers		
Key Activities & Resources	Front-end	Intermediary	Back-end
	User toolkits for: mas-customization, personalization and participatory engineering	Broker toolkit for: • Opportunity characterization • Partners search and selection • Topology set-up • Schedule activities • Assign tasks • Allocate budget • Define KPIs • Identify risks	Networked Enterprise toolkit for: • Monitor activities • Monitor finance • Monitor KPIs • Measure indicators • Manage exceptions • Monitor risks • Liability (guarantees)
	e-Marketplace Platform: An interactive environment for value co-creation and collaborative supply chain management.		
Cost Structure	• Costing models (e.g. variables costs + economies of scope).		
Revenue Streams	• Profit models (e.g. subscription fees + brokerage fees).		

GVE creation tools will support *GVE-brokers* to find glocally (globally and locally) the right GVE partners considering the availability of their green capabilities and capacities, cost, and localization in order to build the best supply chain possible with the shortest lead time, cost and environmental footprint. Within the *GVE creation tools,* those related to GVE partners search and suggestion will play a vital role to help *GVE-brokers* to find and evaluate different feasible GVE configurations with respect to customer-, economic-, social- and environmental- oriented criteria (e.g. customer preferences, production cost, delivery cost, lead time, footprint, green technologies, etc.) [23] [24] [25].

Thus, *GVE-brokers* capability to dynamically create *BTO supply chains,* tailored within a *glocal networked enterprise,* seems to be the most promising sustainable strategy to support 'glocal markets' and respond to the quality-, time-, cost- and environmental- frames demanded by the consumers of customized and small series production products that want a premium customer service (attention) and the feel of proximity (near-by store) when it comes to the services associated to their products. In this scenario (see Fig. 1), *glocal networked enterprises* are an encouraging organizational model to enable agile, lean, and reasonably priced production and services activities glocally-wide [27].

GVE management tools will support *GVE coordinators* in their main activity of orchestrating the *glocal networked enterprise's* product development and servicing networks to strengthen a structure for 'glocal operations'[5] that responds to individual

---

[5] *Glocal operations* can be defined as strategies for providing a global offer while taking local related issues into account and therefore meeting certain local/particular needs or preferences, at lower costs due to the global edge of the networked enterprise [30].

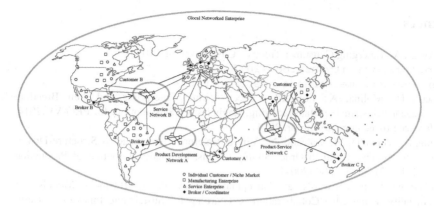

Fig. 1. Glocal Networked Enterprise World-Wide Operations

and niche customers' needs on a global scale with the shortest lead time, cost and environmental footprint possible [23] [26]. *GVE coordinators* will formulate 'glocal strategies' to incorporate the adaptation of the network glocal core-competences and resources, business opportunities characteristics, and location of the *glocal networked member enterprises* to suit the requirements of a local customer and attain a new competitive advantage. *GVE coordinators* will utilize the glocal network experience for customizing products and services in such way that appeal to local/niche markets (small series productions) and single customers (personalization) [28] [29] [30].

5   Conclusions and Future Work

Glocal Networked Enterprises are becoming a needed reality in a globalized marketplace (e.g. e-commerce), aided by an emerging consumer trend for customized products, and supported by the progress in information, communication and production technologies (e.g. Big Data, Internet of Things, 3D printing). Furthermore, future *glocal networked solutions* will have to face the constraints to achieve an economically, socially and environmentally sustainable industrial landscape and marketplace in a global perspective [18].

Green Virtual Enterprise Brokers and their Glocal Networked Enterprises offer an encouraging organizational model for managing 'glocal operations' by means of the cooperation of manufacturing and service enterprises to fulfill world-wide various production and service provision needs. Hence, new markets are opening up for customized and small series production products and their related services but require new collaborative supply chain and business models [30].

Further work is needed to develop not only new collaborative supply chain and business models but also new methods and (ICT) tools to enable 'BTO supply chains for sustainable customer-driven small series productions'.

References

1. Markwart, A.: Emerging Consumer Trends – Customization (2013),
   http://www.vancitybuzz.com/2013/11/
   emerging-consumer-trends-customization/
2. Romero, D., Molina, A.: Forward - Green Virtual Enterprises and their Breeding Environments: Sustainable Manufacturing, Logistics & Consumption. In: PRO-VE 2014, Conference Proceedings (to appear, 2014)
3. Molina, A., Velandia, M., Galeano, N.: Virtual Enterprise Brokerage: A Structure-Driven Strategy to Achieve Build to Order Supply Chains. International Journal of Production Research 45(17), 3853–3880 (2007)
4. Lüdeke-Freund, F.: Towards a Conceptual Framework of Business Models for Sustainability. Knowledge Collaboration & Learning for Sustainable Innovation, Delft, The Netherlands (2010)
5. Short, S.W., Bocken, N.M.P., Rana, P., Evans, S.: Business Model Innovation for Embedding Sustainability - A Practice-Based Approach Introducing Business Model Archetypes. In: 10th Global Conference on Sustainable Manufacturing (2012)
6. Stubbs, W., Cocklin, C.: Conceptualizing a "Sustainability Business Model". Organization & Environment 21(2), 103–127 (2008)
7. Bartolomeo, M., et al.: Eco-Efficient Services - What are they, How do they Benefit Customers and the Environment and How likely are they to Develop and be Extensively Utilized. Journal of Cleaner Production 11(8), 829–837 (2003)
8. Bowman, C., Ambrosini, V.: Value Creation versus Value Capture: Towards a Coherent Definition of Value in Strategy. British Journal of Management 11, 1–15 (2000)
9. Pynnönen, M.: Customer Driven Business Model – Connecting Customer Value to Firm Resources in ICT Value Networks. PhD Thesis, Universitatis Lappeenrantaensis (2008)
10. Cavalieri, S., Pezzotta, G.: Product–Service Systems Engineering: State of the Art and Research Challenges. Computers in Industry 63(4), 278–288 (2012)
11. Botsman, R., Roger, R.: What's Mine Is Yours: The Rise of Collaborative Consumption. Harper Business (2010)
12. Camarinha-Matos, L.M., Macedo, P., Ferrada, F., Oliveira, A.I.: Collaborative Business Scenarios in a Service-Enhanced Products Ecosystem. In: Camarinha-Matos, L.M., Xu, L., Afsarmanesh, H. (eds.) Collaborative Networks in the Internet of Services. IFIP AICT, vol. 380, pp. 13–25. Springer, Heidelberg (2012)
13. Camarinha-Matos, L.M., Ferrada, F., Oliveira, A.I.: Interplay of Collaborative Networks in Product Servicing. In: Camarinha-Matos, L.M., Scherer, R.J. (eds.) PRO-VE 2013. IFIP Advances in Information and Communication Technology, vol. 408, pp. 51–60. Springer, Heidelberg (2013)
14. Lödding, H.: Handbook of Manufacturing Control: Fundamentals, Description, Configuration, pp. 101–103. Springer (2013)
15. Hesselbach, J., Herrmann, C.: Glocalized Solutions for Sustainability in Manufacturing - Preface. Springer (2011)
16. Romero, D., Molina, A.: Collaborative Networked Organisations and Customer Communities: Value Co-creation and Co-innovation in the Networking Era. Journal of Production Planning & Control 22(5-6), 447–472 (2011)
17. Cavusgil, T.S., Knight, G., Riesenberger, J.R.: International Business Strategy, Management and New Realities. Pearsons Prentice Hall, USA (2008)

18. Hau, L.: Aligning Supply Chain Strategies with Product Uncertainties. California Management Review, 44(3), 105–119, (2002); Hesselbach, J., Herrmann, C.: Glocalized Solutions for Sustainability in Manufacturing - Preface. Springer (2011)
19. von Hippel, E.: Perspectives: User Toolkits for Innovation. Journal of Product Innovation Management 18(4), 247–257 (2001)
20. von Hippel, E., Katz, R.: Shifting Innovation to Users via Toolkits. Management Science 48(7), 821–833 (2002)
21. Franke, N., Piller, F.: Key Research Issues in User Interaction with User Toolkits in a Mass Customisation System. International Journal of Technology Management 26(5), 578–599 (2003)
22. Hermans, G.: A Model for Evaluating the Solution Space of Mass Customization Toolkits. International Journal of Industrial Engineering and Management 3(4), 205–214 (2012)
23. Romero, D., Molina, A.: Green Virtual Enterprise Breeding Environment Reference Framework. In: Camarinha-Matos, L.M., Pereira-Klen, A., Afsarmanesh, H. (eds.) PRO-VE 2011. IFIP AICT, vol. 362, pp. 545–555. Springer, Heidelberg (2011)
24. Camarinha-Matos, L.M., et al.: VO Creation Assistance Services. Methods and Tools for Collaborative Networked Organizations, pp. 155–190. Springer, Heidelberg (2008)
25. Wang, X., Wonga, T.N., Wang, G.: An Ontological Intelligent Agent Platform to Establish an Ecological Virtual Enterprise. Expert Systems with Applications 39, 7050–7061 (2012)
26. Negretto, U., et al.: VO Management Solutions - VO Management e-Services. Methods and Tools for Collaborative Networked Organizations, pp. 257–274. Springer (2008)
27. Hartel, I., Billinger, S., Burger, G., Kamio, Y.: Virtual Organization of After-Sales Service in the One-of-a-Kind Industry. In: Camarinha-Matos, L.M., et al. (eds.) Collaborative Business Ecosystems and Virtual Enterprises, pp. 405–420. Kluwer Academic Publishers (2002)
28. Dumitrescu, L., Vinerean, S.: The Glocal Strategy of Global Brands. Journal Studies in Business and Economics 5(3), 147–155 (2010)
29. Foglio, A., Stanevicius, V.: Scenario of Glocal Marketing as an Answer to the Market Globalization and Localization. Part I: Strategy Scenario and Market, Vadyba/Managemt, pp. 26–38 (2007)
30. Johanisson, B.: Building a "Glocal" Strategy – Internationalizing Small Firms through Local Networking. In: 39ème Conférence Mondiale de l'ICSB: "Les PME/PMI et leur contribution au développement régional et international", pp. 127–135 (1994)

Towards a Green and Sustainable Manufacturing Planning and Control Paradigm Using APS Technology

Kenn Steger-Jensen[1], Heidi Dreyer[2], Hans-Henrik Hvolby[1], and Ola Strandhagen[2]

[1] Centre for Logistics, Department of Mechanical and Manufacturing Engineering,
Aalborg University, Fibigerstrede 16, 9220 Aalborg, Denmark
[2] Department of Production and Quality Engineering, NTNU,
S P Andersensvej 5, Trondheim, Norway
{hhh,kenn}@celog.dk,
{heidi.c.dreyer,ola.strandhagen}@ntnu.no

Abstract. This research aims at integrating a green perspective into manufacturing operations of companies through a new sustainable performance objective. The paper highlights the current trends in green and sustainable manufacturing and lines up different options for supporting this in current Advanced Planning and Scheduling Systems. Finally, requirements for future APS functionality is presented.

Keywords: Green, Sustainable, Manufacturing, Planning, Advanced Planning and Scheduling Systems, APS; Optimisation.

1 Introduction

Manufacturing and production operations are considered the most substantial contributor to climate challenges and environmental degradation, for which reason manufacturing firms must be held responsible as well [1]. The basic initiatives in dealing with climate challenges and environmental degradation have until recently mainly been green investments, which by experts have been referred to as 'business-as-usual' investments nowhere near what is perceived adequate. According to the World Economic Forum new approaches are necessary for creating and ensuring economic growth, sustainability and a stable future [2]. One approach which is addressed in the literature and perceived as a necessity to achieve the environmental and sustainable goals, is changing businesses' manufacturing philosophy [1,3].

Changing a manufacturing philosophy entails a shift in the way production systems are operated and managed and contains strategies, principles and techniques on how to achieve one or more objectives. Historically, manufacturing philosophies have changed concurrently with the industrial evolution from the industrial revolution and Adam Smith's division of labor over the Lean and just-in-time principles derived in the early 20th century, to the quality revolution of the 1980s and the supply-chain revolution of the 1990s [4]. Along with the evolution in production philosophies, there has been a natural progression in the way operational performance have been

B. Grabot et al. (Eds.): APMS 2014, Part II, IFIP AICT 439, pp. 442–449, 2014.

evaluated, where the main focus in the early stages of the industrial revolution was primarily on cost [5]. As competition has grown, the subsequent manufacturing philosophies have expanded this view, describing trade-offs between what have later been defined as the five performance objectives; quality, speed, dependability, flexibility and cost [5,6].

As indicated, environmental management has not been considered an integral entity of operational performance in any of the production philosophies [1]. Instead, environmental management was commenced in the 1970s as risk management with focus on waste and pollution. With profitability as a continued driver, the agenda of the 1980s and 1990s addressed product and process management to reduce waste and ensure reusability using life cycle assessments [1].

In recent years, as the industrial evolution has become more and more influenced by the deterioration of the environment, overflowing waste, and increasing levels of pollution, a new paradigm has emerged within the manufacturing philosophy literature [4]. According to Deif [7] we see the rise of a green manufacturing paradigm, which includes eco-efficient strategies, that consumes less material and energy, substituting to cleaner and renewable input materials, reduces unwanted outputs and converting output to inputs. It is the manufacturing managers' awareness of its the production/product impact on the environment and the implementation of the green aspects into the planning and control models which are now necessary if realizing the green objectives in practice.

2   Literature Study

The sustainability of the industrial sector has become one of the most significant societal, political and business issues due to the fact that the manufacturing sector has a huge impact on the environment, economy and the quality of human life. The focus on the impact of manufacturing and supply chain activities including logistics and transportation has captured a huge academic and industrial interest which has led to significant contributions regarding figures and measures [8,9], concepts and strategies and methodologies and tools such as Life-Cycle Assessment (LCA) and Corporate Social Responsibility (CSR). Since first formulated in the Bruntland report in 1987 [10] it seems like the literature agrees on the understanding of sustainability as being the industrial sector's ability to create its outcome in a way that minimizes the impact on the environment, within secure social and ethical condition and contribute to economy and value creating [11].

Looking into the literature that focus on the negative externalities from the manufacturing industry it is the toxic chemicals, waste, energy and water consumption and greenhouse gas emissions and carbon footprint which is the main negative environmental impact from the industry ([8,12,13]. According to the U.S. Toxic Release Inventory [14] the manufacturing industry is the second largest contributor in US of air emission, surface water discharges, land release and underground injections are the toxic chemicals [8]. Furthermore the industry generates a large amount of waste, mainly in the form of solid and water waste but also other categories such as materials, and the amount of waste is more than the sum of all other sectors combined.

The energy consumption is high and is mainly supplied from fossil fuels which contain various polluting elements such as carbon, sulfur and nitrogen that causes greenhouse gases and global warming. With this impact on the environment, and, manufacturers' profitability, the importance of improving the environmental performance is high.

Deif [7] considers sustainability to be the concept and strategy while green manufacturing is the methodology, toolset and the way to dispose sustainability. Green manufacturing is regarded as the first step towards sustainable production and the ability to develop advanced manufacturing capabilities by involve the design and engineering activities in product development and/or the operations of production is critical for improving the environmentally performance of the manufacturing industry [15]. According to Deif [7] the existing literature consists of two types of contributions.

- The first type provides knowledge about the concept of green manufacturing covering topics as waste reduction activities, elimination of causal factors, and, green productivity measures, business models for using new material technologies and the use of sustainability information in decision support.
- The second category is analytical tools and methods that have been developed in order to realize green manufacturing at different levels. Tools for product/process design analyses such as life cycle assessment (LCA) and life cycle costing (LCA) used to evaluate the environmental impact of assets over the entire life cycle and Corporate social responsibility (CSR) used for taking the responsibility for the impact of their activities on customers, suppliers, employers, shareholders, community and the environment in all aspect of their operations.

Important contributions have been made but interestingly very few studies seem to have focused on operations management and how production is planned and controlled and how the green elements actually could be taken into consideration in the higher and lower production planning levels. There is one exception and that is the work by Melnyk et al [16], who has developed a tool that integrates environmental concerns into the material planning activities. By using this kind of tools one does not only make managers aware of the environmental and emission effects associated with the production strategy, plan and schedule, it also triggers action such as changing the plan and the schedule. We have identified a gap in the current literature and a need for developing tools that allow managers to embed green aspects into the higher and lower production and control planning levels and by doing so to be able to take the right decisions in order to actually become more sustainable by simultaneously taking environmental and profit optimizing aspects into account.

3   Towards a Green Manufacturing Planning and Control Paradigm

Pursuing sustainability as a performance objective for manufacturing operations requires primary changes to the manufacturing planning and control system. This is chosen as a point of departure because such systems contain all essential activities that are used within a company for planning and controlling its manufacturing operations [17].

The main goal of developing a "green" manufacturing planning and control framework is to include green parameters into the planning process alongside materials and resources (typically machines and operators) with the aim of reducing the amount of green sources used such as materials, energy and water. Melnyk [16] includes materials waste in the materials requirement planning (MRP) process by implementing a "Bill-Of-Waste", but although their paper is titled "Green MRP" the goal is not to reduce waste but merely to identify the waste created. In the literature study we have identified a list of authors dealing with Green Supply Chains, Green Manufacturing and Green Planning. However, none of these studies discuss how to include green parameters in the planning process.

Traditional enterprise resource planning (ERP) systems do not optimize materials and resource usage but merely calculate the requirement for materials and resources. Therefore, ERP-systems are not able to support our definition of "Green Planning" in terms of optimized planning taking all resources such as materials, operators, energy and water into consideration. This is, however, partly possible in advanced planning and scheduling (APS) systems. In the following we will discuss how this is possible in existing implementations of APS and how to bring APS further towards green manufacturing.

3.1   Advanced Planning and Scheduling (APS) Systems

APS systems use complex mathematical algorithms to plan and schedule production within specified constraints and to derive optimal product-mix solutions. APS-systems aim at reducing costs of goods sold and to increase customer satisfaction by making the right products at the right times, using an optimal combination of manufacturing resources. APS systems are hence able to generate far more realistic and reliable production plans than ERP systems [18,19].

When multiple objectives exist in a manufacturing environment, and most of these are in conflict with each another, an approach is needed for modelling and evaluating the trade-off among the conflicting objectives. Here two options exist: Constraint based planning and optimization. The two approaches are discussed in the following.

3.2   Constraint Based Planning

Constrained based planning is based on hard and soft (or goal) constraints. Its distinguished feature is that the objectives can be stated as minimising deviations from pre-specified goals. Hard constraints are not overruled, whereas soft constraints are overruled, if necessary. As no plan optimisation objectives or criteria are considered this option produces a feasible but not necessarily an optimal plan. Therefore, APS-systems use a hidden plan objective function, which drives the planning and trade-off among the soft constraints. The hidden plan objective function is defined as minimizing plan cost.

It is possible to select one and only one "domain", either *demand* or *supply*, to be a hard constraint. If the *demand* domain is selected as a hard constraint, customer due dates are enforced while material and capacity availability become soft constraints.

If the *supply* domain is selected as a hard constraint, the capacity constraints are enforced, while demand due dates might be overruled. At the same time there is an option to determine whether the constrained plan enforces material, resource capacity or both. Resource capacity constraints are subdivided into operation resources, sourcing resources (supplier, inventory) and transportation resources.

In addition to hard and soft constraints it is possible to use business rules and demand priorities. Business rules are part of the master data and used as explicit decisions made on the supply domain when there are more options to choose among in the plan generation. Business rules are ranked by use of priorities of given topics such as sourcing of capacity, supplier and items. As an example, material requirements are fulfilled from rank 1 suppliers before sourcing from lower ranking suppliers independent of costs.

Rules play an important role in constraint based planning systems by avoiding the traditional (time-consuming) re-planning and re-scheduling after plan generation. If environmental factors are included in the master data and used as well in the business rules and demand priorities it will be possible to support green planning parameters.

3.3   Optimisation

Optimised plans are generated based on plan objectives, penalty factors and constraints beside the hard and soft constraints. The constraint-based rules are exchanged with decision variables and penalty factors, instead of the hidden object function and business rules and demand priorities. To optimise a total plan the APS engine needs one single mutual measure - money - in terms of costs and on profits. In the optimisation the soft constraints might be overruled if this reduces the total costs. For example, demand priority and supplier allocation ranks could be overruled to reach the best profit. If a rank 2 supplier results in lower cost than a rank 1 supplier does, orders will be allocated to the rank 2 supplier(s).

In connection with the objective function, three parameters can be weighted: on-time delivery, inventory turns and plan profit. Besides the objectives, a number of decision variables can be used to achieve the wanted business goals. A planner can use multiple objective criteria to evaluate plans for an unlimited number of decision variables. The decision variables are almost the same as the rules used in CBP without objectives, but in CBP with objectives there are alternative and substitutional conditions considered according to bills and routes.

The decision variables are all time-phased and include supplier sources, routings, BOM's, items, resources, production and purchasing quantities, transportation and safety stock levels. The optimisation seeks the best combination of these decisions.

The optimisation satisfies weighted objectives and takes the penalty factors related to these decision variables into consideration. The following penalty cost factors are used explicitly in relation to decision variables: late demand, safety stock level, exceeding material, exceeding resource capacity and exceeding transportation resource capacity. A planner enters percentages to indicate how important it is that those outcomes do not occur in your plan. The optimisation process drives penalties out of the solution, and tends to drive the most costly penalty factors out first. A high degree of accuracy in setting penalty factors is not as important as the relationship between penalty factors.

When the APS system makes decisions to avoid late demand, it will place higher priority to keeping large sales orders on time. When the penalty for late demand is higher than the penalty for exceeding resource capacity (factor times work order resource cost), the solution will tend to plan overtime work in order to avoid late delivery. In general, all penalty factors work this way.

3.4   Including Green Objectives

The optimised planning as described above is based on a cost perspective, whereas the constraint based planning is based on business rules and demand priorities. When performing its optimization, the APS system has one unique measure: costs ($). One can discuss whether it is possible to measure green (environmental) factors in terms of costs. Some measures, such as water and CO2, may be directly linked to costs whereas outlet of detergents may have specific requirements as to what level is accepted by the government. The latter (here defined as "environmental related factors") is therefore more difficult to include in a financial-based optimization.

Current APS systems have some opportunities for supporting green planning. The most obvious solution is to include green factors in the bill-of-materials (BOM) and the routings. This could for example be done by adding a "CO2" or "WATER" component in the BOM and an "ENERGY" resource in the routing. As APS can handle alternative routings and BOM's it would be possible to offer some kind of environmental optimisation. This approach works for cost related factors but not for environmental related factors. Currently, APS enables a configuration of the plan optimization in terms of weighting the following objectives:
-    Plan profit
-    Inventory turns
-    On-time delivery

One obvious improvement option is to add one more objective to satisfy environmental issues, especially to enable an optimisation of the non-cost related factors. In the following table the options in current APS systems are highlighted.

	Constraints based Planning	Optimization based Planning
Objectives/ Decisions variables	*Hidden objective function containing cost related to pollution factors:* Requirement on environment factors (air, water and energy) is need in the master data, to calculate the sustainability	*Profit based optimisation:* As for CBP, requirements on environment factors is need in the master data
		Sustainability based optimisation: Not possible today, but environment impact of pollution factors in the current object function is need or a unique objective for total pollution of environment in the object function is need to calculate the sustainability.

Constraints	Demand priorities: Where delivery to customer contain less pollution factors	Hard constraints: As today, but since environment impact of pollution factors is not discrete and unique defined, they are modelled as resources in the master data.
	Business Rules: Where sourcing contain less pollution factors	Soft constraints: Not possible today, since environment impact of pollution factors is not discrete and unique defined.
Penalty Factors	None as constraints are not overruled	Late demand and Exceeding material, inventory, transportation, machine and labour capacity. As today, but modelled as resources in the master data.
		Sustainability based penalty: Not possible today, since environment impact of pollution factors is not discrete and unique defined.

4   Conclusion

The effective use of Advanced Planning and Scheduling Systems is a step in the right direction towards generating more realistic and reliable plans. However, optimisation and its objectives and penalty factors within manufacturing systems do not yet support 'green planning' from a sustainability point of view. The optimised plan is based on a cost perspective, which does not always lead to a sustainable plan whereas the constraint based plan is based on business rules and priority, which for the current release is too simple for green planning.

The planner has to know a lot about green production conditions and cost structures to be capable of using optimization. The optimisation is based on a data structure, which does not directly support green planning parameters. The gap between current models and methods in APS systems and models and methods directly supporting green planning is an area for further research.

Acknowledgements. The authors would like to express their gratitude to the Danish Business Innovation Fund for supporting the project which this research is a part of and to Chris Martin for assistance in editing.

References

1. Beamon, B.M.: Designing the green supply chain. Logistics Information Management 12(4), 332–342 (1999)
2. World Economic Forum, "The Green Investment Report The ways and means to unlock private finance for green growth" (2013)
3. de Burgos Jiménez, J., Lorente, J.: Environmental performance as an operations objective. International Journal of Operations & Production Management 21(12), 1553–1572 (2001)
4. Srivastava, S.K.: "Green supply-chain management - A state-of-the-art literature review". International Journal of Management Reviews (2007)
5. Sarkis, J., Qinghua, Z., Kee-Hung, L.: An organizational theoretic review of green supply chain management literature. International Journal - Production Economics 130(2011), 1–15 (2010)
6. Slack, N., Chambers, S., Johnston, R.: Operations Management. 5. Prentice Hall (2007)
7. Deif, A.M.: A system model for green manufacturing. Journal of Cleaner Production 19, 1553–1559 (2011)
8. Dornfeld, D.A.: Green Manufacturing: Fundamentals and Applications. Springer, New York (2013)
9. Bunse, K., Vodicka, M., Schönsleben, P., Brülhart, M., Ernst, F.: Integrating energy efficiency performance in production management – gap analysis between industrial needs and scientific literature. Journal of Cleaner Production 19(6-7), 667–679 (2011)
10. Brundtland Commission, i.e. World Commission on Environment and Development, WCED (1993)
11. Manzan, R., Miyake, D.: A Study on Alternative Approaches to Instill Environmental Concerns in the Domain of Production Management of Industrial Firms. Journal of Technology management & Innovation 8(3), 198–207 (2013)
12. Despeisse, M., Ball, P.D., Evans, S., Levers, A.: Industrial ecology at factory level – a conceptual model. Journal of Cleaner Production 13, 30–39 (2012)
13. Garetti, M., Taisch, M.: Sustainable manufacturing: trends and research challenges. Production Planning and Control 23(2-3), 88–104 (2012)
14. US Toxic Release Inventory Program. Last accessed (June 2014), http://www2.epa.gov/toxics-release-inventory-tri-program/2011-tri-national-analysis
15. Klassen, R.D., Whybark, D.C.: The impact of environmental technologies on manufacturing performance. Academy of Management Journal 42(6), 599–614 (1999)
16. Melnyk, S.A., Sroufe, R.P., Montabon, F.L., Hinds, J.: International Journal Production Research 39(8), 1559–1573 (2001)
17. Silver, E., Pyke, D., Petersen, R.: Inventory management and production planning and scheduling. John Wiley & Sons (1998)
18. Jacobs, F., Weston, F.C.: Enterprise resource planning (ERP) - A brief history. Journal of Operations Management 31, 357–363 (2007)
19. Hvolby, H.-H., Steger-Jensen, K.: Technical and Industrial Issues of Advanced Planning and Scheduling (APS) Systems. Computers in Industry 61(9), 845–851 (2010)

A Comparison of Homogeneous and Heterogeneous Vehicle Fleet Size in Green Vehicle Routing Problem

Abdelhamid Moutaoukil[1], Gilles Neubert[2], and Ridha Derrouiche[2]

[1] Institut Fayol- UMR-5600, EMSE, 158 cours fauriel, 42000 Saint-Etienne, France
[2] UMR-5600, ESC Saint-Etienne 51 cours Fauriel, CS 80029- 42009 Saint-Etienne, France

Abstract. To balance a fragmented logistics organization, Small and Medium Enterprises have to find collective solutions to decrease their environmental impact. Especially when the demand at each producer takes the form of small packages and low quantities this paper examines the effect of the introduction of a consolidation center on the environmental issue. Therefore, the Fleet Size and Mix Vehicle Routing Problem (FSMVRP) was adapted in order to minimize CO_2 emission. An exact mathematical formulation of the extended problem was developed to investigate the difference between homogeneous and heterogeneous fleet size on the environmental issue. Computational experiments for the problem formulation are performed using CPLEX and give a solution of a small instance to illustrate the problem. A case study focuses on optimal parcel picking up, from many producers to a common depot in the agri-food sector.

Keywords: Sustainable routing problem, Fleet Size and Mix Vehicle Routing Problem, Environmental objectives, Pickup optimization, Agri-food sector.

Introduction

By enabling a closer relationship between all supply-chain partners, Supply Chain Management (SCM) achieves cost reductions and revenue enhancements, as well as flexibility in dealing with supply and demand uncertainties [1, 2]. Due to the market evolution and a constant pressure of European regulations companies are pushed now to integrate environmental concerns in their supply chains in line with sustainable objectives [3, 4]. At the same time, new logistics requirement, such as quick response, high delivery frequency and small quantities increase the complexity of flow management and explode logistics costs.

In this situation, SME's with a lower maturity level in supply chain, have difficulties to integrate green approach in their logistics activities. This is why the consolidation of goods appears as a good way to improve the economic and environmental efficiency of flow management and emphasizes the importance of the Vehicle Routing Problem-VRP [3]. The traditional VRP is usually based on a homogeneous fleet size problem and becomes more complex when the vehicle fleet is heterogeneous [5]. Vehicles of different carrying capacities provide capacity according to the customers' varying demand, in a more cost effective way [6, 7], and this configuration has multiple advantages in real life [8].

B. Grabot et al. (Eds.): APMS 2014, Part II, IFIP AICT 439, pp. 450–457, 2014.

The objective of this research is to optimize the logistics' environmental impact of a set of small producers in the agri-food sector. Depending on the amount of products to be collected from these different producers and transported to a common distribution center, this paper investigates the difference between homogeneous and heterogeneous fleet size on the CO2 emission. Thus, the problem that is considered in this paper is a Fleet Size and Mix Vehicle Routing Problem (FSMVRP) that is adapted to take into account the environmental objectives, while focusing on the collect of products from several manufacturers to a common depot.

1   FSMVRP Problem: Definition and Overview

The VRP assumes that there is a limited fleet, each vehicle with the same capacity, whereas the FSMVRP determines the number and the type of vehicles in an unlimited fleet [9]. Thus, the usual objective is to minimize the sum of vehicle acquiring costs (Fixed Cost) and the routing costs (Variable Cost) [7]. Generally, the environmental aspects have been addressed in the literature in some variants of VRP, namely, Green VRP (G-VRP) [10], Pollution Routing Problem (PRP) [11] and Emissions VRP (E-VRP) [12], and consider two main objectives: the minimization of energy (fuel) consumption and CO2 emissions. Since our research mainly focuses on the environmental issues of routing problem while using heterogeneous fleet, a review of literature that deals with vehicles of different types and environmental aspects has been conducted

1.1   Overview of FSMVRP Problem with Green Objectives

Recent research on FSMVRP attempts to assimilate so called "environmental" aspects into normal routing models. Minimizing transportation related emission (especially CO2) and energy consumption instead of the driving distances are significant integration approaches [13]. In their work [14], authors showed how changes in fleet management were introduced as well as the implementation of a methodology to solve vehicle routing problems with environmental criteria minimization but limited to vehicle types with the same characteristics. In their case, as the payload carried on arcs cannot be known in advance, the authors have to settle for estimated values of the emission factors.

In another way, authors in [15] employ the COPERT model presented in [16] to estimate the fuel consumption. Their model is based on the payload and gradient correction factor for heavy duty vehicles. These authors define different vehicle classes and discuss the influence of gradient and payload on CO2 emissions for each vehicle class. Nevertheless, there is no mixed fleet considered in this paper since the analysis is done for several vehicle classes independently.

Unlike the previous scientific work, [13] introduced the fuel consumption minimization of vehicle routing problem with different vehicle classes. Their model minimizes fuel consumption instead of driving distance by offering the possibility of using several types of vehicles. The authors compared their model to the traditional VRP. They found that a significant amount of reduction is possible through the use of a heterogeneous fleet of vehicles and established a direct link between fuel consumption and CO2 emissions. However their model did not provide a minimization function of CO2 emissions in the routing problem.

A detailed literature review leads to conclude that there is need to define a FSMVRP that integrate green objectives, which will be stated in following section.

2   Modeling of FSMVR with Green Objectives

This section presents a new version of the traditional approach of the fleet size and mix vehicle routing problem. This new model reduces environmental costs by enhancing the use of different vehicles types.

2.1   General Assumptions and Problem Formulation

As in normal VRPs, we assume that there is only one depot in our system. The schedules are one-time plans and the time horizon is assumed to be a single period e.g. one day. It is assumed that all goods are conditioned in parcels with different volumes and weights. The fleet consists of vehicles of various types with differing curb weights and load capacities.

All vehicles start their routes at time zero. Each vehicle starts and returns to the depot upon completing its respective trips. At each stop, the vehicle has a loading time which is relative to the vehicle type. There is a restriction on the duration of each route. There is limitation on the vehicle speeds, for regional delivery, average vehicle speed of 45 km/h is considered.

The problem is defined as complete graph $G(N, A)$ where $N=\{0\}U\{1,...,n\}U\{n+1\}$ defines the set of different nodes and $\{0\}$ and $\{n+1\}$ represent the depot and A is the set of arcs between each pair of nodes. The set of manufacturers is represented by N_c $=\{1,...,n\}$. For every arc (i,j) in A, the distance between nodes i and j is defined as d_{ij}. For all $i \in N_c$, there is a positive demand of q_i to be satisfied. For each manufacturer, there is an associated loading time which is directly proportional to the vehicle type but not to the demand of that manufacturer, because we are dealing with very small demands which are delivered in parcels. The demand at the depot is considered to be zero ($q_0 = 0$; $q_{n+1} = 0$). Each manufacturer should be visited once by one vehicle and routes must start and finish at the depot. An unlimited heterogeneous fleet of vehicles is available. This fleet is composed of $V = \{1,..., K\}$ different vehicle types, each with a different capacity (weight and volume) that must not be exceeded.

2.2   Environmental Objective

As point out by [12] and [14], CO_2 emissions depend on distance traveled, the weight carried by the vehicle, curb weight of the vehicle and its average speed. This indicates that using vehicles of adequate size reduces CO_2 emissions. Further, to calculate CO_2 emissions, the distance in the whole logistics network must be modeled: among producers themselves, as well as the distances between depot and producers. The formula given by [17- 19] was adapted to calculate the CO_2 emissions based on vehicle type k and average speed.

$$\varepsilon(d, X^P, k) = d * \left[(E_{full}^k - E_{empty}^k) * \frac{X^P}{C_k^P} + E_{empty}^k \right] \quad (1)$$

With:

d : distance traveled ; X^P : Total weight of transported parcels

C_k^P: Weight capacity of type k vehicle.

E_{full}^k : Emission of type k vehicle in full load

E_{empty}^k : Emission of empty type k vehicle.

The calculation of emission E_{full}^k and E_{empty}^k according to different transport capacity are based on the data provided by [18, 19] and can be calculated by knowing the value of the average speed of a route.

To consider the emission due to a vehicle manufacturing, we have developed a formula to calculate CO2 emissions:

$$\varepsilon(d, X^P, k) = d * \left[(E_{full}^k - E_{empty}^k) * \frac{X^P}{C_k^P} + E_{empty}^k + \frac{E_{manufacturing}(k)}{D(k)} \right] \quad (2)$$

Where:

$\boldsymbol{E}_{manufacturing}$: CO2 emission issued from manufacturing type k vehicle [18].

$\boldsymbol{D}$ (k) : maximum number of kilometers of type k vehicle in its whole life.

From emission function (equation 2), we define the objective function to optimize:

$$Minimize \sum_{k \in V} \sum_{(i,j) \in A} d_{ij} a_k x_{ij}^k + d_{ij} b_k y_{ij}^k \quad (3)$$

Where: $a_k = \left[E_{empty}^k + \frac{E_{manufacturing}(k)}{D(k)} \right]$; $b_k = \left[\frac{E_{full}^k - E_{empty}^k}{C_k^P} \right]$

This objective is divided into two parts: the first determines the CO2 emissions related to the movement of an empty vehicle while the second calculates emissions related to the weight loaded. The CO2 emissions are calculated with the travel distance, and vehicle specific conditions such as the gross weight of the vehicle (including the curb weight and the load carried) and the vehicle speed. Note that the factor "load" plays a significant role in our environmental model and it is this factor which determines the direction of vehicle route.

To assess economic and social costs of environmental optimization solutions, we adopted these equations:

-    Economic function:

$$Cost(\text{€}) = \sum_{k \in V} \sum_{j \in N} f_k x_{0j}^k + \sum_{k \in V} \sum_{(i,j) \in A} \alpha_k d_{ij} y_{ij}^k$$

$$+ \sum_{k \in V} \sum_{(i,j) \in A} \beta_k d_{ij} x_{ij}^k + \sum_{k \in V} \sum_{(i,j) \in A} \delta_k y_{ij}^k \quad (14)$$

-    Social function:

$$Social\ cost = \sum_{j=1}^N Q_k x_{0j}^k * \sum_{k \in V} \sum_{(i,j) \in A} d_{ij} x_{ij}^k$$

With:

y_{ij}^k : flows on arc (i, j) loaded on type k vehicle; d_{ij}= distance of the arc (i, j)

$x_{ij}^k = 1$ if type k vehicle is assigned to (i, j), and 0 otherwise.

n = number of manufacturers (nodes)   ; K = number of vehicle types;
Q_k = Total authorized weight of a type k vehicle ($Q_1 < ... < Q_K$);
f_k = fixed cost of a type k vehicle ($f_1 < ... < f_k$) ; β_k = cost /km of a type k vehicle;
α_k = cost /ton.km of a type k vehicle   ; δ_k = cost /ton of a type k vehicle;

The first part of the economic function gives the total fixed cost of the vehicles used and the others parts give the total variable routing cost. To appraise social impacts in our model, we consider parameters like traveled distance and the number and the size of used vehicles in the routing plan as a social indicator that can give us an idea of the non-measurable social indicators (Accident risk, noise and congestion).

3   Case Study

In order to test the model, we define a case study based on the data coming from the field. A collect center located in Saint-Etienne processes every day a pickup of parcels from different manufacturers. In a given day, 10 addresses are visited, located around the depot. The demand vector is given by table 1.

Table 1. Manufacturer's demand

Manufacturer	1	2	3	4	5	6	7	8	9	10
Demand (Ton)	0.09	0.11	0.07	0.5	0.7	0.03	0.11	0.06	0.05	0.6

3.1   Optimization Approach

First, the mathematical model is programmed in CPLEX. Then, MAPPOINT software is used to represent manufacturers and depot locations geographically. Then, the software provides a distance matrix between the various locations according to their address. Then, this distance matrix with other data from the case study are introduced in the model in the optimization software CPLEX. The execution of our optimization program provides the optimal routes according to environmental criteria. To operate our case study, we used a set of parameters, summarized in table 2:

Table 2. Parameters of optimization (adapted from [18])

Category	Type of vehicles	Total authorized weight (ton)	Useful load (ton)	Cost/km	Cost/ton	Fixed Cost	E_{Empty}^k (g/CO2)	E_{full}^k (g/CO2)	$E_{manufacturing}$ /km	Unloading time (min)
LDV*	1	1.5-2.5	0.7	0.15	0.04	104.84	68.4	68.4	8.3	7
HDV**	2	3.5	1.4	0.23	0.05	111.58	100.9	101	10.5	10
HDV**	3	5-6	2.84	0.25	0.07	111.58	107	154	14.2	17

*LDV: light duty vehicles   ** HDV: heavy duty vehicles

We would like to point out that only diesel engines conforming to the most recent engine standards were considered. To ensure optimal service to producers, the constraint of maximum duration of 4 hours was introduced for vehicle excursions.

3.1   Results

Our environmental optimization model in this case study presents the following results depending on fleet composition:

Table 3. Summary of results

	Fleet	DC	Environmental optimization			
		Type 1 (Best	Heterogeneous	Homogeneous		
		fleet)	Type (1; 2; 3)	Type 1	Type 2	Type 3
Assessment	Economic	262.2	110.73	129.97	91.158	117.52
	Environmental	17106	11142	11237	13665	14282
	Social	4460.6	524.3	1173.6	859.39	1225.9
	Distance	223.03	134.3	146.7	122.77	111.45
	Number of routes	10	3 : 2 of type 1 and 1 of type 2	4	2	2

Routes relevant to the use of different fleets are summarized in the following table:

Table 4. Routes of various scenarios

Fleet	Composition	Routes
Homoge-neous	Type 1	Route 1: (0,5,0); Route 2: (0,10,0); Route 3: (0,1,4,3,0); Route 4: (0,9,2,7,6,8,0);
	Type 2	Route 1: (0,2,7,6,8,5,0); Route 2: (0,9,3,1,4,10,0)
	Type 3	Route 1: (0,9,3,1,4,10,5,0); Route 2: (0,2,7,6,8,0)
Hetero-geneous	Type (1; 2; 3)	Type 1: Route 1 (0,9,2,7,6,8,0); Route 2 (0,1,4,3,0)
		Type 2: Route 1 (0,10,5,0)
		Type 3: No Route (Type not used)

For the case study discussed, the model gives different results depending on the fleet composition. First, the basic scenario with direct collect (DC) from the producers to the depot has to be assessed. In direct collect scenario, the use of a homogeneous fleet of type 1 vehicles gives better results than homogeneous fleets that consist sequentially of type 2 and type 3 vehicles.

The first finding is that environmental optimization for vehicle routing gives best results than direct collection scenario, whatever the composition of the fleet used and whatever the assessment criterion. This is explained by the fact that direct collection scenario requires more vehicles (10 vehicles) and travels longer distances.

The second important point with this model is that the use of a heterogeneous fleet gives the best environmental results and a good compromise of economic and social cost than the use of homogeneous fleet. Indeed, the use of a homogeneous fleet of type 2 vehicles significantly decreases the economic cost, but explodes at the same time the environmental and social costs. And in the same way, using a fleet of type 1 vehicles reduces the environmental cost but not the economic and social costs. The same remark can be made for the use of a fleet vehicle with type 3. Whereas the use of a heterogeneous fleet minimizes the environmental cost, while providing a great compromise for the economic and social cost. Another observation concerning environmental optimization is that routes to take depend on fleet composition.

4   Conclusion

The optimization of freight distribution for Small and Very Small Enterprises needs an improved shared logistics scheme to meet sustainable development requirements. This is especially true for agri-food supply chains, where the logistics flows of each company are characterized by small quantities, low volumes, and required to be delivered quickly. Most of the time, vehicles used for delivery are not adapted, too big, with a very low load rate, and therefore, the performance of their upstream logistics are not in line with the green objectives.

In this paper, the distribution network was designed with a single distribution center and the routing problem was solved taking into consideration the environmental pillar of sustainable development. Due to the constraints of low volume and limited time for delivery, the Fleet Size and Mix Vehicle Routing Problem (FSMVRP) was studied. Starting from the literature on this topic, new green objective functions were developed: the aim was to focus on CO_2 emissions minimization. Based on literature, a new function was developed to take into consideration the type of vehicle and the transported weight.

The aim of this paper was to prove the importance of the choice of the type and number of vehicles in environmental optimization, and that routes depend on fleet composition. Instead of having a sole assessment criterion, this paper suggests to evaluate results on three criteria, economic, environmental and social.

A linear multi-objective programming optimization model was developed that compare optimal environmental solutions depending on the fleet composition. Unfortunately, due to long computational delays, this model can support only small instances. Clearly, this difficulty should be dealt with in future work. This work represents the first step to designing shared logistics schemes that fulfill the requirements of sustainable development.

Acknowledgment. Authors would like to thank Region Rhône-Alpes for its financial support (Research Cluster GOSPI).

References

1. Lee, H.L., Padmanabhan, V., Whang, S.: The Bullwhip Effect in Supply Chain. Sloan Management Review, 93–102 (Spring 1997)
2. Bowersox, D.J., Closs, D.J., Keller, S.B.: How supply chain competency leads to business success. Supply Chain Management Review 4(4), 70–78 (2000)

3. Moutaoukil, A., Derrouiche, R., Neubert, G.: Modeling a logistics pooling strategy for agri-food sMEs. In: Camarinha-Matos, L.M., Scherer, R.J. (eds.) PRO-VE 2013. IFIP AICT, vol. 408, pp. 621–630. Springer, Heidelberg (2013)
4. Yakovleva, N., Sarkis, J., Sloan, T.: Sustainable benchmarking of supply chains: case of food industry. International Journal of Production Research 50 (2012)
5. Hasle, G., Kloster, O.: Industrial Vehicle Routing. In: Hasle, G., Lie, K.-A., Quak, E. (eds.) Geometric Modelling, Numerical Simulation, and Optimization, pp. 397–435. Springer, Heidelberg (2007)
6. Tarantilis, C.D., Kiranoudis, C.T., Vassiliadis, V.S.: A threshold accepting metaheuristic for the heterogeneous fixed fleet vehicle routing problem. European Journal of Operational Research 152, 148–158 (2004)
7. Bräysy, O., Dullaert, W., Hasle, G., Mester, D., Gendreau, M.: An Effective Multirestart Deterministic Annealing Metaheuristic for the Fleet Size and Mix Vehicle-Routing Problem with Time Windows. Transportation Science 42, 371–386 (2008)
8. Pasha, U., Hoff, A., Løkketangen, A.: The Shrinking and Expanding Heuristic for the Fleet Size and Mix Vehicle Routing Problem. Presented at the Communications – Scientific Letters, University of Zilina, pp. 6–13 (2013)
9. Gheysens, F., Golden, B., Assad, A.: A new heuristic for determining fleet size and composition. In: Gallo, G., Sandi, C. (eds.) Netflow at Pisa. Mathematical Programming Studies, pp. 233–236. Springer, Heidelberg (1986)
10. Erdoğan, S., Miller-Hooks, E.: A Green Vehicle Routing Problem. Transportation Research Part E: Logistics and Transportation Review 48, 100–114 (2012)
11. Bektaş, T., Laporte, G.: The Pollution-Routing Problem. Transportation Research Part B: Methodological 45, 1232–1250 (2011)
12. Figliozzi, M.: Vehicle Routing Problem for Emissions Minimization. Journal of the Transportation Research Board 2197, 1–7 (2010)
13. Kopfer, H.W., Schönberger, J., Kopfer, H.: Reducing greenhouse gas emissions of a heterogeneous vehicle fleet. Flex. Serv. Manuf. J. 26, 221–248 (2014)
14. Ubeda, S., Arcelus, F.J., Faulin, J.: Green logistics at Eroski: A case study. International Journal of Production Economics 131, 44–51 (2011)
15. Scott, C., Urquhart, N., Hart, E.: Influence of topology and payload on CO_2 optimised vehicle routing. In: Di Chio, C., Brabazon, A., Di Caro, G.A., Ebner, M., Farooq, M., Fink, A., Grahl, J., Greenfield, G., Machado, P., O'Neill, M., Tarantino, E., Urquhart, N. (eds.) EvoApplications 2010, Part II. LNCS, vol. 6025, pp. 141–150. Springer, Heidelberg (2010)
16. Ntziachristos, L., Samaras, Z.: COPERT III Computer programme to calculate emissions from road transport - Methodology and emission factors — European Environment Agency (EEA) (Publication No. 49), Copenhagen, Denmark (2000)
17. Pan, S., Ballot, E., Fontane, F.: The reduction of greenhouse gas emissions from freight transport by pooling supply chains. International Journal of Production Economics 143, 86–94 (2013)
18. Jancovici, M.: Bilan carbone. Guide des facteurs d'émissions - Calcul des facteurs d'émissions et sources bibliographiques utilisées. ADEME France (2007)
19. Hickman, J., Hassel, D., Joumard, R., Samaras, Z., Sorenson, S.: Methodology for calculating transport emissions and energy consumption (1999)

The Domestication of Global
XPS at Local Production Sites

Hanne O. Finnestrand and Kristoffer Magerøy

SINTEF Technology and Society, Industrial Management, Trondheim, Norway
{hanne.o.finnestrand,kristoffer.mageroy}@sintef.no

Abstract. Inspired by the success created by Toyota and its Toyota Production System (TPS), many large multinational corporations have developed their own company-specific production systems (XPSs). However, it varies to what degree local production sites have made use of the global corporate's PS and in what way it has had any effect on the local site's work practice. In this paper we discuss the technical, social, and cultural factors of the implementation of XPS through the lenses of domestication theory. This study indicates that a rational implementation of global XPS' is all practical, symbolic, and cognitive, and that development of new technology as well as production systems is a multi-sited process. Hence, corporates as well as local sites need to take account for how local managers and employees are involved in the implementation process.

Keywords: XPS, domestication, case study, operations management.

1 Introduction

Inspired by the success created and maintained by Toyota and its Toyota Production System (TPS), many large multinational corporations have developed their own company-specific production systems (XPSs) [1]. Examples are Boing Production System, Electrolux Manufacturing System, Elkem Business System and Volvo Production System. While 'PS' is an abbreviation for 'production system' or something similar (e.g. TPS), the 'X' stands for the company name.

The amount of foreign investments in the Norwegian industry have grown substantially the last decade, and today foreign owned firms constitute 30% of the employment in the industry [2]. In numbers it has nearly been a doubling from just above 800 companies in 2003 to nearly 1600 companies in 2010. Combined with the growing numbers of XPSs, this leads to an increase of Norwegian manufacturing firms facing the challenge of implementing such a system. However, it varies to what degree local production sites have made use of the corporates' production systems and in what way it has had any effect on the local sites' work practice. Hence, an emerging and important question is: How can we understand the process of implementing global XPS in local production companies? In order to study this, we have made use of domestication theory and have addressed this through a multiple case-study of three Norwegian manufacturing companies owned by global corporates.

B. Grabot et al. (Eds.): APMS 2014, Part II, IFIP AICT 439, pp. 458–465, 2014.
© IFIP International Federation for Information Processing 2014

Domestication - A Theoretical Introduction. In order to understand the technical, social, and cultural factors [3] of the implementation of XPS, we make use of domestication theory. Domestication in a figurative sense is to make something taken from an outside world applicable, meaningful and useful to a local world. The concept was taken up by the field of science and technology studies to describe how innovations and new technologies are appropriated by users [4]. Domestication theory holds that technological adoption is an interactive process, opposed to a view where technology forces culture and organization to be reshaped – also called technology determinism.

Within studies of sociology of technology, domestication is a concept developed to describe and analyse processes of technology acceptance, rejection and use [5]. In this paradigm, *technology* is usually understood as a particular artefact such as domestication of the car [6], domestication of multimedia technologies [7], or the domestication of the mobile phone [8]. An XPS is not one specific technology or artefact. It is rather a bundle of technologies and practices, and although several companies have made efforts in designing their own XPSs, there is still a tight relationship between different XPSs today and the technical understanding of the TPS and lean production [1].

When we chose to analyse the implementation processes of XPSs within this framework, it is because domestication theory goes longer than contingency theory [9] or organizational learning theories [10] in including the social dimensions of implementation processes. More specifically, domestication theory focuses on the construction of meaning; hence Sørensen et al. [11] argue that to domesticate technology means to negotiate its meaning and practice in a dynamic, interactive manner. They claim that this negotiation implies that technologies as well as social relations are transformed. Based on this, Sørensen et al. [11] developed three main, generic sets of dimensions when analysing the implementation of technology.

The first dimension is the construction of a set of practices related to the new technology. This could mean *routines* of using the technology, but also the establishment and development of institutions to support and regulate this. Second, the *construction of meaning* of the technology, including the role the technology eventually could play in relation to the identities of the actors involved, and finally, the cognitive processes related to *learning of practice* as well as meaning [8], [11]. The latter dimension requires that the practice or system is integrated into social practice of action. We will make use of these three features when analysing the empirical material.

2   Methodology

We have carried out instrumental case studies in three different manufacturing companies in order to develop an understanding of domestication of XPS. An instrumental case study provides insight into a particular issue, redraw generalizations, or build theory [12]. As with most instrumental case studies, the research team wanted to build new theory by building on and testing existing theory – namely how domestication theory known from science and technology studies [4] informs the implementation of a company specific production system, also called XPS. The multiple case study design enables us to reveal complementary aspects of the phenomenon.

The research team has made individual case reports for all three companies based on mainly three data sources: (1) semi-structural interviews with key personnel such as production managers, shop stewards, HR-managers, and blue collar operators; (2) informal conversations with operators when visiting the production; and (3) available information on the companies' web pages and other written materials developed mainly in order to promote the company and the company group.

3   Case Studies

The presentation of each case study starts with a short introduction to the company, followed by a summary of the most relevant findings. In order to anonymize the companies, we have named them company A, B, and C.

Company A. Company A has about 115 employees and develops and produces advanced tools for a world-wide market within mechanical and petroleum industry. Some years ago the company was bought by its exclusive sale channel; a high-technology, engineering group with advanced products and representations in more than 130 countries. First, this change did not cause any implementation of an XPS, however later the corporate launched a common improvement program.

The company has gone through many changes over the last years, also before becoming part of the corporate. For many years they invested in organizational factors such as establishment of autonomous teams, improved communication within and between production teams, some of the lean principles, and widespread union-management cooperation. The way company A has chosen to involve both the union and production workers as a development partner is quite unique. Their organizational approach has led to a number of extensive development projects with the aim to decentralize decision making to the shop floor in order to be more efficient and flexible. Clearly, the corporate bought a flexible organization capable and used to change.

Also, just before company A merged with the corporate, the company moved into totally new premises. When moving from dark and crowded premises at the old production site, the production workers could suddenly enjoy panoramic view through enormous windows and eat delicious lunch in the company's cafeteria.

In the beginning, both employees and managers found the transition of ownership to be quite smooth. The difference was in most cases described as positive. The managers claimed that the corporate offers a world market for their core product and increases the general robustness of the plant. The employees emphasized that being part of a larger corporate gives them the opportunity to work at other facilities.

Also, in the first two-three years after the transition company A was allowed to operate pretty much as they wanted – or at least the same way as prior to the acquisition. The HR-manager described the autonomy and freedom like this: *"I went to a crash course at the [corporate] in 2009 where we went through the HR-practices at [corporate]. They advised us to make use of those things we liked. They had extensive experience and many good work practices, but we didn't have to copy everything"*. However, later on this changed quite a lot when the company group decided to implement a corporate production system and we received the following e-mail from the production manager: *"We will increase the speed of Lean production implementation; this will be done through a global [corporate] production system"*. The HR-manager explained that she experienced much more standardization within the corporate through this process and now everything had to be related to the corporate's visions. Also, because she had to follow up all the new systems, and even participate in developing them, she felt that she was not as available in the production area as before. She said: *"the ambition is to be more available for the employees, but in practice I'm not"*.

Company B. Company B is a first tier supplier to the global aviation industry, manufacturing highly complex engine products and employs approximately 600 people. As the company has been introduced to a new XPS twice the last decade, this case study provides interesting findings in that respect. The last change was a result of shifting ownership, which also led to increased attention from the head quarter as the company is now part of a major business area within the corporate, in opposite to being part of a business area only constituting a few percent of the total activity.

When introduced to the first XPS, the company experienced that they did not get any clear advice on how and where to start the implementation process. However, they ended up with a quick fix implementation upfront due to a scheduled assessment. The result was that the assessment got a lot more attention than the long term continuous work improvement. The former COO named this way of working as *"a Norwegian manufacturing culture – one based on quick fixes"*. This working culture can be further explained as a task force of engineers moving continuously around in the factory to solve present challenges regarding quality, delivery, etc.

Another visible characteristic of the first attempt was the lack of commitment among leaders. They did not oppose it, but could indisputable been more supportive. It is reasonable to believe that the lack of commitment is in coherence to the little focus put on training. Only a couple of white-collar employees were sent to the corporate academy. In contrast, the implementation of the second XPS involved an extensive training program embracing everyone within the factory and starting with the top management. The program was mandatory and ended with an evaluation focused on productivity. Increased training has resulted in a management team more dedicated to lean than previously. In addition, each site in the corporate needs to assign one continuous improvement leader, providing even more focus and leadership.

As a consequence of the increased focus at productivity, there are now much higher expectations to short-term results. One manager shares his concern: *"We have an increased focus on on-time delivery and details regarding flow, quality etc., this is to such an extent that I'm afraid it overruns the need for also maintaining a long term focus"*. He experiences an anglo-american style of leadership within the corporate, and explains that *"it is taken for granted that manager at the top has detailed insight into everything"*. This is quite opposite to the Scandinavian management practice.

Company C. Company C has recently been in a situation very much like to company B, as a change of ownership have led to the introduction of a new XPS. The company counts around 550 employees and operates in the automotive industry, now as a part of a global division within that field.

A couple of years after introducing the new XPS, company C experienced that the implementation varied extensively among departments. People in many departments did not feel a belonging to the lean based regime and some related to it as one specific tool, e.g. 5S, the visual boards or even cleaning. *"For many of us out here, the corporate system is equal with cleaning"* one shop-floor worker commented. The company therefore developed a roadmap for further implementation to secure a more standardized way, and many employees have recently gone through a course. While interviewees holding administrative or support positions regard the course valuable, operators regard it less valuable and say they lack follow-up and do not clearly see how to utilize their new knowledge into their daily work. One respondent puts it this way: *"The course has little to do with our everyday work. It would be better if we looked upon and focused at what we do daily."*

Not only do the employees struggle with getting a grasp of the content of the new XPS, they are also struggling with seeing the differences compared to the previous, and more self-developed operating system. One experienced worker comments: *"To my understanding it is pretty much the same. It just changes name from year to year."*

Another issue that appeared through the interviews was management involvement. Shop floor workers have experienced less commitment among team leaders and top managers than before introducing the latest XPS. One comments that *"they [managers] must be out here in the production and look at what we do. [...] it is important that they [managers] are visible in the production from time to time"*.

4   Discussion

Routines. Introduced to a new XPS, companies need new practices, routines and institutions to domesticate the system effectively. Basically, the corporate system must be acquired and placed in the company [11]. As an XPS normally contains a vast amount of principles, tools and techniques, the local production unit "receives" a large package of such elements when introduced to an XPS. However, as the case studies show, both company B and C have received this package without a following guideline or a schedule for how to grasp it. In company B this resulted in a shallow implementation only due to some assessments, while in company C the degree of implementation varied extensively among departments leading them to make their own roadmap for further work. Such a roadmap would probably have been the solution for company B as well, if they were not introduced to a new XPS that early.

Furthermore, the findings reveal that the commitment to the previous self-developed operating system in company C was higher than the commitment to the [corporate] operating system. A locally developed roadmap for further implementation will probably help on this, but the effects still remains to be observed. The diverging perception among employees regarding the recently given courses indicates that the implementation process needs to be adapted even at a department level. All together this shows the importance of local adjustments and adaptation.

Construction of Meaning. Leaning on domestication theory, the actors that must relate to the XPS usually negotiate the meaning of it and practice in a dynamic, interactive manner. This negotiation implies that the XPS or work systems, as well as social relations are transformed. People read their previous experiences and agendas into new experiences, and the way they talk about it, use it or even misuse it influences the character of the XPS. In other words, the cultural appropriation of the XPS in a local setting is a multidimensional process. We see interesting and informing examples of this process in our cases. In company A, the transition from local own company with its own system to the global corporate system was described as "smooth" by the local managers. It is likely that their freedom and permission to choose practices from the corporate's "tool box" explains this quite seamless merging. However, it is not unlikely that the positive experience and attitude toward the takeover was more a result of new facilities. As one of the production workers said: *"We moved right before we became part of [corporate], and those things we were negative towards before was the facilities at the old place. The new place was like a dream".* She continues by saying: *"It is difficult to say what's a result of what; the new facility or being part of [the corporate]".* This illustrates well how seemingly random events have great influence on well-planned strategies – events that can turn plans and strategies in wanted directions or in undesirable directions just because the local company with its employees ascribe certain meaning to the corporate's new strategy.

The construction of meaning is also evident in company C. For instance, it varied to what degree the different departments in the company had made use of the XPS although they were actually offered the same XPS. Of course, the implementation phase in itself is important here; employees who do not have any or limited knowledge of the XPS will not be able to make use of the tools and work forms. However, this doesn't seem to be the case with company C as the employees had experienced with an earlier XPS. But the previous experiences influence how the company see or understand the new XPS, and in this case primarily two practices of action are evident. First how the XPS, as based on lean manufacturing, is interpreted as a collection of tools such as 5S only, and responded to accordingly, and second that the employees interpret it as *"pretty much the same"* and therefore continue the same way as before. The employees lack of ownership and ignorance of the XPS both undermine it as a useful system and in some cases turns it into something it was not meant to be by the designers, such as a *"corporate system equal with cleaning"* or local practices just with a different name.

Learning of Practice. Domestication is both pragmatic and a potential issue of conflict. New technology and "know-how" must be domesticated in order to be integrated into local culture, but not all new technology and work forms are domesticated, and different people domesticate different kinds of knowledge and technology [11]. Conflicts arising from domestication may be related to different local interests and roles such as gender, age, and managers versus subordinates. Furthermore, conflicts may be related to the relationship between the XPS designers on the one hand and the local actors' creativity and ability to make use of the new system on the other. The implementation and use of the XPS is understood in relation to the company's social practice of action or culture such as how the company carries out leadership, their values, and company specific "do and don'ts". These may or may not be explicit and articulated by the managers and the employees. In other words, in what way the XPS eventually is embedded in the local site's social practice of action is dependent on how well it fits with the actors' self-understanding and culture.

In both company A and B, potential conflicts in the domestication process seem to be ascribed in what the companies describe as a Scandinavian work form. In company B, the corporate's management style with *"increased focus on on-time delivery and everyday details"*, may fit badly with the local company's self-understanding as highly autonomous on all levels. The same is valid for company A which in addition to an autonomous work force has invested a lot of time, effort and pride in involving both union and production workers as development partners. It is possible that the XPS must be adapted to this social practice of action or that the local enterprise ascribes the XPS new meaning previously described as construction of meaning. In any case, the domestication of XPS will not leave it unchanged, and it is reasonable that the local company with its employees will make use of it differently as a result of the company's routines and institutions. Furthermore, such will affect how the users interpret the new system and give new meaning or re-construct it, and finally how well the XPS fit with the users' self-understanding, culture, or social practice of action.

5   Implications

In this paper we have made use of domestication theory in order to understand the technical, social, and cultural factors regarding the implementation of XPSs in three different production companies. Etymologically speaking, domestication is related to the home, the domestic setting. However, we have used the word as an analytical concept in order to bring new understanding into the implementation process of new work- and production systems designed by somebody who is not the end user of the system. There is however some differences between the domestication of technology in a broader sense at home and in the work place. The implementation of XPSs in companies are usually acquired by managers and support functions in the corporate in order to achieve some goals [1], and even if the process of implementation may not be as rational as many managers and consultants want it to be, managers are usually able to influence the outcome by controlling the information and training offered to employees [11].

In line with theory and empirical work on domestication of technology and the analysis of the three cases in this paper, we will emphasize particularly three implications when implementing global XPSs in companies. First, this study indicates that a rational implementation is not solely an instrumental action. The implementation phase is practical, symbolic, and cognitive. Second, in many cases the local use of an XPS is embedded in an asymmetric relationship between the assumed expertise of its designers and the assumed non-expertise of its users. In other words, there exists an idea of correct and incorrect usage that is predefined by the designers and the corporate. In principle, users are supposed to acquire knowledge from the designer in order to be able to use the XPS in the correct manner. Domestication theory represented by Sørensen et al [11] confronts this linear understanding of design and implementation and stress that the end product is designed through a multi-sited process.

Finally, because an implementation process is all practical, symbolic, and cognitive, and because development of new technology as well as production systems is a multi-sited process, corporates as well as local sites need to take account for how local managers and employees are involved in the implementation process. One way of achieving this could be by making the multi-sited process explicit and involve employees and unions early on in developing a roadmap and a training program specific for the local production site. Hence the effects of such could be of interest to further research.

References

1. Netland, T.H.: Exploring the phenomenon of company-specific production systems: One-best-way or own-best-way? International Journal of Production Research 51, 1084–1097 (2012)
2. Ulstein, H., Günfeld, L.A., Ekrann, G.: Indutrielt eierskap i Norge. Menon Business Economics (11) (2012)
3. Bakardjieva, M., Smith, R.: The Internet in Everyday Life: Computer Networking from the Standpoint of the Domestic User. New Media & Society 3, 67–83 (2001)
4. Hirsch, E., Silverstone, R.: Introduction. In: Hirsch, E., Silverstone, R. (eds.) Consuming Technologies: Media and Information in Domestic Spaces. Routledge, London (1992)
5. Berker, T., Hartmann, M., Punie, Y., Ward, K.: Introduction. In: Berker, T., Hartmann, M., Punie, Y., Ward, K. (eds.) Domestication of Media and Technology, McGraw-Hill International (2006)
6. Østby, P.: Flukten fra Detroit: Bilens integrasjon i det norske samfunnet. Universitetet i Trondheim. Senter for teknologi og samfunn (1995)
7. Brosveet, J., Sørensen, K.H.: Fishing for fun and profit? National domestication of multimedia: the case of Norway. The Information Society 16, 263–276 (2000)
8. Sørensen, K.: Domestication: the enactment of technology. In: Berker, T., Hartmann, M., Punie, Y., Ward, K. (eds.) Domestication of Media and Technology. McGraw-Hill International (2006)
9. Swink, M., Nair, A.: Capturing the competitive advantages of AMT: Design–manufacturing integration as a complementary asset. Journal of Operations Management 25, 736–754 (2007)
10. Argyris, C., Schön, D.: Organizational Learning: A theory of action perspective. Addison-Wesley, Reading (1978)
11. Sørensen, K., Aune, M., Hatling, M.: Against linearity – On the Cultural Appropriation of Science and Technology. In: Dierkes, M., Grote, C. (eds.) Between Understanding and Trust: The Public, Science and Technology, Harwood, Amsterdam (2000)
12. Stake, R.E.: Multiple Case Study Analysis. The Guilford Press, New York (2005)

An Innovative Production Paradigm to Offer Customized and Sustainable Wood Furniture Solutions Exploiting the Mini-Factory Concept

Paolo Pedrazzoli[1], Franco Antonio Cavadini[2], Donatella Corti[1],
Andrea Barni[1], and Tommaso Luvini[1]

[1] University of Applied Sciences and Arts of Southern Switzerland, ISTePS, Manno, Switzerland
{donatella.corti,luca.canetta,alessandro.fontana}@supsi.ch
[2] Synesis, Lomazzo, Italy
franco.cavadini@synesis-consortium.eu

Abstract. To face increasing competitive pressures, European industry must develop methods and enabling technologies towards a personalized, customer oriented and sustainable manufacturing. This statement is well understood by many companies, shared by policy maker at the European Commission (e.g. as per the "Factory of the Future" multi-annual road-map), and empowered by the current funding programmes for industrial research (Horizon2020). Manufacturers are demanded to merge the need to be reactive towards customer needs and wishes (customized products), with the requisite to be proactive towards ecological and social impact (sustainable products). This concept points out two key elements whose impact on manufacturing is complex and interdepended: Customization and Sustainability. Within the CTC 3-year project methods and innovative enabling technologies are developed and integrated to enable a local flexible manufacturing of green personalized furniture close to the customer.

Keywords: furniture sector, mini-factory, short supply chain, green label, customization.

1 Production System Innovation in the Furniture Sector

Europe is a major player in furniture on a global scale, with a total of more than 151.000 companies of which 95% are SMEs. Despite increasingly fierce global competition and significant relocation of manufacturing to low-wage countries, furniture continues to represent one of Europe's major industrial sectors with an annual turnover of more than 130 Billion Euro, and a total workforce of 1,4 million. Manufacturers in this sectors have 1) to become more agile and flexible, in response to the fast rate in which market trends change, demanding manufacturing infrastructures that can produce higher variations in smaller quantities and 2) to introduce personalized products and services whose added value can trigger market acceptance. In this framework, environment intangibles (such as environmental pollution, waste and energy consumption) are also recognized as urgent and the furniture sector faces the

B. Grabot et al. (Eds.): APMS 2014, Part II, IFIP AICT 439, pp. 466–473, 2014.

challenge to actively consider and control those factors as well. This is because both customers demand sustainable products and governments are willing to sharpen regulations to commit companies to improve.

An innovative production paradigm aimed at supporting the European Industry to adapt to global competitive pressures is being developed by the European-funded project CTC. Within this the three-year project started in 2013, methods and innovative enabling technologies are developed and integrated to enable a local flexible manufacturing of green personalized products close to the customer in terms of features offered, place of fabrication, time to deliver, and cost. The integration of sustainability and customization issues is a promising strategy as stressed in recent works (e.g. [1]). This vision is implemented and demonstrated within a European industrial sector of excellence: the furniture sector. The ultimate implementation envisions a *"green factory behind a glass pane"* directly in the shopping mall, where the customer witnesses the manufacturing of its personalized furniture.

In this paper the foreseen system and its impacts are described. First, the pillars the new production paradigm will be based on are introduced highlighting how they go beyond existing solutions. Then, an overview of the foreseen mini-factory layout and functioning is described before presenting the actors who will interact with it. Expected impacts of the proposed concept are discussed before drawing conclusions.

2   The Production Paradigm's Pillars

Main pillars shaping the new production paradigm and their corresponding innovativeness are summarized in the following points:

Formalized Design Approach (and related software technologies) to empower "design to manufacturing in one step" (which also includes the design finalization carried out by the customer himself). The development of a formalized furniture design approach refers to the tools and engineering methods to make the design seamlessly compatible with the manufacturing phase (fostering a design approach standardization), and must not be mistaken for the imposition of a common design style: distinctiveness of styles must be preserved as a key added value. CTC tools are meant to approach product design from a holistic perspective, integrating design methodologies in plug in software for currently available technologies in the woodworking sector. The integration of 3DCE and DfX methodologies promoted by CTC in current software tools and the reduction of complexity in the transition from CAD to CAM will foster a simplified approach to product definition according with an efficient product manufacturing. Starting from the analysis of the state-of-the-art in design methodologies ([2]; [3]; [4]; [5]) and tools (e.g. [6] and [7] for configurators), a process will be developed allowing the simultaneous generation of product design and reliable manufacturing data leading to a 50% reduction of "design to production" time of 50% and a 80% reduction of the time to market for new products development.

Mini-factory Production System Model that can be easily and quickly instantiated in local green factories, and whose processes and machines can be driven directly by the formalized design process. This model represents the factory "to be" blueprints, its logistic structure and short JIT supply chain management approach that takes into consideration existing example of mini-factory (e.g. [8]). It can be regarded as the basis for the "factory franchising" concept, where the manufacturing system can be instantiated locally with minimal production design effort. Thanks to this new system a 60% decrease in throughput time in production is expected as well as an increased ability to rapidly follow market by means of fast production and delivery of customised furniture. Reduced environmental impact because of no unsold or long term storage of products and reduction of work in progress thanks to smart order management and responsive supply chain are also interesting improvements from both economic and sustainable point of view.

Woodwork machining system able to empower the "Close to the Customer" concept. Main target is the development of a next generation woodworking system with high flexibility, high safety standards and ease of use with low production cost and low environmental impact, in particular for very small batches and JIT production, ultimately delivering very quickly to the customer. The system will be empowered by advanced HMI control and automatic machine set-up, and will then run continuously as in flow- like production. As the factory is meant to be instantiated "close to the customer", the machining system must specifically tackle issues such as dust extraction and noise control. Technological advances will allow the achievement of a reduction of CO_2 emissions, lower training time and a safer working environment.

A *CTC Green Label* in order to bring to customer awareness of the uniqueness and advantages of the production process, based on ISO 14955 extension to woodworking machines and on the FSC (Forest Stewardship Council), a certificate label will be developed. The label, also taking advantage of the development of a proper assessment model, is meant to be recognizable and unified, but still articulated and capable of highlighting local peculiarity.

The most challenging aspect of the CTC project is the need for a deep integration between the different modules that expose its multifaceted functionalities. The focus of the validation and demonstration activities will be therefore towards an effective integration of all CTC reference framework modules, because it is in their completed coordination that resides the success of the project. If any of the composing elements is innovative in of its specific characteristics, it is the coordinated effort for creating a much shorter production chain that really transforms the mini-factory into a major technological breakthrough. The success of the proposed production paradigm will be thus based on the exploitation of the above-mentioned innovations, but, above all, from the integration of all of them in an innovative business model delivering value through a local flexible manufacturing of green personalized products close to the customer. The economic potential of this concept lays in the possibility of instantiating several mini-factories all over Europe creating a franchising network.

3   The Reference Architecture

The foreseen functioning of a CTC mini-factory is introduced to give an idea of how the innovative elements will be interacting with each other to enable production and sale of sustainable and customized pieces of furniture close to the customers. The description tells how the CTC mini-factory will look like to a potential visitor once it will be running. Peculiarities of the CTC system at both factory and supply chain level are pointed out to provide an overview of what are the envisioned results upon project completion. A schematic representation of what is being presented is shown in Figure 1. The CTC mini-factory finds its ideal location in a shopping mall where both the sales area (CTC-shop) and the production area (CTC-factory) are located next to each other and are accessible by people visiting the mall. The CTC-system gets started when the Customer enters the CTC-shop and, with the support of a trained CTC-operator, customizes the furniture he/she is interested in using a user-friendly configurator. The design of furniture is driven by a parametric portfolio of products that has been predefined by CTC designers coherently with the functional constraints of the mini-factory. Once the furniture project (a single piece of furniture or a complete room) is finalized and the customer is satisfied with the offer, an order is generated and sent to the CTC-factory. Machine instructions are automatically created to command the behavior of the mini-factory. A real-time update of production data allows the customer to monitor the processing status of his/her order other than to increase the efficiency of the production system itself. A high level of integration of informative systems is one of the main features the CTC-system will rely on. In fact, a smooth flow of information from the idea generation to the production will allow a lean fulfillment of orders in short times. The details of the factory have to be carefully designed along with the supporting supply chain and material handling system. The idea is to have a short supply chain in order to favor the creation of a local suppliers base and to keep the level of inventories within the factory as low as possible. Raw material suppliers will be constantly managed by CTC mini-factory, coherently with short-term planning of the production, in order to grant adequate replenishment of stocks. Strong agreements with fast couriers are exploited for quick logistics. In so doing, a small inbound warehouse able to cover the needs of a few orders is enough. An automated warehouse will be set up in this place so that raw materials (panels) will be moved directly to the production line coherently with the production plan. At the end of the production line a packaging area is setup that will act also as outbound warehouse. So at this point the material is ready to be collected by local couriers for fast delivery to the customer. For the assembly phase, the idea of the project, is to leave the customer the possibility to choose between a specialized operator or the kit for Do-It-Yourself. Finally, it is worth of mention the attention that in the CTC-system it will be paid to the waste management. Production waste has to be managed in a life-cycle conscious way, considering main potential way of treatment: re-cycled through direct agreement with raw material suppliers, burnt for energy generation, or sent to local landfills. To sum up it can be said that a compact and lean system is envisioned that will guarantee the achievement of excellent performance in terms of both customer service (short delivery time and high level of customization) and production efficiency. The design of a proper supply chain is important as well to reach this level of performance.

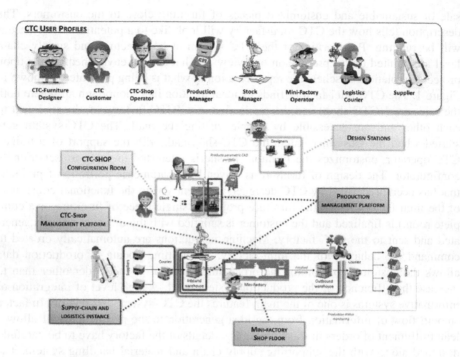

Fig. 1. Reference architecture of the CTC mini-factory, and corresponding users

The CTC Users

Complementary to the innovative modules of CTC, and taking into account that they become the principal interface between the mini-factory as a system on one side, and its users on the other one, a certain set of "CTC user profiles" has been defined. These roles have been selected as those strictly necessary for the good operation of the mini-factory. They are:

- The CTC-Furniture Designer, who will prepare the parametric product portfolio;
- The CTC Customer, interacting with the mini-factory to obtain a customized furniture element;
- The CTC-Shop Operator, interacting with the customer for the product design;
- The Production Manager, supervising the whole mini-factory;
- The Stock Manager, specialized in managing inventory;
- The Mini-factory Operator, capable of operating the whole shop-floor;
- The Logistics Courier, to grant fast delivery of packages;
- The Supplier, to create a really short and integrated supply chain.

The term "user profiles" has been adopted because it is not conceived to represent the physical people who will interact with the CTC pilot, but the roles needed to make the factory work.

4   Impacts Generated by the Implementation of the Concept

The basic idea of CTC is to move the factory directly where the customer is used to shopping: a green mini-factory is set up behind a glass pane in the shopping mall. The main target of the project is a customer segment with an average money availability who is willing to pay for a higher level of customization and who is aware of sustainability issues. The type of selected items and the location of the factory make the young and middle-aged people with children the most interested customers category. The pilot mini-factory will offer pieces of furniture for bedrooms for children and living rooms. The business model behind the diffusion of the CTC mini-factory is based on the idea that the same factory model is installed in shopping malls in different European countries. Local tastes and needs can be taken into account when the product is designed in the point-of-sale, yet the production system is a common one (not its supply chain, though). As a whole, expected benefits from the CTC project will have a significant impact on the European economy, also considering the high number of involved actors in the sector. Implementation of the CTC Mini-Factory will have a major impact on the wood furniture sector for both customers and manufacturers: the creation of a franchising network, for example, could reshape the traditional supply chain and leading to benefits not only in economic terms, but also from the sustainability perspective. The mini-factory is characterized by a set of machines and equipment strictly close to each other not only for the physical proximity, but also from the management point of view. The factory can work without work-in-progress since single orders are moved along the production system. The level of automation is high: the design software is linked with the production resources and the working instructions are automatically sent to machines that are reconfigured automatically with almost null setup times. The system thus works continuously avoiding time losses due to non-productive times - like queues or set ups- that are typical in the current production environment of this sector. The level of embedded technology is so advanced that in the best performing mini-factory a single operator is needed to run the whole system and he does not need to be skilled. In order for the operator to monitor the system, it will be possible to rely on a centralized control panel that do not requires specific knowledge of the single machine. Such configuration of the production system will allow the promising short delivery times (48 hours) and the offer of high level of level of customization.

The initial investment to set up one CTC mini- factory is expected to vary from a minimum of 330.000 Euro and a maximum of 580.000 Euro. In an IKEA shop, the price for a set of pieces of wooden furniture for a living room including TV and media furniture combined with storage units, a bookshelf, a desk and a coffee table could range approximately between 350 and 1900 Euro. A reasonable price for a living room offered under the CTC label should be around 2500 Euro.

A possible average price for a CTC bedroom for children including one single bed, a desk, one armoire with 3 doors, 2 shelves, a bookshelf and a chest of drawers could be set equal to 2000 Euro, whilst a rough estimation for a living room offered under the CTC label including TV and media furniture combined with storage units, a bookshelf, a desk and a coffee table should be around 2500 Euro.

A Network of Mini-factory

The CTC mini-factory finds its ideal location in the European shopping malls. The evolution of the European retail environment calls for more shopping centre space in the near future: it was estimated by Experian [9] that the retail industry would have been the third fastest growing industry between 2005 and 2016 with an average growing rate of 2.6% per year. Considering both their current base and the developing potentialities, the malls can be considered as a fertile ground for the propagation of the CTC mini-factory production model in Europe. The selection of the location for installing the first mini-factories is crucial to get the expected results. Italy, UK and France are the best candidates: their high number of shopping malls [10] is a proof that customers are more used to visit shopping malls and are probably more enthusiastic to experience shopping-related novelties.

In order to identify a reasonable numbers of mini-factories in the hypothetical franchising network that could make the business model a profitable and successful one, the main chains competing in the consumer "do-it-yourself" market sector at the European level have been used as a reference point (i.e. Bricocenter, Leroy Merlin, Obi center, Castorama). On the one hand, the production and delivery mode used by the CTC concept is unique: companies considered as competitors in terms of product types and volumes use different sale channels and their network structure couldn't represent a valid reference. On the other hand, the choice of basing the factory in the shopping mall makes it necessary to take into consideration features characterizing the retail world and their adaptation to the CTC concept. Using the specialized chains based on the "do-it-yourself" mode seems a good choice since, though their offer is based on catalogues, it could be assumed that their customers share some interests with the ones targeted by the CTC mini-factory. Customers who like the "do-it-yourself" products pay attention to the sustainability aspect and are willing to spend time to choose single components and to put their own efforts to get the product that at the best fits with their needs. Considering the level of diffusion of the "do-it-yourself" chains in Europe and assuming that the CTC mini-factory network will be, at least in the medium term, it is reasonable to assume that, in 5-year time, an overall number of 150-180 CTC mini factories will be operating in different European countries. The opening of an average of 30 centres per year is aligned with the expected efforts to install a new mini factory. The overall expected economic impact can be quantified approximately in 360 mln Euro of early turnover generated by a mini-factory network of 150 units. This value corresponds to a 3% market share in value of the European market for the two segments of interest (bedrooms and living rooms). This esteem is likely to underestimate the business of the mini-factory since a smart capacity management policy could generate additional turnover by saturating the available capacity producing pieces of furniture for third parties. Widening the scope, a less easily quantifiable, yet important, business volume is induced in the supply chain. In this phase of the analysis it is not possible to provide precise values, but, for sure, it will contribute to amplify the CTC impact at the European level.

5   Conclusion

This paper first provided an overall understanding of a new paradigm in furniture production, based on the local flexible manufacturing of green personalized furniture close to the customer in terms of features offered (customization), place of fabrication (mini-factory in the shopping-mall), time to deliver (logistics arrangements), and cost (from customization to mass-customization). It then focused on the impact that such a paradigm will have on European economy once implemented. While still enduring fierce competition and relocation, Europe is nonetheless a major player in furniture on a global scale, where personalization and sustainability will represent a key strategy for its future development and success. Whereas the CTC paradigm is implemented and tested in the wood-working sector, the project consortium firmly believes that new business solutions meant to empower consumers as designers, manufacturers to produce in a distributed and small scale manner, and suppliers to be more flexible and demand-driven will be mandatory for most European industrial sectors.

References

1. Boër, C.R., Pedrazzoli, P., Bettoni, A., Sorlini, M.: Mass Customization and Sustainability. An assessment framework and industrial implementation.Springer (2013)
2. Herrmann, J.W., Cooper, J., Gupta, S.K., Hayes, C.C.: Ishii K., Kazmer D., Sandborn P.A., Wood W.H, New directions in design for manufacturing. Salt Lake City, Utah USA. In: ASME, Design Engineering Technical Conferences and Computers and Information in Engineering Conference (2004)
3. Ellram, L.M., Tate, W.L., Carter, C.R.: Product-process-supply chain: an integrative approach to three-dimensional concurrent engineering. International Journal of Physical Distribution & Logistics Management 37 (2007)
4. Addo-Tenkorang, R.: Concurrent Engineering (CE): A Review Literature Report. In: Proceedings of the World Congress on Engineering and Computer Science, San Francisco, USA, vol. II (2011)
5. Tolouei-Rad, M.: An approach towards fully integration of CAD and CAM technologies. Journal of Achievements in Materials and Manufacturing Engineering 18(1-2), 31–36 (2006)
6. Walcher, D., Piller, F.: The customization 500 - An international Benchmark Study on Mass Customization and Personalization in Consume E-Commerce (2012)
7. cyLEDGE-Media, GmbH. Configurator Database. Configurator-Database, http://www.configurator-database.com/ (Cited: November 20, 2012)
8. Jackson, M., Zaman, A.: Factory-In-a-Box – Mobile Production Capacity on Demand. In: IJME - INTERTECH Conference, ENT 104-045 (2006)
9. ESCT The importance of shopping centres to the European economy (March 2008), http://www.icsc.org/srch/rsrch/wp/FINAL_Mar08_Complete%20WIT H%20new%20cover%20and%20charts%20and%20tables.pdf
10. Lambert, J.: One step closer to a pan-European shopping enter standard. Research Review 13(2) (2006), http://www.icsc.org/srch/lib/euro_standard_only.pdf

Socially Sustainable Manufacturing: Exploring the European Landscape

Paola Fantini[1], Claudio Palasciano[2], Marco Taisch[2],
Cecilia Berlin[3], Caroline Adams[3], and Johan Stahre[3]

[1] Fondazione Politecnico di Milano
[2] Politecnico di Milano, Department of Management,
Economics and Industrial Engineering, Milan, Italy
[3] Chalmers University, Goteborg, Sweden
paola.fantini@fondazione.polimi.it,
{marco.taisch,claudio.palasciano}@polimi.it,
{cecilia.berlin,cadams,johan.stahre}@chalmers.se

Abstract. Sustainable manufacturing has been extensively researched in the last decades, however there is a lack of coherence in literature specifically addressing its social dimension. Within the framework of the Social Sustainability-themed project SO SMART (Socially Sustainable Manufacturing for the Factories of the Future), a preliminary explorative survey and interview study were deployed among manufacturing companies and their stakeholders in Europe to investigate the extent to which they understand and practice social sustainability in relation to their business activities and context. Using an inquiry approach based on the main concepts related to social sustainability found in literature, this paper reports findings on preliminary exploration of the European landscape of social sustainability-related practices from a corporate and societal perspective. Findings contribute to the creation of a basis of shared knowledge as a prerequisite for extending and further developing concepts and models for socially sustainable manufacturing ecosystems.

Keywords: social sustainability, sustainable manufacturing ecosystems.

1 Introduction

Within the framework of the SO SMART (Socially Sustainable Manufacturing for the Factories of the Future) project, this paper reports on a study for exploring the European landscape of social sustainability-related practices and concerns, both from a corporate and societal perspective. The central concept of SO SMART is in fact to investigate social sustainability from a "balanced Eco-system" perspective, taking into account the viewpoints of the individual, industry and society [1].

Sustainability is an anthropocentric value that essentially pursues inter-and intra-generational justice [1]. Modern discourse regarding sustainability propagates a triad view, first discussed at the 1992 Rio de Janeiro earth summit [2] and addressing the three "pillars" of economic, environmental and social sustainability as equal and

B. Grabot et al. (Eds.): APMS 2014, Part II, IFIP AICT 439, pp. 474–481, 2014.
© IFIP International Federation for Information Processing 2014

parallel concerns; however, they have so far not been given the same focus. Particularly the social dimension has not been sufficiently explored [1] [3] and the European Factory of the Future Research Association has indicated that social sustainability in manufacturing is among the main challenges and opportunities of the recently issued 2014-2020 Roadmap. The roadmap promotes research to increase human achievements in future European manufacturing to create sustainable, safe and attractive workplaces for Europe 2020, and to achieve sustainable care and responsibility for employees and citizens in global supply chains [4].

Literature specially referring to social sustainability for manufacturing is rather limited and dispersed over different scopes: the global, super-national and national level for industry, public authorities and academia [5], the engineering field [6], science, engineering and manufacturing and the challenges ahead [7], [8], [9], [10].

The scope of social sustainability for manufacturing still appears insufficiently explored and, considering the substantial socio-economic impact of this sector, further investigations and developments are potentially promising.

2   Research Approach

The approach followed to obtain a preliminary view of the socially sustainable European manufacturing landscape encompasses: a literature study, which is not reported in this paper directly but through the references in the following steps; an analysis framework; an explorative study, including interviews to stakeholders and a survey to manufacturing companies.

2.1   Analysis Framework

The set of relevant topics identified during the literature study paved the way for the development of an analysis framework, addressing three main facets: **A. Profile of social sustainability**, reflecting how sustainability is understood and enacted/interpreted, on the basis of sustainability reporting standard practices (i.e. [11]) and of some innovative concepts related to cultural factors derived from the literature analysis; **B. Practices for social sustainability**, describing the specific actions and practices in place, mostly based on well-established sustainability frameworks; **C. Maturity and measurement of social sustainability**, defining the implementation level, grounded on well-established reporting standards and further tailored to the purpose of the survey, taking into account the sustainability profile and additional concepts derived from the literature study.

The following paragraphs report, for each facet, some of the most significant topics identified to be addressed in the survey, along with the references from the literature research that were used to shape the questionnaires.

A.   Profile of social sustainability
— <u>Dimensions and relevance of sustainability</u>. The survey addressed the relevance attributed to economic, environmental and social sustainability. Among the main references [12], [13](triple bottom line) and [14] (related issues).

— Scope of social sustainability. The survey queried whether broad areas (social themes, labour policies, social equity in the supply chain, community involvement and CSR) are considered in the scope of social sustainability for manufacturing. The topics were adapted from impact categories, i.e. [15] and social sustainability terms and definitions [16], [17].
— Drivers and barriers. The survey investigated the relevance attributed to a list of drivers and barriers that affect social sustainability intentions and performances. References were found in [18] (variety of barriers and enablers), [19] (driving forces towards CSR), [20] (internal and external pressure).
— Orientation towards the stakeholders. The survey aimed at identifying the prevailing attitudes towards stakeholders, distinguishing if the target is the benefit of the company, of the stakeholders or of a wider community, based on [21], [22], [23].
— Philosophy of social responsiveness. The survey researched the prevailing type of commitment towards social requirements along a reactivity - proactivity scale [13]. The extreme of the scale has been tentatively extended to include the representation of the Creating Shared Value perspective [24].

B.   Practices for social sustainability
— Social sustainability Practices. The survey queries about the social sustainability practices deployed. Labor practices: human capital development, work-life balance, learning, talent management, employees' turnover and satisfaction management, temporary work, etc. Stakeholders and communities practices: supply chain code of conduct, customer relationship management, risk and crises management, etc.. See [20], [25], [26], [27], [28], [29], [30].

C.   Maturity and measurement of social sustainability
— Social Sustainability vision and values. The survey aims at determining the degree of clarity, understanding and acceptance of the social sustainability vision within the company, based on [12], [13] (relevance of setting and communicating the vision) and [31] (issues related to disseminating the vision within the organization).
— Implementation of social sustainability in the systems and processes. The questions aim at assessing to what extent social sustainability is integrated into practices and affects activities [32].
— Relationship with the stakeholders. The topic concerns the involvement of different categories of stakeholders in the process of defining, implementing and evaluating sustainable performance. References come for [1], [31], [5] (competitors, suppliers, investors and NGOs) and [6] (current/ prospective workers, local community).
— Social sustainability periodical reporting. Inquiries about the reporting methods, actors and procedures. The questions have taken into account [33] (readers' expectations and following actions and [14] (stakeholders involvement).

2.2   Explorative Study

The study, including a survey and stakeholders' interviews, was intentionally stated to be a pilot effort targeted at the following objectives: a) to verify whether the topics and themes identified by reviewing the scientific literature are adequate to represent social sustainability orientations and practices in manufacturing; and if not, to explore missing concepts or perspectives; b) to obtain a preliminary picture of how social sustainability is currently conceived and implemented in European manufacturing.

The survey consisted of multiple-choice questions structured on the analysis framework described in 2.1, complemented with open questions. The survey was deployed online, targeting a sample of European industrial actors and stakeholders. The first pilot phase reached 9 countries and 8 industrial sectors, eliciting a pilot sample of 21 responses, including small and large enterprises, both national and multinational, with different situations and trends in terms of profitability and employment development.

To gain a multi-level eco-systemic perspective, the interviews were conducted mainly with stakeholders from various societal functions concerned with social sustainability. The interviews were semi-structured and aimed to identify any areas and practices of social collaboration between company and societal stakeholders, again with questions based on the analysis framework. Through the SO SMART project partners' networks, 8 individuals representing local or regional authorities, trade unions and enterprises were interviewed as relevant stakeholders affected by company practices of social sustainability. Interviewed stakeholders represented Public Authorities at NUTS[1] levels 2 and 3, Local Authorities, Industrial Associations and Trade Unions.

3   Preliminary Landscape

Taking into account the previously stated pilot nature of the respondent sample, the survey and the interviews to manufacturing companies shows wide recognition among the respondents of the relevance of the triad of economic, environmental and social dimensions of sustainability; however, the importance of the latter is slightly less perceived. Moreover, the broad social themes are considered partially or not in the scope of social sustainability for manufacturing, ranking below labor policies, community involvement and social equity in the supply chain.

The survey responses also suggested that the most important drivers influencing a company's level of action are: positive pressure exerted both by internal stakeholders (i.e. top management and employees) and external stakeholders (customers and local authorities)[2] and the explicit alignment of social sustainability with the company's strategy. Moreover, the survey, complemented by the interview results, highlighted that some important barriers to social sustainability still need to be addressed in order to progress towards a more extended and fully deployed social sustainability, namely: the difficulty in evaluating the benefits coming from social sustainability practices, in particular the difficulty of translating them into easily measurable and quantifiable terms; the existence of unsupportive cultures, both at the organizational and societal level, that promote values and behaviors not aligned to social sustainability principles; the lack of strong collaborative relationships with stakeholders in order to develop shared visions and strategies to achieve common goals.

---

[1] Nomenclature of Territorial Units for Statistics
http://ec.europa.eu/eurostat/ramon/index.cfm?TargetUrl=DSP_PUB_WELC
[2] For the majority of the enterprises, employees and customers, followed by public authorities and trade unions, are the main stakeholders that enterprises interact with.

Although in the presence of some ambiguities, findings seem to outline a population of manufacturers on the whole who are aware of the relevance of social sustainability; who in most of the cases have developed their vision and culture; who have identified, adopted and implemented practices; and who have set up reporting. However, some heterogeneities and discrepancies require further elaboration. The respondents seem to have different levels of understanding and adhesion with reference to social sustainability, which we may exemplify through two "polar" types. The type of "cold/recent adopters", who seem to start from mere acknowledgement of the relevance of social sustainability with a prevalent inward focus, leading to the definition of a vision that remains fuzzy, not accepted/internalized at all levels of the organization nor incorporated in a planning and control process. This type implements specific practices mostly addressing employees and has them integrated in existing processes, in some cases issuing reports about the activities carried out and the resources employed.

A different type is that of the "warm/mature adopters", who embrace social sustainability, consider a wider scope including external stakeholders whom they approach for collaboration, have clearly defined visions and strategies and have deployed them, or are in the process of deploying them, through an integrated framework and a closed-loop planning and control cycle, using performance indicators, involving external stakeholders and/or leveraging external data sources.

We can draw here some preliminary directions for further research, which most likely has to shed more light on the potential multiplicity of socially sustainable manufacturing types, here preliminarily condensed in the two "polar" types evidenced above. Furthermore it seems some investigation should be performed in more detail on i) the role of the temporal/maturity dimension, in order to better distinguish the degree of interest towards social sustainability from the duration of experience, and ii) the assessment and reporting methodologies enacted and the performance indicators monitored by companies.

4   Discussion

The work presented in this paper constitutes a pilot step supporting a wider research and road-mapping effort aimed at developing new models for sustainable manufacturing ecosystems pursuing social, environmental and economic performance objectives.

In the survey, difficulties occurred in interpreting some results: this may indicate that some sub-categories need to be more clearly defined. In terms of deployment, the survey reached a limited number of actors, so it is not sufficient to represent the manufacturing sector as a whole, but it is still valuable as a preliminary exploration. Further issues to address in continued efforts include better coverage of the variety of stakeholders and industry sectors.

Some deficiencies are intrinsic of the survey format, which helped us to highlight current practices, but could not support the elicitation of needs. The individual interviews, aiming at complementing the survey with the desired richness, provided additional elements useful for interpreting the results and for pointing out preliminary directions for further exploratory activities.

In the prosecution of the research, in order to encourage the emergence and development of novel visions, approaches that better leverage the interaction among groups of people and stimulate new ideas (such as Delphi, focus groups or workshops) will be exploited.

5   Conclusions

In spite of the pilot nature of the study deployment, the research has enabled drawing of a preliminary picture of socially sustainable manufacturing, as currently understood and implemented in Europe. The findings are useful to point out relevant directions and topics for later exploration in collaborative workshop formats and similar. The preliminary results from the survey and interviews appear to confirm the substantial comprehensiveness of the framework obtained from literature.

The findings also contribute to the creation of a basis of shared knowledge as a prerequisite for developing a collective vision for socially sustainable manufacturing ecosystems, requiring the involvement and coordination of multiple organizations. Further work is planned within the SO SMART project to address these challenges.

Acknowledgements. This paper has been developed within the EC funded project SO SMART   (GA.608734).

References

1. Omann, I., Spangenberg, J.H.: Assessing Social Sustainability - The Social Dimension of Sustainability in a Socio-Economic Scenario. In: 7th Biennal Conference of the International Society for Ecological Economics, Soussa, Tunisia (2002)
2. United Nations, Report of The United Nations Conference on Environment and Development, Rio de Janeiro (1992)
3. Colantonio, A.: Social Sustainability: a review and critique of traditional versus emerging themes and assessment methods. In: Sue-Mont Conference 2009: Second International Conference on Whole Life Urban Sustainability and its Assessment, Loughborough, Loughborough University, pp. 865–885 (2009)
4. EFFRA - European Factory of the Future Research Association, Factories of The Future Multiannual Roadmap for The Contractual PPP Under Horizon 2020, Publications Office of the European Union, Luxembourg (2013)
5. Jovane, F., Yoshikawa, H., Alting, L., Boer, C.R., Westkamper, E., Williams, D., Tseng, M., Seliger, G., Paci, A.M.: The incoming global technological and industrial revolution towards competitive sustainable manufacturing. CIRP Annals - Manufacturing Technology (2008)
6. Garetti, M., Taisch, M.: Sustainable manufacturing: trends and research challenges. Production Planning & Control: The Management of Operations, 83–104 (2012)
7. Haapala, K.R., Zhao, F., Camelio, J., Sutherland, J.W., Skerios, S.J., Dornfeld, D.A., Jawahir, I.S., Clarens, A.F., Rickli, J.L.: A Review of Engineering Research in Sustainable Manufacturing. Journal of manufacturing Science and Engineering 135(4) (2013)

8. Lanz, M., Majuri, M., Tuokko, R.: Information flows in future advanced manufacturing ecosystems. In: Prabhu, V., Taisch, M., Kiritsis, D. (eds.) APMS 2013, Part I. IFIP AICT, vol. 414, pp. 70–77. Springer, Heidelberg (2013)

9. Berlin, C., Dedering, C., Jónsdóttir, G.R., Stahre, J.: Social sustainability challenges for european manufacturing industry: Attract, recruit and sustain. In: Prabhu, V., Taisch, M., Kiritsis, D. (eds.) APMS 2013, Part I. IFIP AICT, vol. 414, pp. 78–85. Springer, Heidelberg (2013)

10. Fantini, P., Taisch, M., Palasciano, C.: Social sustainability: Perspectives on the role of manufacturing. In: Prabhu, V., Taisch, M., Kiritsis, D. (eds.) APMS 2013, Part I. IFIP AICT, vol. 414, pp. 62–69. Springer, Heidelberg (2013)

11. Global Reporting Initiative, G4, Reporting Principles and Standard Disclosures, Amsterdam (2013)

12. United Nations General Assembly, 2005 World Summit Outcome, United Nations (2005)

13. Elkington, J.: Partnership from cannibals with forks: The triple bottom line of 21st century business. Environmental Quality Management 8(1), 37–51 (1998)

14. Hubbard, G.: Measuring Organizational Performance: beyond the Triple Bottom Line. Business Strategy and the Environment 18(3), 177–191 (2006)

15. Joung, C.B., Carrell, J., Sarkar, P., Feng, S.C.: Categorization of indicators for sustainable manufacturing. Ecological Indicators 24, 148–157 (2012)

16. McKenzie, S.: Social Sustainability: towards some definitions. Hawke Research Institute - Working Paper Series 27 (2004)

17. Vallance, S., Perkins, H., Dixon, J.: What is social sustainability? A clarification of concepts. Geoforum 42(3), 342–348 (2011)

18. Walker, H., Jones, N.: Sustainable supply chain management across the UK private sector. Supply Chain Management: An International Journal 17(1), 15–28 (2012)

19. Reinmann, F., Ehrgott, M., Kaufmann, L., Carter, C.R.: Local stakeholders and local legitimacy: MNEs' social strategies in emerging economies. Journal of International Management 18, 1–17 (2012)

20. Collins, E., Roper, J., Lawrence, S.: Sustainability Practices: Trends in New Zealand. Business Strategy and the Environment 19, 479–494 (2010)

21. Bingham, J.B., Dyer Jr., W.G., Smith, I., Adams, G.L.: A Stakeholder Identity Orientation Approach to Corporate Social Performance in Family Firms. Journal of Business Ethics 99(4), 565–585 (2011)

22. Searcy, C.: Corporate Sustainability Performance Measurement Systems: A Review and Research Agenda. Journal of Business Ethics 107(3), 239–253 (2012)

23. Perrini, F., Russo, A., Tencati, A., Vurro, C.: Deconstructing the Relationship Between Corporate Social and Financial Performance. Journal of Business Ethics 102(1), 59–76 (2011)

24. Carrol, A.B.: Corporate Social Responsibility Evolution of a Definitional Construct. Business and Society 38(3), 268–293 (1999)

25. Theyel, G., Hofmann, K.: Stakeholders relations and sustainability practices of US small and medium-sized manufacturers. Management Research Review 35(12), 1110–1133 (2012)

26. S&P Dow Jones Indices and RobecoSAM, Dow Jones Sustainability World Index Guide v.12.2, RobecoSAM AG, Zurich (2013)

27. International Organization for Standardization (ISO), Discovering ISO 26000, Geneve (2010)

28. Morali, O., Searcy, C.: A Review of Sustainable Supply Chain Management Practices in Canada. Journal of Business Ethics 117(3), 635–658 (2012)

29. Ameer, R., Othman, R.: Sustainability Practices and Corporate Financial Performance: A Study Based on the Top Global Corporations. Journal of Business Ethics 108(1), 61–79 (2011)
30. SAM Reasearch AG, SAM Research Corporate Sustainability Assessment Questionnaire, SAM Research AG, Zurich (2011)
31. Porter, M.E., Kramer, M.R.: Creating Shared Value. Harvard Business Review 1(2), 2–17 (2011)
32. Hockerts, K.: The SusTainAbility Radar. Greener Management International 99(25), 29–49 (1999)
33. Grauler, M., Freundlieb, M., Ortwerth, K., Teuteberg, F.: Understanding the beliefs, actions and outcomes of sustainability reporting: An experimental approach. Information Systems Frontiers 15(5), 779–797 (2013)
34. SO SMART, Socially Sustainable Manufacturing for the Factories of the Future Coordination and Support Action (2014), http://www.sosmarteu.eu/
35. WCED,Our common future: the Bruntland report, Oxford University Press, New York (1987)
36. Social Accountability International, Social Accountability 8000 International Standard, New York: Social Accountability International (2001)
37. UN Global Compact, United Nations Global Compact - Strategy (2014-2016)
38. Littig, B., Griessler, E.: Social sustainability: a catchword between political pragmatism and social theory. Internation Journal of Sustainable Development 8(1/2), 65–79 (2005)
39. Hodge, R., Hardi, P.: The need for guidelines: the rationale underlying the bellagio principles for assessment, in Assessing Sustainable Development. Principles in Practice, International Institute for Sustainable Development, Winnipeg, Manitoba, pp. 7–20 (1997)

Integrated Procurement–Disassembly Problem

Muhammad Khoirul Khakim Habibi[1], Olga Battaïa[1],
Van-Dat Cung[2], and Alexandre Dolgui[1]

[1] École Nationale Supérieure des Mines de Saint–Étienne,
Lab. LIMOS, CNRS UMR6158, 42023 Saint–Étienne cedex 2, France
[2] Univ. Grenoble Alpes, G-SCOP, F-38000 Grenoble, France,
CNRS, G-SCOP, F-38000 Grenoble, France
{muhammad.habibi,battaia,dolgui}@emse.fr,
van-dat.cung@grenoble-inp.fr

Abstract. This paper proposes a novel problem called integrated procurement–disassembly problem. The problem combines vehicle routing problem and disassembly line balancing problem for collecting and disassembling End-of-Life (EOL) products, respectively. The integration of those problems is motivated by the necessity to reduce total cost in reverse supply chain context. After collecting the EOL products from suppliers, the disassembly process begins to release the demanded parts. The objective function aims to minimize the total cost consisting product collection and opening disassembly workstations. The constraints consider vehicle routing problem to supply the disassembly line with EOL products, disassembly line and balancing inventory coordinating those problems. The decision variables include trips sequences associated to collect the products, disassembly task assignment into workstations, and the inventory level.

Keywords: Vehicle routing, disassembly, line design and balancing, in- ventory control, End-of-Life product.

1 Introduction

Electronic and electrical manufacturing sector are encouraged to consider the environmental aspect of its production process. This condition is caused by the shrinking life cycle of electronic and electrical equipments (EEEs) henceforth increases the amount of waste electrical and electronics equipments (WEEEs). The main reasons are government's mandates to extend the responsability of manufacturer (mainly in EU, USA, Australia, Japan and South Korea), consumers' consciousness [1–3] and the potential worthwhile of EOL products.

The disassembly process is considered to deal with this condition. It is a set of activity for disassembling the EOL product in order to release its precious and hazardous parts. Since it is expensive and time consuming acitivity, optimization is required for attaining the profitable state. Our research focuses on a field of disassembly process known as disassembly line balancing problem (DLBP).

B. Grabot et al. (Eds.): APMS 2014, Part II, IFIP AICT 439, pp. 482–490, 2014.
© IFIP International Federation for Information Processing 2014

DLBP is the assignment of disassembly tasks into a sequence of stations such that the returned product is disassembled based on the desired level of disassembly respecting the disassembly precedence relations and some measure of effectiveness [4]. Researches have been conducted in several related factors such as demanded and hazardous part prioritization, task failure, profit orientation etc.

However, the studies on DLBP are usually not connected with other decisions in reverse supply chain. Since the studies on forward supply chain show that the decisions integration permits the cost reduction [5–8], the same idea should be investigated in the reverse supply chain.

For this purpose, this work is intended to deal with the collection and the disassembly process of EOL products. This research proposes an integrated model for Capacitated Vehicle Routing Problem based waste collection (w-VRP) and DLBP called integrated procurement–disassembly problem. The model minimizes the total cost corresponding to EOL products collection and disassembly process related to w-VRP and DLBP, respectively. During products collection process, we assume only one available vehicle and several suppliers who have EOL product to be collected. The model admits partial disassembly since it aims to release the demanded parts only. To the best of our knowledge, it is the first work proposes the integration between collection process and disassembly balancing problem.

The next sections are organized as follows. Section 2 gives an overview of related literature. Section 3 describes our mixed integer linear programming formulation. Section 4 provides computational results. The last section gives a conclusion and some prospects for future work.

2   Literature Review

DLBP has been investigated by researchers in many cases. Such as assembly line balancing problem (ALBP), one of the objectives is to minimize the number of workstations required to reach a given cycle time [9]. Altekin et al. [4] proposed a profit-oriented partial DLBP model to maximize the earned profits of released part while taking into consideration the cost of performing disassembly task as well as fixed cost caused by opening workstations. Partial disassembly is represented by associating the disassembly task with its incurred cost. Bentaha et al. [10–15] offered novel models of profit-oriented partial DLBP based on transformed AND/OR graph of [16] under stochastic condition. The objective of [11–13] was to minimize the total fixed cost of opening workstations and recourse cost caused by task failure. The revenue of released products was considered in [10, 15]. The cost of handling hazardous parts was taken into account [14].

New issues combining several decisions related DLBP are emerged. Özceylan et al. [17] dealt with closed-loop supply chain (CLSC) and DLBP. The proposed model aims to determine the material distribution in forward and reverse flows as well as to balance disassembly line through tasks assignment. Özceylan et al. [18] proposed a model under undeterministic condition concerning task cost, inventory level, demand and reverse rates.

The decisions integration was principally studied for forward supply chain. Boudia et al. [5, 6] and Boudia and Prins [7] worked on IPDP by minimizing the routing and production cost. Bard and Nananukul [8] considered time win- dows into IPDP. Shiguemoto and Armentano [19] considered the cost of produc- tion and inventory at the production facility as well as consumers. Varthanan et al. [20] proposed IPDP model under stochastic demand. Gharehyakeh and Tavakkoli-Moghaddam [21] took into consideration the uncertainty of demand, machine and labor level with time windows. However, no study proposes a model integrating procurement - disassembly problem although these problems are in- terdependent due to their sequential decisions.

3 Problem Description

Before being disassembled, the EOL products are collected from suppliers to disassembly plant. Subsequently, the products are stored at the inventory and will be disassembled in order to release the demanded parts. A single vehicle and a product type are considered. The data concerning product collection and disassembly process are known and deterministic.

In this section, a mixed integer linear programming (MILP) model of inte-grated procurement–disassembly problem is presented. The problem is defined on weighted and undirected graph network $G = (N, E, D)$. N is the set of node denoting the considered suppliers and the inventory of facility plant. This inven-tory is denoted as node 1. E is the set of edges and D_{ab} is the distance between node a and node b where $D_{ab} = D_{ba}$, $a \in N$, $b \in N$. The plant disassemblies a single product type during planning horizon T. A single vehicle with capacity C and unit running cost RC is used for collecting EOL products from suppliers. A supplier a has certain amount of EOL products at period t denoted as S_{at}. A single vehicle visits each supplier at most once for each period. The collected products are stored at the inventory with unlimited capacity where the inventory level at the end of period t is denoted as I_t, $t \in T$.

At the beginning of period t, the disassembly process begins based on the required demand of part 1 denoted by d_{1t}, $1 \in L, t \in T$. Our model requires binary variable d^b, $1 \in L$, $t \in T$ which is equal to 1 if d_{1t} is greater than 0. Since it is assumed that each product consists of exactly one part of type 1, the minimum amount of products stored at inventory d^{max}, $t \in T$, before performing disassembly process at the beginning of period is the biggest amount for all required part at period t.

Our model adopts the AND/OR graph (AOG) in [16] where auxiliary node A_k, $k \in K$ represents subassembly and basic node B_i, $i \in I$ denotes disassembly task. The relations between subassemblies and disassembly tasks are presented in AOG. The dummy task s is introduced to indicate that disassembly process at period t is finished due to the consideration of partial disassembly. P_k is the set of tasks which preceedes subassembly A_k, $k \in K$. S_k, $k \in K$, denotes the set of tasks which succeeds A_k, $k \in K$. Our model requires the set of tasks which permits to release part 1, $1 \in L$, denoted as P_1.

Disassembly task times time$_i$ are known where the time of dummy task s, time$_s$ is 0. At period t, each required disassembly is assigned to a workstation. Workstation time is less than the given cycle time CT. FC denotes the fixed cost of opening a workstation. In our model, the decision variables are:

- I_t inventory level at the end of period t;
- Y_{at} cumulative load of vehicle after visiting node a at period t;
- $X_{abt} = \begin{cases} 1 & \text{if the vehicle visits node } a \text{ just before node } b \text{ at period } t; \\ 0 & \text{otherwise.} \end{cases}$
- $x_{ijt} = \begin{cases} 1 & \text{if disassembly task } i \text{ is assigned to workstation } j \text{ at period } t; \\ 0 & \text{otherwise.} \end{cases}$
- $z_{jt} = \begin{cases} \text{CT} & \text{if } x_{sjt} = 1 \text{ ;} \\ 0 & \text{otherwise.} \end{cases}$

$$\textbf{Minimize} \quad Z = RC \sum_{t \in T} \sum_{b \in N} \sum_{a \in N} D_{ab} \cdot X_{abt} + FC \sum_{t \in T} \sum_{j \in J} j \cdot z_{jt} \qquad (1)$$

Subject to:

$$I_t = I_{t-1} + \sum_{b \in N} \sum_{a \in N \setminus \{1\}} X_{abt} \cdot S_{at} - d_t^{max} \qquad \forall t \in T, a \neq b; \qquad (2)$$

$$\sum_{a \in N} X_{abt} \leq 1 \qquad \forall b \in N \setminus \{1\}, \forall t \in T, a \neq b; \qquad (3)$$

$$\sum_{a \in N} X_{act} = \sum_{b \in N} X_{cbt} \qquad \forall c \in N, \forall t \in T, c \neq a, c \neq b; \qquad (4)$$

$$\sum_{a \in S} \sum_{b \in S} X_{abt} \leq |S| - 1 \qquad \forall t \in T, \forall S \subseteq N \setminus \{1\} : |S| \geq 2; \qquad (5)$$

$$Y_{bt} - S_{bt} - Y_{at} \geq - \left(\sum_{l \in L} d_{lt} \right) \cdot (1 - X_{abt}) \qquad \forall a \in N, \forall b \in N \setminus \{1\}, \forall t \in T, a \neq b; \qquad (6)$$

$$Y_{bt} - S_{bt} - Y_{at} \leq \left(\sum_{l \in L} d_{lt} \right) \cdot (1 - X_{abt}) \qquad \forall a \in N, \forall b \in N \setminus \{1\}, \forall t \in T, a \neq b; \qquad (7)$$

$$Y_{at} \leq C \qquad \forall a \in N, \forall t \in T; \qquad (8)$$

$$Y_{1t} = 0 \qquad \forall t \in T; \qquad (9)$$

$$\sum_{j \in J} \sum_{i \in P_l} x_{ijt} \geq d_{lt}^b \qquad \forall l \in L, t \in T; \qquad (10)$$

$$\sum_{j \in J} \sum_{i \in S_0} x_{ijt} = 1 \qquad \forall t \in T; \qquad (11)$$

$$\sum_{j \in J} x_{ijt} \leq 1 \qquad\qquad \forall i \in I, \forall t \in T; \qquad (12)$$

$$\sum_{i \in S_k} x_{ivt} \leq \sum_{i \in P_k} \sum_{j=1}^{v} x_{ijt} \qquad\qquad \forall k \in K \setminus \{0\}, \forall v \in J, \forall t \in T; \qquad (13)$$

$$\sum_{i \in S_k} \sum_{j \in J} x_{ijt} \leq \sum_{i \in P_k} \sum_{j \in J} x_{ijt} \qquad\qquad \forall k \in K \setminus \{0\}, \forall t \in T; \qquad (14)$$

$$\sum_{j \in J} x_{sjt} = 1 \qquad\qquad \forall t \in T; \qquad (15)$$

$$\sum_{j \in J} j \cdot x_{ijt} \leq \sum_{j \in J} j \cdot x_{sjt} \qquad\qquad \forall i \in I, \forall t \in T; \qquad (16)$$

$$z_{jt} = CT \cdot x_{sjt} \qquad\qquad \forall j \in J, \forall t \in T; \qquad (17)$$

$$\sum_{i \in I} x_{ijt} \cdot time_i \leq CT \qquad\qquad \forall j \in J, \forall t \in T; \qquad (18)$$

$$I_t \geq 0 \qquad\qquad \forall t \in T; \qquad (19)$$

$$X_{abt} \in \{0,1\} \qquad\qquad \forall a \in N, \forall b \in N, \forall t \in T, a \neq b; \qquad (20)$$

$$Y_{at} \geq 0 \qquad\qquad \forall a \in N, \forall t \in T; \qquad (21)$$

$$x_{sjt}, x_{ijt}, \in \{0,1\} \qquad\qquad \forall i \in I, \forall j \in J, \forall t \in T; \qquad (22)$$

$$z_{jt} \in \{0, CT\} \qquad\qquad \forall j \in J, \forall t \in T; \qquad (23)$$

The objective function (1) aims to minimize the total cost consisting to- tal procurement cost and total cost of opening workstations for entire planning horizon. Constraint set (2) balances the plant inventory at each period. At each period, constraint set (3) imposes that each supplier is visited at most once. Constraint set (4) guarantees that the vehicle leaves a node after visiting it. Constraint set (5) eliminates the subtour occurrence. Constraint sets (6–7) update the vehicle load after visiting a node at each period. Constraint set (8) limits the vehicle load during its trips. After leaving the plant as depot of the trip, constraint set (9) resets the vehicle load as zero. Constraints sets (10) de- scribe the relation between part demand and its predecessors. Constraint sets (11–18) are simplification of the model in [12]. Constraint set (11) selects the first tasks succeeding EOL product. Constraint set (12) assigns the disassembly task into at most a workstation. The precedence relations between disassembly tasks and subassemblies are described by contraint set (13). Constraint set (14) selects only one OR successor. Constraint set (15) assigns sink node into a work-station. Constraint set (16) guarantees that each disassembly task is assigned into a workstation with lower or equal index of sink node's workstation. The value of z_{jt} is determined by constraints set (17). Constraint set (18) denotes the limitation of workstation time. Contraint sets (19–23) describe the nature of decision variables.

4   Computational Results

Since no benchmark instance exists for our problem, we considered the following example based on [13]. A compass consisting seven parts is studied. Ten tasks permits to release one or some parts. At first period, the plant has 20 products available in the inventory. The cycle time is 0.61 second. The opening cost of workstation is 7 euros/second. A vehicle with 5000 capacity is used with running cost as 5 euro/km. Table 1 and 2 present the data of demand, part and supplier.

Table 1. Part and Demand Data

Part	Predecessor	Demand(*1000)			
		t = 1	t = 2	t = 3	t = 4
1	3,5,7,9	2	6	2	2
2	7,9	0	3	6	0
3	3,9,10	4	0	5	2
4	2,4,8	1	4	0	1
5	2,4,8	2	7	3	7
6	1,6,10	0	1	0	0
7	1,6,10	4	2	6	2

The model was implemented in Java 7 using GNU Linear Programming Kit(GLPK) 4.9 on a PC with processor Intel® Core™ i7 CPU 2.9 GHz and 4 Go RAM under Windows 7 Professional.

Table 2. Supplier Data

Node	Coordinate		Supply(*1000)			
	X	Y	t = 1	t = 2	t = 3	t = 4
Depot	30	40	-	-	-	-
Supplier 1	37	52	1	1	4	4
Supplier 2	49	49	5	3	1	1
Supplier 3	52	64	4	1	2	2
Supplier 4	20	26	1	1	3	3

The optimal solution is obtained in 85.25 seconds with the total cost 1232.83 euros. Only 2 workstations are opened during four periods considered. The vehicle's trips and disassembly tasks assignment are presented in table 3 and 4, respectively.

Table 3. Vehicle Trip

Vehicle Trip	Period			
	1	2	3	4
First trip	1, 4, 2, 1	1, 3, 1	1, 2, 1	1, 2, 1
Second trip	1, 3, 1	-	1, 4, 1	-

Table 4. Task Assignment

Workstation	Period			
	1	2	3	4
1	2,6	1	1	2,6
2	9	4,9	4,9	9

5   Conclusion

This work addresses integrated procurement–disassembly problem. It combines w-VRP and DLBP for collecting and disassembling the EOL product. A capacitated vehicle collects EOL product from suppliers. The vehicle begins its trip with zero load. Its capacity forces the vehicle to return back into the inventory for disposing its load. If the invetory level of EOL products is sufficient, the disassembly process begins releasing the demanded parts. The proposed model considers partial DLBP under deterministic condition with single product type.

The objective function minimizes the total cost of product colletion and disassembly process through vehicle routing determination and disassembly task assignment. The model takes into account the constraints of DLBP, w-VRP and the balancing constraints coordinating these problems.

Some prospects concerning the proposed model are derived in order to approach the reality. For the next step, the model should be extended to the case of multiple products and multiple vehicles. Then, it should be tested on the industrial data. Moreover, since the uncertainty is major in disassembly process as well as EOL products collection, this factor has to be taken into account.

Acknowledgement. This work has been supported by Région Rhone–Alpes, France.

References

1. Sasikumar, P., Kannan, G.: Issues in Reverse Supply Chains, Part I: End-of-Life Product Recovery and Inventory Management-an Overview. International Journal of Sustainable Engineering 1, 154–172 (2008)
2. Yang, G., Wang, Z., Li, X.: The Optimization of the Closed-Loop Supply Chain Network. Transportation Research Part E: Logistics and Transportation Review 45, 16–28 (2009)
3. Ilgin, M.A., Gupta, S.M.: Performance Improvement Potential of Sensor Embedded Products in Environmental Supply Chains. Resources, Conservation and Recycling 55, 580–592 (2011)
4. Altekin, F.T., Kandiller, L., Ozdemirel, N.E.: Profit-oriented Disassembly Line Balancing. International Journal of Production Research 46, 2675–2693 (2008)

5. Boudia, M., Dauzere-Peres, S., Prins, C., Louly, M.A.O.: Integrated Optimization of Production and Distribution for Several Products. In: International Conference on Service Systems and Service Management 2006, Troyes, pp. 272–277 (2006)
6. Boudia, M., Louly, M.A.O., Prins, C.: A Reactive GRASP and Path Relinking for Combined Production–Distribution Problem. Computers & Operations Research 34, 3402–3419 (2007)
7. Boudia, M., Prins, C.: A Memetic Algorithm with Dynamic Population Management for an Integrated Production–Distribution Problem. European Journal of Operational Research 195, 703–715 (2009)
8. Bard, J.F., Nananukul, N.: A Branch–and–Price a Algorithm for an Integrated Production and Inventory Routing Problem. Computers & Operations Research 37, 2202–2217 (2010)
9. Dolgui, A., Proth, J.: Supply Chain Engineering: Useful Methods and Techniques. Springer, London (2010)
10. Bentaha, M.L., Battaïa, O., Dolgui, A.: A Decomposition Method for Stochastic Partial Disassembly Line Balancing with Profit Maximization. In: IEEE International Conference on Automation Science and Engineering 2013, pp. 404–409 (2013)
11. Bentaha, M.L., Battaïa, O., Dolgui, A.: A Sample Average Approximation Method for Disassembly Line Balancing Problem under Uncertainty. Computers & Operations Research 51, 111–122 (2014)
12. Bentaha, M.L., Battaïa, O., Dolgui, A.: L–Shaped Algorithm for Stochastic Disassembly Line Balancing Problem. In: 7th IFAC Conference on Modelling, Management, and Control, Saint Petersburg, pp. 407–411 (2013)
13. Bentaha, M.L., Battaïa, O., Dolgui, A.: A Stochastic Formulation of the Disassembly Line Balancing Problem. In: Emmanouilidis, C., Taisch, M., Kiritsis, D. (eds.) Advances in Production Management Systems. IFIP AICT, vol. 397, pp. 397–404. Springer, Heidelberg (2013)
14. Bentaha, M.L., Battaïa, O., Dolgui, A.: Chance constrained programming model for stochastic profit–oriented disassembly line balancing in the presence of hazardous parts. In: Prabhu, V., Taisch, M., Kiritsis, D. (eds.) APMS 2013, Part I. IFIP AICT, vol. 414, pp. 103–110. Springer, Heidelberg (2013)
15. Bentaha, M.L., Battaïa, O., Dolgui, A.: Dealing with Uncertainty in Disassembly Line Design. CIRP Annals - Manufacturing Technology 63, 21–24 (2014)
16. Koc, A., Sabuncuoglu, I., Erel, E.: Two Exact Formulations for Disassembly Line Balancing Problems with Task Precedence Diagram Construction using An AND/OR Graph. IIE Transactions 41, 866–881 (2009)
17. Özceylan, E., Paksoy, T., Bekta͟s, T.: Modeling and Optimizing the Integrated Problem of Closed–Loop Supply Chain Network Design and Disassembly Line Balancing. Transportation Research Part E: Logistics and Transportation Review 61, 142–164 (2014)
18. Özceylan, E., Paksoy, T.: Interactive fuzzy programming approaches to the strategic and tactical planning of a closed-loop supply chain under uncertainty. International Journal of Production Research, 1–25 (2013)
19. Shiguemoto, A., Armentano, V.A.: A Tabu Search Procedure for Coordinating Production, Inventory and Distribution Routing Problems. International Transactions in Operational Research 17, 179–195 (2010)

20. Varthanan, P.A., Murugan, N., Kumar, G.M.: A Simulation Based Heuristic Discrete Particle Swarm Algorithm for Generating Integrated Production–Distribution Plan. Applied Soft Computing 12, 3034–3050 (2012)
21. Gharehyakheh, A., Tavakkoli-Moghaddam, R.: A Fuzzy Solution Approach for A Multi–ob jective Integrated Production–Distribution Model with Multi Products and Multi Periods Under Uncertainty. Management Science Letters 2, 2425–2434 (2012)

Collaborative Serious Games for Awareness on Shared Resources in Supply Chain Management

Jannicke Baalsrud Hauge[1], Matthias Kalverkamp[2], Margherita Forcolin[3], Hans Westerheim[4], Marco Franke[1], and Klaus-Dieter Thoben[1]

[1] Bremer Institut für Produktion und Logistik, Bremen, Germany
{baa,tho,fma}@biba.uni-bremen.de
[2] Research Group Cascade Use, Carl von Ossietzky Universität Oldenburg, Germany
matthias.kalverkamp@uni-oldenburg.de
[3] Cetim, Leiden, The Netherlands
Margherita.forcolin@cetim.org
[4] Department of Computer and Information Sciences, NTNU, Trondheim, Norway
hansw@idi.ntnu.no

Abstract. Today manufacturing is a complex process often resulting in long brittle supply chains with considerable contributions to the global resource demand also posing a negative environmental impact (CO_2 emissions, raw material supply, etc.). Reducing the waste of resources and being more sustainable are objectives incentivized by materials in short supply and customer requirements. Thus, the ability to share resources, innovate and to implement emergent ICT will play a key role for companies' competitiveness and their sustainability. However, sharing resources puts high requirements on trust and gain sharing, amongst others. Although well known in supply chain management, the logistics sector is struggling to increase their shared resources. The authors found serious games (SG) to be a promising tool for awareness rising on shared resource. Existing supply chain games are analysed and their potential and weaknesses for the topic are examined, resulting in an outlook on the research needs in SGs for awareness on shared resources.

Keywords: Serious Games, Shared resources, Logistics, CPS.

1 Introduction

Today manufacturing is often a complex process involving several partners around the world [1] and based on economy of scale principles [2]. It results in long brittle supply chains with a considerable contribution to the CO_2 emissions [3]. The supply chain can be seen as an ecosystem of different actors with different needs, acting in a dynamic environment [4]. Customer response, exception management, scheduling, prediction and forecasting are some of the key factors that have to be continuously improved and monitored [5], thus, monitoring the quality of service, supply chain visibility and security have becoming major factors determining logistics processes besides e.g. costs, duration, and carbon footprint [3, 4, 5].

B. Grabot et al. (Eds.): APMS 2014, Part II, IFIP AICT 439, pp. 491–499, 2014.
© IFIP International Federation for Information Processing 2014

The European manufacturing industry's basis is build by innovative SMEs with an excellent R&D base that allows them to thrive on the world market. However, due to the trend toward more customized products with shorter life-cycle the marginal cost per product is increasing and low efficiency of the logistics system is a challenge to overcome for reducing the costs and emissions. Studies reveal that the utilization of e.g. trucks on the roads vary between 30 to 50% [7], partly caused by the reduced size of each product and more efficient packaging, but also because the transport capacity was not adjusted correspondingly [8, 9]. The trend to reduce the waste of resources is not specific to the manufacturing industry, but combined with the increasing world market prices for raw materials the incentives to be as sustainable as possible are stronger. Thus, the ability to share resources, innovate and to drive the implementation and deployment of emergent ICT will play a key role for their competitiveness.

In comparison to the manufacturing area where more and more strategic partnerships are (e.g. extended/virtual enterprises) formed along the supply chain, similar concepts are hardly deployed in the logistics field, even though a better utilisation would lead to cost savings, improved environmental balance and a more sustainable business models, but it also requires trust, coordination, joint planning and problem solving [10]. Business to business (B2B) technology enables a set of complex business processes across distinct operating entities. This allows participants along the entire supply chain to share decision-making, workflow, and capabilities. Furthermore, the technology enables participants to collaboratively design, build, sell and service products faster, more efficiently, and more cost effectively on a global scale. The cooperation can be described in terms of integration within the scope of the network as well as in terms of the strength of the inter-organisational bond [11, 12]. This paper aims at identifying and analysing different barriers for an increased access to shared resource. The second part of the paper deals with potential means to reduce and overcome some of these barriers by providing teaching concepts for awareness raising of the opportunities shared resources may give.

2   A Need for a Shift Towards Production Ecosystems

The traditional supply chain is product-centric, mostly focusing more on production cost reduction than on also including environmental and societal impacts into the optimisation strategy (i.e. using multi-criteria strategies). Consequently, for many years production was delocalized in remote low labour cost countries far from the market. This strategy worked well as long as the transport costs were low and the customer did not care so much about environmental and societal impact in the countries of production or for the environmental impact of transport.

This perception has been slightly changed, and both customers and low cost countries' governments pay more attention to the societal and environmental impacts of the transportation. In addition, most of these countries are now facing increasing wealth, and thus also increasing wages. Thus, there is a need for new production strategies and, thanks to enhancements in ICT technologies; demand driven optimization strategies have been developed [13] both considering new production possibilities (i.e. 3D printing) and local sourcing trends.

Looking ahead, these trends will enforce changes at different levels. On the supply side a market transformation is foreseeable towards more operational cooperation between the different players in the logistics field. Current resistance factors, mostly market protection and lack of trust, will have to be overcome. On the demand side, further globalisation, increases in product variants, personalized solutions and e-commerce might lead to a future establishment of "selling less of more" practices. For the logistics and manufacturing sectors, this will mean that environment-sensitive clients will be at the same time demanding fast and highly customised services. Both producer and the suppliers will profit from collaborative production by sharing resources and access to information through less inventory, less transport costs and improved resource utilisation as well as through a better environmental balance, but it has a negative influence on their flexibility: The requested delivery date by the customer strongly depends on the agreement with suppliers when they can deliver the needed components, which again depends on their production capacity. Sharing resources leads to less flexibility, since the access to the production means or logistics transport means is not only depending on in-house priorities but also on agreements with other collaboration partners. In addition, use of shared resources does increase the complexity of planning and reduces the freedom in the decision making process. This, in combination with the increasing pressure from customers and suppliers for transparent communication and information provision of product properties (e.g. process parameters used, components included) and related information (e.g. on-time according to plan, quality aspects), forces manufacturing companies to think of new ways to utilize the available infrastructure and intelligently add new technological applications. In order to enable innovative cost- and resource-effective product solutions, with a minimal ecological footprint throughout the lifecycle, a holistic view on the supply chain and all its stakeholders (i.e. also the LSPs, transports companies and customs etc as well as manufacturer) should be considered. The challenge of mastering the complexity of applying a shared resource concept in a supply chain context can be envisaged from Ousterhouts layered model, showing the goods and information flow as well as the interaction among stakeholders at different layers in the supply chain (fig. 1).

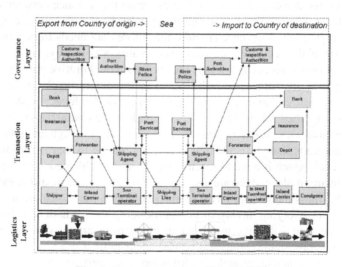

Fig. 1. Oosterhouts layered Model [14]

Based on fig. 1, it appears that the shared resource approach puts several complex requirements both on the collaboration between the stakeholders as well as on the ICT infrastructure, and thus may be a source for the low deployment and many of the existing barriers.

3   Challenges and Barriers for Improved Cooperation and the Access to Shared Resources

The hard global competition, inter-dependencies among stakeholders, tight schedules leads to need for better utilization of available resources. The innovation in the use of shared resources consists of bringing together the resources and capabilities of different stakeholders in a supply chain (e.g. logistics services, providers and shippers) to address the optimisation and sustainability challenges faced by the logistics and transport domain. In Europe, several manufacturers, suppliers and logistics and transport service providers are micro and small enterprises. These companies possess profound, specialized competences [15], but do often face a shortage in access to resources, in terms of human resources, funding as well as complementary assets and technologies [16]. Collaboration giving access to new, shared resources will ensure a better overall utilization [17]. A better utilitsation of resources can be realized today, by adding more intelligence in the existing ICT solutions as well as by increasing the adoption and integration of on-cargo and on-vehicle technologies as well as by using existing SCM tools for planning and execution, but is scarcely adopted. Thus in order to understand the low use, a survey was carried out in order to identify barriers that can limit uptake of new ways of sharing or using innovative solutions. When analyzing the limitation regarding the sharing of information, it was clear that a main problem is the lack of trust among the stakeholders [4]. **Trust** between the involved organizations is however a pre-requisite and can only be achieved through long-term relationships between the actors and contracts that decrease the distance between the companies. Looking at common practice within the supply chain today, the use of short-term contracts is high. Shared resources require that more data needs to be **processed and analyzed** than if the resources are only used within a company, since the planning comprises not only own needs but also those of the collaborative partners. This leads the need for **systems interoperability** between the actors involved and a need for single, easy to use collaborative platforms, linked to the legacy systems. This becomes more important when the number of smaller-size organizations involved (e.g. such as smallholders, consumers purchasing groups, etc.) is high and when the logistics infrastructure is shared. In addition to barriers related to sharing of information at a technical level, which is a well-known barrier, and for which concepts like federated platforms etc are in place, there are also barriers related to the **business models**. Most innovative business models are based on the perception that collaboration can lead to better results for everyone involved. For introducing them, models of how these results are to be split will have to be put in place from an early stage Such models should lead to quantifiable results and be very clear in their use and they should allow for synergy gain calculation and redistribution. Furthermore, business models that involve the collaboration of various actors during the physical delivery process require common or compatible operational practices among the actors involved. This is a typical barrier found in most cases of horizontal or vertical cooperation in the supply chain. In addition, as mentioned above sharing resources has a direct influence on the flexibility, thus sharing infrastructure (especially physical one) among various partners requires clearly defined practices. Finally, the last area analyzed is related to organizational issues - the decision making process differs among the different stakeholders. This in turn, increases the complexity as well as the challenge to keep the decision-making process transparent (local, central, management level etc.); in addition the concept of shared resources can only be realized throughout the supply chain by implementing advances ICT. The adoption of innovative technologies implies changes in the workforce of an organization. New expertise is required while skills acquired previously may become obsolete. In emerging technologies there are few people with the necessary competences. Additionally, the adoption of innovative technologies may result in frustration to the employees that have to change the way they normally used to do their job. All in all, so far it has not been possible to measure/assess the positive effect of the shared resources concepts in across the supply chain to such an extent that it has broadly uptaken and implemented. The next section will therefore discuss approaches based on experiential learning that might be used in order to create the required understanding of advantages and limitations of shared resources.

4   Why Use Serious Games

General trends supporting the use of shared resources like the Internet of Things will impact significantly on the supply chain as a whole. On the one side allowing, monitoring and handling goods through distributed computing infrastructures and, on the other side, allowing easy publication, retrieval and composition of freight information service.

A successful introduction, implementation and operation of advanced technical solutions necessary for using share resources is not only a matter of hardware and software, but it does imply changes both in the organizational structure of the stakeholders' organizations as well as in the working environment of the employees. Thus, a key to a successful implementation of shared resources concept in supply chains is to increase the awareness [18]. Due to its high motivation factor and the possibility to let the participants play an active role, the use of experiential learning forms has been increasing within education at all levels [19, 20, 21]. With SCM and OR education, serious games are regularly used to overcome the gap between theory and practices. The most famous one is still the Beer Game [23] was developed by MIT to simulate the dynamics of a supply chain explaining the bullwhip effect which has been digitalized into online gaming format and systems thinking [23]. Games focusing at different areas of SCM including manufacturing can be found in [19, 20, 21, 25, 26].

Within the vocational training, there are several examples on how SG are used in the executive training for decades as well as examples on how games can be used in the training of operational personnel [27, 28]. Most of these games are multi-player games, not only focussing on the specific problem, but also aiming at conveying the players the importance of communication and collaboration in a supply chain context through their own experience in the gaming environment. Through such games, the players also experience that information sharing and trust are key factors for successful and sustainable collaboration in supply chains.

The above discussed challenges and barriers for implementing shared resources in the supply chain require knowledge and skills about the mid- and long-term impact of collaboration decisions on security, trust, operational practices and gain-share. Looking at available games used for SCM [21, 24] the collaboration and trust raising aspect is covered in several games, and games like the Fresh Connection, also take business consideration into account at a certain level. But a thorough analysis also reveals that they do not cover all barriers like the challenge visualising gain sharing models as well as how to optimise the utilisation of machine and transport capabilities by a high degree of flexibility. Depending on how games like Shortfall and the Lean Leap Logistics Games, the Beer game [25, 26] are embedded in a learning unit, these games can be used to discuss and make the players aware and able to understand how these barriers are related, but their simulation models does not mirror the complexity well enough for the topic of shared resources and therefore need to be extended in order to fully cover the complexity. Still unsolved is the question on how to develop simulation models mirroring the reality of the complex interaction better, and thus able to demonstrate the challenges of ownership of a shared resource etc. (what happens if a partner needs access to a shared resource while it is occupied?), still being so transparent that the players understand the inter-dependencies between their decision and the impact this have in the game? In addition to the knowledge about potential collaboration benefits, game solutions would need to incorporate strategic (and operative) decisions and their impact on the benefits of shared resources. Furthermore, it is important for an awareness raising game, that the player experience the boundaries being able to discover that these change in different environment. This requires that multi-criteria decision making processes in highly dynamic systems can be simplified in different levels and be adapted to be applied in different scenarios/settings. This again however requires a high degree of field specific knowledge and a flexible simulation model.

However, these requirements would increase the complexity of games which often may contradict the learning outcome because it may undermine the transmission of the learning objectives by causing confusion. The players may not have the ability anymore, to comprehend their actions and decisions and to reflect them in front of the game results. In order to avioid this and to take the indivdual learning and awareness raising need into account, we use a concept based on scaffolding principle, In a first step we intend to realise a prototype by using a game engine with an authoring tool allowing constructing several scenarios focussing on different aspects and with different levels (both related to complexity and prior need of knowledge). This will require use of learning analytics in order to monitor and trace the gained skills and also for giving the players and the system feedback.

5   Conclusion

Manufacturing has become a complex process resulting in long brittle supply chains with considerable contributions to the global resource demand and its environmental impact. Materials in short supply and customer requirements trigger market stakeholders to reduce the waste of resources and to be more sustainable. Therefore, the ability to share resources, innovate and to implement emergent ICT becomes more important for the competitiveness and sustainability of businesses and companies. Sharing resources puts high standards on trust, gain-sharing, the use of ICT etc. Furthermore, although well known in supply chain management, the logistics sector is struggling to find approaches to collaborate and to share.

Among the identified barriers trust, the management of big data, interoperability issues and the costs of integration seems to be of high importance, but also the lack of understanding of the concept and its advantages contributes to the low penetration rate. This paper looked at the use of SG as a tool for increasing this awareness, and several games that cover some of the aspects and that could be used for overcoming the barrier were identified. This analysis of existing supply chain games revealed their potential but also remaining weaknesses and gaps, both related to the lack of accurate simulation models, as well as suitable ways of balance the reality of the real world with the simplification necessary for awareness raising of complex systems. Here, more research has to be carried out. New games for the discussed purpose would have gone ahead profound research to balance complexity and learning objectives. This research is complemented by the development of advanced serious game (engines), able to handle more indicators and providing substantial feedback and analysis of the game progress. Improved learning analytics will help to develop and evaluate such advanced environments.

Acknowledgements. The research reported in this paper has been partially supported by the European Union, particularly through the projects: GaLA: The European Network of Excellence on Serious Games (FP7-ICT-2009.4.2-258169) www.galanoe.eu and LOGINN (GA 314338).

References

1. D'Aveni, R.A., Dagnino, G.B., Smith, K.G.: The age of temporary competitive advantage. Strategic Management Journal 31(13), 1371–1385 (2010)
2. Reichwald, R., Piller, F.: Interaktive Wertschöpfung. Gabler Verlag, Wiesbaden (2009)
3. World Economic Forum, Supply Chain Decarbonization: The Role of Logistics and Transport in Reducing Supply Chain Carbon Emissions. Geneva (2009)
4. Cassandra 2012 Cassandra project (2012), Compendium, Download (August 2012), http://www.cassandra-project.eu
5. DHL 2009 Deutsche Post AG, "Delivering Tomorrow, Customer Needs in 2020 and Beyond - A Global Delphi Study", Deutsche Post AG (June 2009)

6. Autry, C.W., Michelle Bobbitt, L.: Supply chain security orientation: conceptual development and a proposed framework. The International Journal of Logistics Management 19(1), 42–64 (2008)
7. Ackermann, Ackermann, H, Mitfahrzentrale für Frachtgüter. Fraunhofer ITWM (2011), http://www.itwm.fraunhofer.de/presse-und-publikationen/pressearchiv/pressearchiv-2011/15052011-mitfahrzentrale-fuer-frachtgueter.html (retreived November 3, 2011)
8. Simchi-Levi, D., Peruvankal, J.P., Mulani, N., Read, B., Ferreira, J.: Is It Time to Rethink Your Manufacturing Stratgy. MIT Sloan Management Review 21 (December 2011)
9. WorldTradeOrganization, International Trade Statistics (2013), Retrieved from http://www.wto.org/english/res_e/statis_e/its2013_e/its2013_e.pdf
10. Min, S., Roath, A.S., Daugherty, P.J., Genchev, S.E., Chen, H., Arndt, A.D.: SC collaboration: what's happening? The International Journal of Logistics Management 16(2), 237–256 (2005)
11. Jagdev, H.S., Thoben, K.: Production Planning & Control – Anatomy of enterprise collaborations 12(5), 437–445 (2001)
12. Braziotis, C., Tannock, J.: Building the extended enterprise: key collaboration factors. The International Journal of Logistics Management 22(3), 349–372 (2011)
13. Hesmer, A., Hribernik, K., Baalsrud Hauge, J., Thoben, K.-D.: Supporting the ideation processes by a collaborative online based toolset. International Journal of Technology Management 55(3/4), 218–225 (2011)
14. Van Oosterhout, M.P.A., et al.: Visibility Platforms for Enhancing Supply Chain Security: a Case Study in the Port of Rotterdam. In: The International Symposium on Maritime Safety, Security and Enviromental Protection, Athens, Greece (2007)
15. Lee, S., Park, G., Yoon, B., Park, J.: Open innovation in SMEs: An intermediated network model. Research Policy 39(2), 290–300 (2010)
16. Madrid-Guijarro, A., Garcia, D., Van Auken, H.: Barriers to innovation among Spanish manufacturing SMEs. Journal of Small Business Management 47(4), 465–488 (2009)
17. Alter, S.: Metamodel for Service Analysis and Design Based on an Operational View of Service and Service Systems. Service Science 4(3), 218–235 (2012)
18. Fawcett, S.E., Waller, M.A.: Mitigating the Myopia of Dominant Logics: On Differential Performance and Strategic Supply Chain Research. Journal of Business Logistics 33(3), 173–180 (2012)
19. Baalsrud Hauge, J., Bellotti, F., Nadolski, R., Kickmeier-Rust, M.D., Berta, R., Carvalho, M.: Deploying serious games for management in higher education: Lessons learned and good practices. In: Escudeiro, P., Vaz de Carvalho, C. (eds.) Proc. 7th European Conf. on Games based Learning (pp, Porto, Portugal, October 2-3, pp. 225–234 (2013)
20. Campbell, A., Gontzel, J., Savelsbergh, M.: Experiences with the use of supply chain software in education. Production and Operation Management 9(1), 66–80 (1999)
21. Lewis, M.A., Maylor, H.: Game playing and operations management education. Int. J. Production Economics 105(2007), 134–149 (2007)
22. Anderson, S., et al.: Urban logistics - how can it meet policy makers' sustainability objectives? Journal of Transport Geography 13(1), 71–81 (2005)
23. Forrester, J.W.: Industrial Dynamics. A major breakthrough for decision makers. Harvard Business Review 36(4), 37–66 (1958)
24. Macdonald, J.R., Frommer, I.D., Karaesmen, I.Z.: Decision making in the beer game and supply chain performance. Operations Management Research 6(3-4), 119–126 (2013)

25. Zhou, L., Xie, Y., Wild, N., Hunt, C.: Learning and practising supply chain management strategies from a business simulation game: a comprehensive supply chain simulation. In: Proc. of IEEE Simulation Conf., WSC 2008, pp. 2534–2542 (2008)
26. Corriere, J.D.: Shortfall: An Educational Game on Environmental Issues in Supply Chain Management. M.S. Thesis. Mechanical & Industrial Engineering. Northeastern University, Boston, MA (2003)
27. Azadegan, A., Riedel, J.C.K.H., Baalsrud Hauge, J.: Serious games adoption in corporate training. In: Ma, M., Oliveira, M.F., Hauge, J.B., Duin, H., Thoben, K.-D. (eds.) SGDA 2012. LNCS (LNAI), vol. 7528, pp. 74–85. Springer, Heidelberg (2012)
28. Gala NoE: D3.3 Serious Games Application Fields report (2013)

The Cornerstone of Sustainability Strategy in Manufacturing Enterprises

David Opresnik, Marco Seregni, and Marco Taisch

Department of Management, Economics and Industrial Engineering, Politecnico di Milano,
Piazza Leonardo Da Vinci 32, 20133, Milano, Italy
{david.opresnik,marco.seregni,marco.taisch}@polimi.it

Abstract. Sustainability has already been seen to impact positively the competitive advantage of an enterprise. Nonetheless managing sustainability still too often represents a conundrum. Consequently, the aim of this article is to help managers of manufacturing enterprises to understand, from an integrative perspective, the impact of the concept of sustainability onto their enterprise, with the objective to increase their long-term success. Thus, it was first assayed, if sustainability is a strategy and what are its main characteristics. To ensure validity, we leaned on the most renowned definitions of "strategy". Secondly, an integrative framework for sustainability in manufacturing enterprises was designed, depicting the interrelations among the enterprise's core elements (strategies, tactics, operations) and also with the environment (legislature and market), while dedicating special attention the concept of "fit". The results altogether creates the cornerstone of the strategy of sustainability for manufacturing enterprises.

Keywords: sustainability, strategy, manufacturing, sustainable manufacturing.

1   Introduction

According to the National Association of Manufacturers, the manufacturing sector has the highest economic multiplier effect of all sectors [1]. Thus, manufacturing plays one of the key roles not only from an economic, but also from a social perspective, as it is a crucial provider of jobs. However, due to an increasing global competition, manufacturing enterprises in mature economies are facing a challenge how to grow on the long-term, while providing high quality jobs within a much stricter legislative environment then some of their peer countries. Thus, they are forced to define new sustainable but competitive growth alternatives. Namely, a single-minded focus on economic sustainability can succeed only in the short run; though, while long-term success requires all three dimensions of sustainability - economic, society and environment [2], [3]. Those three dimensions of sustainability are called the Triple Bottom Line (TBL) [4] through which an enterprise can create more long term value and achieve a higher long term competitive advantage, while encountering fewer risks [2], [5]–[7]. However, sustainability brings many challenges. Namely, managers are realizing that sustainability is becoming part of their business, but they fear the risk of

B. Grabot et al. (Eds.): APMS 2014, Part II, IFIP AICT 439, pp. 500–507, 2014.
© IFIP International Federation for Information Processing 2014

failing in dealing with it [8]. They have trouble understanding the incorporation of sustainability and the implications of their actions on long-term success [9]. Thus the difficulty is no longer whether to implement sustainability, but how [10]. Hence, as sustainability in enterprises still represents a conundrum, the aim of this article is to help managers of manufacturing enterprises understand, from an integrative perspective, the integration of sustainability, in order to enable them to exploit it as a new basis for long-term competitive advantage. Consequently, the following research questions are set: a) is sustainability in a manufacturing enterprise really a strategy and if it is so, which are its main characteristics, b) in which elements of the enterprise (strategic, tactical, operational) is sustainability applicable and what are the interrelations among them, c) what is the impact of the environment (legislature and market)? The results will be twofold: first depicting the main characteristics of sustainability as a strategy and secondly, through an integrative sustainability framework, identifying and assaying the main previously mentioned interrelations. Those two sets of results together represents the cornerstone of sustainability in manufacturing enterprises.

The value of this work for managers of manufacturing enterprises lies in helping them optimize their market position by using sustainability and to optimize its management. As for theory, it offers the first integrative framework for sustainability as a strategy for a manufacturing enterprise, taking into account the concept of fit. The article goes as following. After the literature review, the main definitions of the term "strategy" are assayed and applied on the concept of sustainability. In the next step, the main results are synthesized into an integrative framework.

2   Literature Review

Following the concept of sustainability science [11], this article is *per se* transdisciplinary, gathering the main pillars steaming from manufacturing, sustainability and strategy. Sustainable development goes back to Agenda 21 [12], an important policy document for sustainable development that was adopted at the Rio World Summit in 1992. Sustainability has many definitions, though the most famous is probably from Brundtland's report [13]: *"... the ability to meet the needs of the present without compromising the ability of future generations to meet their own needs"*. Though there are many other definitions of suitability, the framework of the TBL [4] is chosen to work with in this article, as it is depicting the economic, social and environmental aspect of sustainability. Regardless of its high-level principal, sustainability can still be monitored, assessed and reported. An organization's performance in the wider context of sustainability is presented via reporting, using e.g. GRIG4 reporting guidelines. Another possibility to identify in more detail relevant elements of sustainability is to use a priority matrix [14]. Nonetheless, sustainability comes down to subjective rating, as the criteria and their indicators are mostly chosen and calculated based on opinion of experts, although much more exact techniques are also employed in the context of environmental sustainability like the Life Cycle Assessment technique [15].

Sustainability on the enterprise level is most often referred to as corporate sustainability. According to the Dow Jones Sustainability Index – it is a business approach that creates long-term shareholder value [9]. Interestingly sustainability within an enterprise seems to enable an early-mover advantage in international markets [16] or should even go as far as underpinning the current business models that are based on the idea to sell as much products as possible [17]. Sustainability has also been linked with the strategic management tool the Balanced Scored Board [18], resulting in a Sustainability Balanced Scorecard encompassing a perspective of the three pillars of sustainability [19]. Sustainability, the social part, has been also scrutinized in relation to manufacturing [20]. Regardless of its positive impact, sustainability is also criticized. It is argued that the concept is useless because it cannot be adequately defined [21] or that the term "sustainable development" is oxymoronic; how can something develop if it is to remain the same (i.e. "sustainable")? [22]. As identified, sustainability represents a high-level guidance that is certainly useful to some extent, however do not meet the rigid requirements to fully operationalize sustainable development in all the levels of the enterprise integrally, while taking into account the specificities of a manufacturing enterprise.

3   Methodology

This article conceptualizes the strategy of sustainability within a manufacturing enterprise. The dependent variable is long-term competitive advantage of a manufacturing enterprise. The independent variable is the strategy of sustainability. In this context, it is first delved if sustainability can even be considered as a strategy, by benchmarking it against the most renowned definitions of this term. Basing the conceptualization of the strategy of sustainability on rigid criteria in intermediate steps, it allow us to avoid the "problem of demarcation"; thus the article draws on Karl Popper's philosophy and onto its "falsificationism", claiming that "a hypothesis is scientific if and only if it has the potential to be refuted by some possible observation" [23]. In the spirit of this philosophy, we included strict criteria enabling us to critically refute the propositions made in this article.

4   Model Development

In order to identify the cornerstones of the strategy of sustainability for a manufacturing enterprise, the following conceptualization steps are followed. First, in order to position with validity sustainability into a manufacturing enterprise, it has to be reviewed if it can be treated as a strategy and what are its main characteristics. To scrutinize this, the main definitions of strategy are assayed, from which its most relevant characteristics are then derived, representing the next step. Finally, based on the results, an integrative framework depicting all the main interrelations relevant for the strategy of sustainability is designed.

Sustainability has already in some cases been recognized as a strategy [24], [25], in some cases as a perspective of a strategy [19].The need for its management has been also widely acknowledged at different levels of the enterprise [26], [27]. The first definition of strategy is presented according to Porter [28], stating that strategy is the creation of a unique and valuable position, the way a firm chooses activities that differ from those of the competitors. If sustainability is able to create such position and choose differently its activities, it can be seen as a strategy. In addition, it would mean that it does not have only to position itself with a unique and/or valuable position, but it also has to relate this position to some operations within the enterprise. Namely, Porter [29] defines operational effectiveness and the choice of strategic positioning essential for a performance on the longer term. According to the second definition from Quinn [30], strategy is: "The pattern or plan that integrates an organization's major goals, policies, and action sequences into a cohesive whole." This would indicate sustainability to be a viable strategy that has to encompass the enterprise as a cohesive whole, thus indicating the urge for an internal fit. The concept of fit has been viewed as an internal consistency among key strategic decisions or the alignment between strategic choices and critical contingencies with the environment (external) [31], being essential for long-term success [32]. The third definition of strategy defines it as the pattern of decisions that determines and reveals its objectives and produces the principal policies and plans for achieving those goals. It also defines the range of business the company is to pursue, the kind of economic and human organization it intends to be, and the nature of the contributions to various stakeholders [33]. Such patterns and principal policies can also represent the integration of sustainability into the enterprise. According to this definition of strategy, priorities from the economic and human perspectives have to be assumed, as also to which stakeholders and to what extent the strategy should take into account those elements. Finally, according to Barney [34] "a good strategy ... neutralizes threats and exploits opportunities while capitalizing on strengths and avoiding or fixing weaknesses." This would indicate that sustainability within a manufacturing enterprise should be applied selectively, depending at least of the environment (legislative and market) and the relative position of the manufacturing enterprise itself. Hence, this means that sustainability is a viable strategy only when it presents itself as an opportunity to be exploited or as a threat that can be converted into an opportunity. However each business strategy is unique [35], therefore contingent upon many factors.

4.1   The Cornerstones of the Strategy of Sustainability

In the previous section, the main characteristics of a strategy in general were presented. In this subsection, four main characteristics are chosen, from which the main characteristics of sustainability strategy are derived. Afterwards the integrative framework for sustainability is depicted. Those two results constitute the cornerstone of sustainability for a manufacturing enterprise. The four main characteristics are the following (*note*: after each characteristic that is listed, it is then explained how it relates to sustainability).

First strategic characteristic. A strategy enables the manufacturing enterprise to position itself with a unique and/or valuable proposition [28], [36]. Sustainability can enable to change the strategic positioning of an enterprise (e.g. accessing a new customer segment). This positioning depends on the internal as well as on the external context, which is the market (i.e. industry, competition, trends etc.), and the legislative environment that is defining among others incentives for sustainability in manufacturing. Therefore, the positioning of a manufacturing enterprise based on the strategy of sustainability is contingent upon external context, which are the market and the legislative environment (see Fig. 1).

Second strategic characteristic. A strategy neutralizes threats and exploits opportunities while capitalizing on strengths and avoiding or fixing weaknesses [34]. Hence, the strategy of sustainability *per se* can represent itself as an opportunity or as a threat, thus how sustainability is perceived by an enterprise is contingent upon multiple factors. In a supportive environment for sustainability, moreover a supportive legislative (e.g. incentives for environment and social inclusiveness) and a supportive business environment (e.g. consumers are willing to pay a premium for sustainability related product-services), sustainability can represent a threat or an opportunity. Instances of both presented. Firstly, it represents a threat to the focal enterprise, if it cannot take advantage of the opportunities arising from the environment, while its competitors can. For instance, the focal enterprise has to close down its production plant due to a CO_2 emission excess or cannot take advantage of development funds related to sustainability activities or cannot satisfy the new consumer trends, while its competitor can. However, secondly, if the focal enterprise has the internal capabilities to deploy the strategy of sustainability throughout its value chain and thus take advantage of the opportunities arising from such environment, then sustainability presents itself as an opportunity. It is even greater, if its competitors, on the other hand, are not able to take advantage of them. This would indicate that the focal enterprise is deploying a new basis for their long-term competitive advantage. Thirdly, if the focal enterprise intends to take advantage of the opportunities arising from sustainability, but it has assessed poorly its own internal capabilities for deploying such a complex strategy, than this strategy is seen as a threat. The application of such strategy would then impede the growth of its long-term competitive advantage. This case can be classified as a threat and not a weakness, because the sustainability strategy arise from the environment and not from the enterprise, however, it is also true that is transforming itself into a weakness after its integration.

Third strategic characteristic. After positioning itself in relation to sustainability, the manufacturing enterprise must choose activities that differ from the competitors and relate them to the newly chosen position [28]. Based on the strategy of sustainability, the enterprise must define its priorities in sustainability. They have to arise from the strategy and reflect onto the operations, for which the adequate manufacturing tactics have to be chosen.

Forth strategic characteristic. In order to be able to align the strategy with its tactics and operations on one hand and to align them with the environment afterwards, managers must encompass the enterprise as a cohesive whole, while indicating the urge for an internal fit [30]. Thus, two fits must exist. One that aligns the strategy with the tactical and operational level and the second that aligns the internal strategy with the environment. The former fit is essential, because according to a strategy of sustainability, specific tactics and operations have to be chosen and well aligned. It means, for

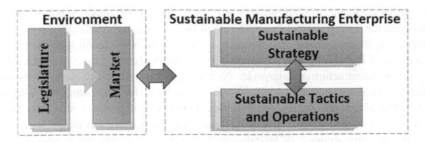

Fig. 1. The Strategy of Sustainability – fit and positioning

example, that if at the operational level a production line is optimized in terms of energy efficiency, also sustainability related improvements should be undertaken at the tactical level (e.g. product-services for sustainable consumption) as also should be aligned with the strategy. Only at the point when the two fits exist (internal and with the environment), a manufacturing enterprise can be seen as an optimized sustainable system. Otherwise, inefficiencies and opportunity costs arise, that in turn does not increase maximally its long-term competitive advantage. As for the second fit, the one between the enterprise and the environment is also crucial. Namely, if the legislative and business environments are not supportive towards the application of sustainability in manufacturing, which is the case for countries where industrialization has just begun or is still undergoing, then the strategy of sustainability for an enterprise in such an environment has no meaning. It can even become a threat, if the focal enterprise invests considerable amounts of resources into implementing sustainability, while no new business opportunities open up due to this investment.

The integrative model for sustainability of manufacturing is depicted on Figure 1. One component is the environment, constituted by the legislation and market, while the second segment is the enterprise. It has three main sub-segments, commencing with the strategy, going down to tactics and operations that are critical for manufacturing, while all are supported and performed by managerial processes. Each element is made of three layers, representing the TBL. Furthermore, the two fits can be seen with the two darker arrows, one among internal elements in the enterprise (strategy, tactics, operations) and the second between the enterprise and the environment. In the next research steps, it should be identified what exactly constitutes a sustainability strategy, to go another step closer to operationalize sustainability in an enterprise.

5   Conclusion

Sustainability through the perspective of a manager in a manufacturing enterprise was delved. In order to do so, it was first assayed if sustainability was a viable strategy for manufacturers, by leaning on the most renowned definition of the term "strategy". After confirmation, the key characteristics of the strategy of sustainability were derived. During the analysis, it was identified that sustainability is omnipresent in the enterprise as well as in the environment. Hence, managers must manage the strategy of sustainability integrally, taking into account all of its components within the enterprise (strategy, tactics, operations and management), the fit among them, as also the fit between the enterprise and its environment (legislature and market).

Managing those complex and dynamic interrelations, while leaning on the key characteristics of the strategy of sustainability formed the cornerstone of sustainability strategy in manufacturing enterprise. Nonetheless, sustainability strategy is not a standalone strategy, but represents an additional basis for increasing the long-term competitive advantage. As it quite complex to manage, it is hence also very hard to imitate it, consequently being able to sustain such competitive advantage for a longer time, making the strategy of sustainability a sustainable one for a manufacturing enterprise.

Acknowledgement. This work has been partly funded by the European Commission through the FoF-ICT Project *MSEE: Manufacturing SErvice Ecosystem (No. 284860)*. The authors wish to acknowledge the European Commission.

References

1. "Global Agenda Council on Advanced Manufacturing 2012-2014,". World Economic Forum (2012)
2. Dyllick, T., Hockerts, K.: Beyond the business case for corporate sustainability. Bus. Strateg. Environ. 11(2), 130–141 (2002)
3. Gladwin, T.N., Kennelly, J.J., Krause, T.-S.: Shifting paradigms for sustainable development: Implications for management theory and research. Acad. Manag. Rev. 20(4), 874–907 (1995)
4. Elkington, J.: Partnerships from cannibals with forks: The triple bottom line of 21st-century business. Environ. Qual. Manag. 8(1), 37–51 (1998)
5. Michael, B., Gross, R.: Running business like a government in the new economy: lessons for organizational design and corporate governance. Corp. Gov. 4(3), 32–46 (2004)
6. Salzmann, O., Ionescu-somers, A., Steger, U.: The Business Case for Corporate Sustainability: Literature Review and Research Options. Eur. Manag. J. 23(1), 27–36 (2005)
7. Valente, M.: Theorizing Firm Adoption of Sustaincentrism. Organ. Stud. 33(4), 563–591 (2012)
8. Berns, M., Townend, A., Khayat, Z., Balagopal, B., Reeves, M., Hopkins, M.S., Kruschwitz, N.: The business of sustainability: what it means to managers now. MIT Sloan Manag. Rev. 51(1), 20–26 (2009)
9. Epstein, M.J., Roy, M.-J.: Making the business case for sustainability. J. Corp. Citizsh. 2003(9), 79–96 (2003)
10. Epstein, M.J., Roy, M.-J.: Sustainability in action: Identifying and measuring the key performance drivers. Long Range Plann. 34(5), 585–604 (2001)
11. Clark, W.C., Dickson, N.M.: Sustainability science: the emerging research program. Proc. Natl. Acad. Sci. 100(14), 8059–8061 (2003)
12. Sitarz, D.: Agenda 21: The earth summit strategy to save our planet. Earth Press (1993)
13. Brundtland, G.H.: World commission on environment and development. Our Common Futur., 8–9 (1987)
14. Bordt, M.: OECD Sustainable Manufacturing Toolkit. Sustain. US Compet. Summit, US Dep. Commer., vol. 8 (2009)

15. Ibáñez-Forés, V., Bovea, M.D., Pérez-Belis, V.: A holistic review of applied methodologies for assessing and selecting the optimal technological alternative from a sustainability perspective. J. Clean. Prod. 70, 259–281 (2014)
16. Porter, M.E., der Linde, C.: Green and competitive: ending the stalemate. Harv. Bus. Rev. 73(5), 120–134 (1995)
17. Garetti, M., Taisch, M.: Sustainable manufacturing: trends and research challenges. Prod. Plan. Control 23(2–3), 83–104 (2012)
18. Kaplan, R.S., Norton, D.P.: Linking the balanced scorecard to strategy. Calif. Manage. Rev. 39(1) (1996)
19. Figge, F., Hahn, T., Schaltegger, S., Wagner, M.: The Sustainability Balanced Scorecard – linking sustainability management to business strategy. Bus. Strateg. Environ. 11(5), 269–284 (2002)
20. Fantini, P., Taisch, M., Palasciano, C.: Social Sustainability: Perspectives on the Role of Manufacturing. In: Prabhu, V., Taisch, M., Kiritsis, D. (eds.) APMS 2013, Part I. IFIP AICT, vol. 414, pp. 62–69. Springer, Heidelberg (2013)
21. Costanza, R., Patten, B.C.: Defining and predicting sustainability. Ecol. Econ. 15(3), 193–196 (1995)
22. White, M.A.: Sustainability: I know it when I see it. Ecol. Econ. 86, 213–217 (2013)
23. Godfrey-Smith, P.: An introduction to the philosophy of science: Theory and reality. University of Chicago Press, Chicago (2003)
24. Epstein, M.J., Wisner, P.S.: Using a Balanced Scorecard to Implement Sustainability. Environ. Qual. Manag. 11(2), 1–10 (2001)
25. Unruh, G.: The Sweet Spot of Sustainability Strategy. MIT Sloan Manag. Rev. 55(1), 15–20 (2013)
26. Asif, M., Searcy, C., Garvare, R., Ahmad, N.: Including sustainability in business excellence models. Total Qual. Manag. Bus. Excell. 22(7), 773–786 (2011)
27. Corbett, L.M.: Sustainable operations management: A typological approach. J. Ind. Eng. Manag. 2(1), 10–30 (2009)
28. Porter, M.E.: What is strategy? Publ. (November 1996)
29. Porter, M.E., Kramer, M.R.: The competitive advantage of corporate philanthropy. Harv. Bus. Rev. 80(12), 56–68 (2002)
30. Quinn, J.B.: Strategies for change: logical incrementalism. R.D. Irwin (1980)
31. Ensign, P.: The concept of fit in organizational research. Int. J. Organ. Theory Behav. (Marcel Dekker) 4(3/4), 287 (2001)
32. Govindarajan, V.: Implementing competitive strategies at the business unit level: implications of matching managers to strategies. Strateg. Manag. J. 10(3), 251–269 (1989)
33. Foss, N.J.: Resources, Firms, and Strategies: A Reader in the Resource-based Perspective. Oxford University Press (1997)
34. Barney, J.B.: Gaining and sustaining competitive advantage. Addison-Wesley, Reading (1997)
35. Rumelt, R.P.: Evaluating business strategy. In: Mintzb, H., Quinn, J.B., Ghoshal, S. (eds.) Strateg. Process. Revis., Ed. Prentice Hall Eur. (1998)
36. Mintzberg, H.: The Strategy Concept 1: Five P's for Strategy. U. of California (1987)

Investigating Lean Methodology
for Energy Efficient Manufacturing

Alice Bush[1], Claudio Palasciano[1], Alberto Portioli Staudacher[1],
Marco Taisch[1], and Stefano Vitali[2]

[1] Politecnico di Milano, and Milano Italy
{alice.bush,claudio.palasciano,
alberto.portioli,marco.taisch}@ polimi.it
[2] BorgWarner Morse TEC Europe,Arcore, Milano Italy
stefano.vitali@morseTEC.it

Abstract. Due to the growing globalization and the increasing interest in environmental concerns, together with the changing legal and regulations landscape, manufacturers need to change their approach to competition, enhancing their knowledge of the manufacturing systems and of the network of interconnections among physical flows and management and control information flows, while developing systemic methodologies that enable waste reduction of manufacturing resources usage (such as energy). Furthermore, companies are increasingly involved in managing the environment as an opportunity for competitive advantage, which establishes the need to highlight the relationships between environmental impact of their processes and company strategy and objectives. This paper presents a proposal for a lean methodology, called Transformation Distribution and Utilization (namely, T.D.U.) methodology, which allows future factories to identify Value Added energy usage, paving the way to activities that can reduce the related inefficiencies and wastes. The T.D.U. methodology has been tested in real company, MorseTEC Europe, a supplier of systems for European car manufacturers.

Keywords: energy efficiency, sustainable manufacturing, continuous improvement, CIP, lean manufacturing, green manufacturing, energy value stream analysis, EVSA, energy value stream mapping, EVSM.

1   Introduction

Due to the growing globalization and the increasing interest in environmental concerns, together with the changing legal and regulations landscape, manufacturers need to change their approach to competition, enhancing their knowledge of the manufacturing system and of the network of interconnections among physical flows and management and control information flows, while developing systemic methodologies that enable waste reduction of manufacturing resources usage (such as energy). We want to propose a new lean approach, the new Transformation Distribution and Utilization (T.D.U.) methodology with the objective to reduce

B. Grabot et al. (Eds.): APMS 2014, Part II, IFIP AICT 439, pp. 508–517, 2014.
© IFIP International Federation for Information Processing 2014

wasted energy within manufacturing processes and in particular presenting and testing it in a real case study in MorseTEC Europe, a supplier of systems for many European car manufacturers.

2   Related Work

The role of energy management in manufacturing is vital and has greatly found application in industry, see for instance [1]. Anyway, there is a wide implementation gap between practice and theory, especially concerning tools for measurement, assessment, control and improvement of energy efficiency in manufacturing companies [2].

Many authors have investigated the aspects concerning the need to enhance manufacturing modeling frameworks and tools to enable energy and resource efficient manufacturing. For instance ISA 95 [3] standard includes process and information flow models enabling representation of additional elements beyond the usual material flows, such as energy consumption, carbon dioxide, emissions, wastes. Various works, such as [4], [5], [6], [7] and [8] extend ISA 95 reasoning by proposing the development of manufacturing modeling frameworks able to capture the complex network of dynamic interactions among the physical flows in the factory, input flows (materials and parts , energy, human resources, etc.) and output flows (products, scrap and solid wastes, emissions, heat, noise etc.), at the different level of the factory, from machine to lines, up to plant/sites.

Other authors have studied modeling concept and methods starting from the observation that machines and other production systems can be in different operating modes (such as "on", "stand by", "processing", etc.) to which correspond different energy consumption profiles. These studies have leveraged on the operating modes concept in many ways, such as supporting manufacturing planning [9] , identifying energy saving machine control policies [10] , energy monitoring [11] . All these contributions show how energy efficiency can depend on both technical design choices and organizational decisions, such as production planning and control and machine control. Anyway, in literature there is no clear method to extend this approach from the machine/component level to the whole factory.

Furthermore, some authors report that enterprises are increasingly involved in managing the environment as an opportunity for competitive advantage, that requires highlighting the relationships between environmental impact of their processes and company strategy and objectives [12]. Finally we highlight the most interesting related works, which confirm the above mentioned need of energy and resource efficient analysis methods and tools.

Drechsel et al. [13] draw the first steps towards the development of an Energy Value Stream Analysis (EVSA), a new approach extending Value Stream Mapping (VSM), a technique for lean manufacturing, developed to support the identification of productive and non-productive usage of manufacturing resources, for a holistic analysis of energy productivity. The contribution describes how to integrate the EVSA in a Continuous Improvement Process (CIP) in which energy saving potentials are identified by a team involving managers/experts of the various production process steps under analysis. Plehn et al. [14] explore the basic structure of a proposed

Environmental Value Stream Mapping (EVSM) as an interface between a multi-criteria performance measurement system and the environmental and economic process flows of a manufacturing system. The main point of the proposed EVSM is the identification of usage of resource flows in different states in time (processing, set-up, stand-by etc.). Fantini et al. [15] propose novel modeling features for each element in the manufacturing systems, features capable to describe their behaviour in terms of resource consumption and release of produced products and parts as well as waste and emissions. The authors propose a systemic approach to manufacturing modeling under a holistic perspective, which includes all elements in a factory such as production systems, technical building services (TBS) and building shell and their network of interconnections with factory management and control levels. To address both manufacturing and environmental performance, the specification of manufacturing elements requires in fact the description of the whole transformation process enacted by the production systems and the systems supplying them and the dynamics of the material and energy flows in input and of the parts and waste in output.

To summarize, academia and industry experts recognize the widespread need for energy efficiency modeling frameworks and methodologies, able to support collaborative teams in their continuous improvement analysis and programs with the integration of proper KPIs and performance indicators systems.

3 Approach: Lean Methodology for Energy Efficient Manufacturing

3.1 Identification of Value and Non Value Added Energy

It is estimated that in most of the companies, 40-70% of total activities are carried out without adding value to the customer. These activities are considered as waste and competitive advantage can be achieved through these waste reduction [16], [17]. The Lean Production is Toyota Production System approach that that focuses on waste reduction to improve operations' performances, and gave quite interesting results in many implementations (e.g. Womack and Jones [18]; [19]; Lean Enterprise Institute www.lean.org) and therefore it is possible to use this approach also with the aim of identifying the energy wastes and remove them.

One of the most important concepts of the Lean Approach is the distinction between Value Added Activities (VAA) and Non Value Added Activities (NVAA). Especially, VAA are all those activities required for the customers, for which they are willing to pay in achieving the final product. The NVAA activities are those not strictly required such as material handling or inventory holding.

The concept of value added can be applied also in energy management field. According to Frazier [20] the Value Added Energy (V.A.E.)is the energy used for all the activities that create value for costumers, and the Non Value Added Energy (N.V.A.E.), the energy consumption related to the Non Value Added Activities.

$$V.A.E. = T.E.$$
$$N.V.A.E = Actual\ Energy - T.E.$$

where:
- Theoretical energy (T.E.): the minimum energy required to produce the desired transformation;
- Actual Energy: the energy really used for the desired transformation.

Seow and Rahimifard [21] propose a different point of view, in which they identify three energy typologies:

- Theoretical Energy (T.E.): the minimum energy required to carry out the production process.
- Auxiliary Energy (A.E.): the Energy required by the supporting activities and auxiliary equipment for the process. A.E. also includes non-productive modules such as machine tool change, start-up, stand by and cleaning.
- Indirect Energy (I.E.): the energy consumed to ensure the correct workplace conditions for the productive processes such as lighting, heating and ventilation.

Integrating and extending these three different point of views   and the aforementioned holistic perspective (11) we propose here as a starting point an high level framework that enables a thorough and systematic assessment of performance of manufacturing systems along multiple dimensions in terms of production performance, economic performance and environ mental impact, suited in particular to identify energy flows, that may happen in production systems and in the services systems (TBS for instance) as well.

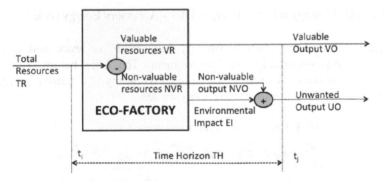

Fig. 1. Valuable, Non Valuable, Un-wanted Flows

Focusing on the physical flows in the system, in Figure 1 we show how Total Resources (TR), such as raw materials, energy, human resources, consumables, etc., can be used:

- partially - the Valuable Resources VR - to produce non-defective final products (valuable output VO);
- partially - namely, the non-valuable resources NVR - can be wasted d u r i n g non-valuable adding activities or while producing defective products, therefore becoming "NonValuable" Output NVO. These wasted resources can be considered "Unwanted" Output (UO), together with all environmental impacts (EI).

The main idea of this paper is finding valuable and non-valuable usage of resources along their whole physical flows, in particular concerning how to identify Value Added Energy, instead that along the traditional transformation flow, for instance from raw materials to product/part produced. Based on the aforementioned three different point of views proposed by literature, Theoretical Energy is the proxy for the Value Added Energy, but under the holistic perspective we can see that this is not enough, as it does not include all energy flows that allow a quality compliant production. We want to introduce in this paper a new concept of VAE, considering the concept of value related to what the customer is willing to pay for the final product compliant with the desired quality level.

Therefore we propose to classify energy into three different typologies:

- Direct Energy (D.E.): VAE for the final clients, that is the theoretical energy used for all the activities that create value for costumers.
- Accessory Energy (A.E): VAE for the internal client, that is the theoretical energy used to allow the factory operators to perform their work in comfortable conditions, (for instance, comfort temperature and lighting level).
- Actual Energy: the energy actually used for the desired transformation.

Based on this classification we can compute the VAE is:

Value Added Energy = Direct Energy (DE) + Accessory Energy (A.E.)

The difference between Actual Energy and VAE is waste and can be considered a potential opportunity for improvement. The table below (Table 1) presents some improvement areas for energy efficiency, by translating the 7 wastes, considered in Lean Philosophy, in energy wastes.

Table 1. Energy Wastes and Improvement Areas

7 Wastes	Energy Wasted connected with production
Transport	Energy used for transport inside / out the warehouse, plant and factory
Inventory	Heating, cooling and lighting inventory storage and warehouse
Motion	Heating, cooling and lighting inventory storage and warehouse
Waiting	Heating, cooling, and lighting during production downtime
Overproduction	Energy consumed in operating equipment to make un-necessary products
Over-processing	Energy to unnecessary processing
Defects	Energy used to process defective products

3.2   T.D.U. Methodology

The Transformation, Distribution and Utilization (T.D.U.) methodology we propose is based on identification of Value Added Energy flows in three phases:

- *Transformation phase*: the energy sources are transformed, if needed, in the energy used directly in the production processes.
- *Distribution phase:* the energy and related transformed vectors (such as compressed air) are brought where the transformation takes place.
- *Utilization phase:* the energy is finally consumed on the shop floor in the production processes (compressed air and thermal energy; electrical driving force and fuel etc.) and on the work place (lighting and heating ventilation and air conditioning systems).

This methodology is simple enough to be used in SMEs, as it is based on a checklist approach that drives the user in identifying which kinds of utilities (production systems, TBS etc.) are involved, in particular focusing on each different phase.

Once defined all the utilities involved in each phase, for each of them a checklist is provided, that encloses all the energy saving activities that can be implemented in that specific utility.

This checklist was obtained by the analysis of scientific publications, documentations prepared by the E.N.E.A. (Italian national agency of new technologies, energy efficiency and sustainable development), reports published by the U.S. Environmental Protection Agency, real case studies of success ful applications of energy efficiency activities and direct evidence of meetings and conferences. In this way users of the T.D.U. methodology have in few pages the summary of the state of art of the industrial energy efficiency and can identify in a few minutes which activities can be implemented for improving the energy efficiency of their processes.

The energy flow is designed as follow:

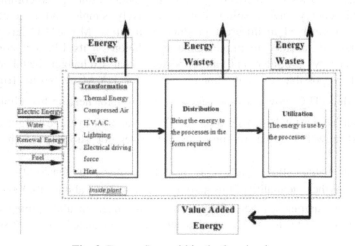

Fig. 2. Energy flow within the 3 main phases

This methodology has been applied and tested with a great success in MorseTEC Europe, the European division of BorgWarner Group.

Application Case Study

MorseTEC Europe has represented for over 15 years the expression of the European division of BorgWarner Group. Located in Arcore, 20 km northeast of Milan, MorseTEC Europe is a partner of absolute importance as a supplier of systems for most European car manufacturers (Ford, Audi, General Motors, Fiat, Volkswagen, Jaguar and PSA) by offering exclusive service, competence and experience in the development and production of distribution systems and transmission chain.

In this section there will be presented some activities implemented in the plant of Arcore of the BorgWarner MorseTEC Europe after the application of the T.D.U. methodology.

Specifically are reported two examples of the activities implemented in the Morse-TEC plant: heat recovery from compressors and energy consumption reduction by equipping compressor with an inverter.

Energy Saving Activity #1: heat recovery from compressors

- T.D.U. Phase: Transformation_compressed air
- Checklist question: Is the heat emitted by your compressors recovered?
- Answer: No
- Solution: Purchase of Heat exchanger for compressors
- Type of activity: Opportunity
- Status: Completed

This activity consists in recovering the heat generated during the compression of the air. This energy saving solution is a relatively simple and in recent years has been implemented in different production realities. MorseTEC has three big compressors and decided to implement this solution on its 135 kW compressor. With this energy available and an opportune heat exchanger installed in this machine it is possible to heat enough water for HVAC system for heating 1000 m^2. MorseTEC now uses the recovered power for heating his administrative offices, with have a total surface area of 900 m^2 and an average height of 2.8 m. The excess power is used to produce hot water for showers of the workers restrooms.

For implementing this solution it has been made a feasibility study for understanding the potentiality of this activity and have spent about 40.000 € for the heat recovery equipment made off by an heat exchanger, insulate piping necessary to bring the hot water to the H.V.A.C. system and 2 insulated tanks for storing the hot water.

Most part of this investment has been financed by other energy saving activities: it has been calculated that the economic saving generated by this solution amounts to 18.000 €/year. MorseTEC buys externally the heating water service and this saving represents the thermal energy consumption that the company is able to recover from its compressor . The expected payback time of this investment is equal to 2 years and 3 months.

Energy Saving Activity # 6: Compressor Equipped with an Inverter

- T.D.U. phase: Transformation_compressed air
- Check list question: Is your compressor equipped with an inverter?
- Answer: No
- Solution: Purchase of a compressor with an Inverter
- Type of activity: Opportunity
- Identified NVA energy: 98.500 kWh / year
- Status : Completed

4   Conclusions

As we stated before, putting effort in improving energy efficiency process is becoming more and more relevant for Companies, to reach a higher competition level. Lean Approach concept of waste management is not only related to products and time, but also can be translated to energy. The approach proposed for improving energy efficiency in manufacturing takes into account many contributions   from literature, however its innovation is on how to identify Value Added Energy, based on the classification of energy in three different categories. Then we proposed a methodology, called T.D.U. methodology with the main objective to identify three main different phases in which applying a checklist for each facility used in every phase. The checklist is formed by several standard questions, and answering to that questions leads to implement specific activities for removing part of NVAE. MorseTec Europe (European level manufacturer system provider) applied the T.D.U. methodology and we briefly reported the results of the activities done: in the table below costs and benefits obtained by the two activities are summarized :

Table 2. MorseTEC case study: cost benefit analysis

Activity	T.D.U. Phase	Yearly Saving €/y.	Status
Heat Recover from Compressor	T	18.000	100%
Compressor with Inverter	T	13.500	100%

By applying this easy methodology is possible to reach high economic and environmental results. The next step of this work is to better and deeper relate economical performances to environmental ones.

Acknowledgments. The research work has been developed with the helpful and very appreciated availability of MorseTEC Europe, in particular thanks to Ing. Vitali.

References

[1] Abdelaziz, E.A., Saidur, R., Mekhilef, S.: A review on energy saving strategies in industrial sector. Renewable and Sustainable Energy Reviews 15(1), 150–168 (2011)

[2] Bunse, K., Vodicka, M., Schlonsleben, P., Brulhart, M., Ernst, F.O.: Integrating energy efficiency performance in production management - gap analysis between industrial needs nad scientific literature. Journal of Cleaner Production 19(6-7), 667–679 (2011)

[3] ISA-95 International standard for the integration of enterprise and control systems (2013), http://www.isa-95.com

[4] Choi, A.C.K., Kaebenick, H., Lai, W.H.: Manufacturing process modelling for environmental impact assessment. Journal of Material Processing Technology (70), 231–238 (1997)

[5] Shao, G., Bengtsson, N., Johansson, B.: Interoperability for simulation of sustainable manufacturing. In: Proceedings SpringSim 2010 Proceedings of the 2010 Spring Simulation Multiconference, Sponsored by The Society for Modeling and Simulation International, Orlando, USA, April 11-15 (2010)

[6] Thiede, S., Hermann, C.: Process chain simulation to foster energy efficiency in manufacturing. CIRP Journal of Manufacturing Science and Technology 1(4), 221–229 (2009)

[7] Fysikopoulos, A., Pastras, G., Alexopoulos, T., Cryssolouris, G.: On a generalized approach to manufacturing energy efficiency. The International Journal of Advanced Manufacturing Technology (May 2014)

[8] Duflou, J.R., et al.: Towards Energy and Resource Efficient Manufacturing: A processes and systems approach. CIRP Ann. Manufacturing Technology 61(2), 587–609 (2012)

[9] Weinert, N., Chiotellis, S., Seliger, G.: Methodology for planning and operating energy-efficient production systems. CIRP Ann. Manuf. Technol. 60, 41–44 (2011)

[10] Prabhu, V.V., Jeon, H.W., Taisch, M.: Modeling green factory physics — An analytical approach. In: 2012 IEEE International Conference Automation Science and Engineering (CASE, Seoul, Korea (South), August 20-24, pp. 46–51 (2012)

[11] Vijayaraghavan, A., Dornfeld, D.: Automated energy monitoring of machine tools. CIRP Annals of Manufacturing Technology 59, 21–24 (2010)

[12] Garetti, M., Taisch, M.: Sustainable manufacturing: trends and research challenges. Production Planning and Control 23(2-3), 83–104 (2012)

[13] Drechsel, M., Bornschlegl, M., Spreng, S., Bregulla, M., Franke, J.: A New Approach to Integrate Value Stream Analysis into a Continuous Energy Efficiency Improvement Process. In: 39th Annual Conference of the IEEE Industrial Electronics Society (IECON 2013), Vienna, Austria, pp. 7502–7507 (2013)

[14] Plehn, J., Sproedt, A., Gontarz, A.: From Strategic Goals to focused Eco-efficiency Improvement in Production - Bridging the gap using Environmental Value Stream Mapping. In: The 10th Global Conference on Sustainable Manufacturing, Istanbul, Turkey, October 31-November 2 (2012)

[15] Fantini, P., et al.: Towards Environmental Conscious Manufacturing. In: IEEE Conference on ICE 2014, Bergamo, Italy (to be published, 2014)

[16] Ohno, T.: Toyota Production System: beyond large-scale production. Productivity Press (1988)

[17] Womack, J.P., Jones, D.T.: Beyond Toyota: How to Root Waste and Pursue Perfection (September-October 1996)

[18] Womack, J.P., Jones, D.T.: Lean Thinking. Free Press (1996)

[19] Soahl, A.S.: Developing a lean production organization: an Australian case study 16(2) (1996)

[20] Frazier, R.S.: Bandwidth analysis, lean methods and decision science to select energy management projects in manufacturing. Energy Engineering, 24–45 (2008)

[21] Seow, Y., Rahimifard, S.: A framework for modelling energy consumption within manufacturing systems. CIRP Journal of Manufacturing Science and Technology 4(3)

Stakeholder Mapping in a Collaborative Project for a Sustainable Development

Mohamed Mabrouk, Severine Sperandio, and Philippe Girard

IMS - University of Bordeaux,
33401 TALENCE cedex, France
{Mohamed.mabrouk,severine.sperandio,
philippe.girard}@ims-bordeaux.fr

Abstract. Sustainable development is an approach to development which consists in balancing the different environmental, social and economic needs, where many stakeholders are involved. The collaboration about the objectives set by the business members of the project-leading is decisive, but it can prove to be complicated, since each of the stakeholders can adopt various sustainability strategies and practices. This paper proposes an approach for applying stakeholder map for collaborative strategies in order to support the identification of significant partners and thus their involvement within the projects. A certain focus is provided on sustainability issues. The approach is based upon the audit of the different partners of a network in order to know their sustainable expectations and priorities, and their degrees of influence and dependency. It leads to the identification of eight stakeholders families or types, following their involvement, voluntary or not, faced with sustainable development.

Keywords: Sustainable Development, Corporate Social Responsibility, Stakeholder map.

1 Introduction

More than one hundred definitions of sustainable development exist, but the most widely used one is from the World Commission on Environment and Development (1987): it states that sustainable development is a "development that meets the needs of the present without compromising the ability of future generations to meet their own needs" [1]. In the same way, Corporate Social Responsibility (CSR) is the implementation of sustainable development by companies: it represents the company's sense of responsibility towards the community in which it operates. In other words, a company has to increase its profitability and ensure its durability, but has to also consider the needs and interests of all its stakeholders in order to improve their economic, social and environmental performances. This research aims to establish a procedure for developing a stakeholder map for strategic projects in order to facilitate decision making of senior managers in a sustainable context: by taking into account needs and expectations of their partners early in the project, they can more easily ensure satisfaction and performance of these partners and therefore allow the success of the strategy. With this intention, the paper is organized as follows. In Section 2, general points

B. Grabot et al. (Eds.): APMS 2014, Part II, IFIP AICT 439, pp. 518–525, 2014.

of stakeholder theory and its impact on a collaborative project are introduced. In Section 3, we develop a methodology to create a stakeholder map in a collaborative project, with sustainable constraints. Finally, some conclusion remarks and discussions are provided in the last section.

2   What about Stakeholder Theory

The collaboration between stakeholders is decisive for the success of any project, particularly in the fields of Sustainable Development (SD) and Corporate Social Responsibility (CSR), where the taking into account of stakeholders' opinions is central in their guidelines. However, all stakeholders belonging to a same system share not necessarily the same concerns and have most of the time different and heterogeneous expectations and priorities. For this, the opportunity to identify and analyze the behavior of these stakeholders can change strategic directions of future development projects. What are the relationships between the different stakeholders? What relative influence do they have? Such an analysis enables the identification of institutions and relationships which need to be developed or dealt with to avoid negative outcomes and enhance positive ones [2]. Of course, the literature overflows with stakeholders' categorizations. The authors note that this theory contributes to understand projects by highlighting the importance of considerations of the stakeholders during planning, due principally to their influence on the project. It can also assist to classify the stakeholders as internal and external [3], primary and secondary [4], according to they are immediately affected by, or can immediately affect the system. The major contribution about relationships between managers and stakeholders and the way to categorize them comes from Mitchell, Agle and Wood [5]. The authors tried to provide a dynamic model allowing to explain how a stakeholder should order its relationships. Their multi-attribute approach is based on three criterions allowing to categorize stakeholders on an organization: the power of the stakeholder to influence the organization, the legitimacy of the relationships in terms of desirability or appropriateness, the urgency (expectations of the stakeholder in terms of criticality and time-sensitivity). Such an analysis is very interesting, since the power or influence analysis between all the stakeholders is paramount in collaborative projects. However, we think that a simple classification is not sufficient when it comes to share and collaborate in the long term. Indeed, the theory does not give a clear guidance on how to exactly understand the settings and implementation, and dialogue aspects and consideration of stakeholders' expectations are not clearly identified. We decide to inspire from this approach to develop a model for applying stakeholder map for collaborative projects in order to support strategies and associated projects to be implemented. A certain focus is provided on sustainability issues. The model is based upon the audit of the different partners of a network in order to know their sustainable expectations and priorities, and their degrees of influence or dependency.

3   Aid to Stakeholder Mapping in a Collaborative Project, with Sustainable Issues

The performance of sustainable strategies depends in a large part to issues related to some actions to be implemented as: establish a constructive dialogue and a transparent communication with its stakeholders; share expertise with its partners; better determine the expectations from the various stakeholders; communicate its commitments and objectives with stakeholders; enhance the structure of the dialogue and adapt it to the needs of different issues. Thus, identify the stakeholders responsible for implementing and contribution of some objectives is a difficult and complex task. We also want to aid decision makings of senior managers by a procedure enabling to identify the "Sphere Of Influence" (SOI), which defines the scope of a company's social responsibility (ISO 26 000). We base this research on the actors' strategy and on the structural analysis [6], which are two methodologies enabling, by studying relations between the different elements of a same system (organization, network of companies …), to underline the variables that are essential to the system's evolution. They have the advantage of stimulating reflection within a group, and leading it to think about certain aspects, which are sometimes counterintuitive. Our approach consists in laying down and analyzing the relations between stakeholders: it focuses on issues of sustainable development which represent stakes for the future and around which the actors could build their strategies. However, before beginning any project of development, a company has to know the involvement of its stakeholders and has to recognize stakeholders that can help or impede the completion of the project, depending of the impacts of this project on their own strategies: operational impacts (changes in operating activities), structural impacts (changes of capacities and / or competences of human and technical resources), functional impacts (integration of new technologies, modification of the supply chain, etc.). The associated computer tool is developed under Microsoft Visual Basic for Applications (VBA).

3.1   Stage 1: Strategic Sustainable Issues of the Company and Associated Objectives

This stage, which is the least formal, is crucial: it allows to identify and analyze the strategic vision of the company by the selection of the objectives, for a sustainable development. This multi-objective vision of a sustainable development has been developed by John Elkington (notion of triple bottom line or Triple-P (People, Planet, Profit)) when he has defined sustainability as the balance between economic, social and environmental performances [7]. Here, we consider generic objectives associated to these performances, but also the objectives associated to the performances of bearable aspects (intersection of the environment and the social), viable aspects (intersection of the environment and the economy) and equitable aspects (intersection of the social and the economy) (Table 1).

Table 1. Strategic objectives for a sustainable development

Dimensions	Objectives
Social	Improve wellness and security of the employees
	Facilitate the participation
	Create or maintain a social implication
Bearable	Promote a local development
	Register a collective responsibility approach
	Respect the best practices with external stakeholders
Environme nt	Preserve the natural resources
	Reduce negative environmental impacts
	Communicate on environmental management
Viable	Optimize the means of transport
	Educate new kinds of consumption and sustainable consumption
Economic	Ensure customer satisfaction
	Be more flexible and responsive
	Ensure economic and financial performance
Equitable	Ensure accessibility and social diversity in the work
	Ensure a better socio-economic balance

3.2 Stage 2: Relationships between the Different Stakeholders

In this stage, the different stakeholders (or actors) of a company for a project of sustainable development are identified. In this case, for example, we shall consider 6 actors ($n=6$: A_1, A_2..., A_6) corresponding to the customers, suppliers, subcontractors, banks, organisms, co-workers..., interacting with the company. The actor's strategy is also analyzed, as follows:

Matrix of Direct Influences (MDI). The matrix of Direct Influences is a square matrix of order 6 (Actors x Actors). It highlights the direct influences that each actor has on the others (Fig.1). For each cell of the matrix, a score "$x_{i,j}$" is assigned, depending to the influence that the row variable "i" has on the column variable "j". By definition, there is no impact of an Actor on itself (score = 0 when i=j). We will use for the different scores the values 0, 1, 2 and 3 (no influence, weak influence, medium influence, strong influence), so $x_{i,j} \in [0, 3]$.

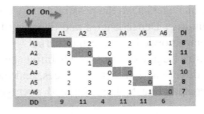

Fig. 1. Matrix of Direct Influences (*MDI*)

522   M. Mabrouk, S. Sperandio, and P. Girard

Once the *MDI* matrix completed, we calculate the degrees of Direct Influences (*DI*) and Direct Dependencies (*DD*), for each Actor "*A_i*", as follows:

$$DI_i = \sum_{j=1}^{n} x_{i,j} \quad \text{The scores assigned to the row for the } A_i \tag{1}$$

$$DD_j = \sum_{i=1}^{n} x_{i,j} \quad \text{The scores assigned to the column for the } A_j \tag{2}$$

In this example, the Actor "*A_2*" seems to be in a dominant position because it is the more influent (*DI* = 11), but it is also very dependent of the others (*DD* = 11). However, such a study doesn't enable to conclude on the actors' strategy in the network of partners because an actor can also influence other actors via transitional actors (this is the domino effect). Consequently, we cannot restrict ourselves to the analysis of direct influences, and the following paragraph focuses on the analysis of indirect influences between the different actors.

Matrix of Indirect Influences (MII). The *MII* matrix allows considering indirect influences of each actor on the others. The $MII_{i,j}$ matrix, which analyses the impact of the Actor "*i*" on the Actor "*j*" via "*n*" other Actors, is obtained in "$v_{i,j}$" as follows:

$$V_{i,j} = Min(MDI_{i,1}; MDI_{1,j}) + Min(MDI_{i,2}; MDI_{2,j}) + \ldots + Min(MDI_{i,n}; MDI_{n,j}) = \sum_{k=1}^{n} Min(MDI_{i,k}; MDI_{k,j})$$

where $k \neq i$ and $k \neq j$. Thus, the degrees of Indirect Influences (*InI*) and Indirect Dependencies (*InD*), for an Actor "*i*", are:

$$InI_i = \sum_{j=1}^{n} v_{i,j} \quad \text{The scores assigned to the row for the } A_i \tag{3}$$

$$InD_j = \sum_{i=1}^{n} v_{i,j} \quad \text{The scores assigned to the column for the } A_j \tag{4}$$

Synthesis. At this point, managers have the possibility to weight the different degrees (degrees of Direct and Indirect Dependencies and degrees of Direct and Indirect Influences) according to their knowledge about the market (Fig.2). Then, two synthesis elements are calculated: the Degree of the Overall Influence (*DOI*) corresponding to the weighted average of direct and indirect influences, and the Degree of the Overall Dependence (*DOD*) corresponding to the weighted average of direct and indirect dependences.

Weighting	1,5	▼	1	1,5	1		
Actors	0,5		DD	InI	InD	DOI	DOD
A1	1,5		9	45	35	26,5	22
A2	2		11	49,5	37	30,25	24
A3	8		4	40,5	13	24,25	8,5
A4	10		11	48	35	29	23
A5	8		11	46,5	35	27,25	23
A6	7		6	40,5	25	23,75	15,5

Fig. 2. Synthesis

These to synthesis elements enable to know the stakeholders to be considered for future collaborations. However, considering that each project has its own characteristics related to one or several strategic objectives (cf. Table 1), they are not sufficient to build precisely the Sphere Of Influence since the positioning of the actors in relation to these objectives is not clarified.

3.3   Stage 3: Positioning of the Actors in Relation to the Strategic Objectives

Here we research the possible convergences and divergences of the different actors relative to the objectives of the project. Of course, they are different from one objective to another: it is also very important to collect the opinions of the different stakeholders in relation to each objective, in order to understand their positioning towards the project. The Matrix of Actors and Objectives (*MAO*, Fig. 3) shows this positioning according to a qualitative scale (-1, 0 and +1 corresponding to the fact that the actor is against, without opinion or favorable to the achievement of the objective).

	O1	O2	O3	O4	O5	O6	O7	O8	O9	Supp	Opp	DIN
A1	1	1	0	1	1	-1	1	1	-1	6	-2	8
A2	0	-1	1	1	-1	0	-1	-1	1	3	-4	7
A3	-1	-1	-1	0	-1	1	1	0	-1	2	-5	7
A4	-1	-1	0	0	0	1	-1	0	-1	1	-4	5
A5	-1	0	-1	0	1	-1	1	0	-1	2	-4	6
A6	1	0	0	0	-1	0	1	1	1	4	-1	5
Agreements	2	1	1	2	2	2	4	2	2			
Disagreements	-3	-3	-2	0	-3	-2	-2	-1	-4			

Fig. 3. The MAO matrix

Thanks to the *MAO* matrix, we can now calculate the Degree of INvolvement (*DIN*) of the different actors. Therefore, for the Actor "*i*":

$$DIN_i = Supp_i + \mid Opp_i \mid$$ where $Supp_i$ is the support level of the Actor "i" (corresponding to the sum of the positive scores assigned to the row of this actor) and Opp_i is the opposition level of the Actor "i" (corresponding to the sum of the negative scores assigned to the row of this actor).

Moreover, the matrix enables to know the number of agreements and disagreements for each objective, which can be interesting information to help the decision making of managers.

3.4   Stage 4: Stakeholder Map

Here we propose a generic table including eight families of stakeholders, corresponding to the eight possible combinations between the three main attributes (*DIN*, *DOI* and *DOD*: see Table 2).

Table 2. Stakeholders Classifications

SH Mapping / Attribute	(1)	(2)	(3)	(4)	(5)	(6)	(7)	(8)
DIN	-	-	-	-	+	+	+	+
DOI	-	-	+	+	-	-	+	+
DOD	-	+	-	+	-	+	-	+

(1) The Dormant Stakeholders: they have no power (or a weak power) and are neither dependent nor involved (low level of the three attributes). They don't need a special attention and need only a minimum monitoring.

(2) The Dependent Stakeholders: They have a high level of dependency but low levels of influence and involvement (follower stakeholders). The existence of a contract with them leads to the necessity for the managers to follow their activities.

(3) The Influential Stakeholders: their interest for the project is low but they are powerful. No emergency action is requested because they aren't a part of the project, but managers must satisfy their possible requirements.

(4): The Influential and Dependent Stakeholders: they are both powerful and dependent. They have their own ways to carry out their projects, but are also influenced by the actions of the other stakeholders. Such a category of actors has to be seriously monitored.

(5) The Interested Stakeholders: They have a high level of involvement but are neither influential nor dependent. They can't engage a pressure on the company but it's necessary to keep them informed since they can be considered as potential collaborators (for example: associations, consulting firm).

(6) The Involved and Dependent Stakeholders: they are involved but dependent. They aren't powerful (subcontractor for example): they also can't engage pressures on the company, but it's necessary to inform them for any progression in the project.

(7) The Dominant and Involved Stakeholders: they are both powerful and interested in the project. Their cooperation is essential to ensure the feasibility of the project.

(8) The Primordial Stakeholders: they are powerful, interested in the project, and dependent. Managers are obliged to establish a privileged relationship for responding to their needs and expectations.

We will consider that the Sphere of Influence to be considered for a project includes all the actors interested in the project and can help its completion: these are the categories (6), (7) and (8).

4   Conclusion

Stakeholder theory has its roots from management literature and was developed as a response to the needs to successfully carry out strategic processes in the context of profit-organizations. Here, the approach of stakeholder analysis has been completed and oriented towards sustainable development issues. The existence of an approach that allows collecting different opinions and strengthening the dialogue between the different stakeholders is critical to a long-term success. Resource managers can thus intervene in the interest of development and improvement of future projects, in order to re-evaluate the strategic objectives initially set, revise the different contracts with stakeholders, regularly maintain and update the different classes of stakeholders. In this paper, we have tried to overcome many limits related to stakeholder theory and have created a model for decision making in a collaborative and sustainable context: this model enables to identify the stakeholders with whom it is recommended to collaborate. The purpose is also to build the strategies to be implemented, taking into account the expectations of the different stakeholders, in order to ensure the satisfaction of these partners and therefore allow the success of future collaborations. Our work has demonstrated its ability to not only contribute to select suitable stakeholders, but also provide a guide to strategic management for sustainable development issues. However, we cannot neglect some weaknesses of this theory which can be ambiguous and subjective. Indeed, the categorization process depends on the evaluators and their analysis can be influenced by their backgrounds, environment or people involved in the process. It is also subject to indirect aspects such as honesty and reliability of the collected information.

References

1. Brundtland Commission.Report of the World Commission on Environment and Development. United Nations (1987)
2. Mayer, J.: Stakeholder power analysis. Power Tools Series. International Institute for Environment and Development, London (2005)
3. Clarkson, M.B.E.: A Stakeholder framework for Analysing and Evaluating Corporate Social Performance. Academy of Management Review 20(1), 92–117 (1995)
4. Caroll, A.B.: Business and Society: Ethics and Stakeholder Management, O.H., South-Western, Cincinatti (1989)
5. Mitchell, R.K., Agle, B.R., Wood, D.J.: Toward a Theory of Stakeholders Identification and Salience: Defining the Principles of who and what really Counts. Academy of Management Review 22(2), 833–886 (1997)
6. Arcade, J., Godet, M., Meunier, F., Roubelat, F.: Structural analysis with the MICMAC method & Actors strategywith MACTOR method, Futures Research Methodology, American Council for the United Nations University: The Millennium Project (1999)
7. Elkington, J.: Cannibals with Forks: The triple bottom line of 21st century business. Capstone, Oxford (1997)

Environmental and Social Impacts of Mass Customization: An Analysis of Beginning-of-Life Phases

Golboo Pourabdollahian[1] and Frank Steiner[2]

[1] CNR-ITIA, Via Bassini 15, 20133, Milan, Italy
[2] RWTH Aachen University, Technology and Innovation Management Group,
Aachen, Germany
golboo.pourabdollahian@itia.cnr.it, steiner@tim.rwth-aachen.de

Abstract. For about two decades Mass customization (MC) has been broadly discussed as a proper business model to satisfy heteregenous needs of customers in an efficient manner.However, the increasing importance of other trends such as sustainability make it inevitable for MC companies to operate in an eco-friendly and socially-friendly way. This paper aims investigating and identifying of potential impact factors of Mass Customization on environmental and social sustainability following a Product Lifecycle management (PLM) approach.

Keywords: Mass Customization (MC), Sustainability, Beginning of Life (BOL).

1 Introduction

From its early introduction as a strategy, Mass Customization (MC) has significantly changed the market offer and value proposition for customers. The concept of Mass Customization emerged to deal with high levels of heterogeneity of the customers' needs [1]. In the other words, Mass Customization can be seen as a hybrid competitive strategy attempting to provide customers with individualized products in a cost-efficient manner [2]. Accordingly MC benefits the firm through profit generation thanks to the premium price. Mass Customization can be considered as an economically viable strategy since it create revenues and thus profit through turning heterogeneities of customers' needs to an opportunity to create value [3] while the cost level can be kept in a level comparable to mass produced products thanks to implementation of flexible manufacturing processes and suitable customer interaction tools.

Although evaluation of MC from an economic point of view is crucial for success of a MC firm but it is not sufficient considering other challenges that the global community face today. In this regard sustainability is considered as one of the main concerns of manufacturing companies operating in different sectors and applying different strategies. Accordingly, MC enterprises need to take steps toward being more sustainable through development of a "Win-Win-Win" strategy which is sustainable not only from economic point of view but also from social and environmental perspectives [4].

B. Grabot et al. (Eds.): APMS 2014, Part II, IFIP AICT 439, pp. 526–532, 2014.

Nevertheless, the existing body of literature concerning MC and sustainability is extremely narrow and non-mature. There are very few studies, mainly conceptual, investigating the role of MC for environmental and social sustainability [5, 6, 7]. The existing gap in this regard opens up interesting research streams that can be studied to support companies in implementing MC in a more sustainable manner. Accordingly, this paper aims at investigating and identifying of potential impact factors of Mass Customization on environmental and social sustainability following a Product Life-cycle management (PLM) approach. The paper is specifically focused on potential environmental and social impacts of MC during the three main phases of beginning of life of a product life cycle namely design, manufacturing and distribution.

2 Beginning of Life within the Product Lifecycle Approach

The main objective of Product Lifecycle Management (PLM) is to all the activities and processes along the whole product lifecycle phases which consists of three phases: Beginning of Life (BOL) concerning design, manufacturing, and distribution; Middle of Life (MOL) concerning usage and maintenance; and End of Life (EOL) concerning waste management strategies [8]. Within the product lifecycle, the BOL phase is considered as a critical phase due to its future impacts on the two other phases of MOL and EOL. The decisions which are made during the beginning of life (e.g. design phase) affect significantly on both MOL and EOL of a product. On one hand the final peformance of the product during its use phase is extremely dependent on its design [9], while on the other hand the proper waste management strategy depends on structure of the product the way it is manufactured.

Considering the importance of BOL, in this paper we invetigate the potential influences of MC on environmental and social sustainability during the beginning of life. In particular the impact factors are identified within the three phases of design, manufacturing and distribution. It should be noticed that the impact factors include both positive and negative ones considering that while some aspects of MC can be beneficial for sustainability, there are some other aspects which might affect negatively the environmental and social performance.

2.1   Impact Factors in the Design Phase

In the context of Mass Customization, the approach to product design differs rather strongly from the design of mass produced goods: the strategy of MC aims at integrating the customer throughout all phases of the PLC and thus includes a strong firm-customer-collaboration during the design phase. This process of co-designing products enables the customers to articulate their individual needs and specifications for the respective product [10]. The involvement of the customer in the design phase potentially enhances social and environmental aspects of sustainability: from a social perspective, this early integration of customers may enable a better consideration of the functional needs of specific interest groups such as elderly users or disabled people, etc. From an environmental perspective, the collaboration with customers in the design phase bears two major impact factors: firstly, being part of the product configuration process provides customers with a learning opportunity concerning the environmental impacts of their feature selection and thus increases the customer awareness of environmental sustainability [11]. Consequently, providing customers with enough information on the environmental impact of certain product attributes during the co-design process can help the users to understand the sustainability impact of their individual choices and thus ultimately supports the design of more eco-friendly products. Secondly, the integration of customers in the design phase, protects manufacturers from implementing an excessive feature load in their products: The co-design process helps to select product attributes, which are strongly aligned with the specific customer needs in a respective market. Subsequently, co-designing with customers helps MC companies to manufacture only such products that are needed and requested by the customers and thereby avoids wasting resources for the integration of unnecessary product features [11].

Beside the co-design process itself, the aspect of modularity has to be considered in the context of the product design phase. MC products are usually characterized by the use of modular product architectures, as modularity serves as one of the main operational enablers of Mass Customization. A modular architecture enables manufacturers to produce a large number of varieties by using different combinations of product modules. That way, modularity allows manufacturers to benefit from economies of scale and reductions in production lead-time, even though mass customization typically requires firms to reduce lot sizes and standardization [12]. However, besides this large economic benefit of modularity, the use of modular product architectures also carries environmental implications: whereas a modular product might be more environmentally-friendly in terms of maintenance and its end-of-life treatment, it carries negative environmental impacts for the product design. Modular products are always inferior to integrated product designs in terms of weight and performance. Hence, more material resources are required for a product that is designed in a modular way [13, 14].

Lastly, an additional negative effect of MC can be assumed with regard to product design: the design phase is not only the initial stage of a product lifecycle, but can also be regarded as an essential step in a closed-loop lifecycle that merges the BOL of a new product with the end of life of a former product [15]. In this context, the implementation of a closed-loop lifecycle can be realized more easily in a mass production system than in the context of MC, as mass production deals with more standardized products. Whereas the combination of the EOL product and the new product is standardized in mass production, a mass customizer will be confronted with new combinations of old and new products with every customer.

2.2   Impact Factors in the Manufacturing Phase

Typically, manufacturing companies focus on waste reduction during production, when they pursue the issues of environmental and social sustainability for the first time. According to the National Council of Advanced Manufacturing (2009) sustainable manufacturing refers to the "creation of manufactured products that use processes that are non-polluting, conserve energy and natural resources, and are economically sound and safe for employees, communities, and consumers" [16].

Similar to the situation in the design phase, the implementation of Mass Customization shows controversial effects on the manufacturing processes in terms of environmental and social sustainability. However, it has to be noted, that the most important environmental impact factor of MC can be observed in the context of manufacturing: most MC companies operate a so-called X-to-order fulfillment strategy. This means that products are produced only after a respective order has been received from the customer. This approach prevents overproduction, as only those goods are manufactured that are actually needed by the customers. This results not only in a significant decrease of waste in terms of unwanted products, but also in a much lower level of energy consumption for the overall production. According to a 2009 estimation, 300 million pairs of shoes are over produced each year. Considering the energy required to produce each pair of shoes, the total energy consumption to manufacture all these unsold pairs of shoes equals 14% of the annual energy consumption of Switzerland [17]. This study shows that Mass Customization indeed has a major beneficial impact on sustainability in terms of manufacturing.

On the other hand – as mentioned above – there are also negative aspects to MC manufacturing. For example, it has to be acknowledged that the realization of customized goods typically consumes more energy and resources than the manufacturing of mass-produced products. Coming back to the example of shoes, every customized pair requires an individual type and cut of the leather, while for a standard pair of shoes the same type and cut of leather can be used. In consequence, manufacturing processes and the usage of raw material can be optimized in mass production and overall a lower consumption of raw materials and energy can be realized [18]. Hence, the increase of manufacturing complexity that results from an increase in product variety leads to a negative environmental impact of MC.

Besides these environmental aspects, the implementation of Mass Customization also shows social impacts in the manufacturing phase: whereas the rise of mass production has led to an increased used of offshoring of manufacturing, it can be observed that MC oftentimes goes along with more localized manufacturing concepts. As the products in MC are highly customized, fast response times and local distribution channels are of higher importance for manufacturers than in the context of mass production. Therefore, the implementation of Mass Customization carries the beneficial social impact factor of building and protecting a healthy, local job base.

2.3   Impact Factors in the Distribution Phase

Due to its typical x-to-order fulfillment strategies, the implementation of MC also requires new approaches for the distribution of final products, which in turn result in particular impacts on environmental sustainability. As in most cases of MC production can only start after the customer order has been placed, the customer cannot directly receive the product at the point of sale. Thus – irrespective of whether the order was placed in a store or via an online sales channel – most MC companies have to realize home delivery for individual products. Naturally, such individual shipments of products require additional resources in terms of packaging and energy consumption [18, 14]. Moreover, this single batch delivery also leads to the consequence that each product is shipped individually, instead of transporting a larger batch of products to a store or distribution warehouse. Subsequently, a higher number of delivery operations is needed and hence more transportation emissions have to be expected. On the other hand, if MC was realized as an online retail business, customers do not have to travel to a store for picking up the final product. This suggests that MC may also have a positive environmental effect in terms of the distribution phase [18].

Additionally, the overall environmental impact of the distribution phase depends largely on the distance between the production site and the respective customers. A study by Kleer and Steiner, for example, shows that for a manufacturer of individualized shoes the individual shipment of products from the production site in China to the customers in Europe makes up a considerable part of the overall CO_2 emissions of this specific business model [6]. However, if MC is realized in combination with a localized production – for example in the form of so called micro factories [39] – the negative environmental effect of individual distribution can be strongly mitigated. In such a case, the distribution distance could be reduced significantly and would result in lower energy consumption and less emissions during the distribution phase [20].

Lastly, the impact of reverse logistics is a critical point with regard to the distribution phase. Generally speaking, MC companies enjoy a less complicated distribution system in terms of reverse logistics: as MC products are tailored to the specific needs of individual customers, it is rather difficult to apply a return policy for these products. The lack of such a return policy has its own controversial impacts in terms of environmental sustainability: on one hand, companies do not have to deal with reverse logistics, as customers cannot return the goods. This significantly reduces the level of energy consumption and transportation emissions. On the other hand, the lack of a return policy could also result in an increase in the level of waste: a customized product that does not meet the expectations of the customer, for whom it was customized, will most likely be disposed without being used, because it simply is not compatible with the needs of any other customer. This limitation towards re-use of the product may thus be regarded as a negative impact that results from the specific role of reverse logistics in mass customization.

3   Conclusion

Mass customization is mainly recognized as strategy to fulfill the individual needs of the customers in an efficient manner. The increasing interest of customers in involvement in the design phase and creating a customized product has made MC a proper business model and an attractive trend for many companies. Nevertheless for most companies, specially manufacturing companies, it is not the only trend to be followed. The increasing importance of sustainability both among customers and governments has pinpointed it as a critical point of attention for manufacturing companies including MC firms. In this paper we try to target this topic by having a closer look to the concept of Mass Customization from the sustainability point of view, both environmental and social. The paper tries to discover the potential interdependencies between MC and sustainability and eventually explore the environmental and social impacts of Mass customization. Following the product lifecycle management approach, the study is particularly focused on the beginning of life of MC products consisting of three main stages namely, design, manufacturing, and distribution.

The analysis reveals that while in some aspects MC can act as a positive driving force for sustainability, in some another aspects it could cause challenges for sustainability. For instance, from an environmental point of view, the modular architecture of a MC product can be seen as a significant positive driver for sustainability positive impact factor for sustainability due to facilitating of disassembly and therefore implementation of sustainable waste management strategies such as re-manufacturing and re-design at the end of the life of the product. However, from a different perspective, the customized nature of MC products makes them very single customer oriented and approximately impossible to be re-used by another customer. The elimination of re-using as a proper waste management strategy at the EOL phase, would lead to an increase in waste and a shorter lifespan of the MC products.

On the other hand, from a social perspective MC seems to be a more a positive driving force. Thanks to the co-design process, the strategy benefits customers, especially those with special needs (i.e. disabled customers), through providing them with products which are designed to satisfy their specific requirements in terms of function, performance or aesthetic. Meanwhile it would result in creation of more local jobs.

Consequently, it is not possible to label Mass Customization as a sustainable or non-sustainable strategy. The environmental and social impacts of Mass Customization mark it as a bilateral business model. In fact, the challenge for the MC enterprise is to realize the trade-off and try to implement MC in a more sustainable manner.

References

[1] Davis, S.M.: Future Perfect. Addison-Wesley, Reading (1987)
[2] Piller, F.T.: Mass Customization: einwettbewerbsstrategischesKonzeptimInformationszeitalter, 2nd edn. Gabler, Wiesbaden (2001)
[3] Piller, F.T., Steiner, F.: Mass Customizationas an Enabler of Network Resilience. In: Poler, R., et al. (eds.) Intelligent Non-hierarchical Manufacturing Networks, pp. 3–22. John Wiley&Sons, Hoboken (2013)
[4] Elkington, J.: Towards the Sustainable Corporation: Win-Win-Win Business Strategies for Sustainable Development. California Management Review 36(2), 90–100 (1994)
[5] Pollard, D., Chuo, S., Lee, B.: Strategies For Mass Customization. Journal of Business &Economics Research 6(7), 77–86 (2008)
[6] Kleer, R., Steiner, F.: Mass Customization: BridgingCustomer Integration and Sustainability (WorkingPaper), Availableat SSRN: http://ssrn.com/abstract=2245622
[7] Boër, C.R., Pedrazzoli, P., Bettoni, A., Sorlini, M.: Mass customization and sustainability: an assessmentframework and industrial implementation. Springer, London (2013)
[8] Matsokis, A., Kiristis, D.: An ontology-basedapproach for Product Lifecycle Management. Computer in Industry 61, 787–797 (2010)

[9] Maropoulos, P.G., Ceglarek, D.: Design verification and validation in productlifecycle. CIRP Annals - Manufacturing Technology 59(2), 740–759 (2010)

[10] Piller, F.T., Schubert, P., Koch, M., Möslein, K.M.: From mass customization to collaborative co-design. In: Proceedings of the European Conference on Information Systems (ECIS), Turku, Finland (2004)

[11] Badurdeen, F., Liyanage, J.P.: Sustainablevalue co-creationthrough mass customisation: a framework. International Journal of Sustainable Manufacturing 2(2/3), 180–203 (2011)

[12] Blecker, T., Friedrich, G.: Mass customization: challenges and solutions. Springer International Series, Boston (2006)

[13] Ulrich, K.T., Eppinger, S.D.: Product design and development, 3rd edn. McGraw Hill, New York (2004)

[14] Petersen, T.D., Nielsen, K., Taps, S., Jørgensen, K.A.: Is mass customization sustainable? In: Proceedings of the 6th International Conference on Mass Customization, Personalization and co-creation (MCPC 2011), San Francisco, US (2011)

[15] Clark, G., Kosoris, J., Hong, L.N., Crul, M.: Design for Sustainability: Current Trends in Sustainable Product Design and Development. Journal of Sustainability 1(3), 409–424 (2009)

[16] National Council for Advanced Manufacturing, Sustainable Manufacturing (2009), http://www.nacfam.org/

[17] Boer, C.: International cooperation on sustainable manufacturing. Presentation at the ICT for Energy Efficiency Conference, Brussels, Belgium, March 19-20 (2009)

[18] Brunø, T.D., Nielsen, K., Taps, S.B., Jørgensen, K.A.: Sustainability evaluation of mass customization. In: Prabhu, V., Taisch, M., Kiritsis, D. (eds.) APMS 2013, Part I. IFIP AICT, vol. 414, pp. 175–182. Springer, Heidelberg (2013)

[19] Pourabdollahian, G., Taisch, M., Tepe, G.: Exploring different faces of mass customization in manufacturing. In: Prabhu, V., Taisch, M., Kiritsis, D. (eds.) APMS 2013, Part I. IFIP AICT, vol. 414, pp. 13–20. Springer, Heidelberg (2013)

[20] Reichwald, R., Stokto, C.M., Piller, F.T.: Distributed mini-factory networks as a real-time enterprise: concept, flexibility potential and case studies. In: The Practical Real Time Enterprise, pp. 403–434. Springer, Berlin (2005)

Knowledge-Based Services

Capacity Planning at a Tactical Level in Hospital Departments

Agneta Sara Larsson[1] and Anna Fredriksson[2]

[1] Chalmers University of Technology, Gothenburg, Sweden
[2] Linköping University, Linköping, Sweden

Abstract. The purpose is to describe the essential components and output of the tactical planning process and to explore context-related variations in the applicability of the planning process for hospital departments. The paper is based on a multiple-case study of three hospital departments' planning processes at a tactical level, wherein the department manager's[1] support of the planning process was found to be essential. This study illustrates how an active tactical planning process can provide for numerous potential measures to adjust capacity and how they may vary in different contexts. An active tactical planning process provides the ability to move from current short-term, costly fire-fighting measures to more proactive capacity adjustments within hospital departments, which allow the department to stay under budget while keeping waiting times and queues within limits.

Keywords: Capacity planning, Healthcare, Tactical level, Planning process.

1 Introduction

Over the years, capacity management challenges of healthcare organizations [7, 8] have been reported in England [e.g., 2], Holland [e.g., 3, 4], Australia, Canada, England, New Zealand, Wales and Belgium [5, 6]. Silvester and Lendon [2] suggest that these challenges should be met by more accurate match between demand and supply of resources. The matching between resource supply and demand is made in the organizations' capacity planning processes, where tactical-level planning dictates how operational-level matching is accomplished. Several authors (i.e., Larsson and Johansson [9], Roth and van Dierdonk [10] and Hand et al. [4]) report on operational challenges due to insufficient planning at the tactical level. As a result, high-resource utilization and long wait times for some patient groups are dealt with through "fire-fighting" measures, such as engaging costly excess resources [4]. These issues illustrate the need for increased tactical capacity planning within healthcare organizations.

Previous research regarding capacity management within hospital departments has focused on operational planning level [e.g., 11, 12-14], such as the patient mix [14] or

---

[1] The department manager is responsible for the provision of hospital specialty care. In this paper, the relevant individuals manage the Urology, Cardiology and Psychiatry (affectionate disorders) departments.

B. Grabot et al. (Eds.): APMS 2014, Part II, IFIP AICT 439, pp. 535–547, 2014.

scheduling practices [12]. Literature that deals with the managerial aspect of the hospital planning process mainly presents planning and control frameworks that structures all planning levels [e.g., 3, 4, 8]). However, these studies do not describe the step-by-step planning process to assist hospital managers in matching the supply of resources with the demand for resources. There remains a need for understanding how to balance supply and demand in the tactical planning process within hospital departments. Thus, the purpose of this paper is to *describe what components and output of the tactical planning process are essential and to explore context-related variations in the applicability of the planning process for hospital departments*. The study is based on the tactical planning process within three hospital departments at a Swedish University hospital. The study will contribute to the understanding of tactical capacity planning by studying the required input, activities performed, measures used to adjust capacity and demand and the desired output within these three cases.

2   Theoretical Framework

This section will answer to the first part of the purpose stated above. It presents the included components of the planning process and the content of each component. A descriptive summary of theoretical planning process is stated at the end of the section, Table 1.

Production planning is often described as a hierarchal structure of processes, at the *strategic*, *tactical* and *operational* levels [8, 10, 13, 15]. Planning processes on the tactical level are the sales and operations planning (S&OP) process and the master production schedule (MPS) process [16]. In some organizations, S&OP and MPS are not separated into two different processes, but are called Master Planning [16, 17]. The responsibility for the tactical planning in hospital lies on the middle managers, however, it sometimes relies on interaction with top management [3].

The tactical planning process consists of different activities, including estimating the demand for products or services, deciding on a preliminary delivery plan and generating a preliminary master production schedule, reconciliation of plans and conditions and adaption of plans, as needed [17, 18]. When the demand and supply of capacity is balanced, the next step is to settle the prepared plans. The task of reconciling plans and conditions, and focus of this paper, is capacity planning, which at this planning level is often referred to as a rough-cut capacity plan (RCCP) [19], in which the anticipated capacity variations are included [2]. According to the works of Tavares Thomé, Scavarda [16], the planning processes can be divided into the following four parts: the planning process structure and activities, planning process input, measures that are available for balancing demand and supply, and the process delivery output.

Structure and Activities. The form in which a planning process is performed can be described as the structure and activities [16], which is denoted as managerial aspects consisting of meetings, activities and methods used to analyze data. The meetings can be characterized by the frequency and participants of meetings [16, 19]. The planning object at the tactical level is a product or service group. The planning horizon may vary between organizations, depending on product or service lead-times [18] and may span from less than six months to over 18 months [16]. The frequency of tactical planning is usually monthly or quarterly [17].

The activities of capacity planning are described by Jonsson and Mattsson [17] as calculating required and available capacity, performing capacity adjustments and making alternative actions. The manner in which data is analyzed and combined varies among organizations. Advanced IT system spreadsheets or mathematical models are analytical tools used to support capacity planning, where even the simplest method may be sufficient to fill its purpose [20]. Present methods and calculations models can roughly be described as either focusing on how to utilize resources in an effective way [14] or how to re-design resources to create a better flow of patients through the resources [e.g., 21, 22]. Furthermore, literature presents different kinds of tools supporting the decision-making in the capacity planning process [e.g., 11, 21, 22, 23].

Input. Input to the capacity planning process is necessary to determine future needs, such as demand, available resources, restrictions placed on the system, targets and to what extent production will be allowed to deviate from plans. Information about the future demand in hospitals should be unconstrained [19] and should describe the variations [2, 3]. Future demand consists of both known and unknown demand [4]. The unknown demand is forecasted demand, often based on historical data, whereas known demand includes waiting list information and "downstream" demand of patients currently under treatment [4]. Demand variation in healthcare is to be found both in volume [23, 24] and mix of resource requirements [14, 22]. Furthermore, the urgency and patient-throughput time create variations regarding the required timing of resource supply. Input regarding hospital capacity generally consist of the following resources: facilities, workforce and equipment [13]. Resource properties influence the available capacity (i.e., whether a resource is multifunctional [15] or specialized, if the resource is cost-intensive, resource availability [3] and if the resource is a shared resource or a dedicated resource [3, 14]). The available capacity is often formulated in terms of available hours and number of entities.

Tactical-level planning is restricted by decisions made at the strategic level and the feasibility of options at the operational level [14]. Strategic decisions may include the available number of units or time at the units. Other restrictions may be financial, such as budgeting or if the hospital is operating in a contracting market under planning restrictions [3]. Planning targets are formulated in terms of patient through-put (time, volume) [14], patient waiting time, length of waiting lists, resource utilization rate [14], production costs [15] or level of bed occupancy [21], etc. As input to the planning process, tolerance levels may also be provided.

Measures. Measures taken to balance demand and supply include adjustments to both the demand side and the supply side [25]. In the healthcare setting, measures adjusting capacity involve decisions concerning the acquisition and allocation of three types of resources: work force, equipment and facilities [7, 23]. A resource acquisition at the tactical level involves, for example, decisions concerning work force changes, overtime and subcontracting [7, 25], as well as the use of innovative shift schedules and employee cross-training to allow for movement between units [24]. Measures used to adjust patient demand is include prioritizing patients according to medical condition, re-scheduling, building queues, admissions planning and using scheduling rules [14].

Output. According to Tenhiälä [26], the primary objective of capacity planning is to ensure the feasibility of production plans. Besides the production plan per se, the output should link lower planning levels with higher by providing feedback regarding tactical plan feasibility, which helps improve hospital management performance [1] and the effectiveness and efficiency of healthcare delivery [4]. Linking the lower planning levels to the higher results in changing the role of managers from one that is reactive to one that is more pro-active [1].

Table 1. Summary of analytical framework based on theory

Structure and Activities	Input	Measures	Output
Meetings Frequency Participants Planning horizon Planning object **Activities** Calculate available and required capacity Compare available capacity with required capacity Choose suitable measure/-s considering targets Adapt the delivery plan and/or the production plan Establish delivery plan, production plan and actions taken at the tolerance levels **Analytical methods** Spreadsheet IT system support Mathematical models	**Future demand** Production plan based on: Unconstrained and consensus-based forecast Downstream demand Backlog/waiting lists **Available capacity** RCCP – including anticipated capacity cut downs (e.g. further training of staff) **Restrictions** Budget (available funding) Strategic planning Operational constrains **Targets** Through-put (time and volume) Waiting time Length of waiting lists Resources utilization Costs (change in budget) **Tolerance levels**	**Capacity adjustments** Overtime Extra staff Sub-suppliers, i.e. Buy care from other health care provider Moving capacity Cross-training **Demand adjustments** Medical priority Re-scheduling Building queues Admissions planning Scheduling rules	**Feasible production plan** **Feedback** To upper planning level To the next round of planning

3   Methodology

The authors of this paper selected an exploratory multiple-case research design to explain the phenomenon under investigation. The research started with constructing an analysis framework of the capacity planning at the tactical level based on existing literature [27]. The analytical framework was built on literature from both the healthcare and manufacturing domains; thereby forming a foundation of previously developed theoretical frameworks on which to build this study [16, 20], while systematically verifying their applicability in a new setting. The data collection was made through semi-structured interviews. An interview guide based on the analytical framework was used [28]. The studied departments were selected based on their differences in service, demand and manufacturing processes, which were chosen to obtain a wider understanding of the tactical capacity planning process within different contexts. The data collection focused on identifying the main structure and activities, input, output and measures used in the tactical capacity planning process at the studied departments. A cross-case analysis was performed to compare the ways that tactical capacity planning was conducted in the cases.

4   Empirical Data

4.1   Cardiology

Approximately 40 physicians, 250 nurses and administrative staff in the Cardiology department treat an average of 16,900 outpatients and 6,000 inpatients each year. The department consists of three wards, six laboratories, an outpatient policlinic, divisions that treat heart problems and patients undergoing smoking cessation as well as a teaching unit.

Structure and Activities. There is no set planning process structure, and the focus is on costs. As such, the frequency of meetings follows the yearly budget process. The planning of available resources is not synchronized with the yearly production planning, rather the status of consumed financial means is controlled on a monthly basis, and the staff is scheduled on a quarterly basis. As a result, there is minimal connection between demand and available resources, as there is a continuous inflow of patients with treatment processes measured in days and weeks. Meeting participants represent all relevant parties for the treatment processes and financial and organizational units, including the department[2] manager, the unit[3] managers, the section[4] manager, operational developer,[5] accountant and human resources representative. During planning, patient groups are formed according to their resource requirements, and spreadsheets facilitate the understanding of required and available capacity; however, spreadsheets are not used for all patient groups.

Input. The anticipated demand and allocation of capacity between patient groups are based on the previous year's outcome. Data regarding patient demand and available capacity is, to some extent, available in the IT systems but is not systematically used. For example, the waiting lists are recorded and viewed by the manager, but are not used during the planning process by including the backlog in the demand. Restrictions

---

[2] The department manager is responsible for the provision of hospital specialty care (e.g., Cardiology, Urology and Psychiatry. Psychiatry, which in this case includes affectionate disorders.)

[3] The unit being an organisational part of the production system, such as a ward unit or a clinic

[4] The section is a subdivision according to speciality of care within the department, defined by the competence of the physicians

[5] The hospital's support function for improving the production performance of the hospital

are formulated in financial terms as limits where new funding is required and as patient waiting times. The limit is used to notify upper organizational levels that the budget is insufficient. Patient waiting times are measured but are not actively used in the planning process; rather, the patient waiting time restriction is used to depict when patients are redirected to costly sub-contractors. The objectives of the planning process are to achieve the performance measures, patient waiting time and delivered number of patients and medical priority of patients. The tolerance levels are expressed by the department as patient waiting time but, when interpreting the priority of planning focus, one could suggest that they also have indirect tolerance levels regarding costs.

Measures. The measures taken to balance demand and supply adjust capacity by utilizing extra staff, approving overtime, and using sub-suppliers and cross training. Demand is adjusted by building queues, prioritizing patients according to medical condition and re-scheduling patients. Moving capacity between points of use (e.g., relocating surgery equipment between operating rooms) is rarely used as a measure of adjusting capacity because each department's equipment is typically stationary and requires specialized staffing. However, relocating resources does occur with some nurses and physicians when the required competence is the same. The admission planning and scheduling rules are not used due to the large number of emergency patients.

Output. The output of the existing planning process is not a production plan, but rather a set of recommendations regarding what to produce. Existing planning activities provide feedback to the strategic level regarding the consumption of the budget and what the production process has achieved to deliver.

4.2   Urology

The Urology department treats approximately 22,000 patients each year and performs about 1,300 inpatient and 5,000 polyclinic operations, with the largest patient group being cancer patients. The department comprises two ward units and one outpatient clinic, which consists of eight nurse receptions, each one specializing in distinct specialties, such as prostate cancer, colostomy, kidney cancer or kidney stones.

Structure and Activities. Planning process activities include calculation of available and required capacity, comparison of available capacity and required capacity, establishing measures to adjust the two, adaption of a production plan and establishing the production plan. The activities are treated at the monthly planning meetings. The planning process is heavily dependent on the department manager and a spreadsheet-based planning tool supports the planning. The established plan is locked for changes 3-5 weeks ahead, with built-in slack for emergency patients. The planning process is divided into two separate parts: clinic planning and surgery and wards (inpatient) planning. The reason for combining the surgery and wards planning is the strong dependency between surgery and wards. However, the separation between clinic and inpatient planning make the planning of the inpatient treatment process fragmented by decoupling one patient's clinical treatment from the inpatient part of the treatment. The planning meetings include department manager,[6] unit managers[7] and administrator[8]. The planning horizon is a 12-month rolling period that bridges the budget year. The planning objective is to form patient groups for the two separate planning processes that are quantified differently. At the surgery unit, the resource requirements of the patient groups are measured in multiples of required surgery time (minutes), while the requirements at the ward unit are measured in days (or sometimes in beds). Clinical planning focuses on patient groups and the required number of visits (one patient one visit, and days include a number of visits), allowing adjusting resources according to the varying requirements of a specific patient group.

Input. The department makes use of available data from the IT systems regarding patient demand. Demand is forecast by factoring the amount of demand met during the previous year (hospital days, number of visits and discharges) and patient waiting lists. The forecast is adjusted with tacit knowledge, such as experience and other relevant information. The number of referrals is not directly used in the planning due to the department's ability to admit all referred patients at the clinic within a reasonable time.

Available capacity is estimated based on previously used capacity (i.e., the volume of capacity that each treatment unit (e.g., lab or surgery) provided last year. This method is preferable due to generally small changes in staff, facilities and equipment. Capacity is measured in the same way as demand (i.e., number of patients per patient group, days at the ward or surgery unit, visits). Restrictions on the planning process are derived from strategic decisions made by hospital management and factor in the allocated budget and the maximum patient waiting time for new and return visits. The strategic decisions are also used to formulate targets for the production system, such as patient waiting time for new and return visits and the yearly number of surgeries. Other targets are to prioritize patients according to medical priority and to treat critical conditions within an adequate timeframe.

Measures. Measures taken for capacity adjustments include the following: overtime and moving workforce and ambulatory equipment. In general, there is a lack of urologists in Sweden; therefore, overtime at evening clinics is frequently used. The department manager has limited authority to make changes outside of the budget and, when required changes are outside his authority, they are passed higher up in the hierarchy. Measures taken to adjust the demand to better fit the capacity abide by scheduling rules. The surgery unit is perceived as the bottleneck of the production system, and the purpose of using scheduling rules is to make better use of available capacity at the surgery unit. Medical priority is not articulated as a measure to adjust demand. However, dedicating slack time to treating emergency patients can indirectly priorit-

---

[6] See footnote 2
[7] See footnote 3
[8] Staff with insight into the historic data of the department

ize urgent medical conditions. While queues and admissions planning are not intentionally used, queue length varies as a natural consequence of patient inflow.

Output. The output of the planning process is actively used to create production support on both a weekly and monthly basis. The feedback the planning process provides is regarding insufficient capacity and how well the system produces according to targets.

4.3   Psychiatry

The studied Psychiatry department specializes in affective disorders and is comprised of nine outpatient clinics at different geographic locations with varying specializations. The department also consists of five ward units for inpatient care and one unit for research and teaching.

Structure and Activities. Planning activities include estimating the required and available capacity, comparing the two types of capacity and choosing suitable measures that will adjust the balance, thereby establishing a production plan. First, the forecast from the previous planning period is evaluated and compared with the outcome (i.e., number of referrals, accepted referrals, first visits, return visits and discharges). The meeting also includes follow-ups on tasks discussed during the previous meeting. Second, production plans for each clinic are established, and then combined into an overall plan for the whole department. Third, capacity and demand adjustments are made within or between clinics, if needed. Fourth, the plan is frozen one month prior to the planning meeting, with changes allowed only when forecasted patient waiting times exceed three months. The department manager, unit managers, administrator,[9] and operational developer[10] take part in the monthly meetings. The planning objective is patient visits over a rolling 12-month planning horizon. The majority of the treatment process is based on visits, with the exception of an inpatient resource demand of beds and the rare need for radiology equipment. New visits are given priority over return visits because this is the politically stated performance measure used. Spreadsheets are used to support planning and to control production.

Input. Demand input consists of data from the patient process at an aggregated level: total number of incoming patients, total number of visits and discharges. The available capacity is the number of employees and their competence. According to hospital management, each treating staff member (e.g., psychiatrist or therapist) is expected to provide 800 hours of patient treatment time per year, which is less than 50% of full-time employment. How the number of patients in the production system translates into capacity requirements is not known and is thereby not used as input when planning.

---

[9] Staff with insight into the historic data of the department
[10] Hospital support function for improving the production performance of the hospital

The expressed restrictions are the allocated budget; however, there are also capacity adjustment restrictions (i.e., the possibility of hiring additional staff members). Targets of the capacity planning process are the length of patient waiting time, the number of new visits and the number of discharged patients. All of the targets are related to performance measures by which the production is evaluated. The tolerance level and targets are formulated according to the number of new visits and maximum patient waiting time.

Measures. Measures used for adjusting the capacity of the production system include overtime and moving capacity. The movement of capacity is usually in the form of physicians and psychiatrists, while nursing staff is seldom moved. Measures for adjusting demand include admissions planning and rescheduling. Admissions planning is accomplished by redirecting referrals between units that have equal supplies of competence, with a goal of balancing the numbers of new and return visits. To adjust the demand to meet capacity, the frequency of visits is decreased from four visits per month to three visits. However, when the treatment process becomes ineffective due to scarce visits with the therapist, a frequency limit must be considered when scheduling patients' return visits. Patients may also be rescheduled to alternative, similar treatment resources. Lastly, the department also adjusts the demand for resources by reducing the number of patients in the production system.

Output. The output of the planning process is a monthly production plan for all eight clinics, providing planning support on two levels: the individual clinic production and the total amount of psychiatric care production for the hospital region. The output of the planning process also provides feedback regarding the forecast accuracy, which is invaluable for strategic planning by hospital management. Feedback is made by signaling when production is about to violate the tolerance levels for maximum patient waiting time. In this case, tolerance levels are formulated according to how many visits are required to reach the target of maximum patient waiting time, rather than being based on patient throughput time or the number of patients that must be rebooked due to lack of capacity.

5   Analysis

Table 2. Cross-case analysis of planning processes at Cardiology, Urology and Psychiatry departments

Structure and Activities	Cardiology	Urology	Psychiatry	Cross-Case Analysis
Structured capacity planning process	No	Yes	Yes	There is no hospital wide standardized planning when it comes to structure and activities, which forces the department managers to form the process themselves. In the **Cardiology** department the capacity planning process is under development and, therefore, not used as a tool for pro-active actions. The **Psychiatry** department is starting to make use of the planning process for better balance between supply and demand. However, lack of relevant data (e.g., proper patient care plans) complicates the planning and evaluation of production outcome. The **Urology** planning process is actively used to plan and control department operations; however, there are still potential for improvements when bureaucracy delays the timing of proper measures.

Table 2. *(continued)*

Structure and Activities	Cardiology	Urology	Psychiatry	Cross-Case Analysis
Frequency of meetings	Yearly (Quarterly)	Monthly	Monthly	The frequency of **Urology** and **Psychiatry** department meetings is similar to the frequency of theory, but not for **Cardiology,** for which there are fewer opportunities to react to changes due to infrequent planning meetings. The scheduling of staff is made quarterly.
Meeting participants	Cross-functional	Cross-functional	Cross-functional	**All three departments** use a cross-functional process in which meeting participants include a department manager, unit and section (when applicable) managers, and a representative providing data. Since the **Cardiology** department planning meeting is mainly a budget meeting, the human resource representative and the economist are also present. The **Cardiology** and **Psychiatry** departments are both developing their capacity planning processes and, therefore, include a planning support function at the meetings.
Planning horizon	Year	Rolling year	Rolling year	**All three departments** have a planning horizon of 12 months. However, the **Urology** and **Psychiatry** departments utilize a rolling horizon, which results in static planning perspective, while the **Cardiology** department's planning horizon decreases during the fiscal year.
Planning object	Some pat groups	Pat groups	Total amount of visits	The focus on patient groups makes it possible for the **Urology** department to adjust resources according to the varying requirements. However, in the **Psychiatry** department, all patients are aggregated and the focus lies on the total number of new and return visits, which has led to the inability of capacity planning to provide improvements for specific patients groups. The **Cardiology** department has been better able to provide appropriate care since it began to focus on the number of visits to patient groups. Planning based on patient groups is not currently utilized for all patient groups but is a first step in creating a capacity planning process.
Activities	No	Yes	Yes	Since **Cardiology** has only one yearly meeting with random check-ups during the year, it has little knowledge of the performance of the production system during the year. **Urology** is the most updated of current state among the departments and controls the production through its planning activities and adjustments of activities according to capacity and demand. **Psychiatry** has a functioning system of activities but requires better input to improve planning performance.
Analytical methods	Partly	Yes	Yes	For **all three departments**, simple comparisons of numbers in Excel are the only analytical method used; there is no use of optimization calculations The use of spreadsheets is probably suitable for its purpose. Generally, the available data has a low level of detail, which reduces the potential for the exploitation of a more sophisticated planning tool.
Input				
Future demand	Historical data	Historical data and tacit knowledge	Historical data	**All three departments** use the historical data of treated patients as forecasts, but use the data differently. Since the department treats all referred patients, **Urology** forecasts demand using historical data and adding tacit adjustments when it is needed. **Psychiatry** forecasts demand using historical data, but does not know how to interpret the number of patients as resource requirements due to undefined patient care processes. **Cardiology** uses the data as forecasts but is unaware how it corresponds to the actual patient demand and whether it has changed.
Available capacity	Yes	Yes	No	**All three departments** estimate capacity based on the previous year. This method is consciously chosen for **Urology** since there is little variation in staff, equipment and facilities between years. **Cardiology** strictly uses the data from previous year out of tradition. **Psychiatry** has no active way of measuring capacity and uses the performance of the previous year as guidance, without making adjustments. **Psychiatry** uses capacity levels garnered from hospital management, which is based on negotiations between management and staff representatives rather than time measures and treatment plans.

Table 2. *(continued)*

Struc-ture and Activities	Cardiology	Urology	Psychiatry	Cross-Case Analysis
Restrictions	Yes	Yes	Yes	Budget is a restriction used by **all three departments**. In addition, **Cardiology** and **Urology** use patient waiting time as a restriction. In the **Psychiatry** department, the patient waiting time is classified as a target. For the departments that use patient waiting time as restriction, the waiting time is also used as target.
Targets	Yes	Yes	Yes	Department targets (e.g., patient waiting time, number of visits or number of discharges) are generally formulated according to the KPIs (key performance indexes) by which the production is evaluated. The targets are also formulated in efficiency terms (i.e., number of patients delivered for a certain amount of money and number of surgeries per year).
Tolerance levels	Yes	Yes	Yes	At both **Cardiology** and **Urology**, the department manager oversees that production delivers within tolerance levels and according to targets. In the case of **Psychiatry**, tolerance levels are set by and supervised by hospital management. Thereafter, hospital management provides feedback on production performance.
Measures				
Capacity adjustments	Yes	Yes, focus	Yes, limited	Capacity measures made by **Cardiology** focus on using extra resources (e.g., sub-suppliers and extra staff), and adjustments made within current resources are by via cross-training and overtime usage. **Urology** focuses on adjusting capacity according to demand. The adjustments are made within current resources with no addition of sub-suppliers or extra staff. **Psychiatry** adjusts both demand and capacity whenever possible. Capacity adjustments for Psychiatry are, however, limited by the supply of qualified staff and regulations of hiring temporary psychiatrists.
Demand adjustments	Yes	Yes, minor	Yes	**Urology** has created measures on the demand side to schedule surgeries and better utilize the operation theatre. While the **Urology** department focuses on capacity measures, the **Cardiology** department makes increased use of demand measures as well as **Psychiatry,** which focuses on making adjustments at the demand side.
Output				
Feasible production plan	Recommendation	MP	MP	**Cardiology** does not use a planning process to obtain a feasible production plan. The scarce output of planning is a recommendation for next year's production. The planning processes of both Urology and Psychiatry provide a feasible master production plan. For the **Psychiatry** department, the plan is given on two levels.
Feedback	Yes	Yes	Yes	The feedback that **Cardiology** is utilizing for planning is the status on consumed budget. **Urology** frequently uses the planning process for continuous feedback on production performance, which is used in the next round of planning. The feedback of the **Psychiatry** planning process is based on patient waiting time and delivered to upper hospital management. The planning process also provides the manager with feedback on forecast accuracy.

6   Discussion and Conclusions

The purpose of this paper is to describe the essential components and output of the tactical planning process and to explore context-related variations in relation to the applicability of the planning process for hospital departments. The components and the output that this study has identified are summarized in Table 1. Regarding the context related variation, presented in Table 2, the devotion of the manager was superior for the performance of the planning process. It was foremost decisive of the activities performed, the frequency of meetings, the planning targets and tolerance levels, the choice of measures and the use of the planning process output. The planning process at the Urology department showed to be the most developed process, followed by the Psychiatry department and Cardiology. Urology shows a pro-active planning process, which focuses on providing the most care with the given capacity. The planning object is patient-groups but complements with an overall target of total number of visits and surgeries. Compared to Psychiatry, which also measure total number of visits, the Urology planning process are able to proactively provide measures for patients groups when required while the Psychiatry planning process is dull in its measures with its overall number of visits. The planning at the Cardiology department has improved by introducing patient groups as planning object.

Context related variations regarding the process input were evident in the available data at the Psychiatry department. There were no care plans specified for patient groups and the IT systems were lacking relevant data. Deficient input on required capacity and limited options for adjusting capacity resulted in a re-active capacity planning, with focus on demand adjustments. The cost intense production system of Cardiology along with the immature planning process has lead to a planning process that is more of a budget tool than a support system, where the output is a budget consumption indicator. The way Psychiatry uses the process output enlarge the utility planning process output, from providing production plans and feedback on tolerance levels to include evaluation of previously made forecasts.

This study illustrates the possibilities that an active tactical planning process can provide regarding the number of possible measures to adjust capacity. An active tactical planning process enables the potential to move away from the current short-term, costly fire-fighting measures to a more proactive manner of capacity adjustments within hospital departments that allow the department to maintain the budget while keeping waiting times and queues within limits and, perhaps, shortened.

References

1. Butler, T., Leong, Everett, L.: The operations management role in hospital strategic planning. Journal of Operations Management 14, 137–156 (1996)
2. Silvester, K., et al.: Reducing waiting times at the NHS: Is lack of capacity the problem? Clinician in Management 12(3), 105–111 (2004)
3. Vissers, J., Bertrand, J., De Vries, G.: A framework for production control in health care organizations. Production Planning and Control 12(6), 591–604 (2001)
4. Hans, E.W., Van Houdenhoven, M., Hulshof, P.J.H.: A framework for health care planning and control. Memorandum, 1938 (2011)
5. Willcox, S., et al.: Measuring and reducing waiting times: a cross-national comparison of strategies. Health Affaires 26(4), 1078–1087 (2007)
6. Cardoen, B., Demeulemeester, E., Van der Hoeven, J.: On the use of planning models in the operating theatre: results of a survey in Flanders. International Journal of Health Planning and Management 25, 400–414 (2010)

7. Smith-Daniels, V., Schweikhart, S., Smith-Daniels, D.: Capacity management in health care services: Review and future research directions. Decisions Sciences 19(4), 889–919 (1988)
8. Rhyne, D., Jupp, D.: Health care requirements planning: A conceptual framework. Health Care Management Review 13(1), 17–27 (1988)
9. Larsson, A., Johansson, M.I.: Health Care Planning–a case study of a surgery clinic. In: PLANs forsknings-och tilläpnings konferens 2007, Jönköping, Sweden (2007)
10. Roth, A., van Dierdonk, R.: Hospital resource planning concepts, feasibility and framework. Production and Operations Management 4(1), 2–29 (1995)
11. Ridge, J., et al.: Capacity planning for intensive care units. European Journal of Operational Research 105, 346–355 (1998)
12. Cardoen, B., Demeulemeester, E., Beliën, J.: Operating room planning and scheduling: A literature review. E uropean Journal of Operational Research 201, 921–932 (2010)
13. Jack, E.P., Powers, T.L.: A review and synthesis of demand management, capacity management and performance in health-care services. International Journal of Management Reviews 11(2), 149–174 (2009)
14. Adan, I., Vissers, J.: Patient mix optimisation in hospital admission planning: a case study. International Journal of Operations and Production Management 22(4), 445–461 (2002)
15. de Vries, G., Bertrand, J., Vissers, J.: Design requirements for health care production control systems. Production Planning and Control 10(6), 559–569 (1999)
16. Tavares Thomé, A., et al.: Sales and operations planning: A research synthesis. International Journal of Production Economics 138, 1–13 (2012)
17. Jonsson, P., Mattsson, S.A.: Manufacturing Planning and Control. McGraw-Hill Education, Berkshire (2009)
18. Grimson, A., Pyke, D.: Sales and operations planning: an exploratory study and framework. International Journal of Logistics Management 18(3), 322–346 (2007)
19. Lapide, L.: Sales and operations planning part I: the process. The Journal of Business Forecasting 23(3), 17–19 (2004)
20. Jonsson, P., Mattsson, S.A.: The implications of fit between planning environment and manufacturing planning and control methods. International Journal of Operations and Production Management 23(8), 872–900 (2003)
21. Beliën, J., Demeulemeester, E.: Building cyclic master surgery schedules with leveled resulting bed occupancy. European Journal of Operational Research 176, 1185–1204 (2007)
22. Tai, G., Williams, O.: Product line management for health care system: Theoretic capacity planning over various resources. In: IEEM, Singapore (2008)
23. Utley, M., Worthington, D.: Capacity Planning. In: Handbook of Healthcare System Scheduling, pp. 11–30. Springer (2012)
24. Jack, E.P., Powers, T.L.: Volume flexible strategies in health services: A research framework. Production and Operations Management 13(3), 230–244 (2004)
25. Olhager, J., Rudberg, M., Wikner, J.: Long-term capacity management: linking the perspectives from manufacturing strategy and sales and operations planning. International Journal of Production Economics 69, 215–225 (2001)
26. Tenhiälä, A.: Contingency theory of capacity planning: The link between process types and planning methods. Journal of Operations Management 29, 65–77 (2011)
27. Voss, C., Tsikriktsis, N., Frohlich, M.: Case research in operation managment. International Journal of Operations and Production Management 22(2), 195–219 (2002)
28. Halvorsen, K.: Samhällsvetenskaplig method. Studentlitteratur, Lund (1992)

The Influence of the Customer in Service Production

Günther Schuh, Christian Fabry, and Philipp Jussen

Institute for Industrial Management (FIR), Campus-Boulevard 55, 52074 Aachen, Germany
{G.Schuh,Christian.Fabry,Philipp.Jussen}@fir.rwth-aachen.de

Abstract. Increasing productivity in product-service systems is a vital success factor for industrialized economies and individual businesses. The service production is typically described as an integrated value chain setting, in which the provider and the customer are co-creators. This paper embraces a characteristic curve model in order to illustrate the influence of the customer on the productivity of service production. The characteristic curves are derived from a system dynamics simulation model for a synchronized takt-based service production. In conclusion this research leads to designs recommendations for service production systems in order to reduce lead times and increase adherence to delivery dates.

Keywords: Service production, productivity, characteristic curves, customer productivity, external factor.

1 Introduction

Due to an increase in competition and the need to generate additional value for the customer the manufacturers of tangible goods expand their portfolio with supplementary industrial services thus creating innovative product-service-system [1]. Increasing operational productivity for these Product-Service-Systems is different from regular production of tangible goods due to the characteristics of services. The intangibility of services [2] and the interaction with the customer [3] require a separate set of management concepts [4]. This paper focuses on the interaction with the customer and the customer's role as an external production factor in product-service-systems. Due to the integration in the service production process the customer has a determining effect on the productivity of the process.

2 The Customer as an External Factor in Production-Service-Systems

"Services are production processes wherein each customer supplies one or more input components…" [5]. The service customer therefore is characterized by being part of the service production process [2]. This is illustrated in figure 1.

B. Grabot et al. (Eds.): APMS 2014, Part II, IFIP AICT 439, pp. 548–555, 2014.

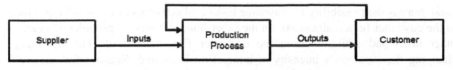

Fig. 1. Service Input/Output Model [5]

The customer can bring himself or an object in his possession as an external production factor into the process [6]. The involvement of the customer can range from a passive role regarding the provision of own production factors to an active participation in the production process [7]. Thus the external factor can have different characteristics, which can be differentiated into tangible good, immaterial good and human participation [8].

Tangible goods appear as mobile or immobile goods of the service customer. They are objects in the possession of the customer. From a production theory point of view the juridical component is sometimes considered not relevant. But the inability for the service provider to freely dispose makes it a matter of productivity as the timely and locally correct disposal determines duration of the service delivery process and therefore is an important factor in the consideration of service productivity [8]. *Immaterial goods* can be information, risks or patents. They can be an important factor in the planning and control of a service production process. The *human participation* describes the case when division of labor between the provider and the customer exists and the customer is integrated in the service production process as a co-creator [9]. In Product-Service Systems, the external factor usually is a combination of the three types.

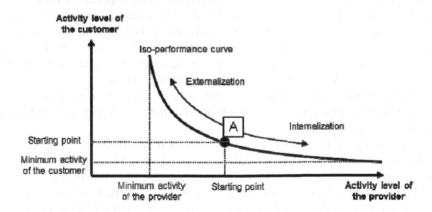

Fig. 2. Intensity of integration of the customer in service production [11]

The service production requires a synchronous concurrence of the internal and external production factors [2]. The intensity of integration, sometimes defined as customer integration level, describes how far the external factor is involved in the production process of a service [10]. There are two different development paths to diversify the intensity of integration for the service provider (figure 3). On the one hand there is the possibility to outsource tasks and activities of the service production to the customer (externalization), on the other hand the service provider can carry out other tasks and activities from the customer (internalization). The flexibility of changing the customer's intensity of integration is limited. Reasons for this are that quantitative and qualitative resource capacities on both sides are limited and that the execution of the service requires a minimum activity on both sides [11].

For the service production process different characteristics and features of the external factor have an impact on the productivity. The **ability to dispose** the external factor describes to what extent the service producer can autonomously access the external factor. The external factor can remain in the command of the customer or switch to the command of the service provider during the production. If the external factor remains in command of the customer timing and synchronization between the consumer and the provider is required. If the external factor changes to the area of disposition of the service provider, the provider can arrange the external factor autonomously. Closely related to the ability to dispose the external factor is the ability of the service provider to control the time window for the service delivery. The customer can set dates for access to the external factor or for the interaction in the service production process, if these are necessary requirements for the customer. This limits the freedom of action for the service provider. A typical case is a time critical repair service. If there are no restrictions on customer side for the date of the service provision, the customer can specify a time window or can get a time slot from the provider. An example for this case is a maintenance service, if the customer does not specify a date, but only a time window for the procedure.

The **localization** of the external factor describes the accessibility of the external factor. Immobile external factors are characterized by their dependency on a location. In combination with the requirement to involve the external factor in the service production process, this leads to a service provision at the site of the external factor. Mobile external factors are characterized by their ability to vary their location. A special type of mobile external factor exists, if the access to the factor can be done virtually anywhere. An example for this is typically information.

The **need of the areal coincidence** describes if service provider and customer must come together for production. A differentiation can be made between located and separated services [12].

The knowledge of the service provider of **detailed features** of the external factor and the knowledge of the **current state** at the beginning of the service production process can vary. In the best case the service provider has detailed information to describe the external factor and its current state before the actual provision. In reality however, the characteristics and the current state of the external factor are typically only partially known in advance or become clear during the service delivery [7].

In summary the following features can be differentiated:

- **Type of external factor**: Human; Object; Information
- **Type of integration**: passive; access of the external factor; Co-Production
- **Ability to dispose**: deadline by customer; matching of a time window the customer; autonomously by the service provider

- **Local dimension and accessibility**: immobile; mobile; independent of location
- **Areal coincidence of customer and service provider**: necessary; not necessary
- **Information about the external factor**: completely available; partly available; get clear during the provision

3   Methodology

In order to research the influence of the external factor in the service-production process a system theory approach is taken in order to create a simulation model. System theory is used for modeling relationships in complex organizational structures such as productions systems [13]. System dynamics is used as simulation method. The system dynamics methodology is specifically suitable to explain behavior system by analyzing the structure of cause-effect relationships between the system elements. On the basis of delayed or back coupled effects non-linear or counter-intuitive system behavior can be modeled, simulated and analyzed [14]. A holistic model for service production was created. The simulation model was validated with respect to its structure, the parameters and the model behavior [15]. The validation with respect to structure and parameters was conducted in workshops with experts from research and from the industry. In order to evaluate the model behavior a sensitivity analysis and extreme-conditions tests were conducted. The validation showed that the developed system-dynamic model is robust and suitable for the stated problem. The part which concerns the external factor is introduced in detail in this paper.

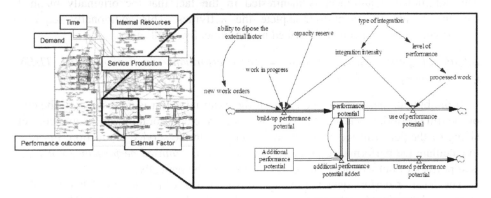

Fig. 3. Simulation Model for the performance potential of the external factor

From the perspective of the service producer the activities of the customers, which are connected to the internal activities of the service producer and its internal production factors, are relevant to the production process. Autonomous activities of the customer are beyond influence of the service provider. For the production process it is only relevant that the required performance potential of the external factor is available and whether the activities were carried out as previously intended.

The *build-up performance potential* of the external factor arises from the amount of *pending work* orders, the *integration intensity* as well as the planned *capacity reserve* of the external factor. The pending work describes the within the next time period generally pending activities. The pending work is the sum of the work still in process plus the newly released work orders. The integration intensity is a factor for the degree of contribution of the external factor to the service provision.

The co-producing external factor can accumulate for a smaller or bigger share of the work. The integration intensity ultimately is the ratio of amount of work between the service provider and the external factor. The reserve capacity reflects the fact that the customer anticipates deviations in required potential during the service production process and holds available additional capacity.

Build-up performance potential = (New work orders + work in progress) * integration intensity * capacity reserve

The *performance potential* of the external factor is used in the course of the production of services to combine with the capacities introduced by the service provider and add value. The *use of performance potential* results from the amount of *processed work* in general. The specifically retrieved potential of the external factor is proportionally dependent on the degree of integration.

Use of performance potential = processed work * integration intensity

If there are deviations in the service production process, this may lead to more or less work compared to what was planned. In the first case this requires the provision of *additional performance potential* to fully perform the required work performance. This additional requirement is manifested in the fact that the originally planned capacity is not sufficient to complete the activities. This additionally required performance potential can be described mathematically as follows:

Additional performance potential = IF (performance potential < 0) THEN (performance potential) ELSE (0)

If the buildup performance potential of the external factor is not used until the end of the time period, it deteriorates. The reasons for the deterioration can be an incorrect sizing of the performance potential and variations in the service production. In order to calculate the performance of the external factor, the *unused performance potential* is kept track of but will not be described further mathematically.

The *level of performance* is (amongst other factors which are not debated in this paper) a determining factor of the *processed work* of each time period. The *type of integration* of the external factor can be the provision of information, the provision of access or co-production. If the integration of the external factor includes only the provision of information or the granting of access to an object in the possession of the customer, the level of performance of the external factor is assumed constant. An impairment of service production due to inadequate information or limited accessibility manifests itself in a disposition related error or hold-up and thus leads to interruption or slowing of production. In the case of co-production it is assumed that the external factor mainly consists of human workforce. The performance level of staff is determined by the factors performance conditions, performance requirements, performance ability and motivation. These factors are assumed constant but can be varied and adapted for a specific organization.

The *ability to dispose* the external factor describes the extent to which the service provider can influence the customer to confirm the date of service provision. By controlling the amount of work orders the ability to dispose indirectly determines the amount of work in a specific time period. The service production planning and control algorithms distribute the amount of work over different time periods in order to achieve a constant degree of capacity utilization. If there is no ability to dispose the external factor, i.e. there is a fixed period for the service production, the fluctuations of the amount of work will be bigger over different time periods.

4   Results and Discussion

The system-dynamic model reveals the influence of external factors on the service production performance.

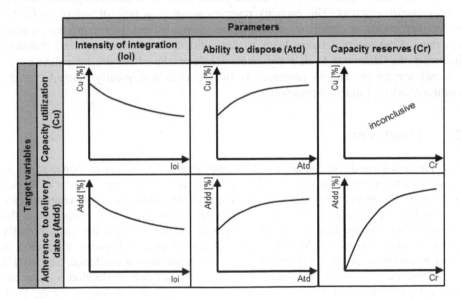

Fig. 4. Characteristic curves for the influence of the external factor in service production

In order to generate the results simulation runs were conducted in each of which the set-up of the parameters of the simulation model was kept constant, expect for one parameter. The parameters varied were *intensity of integration*, *ability to dispose* the external factor and the *capacity reserves* of the external factor. For each value of the parameters the resulting averages for the target variables were calculated over the time periods. In order to illustrate the effect of the parameter changes, the dependent target variables *capacity utilization* and *adherence to delivery dates* were used. By plotting the parameter on one scale and the resulting target variable on the other a characteristic curve is obtained (see figure 5).

With increasing *intensity of integration* of the external factor, the influence of the customer on the service production process increases. This results in increased process interferences, which leads to fluctuating process durations. Accordingly the utilization of the internal resources of the service provider decreases with the increasing influence of the customer. When the customer only provides information, the integration and influence of the external factor is limited. The influence on the production process increases when the customer has to grant accessibility. In a scenario of co-production the influence of the external factor is largest.

With an increase in *ability to dispose* the external factor the utilization of the internal resources of the service provider increases. When the service provider has only a slight possibility of coordinating the point of service production with the customer, not all work orders can be started on time. This leads to a poorer utilization of the service production system. This effect is enhanced in the presence of a high proportion of short-term work orders, which must be either served at the time or rejected.

The customer impacts the performance of the service production system with his own *capacity reserves*. The capacity reserves serve as a type of safety buffer for unforeseen events or complications in the service production. Increasing the capacity reserves of the external factor helps to deal with those disturbances and therefore increases the adherence to delivery dates. However the effect on the utilization of internal service production resources is inconclusive and greatly depends on the outline of other production parameters.

5   Conclusion

This paper discussed and characterized the customer in service production systems as an active part in service production. A simulation model was used in order to further investigate the effects and illustrate cause-effect relationships using characteristic curves. Two major implications can be derived from this research. First because of the immateriality and the lack of storability service production systems are especially prone to utilization issues. Maintaining a constant degree of capacity utilization in order to maximize productivity therefore is a key management challenge. Secondly it is evident that to ensure high performance of the service production system the relevant parameters of influence have to be tuned together with the customer. With respect to existing research on the topic, this paper shows the effects of the customer as an external production factor in service production for the first time using characteristic curves. Further research may include finding a way to parameterize the curves in mathematical equations, so that the concept can be applied to specific practical use cases in order to find optimal solutions.

Acknowledgements. The research presented in this paper was partly developed in the work of the research project SERVSYNC. This project is sponsored by the AiF under the program for the promotion of industrial research and development (IGF) by the Federal Ministry of Economics and Technology under the number 17743 N.

References

1. Baines, T.S., Lightfoot, H.W., Evans, S., Neely, A., Greenough, R., Peppard, J., et al.: State-of-the-art in product-service systems. Proceedings of the Institution of Mechanical Engineers, Part B: Journal of Engineering Manufacture 221(10), S.1543–S.1552 (2007)
2. Frietsche, U., Maleri, R.: Dienstleistungsproduktion. In: Bullinger, H.-J., Scheer, A.-W. (eds.) Service Engineering, pp. 195–225. Springer, Heidelberg (2006)
3. Meier, H., Roy, R., Seliger, G.: Industrial Product-Service Systems – IPS2. Annals of the CIRP – Manufacturing Technology 59, 607–627 (2010)
4. Grönroos, C., Ojasalo, K.: Service Productivity. Towards a conceptualization of the transformation of inputs into economic results in services. Journal of Business Research 57(4), 414–423 (2004)
5. Sampson, S.E.: The Unified Service Theory. A Paradigm for Service Science. In: Kieliszewski, C.A., Maglio, P.P., Spohrer, J.C. (Hg.) Handbook of Service Science, pp. S107–S131. Springer, New York (2010)
6. Haller, S.: Dienstleistungsmanagement. Grundlagen - Konzepte - Instrumente. 5. Aufl. Wiesbaden: Gabler, Gabler Lehrbuch (2012)
7. Fitzsimmons, J., Fitzsimmons, M.: Service Management. McGraw-Hill/Irwin, Boston (2008)
8. Frietzsche, U., Scheuch, F.:: Externe Faktoren in der Dienstleistungsproduktion. Ansätze zur Lösung von Erfassungs- und Bewertungsproblemen. 1. Aufl. Wiesbaden: Dt. Univ.-Verl. (Gabler Edition Wissenschaft) (2001)
9. Dunkel, W., Weihrich, M.: Interactive Work: A Theoretical and Emipircal Approach to the Study of Service Interactions. In: Wolfgang Dunkel und Frank Kleemann (Hg.): Customers at work. New perspectives on interactive service work, pp. S49–S75. Palgrave Macmillan, Houndmills (2013)
10. Kleinaltenkamp, M., Bach, T., Griese, I.: Der Kundenintegrationsbegriff im (Dienstleistungs-) Marketing. In: Bruhn, M., Stauss, B. (Hg.) Kundenintegration, pp. S35–S62. Forum Dienstleistungsmanagement, Gabler (2009)
11. Meffert, H., Bruhn, M.: Dienstleistungsmarketing. Grundlagen - Konzepte - Methoden. 7. Aufl. Wiesbaden: Gabler (Meffert-Marketing-Edition) (2012)
12. Kulke, E.: Wirtschaftsgeographie. 5., überarb. Aufl. Paderborn: UTB; Schöningh (Grundriss Allgemeine Geographie) (2013)
13. Wiendahl, H.: Betriebsorganisation für Ingenieure. Carl Hanser, München (2010)
14. Oliva, R., Bean, M.: Developing operational understanding of service quality through a simulation environment. International Journal of Service Industry Management 19(2), S160–S175 (2008)
15. Fabry, C.: Service Excellence durch Lean Services. Service Today 1, S34–S35 (2012)

Using a Cooking Operation Simulator to Improve Cooking Speed in a Multiproduct Japanese Cuisine Restaurant

Takeshi Shimamura[1,2,], Yoshihiro Hisano[2], Syuichi Oura[2], Tomoyuki Asakawa[2]
Toshiya Kaihara[3], Nobutada Fujii[3], and Tomomi Nonaka[3]

[1] Center for Service Research,
National Institute of Advanced Industrial Science and Technology, Tokyo, Japan
[2] Ganko Food Service Co. Ltd., Osaka, Japan
[3] Graduate School of System Informatics, Kobe University Kobe, Japan
t-shimmura@aist.go.jp

Abstract. This study was conducted to improve the cooking speed in multiproduct Japanese cuisine restaurants using a cooking operation simulator. Traditionally, restaurants improve cooking speed through menu and cooking operation simplification because the cooking speed depends strongly on customer satisfaction and productivity. In recent years, customer requirements for restaurant menus have become diverse. A restaurant must evolve the menu and cooking operations to adapt to customer needs. Cooking systems of multiproduct restaurants can produce diverse menus, but the cooking speed is low. They should improve the cooking speed to improve customer satisfaction and productivity.

A cooking operation simulation was conducted to improve cooking speed by improving the kitchen layout, cooking machine capacity, and work plans. Simulation results show that cooking speed can improve: 1) working habits of crew chiefs should be changed to improve cooperation; 2) IE and QC should be introduced to resolve problems such as staff fatigue; 3) simulations should be conducted frequently to adapt to changing customer needs and changing contents of orders.

1   Introduction

Until the 1960s, dining out was a luxury enjoyed by wealthy people. Restaurants provided fine dishes to satisfy wealthy customers. For such occasions, they hired skillful chefs at high salaries to compete with other restaurants by offering fine dishes. Consequently, fine dining was expensive. The restaurant market remained small.

In the 1970s, some innovative Japanese restaurant companies introduced chain store operation systems to reduce restaurant costs and therefore prices. The system introduced factory production systems with a so-called "central kitchen" to reduce the number of kitchen staff members. In addition, the central kitchen was able to reduce the dependence on skillful chefs because demanding cooking processes were done at

B. Grabot et al. (Eds.): APMS 2014, Part II, IFIP AICT 439, pp. 556–563, 2014.
© IFIP International Federation for Information Processing 2014

a central kitchen. In addition, chain store restaurants reduced the total menu items to simplify cooking processes [1] [2]. Especially, fast food and family restaurants made strong efforts to introduce systems providing ordered items quickly because the cooking speed strongly affects customer satisfaction and productivity [3] [4].

In the 1980s, Japanese restaurants introduced information systems to improve cooking speeds further. For instance, point of sale (POS) systems that had been introduced into the CVS industry were introduced in restaurants [5] [6]. Until the introduction of POS systems, order information was written down on order sheets by service staff. Sheets were handed to the kitchen staff. A worker had to input each ordered item and a price when a customer checked out. In contrast, the POS system records order information, stores it on a POS server using a small order-entry device, and transmits it to the kitchen. A kitchen printer immediately issues an order sheet and a kitchen staff member cooks after referring to it. In addition, the POS cashier sums up the total of price using order information. Therefore, a service staff member need not convey an order sheet when receiving an order, and need not input a price when a customer checks out [5] [6].

The restaurant industry introduced cooking machines to simplify cooking operations. Sushi companies developed sushi makers. Before introduction of such machines, sushi was prepared by an experienced sushi chef. For that reason, sushi was expensive and preparation was slow. By contrast, a sushi maker prepares sushi automatically (a part time employee merely inserts raw fish), and serves it on a belt conveyer. The price of sushi dropped to that of fast food. Today, sushi has become a popular food for restaurant diners [7].

Dining out had become not a luxury but light leisure for Japanese customers by the introduction of new systems and technologies. As a result, the restaurant industry market size expanded rapidly. By the early 1990s, the restaurant industry had become a key industry in the Japanese economy. The Japanese restaurant market was approximately 30 trillion yen (300 billion US dollars), employing approx. 4 million staff workers [8].

However, as the market has expanded, the gap separating production systems and customer requirements has widened. As customers have experienced various dining experiences, their requirements have become diverse [9]. The chain store system has simplified menus and cooking operations. Restaurant companies understand the gap, but they cannot change or diversify menus because changing production systems and menus entails abandonment of the chain store system and production system.

Instead, Japanese restaurant companies have introduced low-price strategies to achieve breakthroughs. They accelerated investigation of restaurants to realize economies of scale, not introducing new production systems and menus to adapt to customer needs. That strategy saturated the Japanese restaurant market with many competitors. Many restaurant companies were bankrupted during the 1990s.

In the 2000s, the Japanese restaurant industry changed its policy from a "low price strategy" to "menu diversification". For instance, the largest providers increase menus from 3 to 21 categories [10]. That strategy satisfied customer requirements, but productivity declined because increased cooking speeds aggravated the sheet turnover ratio and increased the number of cooking staff. The restaurant industry must introduce new production systems.

The authors have introduced a cell production system to reduce labor costs and to reduce food production amounts at multiproduct Japanese restaurants [11]. The system concept combines machine production and manual work. In addition, the system is intended to reduce labor costs by enhancing labor elasticity. When a restaurant is rushed, many staff members work in the kitchen to prepare numerous and diverse orders. When the order number is reduced, a multi-skilled worker prepares dishes using cell equipment.

However, previous studies have revealed some problems. For instance, the study did not change the basic kitchen layout. The cell was placed in a vacant area to improve cooking operations but optimization of the kitchen layout was not considered. The entire kitchen layout is regarded as improving cooking operations. Moreover, the study did not measure cooking speed, although it is necessary for customer satisfaction, turnover ratio of table, and labor input.

To resolve the problems, a cooking operation simulator was developed to optimize the kitchen layout based on a food factory simulator [12]. The system simulates the cooking time of individual orders. Simulations are run several times using order data, labor input data, cooking-operation database, and a kitchen-layout database. Some kitchen layouts are designed based on the simulation results. A method of kitchen layout design using the simulator is demonstrated and discussed.

2   Simulating Cooking Operation

2.1   Cooking Operation Simulator

The cooking simulator system is developed to simulate the cooking time of orders using actual order information (Fig. 1). The system comprises a POS system, an attendance management system, a cooking-operation database, and a kitchen-layout database. Order information (Demand) is recorded by the POS system; the labor input (Supply) is measured by the attendance management system.

The cooking time of the multiproduct Japanese cuisine restaurant A (6 floors, 500 sheets, 2 washoku kitchens on the first floor and sixth floor, 1 sushi kitchen on the first floor, and 210 menu items) managed by restaurant company B (operating 100 Japanese cuisine restaurants in Osaka, Japan) is simulated. The average cooking time of orders at each cooking position (T_p) and total orders (T_a) are simulated as KPI of [3][4][13].

Cooking times of 210 menus are measured by 22 cooking staff members and scorers to create a cooking-operation database of restaurant A. To create the present kitchen layout database of restaurant A, the location, size, front, and production capacity of the cooking machine are measured using a drawing sheet of restaurant A. Customer orders (484 orders), working hours (128 hours), and places of staff members (20 staff members) of restaurant A on 12, 8, 2013 are recorded by the POS system and the attendance management system to simulate the cooking time at restaurant A.

Based on these results, problems of the present kitchen layout are discussed by an experienced store manager (41 years old, 19 years of service at B), a grand chef (52 years old, 34 years of service at B) of restaurant A, and a kitchen planner (43 years old, 15 years of service at B). Two ideas for kitchen layout improvement at restaurant A were planned based on the results (plan A, plan B). Plan A maintains the present kitchens (2 washoku kitchens, 1 sushi kitchen). Plan B consolidates the 2 washoku kitchens to 1 kitchen on the first floor. T_p and T_a of plan A and B are simulated by the system to confirm the efficacy of plans A and B.

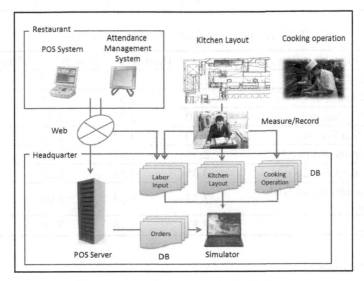

Fig. 1. Layout of the restaurant A's kitchen.

Based on those results, they again discussed effects and problems of the respective plans and designed a more efficient kitchen layout (plan C). The T_p and T_a of plan C are simulated to confirm the efficacy of plan C. Then they were compared to the present layout, plan A, and plan B.

3   Results and Discussion

3.1   Results

Table 1 and Table 2 present results of simulations. T_a of the present layout was 4.22 min (SD=3.51 min). Plan A was 4.81 min (SD=3.18 min). Plan B was 5.31 min (SD=3.28 min). Plan C was 3.75 min (SD= 2.67 min).

Table 1. Average cooking time of simulations (min)

	Cooking Position	Present	Plan A	Plan B	Plan C
	Sushi, Sashimi	3.73	5.06	5.08	3.47
	Noodles	4.79	4.47	4.36	4.11
	Tray Service	2.08	2.79	3.68	2.18
T_p	Fried Foods	4.76	5.93	6.51	5.00
	Simmered Foods	4.93	5.48	6.38	4.88
	Baked Foods	5.31	5.13	5.96	4.78
	Salads, Small Dishes	6.50	4.34	6.37	3.74
T_a		4.22	4.81	5.31	3.75

Table 2. Standard deviation of the simulation (min)

	Cooking Position	Present	Plan A	Plan B	Plan C
	Sushi, Sashimi	2.28	3.47	3.03	1.85
	Noodles	1.80	1.39	1.05	1.35
	Tray Service	1.60	2.33	3.19	1.75
T_p	Fried Foods	3.30	2.24	2.74	2.34
	Simmered Foods	2.35	2.53	3.37	2.80
	Baked Foods	0.35	0.58	1.25	0.56
	Salads, Small Dishes	7.33	4.35	4.90	5.22
T_a		3.51	3.18	3.28	2.67

3.2   Discussions

First, the respective problems and efficacies of plan A and plan B are discussed. Both plans A and B were insufficient to improve T_a, although the plans were designed by experienced staff members. Long experience and diverse skills are important factors supporting layout design, but both plans based on their heuristics were insufficient to enhance cooking time.

Three reasons explain why T_a of plans A and B worsened compared to the present layout: 1) reduction of cooking positions, 2) increasing work-load ratio because of changing work plans, and 3) increasing work-load ratio because of changing cooking equipment.

1) T_p of sushi and sashimi worsened because of the reduction of cooking positions. Both plans A and B reduced 1 sushi and sashimi cooking position because both plans were aimed at consolidating the washoku kitchen located at the first floor. The main washoku kitchen of restaurant A is located on the sixth floor. The sub washoku kitchen is located at the first floor, although the main floor of restaurant A is located on the first floor.

2) T_p of the tray service worsened because of increasing work load. Both plan A and B added noodle-cooking operation to tray service staff because T_p of noodles was

sluggish compared to tray service, and tray service of sub washoku kitchen was placed next to noodle boiler.

Instead, T_p of noodle of both plans A and B was improved compared to the present layout because of the work plan redesign. However, T_p will worsen if staff members of tray service do not help with noodle cooking. An alternative solution should be introduced to improve T_p of the position.

3) T_p of both simmered and fried foods worsened because of cooking machine replacement. Both plan A and B moved the fryer and stove burner from the sixth floor to the first floor to save conveyance operations from the sixth floor to the first floor by lift. Although the conveyance process was eliminated, the work load of staff members of both positions worsened because the work loads of staff members at simmered food and fried food areas increased.

However, T_p of salads and small dishes of both plans A and B were improved. Both plans A and B moved the position to the first floor to save conveyance operations from the sixth floor to the first floor by lift. Different from simmered and fried foods, salads and small dishes can cook and stock using idle time. Therefore, they need not cook when they receive orders.

Second, the efficacy and problems of plan C are discussed based on the problem categories. Plan C improved T_a compared to the present layout, and plans A and B. Plan C was designed based on the simulation results. Therefore, plan C was redeemed to resolve problems of plans A and B.

1) T_p of sushi and sashimi improved compared to present layout, plan A, and plan B. Plan C did not reduce sushi and sashimi cooking positions to maintain T_p of sushi and sashimi. Moreover, Plan C moved the sashimi cooking position from the washoku kitchen at the sixth floor to sushi kitchen to improve its T_p. Results show that staff members of sushi and sashimi cooking positions increased from 3 to 4; their work load was reduced.

2) T_p of noodles maintained improvement compared to present layout, and plans A and B. Plan C replaced the work plan of tray service staff, and changed the kind of noodle boiler to enhance T_p of noodles. Results show that improvement of T_p was retained, although plan C stopped noodle-cooking support by tray service staff.

Nevertheless, T_p of tray service was not improved despite work plan replacements. The work load of tray service seemed to increase because T_p of sushi, sashimi, noodles, simmered foods, baked foods, salads, and small dishes were improved, and dishes flooded to the position of plan C did not increase the total number of staff members.

3) T_p of simmered foods improved compared to the present layout. Plan C increased the number of stove burners compared to the present layout to enhance cooking capacity. In addition, Plan C cleared the wall located between the sushi and washoku kitchen on the first floor to enhance cooperation between sushi and washoku staff members to assist one another when they had free time. Changing the layout, work plans, and increasing the cooking capacity are measures that boost the T_p of both positions.

However, T_p of fried foods was not improved even though plan C increased the number of fryers, and cleared the wall separating the sushi and washoku kitchen areas. Simmered foods are cooked dish-by-dish using a pan. Therefore, the cooking time depends strongly on the total number of stove boilers and staff members. Different from simmered foods, many fried foods are cooked simultaneously using fryers. Therefore, the cooking time has nothing to do with the total number of staff members. Moreover, the cooking speed depends strongly on ingredients. For instance, the cooking time of sliced vegetables such as pumpkin for fried foods is 3 min, that of eggplant is 2 min, and that of shrimp is 1.5 min. Extension of fryers does not necessarily improve the cooking speed of fried foods.

As discussed above, kitchen design based on simulator results can improve the cooking time of multiproduct Japanese cuisine restaurant, but some critical problems remain.

First, Japanese cuisine chefs shun mutual cooperation because of their pride and habits. They believe that if a chef is supported by another chef, then the former must be regarded as "less-skilled" [12]. Moreover, sushi and washoku chefs dislike working together because they belong to different guilds. In Japan, sushi and washoku guilds have existed for more than 300 years. They have avoided copying and sharing their respective techniques. Such a historical reason prevents them from working together. They should be educated to change from a pride-based working system to a CS-based working system. Restaurant companies should produce a new training system for staff members, instead of a guild-based training system.

Second, results of simulation should be applied to actual restaurants. Although plan C improves T_a, and T_p of sushi, sashimi, noodles, simmered foods, baked foods, salads, and small dishes, the results are only reflective of the simulation. Other factors affect the cooking speed such as the total number of available kitchenware such as dishes and pots, and operational impediments such as complaints and mistakes, and fatigue of staff members. Appropriate methods such as IE methods, behavior measures, and QC activities must be introduced to resolve those problems [14],[15].

Third, the redesign of work plans and work scheduling should be conducted each time the menu is changed. Multiproduct restaurants frequently change menus to tune the line up for customer requirements. For instance, the Japanese cuisine course "Kaiseki" changes the menu every month. In addition, the operation change should be discussed at turn of the year because contents of orders differ among seasons.

4   Conclusions

This study was undertaken to improve cooking times at multiproduct Japanese cuisine restaurants by introducing a cooking operation simulator. The cooking times of dishes at restaurant A were simulated using order data recorded by a POS system of restaurant A, with labor input recorded by input attendance management system of restaurant A. Results show that the cooking times of dishes can improve the work plan redesign, cooking machine placement, and changing kitchen layout. To realize simulation results at an actual restaurant, 1) working habits of chefs should be changed, 2) some other methodology such as IE and QC should be introduced to resolve some other problems, and 3) simulations should be conducted frequently to adapt to changing customer needs and changing order contents.

Acknowledgements. This study was partially supported by the Project of Service Science from JST/RISTEX for Service Science in 2013, and as a joint study with the Center for Service Research, National institute of Advanced Industrial Science and Technology (AIST).

References

1. Mariani, J.F.: America Eats Out, An Illustrated History of Restaurants, Tav-erns, Coffee Shops, Speakeasies, and Other Establishments That Have Fed Us for 350 Years. William Morrow and Co. (1991)
2. Chase, R.B., Apte, U.M.: A history of research in service operations: What's the big idea? Journal of Operations Management 25(2), 375–386 (2007)
3. Davis, M.M., Maggard, M.J.: An analysis of customer satisfaction with wait-ing times in a two-stage service process. Journal of Operations Management 9(3), 324–334 (1990)
4. Luo, W., Liberatore, M.J., Nydick, R.L., Chung, Q.B., Sloane, E.: Impact of process change on customer perception of waiting time: a field study. Omega 32(1), 77–83 (2004)
5. Swart, W.: A microcomputer network to enhance restaurant productivity. Computers & Industrial Engineering 11(1), 430–433 (1986)
6. Stein, K.: Point-of-sales systems for foodservice. Journal of the American Dietetic Association 105(12), 1861–1863 (2005)
7. Ngai, E.W.T., Suk, F.F.C., Lo, S.Y.Y.: Development of an RFID-based sushi management system: the case of a conveyor-belt sushi restaurant. International Journal of Production Economics 112(2), 630–645 (2008)
8. Takenaka, T.: Shimmura. T., Ishigaki, T., Motomura, Y., Ohura, S.: Process management in restaurant service – a case study of Japanese restaurant chain. In: Proceeding of International Symposium on Scheduling, pp. 191–194 (2011)
9. Takenaka, T., Shimmura, T.: Practical and Interactive Demand Forecasting Method for Retail and Restaurant Services. In: Proceeding of International Conference Advances in Production Management Systems, vol. 2, pp. 3–4 (2011)
10. Yoshinoya HP Retrieved from (April 19, 2014),
    http://www.yoshinoya.com/menu/
11. Shimamura, T., Takenaka, T., Ohura, S.: Improving labor productivity and labor elasticity at multiproduct japanese cuisine restaurant introducing cell-production system. In: Prabhu, V., Taisch, M., Kiritsis, D. (eds.) APMS 2013, Part II. IFIP AICT, vol. 415, pp. 11–17. Springer, Heidelberg (2013)
12. Fujii, N., Kaihara, T., Uemura, M., Nonaka, T., Shimmura, T.: Facility layout planning of central kitchen in food service industry: Application to the real-scale problem. In: Prabhu, V., Taisch, M., Kiritsis, D. (eds.) APMS 2013, Part II. IFIP AICT, vol. 415, pp. 33–40. Springer, Heidelberg (2013)
13. Shimmura, T., Takenaka, T., Akamatsu, M.: Real-time process management system in a restaurant by sharing food order information. In: Proceeding of International Conference on Soft Computing and Pattern Recognition, pp. 703–706 (2009)
14. Ueoka, R., Shimmura, T., Tenmoku, R., Okuma, T., Kurata, T.: Introduction of Computer Supported Quality Control Circle in Japanese Cuisine Restaurant. In: First International Conference on Human Side of Service, pp. 6632–6641 (2012)
15. Tenmoku, R., Ueoka, R., Makita, T., Shimmura, T., Takehara, M., Tamura, S., Hayamizu, S., Kurata, T.: Service-Operation Estimation in a Japanese Restaurant Using Multi-Sensor and POS Data. In: Proceeding of International Conference Advances in Production Management Systems, vol. 3–4, 1 (2011)

An Analysis of the Advantages, Challenges and Obstacles of Cloud Computing Adoption to an Academic Control System

Eduardo Zied Milian, Mauro M. Spinola,
Rodrigo F. Gonçalves, and André Leme Fleury

Production Engineering Department,
Polytechnic School of São Paulo University, São Paulo, Brazil
{eduardo.zied,mauro.spinola}@usp.br
rofranco@osite.com.br, andreleme.fleury@gmail.com

Abstract. The evolution of cloud computing (CC) over the past few years is certainly one of the greatest advancements in the history of computing. However, for this technology to reach its potential there must be a clear understanding of the issues involved in its adoption. The purpose of this exploratory case study is to build an evaluation model that takes into account aspects such as the advantages, challenges and obstacles of adopting CC. To assess the feasibility and usefulness of such model, an Academic Control System (ACS) from an International School was analyzed. Such analysis enabled the development of recommendations, the provision of inputs and the suggestion of actions necessary to launch the ACS as a cloud service. The model revealed challenges regarding governance, human resources (HR) management, project management and organizational culture to deal with innovations and changes. Such challenges shall be taken into account in the cloud strategy. Also, security issues, business models, technical capacity, performance, service level agreements (SLA) are obstacles that organizations willing to provide such services must face. According to the model, the recommendations to overcome such challenges and obstacles include HR management good practices, risk management processes and well-defined decision making instances.

Keywords: Cloud Computing, Software as a Service, Product Management.

1   Introduction

Considered one of the greatest developments in the history of computing [1], Cloud Computing (CC) has been gaining ground as a successful model as it promises economic savings, easiness of use and greater flexibility in the control of resource use, anytime and anywhere, while delivering the required computing power. The model's value proposition is that resources are no longer idle, as they almost used to the fullest (with lower unit costs) [2]. However, for this technology to reach its potential there must be a clear understanding of the various issues involved in its adoption, from the point of view of both providers and customers [2].

B. Grabot et al. (Eds.): APMS 2014, Part II, IFIP AICT 439, pp. 564–571, 2014.
© IFIP International Federation for Information Processing 2014

The purpose of this research is to investigate the applicability and usefulness of an evaluation model for the CC adoption, built under the scope of the study. The model considers aspects such challenges, obstacles and advantages of CC. Supported by the literature, these aspects were unfolded into issues involving governance, people management, project management, risk management and forms of investments, as well as into other topics related to design, development and marketing of software products to be offered with a service, within this new paradigm of computing.

Having started its operation in 2003, an International Education institution began modernizing its Information Technology (IT) area in 2009. As its growth exceeded 100% per year, the department, initially directed to academic needs, started meeting business requirements through the adoption of specific ERP modules and development of an Academic Control System (ACS), aiming at improving organizational processes and controls.

In light of the challenges to maintain the hardware and software infrastructure updated and secure and with the required availability, IT management currently rethinks the way in which these computing resources are acquired, developed and used, studying the feasibility of the adoption of CC.

IT managers believe that the internally developed ACS, as part of efforts to improve processes and controls, could become a product to meet common needs of international schools. As with the IT infrastructure, the International School is assessing the possibility of using CC. The ACS would open a new business opportunity for the organization, currently focused exclusively on the education segment, possibly with the setting up of a company with this specific purpose. Thus, this new product would be developed for the cloud, and it would be necessary to assess the issues inherent to this decision.

The main motivation of this case study was to examine the robustness of the proposed evaluation model, as well as to assist the International School in making decisions regarding the release of the ACS, seeking to identify the key advantages and potential obstacles for the adoption of CC, so that organizations can offer competitive, updated and effective products, with the most efficient use of its resources.

2   Literature Review

To achieve the proposed objective to work (construction of an evaluation model for the adoption of CC, investigating its applicability and its usefulness for the launch of the ACS as a cloud service), the authors searched the literature that examine major issues concerning the subject, as follow.

Definition of Cloud Computing. Although many formal definitions have been proposed by academia and industry [3,4,5,6], the definition provided by NIST (National Institute of Standards and Technology) [7] includes the main concepts commonly used in the CC community. According to NIST, "cloud computing is a model for enabling ubiquitous, convenient, on-demand network access to a shared pool of configurable computing resources (e.g., networks, servers, storage, applications and services) that can be rapidly provisioned and released with minimal management effort or service provider interaction."

Table 1. Advantages of Cloud Computing

ADVANTAGES	DESCRIPTION
A1	**Lower cost of customers' capital:** Customers do not buy software or infrastructure (hardware and operating system, for example) in advance, but they pay for the access to those services over time [1].
A2	**Lower cost of providers' capital:** CC can provide an almost immediate access to hardware resources with no upfront investments to its users, reducing the "time to market" for products from many companies [1].
A3	**Reduces deployment cycle:** since applications are already deployed in *SaaS* vendors' sites. The SaaS model also allows cost savings in the large-scale operation of standardized business components [9].
A4	**Reduces cost of entry into new business:** significantly reduces the cost of entry for small companies that can benefit from the business applications, previously available only to large corporations [1].
A5	**Reduces cost of business expansion or entry into new markets:** CC makes it easier for businesses to expand their services according to customers' demands, since computing resources can be deployed very quickly and in accordance with needs [1].
A6	**Easier maintenance:** the IS provider has greater flexibility to correct, improve or add new features as it has greater control of the application's configuration [10].

Table 2. Challenges of Cloud Computing adapted from [12]

CHALLENGES	DESCRIPTION
C1	**Human Resources:** in practice, the recruitment and retention of a high quality team, albeit small, is one of the biggest challenges of HR management. In general, there is a lot of demand for staff skilled to work with CC resources, requiring organizations to pay them slightly more than competitors, within a career plan, keeping them always challenged and stimulated.
C2	**Changes in culture, values, guiding principles, beliefs:** CC allows a change in the vision of the IT function. Traditionally, IT departments spend 60% to 80% of their efforts to keep their infrastructure running, resulting in little time to focus on business needs. With CC, IT can be quicker to respond to changing needs in business requirements. This challenge is enabling the change in the current situation of organizations, to achieve the skills to meet the business needs and the functions of architects and experts in CC.
C3	**Project Management:** it must be a core skill of the organization and not just the maintenance of a business resource. Candidates for the role of project manager are most likely found among relationship builders and technology evangelists. The creators of business systems, leaders, architects and specialized buyers must have an active role in projects with a strong technology or component of CC.
C4	**Innovation:** IT areas shall be designed to handle dynamic business contexts, which, among other tasks, are designed to innovate. Organizations still need to make big changes if they want to take advantage of the great innovations of technology/service providers in the cloud. Fundamental practices such as support the effective collaborative innovation and deepen the collaboration between areas of the organization can offer not only an operational IT but also business process and strategic innovations.
C5	**Cloud evolution:** IT executives need to focus on the reality of technical expertise and services, while ensuring that business managers have the correct perception of the necessary improvements to IT performance. Capacities to plan architecture, correct technical errors and facilitate contract management are particularly important. A greater pro-activity in the delivery of strategic technologies for business and increased focus on needs are required.

Cloud Computing Services. Also according to NIST [7], the definition of CC includes three different service models: Infrastructure as a Service (*IaaS*), Platform as a

Service (*PaaS*), and Software as a Service (*SaaS*). In the IaaS model, customers are allocated computing resources in order to run virtual machines consisting of operating systems and applications [8]. In the *PaaS*, consumers are allowed to write applications that run on the service provider's environment. The third model, *SaaS*, provide consumers with typical software applications running over the Internet. *Google Apps Engine* and *Google Docs* are, respectively, examples of PaaS and SaaS [3]. The paradigm of cloud computing reinforces the assertion of Delone [11], which to measure the overall success of IT, the service quality is more important than the quality of the information or the quality of the systems themselves.

Table 3. Obstacles for Cloud Computing adoption

OBSTACLES	DESCRIPTION
O1	**Strategic feasibility of procurement or provision of services:** organizations may believe that certain information systems, depending on their criticality to the business and on the need to maintain them under their control, cannot be hired or offered in the cloud. This may occur when the system business rules can offer a competitive business advantage for that organization within the segment in which it operates. [15].
O2	**Lack of technical capacity:** implementing a CC environment is a major technical challenge. Complex software solutions have to be developed and available 24x7 [13].
O3	**Business model deficiencies:** the economic viability of provider, its ability to thrive and continue in the activity may inhibit customers' willingness to use cloud products [13].
O4	**Security issues:** Migration to any of CC models presents many security risks. In addition to physical security and to the security of organizations' data, there are technical, legal and policy issues [16]. The risk model must cover all aspects of security requirements, including physical security, data security and policy, technical and legal issues [16].
O5	**Behavioral Tradition - Abandoning the traditional IT model:** There is an important cultural obstacle, which can generate mistrusts and uncertainties. This obstacle can be represented by customers' need to abandon the traditional IT model, in which physical and logical IT resources to support business organizations are more tangible [13].
O6	**Availability:** services require an internet connection constantly available. Otherwise, these connection failures may result in the application unavailability [10] [13].
O7	**Performance:** applications may not work well with low-speed connections: which will result in the downtime or slowdown of the application or of some of its resources due to possible latency in the target analysis application data transfers [10] [13].
O8	**Governance:** As a result of technical and contractual complexity, consumers fear that unheard-of situations and consequent short time of maturations, providers are not prepared to deal with them satisfactorily, causing difficulties in the relationship [14].
O9	**Service level agreements (SLAs) and quality:** these refer to providers' ability to ensure availability and have the resources to meet contingencies. They are provided for in the SLA, where compliance standards and penalties are defined [14].
O10	**Reliability:** consumers expect CC environments to be reliable and that the availability of services and resources offered fully meet their needs, especially those related to critical business aspects. Thus, CC crucially depends on reliability; if consumers feel the system is not fully reliable, they become reluctant to use this service model [14].

Advantages, Challenges and Obstacles to the Adoption of CC. Marston [1] considers that CC, by enabling the convergence to an environment where information can be accessed, notwithstanding the device used and the location, represents a major shift in computing and can offer significant advantages to adopting organizations. Table 1 shown the main advantages of CC, identified as A1 to A6, to facilitate the understanding of the recommendations presented in 4.

According to Willcocks *et al.* [12], there are five major challenges that must be faced by those who currently use the traditional IT infrastructure model and who want to switch to CC. Challenges were identified as C1 to C5 in Table 2, in order to facilitate the understanding of the recommendations presented in 4.

The literature on CC offers studies [13,14,15] which mention the difficulties to its adoption, represented by obstacles inherent to the computing model. The main obstacles, listed from O1 to O10, are shown in Table 3.

3   Research Methodology

Research Method. The research consisted of an exploratory case study. Based on the literature review, was identified advantages, challenges and obstacles relevant to the development of an evaluation model for the adoption of CC. These aspects are the basis for building the model, in which challenges and obstacles were grouped into four correlated action foci: organization, business model, human resources and security. These action foci grouped the recommendations of the action plan (Table 5), facilitating the understanding and its unfolding in the actions themselves.

Questionnaires were used to implement the analysis model. They were designed to investigate the qualitative aspects (advantages, challenges and obstacles) of the evaluation model. The result of these questionnaires applying, called Case Narrative (Fig. 1), were analyzed using knowledge of literature bounded by the model. The result of the analysis is a set of recommendations, which unfolds in the proposed action plan.

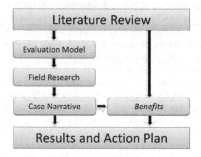

Fig. 1. Schematic diagram of the construction of results.

Characterization of the Target Organization. The unit of analysis is an International School that started its activities in 2003 with just over 70 students and a few staff, and grows exponentially since then. It currently has about 1,000 students, approximately 250 employees and its revenue is of approximately R$ 48 million/year.

In addition, the organization and its IT environment (personnel, systems, processes, etc.) have the relevant characteristics to enable the study. Following the definition of issues and research project, interviews were held with people who hold the following positions: IT manager, process and authorship engineer (manager), development coordinator (manager) and development analyst (coordinator).

Description of the Target Application. The IT infrastructure currently has ERP (Financial - billing) systems and the Academic Control System (ACS), which becomes, every day, more important in the operation of the organization. The application that will be the object of analysis is the ACS (candidate to move to the cloud).

4   Results and Action Plan

The construction of the Case Narrative (Fig. 1) resulted from the application of questionnaires to investigate the relevant topics of the target organization and the target application. Table 4 presents the advantages of using the CC found in the literature and adapted by the author based on what can be extracted from the Field Research and recorded in the Case Narrative.

Table 4. Recommendations for taking advantages of CC

ADVANTAGES	RECOMMENDATIONS
A1 & A3	**Lower customer capital:** ACS provider shall promote its product to customers in the SaaS model, arguing that they will not need to purchase software or infrastructure, but will pay for access to services over time. This will result in reduced cost of fixed capital, dilution of service costs over time, allowing a quicker return on investment, and potentially, bringing significant cost savings.
A2	**Lower providers' capital cost:** CC, by providing almost immediate access to hardware resources with no initial investment for ASC provider, improving its "time to market". As it is an operating expense, it also helps drastically reducing the necessary investments to product launching.
A3	**Reduces deployment cycle**: ACS provider shall promote its product arguing that it is already deployed under the SaaS delivery model, reducing deployment time, parameterization and system "tuning" (ACS).
A4	**Cost of entry into new business:** ACS provider shall promote its product arguing that customers can drastically reduce the cost of entry into the market for international schools that benefit from the knowledge of existing ACS business rules.
A5	**Cost of business expansion or entry into new markets:** ACS provider shall promote its product arguing that CC makes it easier for customers to expand their services for purposes of business expansion or entry into new markets according to their strategic plan. This is because computational resources can be deployed very quickly, according to new needs, scaling them up or down dynamically, depending on customer's load, with minimal interaction with service providers (self-service).
A6	**Easy maintenance:** ACS provider has greater flexibility to correct, improve or include new features, as it has a greater control on the distribution and management of its applications, enabling agility in meeting the business needs of customers.

The recommendations were grouped in into four foci of correlated actions summarized in a preliminary action plan (Table 5) for further detail, with the definition of responsible parties, timeframes and indicators for monitoring and control.

Table 5. Action Plan to implement recommendations

ACTION FOCUS	ASPECT	ACTION TO BE PLANNED
Organization	C2, C4, C5 & O8	- Share organizational values, such as, for example, keeping channels of communication that promote improvements, seeking greater efficiency and effectiveness. - Practice effective **collaborative innovation** between different areas involved with CC, such as development, marketing, human resources and interfaces with providers. - Demonstrate the commitment to develop, implement and improve the ability to offer ACS as a service, within the organization's business context and customers' needs. - Inform customers of sustainable strategies through decisions (medium and long terms) involving CC.
Business Model	C5, O1, O3 & O5	- Improve processes for the selection of providers based on technical and commercial criteria. - Rely on outside legal assistance for the preparation of procurement contracts and offering of services associated with ACS. - Solidly rely on technology partners and infrastructure providers, which shall preferably be large organizations, well known in the market, to be presented to business plan partners for the development and commercialization of the product.
(HR) Human Resources	C1 & O2	- Promote measures to reduce turnover of highly skilled people in CC. - Promote training in CC key technologies.
Product Development	C3, C4, C5, O7, O9 & O10	- Define processes, records and documentation of projects. - Plan, design and implement activities directly focused on the performance of ACS. - Establish metrics (indicators) to monitor and control the expected performance. - Develop a plan to identify and mitigate risks inherent to the selected service model (own or outsourced infrastructure under the *PaaS* model).
Security	C5 & O4	- Deploy an IT risk management through a set of processes, policies and structures, providing an insight into the organization of all risks involved in the service provision.

5   Conclusions

The analysis model proved to be robust enough to capture the peculiarities (and de-sires) of the organization and compare them with literature. Its application enabled the formulation of recommendations, giving subsidies and presenting an action plan for the International School to be able to guide and implement its decisions, regarding the development and marketing of ACS as an application for CC.

Although CC is a relatively new model for the delivery of IT resources, based on its proposal and use, is possible to see that the main issues addressed are the same of the traditional IT model found in organizations. Issues such as organizational strategy, governance, technical and legal training, information security, personnel manage-ment, project management, contract management are present and are the same as the vastly used IT model, although here seen from the perspective of CC.

The model identified good management practices, such as establishing communi-cation channels between the hierarchical levels and owners, promoting innovation through collaboration between areas, establishing strategic and long-term partnerships with providers, establishing payment policies to retain people, setting processes and metrics for the development and performance of the product and treatment of risks as a structured process with clearly defined responsibilities and methods. These aspects should be taken into account by organizations wishing to offer cloud services.

Difficulties encountered in applying the model result from the different nature of the issues involved (for ex., governance, HR, security, etc.). Thus, applicator must have specific knowledge of these aspects, so that, when raised and analyzed, they produce the appropriate result.

Any generalization is limited since the study's focus is on a single application in a single organization. Aiming to generalize the findings of this work, further study of the model can be performed in different countries and with software vendors or service providers willing to use the cloud to offer their applications.

References

1. Marston, S., Li, Z., Bandyopadhyay, S.: Cloud computing – The business perspective. Decision Support Systems 51(1), 176–189 (2011)
2. Kaisler, S., Money, W.H., Cohen, S.J.: A Decision Framework for Cloud Computing. In: 45th Hawaii Int. Conf. Syst. Sci., pp. 1553–1562 (2012)
3. Vaquero, L., Rodero-Merino, L.: A break in the clouds: towards a cloud definition. ACM SIGCOMM Computer Communication Review 39(1), 50–55 (2008)
4. Taurion, C.: Cloud Computing: Transforming the World of Information Technology, 1st edn. Brasport, Rio de Janeiro (2009)
5. Veras, M.: Datacenter: Central component of the IT Infrastructure, 1st edn. Brasport, Rio de Janeiro (2009)
6. Linthicum, D.S.: Cloud computing and SOA convergence in your enterprise: a step-by-step guide. Pearson Education (2009)
7. Mell, P., Grance, T.: The NIST Definition of Cloud Computing – Recommendations of the National Institute of Standards and Technology (2011),
   http://csrc.nist.gov/publications/nistpubs/800-145/
   SP800-145.pdf (March 12, 2013)
8. Chudnov, D.: A view from the clouds. Computers in Libraries 30(3), 33–35 (2010)
9. Xin, M., Levina, N.: Software-as-a-Service Model: Elaborating Client-side Adoption Factors. In: Proceedings of the 29th International Conference on Information Systems, Paris, France, December 14-17 (2008)
10. Sommerville, I.: Software engineering, 9th edn. Pearson/Addison-Wesley (2011)
11. Delone, W.: The DeLone and McLean model of information systems success: a ten-year update. Journal of Management Information Systems 19(4), 9–30 (2003)
12. Willcocks, L., Venters, W., Whitley, E.: Cloud Sourcing: Implications for Managing the IT Function. The Dynamics of Global Sourcing 130, 142–163 (2012)
13. Miller, M.: Cloud computing: web-based applications that change the way you work and collaborate online. Que Publishing, Indianapolis (2008)
14. Marks, E.A., Lozano, R.R.: Executive's guide to cloud computing. John Wiley, Hoboken (2010)
15. Chaves, S., Souza, C.: Obstacles to Cloud Computing Adoption: A Delphi Study Conducted with Brazilian Professionals and Academics. In: CONF-IRM 2012 Proceedings (2012), http://aisel.aisnet.org/confirm2012/62 (March 15, 2013)
16. Mather, T., Subra, K., Shahed, L.: Cloud security and privacy: an enterprise perspective on risks and compliance. O'Reilly Media, Inc. (2009)

Improving Transport and Accessibility through New Communication Technologies

Jan Frick

University of Stavanger, Stavanger, Norway
jan.frick@uis.no

Abstract. The accessibility of regions regarding transport is a clear advantage in terms of their social-economic development. New technologies may improve the utilization and usability of public transport on a large scale. The ITRACT project investigates this by developing and testing applications for wireless communication regarding public transport.

Keywords: public transport, usability, wireless communication.

1 Introduction

Regions want to develop, and the accessibility of regions is a clear advantage in terms of their social-economic development. With new technologies, such as satellite and integrated sensor networks, transport and accessibility of remote areas and functionality of transport in urban areas can be improved in innovative ways. This is a development that is going on in many regions. (Emmanouilidis et al., 2013) It is partly related to and dependent of the local access of wireless communication in the region and partly to the availability of Internet access in general.

There is also a clear difference on wanted functionality in urban versus rural areas. The urban issues might focus on reducing the effect of rush-hours, where the rural issues will focus more on how to make best use of less frequent public transportation. There is also a difference in need in the population as people commuting to work or studies will have different needs than other groups as retired people or tourists.

This is not a new concept as futuristic writers have written about such functionality in several decades. One of the most famous is Isaac Asimov that wrote for the World Fair in 1964 on prediction for the future 40 years ahead.

(Asimov, 1964) But now personalized interconnected mobile gadgets are available with a fast increasing functionality.(Klein, 2014, Gubbi, 2013)

2 The ITRACT Project

The ITRACT project (Frick, 2014) was started in January 2012. It develops and test innovative tools for efficient, user- and environment-friendly transport networks across the North Sea Region. The aim is to create sustainable and inclusive regional

B. Grabot et al. (Eds.): APMS 2014, Part II, IFIP AICT 439, pp. 572–578, 2014.

economies and communities throughout the North Sea Region by improving the virtual and physical modes of transport on a large scale. The project is funded by the European Union "InterReg IVb NorthSea". (Interreg-IVb-NorthSea, 2014) The regions that participate are Groningen in Netherlands, Värmland in Sweden, Ems-Jade in Germany, Yorkshire in UK, and Rogaland in Norway. All regions participate with both county/ public transport administrator and university, except UK that have public transport administration only.

The project started out with a process to involve users of public transport and through workshops establishing priorities in each region. These were then grouped by functionality and programs (apps) to be developed were decided. Then some of the universities developed an architecture and following database to provide the different apps with a common backbone and thus achieve a higher functionality that what stand-alone apps might alone. The regions then defined how apps could be grouped in tests for functionality and usability, and these tests are due late 2014. (Frick, 2014)

The ITRACT project has during 2013 moved from the early stage of describing the need of the regions and brainstorming how to answer the prioritized issues. Now apps designed to be building blocks are under development and will be available for all regions as described in the defined priorities. These apps shall utilize WIFI communication to improve the public transport issues in the participating regions. The regions will test and utilize the apps in various ways depending on the need in each region.

3   Rogaland

3.1   Scheduling App

When ITRACT project started, it became clear that the public transport administrator in Rogaland County (Kolumbus) had a parallel activity in their own development process. In spring 2012 an app for scheduling was distributed for public use. It is available for iphone, android, and also available as a website.

The scheduling app utilizes Google Maps and Google Transit Feed Spesification Reference, GTFS. The use of GTFS enables the scheduling app to connect to other transport data in other regions. The consequence is that if you want to plan a travel from University of Stavanger to a location at University of Oslo, then the planner tells you where to walk to the bus stop, when next bus is expected due to schedule, when you can transfer from bus to next train to Oslo, when you can transfer to the local Oslo bus, where to stop, and where to walk to final location. All based on where you are and published schedules. Since 2012 the GTFS has become a standard for these types of mobile systems as most public transport companies need to exchange data with neighbouring regions to provide users with transferability options from one location to the next. The scheduling app had so far more than 3000 scheduling request per day in 2014 in a population of 300 000.

3.2   Real-Time App

Then in April 2013 a real-time app was distributed. This one does not plan your travel, but it identifies where you are with bus stops closest to you, and then tells you which busses will connect at that stop and when they are expected including delays. This real time functionality is available for iphone/ ipad, android, and general website. But the real-time information is also on screens at bus stops and on a screen in the busses. The real-time app is the most popular app as it enables its users to optimize their time due to better knowledge on actual transport options.

Fig. 1. 3 iphone screen captures from Kolumbus scheduling app

From the bus administrator, it can be seen as "High Resolution Supply Chain Management" similar to the model suggested by Volker Stich et al. (Volker Stich et al., 2011). Users tend to forget that a mobile app like this one includes much more that the map, locations, and time estimates that they see. Behind the scene are databases with schedules, locations, map references, historic data, and a continuous analysis of data and forecast of each bus that is in use. So included to the forecast presented to users, the drivers have a similar feedback on status versus schedule, and the bus administrators have a framework for allocating and optimizing all activities within the focus of published schedule.

The scheduling app is a simple case compared to the infrastructure behind the real-time app. In the scheduling app we have a schedule plan with its locations a related expected time and map references, but in the real-time app we have added dynamic collection of data, historic comparison, and a continuous analysis to be presented to users depending on their location. It is a complex cybernetic system.

The real-time app reached up to 220 000 update clicks per week in April 2014.

Fig. 2. 2 iphone screen captures from Kolumbus real-time app

3.3   Flexible Payment App

The flexible payment app was released in September 2013. It enables people with to enter a bus, pay with an iphone or android, and then show it to the bus-driver as one would do with a prepaid ticket.

This sounds easy, but the price to pay depends on zones included in the travel. So locations of start and end points and the identification of the bus-route are included in the calculation. In the future, a development to move most or all passengers to cash free system may be provided, but for the moment only a single ride payment is in place. Users of rebated monthly payment and similar reduced fare options still have to use a traditional ticket or card.

The 3 apps have been very popular with estimated downloads of 80000 up to May 14 in a population of 300000. The local ITRACT project group used a group of students in 2013 with a questionnaire to look for feedback about functionality and usability. This gave surprisingly little negative comments on functionality or usability. A survey to university employees and students in June 2014 showed > 60% of respondents as transport app users. 60% also indicated that such apps might increase their use of public transport. Next issues will be to further test the usability and functionality of these 3 apps more in detail with both the users in the region and to compare as far as possible with apps developed at the other ITRACT partner universities. The purpose of this is to see if or how functionality and usability can be improved. A possibility is also to merge the apps.

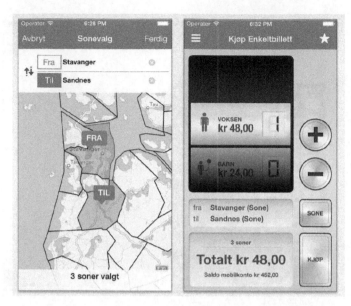

Fig. 3. 2 iphone screen captures from Kolumbus flexible payment app

In addition, Rogaland County will test "Bus on Demand" or "Shared Ride" apps developed at the ITRACT partner universities. This is assumed to be able to offer an improved service for rural areas in periods of the day when busses have a lower frequency. A "Bus on Demand" app is supposed to run a planned route but collect and deliver passengers within an area close to the route. The route will then be run when a number of passengers have accumulated and passengers will get a response on when to expect to be collected. So this may become an app demanding to-way dialogue to group passengers and keep the flexibility. If this will work remains to see, but such an app is in development at ITRACT partners, and Rogaland county has such a functionality based on phones in a rural area of the county.

Other results from the June 2014 survey are that 60% would like that their employer might prepay their travel so an payment app could confirm this, and that 40% would like automatic payment from the app when they boarded the bus. This is technical feasible as the mobile phones can be identified in a similar way as RFID tags. RFID has two main tag technologies, which is active with a battery or inactive without. (Jones and Chung, 2011) The bus tickets or cards used contain RFID tags, and a similar identification can be made for phones. The registration within a certain distance from a reader is easy, but it may be more complex to register when a user is leaving if there are different zones with their own rate. And there is also a matter of security regarding tracking of user movements. Several comments in the June 2014 survey indicated wishes for better maps included where user location, the bus to take, and their destination could be seen in real-time.   And this also relates to the possibility to track people issue.

4   IBeacon

New technologies with possible impact on communication and public transport arrive quite often. New this year is the IBEACON technologies that Apple computer implemented in its operation system 7 for iphone and ipad units. (McFarland, 2014) It is a bluetooth based location recognition service. It enable mobile units to provide users to get relevant information when they come close to a sender.(Griffin, 2013)

Rogaland County made a similar "virtual reality" route in 2012. A scenic tourist route got signs along the road telling tourists which address to type on their phone, and then they could get a voice telling them about that location in several languages. The recent IBeacon technology can make such signs obsolete as the location of the user may push a similar message to the user provide the gadget have an app that is open for such information. Like a tourist may be told where to look for food or accommodation when approaching such offers. The IBeacon technology and similar may change or automate several functions in our surroundings. Examples may be automated payment as people access a bus or walk into a theatre, or registration as products in a supply-chain are passing a control-point. Location based apps may also be seen as a component in virtual reality and utilised in education. (Willem et al., 2012)

5   Conclusion

The rapid changing technologies in communication and related software provide us as users with more information at hand. This enables us to optimize our travels and thus may increase the use of public transport as waste of time in waiting may become reduced. Payment apps may also reduce the need for cash on busses and thus enable more efficient travels as seen from the driver.

We may expect several new location oriented apps that can inform tourists, students, or citizens about what to see and what to do, even inform about the offers of the day in next shop. This functionality may also change other software tools that do not include location relation now.

The perhaps most interesting issue is how these developments and their massive acceptance of the public may change public strategies from politicians or public planners. Related to public transport we may ask: Will such gadgets encourage more people to utilize public transport and therefore reduce rush-hour problems in urban areas and enable more frequent busses in rural areas?

References

Asimov, I.: Visit to the World's Fair of 2014. New York Times (August 16, 1964)

Emmanouilidis, C., Koutsiamanis, R.-A., Tasidou, A.: Mobile guides: Taxonomy of architectures, context awareness, technologies and applications. Journal of Network and Computer Applications 36, 103–125 (2013)

Frick, J.: ITRACT (2014), http://www.itract-project.eu (accessed April 30, 2014)

Griffin, D.E.T.: Understanding tourists' spatial behaviour: GPS tracking as an aid to sustainable destination management. Journal of Sustainable Tourism 21, 580–595 (2013)

Gubbi, J.: Internet of Things (IoT): A vision, architectural elements, and future directions. Future Generation Computer Systems 29, 1645–1660 (2013)

INTERREG-IVB-NORTHSEA North Sea Region Programme 2007-2013 (2014), http://www.northsearegion.eu/ivb/projects/details/&tid=132:; Interreg IVb North Sea

Jones, E.C., Chung, C.A.: RFID and AUTO-ID in Planning and Logistics. CRC Press, Boca Raton (2011)

Klein, B.: User-Aware Management of Prosumed Micro-services. Interacting with Computers 26, 118–134 (2014)

Mcfarland, M.: 2014. How iBeacons could change the world forever. Washington Post (January 7, 2014)

Stich, V., Brosze, T., Bauhoff, F., Gläsner, F., Runge, S., Groten, M.: High Resolution Supply Chain Management – A Structural Model for Optimized Planning Processes Based on Real-Time Data. In: Frick, J., Laugen, B.T. (eds.) Advances in Production Management Systems. IFIP AICT, vol. 384, pp. 123–131. Springer, Heidelberg (2012)

Willem, C., Bartolomé, A., Steffens, K., Frick, J., Bouwel, S.V., Kędzierska, B., DéTienne, F., Cawston, J., Ibrahim, S., Martínez, J., Hugger, K.-U., Grané, M.: Avar+: Audio-Visual Augmented Reality for Creative Learning. Work programme topic addressed ICT-2011.8.1 Technology-enhanced learning, d) Computational tools fostering creativity in learning processes. University of Barcelona, Barcelona (2012)

Health Tourism in Brazil: The City of Teresina Case

Átila Melo de Lira, Herbert Gonçalves Espuny, Pedro Luiz de Oliveira Costa Neto,
Reinaldo de Araújo Lopes, and Josimar Alcantara de Oliveira

Paulista University – UNIP, Graduate Program in Production Engineering,
Dr. Bacelar St. 1212, São Paulo – SP, Brazil
atilalira@hotmail.com, {hgespuny,politeleia}@uol.com.br,
mestradoua@bol.com.br

Abstract. In recent years, the global growth of the economy contributed to the significant increase of tourism in the world, where the movement of foreign exchange earnings doubled in the last ten years, spreading its effects in Brazil, and particularly, growth in the Northeast region, globalization and other short term changes. This work aims to presents how a Brazilian state, among those with lower income per capita in the Federation, such as Piauí, has a health care system in its capital which is a benchmark in Northeastern Brazil, influencing positively health tourism in this regims. The research deals with issues involving tourism as a product and service, having as a result a cluster of health enterprises in the city of Teresina, whose economic expression justifies its importance as a generator of income, employment, science and technology and a promoter of sustainable development in that city.

Keywords: tourism, public health, sustainable development.

1 Introduction

The State of Piaui in northeastern Brazil, that until recently was considered one of the most backward in the country, has currently been highlighted by actions that project positively it on the national scenario. One of these actions was cited in an article approved at the congress of APMS 2013 [1].

According to the World Tourism Organization [2], the global tourism lifted foreign exchange revenues at approximately U.S. $ 919 billion in 2010. There was a slowdown in this tourism sector in the light of the global economic crisis of 2008, which caused a certain instability of trust for future events. However, despite the crisis, a comparative analysis of the ten years prior to 2010 shows that the foreign exchange earnings with tourism in 2008 (U.S. $ 857.40 billion) was 92.67% higher than in 1999 ($ 445, 00 billion), demonstrating a significant growth. Still according to the OMT, between 1999 and 2010 the international flow of tourism in the world registered a growth of 49%, knocking the mark of 935 million trips in 2010, with an estimated 1.6 billion in 2020. Figure 1 illustrates the growth of the sector over the analyzed period.

B. Grabot et al. (Eds.): APMS 2014, Part II, IFIP AICT 439, pp. 579–586, 2014.
© IFIP International Federation for Information Processing 2014

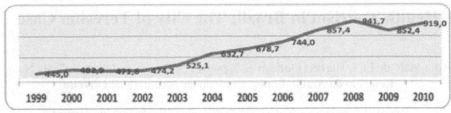

Source: [2]

The same survey by [2] provides important data from tourism sector in Brazil, where, in the same period, foreign exchange earnings have more than tripled from U.S. $ 1.81 billion in 1999 to $ 5.92 billion in 2010.

The Health Pole of Teresina has shown steady growth in recent years, becoming a regional reference center. A first diagnosis made by the Union of the Hospitals of Piauí shows that 30% of attended clients come from six other states of the federation, generating employment and income for the city [3].

The beginning of a health cluster development can be observed with the formation of a production chain and linked services, bringing benefits in terms of cost reduction, quality improvement, training of qualified manpower, capital attraction and increase in employment and income. Such benefit extends to the Private Health Network, increasing its share in serving the population through an investment which reached US $ 47,5 million in 2011 [4].

With this, the main objective of this article is to demonstrate the contribution of health tourism as a tool for the opening and growth of companies, as well as a mechanism to help to ensure that companies efficiently assume their social function, contributing to the improvement of life quality in that region and being immediate inducer of Teresina's growth factor.

Another important point that this paper seeks to demonstrate in that tourism focused on health, especially in this case, allows such activity to be an aspect of good practice as part of the World Tourism Organization's Code of Ethics (ESDT) [5], as a principle for sustainability, because it avoids unnecessary travel. Indeed, the region of Teresina is located in the Northeastern Brazil, in an area where lacks several resources and requires internal migration for various reasons, including health.

2   Methodology

Using the proposition of [6], it is possible to classify this research in two respects: by the final purpose and by the means of investigation.

As for the means of investigation, this research has an important bibliographic emphasis. Bibliographical because it holds a review of the available literature on the subject; a systematic survey of books, journal articles, theses and dissertations, and other publications on the subject, aiming to theoretically justify the thesis and help to analyze the collected data.

As for the purpose, the research is exploratory, descriptive and applied. Exploratory because there is little accumulated knowledge about the subject influencing a determined sector such as it is in Teresina health sector. There are few published works on the identification of variables in Tourism Health and the composition of clusters in the city influenced by Tourism Health.

This research is also descriptive, as it includes the collection and display of data representative of a given situation or phenomenon. According to [7], the purpose of this type of research is "to discover and observe phenomena, trying to describe them, classify them and interpret them." Also in respect of the purpose, it can be classified as applied, since it has practical purpose and is motivated by the need to demonstrate how Health Tourism in a particular geographical area of the country may lead to generation of employment and income.

3   Literature Review

3.1   Definition of Tourism and Its Ratings

Tourism can be defined as a phenomenon that refers to a movement of people in their own country (domestic tourism) or crossing national borders (international tourism). This movement reveals elements, such as interactions, individual and group relationships, human comprehension, feelings, perceptions, motivations, pressure, satisfaction, notion of pleasure, etc. [8].

According to [9], the comprehension of the current touristic phenomenon shall necessarily goes through an analysis of the meaning of travelling throughout history. Usually motivated by economic, political or military reasons, trips are made by people to different regions

A trip is an action that comes from a context in which a determined time of history is inserted. Travelling is one of the components of the economic and social life, as well as of the world it is inserted. Each type of civilization ou society corresponds in a way to how they travel or welcome a traveller.

For [8], the anatomy of the phenomenon is basically composed by the knowledge of three elements: man (human element as performer of tourism), space (physical element, where the act is taking place), and time (temporal element consumed by the trip and the stay). These respresent the conditions for the existence of the phenomenon.

However, other characterizing factors distinguish tourism from the simple act of travelling. These factors are related primarily to the objective and temporary nature of the displacement, and the use of touristic services and equipments, most importantly the notion of pleasure and recreation.[10].

For[11], a revolution in traditional travelling concepts was performed by the tourictic phenomenon since the 19th century, when protestant minister Thomas Cook opened the first tourism agency in England.

Some countries, such as Italy, France and Spain – former colonialist and military powers – were able to stabilize their post-war capital account to a point in which this activity builds a real industry, with proper state organs and specific legislation, that regulates different aspects of tourism, such as social, economic, commercial and cultural, with the objective of expanding the touristic industry.

3.2   Factors that Influence Touristic Decisions

Every person is a potential tourist, but requires the act of travelling for tourism to exist. For that there are some conditions such as the will (animus) and the possibility [11]. The will can be originated by different causes, such as advertisements, status, habit, the physical, moral or intellectual convenience, seduction or interests in commerce, profit and health. Possibilities, however, involve factors that are out of the control of man, such as free time, money, transportation, among others.

Possibilities exist most commonly in higher social classes, therefore there is an association of privileged to tourism. Nowadays, however, with several facilities, social and popular tourism became more common.

Considering this, there are many reasons that lead a person to be a tourist, for example: business, religion, health, culture, education and pleasure.

According to [12], the needs that tourism satisfy can be varied, for the causes are as diverse and subjective as the human body and soul's needs. The touristic motivations or subjective causes, can be classified as primary and secondary causes; direct and indirect; near and remote; individual and social.

• Primary and Secondary Causes

The tourist, when he decided to travel, this usually has more that one cause. There is, however, one that is the most important and determines the trip, called primary. However, there are also secondary causes of less importance. For example, a person who takes a peregrination trip has as his primary cause the spiritual grace, but also has secondary causes, such as the possibilities of knowing new places, visiting famous monuments and resting.

• Direct and Indirect Causes

A trip can occur due to an invitation or the desire to meet new places. Although, it can also involve indirect causes such as the habit of travelling or the social and economic level of the traveller.

• Near and Remote Causes

An example of near cause of a trip is an advertisement of a travel agent, and a remote cause could be the memory of a previous trip.

• Individual and Social Causes

Individual causes act on the person's decision to travel, while the social causes are influenced by some sector of the population. Practicing a sport may be an individual cause, and fashing trends or ideological affinities are social causes.

The search for the healing of a disease is, of course, the primary, direct, near and individual cause that moves Health Tourism, but often other causes come together and reinforce its economic and social importance.

3.3   Tourism Classification

Tourism can be classified due to its modalities – Internal, External, Receptive, Intermediate and Quantitative – and about type – Vacation, Cultural, On Business, Sportive, Health and Religious [13]. The Health Tourism, also known as Therapeutic Tourism, refers to the set of activities which achieve good physical and psychic conditions [7].

In relation to the city of Teresina and its health center in context, the modality to which it belongs, according to [7], is of a regional receptive center for people in health treatment with internal characteristics, because the temporary population flow is typically regional and from the country.

The internal relationship between tourism and economic science is expressed in terms of the touristic contribution to the economic development. With respect to this, [8] wrote:

"Tourism is a phenomenon that moves capital of one country to the other, by people who dislocate to other places in order to consume a product or stay. They are potential consumers of a complex of goods and services that is offered with a specific objective. Tourism, through consumption and investment, affects different sectors of the economic system of a country, and it is believed that its multiplied effect is higher that the one observed in other sectors of economy, such as the industry...".

According to [14], the advantages of tourism for a receptive country or state are :

- Increase in revenue and currency through selling services and goods;
- Creation of new revenues in various economic sectors;
- Low investments in comparison with profit income;
- Integration between different regions and populations, with diverse habits, gestures and languages.

It is possible to verify, with the citation above, that tourism does not only bring currency to a region or country, but also provides integration between different cultures, achievement that is one of the most important in a modern society and civilized world.

The economic impacts generated by a touristic activity may be characterized, as by [15], in:

- Direct impacts: the total profit of touristic sector as a direct results of the product investment;

- Indirect impacts: the total income generated by the investment made by tourism sectors, in goods and services offered by the economy.

- Forced impacts: as a result from indirect and direct impacts of tourism, representing the levels of income increased in the economy; furthermore, part of this profit will be invested in goods and services produced internally, and represent the forced impact.

4   Case Study

Teresina, a city with 836.475 inhabitants, has a complete network of health services, composed by a number of hospitals, clinics, policlinics, mixed units, and health posts and centers that belong to the state, to the city and to the private initiative, which makes the capital of Piaui an important medical center of various areas

Due to these characteristics, as well as its location, 40% of the medical consultations are represented by people from the North and NorthEast, who travel to Teresina for medical care.

This is an increasing tendency in the city, not ony due to the fact that there is a Medical College well known in the country, but also because of the high quality in services by the health professionals. In Teresina, today, surgeries such as heart and organ transplants, and neurologic surgeries, among others, are performed.

Due to its good location, Teresina became a so important Northeast Medical Center. In last years, the capital of Piauí has been highlighted nationally, being the health center that receives the higher number of patients from other regions [16].

The investments in the area are very expressive and, lately, the clinics have doubled in number. According to the city's statistics, there are 663 health establishments; 8 are hospitals, 181 are medical clinics and 170 are practices.

Table 1 shows the importance of the Health Center in the city of Teresina, as a generator of profit and jobs.

Table 1. Establishments on Health Center by sub-area

establishments located on the health center, by subarea				
Sub- area	Center Area	Peripheral área I	Peripheral área II	Total
Hospitals	5	1	2	8
Clinics	163	14	4	181
Practices	133	36	1	170
Laboratories	24	3	-	27
Blood stock	1	-	-	1
Emergency	1	-	-	1
Maternity	-	1	1	2
Direct activities Subtotal	327	55	8	390
Material/Com./H..	3	2	-	5
Medical schools	2	-	-	2
medical companies	39	15	7	61
Health insurance adm.	4	2	-	6
Hostels and hotels	28	-	9	37
food commerce	108	23	-	131
Social assistance unit	1	-	-	1
Indirect activities Sub Total	185	43	17	245
TOTAL	512	97	24	633

Source: [3].

The chart above shows how the Health Center in Teresina has an expressive number of direct and indirect activities, connected to the health sector of the city. It is noted the beginning of health clusters, with the development of a productive chain with interconnected services, that brings benefits in terms of cost reduction, qualification, jobs, and academic formation. According to the regional station of work in Piaui, more them 15,000 jobs are directly involved in the health sector in Teresina.

In Teresina there are two factories of medicine and hospitalar materials: one of serum and one of masks, robes and gloves.

It is very significant that Teresina has respectively 181% and 280% more health establishments per 1,000 inhabitants than the other nearby state capital, as shown in Table 2, what is clearly a consequence of the existence of a health pole established in the Piauí State capital city.

Table 2. Table comparing Piaui and other nearby capital

CITIES INDEXES	TERESINA	SÃO LUÍS	FORTALEZA
Number of Health Establishments	633	283	531
Number of Inhabitants (August 2013 projections)	836.475	1.053.922	2.551.806
Health Establishments/1000 Inhabitants	0,76	0,27	0,20

Source: [16],[17].

Another factor that transforms the capital of Piaui in a Health Reference Center, was the development of the human resources in all levels: graduate, technician, auxiliary and administrative. In the graduate level, the courses offered are medicine, odontology, nursery, nutrition, social service, physical therapy, pharmacy, psychology, radiology and nutrition; in technician level the options are auxiliary in technical nursery, radiology, dental hygiene and consultant in odontology practice.

5   Conclusion

Tourism is generally understood as an activity involving leisure, but can also be associated to other finalities. In this article in particular, the importance of tourism was shown regarding health motivations, and how its management caused profitable and beneficial results to a city located in one of the poorest states in Brazil, away from the sea and lacking specific attractive leisure touristic motivations.

A combination of factors, such as geographic localization, opportunity vision and enterprise, made a new tourism center emerge, regarding health issues, which also represents the development os various activities that generate jobs, income, profit and development.

The main aim of this article was to describe this phenomenon, showing that good results may be obtained in unexpected places and conditions, as for ar a vision and a wish exist which can find possibilities for entrepreneurship in these situations.

It is intended that the example examined in this article can be an example and incentive for other governments and entrepreneurs in the sense that they can develop innovative projects of real utility in places that, in principle, present little or no conditions for these realizations.

References

1. Buccelli, D.O., Espuny, H.G., Cavaleiro, J.C., de Oliveira Costa Neto, P.L., de Araujo Lopes, R., Romano, S.M.V.: Education mediated by technology: Strategy to spread high school learning in piauí state, brazil. In: Prabhu, V., Taisch, M., Kiritsis, D. (eds.) APMS 2013, Part II. IFIP AICT, vol. 415, pp. 334–341. Springer, Heidelberg (2013)
2. WTO – World Tourism Organization – Fecomercio Tourism and Business Council, São Paulo (June 2011)

3. Teresina Municipality Agenda 2015 Review, Teresina (2010)
4. Sindhospi – Piauí Hospitals Syndicate (2010)
5. ESDT. Ethics and Social Dimensions of Tourism. TOURISM WORLD ETHICS CODE., http://ethics.unwto.org/sites/all/files/docpdf/portugal.pdf (acessed: March 18, 2014)
6. Vergara, S.C.: Methods of Research in Management. Atlas, São Paulo (2010)
7. Rudio, F.V.: Introduction to the Scientific Research Project. Petrópolis (RJ): Vozes (2002)
8. Wahab, S.-E.A.: Introduction to Tourism Management. São Paulo: Pioneira (2008)
9. Castelli, G.: Hospitality: Innovation in Management in Service Organizations. São Paulo: Saraiva (2010)
10. Dornelas, J.C.A.: Entrepreneurship. São Paulo: Elsevier (2010)
11. Olímpio, B.N.: Introduction to Tourism Study. São Paulo: Atlas (1984)
12. Arrilaga, J.I.: Introduction to Tourism Study. São Paulo: Atlas (2004)
13. Andrade, J.V.: Tourism: Fundamentals and Dimensions. São Paulo: Ática (2008)
14. Baptista, M.: Tourism: Strategic Management. São Paulo: Atlas (2004)
15. Lage, B.H.G., Milone, P.C.: Economy of Tourism. Campinas: Papirus (2010)
16. Ministry of Health of Brazil National Register of Health Care Facilities, http://cnes.datasus.gov.br/Lista_Tot_Es_Municipio.asp?Estado=22&NomeEstado=P%CDAUI (accessed: March 18, 2014)
17. IBGE – Brazilian Institute of Geography and Statistics, ftp://ftp.ibge.gov.br/Estimativas_de_Populacao/Estimativas_2013/populacoes_estimativas_municipios_TCU_31_10_2013.pdf (acessed: March 18, 2014)

A Customer Satisfaction Model for Effective Fast Fashion Store Service

Tomomi Nonaka[*], Mitsuru Igarashi, and Hajime Mizuyama

Dept. of Industrial and Systems Engineering, Aoyama Gakuin University,
5-10-1 Fuchinobe, Chuo-ku Sagamihara-shi, Kanagawa 252-5258, Japan
nonaka@ise.aoyama.ac.jp

Abstract. This paper proposed a customer satisfaction model to effectively manage staff priorities and service at fast fashion stores. An evaluation model of customer satisfaction was developed through multiple regression analysis of two measures. The first measure considered the difference between actual times and perceived times of customers' behavioural processes while shopping to determine whether or not customers felt dissatisfied. The second measure identified factors which led to customer frustration through a multiple choice questionnaire. The proposed model was applied to multi-agent simulation to compare customer satisfaction levels.

Keywords: customer satisfaction, multiple regression analysis, multi-agent, perceived time.

1 Introduction

The service sector plays a key role in economic activity and the creation of employment opportunities in developed as well as developing countries. The growth of the fashion retail industry, which is part of the service sector, has been increasing as new industry players called 'fast fashion retailers' enter the scene. Fast fashion is used to refer to retailers with strategies to adopt current and emerging trends quickly and effectively [1]. They sell clothes and provide related services at their stores, which is categorised as a business to customer (B to C) service. The importance of customer satisfaction in B to C service has been widely recognised, as it has been found to be a significant determinant of repeat sales, positive word of mouth, and consumer loyalty [2]. Many studies have investigated the relationship between service quality and customer satisfaction [3][4][5][6], where it has been demonstrated [5] that these variables are independent but closely related.

To increase customer satisfaction and, at the same time, be profitable, it is necessary to provide quality service with limited human resources. Therefore, strict task prioritisations and staff assignments are often employed in fast fashion stores. The rules, which are often founded according to customer-first philosophies and prior

---

[*] Corresponding author.

B. Grabot et al. (Eds.): APMS 2014, Part II, IFIP AICT 439, pp. 587–594, 2014.

experience, may make it difficult to adapt to fluctuating customer demands. Furthermore, the effects of prioritisation on customer satisfaction have not yet been revealed.

Thus, a model to evaluate customer satisfaction should be applied to effectively manage task priorities. Customer satisfaction has been evaluated by measuring the customer wait experience [7]-[15], which is described as a pervasive and often unavoidable experience that appears to be a strong determinant of overall satisfaction [9][13]. A negative correlation between wait times and overall customer satisfaction has been shown [15][16]; when time spent waiting increases, satisfaction in general decreases [13][14]. Following these findings, actual wait times compared with perceived wait times have been introduced as indicators of customer satisfaction [8][11][12][15]. An earlier study [8] measured both actual and perceived customer wait times, and then compared these before and after a process change. The effects of a process change on customers' perceptions of wait times and customer satisfaction have also been examined. An earlier study [11] measured the actual and perceived wait times at a restaurant, and found that perceived wait times became shorter with the introduction of a digital signage system that provided interesting menu-related information to customers while waiting for their orders to arrive.

In the aforementioned studies, customer satisfaction has only been evaluated in select situations. However, assessing overall customer satisfaction is needed in order to control staff task prioritisation and improve service quality. Thus, this study proposes a customer satisfaction model using multiple regression analyses of two measures. The first measure was the difference between actual and perceived times spent at each stage of the customer's behavioural process, which indicated the degree of customer dissatisfaction throughout the shopping experience. The second measure aimed to identify key factors which led to customer frustration through a multiple choice questionnaire. The proposed model was then incorporated into a multi-agent simulation to examine customer satisfaction potentials related to different managerial methods under various conditions.

The remainder of this paper will propose an evaluation model and introduce a method to measure customer satisfaction. The paper will then test this proposed model on customer satisfaction levels through a multi-agent simulation analysis. Following the results, the discussion and conclusions are provided.

2   Customer Satisfaction Model

The proposed customer satisfaction model considers the difference between actual and perceived times [8][11][12][15] during the behavioural process of customers at a store as an evaluation method of customer satisfaction. Evaluating customer satisfaction throughout the entire service process rather than at specific stages is required to improve overall service quality.

2.1   Measuring Perceived and Actual Times

Customers' perceived and actual time spent at specific stages during their shopping experience were measured. First, a customer visited a fast fashion store accompanied by an investigator. The customer was required to decide on a product to purchase before entering the shop. The investigator observed the customer's buying behaviour and measured the actual time spent at each stage of the shopping process. Investigators then surveyed customers about the perceived amount of time spent at each stage. The stages were classified as follows:

Stage A: The time it took to enter the shop and find the display cabinet where the predetermined product was kept

Stage B: The time it took to reach the display cabinet and select an item

Stage C: The time it took to use a fitting room

Stage D: The time it took to decide on an item and reach a cash register

Stage E: The time spent waiting in line

Stage F: The time it took to complete the transaction

Next, the differences between the actual measured times and customers' perceived times spent at each stage were evaluated as a dissatisfaction indicator. The indicator was calculated as the proportion of perceived time (T_1) to actual time (T_2). Dissatisfaction levels were evaluated as either 'very dissatisfied': $T_1/T_2 \geq 1.5$, 'dissatisfied': $1.5 > T_1/T_2 \geq 1.0$, or 'slightly dissatisfied or no dissatisfaction': $1.0 > T_1/T_2$. Depending on the second measure described in the next subsection, the answer could also be judged as 'no dissatisfaction' if a customer did not select a frustration factor at a stage.

2.2   Multiple Choice Questionnaire

A multiple choice questionnaire was completed by customers to identify factors which led to frustration during the shopping experience. As shown in Table 1, possible dissatisfaction factors are listed for each stage of the shopping experience, as described in section 2.1. The number of choices for each question ranges from five to eight, and allows for customers to make multiple selections. The answers to the questionnaire were then quantified and converted to either the number 1, which meant selected, or 0, which meant not selected by dummy variables.

2.3   Developing the Customer Satisfaction Model

Multiple regression analysis was used to integrate the results of the two measures discussed in sections 2.1 and 2.2. First, a regression model that linked dissatisfaction levels with dissatisfaction factors was obtained. The model considered each stage separately. The customer satisfaction model is shown in Eq. 1.

$$Y = \beta_0 + \beta_1 x_1 + \beta_2 x_2 + \cdots + \beta_n x_n + \varepsilon \tag{1}$$

The explained variable Y represents the proportion of perceived time (T_1) to actual time (T_2): T_1/T_2. The independent variables $x_1, x_2, ..., x_n$ are known constants that represent the dissatisfaction factor derived from the answers to the questionnaire. The variables are quantified and converted to 1, which means selected, or 0, which means not selected by dummy variables as shown in section 2.2. In this model, the intercept coefficient β_0 is adopted as the value '1'. Therefore, the explained variable Y is '1' when all independent variables are '0', which means customers do not feel any dissatisfaction, as represented by $T_1/T_2 = 1$.

Table 1. Items from the Multiple Choice Questionnaire

Stage	Items from the multiple choice questionnaire
Stage A: The time it took to enter the shop and find the display cabinet where the predetermined product was kept	1. difficulty browsing the store due to crowds (x_1) 2. could not find the predetermined item (x_2) 3. there were no staff around to ask where the predetermined item was located (x_3) 4. could not find the predetermined item due to confusing instructions from staff (x_4) 5. the store was dusty and dirty with many unfolded clothes (x_5) 6. other reasons (x_6)
Stage B: The time it took to reach the display cabinet and select an item	1. could not buy the predetermined item because it was out of stock (x_1) 2. the desired colour, pattern, or size was not readily visible (x_2) 3. could not find the desired design (x_3) 4. more expensive than expected (x_4) 5. unable to decide on an item due to sizing uncertainty (x_5) 6. could not reach the desired item due to crowds (x_6) 7. the store was dusty and dirty with many unfolded clothes (x_7) 8. other reasons (x_8)
Stage C: The time it took to use a fitting room	1. long wait time due to full fitting rooms (x_1) 2. could not judge whether or not one was allowed to use the fitting rooms (x_2) 3. there were no staff around to consult (x_3) 4. there was trash or clothes hangers inside the fitting room (x_4) 5. felt the fitting room was small and uncomfortable (x_5) 6. other reasons (x_6)
Stage D: The time it took to decide on an item and reach a cash register	1. difficulty reaching a cash register due to crowds (x_1) 2. could not find where the cash registers were located (x_2) 3. there were no staff around to ask where the cash registers were located (x_3) 4. could not find the cash registers due to confusing instructions from staff (x_4) 5. the store was dusty and dirty with many unfolded clothes (x_5) 6. other reasons (x_6)
Stage E: The time spent waiting in line	1. the line was long and processed slowly (x_1) 2. could not find the end of the line (x_2) 3. another customer cut the line (x_3) 4. lack of attention to customer care, with no words such as, 'sorry to have kept you waiting' (x_4) 5. the cashier worked slowly (x_5) 6. the counter was dusty and dirty (x_6) 7. too few cash registers (x_7) 8. other reasons (x_8)
Stage F: The time it took to complete the transaction	1. staff were hard to hear (x_1) 2. staff spoke too fast (x_2) 3. artificial service (x_3) 4. the cashier took a long time to pack the bought items (x_4) 5. treated items roughly (x_5) 6. the counter was dirty (x_6) 7. the counter space was small (x_7) 8. other reasons (x_8)

In addition, this paper set the parameters of $\beta_1, \beta_2, \ldots, \beta_n$ as positive values in order to prevent a factor from having unnatural effect of reducing the degree of dissatisfaction. When a parameter was estimated as a negative number, the corresponding dummy variable was removed from the model and the analysis was repeated. The estimation was repeated until all parameters became positive values.

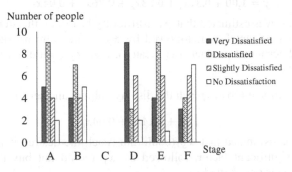

Fig. 1. Dissatisfaction levels at each stage of shopping

3   Field Experiment

3.1   Implementation

This section discusses how the proposed model was tested in an actual experiment at a fast fashion store. The experiment was conducted on weekdays during the busy shopping season between November and December in order to test the model in crowded store situations. A sample size of 20 students aged in their twenties was used. A limited age range was included in the study in order to control for the influence of ageing in the perception of time [17].

First, actual and perceived times were measured. Figure 1 shows the dissatisfaction levels at each stage of shopping, with the vertical axis representing the total number of people. In this experiment, Stage C is removed from further analysis because there was only one consumer who used a fitting room. The results show that Stage D has the most 'very dissatisfied' ratings, although it is also observed in Stages A, B, E, and F. Furthermore, the stages all had similar numbers of 'very dissatisfied' and 'dissatisfied' ratings, the sum of these two values being 14, 11, 12, and 13 in Stages A, B, D, and E, respectively. These results indicate that customers feel dissatisfaction at multiples stages during shopping.

Next, a multiple choice questionnaire was distributed to the target customers.

3.2   Developing the Customer Satisfaction Model

Using the results of the investigation shown in the previous section, a customer satisfaction model was developed using multiple regression analysis. The developed customer satisfaction models derived by Eq. 1 are shown in Eq. 2 to Eq. 6. The model considers each stage separately, as mentioned in section 2.2. The independent variables $x_1, x_2, \ldots, x_n$ correspond with the dissatisfaction factors shown in Table 1.

1. Stage A: The time it took to enter the shop and find the display cabinet where the predetermined product was kept.

$$y = 1.00 + 0.31x_1 + 0.23x_2 + 0.26x_3 + 0.04x_5 \tag{2}$$

As a result, it was estimated that x_1 (difficulty browsing the store due to crowds) was the most significant factor, followed by x_3 (there were no staff around to ask where the predetermined product was located), and x_2 (could not find the predetermined product).

2. Stage B: The time it took to reach the display cabinet and select an item.

$$y = 1.00 + 0.14x_1 + 0.64x_6 \tag{3}$$

The equation estimated that x_6 (could not reach the desired item due to crowds) was the most significant factor, followed by x_1 (could not buy the predetermined item because it was out of stock).

3. Stage C: The time it took to use a fitting room.

There was only one consumer who used a fitting room during the experiment, therefore Stage C was removed from further analysis.

4. Stage D: The time it took to decide on an item and reach a cash register.

$$y = 1.00 + 0.52x_1 \tag{4}$$

The most significant factor was estimated as x_1 (difficulty reaching a cash register due to crowds).

5. Stage E: The time spent waiting in line.

$$y = 1.00 + 0.29x_1 + 0.02x_2 + 0.13x_5 + 0.01x_7 \tag{5}$$

It was estimated that x_1 (the line was long and processed slowly) was the most significant factor, followed by x_5 (the cashier worked slowly).

6. Stage F: The time it took to complete the transaction.

$$y = 1.00 + 0.23x_3 + 0.13x_4 \tag{6}$$

The variable x_3 (artificial service) was the most significant factor, followed by x_4 (the cashier took a long time to pack the purchased items).

The findings regarding Stage E (the time spent waiting in line) supported the findings by [9][13][14]. In addition, the independent factors with the highest parameters were all related to crowded situations, as demonstrated by x_1 (difficulty browsing the store due to crowds) in Stage A, x_6 (could not reach the desired item due to crowds) in Stage B, and x_1 (difficulty reaching a cash register due to crowds) in Stage D. The results indicated that dissatisfaction factors were not only related to waiting, but also other situations encountered while shopping.

4   Multi-agent Simulation

A simulation model was developed on a software named artisoc and the proposed customer satisfaction model was incorporated into a multi-agent simulation model. Figure 2 shows the implemented store layout and item locations. In this paper, customers, store staff, and cabinet agents were implemented and the store space was about 500 squire meters. The action model for customers was determined using the following rules: (1) avoid passing through aisles, (2) exploring desired product categories, and (3) waiting in line at cash registers. Each rule was implemented by the program using the results derived from section 3.

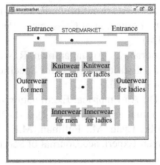

Fig. 2. Store layout and item location implemented by artisoc

This paper examined two conditions. The first considered staff assignments and task priorities as usual. The second changed staff assignments by moving one staff member from the sales floor to the cash register. Additionally, the rule regarding the limitation of working area was removed. The results were then evaluated and compared with the proportion of perceived time (T_1) to actual time (T_2): T_1/T_2. The simulation was repeated 50 times.

The results showed that the value of T_1/T_2 was 1.11 for the first condition and 1.07 for the second condition. This confirmed that changing the priority and assignment rules derived from the proposed model improved customer satisfaction.

5   Conclusion

This paper proposed a customer satisfaction model to effectively manage staff task priorities in fast fashion service. The experiment was conducted at an actual store and validated the model. The results indicated the stages during shopping where customers experienced the greatest dissatisfaction, and which factors caused this dissatisfaction. Furthermore, multi-agent simulation was implemented using the results of the experiment, and confirmed that customer satisfaction levels increased after introducing task prioritisation and staff assignment changes. Applying the proposed evaluation model to other cases and testing it through further simulation are the next steps of this study.

Acknowledgements. This work was partially supported by JSPS KAKENHI Grant-in-Aid for Young Scientists (B) Number 26730159.

References

1. Fernie, J.: Retail Logistics. In: Bruce, M., Moore, C., Birtwistle, G. (eds.) International Retail Marketing, pp. 39–63. Butterworth-Heinemann, Oxford (2004)
2. Bearden, W.O., Teel, J.E.: Selected Determinants of Consumer Satisfaction and Complaint Reports. Journal of Marketing Research 20(1), 21–28 (1983)
3. Iacobucci, D., Ostrom, A.: Distinguishing Service Quality and Customer Satisfaction: The Voice of the Consumer. Journal of Consumer Psychology 4(3), 277–303 (1995)
4. Taylor, S.A., Baker, T.L.: An Assessment of the Relationship between Service Quality and Customer Satisfaction in the Formation of Consumers' Purchase Intentions. Journal of Retailing 70(2), 163–178 (1994)
5. Sureshchandar, G.S., Rajendran, C., Anantharaman, R.N.: The Relationship between Service Quality and Customer Satisfaction - A Factor Specific Approach. The Journal of Service Marketing 16(4), 363–379 (2002)
6. Spreng, R.A., Mackoy, R.D.: An Empirical Examination of a Model of Perceived Service Quality and Satisfaction. Journal of Retailing 70(2), 201–214 (1996)
7. McGuire, K.A., Kimes, S.E., Lynn, M., Pullman, M.E., Lloyd, R.C.: A Framework for Evaluating the Customer Wait Experience. Journal of Service Management 21(3), 269–290 (2010)
8. Luo, W., Liveratore, M.J., Nydick, R.L., Chung, Q.B., Sloane, E.: Impact of Process Change on Customer Perception of Waiting Time: A Field Study. The International Journal of Management Science Omega 32(1), 77–83 (2004)
9. Pruyn, A., Smidts, A.: Effects of Waiting on the Satisfaction with the Service: Beyond Objective Time Measures. International Journal of Research in Marketing 15(4), 321–334 (1998)
10. Kumar, P.: The Competitive Impact of Service Process Improvement: Examining Customers' Waiting Experiences in Retail Markets. Journal of Retailing 81(3), 171–180 (2005)
11. Shimmura, T., Kaihara, T., Fujii, N., Takenaka, T.: Improving Customer's Subjective Waiting Time Introducing Digital Signage. Advances in Production Management Systems. Competitive Manufacturing for Innovative Products and Services, IFIP Advances in Information and Communication Technology. 398, 385–391 (2013)
12. Gail, T., Lucey, S.: A Field Study Investigating the Effect of Waiting Time on Customer Satisfaction. The Journal of Psychology 131(6), 655–660 (1997)
13. Taylor, S.: Waiting for Service: The Relationship between Delays and Evaluations of Service. Journal of Marketing 58(2), 56–69 (1994)
14. Davis, M.M.: A Framework for Relating Waiting Time and Customer Satisfaction in a Service Operation. Journal of Services Marketing 4(1), 61–69 (1990)
15. Chebat, J.C., Filiatrault, P.: The Impact of Waiting in Line on Consumers. The International Journal of Bank Marketing 11(2), 35–40 (1993)
16. Murdick, R.G., Render, B., Russell, R.S.: Service Operations Management. Allyn and Bacon, Boston (1990)
17. Wada, H., Murata, W.: Duration Judgments in Elderly-Hospitalized Persons: Aging and Subjective Time Passages. Annual Report Gerontological Research 17, 79–85 (2001) (in Japanese)

Innovative Solution for Distance Education in a Developing Region

Jean Carlos Cavaleiro, Elisângela Mônaco de Moraes,
Reinaldo de Araújo Lopes, and Pedro Luiz de Oliveira Costa Neto

Paulista University-UNIP, Graduate Program in Production Engineering,
Dr. Bacelar St. 1212, São Paulo, Brazil
ajean@ig.com.br, politeleia@uol.com.br,
mestradoua@bol.com.br, emonaco@unip.br

Abstract. This work is about a project on distance education in a developing country, adapted to the needs of one of the poorest areas in Brazil. The difficulty due to the lack of access to broadband internet has made the government to contract a study for the development of a project to break the barrier of digital exclusion in that region. The article details the technique deployed to distribute materials on a large scale through digital medium, by which the students can develop activities and send them to teachers during attendance classes at study centers. The project is at implementation phase, but it is expected that it be useful also for other Brazilian States.

Keywords: Knowledge, Distance Education, Technological Restriction, Mobility.

1   Introduction

This paper describes one of the advances that the State of Piauí has had in recent years using the practicalities of Distance Education, with emphasis on an innovative solution developed to solve arising problems due to limitation, resulting from the unfeasibility of the use of broadband internet throughout the state and inaccessibility to computing equipment at homes. The State field of research has been for decades among those with the lowest HDI - Human Development Index in the country, with worse per-capita income and low investment in technology and infrastructure. This situation has been changing since 2007 as the State's GDP has grown above the national average, reaching in 2010, 22 billion Reais, and in 2012 reached 24 billion, according to IBGE [1]; amount that represents 0.5% of National GDP. Located in the northeast of Brazil, Piauí has Teresina as its capital city, with an estimated population of 836 thousand people in 2013. It is the third largest state in the region and the tenth of Brazil, with a land area of 251 577 km2, corresponding to 2.9% of the national territory. Borders with five others Brazilian states: Maranhão, Ceará, Pernambuco, Bahia and Tocantins, as [2].

One of the features that put the state among the poorest in the country was the low qualification of labor, which, by the volume of students in rural areas, made it

B. Grabot et al. (Eds.): APMS 2014, Part II, IFIP AICT 439, pp. 595–602, 2014.

difficult the access to education. The Brazilian Institute of Geography and Statistics - IBGE [2], states that the State of Piauí has a population of approximately 3 million people, with 1 million inhabiting the rural area and 2 million in the urban area. In 2010, exactly 829 143 inhabitants were at school age, four to seventeen years old. Enrolled in high school, there were a total of 162 027 inhabitants, of whom 140 481 were students of public schools.

The low offer of regular high school courses occurs mainly by the lack of qualified professionals on most deprived regions and difficult of access in our country, one of them is the Rural Zone and the interior of Piauí. The geographical features and means of transportation available to residents of low density population communities form barriers for students to access the already existing high school.

The development then is conditional on growth of educational quality and the characteristics of the state were not conducive to that. Hence the difficulties require measures that make feasible the amenity to the student, independent of the type of access available to their city or community, thus respecting the express provision in the Federal Constitution, section II of Article 208, which guarantees as duty of the State "progressive universalization of free High School"and in Article 211, paragraphs 3 "the States and the Federal District shall act primarily in elementary and high school" and 4 "in the organization of their education systems, states and municipalities shall establish ways of collaboration in order to ensure the universalization of compulsory education".

To meet this challenge, the Government of Piaui, through the State Department of Education, conducts the implementation of High School Classes with Mediation of Technology, a project presented in APMS - 2013 [3], with the strong purpose of ensuring decent social conditions for these young people, offering them an education that enables the continuity of theirs studies, the construction and reconstruction of knowledge to the exercise of citizenship. The project has now, in 2014, the implementation of a new feature; the integration of virtual mobile learning environment, combined with a solution for distributing files on a large scale.

This project aims to reduce social exclusion, minimize the digital exclusion reducing school dropouts thus expanding the quality of labor available in the region.

2   Methodology

This work has the characteristics of a case study held in Piauí State, aiming to present an innovative solution in distance education due to the existence of a technological constraint. For this, the necessary references were searched and the descriptive method was used for the presentation of the results.

3   DE – Distance Education

The story relates the existence of distance education for many decades, in some secular situations, having as main definition, the education model where the student and teacher are not in the same environment or physical space at the same time, being mediated by technological resources with the assistance of teams prepared for interaction. The concepts are numerous, but follow the same direction, as you can see below the definitions of some authors.

Yarmohammadian et al. [4], in an article published in Science Direct, says that, distance education is a method in which the student is not physically present in educational environments and classrooms. A traditional concept, in keeping with the origins of distance education, where it sought to offer large scale knowledge independent of the distance between students and educational institution. Over time the definition below complete the one mention above.

For Shin et al. [5] , distance education is a teaching model in which students can build knowledge anywhere and anytime, and for this it is enough to have learning objects , be mediated for integration to happen and consequently participate in an environment on which one can have an area of interaction.

This definition can now be considered a reflection of the evolution of information and communication technologies, where the construction and exchange of digital content, i.e. text, video or animations, becoming increasingly cheap and efficient.

Reinforcing this definition, Aretio [6] says that ICT - Information and Communication Technology has supported the main purpose of the distance education, which is decrease physical distance between teacher and student, and still provide competition on a Global level in the area of distance education. Hence the concerns in expanding investments in the area, for not suffer from already established models in the world.

Moore and Kearsley [7] states that, distance education is based on the planned learning that normally occurs in a different location from educational environments, which to the author requires special techniques of creation, organization and management, as well as communication through various technologiesDistance Education has expanded its importance to meet a suppressed demand for qualification of skilled labor, at various levels, free, professional, technical and upper level courses. Distance Education meets needs of countries with similar characteristics that of Brazil, where in some regions there is a lack of physical structures to meet the demands of education, lack of qualified teachers to work and where there are difficulties in locomotion, primarily in agricultural regions, and across the North and Northeast of the country. Consequently Distance Education has a role in social inclusion, bringing wide offer of quality education and flexibility demanded by the characteristics of the country.

4   Project Description and Evaluation

4.1   The Antecedent

As described above, the Distance Education is a teaching model that by the distance between student and teacher requires mediation by various technological resources, and aligned with the characteristics of each region and or groups involved. The Internet has been the basis of the proliferation of distance education in the world, but in Brazil the quality of broadband internet does not meet the needs of the online content transfer. Either by the capability or the costs involved, underserved regions such as the State of Piauí would not be able to make use of this modality in case internet use was essential to its development.

In the already mentioned [3], the authors presented the Project of Implementation of High School Classes with Technology Mediation in the State of Piaui, which constitutes the administrative-pedagogical alternative to attend graduating Elementary School students, from rural communities where there are no high school courses or the demand exceeds the number of places offered. The alternative was summed up in offering a High School course with differentiated and innovative methodology, with implementation of multimedia communication services (data, voice and image) and autonomy to cater the 224 municipalities in the eleven areas of development of the state; configuring a suppressed demand, thus aiming at social inclusion, taking quality education where there was none.

The model operates through a modern telecommunications platform, to offer the placement of modular curriculum series through video conferencing solution, including simultaneous access to Broadband Internet and allocation of multidisciplinary team to support pedagogical coordination in the implementation and operationalization of the project. The technologyconsist of Interactive Digital TV over IP via satellite VSAT (Very Small Aperture Terminal) platform.

The model presented demonstrated the project scope and reinforced its goal, which was to offer regular quality education to the general population, consequently facing the challenge of limited budgets for infrastructure, overcomes the shortage of schools and teachers. The figure 1 describes visually the model:

Fig. 1. (a) Ministering teachers   (b)Assistant teachers and students

In this model presented, ministrant teachers interact remotely with teaching assistants and students, interconnected via satellite by multipoint Interactive Digital TV over IP, with an appropriate and necessary interactivity as illustrated in Figure 2.

The continuity of the learning takes place through the development of activities at home, where students would access the lessons, solve the activities and would send through the platform to be corrected. This activity required that the students had some equipment in their homes, such as a computer with minimal configuration, broadband internet and domain on the use of these technologies.

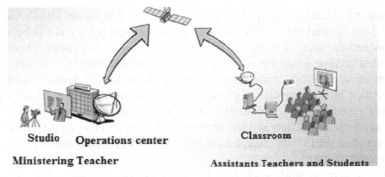

Studio   Operations center   Classroom

Ministering Teacher   Assistants Teachers and Students

Fig. 2. Interaction between teacher and students

These necessities became barriers for the presented model to become even more promising than already was. From this difficulty emerged the second stage of the project, object of this article, which consists in a distribution solution of files in large scale combined with virtual mobile learning environment, more specifically with the use of tablets, associated to the structure available to the courses.

4.2 Tablet Project

The tablet project is a complement to the teaching model mediated by technology, proposed by the Government of the State of Piaui, consisting of a virtual mobile learning environment that will allow the student to access all courses content available on the tablets, even if it does not have internet connection. The student may attend classes, ask questions, contact teachers and do all exercises in offline mode. All data will be saved on the device. When going to the study center or outposts school for the mediated attended classes, students will have access to the wireless network (Wi-Fi), and on that moment, it can, not just download all data stored on the device, which will be sent to teachers, but still download new teaching materials for the next classes.

The project provides to the students of an educational institution in hand pedagogical content of all disciplines studied, gathered into a single mobile device, with a way to supplement regular classes or even a methodology for distance education courses that seeks to bring ways to expand the learning.

In providing education on a large scale, with thousands of students and hundreds of study centers, one of the difficulties is the distribution of educational content, where on Distance Education models, besides traditional texts, involves multimedia such as video files and learning interactive objects. To remedy this difficulty, in the face of lack of broadband internet in much of the state of Piauí, the project presented meets the need to associate the virtual learning environment to a service for the distribution of files on a large scale.

4.3 The Operation of the Model

Technically, the large-scale distribution for mobile is summarized as a multicast data transfer service (distribution to multiple points simultaneously) via satellite including management and scheduling system via web interface. The model allows videos and files to be transmitted via satellite multicast from a central point and can be stored on local concentrator units (a computer in every room at a study center). Therefore, the downloaded content could be accessed locally, after the transfer, without the consumption of satellite interconnection bandwidth. It should be available centralizing units installed in the computers themselves available on each study center with service already configured. Access to data stored in each location can be done by mobile devices available to students and teachers through local wireless connection (WI - FI) to be offered as part of the complementary structural implementation of the educational process platform.

For the system to work, each polo being structured with the following requirements:

- Support for 802.11n 2.4 GHz;
- Interface 1000Base-T RJ-45 connector for LAN connection;
- 128 MB RAM;
- 40 simultaneous accesses;
- Data Rate at 300 Mbps physical layer;
- Support for WPA/WPA2 Enterprise;
- Supports MIMO (multiple-input multiple output) 2x3;
- 3 to 5 dBiomni antennas;
- Desirable support 802.11s (mesh) in the firmware.

Figure 3 illustrates the use of the equipment described.

Fig. 3. Illustration of the use of tablet

The access points must be connected directly to the remote location gigabit switch with CAT6 UTP cables. Rooms far more than 100m from the switch, should use repeaters.

The project will be implemented in 2014, with students from Pronatec a Federal Government program, with technical courses in Administration, Agriculture, Nursing, Technology and Logistics, totaling 19,000 places. The budget for infrastructure of the study centers is estimated at € 923,720, comprising equipment and technologies deployed at the study centers so that they have the ability to access and exchange information on large scale.

5   Expected Results

It is hoped that the project will be one of the options to minimize the barriers to enlarge Distance Education in the country, which is the low level of digital inclusion of the population, especially the focus population of this study, in the rural area of the state of Piauí. At the heart of the 21st century many Brazilians still do not have Internet access, especially broadband. Even with current levels stating that the country is expanding the number of Internet users, the North and Northeast regions do not correspond to that statistic. The problem becomes even more severe in areas of difficult access, in the interior of the country, demanding governments to increase efforts to ensure universalization of the education, as seen throughout the article, and Distance Education as means to that end. The main benefit of the project is precisely to meet the educational deficiency, allowing that students without internet access can be integrated into programs of distance education.

The project intends to assist students of technical courses, minimizing the difficulties of this study model by the absence of necessary equipment such as internet, computer and digital knowledge. As a means of social inclusion, investment in education and improvement in learning processes, has led the state of Piauí to superior outcomes comparing to national average, such as; GDP growth, the results of evaluations of the quality of public education in the state, and its own generation of income and wealth in the State, being boosted by investment in qualified labor.

6   Conclusion

In the present article was presented and discussed a proposal to be implemented in 2014 in the distance education in the state of Piauí, in courses Pronatec of the Federal Government . The project aims to reduce the impacts of the digital exclusion present in some areas, by lack of infrastructure in rural areas and in all North and Northeast of Brazil. The lack of broadband internet is resolved with the large-scale distribution of equipment via mobile digital media, such as the tablet. The model is operated with Wifi access at the supported study centers, where students download the mobile devices with the content of the lessons, such as texts, videos and activities, studying retrospectively in an offline mode, solve the activities and unload it at the study centers, sending them for correction and receive new material. This action brought the possibility of securing access to the study material even without internet access, bringing digital social inclusion by enabling access to quality education and with proven efficacy in the country and in the world.

The expected results are still projections, since the project is in implementation phase, but is expected to improve learning, motivation from the student, reducing school dropout, adding value to the labour force available in the area, attending on a large scale, underserved regions with low cost.

References

1. IBGE. Estado do Piauí. Disponível em,
   http://www.ibge.gov.br/estadosat/perfil.php?sigla=pi
   (Acesso em: 18 March 18, 2013)
2. FUNDAÇÃO CENTRO DE PESQUISAS ECONÔMICAS E SOCIAIS DO PIAUÍ,
   Avaliação das Contas Regionais do Piauí 2010 Disponível em (2010),
   http://www.cepro.pi.gov.br/download/201212/
   CEPRO13_f1e6e3e34a.pdf (Acesso em: March 20, 2013)
3. Buccelli, D.O., Espuny, H.G., Cavaleiro, J.C., de Oliveira Costa Neto, P.L., de Araujo
   Lopes, R., Romano, S.M.V.: Education mediated by technology: Strategy to spread high
   school learning in piauí state, brazil. In: Prabhu, V., Taisch, M., Kiritsis, D. (eds.) APMS
   2013, Part II. IFIP AICT, vol. 415, pp. 334–341. Springer, Heidelberg (2013)
4. Yarmohammadian, M.H., Ahmadi, A., Sadrian, M., Fooladvand, M.: Evaluation of distance
   education programs based on the NADE-TDEC 2009-2010. Procedia - Social and
   Behavioral Sciences 28, 117–119 (2011)
5. Shin, D.H., Shin, Y.J., Choo, H., Beom, K.: Smartphones as smart pedagogical tools:
   Implications for smartphones as u-learning devices. Computers in Human Behavior 27(6),
   2207–2214 (2011)
6. Aretio, L.G.: Educación a Distancia Hoy. Universidad Nacional de Educación a Distancia.
   Madrid (1994)
7. Moore, M., Kearsley, G.: Educação a Distância: uma visão integrada. São Paulo, Thomson
   Learning (2007)
8. Godoy, A.S.: Pesquisa Qualitativa: Tipos fundamentais. Pesquisa Qualitativa: Tipos
   fundamentais 35(3), 20–29 (1995)

Knowledge Management in Public Transportation: Experiences in Brazilian Bus Companies

Hélcio Raymundo, Oduvaldo Vendrametto, and João Gilberto Mendes dos Reis

Paulista University, Postgraduate Studies Program in Production Engineering
Dr. Bacelar 1212, 04026-002 São Paulo, Brazil
{helcioru,oduvaldov}@uol.com.br,
betomendesreis@msn.com.br

Abstract. The Brazilian public transportation system is composed of small and medium size companies. These companies may not be prepared to thrive in a competitive environment because, generally, these firms are managed like a family business. Thus, Knowledge Management (KM) can be defined as an efficient and simple way to solve day-to-day problems and drive the quality of services. Knowledge Management System (KMS) is a business process developed to encompass a basic investigative process, which consists of a synthetic diagnosis of the general conditions and the establishment of programs aimed at the generation of improvements based on the reduction and or elimination of wastefulness. This paper presents KM methodology (KM and KMS) applied in three case studies in Brazilian bus companies. The results indicate that application of this methodology allows companies to reach a competitive advantage. This paper is a result of consulting services in these companies.

Keywords: Bus companies, KM, KMS, Public transportation.

1   Introduction

Brazil is the largest country in Latin America (8.5 million sq. km), with a population of almost 200 million inhabitants. In 2013, Brazil was the 7th economy in the world [1], considering the GNP in purchasing power parity (US 2.5 trillion dollars), behind the US, China, India, Japan, Germany and Russia.

The Brazilian public transportation system encompasses rail services (tram / metro systems and trains) and bus services. In the eight major Brazilian cities, including São Paulo and Rio de Janeiro, there are tram/metro systems, while trains operate, in general, in metropolitan areas. All the rail services are operated by large public companies that carried 2.60 billion passengers in 2012 [2]. On the other hand, bus services are extremely popular and the preferred method of transport in Brazil. Over 19.23 billion passengers are carried per year by around 3,870 operators with a fleet of 183.1 thousand buses. The bus services can be divided into three main categories, as shown in Table 1.

B. Grabot et al. (Eds.): APMS 2014, Part II, IFIP AICT 439, pp. 603–610, 2014.

Table 1. The Brazilian Bus Transportation Systems in Figures of 2011

Services	Passengers Carried (billion)	Companies (units)	Fleet of Buses (thousands)
International and Interstate (a)	0.13	260	18.7
Intercity (b)	1.40	1,810	57.0
City and Metropolitan (c)	17.70	1,800	107.4
Total	19.23	3,870	183.1

Source: Adapt [3], [4] [5], and [6]

The bus services are operated by small and medium size companies, normally family companies. Family businesses are a predominant type of organization in various industries in Brazil, and contribute significantly in economic and social terms, employing over 60% of the available workforce [7]. There are specific traits that are seen as characteristics of Brazilian family companies, such as the trend toward informality, centralism, the non-acceptance of methodical management, tends to paternalism in labor relations and "the aversion to risk and lack of managerial maturity" [7]. As a consequence, family businesses in general and private operators of bus services in particular, face many difficulties in management, failing to adapt to new market demands. This occurs because the business owners tend to centralize decisions and be disinclined to radical changes, especially those that represent a break with traditional culture and work habits.

In this context, considering the several aspects involved and what really matters to solve the day-to-day problems in bus companies, knowledge management (KM) and knowledge management systems (KMS) were tested as useful tools to understand, interpret, analyze and provide feasible solutions. The literature of this field is vast, which, however, does not avoid the establishing of practical applications that can benefit family businesses from the theoretical foundations.

Thus, a strong conceptual basis was found from a comprehensive historical view, in terms of: "knowledge is a broad and abstract notion that has defined the epistemological debate in western philosophy since the classical Greek era" and "in the past few years, however, there has been a raging interest in treating knowledge as a significant organizational resource" [8].

Following this conceptual basis, the state of art of KM and KMS and an organized guide of tangible applications [9]. Additionally, useful elements are shown, teaching how to cope with changes in the business in the everchanging environment and how to apply KM and KMS through technological means [10].

It was also possible to learn the way to apply KMS in different levels of communication technology, even without them, in an eye-to-eye relationship with the "owners" of the knowledge in a company [11]. In turn, by means of a literature review, consolidates and updates the majority of concepts until now found in the above references and allows a broader understanding of the concept of KM [12].

Finally, the practical application of KM is connected with the theoretical basis and [13] while Hislop analyzing it used in business until recently, produces a critical analysis of the importance and benefits of KM [14], serving as one of the guides for the methodology developed and applied in this paper.

Under these conditions, it can be said that the purpose of this paper is to describe a typical application of the KM methodology, according to the concept that KM and KMS can be represented by the strategies and processes designed to identify, capture, structure, value, leverage, and share an organization's intellectual assets to enhance its performance and competitiveness [14]. This methodology is based on two critical activities: (1) capture and documentation of individual explicit and tacit knowledge; and (2) its dissemination within the organization [12].

With the purpose of testing the methodology proposed, three case studies were conducted in Brazilian bus companies. These enterprises operate in the Brazilian public transportation system and this research is a result of a consulting service provided to them.

2 Methodology

Three bus companies were studied to show KM methodology application in operations of Public Transportation. These companies were coded A, B and C. The criterion used to select the enterprises was to choose those to which KM methodology was applied, regardless of type, size and location.

Considering that this research was a result of a consulting service, the five stages of the investigative process were made, following KM techniques: (1) Characterization of the Problems, (2) Diagnosis, (3) Suggested Solutions, (4) Proposed Actions and (5) Analysis of Results.

Characterization of the Problems: this step is sought for troubleshooting, related to problems generally demonstrated through the manifestation of its more harmful effects. Thus arises what here can be called "Fact Generator" or "Main Problem".

Diagnosis: is to find evidence by identifying the origins of problems through their symptomatic manifestations. Similar to a process of determining by examining the nature and circumstances of a problematic condition, Diagnosis also could be defined as: (1) a decision reached from such an examination; (2) an analysis of the cause of a problem or situation; or (3) an answer to a problem situation.

Suggested Solutions: are actionable solutions, applications to be discussed. Sometimes, even adequately proven in the Diagnosis, there are difficulties in evaluation and consolidation of the solutions and their relationship with the Suggested Solutions, due to the incorrect interpretation of the way of combatting the problems. In this step, whenever necessary, the consultant must reiterate the tactical and/or strategic character of the Suggested Solutions.

Proposed Actions: the Suggested Solutions are implemented and monitored in their effective implementation and measurement of qualitative and quantitative indicators of interest. The retrospective evaluation of indicators of interest can then perform analysis "before/after".

Analysis of Results: the results are demonstrated by the evolution of the indicators of interest, confirmation of problems resolution and benefits achieved.

3   Case Studies

The Table 2 shows general information about the companies studied.

Table 2. General Characterization of Selected Bus Companies

Bus Company	Size	Number of Garage	Main Service	Market Share(%)	City or Region (1,000 inhabitants)
(A)	300	1	Urban	10	> 20,000
(B)	30	1	Urban	100	75
(C)	25	1	Urban	10	250

The selected companies are operating in different cities and regions of Brazil. Company A still has its headquarters in São Paulo, whose metropolitan area is the largest in Brazil. Companies B and C are functioning in small and midsize cities located in the countryside of Minas Gerais.

3.1   Case 1

The "Main Problem" of company A was the loss of 10% of the passengers in a few of its lines by the action of illegal transportation. Company A was well organized in a consolidated structure and presented a reasonable level of professionalization. Thus, the Diagnosis phase indicated that in accordance with the results of an opinion poll of passengers and drivers, this pointed to a mismatch between the service provided and the desired service. The Suggested Solution was to change the service in order to provoke direct competition with illegal transportation.

The Government Agency placed itself publicly against the illegal transportation, while maintaining a contradictory policy to "legalize" these services. In doing so, the Government Agency could not approve the Suggested Solution. This would have consisted of, among other actions, the implementation in the lines most effected by the competition of express services with air conditioning minibuses, only for seated passengers at peak hours, in a higher level of offer than the usual. The minibuses would initially be hired for subsequent operation in "leasing" or permanent acquisition.

A pilot test of a week was performed (Test 1) only with the normal company fleet of common buses, as if they were minibuses, resulting in a recovery of about 5% of passengers. The Government Agency, however, did not approve

Test 1. Then another solution was developed (Test 2), consisting of: (1) Maintenance of the official timesheet, rigorously fulfilling the programming; (2) Use of solely brand new vehicles, equipped with "suggestion boxes". (3) Ensuring of a sufficient fleet of vehicles on standby in the garage, in order to fix problems related to congestions, vehicle breakdowns or overcrowding; and (4) Designation of the best drivers and conductors properly uniformed and instructed to treat passengers as preferred customers.

The recovery of demand in the Test 2 was less than the Test 1, reaching a maximum of 2%. The comparison of the tests, however, was revelatory. The Test 1 provoked a small addition of costs, of 1% to 2%. The Test 2, on the other hand, showed an increase of more than 10% of costs.

Under these conditions, another opinion poll was performed and revealed, considering all the suggestions and criticism from passengers, that it was clear that the improvement of quality was welcome, but most of them (more than 50%) wanted in the morning peak hours more speed, agility and comfort. The passengers' opinions also showed that drivers and conductors were attentive and well-intentioned, but seemed not to understand the needs of passengers.

As a result of these tests, the company opened two fronts. An internal one, with extra costs limited to 2%, applying customer service training for drivers and conductors and changing operational procedures to provide increased reliability and regularity to their services. The second front, external, branched out in two actions: (1) addressed to the Government Agency, assisting them in monitoring the services; (2) had an institutional character, and involved the participation of a representative of the Board of Directors at meetings and forums held by the NTU (Brazilian National Association of Urban Transport Companies) and ANTP (National Association of Public Transport) related to discussion and dealing with solutions to illegal transportation.

As a result, the company A, even having not fully recovered the lost demand, has absorbed part of the illegal transportation impacts by reducing costs and is better prepared to face the problem of competition with them. The most important aspect however is that the enterprise had learned a new way of coping with their problems from their own experience and their internal resources.

3.2   Case 2

The "Fact Generator" of the company B was related to the management. The Bus company was a small one, with a low degree of professionalization and a fleet of buses aged between 4 and 5 years. They implemented a computerized system of control, at the request of the minor owner. The senior partner, however, could not "feel" any type of economy generated by the new system, in spite of considering it "revolutionary".

The Diagnosis phase revealed that the computerized system, in fact, did not reduce costs, but accelerated additions of new controls of little or no use. Besides, it was possible to verify that profitability was satisfactory, but had decreased in recent years, due to the adjustment of fares lower than the growth of the costs and due to the growth in the wastefulness level in the company. The latter event was related to their (informal) police, represented by the following beliefs:

- "Old buses serve only to "drink" oil and squander tires and parts" (the words of the head of maintenance); and
- "Drivers and conductors are a breed that there's no way to control" (the words of the head of operations).

Based on the simple principle that there is no administration without controls and controls must generate actions, firstly it was established what should be controlled. Under this principle, the Suggested Solution was to transform the new computerized system into a supporting decision-making system and to implement a program to reduce the wastefulness.

Low-cost programs were also deployed, such as 5S, a supplier management program and some specific training actions for mechanics. In the operational area, the drivers were updated through training in safe driving.

In a second phase, the partners defined which indicators would be monitored and the goals to be pursued. This process was discussed with the head of maintenance, head of operations and staff representatives of each area of the company. In three months, adverse trends were reversed with a reduction of costs between 10% and 20%. Overcoming this phase, the company B implemented a program of fleet renewal and today is experiencing an increase in profitability levels.

3.3   Case 3

The company C operated lines of low profitability. It was also experiencing a lack of resources to pay off short-term commitments and a high level of debt. This was due to the implementation of financial reorganization, which was poorly conducted, and was still in progress. As a result, there were difficulties for the renewal of the fleet (buses with an average age of 7 years).

The Diagnosis phase showed 75% of revenue committed to the operational activities and a vicious circle represented by:

- The aging of the fleet increased the operation and maintenance costs and decreased the cost of depreciation;
- The reduction of depreciation cost was never compensated by the increases in costs of operation and maintenance; and
- The loss of income reflected in the day-by-day of the bus company, represented by high production losses.

As the situation became critical, the company renewed part of the bus fleet using finance in unfavorable terms, paying high interest rates, which made financial costs grow, increasing the pressure of rising costs and preventing future purchases of new. The Suggested Solution recommended was to "break" this vicious circle through:

- Implementation of a recovery program to reduce the debts supported by a complete austerity in the use of resources of the company;

- Monitoring and control of each line in order to improve performance measured by the indicators of (a) passengers carried per distance travelled by the fleet and (b) passengers per bus per day;
- Management actions to improve the schedules of the lines;
- Applying training at all levels of the workforce;
- Management of suppliers in order to obtain price reductions
- Management to reduce indirect costs (insurance, taxes, fees etc.); and
- Implementation of a fleet management system.

These measures should be implemented and evaluated. Every 10% reduction in expenditure meant the possibility of buying a new bus. If the average age was reduced by 3 or 4 years an immediate reduction of 15% of the costs would be obtained.

The enterprise implemented the measures suggested and today has a commitment of 60% of revenue with the operation and the average age of the fleet has dropped to 4.5 years. It was not planned, but there was an increase of 5% in demand for better quality of services and reduction of production losses. A quality program was initiated recently and has revealed opportunities for additional reduction of costs.

4 Conclusion and Outlook

The cases showed the applied methodology of KM. Even in the case of partial implementation of the Suggested Solutions, the application of KM always generates some kind of benefit to the companies, putting them in more favorable positions in terms of corporate training, profitability, competitiveness and reduction of wastefulness.

It's possible to come to the conclusion that KM methodology is a tool which helps to utilize some available resources of bus companies in a smart and efficient way to achieve higher business goals in a productive fashion. It was also shown that it's possible, with low cost or nearly no cost, to reach the development of new opportunities, creating value, obtaining competitive advantages and improving performance to attain the objectives of bus companies and their emerging needs, as indicated in references [9], [10], [11], [12], [13], and [15].

Under these conditions, it is recommended that further studies should be done and more cases should be developed to confirm the results showed here and allow the consolidation of a KM methodology that can be applied to the majority of bus companies in the world.

References

1. Central Intelligence Agency: The world fact book,
   https://www.cia.gov/library/publications/
   the-world-factbook/geos/br.html
2. National Association of Public Transport of Rails, www.anptrilhos.org.br

3. National Agency of Land Transport: Annual Report, 5th edn., vol. 9. ANTT, Brasilia (2009)
4. Brazilian Association of Companies for Road Passenger Transport, http://www.abrati.org.br/page/11728
5. National Association of Public Transport: Relatório comparativo 2003-2011 (2012)
6. Brazilian National Association of Urban Transport Companies: Dados do transporte público por ônibus, http://www.ntu.org.br/novo/AreasInternas.aspx?idArea=7
7. Almeida, E., Melo, M.C.D.L.: Implantação do processo de sucessão em uma empresa familiar de transportes: Desafios e contradições, Resende, pp. 1–17 (2012), http://www.aedb.br/seget/artigos12/511630.pdf
8. Alavi, M., Leidner, D.E.: Knowledge Management and Knowledge Management Systems: Conceptual Foundations and Research Issues. SEAD Working Paper Series, Fontainebleau (1999)
9. Gamble, P.R., Blackwell, J.: Knowledge Management: A State of the Art Guide. Kogan Page Publishers (2001)
10. Botha, D.A., Kourie, D.G., Snyman, R.: Coping With Continuous Change in the Business Environment: Knowledge Management and Knowledge Management Technology. Chandos Publishing (Oxford), Limited (January 2008)
11. Maier, R.: Knowledge Management Systems: Information and Communication Technologies for Knowledge Management. Springer (June 2007)
12. Anand, A., Singh, M.: Understanding knowledge management: a literature review. International Journal of Engineering Science and Technology 3(2), 926–939 (2011)
13. Dalkir, K.: Knowledge Management in Theory and Practice. Elsevier Science (June 2005)
14. Business Dicionary, http://www.businessdictionary.com/definition/knowledge-management.html
15. Hislop, D.: Knowledge Management in Organizations: A Critical Introduction. Oxford University Press (January 2013)

Agricultural Service Center Location Problem: Concept and a MCDM Solution Approach

Morteza Zangeneh[1], Peter Nielsen[2], Asadolah Akram[1], and Alireza Keyhani[1]

[1] Tehran University, Karaj, Iran
{mzangeeh,aakram,akeyhani}@ut.ac.ir
[2] Aalborg University, Aalborg, Denmark
peter@m-tech.aau.dk

Abstract. The main aim of this study is to develop a multi-criteria decision making approach considering all aspects of the agricultural service center location problem (ASCLP). Initially a Delphi Fuzzy-AHP survey has been completed to extract the objectives and attributes of the ASCLP and their local weights. The main novel contribution of this paper is extracting and considering in a comprehensive manner the attributes and objectives for solving the problem of identifying: technical potential of candidate locations and demand and market location. By using the developed attributes, two scores (maxi-min and maxi-max) are computed for each candidate location and non-dominated solutions identified.

Keywords: Attribute, Objective, Service, Location, Agriculture.

1 Introduction

1.1 Agricultural Services

Agriculture is the only major sector that uses the land surface as an essential input into its production function. This wide geographical dispersion of agricultural production has the important economic consequence; transportation becomes essential. Output must be transported for consumption by others and inputs; such as modern seeds, fertilizer, pesticides, or machinery, must be transported to the farm to raise output (Timmer, Falcon et al. 1983). Locating and sizing facilities to serve customers is an aspect of supply chain design that presents a number of challenges. Customers are sensitive to the total cost of interacting with a firm's service, including time and access costs, in addition to price (Pangburn and Stavrulaki 2005). Several services can be provided to the whole agricultural supply chain (ASCH) includes: Input supply, mechanization, advisory, financial, inspection, business and etc. Unfortunately, the majority of supplier companies remains concentrated in urban areas or rural zones with large concentrations of commercial farmers. Therefore millions of poor farmers in rural areas without large commercial farmers do not have access to affordable agricultural inputs such as improved seeds, chemical fertilizers and other agro chemicals

B. Grabot et al. (Eds.): APMS 2014, Part II, IFIP AICT 439, pp. 611–617, 2014.

needed to raise farm productivity (Dorward and Chirwa 2011). The manufacture, distribution, repair, maintenance, management and utilization of agricultural tools, implements and machines are covered under the discipline of mechanization services (Lak and Almasi 2011). The basic indicators for the success of a demand-driven advisory service system in agriculture are: farmers have access to and use agricultural advisory services (Chipeta 2006).

1.2 Agricultural Service Center Location Problem

Location problems (LP) in agriculture exhibit several features, such as their large scope and size, or the consideration of multiple and often conflicting objectives and, thus, implies high levels of complexity (Lucas and Chhajed 2004). Agricultural services have different characteristics than other public services such as health, police or etc., resulting in somehow different location selection procedure. The details of the current LP are shown in Table 1. There are three types of customers in this LP: Customer type A; The number of farms is very large. Any demand point has different types of service requirements. Any demand point may need several services at any given time. Candidate locations and demand points are the same (both are village points). For transport of any product it is enough to reach the demand point and the specific destination is not important in this LP.

Customers type B and C; they want access to the services at their location. This type may be available or not in some rural regions.

Table 1. Services description

Characteristics	Service type						
	Pre-Production	Production			Post Production		
	Input supply	Mechaniza-tion	Consulting for farms	Financial	Consult-ing	Inspection	Busi-ness
Times for each season	Single	Multiple	Multiple	Single	Multiple	Single	Multiple
Customer for each service	A	A	A	A	B,C	B,C	A,B,C
Location of service demand	On farm	On farm	On service center	On service center	On site	On site	On site
Capacity	Unlimited	Limited	Unlimited	Limited	Unlimited	Unlimited	Limited
Demand weight	Weighted	Weighted	Un-weighted	Weighted	Un-weighted	Un-weighted	Weighted
Time criticality	Yes	Yes	No	Yes	No	No	Yes

The layout of the agricultural service center location problem (ASCLP) is shown in Fig. 1. Since there are several services, so more distance functions should be considered.

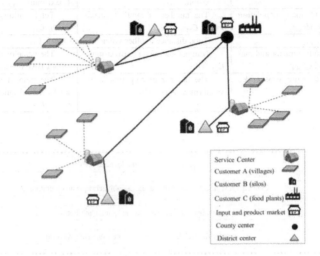

Fig. 1. Layout of the agricultural service network

In this paper, initially a Delphi Fuzzy Analytic Hierarchy Process (Delphi-FAHP) survey has been completed to extract the objectives and attributes of ASCLP. After that, using FAHP the local weight of location attributes for the LP has been computed. In this paper a stepwise approach to solve the ASCLP has been introduced. So the main aim of this study is to develop a multi-attribute decision making approach considering all aspects of this LP. The ideal solution for this problem should satisfy the main objectives, including simultaneously: maximizing service quality, service speed, and service centers profit and minimizing service cost. Widespread demand and the short available time to respond to them is the main distinguishing feature of current LP in compare to classical production systems.

2   Material and Methods

Generally in this research, the FAHP has been used to assess the location indicators (both objectives and attributes) of agricultural service centers (ASC) (Cho and Lee 2013). Using the FAHP method, the ASC location attributes has been prioritized based on objectives which have no differences. Another phase is however added to the framework to address the possible differences between objectives using Multi Choice Goal Programming, i.e. in the case that the priority of objectives is not the same. So this research has five main phases for assessing the location attributes (see Fig. 2). To select the best candidate location for ASC, some sub-attribute for each location attribute which can easily be measured has been defined (see Table 2).

Table 2. The attribute and sub-attribute for ASCLP

Attribute	Sub-attribute	
Easy support: χ_1	Distance to center of county (maxi-min): C_{11}	Distance to center of district (maxi-min): C_{12}
Proximity to more population and cultivated lands: χ_2	The number of families (maxi-max): C_{21}	Total cultivated area (maxi-max): C_{22}
Easy access: χ_3	Total distance to other villages (maxi-min): C_{31}	
Proximity to less tractor and machinery availability: χ_4	Number of tractors (maxi-min): C_{41}	The value of mechanization efficiency (maxi-min): C_{42}
Proximity to more service demand: χ_5	The number of crop type cultivated (maxi-max): C_{51}	The ratio of irrigated cultivated land to dried cultivated land (maxi-max): C_{52}

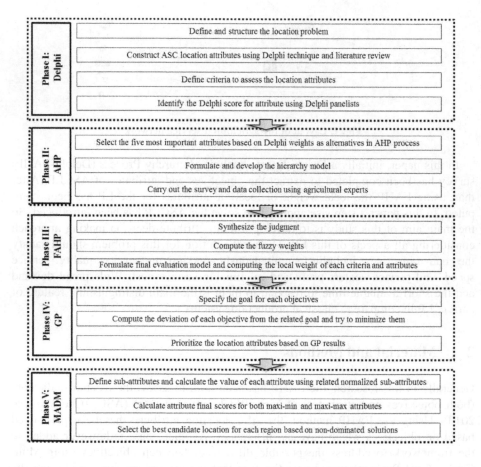

Fig. 2. Summary of proposed MCDM approach

The Eq. 1 can be used to calculate the value of each attribute for each candidate location:

$$\chi_{ij} = \sum_{k=1}^{p} \tilde{C}_k \quad \forall \, i,j \tag{1}$$

Where; k is the index of sub-attribute and $\tilde{C}_k$ is the normalized value of sub-attribute k.

Since the unit of sub-attributes is different, to use them in formulations, they are converted to a normal range between one and zero before calculation of decision parameters using Eq. (2):

$$\tilde{C}_k = \frac{C_k - \min C_k}{\max C_k - \min C_k} \quad \forall \, i,j \tag{2}$$

There are two type of attributes viewpoint of their preferred values, for example lower values of distances (e.g. χ_1) are preferred, while higher values of total cultivated area is outranked to select such a candidate location for establishing an ASC. So, two separate formulations for maxi-min and maxi-max attributes (see Eq. 3 and 4) are defined. These equations will be used to compute the suitability of candidate locations for service center establishment.

$$S_i^{\nabla} = \sum_{i=1}^{n} \gamma_j \left[\chi_{ij} \right] \quad (j = 1,3,4) \tag{3}$$

$$S_i^{\Delta} = \sum_{i=1}^{n} \gamma_j \left[\chi_{ij} \right] \quad (j = 2,5) \tag{4}$$

Where; i is the index of candidate locations and demand points, j is the index of attributes of ASCLP, S_i^{∇} is the final score of candidate location i for attributes where lower values of them are preferred (maxi-min), S_i^{Δ} is the final score of candidate location i for attributes where greater values of them are preferred (maxi-max), γ_j is the importance weight of attribute j obtained from FAHP and χ_{ij} is the value of attribute j for candidate location i.

After calculating the final scores of each candidate location, they will be ranked based on their score values. Then candidate locations which their score of maxi-min (S_i^{∇}) is lower than a threshold ($\alpha\%$ of the selected range which identified by decision maker) and also for maxi-max scores (S_i^{Δ}) which is higher than a threshold ($\beta\%$ of the selected range which identified by decision maker) will be selected and categorized in two set of A_ρ and B_ρ for each region of study (see Eq. 5 and 6).

$$A_\rho = \{i \mid S_i^{\nabla} \leq \alpha\% \text{ of the selected range}\} \tag{5}$$

$$B_\rho = \{i \mid S_i^{\Delta} \geq \beta\% \text{ of the selected range}\} \tag{6}$$

In the last step of this approach, locations are selected which satisfy both selection conditions described previously. The aim of this study is to select at least one location for each region to open a service center, locations will be selected which is in the subset of A_ρ and B_ρ (see Eq. 7):

$$Y_\rho = A_\rho \cap B_\rho \tag{7}$$

Where; ρ is the index of region $\rho = (1, \ldots, 7)$, A_ρ is the set of candidate locations selected by using the minimization selection criteria, B_ρ is the set of candidate locations selected by using the maximization selection criteria, Y_ρ is the final selected locations for region ρ.

After finding the set of Y_ρ, one must propose the best location, because potentially more than one location satisfies the selection conditions. In classic location models the distance function is always used to select the best location. However in this case due to the characteristics of agricultural services, other attributes (technical aspects of the locations) supplementing the distance function should be imported.

3   Results and Discussion

The approach proposed in this paper can quickly lead to the best non-dominated solution, as it utilizes simple calculations and uses measurable attributes. To prove the capability of proposed approach, a case study of Iran has been done.

Using the defined set conditions, candidate location which satisfied the selection condition in each region has been selected and the numbers of selected candidate locations are illustrated in Table 3.

Table 3. The set of selected locations in each region

Region	A_ρ	B_ρ	Y_ρ
Boqrati	{1,3,4,7,8,12}	{4,5,7,11,12,13}	{4,7,12}
Darjazin-Olia	{2,3,4,6,7,8,10,12,13,14,15}	{3,4,6,8,9,10,14,15}	{3,4,6,8,10,14,15}
Darjazin-Sofla	{2,3,4,5,6,9,10}	{1,5,6,9,10,12,14}	{5,6,10}
Kharaqan	{2,3,4,5,6,8,10}	{2,7,8,9,11,12,15}	{2,8}
Razan	{2,3,4,5,7,8,9,10,14,17}	{1,5,6,7,10,13,15,17,20,21}	{5,7,10,17}
Sardrood-Olia	{1,2,3,6,7}	{2,4,6,9,11}	{2,6}
Sardrood-Sofla	{2,3,5,6,7,8,10}	{1,2,4,5,6,13,14}	{2,5,6}

$\alpha = 50\%, \beta = 50\%$

Usually in location decisions, distance and transportation play a very important role. So in this paper the role of maxi-min attributes is highlighted, which contains different distance functions, in selecting the best solutions. As can be seen in fig.3, in Boqrati regions, one of studied regions, there is no unique non-dominated solution. In Boqrati region, S_4^∇ is lower than S_7^∇ while S_7^Δ is higher than S_4^Δ. In this situation no one can dominate the other one. In such cases the decision maker has to propose all non-dominated solutions and this is the main disadvantage of proposed approach, while it has several advantages such as simplicity of calculations, the ability to consider inherent specification of agricultural activities.

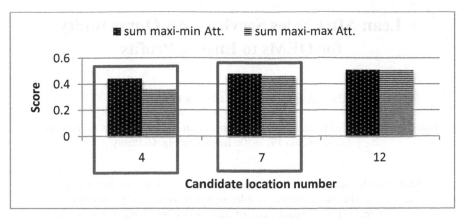

Fig. 3. The chart of selected locations of Boqrati

4   Conclusion

In this paper a concept is presented and a fast and intelligible approach to solve an important agricultural facility location problem is developed. Agricultural services due to their dispersed customers' need to be optimally distributed and be able to supply all required services. The ASCLP also plays an important role in the efficiency of the ASCH. As can be understood from the results of this research, establishing an ASC network can lead to high quality services, low price and cost, fast deliver services, and sustainable service centers able continue their activity due to good estimated customer availability for their services. In this paper all aspects of the ASCLP have been considered, i.e. from the viewpoint of customers and service suppliers, and also technical suitability of candidate location for locating the service center on them.

References

1. Chipeta, S.: Demand driven agricultural advisory services. Neuchatel Group, Denmark (2006)
2. Cho, J., Lee, J.: Development of a new technology product evaluation model for assessing commercialization opportunities using Delphi method and fuzzy AHP approach. Expert Systems with Applications 40, 5314–5330 (2013)
3. Dorward, A., Chirwa, E.: The Malawi agricultural input subsidy programme: 2005/06 to 2008/09. International Journal of Agricultural Sustainability 9(1), 232–247 (2011)
4. Lak, M.B., Almasi, M.: An analytical review of parameters and indices affecting decision making in agricultural mechanization. Australia Journal of Agricultural Engineering 2(5), 140–146 (2011)
5. Lucas, M., Chhajed, D.: Applications of location analysis in agriculture: a survey. Journal of the Operational Research Society 55(6), 561–578 (2004)
6. Pangburn, M.S., Stavrulaki, E.: Service Facility Location and Design with Pricing and Waiting-Time Considerations. Supply Chain Optimization 98, 209–241 (2005)
7. Timmer, C.P., et al.: Food policy analysis. The Johns Hopkins University Press, Baltimore (1983)

Lean After Sales Service – An Opportunity
for OEMs to Ensure Profits

Uwe Dombrowski and Constantin Malorny

Institute for Advanced Industrial Management, Technische Universität Braunschweig,
Langer Kamp 19, 38106 Braunschweig, Germany

Abstract. Original equipment manufacturers (OEM) have recently recognized that offering after sales services enables higher revenues and profits (for example additional services, spare parts or accessories business). For this reason, OEMs have decided to step up efforts to improve or offer additional after sales services in order to achieve competitive advantages. Moreover, offering after sales services combined with primary products is an appropriate instrument to improve customer satisfaction and loyalty. Due to the increasing competitive pressure in the after sales service sector, methods and instruments have to be identified to sustain a profitable business area. In branch of production, the use of lean production systems turned out as a suitable application to secure and improve competitiveness, to reduce waste in production and to realize sustainable profits. Therefore, in this paper a methodical approach to transfer lean production system (LPS) principles to customer service as well as a qualitative applicability of the principles will be described. For transferring LPS principle to customer service, the reference guideline "VDI 2870 – Lean production systems" published by The Association of German Engineers is used.

Keywords: Lean Production Systems, Lean After Sales Service, Customer Service.

1 Introduction

This paper focuses on customer service as one part of the after sales service whereas customer service is understood as support of the primary products [1]. Spare part management, another field of the after sales service, is especially associated with logistics, forecasts, demands and manufacturing. In this field of after sales service a lot of research activities has been performed including approaches of lean logistics but the transfer of lean principles to customer service or even the development of an lean after sales services system focusing on customer service has not been researched sufficiently yet.

To ensure the high profits resulting from after sales service (particularly the customer service), in this paper a guideline for transferring lean production system principles to service is presented. With the help of a lean after sales service-guideline, services can be improved and help to satisfy customers. As a result, lean after sales service improves the customer's feedback with regard to used services and therefore helps to strengthen customer loyalty and promote primary product sales [2].

B. Grabot et al. (Eds.): APMS 2014, Part II, IFIP AICT 439, pp. 618–625, 2014.

2   After Sales Service

Manufacturing enterprises have recently recognized that there is a huge economic potential of offering after sales services in addition to their primary products [3]. This is recognizable by the high number of 60 % of manufacturing companies offering services and supports combined with goods in western countries [4]. These services have become a very successful sector of Original Equipment Manufacturers (OEM) because of being mainly responsible for the gained profits. Companies are able to generate more than 65 % of overall profits by offering services complementary to primary products. Beyond this, it is possible to realize EBIT margins over 10 %. On the contrary, the spare part business, former driver of after sales service, is dealing with declining revenues and profits. [5]

These profits can be generated not only when selling but also during the complete life cycle. But the major advantage of after sales services over primary product sales is the low influence of economic cycles and economic crises. [6] Nevertheless, customer service sector deals with similar problems like the production sector. Customer's expectation is rising so that the quality of services has to be improved by the companies. But offered services still have to be cheaper than comparable offers. This results in revenue and competitive pressure. [7] Above this, customer loyalty as well as customer satisfaction has huge influence on revenues gained by OEM's after sales services which results in the improvement of the offered services [8].

Typically, offered services of OEMs are repair and spare part installation, commissioning, preventive maintenance, inspection, 24-hours-service-contracts, warranty and complaint management, modernization or upgrade of products and staff trainings [9], [10]. This listing demonstrates that the customer service has several different areas of responsibility. In addition, OEMs are also faced with the problem that services are difficult to standardize as well as customize [11]. Combined with an increasing number of variants of offered services and growth of service ranges [12], companies have to implement quality insurance as well as quality improvement sections reducing the profits and profitability [11].

3   Lean Production Systems Principle in Service

For realizing a lean enterprise, business units such as development, production and sales & service need an implementation of lean principles [13]. Therefore, the guideline "lean production system" was created. Furthermore, principles taken from this guideline focusing on production and assembly were transferred to development [14]. Other units like sales & service still need a transformation or a guideline for implementing lean production system principles.

Lean production systems have their origin in lean production, Taylorism and innovative working arrangements [15]. LPS constitute a methodical guideline for enterprises with the aim to focus all production processes on the customer. Furthermore, lean production systems strive for waste reduction and continuous improvement so that LPS-implementation can help to generate profits sustainably. [16] To improve quality and increase transparency in production processes, LPS offer several principles, methods and tools. By implementing an individual developed production system companies are able to adapt and react to new market situations, customer expectations or challenging market conditions. Moreover, processes are transparent and it is possible to manufacture customer individual products high-qualitatively. [17] Typical principles implemented in lean production systems are standardization, zero defects principle, flow principle, pull principle, continuous improvement process, employee orientation and management by objectives, avoidance of waste and visual management [16], also explained and described in context of Toyota Production System respectively Lean Production.

The described objectives of lean production systems cover the same problem areas occurring in after sales services. Customers expect an excellent, individual service as well as individual support during operation of the product. At the same time, customers focus on cheap service performances, otherwise they change to a competitive service provider only specialized on offering services. To react to these customer requirements waste in service processes has to be reduced, service quality has to be improved and service delivery has to be adapted to the customer. [11] Therefore, the hypothesis is based on the assumption that lean production system principles are transferable to after sales service. By realizing this transfer, lean production system principles provide an opportunity to meet these challenges and customer requirements.

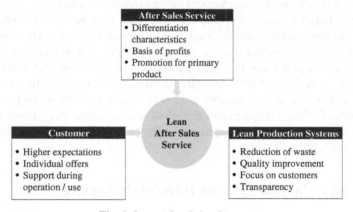

Fig. 1. Lean After Sales Systems

First approaches show that it is possible to transfer LPS-principles to service sector [18]. For example, in financial or insurance sector the use of these principles and methods is practicable because of a high number of similar processes and activities. Other fields of lean application are food service sector [7], hospitals [19] or administration (e.g. controlling or accounting). These sectors include a high number of static processes which are characterized by high repetition rates and low diversity so that processes can be standardized and a flow of information or material is realizable. [20]

4   Transferring LPS Principles to Customer Service

As already described, LPS-principles are not only suitable for production but also for service sector. Therefore, in this section a methodical transfer of the LPS principles is presented including identification of relevant influence factors, analysis and structuring of possible LPS principles. Moreover, individual adjustment and integration into daily routine are briefly described.

4.1   Identification of Relevant Influence Factors and Basic Conditions in Service

The need of the customer has to be identified so that all processes in customer service can be aligned to their requirements [7]. Here, every field of customer service includes own influence factors. For example, customers expect a fast repair of their products, e.g. their cars, and short waiting times at the repair station reception. In case of maintenance of machine tools, the down time has to be minimized and the maintenance process has to be designed effectively.

On service provider side, an analysis of business processes has to be performed to overview all relevant service activities. For example, process mapping or value stream mapping are applicable methods to represent all processes and connection between units or employees in a transparent way. With regard to high numbers of different tasks, varying lead times and fluctuating demand, problems in service processes can be identified. These processes and service-individual challenges build a cluster of influence factors concerning the customer service. On this basis, it is possible to identify possible LPS principles that can be transferred.

4.2   Analysis of Possible Use of Lean Production System Principles

The identification of influence factors and basic condition is necessary for transferring LPS principles to customer service. It is possible that identified principles are not directly adaptable for each after sales service field. This is based on wide range of service variants (e.g. huge number of different repairs) including varying lead times and uncertain demand characteristics [21]. But generally, the implementation of LPS principles is possible. In particular, the principles standardization and continuous improvement possess high potential for an implementation in customer service. [12]

However, as mentioned before, standardization is appropriate for repetitive processes especially taking placing in flow production. These repetitive processes can be found in administrative tasks of the customer service. Therefore, the implementation of standardization in administration or common tasks [22] is noncritical and an effective principle. On the contrary, operational processes differ widely in effort, unspecified and indeterminable lead time and work content. As result, standards either have to be created for every work step leading to an enormous high number of different standards or standards have to be created flexibly to cover all work contents.

An adjustment of a LPS principle takes place for the principle "avoidance of waste". Some kinds of waste, such as overproduction, unnecessary movements or transportation [23], mainly occur in mass production but are unusual in service processes. As a result, these kinds of waste have to be modified. For example, "over-production" could be modified to "too much information", "inefficient work routines" replaces unnecessary movements and transportation in service is represented by "information transfer". "Too much information" in service means that employees get information that is not needed or may confuse them whereas "inefficient work routines" is caused by high level of bureaucracy, unstructured work places or inefficient workshop layouts. Waste in "information transfer" describes non-expedient or slow information flows between employees or departments.

Generally, the principle "continuous improvement process" is directly adaptable. This principle represents the philosophy of simple but steady improvement of processes without high investments for new equipment. To implement this philosophy, a change of employee's mindset is required aiming to improve all process and routines. [24] Moreover, the implementation of key figures systems is necessary to verify improvements and to improve the quality of processes [25]. This philosophy as well as key figure systems are also appropriate and usable in service but the employees have to accept and live this principle. A qualitative evaluation of the possible use of lean production system principle described in VDI 2870 [16] is shown in figure 2.

Principle	Description	Possible use in service
Standardization	• Implementation of stable, repeatable processes and routines	↑/→
Zero defects principle	• Improvement of quality by error prevention and error analysis	↗
Visual management	• Visualization of objectives and achievements • Transparent processes	↑
Continuous improvement	• Philosophy of simple but steady improvement of processes	↑
Employee orientation and management by objectives	• Motivation and training of employees to question processes critically and to improve routines	↗
Flow principle	• Continuous, fast material and information flow	→
Pull principle	• Customer- and demand-orientated material supply	→
Avoidance of waste	• Reduction of non-value adding activities	↑

Fig. 2. Qualitative evaluation of possible use of LPS principle in customer service

"VDI 2870 – Lean Production systems" is used because this reference guideline focuses on producing companies that are attempting to implement an individual lean production system. For this reason, all essential principles are identified as well as fields of application are explained so that this guideline constitutes a good basis for the analysis of a possible use in customer service.

For the identification and adjustment of further, appropriate principles, a comparison between each principle as well as its methods and the relevant influence factors or basic conditions is needed. All useful principles and methods are needed in the next step for structuring a valid guideline.

4.3 Structuring a Holistic Guideline

The structuring of the guideline can be created, analogous to VDI 2870 [16], as a principle catalogue. For each principle several methods and tools have to be listed which are necessary for implementing a lean after sales service. For realizing this step, there are two ways of creating the guideline: either providing one principle catalogue for each field of customer service or providing a single principle catalogue for all fields of customer service including individual information about possible fields of application and necessary adjustments of the principle, method and tool. This catalogue builds a basis for OEMs to select and implement principles depending on their individual conditions. After structuring possible principle an allocation of appropriate methods and tools is needed. At this stage changes or modification of methods and tools to the specifics of after sales service can be necessary as well. In accordance with lean production systems, the developed lean after sales service system is only a guideline listing possible principles but the individual implementation and integration into daily routine requires individual adjustment.

4.4 Individual Adjustment and Integration into Daily Routine

With the help of the developed guideline a company-individual implementation of principles can be performed. It is also possible to eliminate all non-value activities and processes so that the quality of the process will be improved. Moreover, the processes and activities will be created more customer-related as well as transparent. As result of lean after sales services, customer satisfaction and loyalty can be increased and OEMs are able to react faster to changing conditions.

To identify further company-specific influence factors, the execution of customer surveys helps to overview customer expectation. Above this, the implementation of complaint management continuously provides information regarding changing customer's wishes such as pricing of service or further service offers. Additionally, SWOT-analyses give information about strengths, weaknesses, opportunities and threats of the provided services. Based on weaknesses, opportunities and threats, problem fields can be identified and necessary principles can be selected.

Above this, the continuous improvement process is fundamental for lean after sales service systems. This process is based on the fact that operational employees have profound knowledge about the processes performing every day [24]. Thus, these employees know best what kind of problems and errors in service process occur. With their help, inefficient processes or routines can be easily identified and fixed. Additionally, the implementation and tracking of key performance indicator systems helps to secure and improve service process quality.

5   Summary

The present paper deals with the transfer of lean production principles to after sales services. Therefore, the customer service as one field of after sales service is described. To transfer principles as well as methods and tools of lean production systems, an introduction of LPS is given. On this basis, a qualitative approach to analyze and structure lean production system principles is given. This transfer shows that the use of the lean production system principles and methods is appropriate for the customer service.

Nevertheless, in this field of research a lot more research has to be done. For example, a methodical set of rules, only described qualitatively in this paper, has to be developed for OEMs offering after sales services. This includes the identification of further appropriate principles not considered in this paper. To develop this guide line, the execution of a detailed process analysis of the different task areas in customer services is needed. For an individual implementation, an implementation process has to be defined, similar to the LPS implementation process [26].

Moreover, concrete effects and benefits of the lean transfer to customer service have to be examined so that valid conclusions about improvement in efficiency can be made. Nonetheless, implementing and using LPS principles in customer service is a possibility for OEMs to enlarge their margins and increase customer satisfaction and loyalty so that this business unit will still be an effective sector for manufacturing companies.

References

1. Zeithaml, V.Z., Bitner, M.J., Gremler, D.D.: Services marketing – Integrating customer focus across the firm. Mc-Graw-Hill, New York (2013)
2. Kastalli, I.V., Van Looy, B.: Servitization: Disentangling the impact of service business model innovation on manufacturing firm performance. Journal of Operations Management 31(4), 169–180 (2013)
3. Mahmoodzadeh, E., Jalalinia, S., Yazdi, F.N.: A business process outsourcing framework based on business process management and knowledge management. Business Process Management Journal 5(6), 845–864 (2009)
4. Neely, A.: Exploring the financial consequences of the servitization of manufacturing. Operations Management Research 1(2), 103–118 (2008)
5. Roland Berger Strategy Consultants: think: act content - Evolution of service (2013)
6. Dombrowski, U., Schulze, S., Engel, C.: Zukunftsgerechte Gestaltung des After Sales Service. ZWF 106(5), 366–371 (2011)
7. Allway, M., Corbett, S.: Shifting to Lean Service: Stealing a Page from Manufacturers' Playbooks. Journal of Organizational Excellence, 45–54 (Spring 2002)

8. Qi, J.-Y., Zhou, Y.-P., Chen, W.-J., Qu, Q.-X.: Are customer satisfaction and customer loyalty drivers of customer lifetime value in mobile data services: a comparative cross-country study. Information Technology and Management 13(4), 281–296 (2012)
9. Turunen, T.T., Toivonen, M.: Organizing customer-oriented service business in manufacturing. Operations Management Research 4(1-2), 74–84 (2011)
10. Saccani, N., Johansson, P., Perona, M.: Configuring the after-sales service supply chain: A multiple case study. International Journal of Production Economics 110(1-2), 52–69 (2007)
11. Wang, G., Wang, J., Ma, X., Qiu, R.G.: The Effect of Standardization and Customization on Service Satisfaction. Journal of Service Science 2(1), 1–23 (2010)
12. Dombrowski, U., Winnefeld, M.: After Sales Service – Trends und Lösungsansätze – Ergebnisse einer Studie. Shaker Verlag, Aachen (2012)
13. Hoppmann, J., Rebentisch, E., Dombrowski, U., Zahn, T.: A Framework for Organizing Lean Product Development. Engineering Management Journal 23(1), 3–15 (2011)
14. Dombrowski, U., Ebentreich, K., Schmidtchen, K.: Systematic approach to adopt LPS principles in product development. In: Proceedings of 22nd International Conference on Flexible Automation and Intelligent Manufacturing, pp. 901–908 (2011)
15. Korge, A., Lentes, H.-P.: Ganzheitliche Produktionssysteme – Konzepte, Methoden, Erfolgsfaktoren. In: Bullinger, H.-J., Spath, D. (eds.) Handbuch Unternehmensorganisation, pp. 569–574. Springer, Berlin (2009)
16. VDI – Verein Deutscher Ingenieure: Lean production systems – Basic principles, introduction, and review. Beuth Verlag GmbH, Berlin (2012)
17. Spath, D.: Revolution durch Evolution. In: Spath, D.: Ganzheitlich produzieren – Innovative Organisation und Führung. LOG_X Verlag, Stuttgart (2003)
18. Song, W., Tan, K.H., Baranek, A.: Effective toolbox for lean service implementation. International Journal of Service and Standards 5(1), 1–16 (2009)
19. Wesemann, S.: Ganzheitliches Krankenhaussystem (GKS) – Ein Organisations modell für Krankenhäuser. Shaker Verlag, Aachen (2014)
20. Laqua, I.: Lean Administration. ZWF 100(12), 738–742 (2005)
21. Johansson, P., Olhager, J.: Industrial service profiling: Matching service offering and process. International Journal of Production Economics 89(3), 309–320 (2004)
22. Brunt, D.: Applying Lean to Dealers – After Sales Service. 2. German Conference "After Sales Service", Frankfurt (2011)
23. Ohno, T.: Toyota Production System – Beyond Large-Scale Production. Productivity Press, New York (1988)
24. Imai, M.: Gemba Kaizen. McGraw-Hill, New York (1997)
25. Dombrowski, U., Schmidt, S.: Framework for the Planning and Control of Lean Production System Implementation. International Journal on Agile Manufacturing, 146–151 (2008)
26. Dombrowski, U., Schmidt, S., Crespo, I.: Knowledge Management as a Supporting Function in Lean Production System Implementation. In: Proceedings of the 2nd International Conference on Changeable, Agile, Reconfigurable and Virtual Production (CARV), pp. 453–462 (2007)

Attracting Young Talents to Manufacturing: A Holistic Approach

Stefano Perini[1], Manuel Oliveira[2], Joao Costa[3], and Dimitris Kiritsis[4],
Poul Henrik Kyvsgaard Hansen[5], Loukas Rentzos[6], Afroditi Skevi[4],
Hadrien Szigeti[7], and Marco Taisch[1]

[1] Politecnico di Milano, Italy
{stefano.perini,marco.taisch}@polimi.it
[2] SINTEF, Norway
manuel.oliveira@sintef.no
[3] HIGHSKILLZ, Portugal
joao.costa@highskillz.com
[4] Ecole Polytechnique Fédérale de Lausanne, Switzerland
{dimitris.kiritsis,afroditi.skevi}@epfl.ch
[5] Aalborg University, Denmark
kyvs@business.aau.dk
[6] University of Patras, Greece
rentzos@lms.mech.upatras.gr
[7] Dassault Systémes, France
Hadrien.SZIGETI@3ds.com

Abstract. In the last years, despite the global economic crisis, manufacturing is facing a serious difficulty in the recruitment of the brightest high-skilled human resources. National and international institutions have provided important guidelines to combat this skills mismatch and several innovations have been made both in STEM and manufacturing education. However, there is still a lack of concrete strategies harmonizing together delivery mechanisms and pedagogical frameworks throughout the whole student lifecycle. In order to mitigate these urgent needs, ManuSkills innovative approach provides a strong integrated strategy towards attracting young talent to manufacturing, by raising the awareness and providing the acquisition of new manufacturing skills. The key-concepts and the strategy to achieve learning objectives are presented. Finally, ManuSkills Five Pillars, i.e. Interaction with the Experiments, Interaction with real companies, Social networks, Challenges and making real products, Career management and skills orientation, are explained in detail with the support of examples of application.

Keywords: manufacturing education, manufacturing skills, young talents, strategy.

1 Introduction

There are signs of timid improvement in the global economy where manufacturing plays a pivotal role. The persistent reports of skill shortages throughout the recession

B. Grabot et al. (Eds.): APMS 2014, Part II, IFIP AICT 439, pp. 626–633, 2014.
© IFIP International Federation for Information Processing 2014

will only continue, and possibly escalate. Consequently, it has become of strategic interest for manufacturing industry to attract young talent, as also documented by a survey of over 400 CEOs all over the world managed by Deloitte and the U.S. Council on Competitiveness [1]. In fact, evidence suggests that manufacturing is facing more than other sectors an increasing difficulty in the recruitment of the brightest human resources [2]. This general difficulty seems to be clear taking into account also different perspectives, i.e.:

- the countries, facing high unemployment rate despite the increasing number of employers reporting difficulty in filling manufacturing jobs [3];
- the different functions within a single organization, with the engineering/technical ones among the most affected [4];
- the educational attainments, with a more critical shortage of high-skill and medium-skill workers rather than low-skill ones [5].

The above summary of indicators are just the tip of the iceberg concerning the problem of skill shortage in manufacturing, when one submerges beneath the surface, one encounters a more critical set of indicators related to young talent, which has been aptly designated as the STEM (Science, Technology, Engineering and Mathematics) leaking pipeline. This translates in the generalized disinterest of young students (i.e. both primary and secondary schools) in STEM and the disillusionment of young adults at universities leading to drop-outs. In fact, an analysis of the whole student lifecycle shows that the perception and feeling of the youngsters towards STEM is fundamental in order to form and stimulate their possible future involvement in the manufacturing world [6].

Therefore, strong actions are necessary to mitigate the challenge of attracting young talent to manufacturing. For instance, European Commission has supported it by providing guidelines to combat general skills mismatch [2], while the American Society of Manufacturing Engineers (SME) has profiled specific recommendations to solve the manpower crisis in manufacturing [7]. However, it is necessary to go beyond general guidelines, and conceive of more concrete strategies to attract young talent to manufacturing. In particular, there is a need for an integrated approach to harmonize together delivery mechanisms and pedagogical frameworks. Finally, these strategies need to be coordinated to support the students throughout their whole learning lifecycle. This means different actions are necessary across the STEM pipeline (i.e. children, teenagers, young adults), where in the early stages the focus should be on raising awareness towards manufacturing and in the later stages the focus should be the transformative deep learning of individuals, with reduced time-to-competence.

2 Limitations in Current Approaches

It is clear that the recruitment of young talents is crucial for the support and development of the manufacturing world. At the same time, it is evident that the harmonization between their demand and offer in a sector complicated also by the extreme need of multifaceted roles is becoming more and more difficult. Therefore, in this context, structural problems of lack of talents blend in with the need to prepare professionals able to face with success the new challenges of the Factory of the Future.

Pedagogical frameworks and learning theories have been widely addressed in literature, both as stand-alone concepts and taking into account the impact of ICT [8]. However, the contextualization to manufacturing remains largely amiss, although there has been an increase in effort to making STEM more engaging [9]. Some narrow, case in point, contextualized actions in manufacturing have carried out for children and teenagers, but mostly for testing purposes, as in the case e.g. of classroom immersion [10], computer aided systems [11], virtual design [12] and involvement of the students in visits to industrial plants [13]. For university students, there is more evidence of contextualized interventions, with plenty of studies concerning methods to engage students in manufacturing and improve the learning of advanced manufacturing skills. Despite the positive results achieved in the studies, the challenge remains concerning effective change and scale, thus illustrating the absence of a concerted approach to attracting young talent. The different efforts should be orchestrated and coordinated throughout the whole young talents pipeline, allowing the full exploitation of the existing contributions and enabling the continuous creation of innovative ones. Furthermore, it is necessary to collate information on the impact and effectiveness of the different approaches according to a wide range of indicators, such as age, theme, delivery mechanism, etc. Consequently, we believe the following key points should be taken into account:

- A child is faced with key decision points that affect his/her future career path. Because of the extreme complexity to define them from a psychological and evolutionary point of view (they can greatly vary from individual to individual) [14], a method is hence represented by their identification according to the concrete organization and timing of the different educational systems. For instance, a key decision point can be identified in this sense in the age group between 14 and 16 years, where important choices should be taken according to the differentiation occurring in the single educational systems;

- In most initiatives pertaining raising awareness in manufacturing, the impact is temporary and then the child may not be influenced by their past experience, which may have an important event but that would lose strength over time. It is necessary to provide more frequent experiences to young talent to remain positively influenced, thus each event renovates and reinvigorates results of the previous;

- There is evidence that the mainstream perception of manufacturing is antiquated and not aligned with reality, thus one way of changing this perception is by presenting to youngsters the latest trends in manufacturing. It is equally important to demonstrate the interdisciplinary knowledge and competencies required in manufacturing (e.g. digitalization, virtualization, servitization).

3   ManuSkills Approach

The main aim of ManuSkills approach is to provide a strong integrated strategy towards attracting young talent to manufacturing, by raising the awareness and providing the acquisition of new manufacturing skills. With this aim in mind, the role of ICT in ManuSkills is twofold:

- it serves as enabler of the delivery of ManuSkills learning objects, by leveraging the mechanisms preferred by young talent of the generation of digital natives used to gaming, social media, experimentation and rich media;
- it provides the integration needed to collect and offer in a coordinate and efficient way different learning experiences in a gamified manner.

3.1   ManuSkills Experiment

Pivotal to ManuSkills is the concept of an Experiment, which consists of a self-contained educational object conceived for a mixed ratio of creation/increase manufacturing awareness and of learning manufacturing skills. The actual contents of an educational object can be a simulation, video, serious game, animation, hands-on experiment to setup, etc. Consequently the meta-data of an Experiment consists of an Owner, Requirements, Delivery Mechanism, Content and Target Group.

3.2   ManuSkills Target Groups

Although ManuSkills addresses the entire student lifecycle, the creation of experiments is focused on two specific groups, i.e. Teenagers and Young Adults. This choice is rooted in three reasons:

- Focus the Experiments close to one of the most important key decision points of the student lifecycle of around 14-16 years old, i.e. when the different educational systems are differentiated in terms of curricula and types of schools;
- ManuSkills considers the "tweens", i.e. the youngsters between 10 and 12 years of age, that are too old to be children and too young to be teenagers. The reason being the pervasive misconceptions that affect the representative period before the key passage of the 14-16 years old but without deepening into the universe of children;
- ManuSkills considers "young talent" as the youngsters who have chosen a high-level educational path and who are going to access the working world as high-qualified professionals. This group is important due to the phase of disillusionment that leads to dropping out of the STEM pipeline, thus reducing the further the pool of young talent.

3.3   ManuSkills Learning Objectives

ManuSkills applies different strategies for the learning objectives given to the two target groups:

- Teenagers: to drive and support the increase of their Awareness and Interest in manufacturing;
- Young Adults: to drive and support the increase of their Awareness, Interest and Application of manufacturing.

Awareness, Interest and Application represent the three different levels of communication and perception that are needed in order to efficiently involve the two Target Groups. These levels are inspired by Bloom's Taxonomy of Learning Objectives [15]. Bloom's taxonomy refers to a classification of the different objectives that can be set for students to define learning objectives. The lowest level of the Bloom's Taxonomy (remember) refers to basic knowledge: recalling facts, terms, and basic concepts. The second level (understand) refers to ability to understand facts and ideas by organizing, comparing, translating, and interpreting. The two upper levels refer to the ability to apply and use knowledge: application, analyze, evaluate, and create. Consequently, as indicated in Table 1, ManuSkills Learning Objectives reduce the Bloom's Taxonomy to only three levels:

Table 1. Mapping ManuSkills learning objectives to revised Bloom's taxonomy

ManuSkills Learning Objectives	Revised Bloom's Taxonomy [16]
Awareness	Remember
Interest	Understand
Application	Apply, Analyse, Evaluate, Create

When combining the ManuSkills Learning Objectives with the two Target Groups a matrix emerges. This matrix illustrates the challenges of targeting the two groups and fulfilling the Learning Objectives as depicted in Fig. 1.

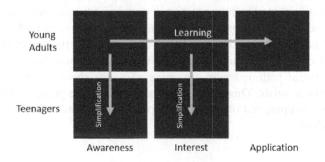

Fig. 1. Matrix of learning objectives strategy and target groups

The challenges can be addressed individually one by one, e.g. how to create Awareness among Teenagers and how to create Awareness among Young Adults, etc. However, this would cause a huge effort and, therefore, ManuSkills approach highlights the importance of defining strategies based on a re-use of Delivery Mechanisms and Content among the different Target Groups and the different Learning Objectives.

3.4   ManuSkills Five Pillars

ManuSkills approach introduces five main pillars to follow in order to achieve the necessary impact in the targeted age groups:

1. **Interaction with the Experiments:** ManuSkills proposes the systematic use of innovative delivery mechanisms, integrated in an ICT platform that allows the dissemination of a wide range of Experiments, from very simple situations to complex challenges using professional manufacturing software. The platform requires a scientific approach in relationship with a curriculum of key subjects and skills to be taught. Each Experiment should bring awareness or understanding on well-defined key subjects, or let young adults apply well-defined manufacturing-related skills. Examples of Experiments are the creation of serious games to explain specific concepts and the development of simulations and quizzes to introduce manufacturing processes.
2. **Interaction with real companies:** ManuSkills identifies as fundamental the interaction of young talent with real companies, leveraging also the opportunity represented by the different Experiments. The interaction is essential in order to engage talents with living problems and situations also allowing manufacturing companies to extract interesting and innovative ideas in a continuous improvement perspective. Examples are the online living interaction between students and manufacturing engineers and the collection of feedbacks on students' work directly from manufacturing companies.
3. **Social networks:** Young talent should be involved by leveraging innovative distribution channels such as social media. The focused use of this kind of systems can capture with appealing situations the attention of the youngsters and enable more direct and up-to-date modalities of interaction among the different stakeholders. Examples are the collection of feedbacks from students by means of social network features and the creation of forums for the discussion of specific manufacturing themes.
4. **Challenges and making real products:** Another important aspect is for young talent to have realistic and scenario-based challenges. Both creation of awareness and development of skills benefit from the anticipated exposition to real-world problems, such as the design of real products. This aspect will further improve the needed relationship among youngsters, schools, universities and manufacturing companies. Examples are the creation of incubators to allow students to prototype their ideas and the definition of contests among students based on the improvement of an everyday product.

5. Career management and skills orientation: Finally, the career management and skills orientation aspects of ManuSkills supports all the other Pillars. This strong effort will help in communicating to the young audience the real essence of manufacturing, allowing the creation of a real and authentic perception of what modern manufacturing is and will be. Examples are the possibility for students to show their talent by means of the platform and the use of engaging ways to present career options in manufacturing online.

4   Conclusions and Next Steps

In this paper, the big issue of attracting young talents to manufacturing is clearly introduced and explained in all its aspects. The available approaches trying to support its solution, both involving and not involving ICT technologies, are reviewed. Therefore, the lack of a holistic approach providing an integrated solution to the problem is highlighted. In this respect, the innovative ManuSkills approach is presented, outlining a concrete strategy that takes into account three fundamental requirements for the success of such kind of concept, i.e. the focus on the key-decision points of the student lifecycle, the correct timing of the different actions to implement and the priority given to youngsters following a high-level educational path. The strategy to involve the two Target Groups identified (i.e. Teenagers and Young Adults) by means of three different levels of communication and perception, i.e. Awareness, Interest and Application, is explained. Finally, the five Pillars of ManuSkills approach to support the development of coordinated actions for the attraction of young talents to manufacturing and their deep learning of manufacturing skills is presented. The main Pillars identified are Interaction with the Experiments, Interaction with real companies, Social networks, Challenges and making real products, Career management and skills orientation. For each of them, proper examples of application are given.

The next steps will be the finalization of ManuSkills ICT platform and of the related Experiments. The different Experiments developed will be subsequently tested in different scenarios with the aim of collecting precious feedbacks from users belonging to the two Target Groups. Further findings will be hence properly used also for the empowerment and refinement of the presented ManuSkills approach in a continuous improvement perspective.

Acknowledgements. The research leading to these results has received funding from the European Community's Seventh Framework Programme (FP7/2007-2013) under grant agreement n° 609147.

References

1. Deloitte U.S. & the Council on Competitiveness, Global Manufacturing Competitiveness Index (2013)
2. European Commission, Employment and Social Developments in Europe 2012 (2013)

3. World Economic Forum, The future of manufacturing - Opportunities to drive economic growth (2012)
4. Economist Intelligence Unit, Plugging the skills gap - Shortages among plenty (2012)
5. McKinsey & Company, Manufacturing the future: The next era of global growth and innovation (2012)
6. Manufacturing Institute, Roadmap to education reform for manufacturing (2010)
7. Society of Manufacturing Engineers, Workforce imperative: a manufacturing education strategy (2012)
8. Klein, H., Noe, R., Wang, C.: Motivation to learn and course outcomes: The impact of delivery mode, learning goal orientation, and perceived barriers and enablers. Personnel Pscyhology, 665–702 (2006)
9. Patterson, D.: Student Awareness and Career Motivation in the STEM Fields. Northwest Association for Biomedical Research (2011)
10. Fralick, B., Kearn, J., Thompson, S.: How Middle Schoolers Draw Engineers and Scientists. Journal of Science Education and Technology, 60–73 (2009)
11. Ziemian, C., Aument, J., Whaley, D.: Manufacturing Technology in Middle School Classrooms: A Collaborative Approach. In: International Conference on Engineering Education, ICEE, Coimbra, Portugal (2007)
12. Howard, M., Washington, N., Shurn, T., Brge, L., Warner, G.: The Tricked-Out Virtual Body Shop: Recruiting African-American High-School Students to STEM through Automotive Design (2011)
13. Prins, R., MacDonald, S., Leech, J., Brumfield, J., Ellis, M., Smith, L., Shaeffer, J.: Techfacturing: A Summer Day Camp Designed to Promote STEM Interest in Middle School Students through Exposure to Local Manufacturing Facilities. In: ASEE Southeast Section Conference (2010)
14. Osborne, J., Dillon, J.: Science Education in Europe: Critical Reflections. King's College, London (2008)
15. Bloom, B.S., Engelhart, M.D., Furst, E.J., Hill, W.H., Krathwohl, D.R.: Taxonomy of educational objectives: The classification of educational goals. David McKay Company, New York (1956)
16. Anderson, L.W., Krathwohl, D.R., Airasian, P.W., Cruikshank, K.A., Mayer, R.E., Pintrich, P.R., Raths, J., Wittrock, M.C.: A taxonomy for learning, teaching, and assessing: A revision of Bloom's taxonomy of educational objectives. Allyn and Bacon (2000)

Eco-process Engineering System for Collaborative Product Process System Optimisation

Juhani Heilala[1], Reino Ruusu[1], Jari Montonen[1], Saija Vatanen[1], Carlos Kavka[2], Fabio Asnicar[2], Sebastian Scholze[3], Alberto Armiojo[4], and Mario Insunza[5]

[1] VTT Technical Research Centre of Finland, PO Box 1000, FI-02044 VTT, Finland
juhani.heilala@vtt.fi
[2] ESTECO, AREA Science Park, Padriciano 99, 34149 Trieste, Italy
[3] ATB, Institut für angewandte Systemtechnik Bremen GmbH,
Wiener Straße 1, 28359 Bremen, Germany
[4] TECNALIA, Parque Científico y Tecnológico de Bizkaia - C/ Geldo.
Edificio 700. E-48160 Derio, Spain
[5] SISTEPLANT, S.L. - Parque Tecnológico de Bizkaia, 607 building, 48160 Derio, Spain

Abstract. Eco-Process engineering system (EPES) means systematic collaborative eco-efficiency and eco-innovation aspects in product service system (PSS) development and management, and covers all life-cycle phases. It is an ICT tool and related application methodology. The development focus on PSS from functional and cost performance is currently enhanced with sustainability aspects. The goal is to create more value with less environmental impact. In the virtual factories, extended enterprises, the collaboration between different stakeholders, engineers, managers, users of the PSS is a must and all actors in the value chain need a common goal. EPES system provides a collaborative space, covering common data and functionalities for knowledge management, multi-objective decision making, simulation and optimisation. Coordinated evolution (co-evolution) of products, processes and services creates competitive advantage. This paper shows a prototype of EPES system. The software building blocks of EPES system are illustrated as well methodology steps in setting up system and using it.

Keywords: product service system, life-cycle optimisation, collaborative space.

1 Introduction

The focus of product, process or service design is currently rapidly widening to include additional goals related to sustainability, especially in the field of energy and energy-intensive industry [1]. In addition to economic, functional performance, product, process and service quality and marketability issues, new social and environmental aspects are increasingly taken into account.

Examples of the drivers of this development are: Cost savings, resource efficiency, regulations set by society, directives, standards, also customer requirements and communication, business reputation and so on. The eco-constraints, e.g. resource

B. Grabot et al. (Eds.): APMS 2014, Part II, IFIP AICT 439, pp. 634–641, 2014.
© IFIP International Federation for Information Processing 2014

efficiency, energy consumption, emission, hazardous waste, etc., need to become a part of the wider assessment of the overall Product, Process and Service (PPS) feasibility analysis, engineering development and management.

The nature of sustainability as a holistic viewpoint presents a need for complex multi-objective decision-making, in which compromises need to be made between mutually exclusive criteria. Additionally all the stages of the life cycle of a product service system need to be taken into account in the development stage. This greatly increases the quantity of good-quality data that needs to be presented to decision-makers. This data is not only hard to collect but subject to continuous change, due to technological development [2].

In order to address complex multi-objective decision-making in a distributed world of the extended enterprise, flexible tools that provide support for knowledge management, communication, co-operation and business process management are needed [3]. Service-oriented ICT tools are one enabler for efficient networking. A need for efficient Business Process Management (BPM) arises to orchestrate the activities carried by the various actors that do not necessarily fit within a single product-oriented organizational structure.

Selection of the best design among a set of alternatives is a very important task in the development stage of a PPS. Modelling and simulation techniques are necessary in order to account for future effects of design decisions.

In most engineering environments, designers need to be encouraged to integrate environmental aspects by increasing the availability of suitable tools and knowledge. Integration of sustainability aspects to various simulation models is still rare [4]. One example of development is shown in [5]. In short, the main requirements should include: A simple and easy to use method; Availability of appropriate data; Clear and easily communicable results; and Traceable conclusions.

Above all, any tools or information deployed as part of Design for Environment (DfE) should be fully integrated in an existing design process, procedures and manuals. Environment aspects should become a new key parameter to consider in decision-making, alongside technical performance, safety and cost [6].

In the EPES project, a software service platform is created for bridging the gap between design-oriented tools, such as CAD and CAE, operations and service planning tools and tools for managing the business decision-making. Partially this is the traditional domain of PLM systems, most of which are, however, quite costly and inflexible.

The idea of EPES is to provide the users with a product-process-service (PPS) development-oriented "collaborative space" that can be organized by its users without customization by a software vendor, but allowing a level of integration of tools and databases that is not available on general purpose collaboration platforms.

2   New way of Working

The EPES project is developing a comprehensive software platform that allows engineering issues to be addressed from the multiple points-of-view of sustainability. The

636   J. Heilala et al.

EPES system is an integrated Enterprise Content Management (ECM) and Business
Process Management (BPM) platform that provides general advantages as an engineering and/or decision-making platform [7, 8, 9, 10]. Its focus is on efficient interdisciplinary co-operation, communication, data collection and management. It also
serves as a tool for communication between the engineering community and the strategic decision-makers, allowing them to make informed decisions at the earliest
stages of the PPS development and management.

The platform provides functionalities for:

- **Knowledge Management**, in the form of an enterprise content management system, which is augmented with a semantic context database for providing additional
  meta-data
- **Business Process Management**, in the form of a BPM platform on which complex
  processes can be modelled using BPMN 2.0.
- **IT service automation** that provides additional support for meta-data collection
  and processing and automating the execution of complex computational processes
  for producing the key performance indicators that are needed for decision-making.
- **Multi-objective simulation and optimization**, in the form of an integrated state-
  of-the art solution.
- **Business Intelligence**, in the form of a data integration and analytics platform.

In order to provide maximum accessibility in a distributed environment, the platform is built to be operated in a strictly browser-based user interface.

In the EPES project business cases, the core eco-efficiency objectives are: Increase
product or service value, optimizing the use of resources, and reduce environmental
impact. The business cases are diverse, and include electric grid design and operation,
wind turbine maintenance operations and aircraft wing design from the point of view
of manufacturability (see chapter 4).

The overall EPES reference architecture schema is illustrated in Figure 1

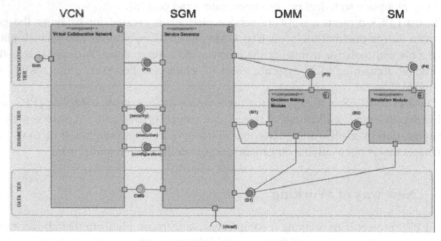

Fig. 1. EPES Architecture Schema

EPES is separated into a three-layered structure that complies in every layer to a service oriented approach. Three layers are: Data tier, Business Tier and Presentation tier (see Fig 1.).

Based on the service-oriented development approach, that represents several different processes as services that are fully interoperable and allow further re-use for specific process reoccurrences. All layers of the EPES system concept are seen as a part of an overall service structure so that every component could interact with each other, but is additionally focused around specific transition services.

The EPES system is built upon the following core services, VCN, SGM, DMM and SM (see Fig 1.).

Virtual Collaborative Network (VCN). The VCN main functionality is to provide a main point of access for non-expert end-users through user interfaces, including capabilities for supporting the aggregated Graphical User Interfaces (GUI) provided by the Service Generator. It provides the technical infrastructure for the distribution of users into groups; content management and sharing mechanisms; workflow engine for contents production, consumption and transformation. In addition, the VCN provides a Knowledge Base, containing actual data, historical data, identified constraints and objectives from collaborative networks, KPIs and Life-Cycle Inventory data.

Service Generator (SG). The Service Generator's main functionality is creating, updating, and deploying configurations for application-specific services. It interacts with the Simulation Module and the Decision Making Module to compute parameters for updated configurations. The SG can also store / retrieve configurations in/from the Virtual Collaborative Network. Finally, the SG allows identification of contextual information about EPES solution operators as well as connected legacy systems.

Simulation Module (SM). The simulation module of the presented platform provides a capability for running numerical analyses related to the life-cycle assessment process. It provides simulation services through an abstract service interface that allows higher-level components of the platform to use simulation as an interchangeable service, according to the principles of the Service Oriented Architecture (SOA) design paradigm. It allows the other modules to present configuration options and numerical parameters of simulation modules without any prior knowledge of the internal structure of the model.

Decision Making Module (DMM). DMM is an interactive system intended to help decision-makers to use data and models to identify and solve problems and to make decisions. On the one hand, there will be some traditional indicators for measuring the overall PSS performance, but on the other hand, there will be new KPIs established and defined in the DMM. These KPIs will be traced to the measured constraints, and the DMM will show, where the constraints are, and how to measure the performance of the organization, in order to take the best decision in a range of values proposed by the SM taking into account the localized constraint. The KPIs taken into consideration will mostly reflect eco constraints. Inputs from the SM will support the decision process, by simulating the potential evolution of relevant KPIs and allowing thus taking informed decisions.

3   EPES Prototype

The existing EPES prototype platform makes use of many existing solutions as parts of its integrated comprehensive platform. These solutions include:

- Alfresco: An Enterprise Content Management (ECM) system
- Activiti: A business process modelling and execution framework
- SOMO by ESTECO: An optimization and simulation integration platform
- Pentaho: A business intelligence platform.

Additional software components have been developed in order to facilitate the integration of these existing solutions. The solution is cloud based and collaborative space user needs just a browser.

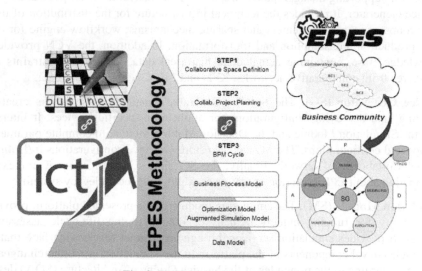

Fig. 2. EPES Methodology main steps

The main steps in the EPES methodology (see Fig. 2.)

1. Collaborative work environment definition, strategic level
2. Collaborative project planning, operative level
3. Business Process Management cycle, operative level

The main concept of organization of work in the EPES platform is the "collaborative space". This is a concept that is quite similar to the concept of workspaces on platforms like Microsoft SharePoint, including both data and business process (or workflow) models, but provides additional functionality in the sense of configured computational services e.g. simulation and optimisation, that can operate directly on structured data files on the underlying content management platform.

Each collaborative space can also contain a customized semantic database of contextual data, which is used for organizing and linking together a possibly complex set of data, users, services and business processes. This context data provides a structured view of the contents of the collaborative space simultaneously from multiple points of view.

Each collaborative space is typically built to manage activities related to a product or a family of products or services. It involves data that is shared between different organizational units, such as marketing, business analytics, design, engineering and use and service e.g. maintenance activities. The goal is to avoid any need to keep data on personal or group-accessible repositories.

A methodology has been developed for managing the collaborative space. It is advisable to establish the collaborative space right at the planning stages of a project, and to maintain it to the end. In the case of product development, the collaborative space can live and adapt to the needs of the organization throughout the stages of the product life-cycle.

All content in a collaborative space is version-controlled. A collaborative space, or parts thereof, can be easily branched by creating a copy. This eases the parallel development of product alternatives, of which the best one can be selected at a later stage.

Some collaborative spaces are not used for projects, but for continuous activities, in which case the methodology proposes a business process management cycle of continuous improvement.

This work environment can be extended beyond the group of people who directly participate in the development processes. This enables, for example, a more direct form of feedback from the users to the engineers. It also connects varies engineering disciplines, group of engineers and managers.

Each of the actors in the defined Collaborative Spaces system has a role. The role could be, for example, an owner of the product, a user of the product, a service provider, a manufacturing or product-related engineer, a sales representative or a business decision-maker. Using the collaborative parts of the EPES system, any group of actors in the product service system community can distribute knowledge, collaborate, pin-point eco-constraints, bottlenecks and solve problems.

4   EPES Use Cases

The presented EPES approach is being applied in three industrial business cases (BC), to validate the proposed decision making solution within different application domains, as listed here.

BC1. Engineering maintenance services for optimizing maintenance and increasing availability of wind turbines. The decision processes involved here deal with the best scheduling of maintenance tasks to be taken for optimal maintenance of multiple wind turbines. The decision making and optimisation constrains include, service and operation history, weather conditions and forecast, availability of service resources and so on.

BC2. Power grid control systems for improved identification of improved monitoring of grid load and safety limits. Smart cable has features for temperature detection and monitoring at any point of the cable. Decision support methods are supporting the user in detecting trends in the grid load, ensuring thus that good load balancing decisions will be taken. Also new cable design is supported, e.g. material saving has multiple impacts on manufacturing, logistics and installation of cable network.

BC3. Support for optimized design and manufacturing of aircraft wings. Here, the decision support system addresses the optimal layout of manufacturing facilities in the conceptual design phase. User can fix some of the parameters of the facility, i.e. work shifts, cycle times and capacity, and the optimization returns the numbers of required facility elements; resources, personnel etc. The production data is aggregated with sustainability data to enable optimization in environmental point of view.

5   Summary

Sustainability-related issues are important and they are adding heavily to the complexity of the design process. The amount of data that is needed for decision-making is growing and multiple parameters and constraints must be considered simultaneously. Because multiple engineering disciplines, multiple actors and multiple life cycle stages are involved in the goal of sustainability, multidisciplinary optimisation (MDO) and multi-objective optimisation (MOO) techniques can seldom be avoided. When these techniques and tools are provided as services, the transparency and traceability of the decision making processes can be improved.

The EPES platform is a tool for managing both technically and organizationally complex tasks in a distributed organizational environment, such as virtual factory. The platform combines existing enterprise IT tools into a platform that is flexible and configurable and supports the simultaneous management of knowledge from multiple viewpoints.

Provision of engineering analyses and optimisation as services is one of the advantage of the EPES platform. When combined with knowledge management, communication and collaboration, business intelligence, and business process modelling and execution, a comprehensive platform is created. Instead of several desktop applications, engineering islands of analysis, the EPES system provides both integration and automation of the assessment methods that are necessary for tackling sustainability aspect.

Instead of directly addressing sustainability, the focus of the platform is on streamlining the processes and integrating the existing tools that are necessary for addressing it. In practice, by reducing the amount of required effort, the application of the solution also results in more sustainable outcomes, by allowing the enterprise to more efficiently use the available engineering resources, both human and computational.

The EPES approach is assessed in three companies from different sectors (wind farm maintenance, cable production and aeronautics), which represent typical examples of companies in need for such highly reconfigurable services to continuously optimize product performance and service delivery.

The maintenance and other services of industrial products, investment goods or design of complex, multi-disciplinary engineering products and collaborative product process service development are promising application areas for the EPES system.

EPES system is an enterprise application, thus it needs customization and integration to existing legacy and other engineering systems. First time service set-up, and integration requires high expertise. Exploitation plans of the development is ongoing

Acknowledgements. The research presented in the paper has been carried out within the frames of the EPES, "Eco-Process Engineering System for Composition of Services to Optimize Product Life-Cycle" collaboration project, (www.epes-project.eu) co-funded by the European Commission under FoF-ICT-2011.7.3-285093 contract. The authors wish to express the acknowledgement to EC for the support and to all project partners for their contributions during the development presented in this paper. This document does not represent the opinion of the European Community, and the European Community is not responsible for any use that might be made of its content.

References

1. Baños, R., Manzano-Agugliaro, F., Montoya, F.G., Gil, C., Alcayde, A., Gómez, J.: Optimization methods applied to renewable and sustainable energy: A review. Renewable and Sustainable Energy Reviews 15(4), 1753–1766 (2011)
2. Seung, J.K., Kara, S., Kayis, B.: Economic and environmental assessment of product life cycle design: volume and technology perspective. Journal of Cleaner Production 75, 75–85 (2014) ISSN 0959-6526
3. Kleindorfer, P.R., Singhal, K., Van Wassenhove, L.N.: Sustainable Operations Management. Production and Operations Management 14(4), 482–492 (2005)
4. Thiede, S., Seow, Y., Andersson, J., Johansson, B.: Environmental aspects in manufacturing system modelling and simulation—State of the art and research perspectives. CIRP Journal of Manufacturing Science and Technology 6, 78–87 (2013)
5. Heilala, J., et al.: Discrete Part Manufacturing Energy Efficiency Improvements with Modelling and Simulation. In: Emmanouilidis, C., Taisch, M., Kiritsis, D. (eds.) APMS 2012, Part I. IFIP AICT, vol. 397, pp. 142–150. Springer, Heidelberg (2013)
6. Design for Environment, Airbus Corporate Answer to Disseminate integrated Environmental Management sYstem (ACADEMY), ISSUE N°1 ACADEMY
7. Sorli, M., Armijo, A.: EPES: Engineering System for Optimization of Product Life-cycle through Adapted Eco-services. Procedia Engineering 63, 310–317 (2013), The Manufacturing Engineering Society International Conference, MESIC 2013
8. Scholze, S., Grama, C., Kotte, O.: Eco Process Engineering System for highly customized industrial products, processes and services. In: International Conference on Sustainable Design and Manufacturing, SDM 2014, Cardiff, Wales, UK, April 28-30 (2014)
9. Heilala, J., Ruusu, R., Montonen, J., Vatanen, S., Bermell-Garcia, P., Astwood, S., Iwhiwhu, C., Kavka, C., Asnicar, F., Ricco, L.: Product Concept Manufacturability and Sustainability Assessment with Eco Process Engineering System. In: International Conference on Sustainable Design and Manufacturing, SDM 2014, Cardiff, Wales, UK, April 28-30 (2014)
10. Scholze, S., Kotte, O., Stokic, D., Grama, C.: Context-sensitive decision support for improved sustainability of product lifecycle. In: 5th International Conference on Intelligent Decision Technologies, KES IDT 2013, Sesimbra Portugal (2013)

Reference Ontologies to Support the Development of New Product-Service Lifecycle Systems

Claire Palmer[1], Esmond Neil Urwin[1], Jose Miguel Pinazo-Sánchez [2],
Francisco Sánchez Cid[3], Sonja Pajkovska-Goceva[4], and Robert Ian Marr Young[1]

[1] Wolfson School of Mechanical and Manufacturing Engineering,
Loughborough University, Loughborough, Leicestershire, UK
{c.palmer3,e.n.urwin,r.i.young}@lboro.ac.uk
[2] Ainia centro tecnológico, Parque tecnológico de Valencia,
Avinguda de Benjamin Franklin, 5-11, 46980 Paterna, Valencia, Spain
jmpinazo@ainia.es
[3] Instituto Tecnológico de Informática,
Camino de Vera s/n, Edif. 8G, Acceso B, CP 46022, Valencia, Spain
cid@iti.es
[4] Fraunhofer Institute for Production Systems and Design Technology IPK, Pascalstraße 8-9,
10587 Berlin, Germany
sonja.pajkovska-goceva@ipk.fraunhofer.de

Abstract. In competitive and time sensitive market places, organisations are tasked with providing Product Lifecycle Management (PLM) approaches to achieve and maintain competitive advantage, react to change and understand the balance of possible options when making decisions on complex multi-faceted problems, Global Production Networks (GPN) is one such domain in which this applies. When designing and configuring GPN to develop, manufacture and deliver product-service provision, information requirements that affect decision making become more complex. The application of reference ontologies to a domain and its related information requirements can enhance and accelerate the development of new product-service lifecycle systems with a view towards the seamless interchange of information or interoperability between systems and domains.

This paper presents (i) preliminary results for the capture and modelling of end-user information and (ii) an initial higher level reference core ontology for the development of reference ontologies to ameliorate product-service lifecycle management for GPN.

Keywords: product lifecycle management, global production networks, reference ontologies, interoperability, product service lifecycle systems.

1   Introduction

The nature of competition dictates rivalry and in the domain of manufacturing industry the act of competing for supremacy in the design, production and selling of products. The 21st century information age is forcing manufacturers to act differently to

B. Grabot et al. (Eds.): APMS 2014, Part II, IFIP AICT 439, pp. 642–649, 2014.
© IFIP International Federation for Information Processing 2014

compete successfully and find different ways in which to not only source and manufacture products but also configure and then sell them to customers.

The servitisation of products i.e. 'the increased offering of fuller market packages or 'bundles' of customer focused combinations of goods, services, support, self-service and knowledge' [1] is proving to be an enticing form of selling products via services to customers. Whilst the benefits can be seemingly apparent and instant, the actuality is that there are many additional components that are necessary.

The challenge for manufacturing industry which is servitising products is, what is the most effective way to design, produce and sell a product together with it associated service components effectively, to form a Product-Service System (PSS)? At the heart of this is how to align and integrate a traditional product lifecycle viewpoint with a more modern service lifecycle to develop a Product-Service Lifecycle System (PSLS). Additional complexity is added to this approach when Global Production Networks (GPN) are to be configured and reconfigured and in the face of rapidly changing product-service requirements. By employing a GPN, organisations can adopt technology at a faster pace, lower costs and be more open to change [12]. But an important aspect must be considered carefully, that of information interoperability between suppliers, manufacturers and service provision mechanisms. This becomes paramount when configuring sizeable and diverse GPN across potentially large geographical areas and between widely varying domains and contexts. It can introduce a wide and varied range of risks and perturbations from diverse system processes and capabilities, to different legislation and laws. One such method that can mitigate these risks to information interoperability is the use and application of ontological reference models.

What can be derived from this is that organisations are tasked with providing product lifecycle management (PLM) approaches and solutions to enable the sharing, use and reuse of information and knowledge, the main objective of this being to achieve and maintain competitive advantage for their Product-Service Systems [3]. They must be able to react to change and understand the balance of possible options when making decisions on complex multi-faceted problems, GPN is one such domain in which this applies.

Two interesting formal reference ontologies for interoperability have been put forward, those of the Interoperable Manufacturing Knowledge Systems (IMKS) project [4] and the Manufacturing Core Ontology (MCO) [5]. These concern the design, manufacturing and assembly of a product, as such they do not include or allow for PSLS nor GPN. What is highlighted by this is the need to develop formal reference ontologies to help develop, implement and ameliorate interoperability within PSLS when employing a GPN.

The premise of this paper is to put forward the notion that the application of formal reference ontologies to a domain and its related information requirements so as to enhance and accelerate the development of new PSLS with a view towards the seamless interchange of information or interoperability between systems and domains. This approach is being developed as part of the research being undertaken in the EU FP7 FLEXINET project.

This paper is structured as follows. Section 2 discusses the FLEXINET project and its purpose. Section 3 sets out the methodological approach and development of reference ontologies for product-service lifecycle systems. Section 4 draws the paper to a close with conclusions and further work.

2   The FLEXINET View

FLEXINET aims to support decision-making in the early design of global production network configurations based on the implementation of new complex technologies. FLEXINET will apply advanced solution techniques to the provision of a set of Intelligent Production Network Configuration Services that can support the design of high quality manufacturing networks, understanding the costs and risks involved in network re-configuration, and then mitigating the impact of system incompatibilities as networks change over time. These are fundamental requirements for high quality decision-making in the early design of intelligent manufacturing system networks. These innovative concepts will enable a fast and efficient response to market variations and be easily adaptable across industrial sectors. The FLEXINET concept is illustrated in Figure 1.

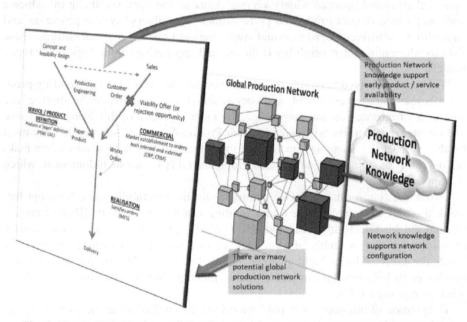

Fig. 1. The FLEXINET Concept: Intelligent Production Network Configuration Services

FLEXINET takes the view that new manufacturing business modelling methods are needed that can model business cases and identify the critical network relations that underlie the business operation. Such methods and models are essential to the ability to define both the production network knowledge that must be captured and the queries that must be made if new business configuration possibilities are to be eva-luated. Product servitisation adds to the complexity of this problem as the relation-ships between product lifecycles and service lifecycles also need to be understood and their impact on production system networks specified within the resulting business models.

The main aims of the FLEXINET ontological research are the following, (i) docu-ment key semantic concepts, knowledge constraints and inter-relationships in the context of globalised production networks, (ii) structure and formally model concepts, relationships, constraints and related facts to provide an underpinning environment against which specific network configuration designs can be evaluated and (iii) devel-op methods for ontology querying from which to evaluate the compliance of potential production network configurations from both OEM and SME perspectives.

3   A Reference Ontology for Product-Service Lifecycle Systems

The starting point for the development of the FLEXINET formal reference ontology for product-service lifecycle systems has been three industrial case studies which have provided a solid base for the elicitation and capture of information and knowledge. In addition to this, the work from the Interoperable Manufacturing Knowledge Systems (IMKS) project, the Manufacturing Service Ecosystem (MSEE) project and the Man-ufacturing Information ontological model set out by Hastilow [6] is being assessed for applicability to the GPN and PSLS domains.

The FLEXINET approach focuses on the intelligent configuration of a network of products or product-service systems, to support interoperability between systems and domains the approach utilises a core foundation ontology. To enable ease of con-struction and to facilitate re-use across domains the FLEXINET ontology is organised into five levels, as illustrated in Figure 2. Each level inherits concepts from and pro-vides additional concepts to the level above, the ontology becoming more domain specific with each level. Five levels are needed to specialise the concepts from the foundation to the specific domains. Figure 2 shows example domains at each level, the scope of FLEXINET being indicated in white.

Level 0 Core consists of foundation concepts applicable to all domains, having nothing to do directly with Product-Service Lifecycle Systems. The foundation con-cepts include time, events, aggregation and lists and are derived from the Highfleet Upper Level Ontology (ULO) [7]. Level 1 contains the few key concepts necessary to model any system. A system transforms inputs into outputs and is defined as "a com-bination of interacting elements organized to achieve one or more stated purposes" [8]. Level 2 uses Banathy's classification [9] to specialise systems into "Natural Systems" and "Designed Systems". Natural systems are living systems of all kinds, the solar system and the Universe. Designed systems are man-made creations, includ-ing fabricated physical systems, conceptual knowledge and purposeful creations. FLEXINET will provide decision support for product lifecycle management and, as this requires human input (i.e. input from a living system), the scope of FLEXINET covers purposeful creations and overlaps into natural systems.

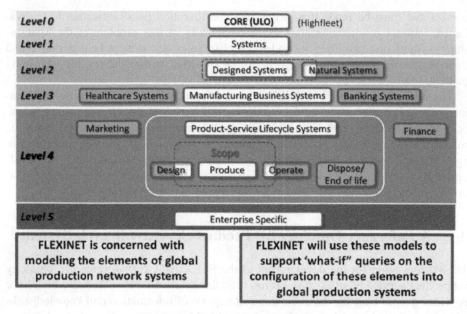

Fig. 2. The FLEXINET ontology levels

Level 3 further differentiates designed systems, FLEXINET being concerned with Manufacturing Business Systems which are specialised within Level 4. At this level FLEXINET considers Product-Service Lifecycle Systems, implemented as Global Production Networks. The lifecycle phases are denoted as design, produce, operate and end of life (including disposal, recycling and remanufacturing). The focus of FLEXINET is how to design a GPN to produce and operate a product-service. The main area FLEXINET considers within the Product-Service Lifecycle is "Produce" (producing the product) but the scope also overlaps into "Design" (of the network) and "Operate" as the operation of the product and the service needs to be considered. Level 5 applies Level 4 to case studies creating enterprise specific domains.

Figure 3 sets out the level 1 ontology. It applies the Unified Modelling Language (UML) [10] technique to describe the details about the concepts and relations necessary to specify a system. This ontology level utilises the concept TimeSpan (inherited from Level 0) and contains two parent concepts: Basic and Role. A TimeSpan includes the first and last instants of a date and all the instances in between [7]. A Basic concept [11] is independent of the system or context, its definition does not depend on another concept and an instance of a Basic always retains its identity as such. Examples of Basic are information and material. A Basic can be comprised of Basics, e.g. "bottled water" is comprised of the materials "bottle", "cap" and "mineral water". A System is subtype of Basic and provides a context for the Roles it contains (shown via the "depends on" relation and the composition filled diamond in the figure).

The definition of a Role depends on a context, an instance of a Role cannot exist without a context and the playsRole relation is transitory. For example, a person Joe has a Role as a lecturer (context "university") and changes Role to a consultant (context "enterprise"), whereas the Basic "bottle" is always a "bottle". It can be seen that a lecturer Role cannot exist without the university context, if the university closes the lecturer role ceases to exist. Roles may be comprised of Roles (e.g. a lecturer Role may be comprised of administration, teaching and staff Roles).

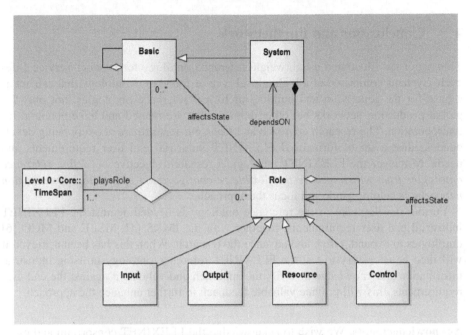

Fig. 3. FLEXINET Level 1 Systems Ontology

A Basic plays a Role for certain TimeSpans, modelled in the ternary relation "playsRole". For example in the context of a manufacturing organization system, the Basic "bottled water" can play the Role of a Product during the TimeSpan of the system. Within a University a person could play the Role of a lecturer for a TimeSpan of five years, become unemployed and then play the Role of a lecturer again for a further TimeSpan.

A Basic can play more than one Role at the same time (e.g. a person could be a lecturer and a parent). A Role can be played by more than one Basic, e.g. the role of a laundry would require a washer and a drier. There is no requirement for a Basic to play a Role (shown by the 0..* multiplicity next to the Role concept in the figure). Role and Basic concepts exist separately and have separate identities. There is also no requirement for a Role to be played by a Basic, enabling empty Roles to be modelled (e.g. if a person Joe left his Role as a lecturer the Role would still exist as a lecturer vacancy).

A Basic may affect the state of a role, e.g. the size of a Basic "bottled water" playing the Role of a product could influence the dimensions required for a packing resource Role. Additionally a Role may affect the state of a Role, e.g. within the lecturer Role more duties allotted to the administration Role would cause duties to be removed from the teaching Role).

The four key Roles which describe a system are input, output, resource and control. An input represents what is brought into and is transformed or consumed by the system to produce outputs. An output represents what is brought out from or is produced by the system. A resource is used by or supports the execution of the system. A control is a condition required to produce correct system output [12,139].

4   Conclusions and Furtherwork

This paper has illustrated a lightweight reference ontology for Product-Service Life-cycle Systems comprised of a higher level core or foundation ontology that can act as a base for the generation and building of formal reference ontologies, not only for global production networks but other domains that are related and have potential for interoperation. The research approach and ideas put forward are actively being developed against a set of formalised FLEXINET industrial end user requirements and needs. Moreover the FLEXINET ontological research objective of *'define reference ontologies from which to base the flexible re-configuration of globalised production networks'* is helping guide and focus the approach.

Further development of the reference ontology is needed against the FLEXINET industrial end user requirements, together with the IMKS [4], MSEE and MCO [6] ontologies to expand, refine and advance the research. When this has been achieved it will then be necessary to test the FLEXINET reference ontology utilising industrial information and knowledge to verify the approach and validate it against the end user requirements, this will provide valuable feedback to further enhance the approach.

Acknowledgements. We wish to acknowledge the FLEXINET consortium and especially the financial support from the European Union Seventh Framework Programme FP7-2013-NMP-ICT-FOF (RTD) under grant agreement no 688627.

References

1. Vandermerwe, S., Rada, J.: Servitization of business: adding value by adding services. European Management Journal 6(4), 314–324 (1988)
2. Coe, N.M., Dicken, P., Hess, M.: Global production networks: realizing the potential. Economic Geography Research Group, Working Paper Series No. 05.07 (2007)
3. Young, R.I.M., Gunendran, A.G., Chungoora, N., Harding, J.A., Case, K.: Enabling interoperable manufacturing knowledge sharing in PLM. In: Proceedings of the Sixth International Conference on Product Life Cycle Management PLM 2009, University of Bath, Bath, UK, July 6-8, pp. 130–138. Inderscience Enterprises Ltd., Switzerland (2009)
4. Chungoora, N., Young, R.I.M.: The configuration of design and manufacture know-ledge models from a heavyweight ontological foundation. International Journal of Production Research 49(15), 4701–4725 (2011)
5. Chungoora, N., Cutting-Decelle, A.-F., Young, R.I.M., Gunendran, G., Usman, Z., Harding, J.A., Case, K.: Towards the ontology-based consolidation of production-centric standards. International Journal of Production Research 51(2), 327–345 (2013a)

6. Hastilow, N.: An Ontological Approach to Manufacturing Systems Interoperability in Dynamic Change Environments. PhD Thesis. School of Mechanical and Manufacturing Engineering, Loughborough University, UK (2013)
7. Highfleet Ontology Library Reference. Highfleet Inc., Baltimore (2014)
8. International Standards Society, ISO/IEC 15288:2008 Systems and Software Engineering – System lifecycle processes. ISO, Genève (2008)
9. Banathy, B.H.: A systems view of education: Concepts and principles for effective practice. Educational Technology (1992)
10. OMG, 2012 OMG unified modeling language (OMG UML), superstructure and infrastructure version 2.4.1 (2012), http://www.omg.org/spec/UML/2.4.1/ (accessed May 9, 2014)
11. Mizoguchi, R., Kozaki, K., Kitamura, Y.: Ontological analyses of roles. In: 2012 Federated Conference on Computer Science and Information Systems (FedCSIS), pp. 489–496. IEEE (September 2012)
12. FIPS PUBs: Integration definition for function modelling (IDEF0). Federal information processing standards publication, 183 (1993)
13. POP* Revised framework Work package – A1.8, Athena European integrated project no. 507849 public deliverable (2006)

Modelling Requirements in Service to PLM for Long Lived Products in the Nuclear Field

Albéric Cornière[1], Virginie Fortineau[1], Thomas Paviot[1], Samir Lamouri[1],
Jean-Louis Goblet[1], Audrey Platon[2], and Cécile Dutertre[2]

[1] Arts et Métiers Paristech, 151 bd de l'hopital, Paris, France
[2] EDF - DIN - projet PLM, 97 av Pierre Brossolette, Montrouge, France

Abstract. Requirements engineering in usually considered a first step before design that is to evolve with each generation or version in a product line. Nuclear plants however, are subject to modifications during their lifetime, in their design and implementation as well as in the requirements they have to satisfy. Economic, technical and safety reasons lead to extending the requirements engineering process through the whole life-cycle of the nuclear plants. This article presents an ontology-based approach to integrating the requirements engineering into a PLM ap- proach for such long-lived, large-scale products.

Keywords: Requirements Engineering, PLM, Ontology, Long Life-Cycle, Large-Scale, System Engineering.

1   Introduction

Requirements engineering in usually considered a first step before design that is to evolve with each generation or version in a product line. Nuclear plants however, are subject to modifications during their lifetime, in their design and implementation as well as in the requirements they are to satisfy. Economic, technical and safety reasons lead to extending the requirements engineering process through the whole life-cycle of the nuclear plants. This article will present the requirements engineering with the goal of setting a frame to the problem, then it presents the different approaches that are used, mainly in the field of computer sciences. In section 4 several particularities in the context of nuclear plants are given, leading in section 5 to a proposition of modelling with the intent to answer the industrial problem.

2   Definitions and Uses of Requirements

Requirements engineering is commonly mentioned in scientific publications, especially in the field of computer sciences. However, there is seldom a definition given for this process, and comparatively few of the articles available treat of requirements engineering itself. Jureta [13] notices "To say that requirements are

B. Grabot et al. (Eds.): APMS 2014, Part II, IFIP AICT 439, pp. 650–657, 2014.
© IFIP International Federation for Information Processing 2014

engineered is currently more of an ideal than the actual state of affairs". We will retain the definition given by [6] : "Requirements engineering is the process producing a coherent set of specifications on a yet-to-be-designed object"

As for requirements, the definition is still heterogeneous depending on the context in which the notion thereof is used: in most situations, the starting point with requirements engineering is the expression of what the product is to accomplish, that is to say the expression of the needs of the stakeholders. The SysML specifications [15] refer to requirements in the fields of computer sciences as thus : "A requirement specifies a capability or condition that must (or should) be satisfied. A requirement may specify a function that a system must perform or a performance condition a system must achieve", while many other consider them as high level specifications of what the product is to accomplish [1]. We were unable to find in the scientific literature a situation presented in which requirements are considered outside the beginning of life of a product, or in which they may change during the product life-cycle.

For the purpose of this article we will consider a requirement as "one or several properties or behaviours of a system that must be satisfied"[15]

3   Requirements Modelling Today

Recent works using requirements engineering are mostly from the field of computer sciences ; about 90% to 95% of the search results on a scientific repository such as Springer link for "requirements engineering" are identified as computer science works. In those works, two main tendencies can be identified : on one hand, works that focus on defining the requirements so as to waive ambiguities, in order to allow design to be based on a reliable transcription of the stakeholders needs; and on the other hand works that focus on analysis of the requirements sets, in order to ensure the requirements set is coherent and satisfiable.

3.1   Eliciting the Requirements

The first goal of requirements engineering is to define what needs the stakeholders express: several studies focus on this task [8, 17, 11]. Goal-driven requirements engineering addresses this question by defining goals to be attained during design, and prioritising them considering which stakeholder expressed it, what importance it has to the main goals, and several other criteria.

The elicitation problem is crucial: even in the nuclear context and considering safety rules and regulations that are not to be interpreted, the requirement still have to be translated into expressions in a model for a computer to manipulate them. The elicitation of requirements is therefore needed to ensure a proper correspondence between expressed requirements and their expression in the model. [13] presents a possible use of the DOLCE ontology (from [14]) for requirements elicitation.

652   A. Cornière et al.

3.2   Analysing the Requirements

As most, if not all requirements define an obligation (or an interdiction) for the system, it has been shown by [2, 6, 7, 12, 13] that a modal logic can be defined that allows to treat requirements as logic expressions expressed in first-order deontic logic. From there on, the whole set of requirements can be analysed through formal logic, manipulated and corrected to render the requirements set consistent if needed.

3.3   Modelling Requirements with Ontologies

Ontologies, especially using OWL2, allow for reasoning in direct logic: an ontology designed for requirements analysis is presented in [13]. This model based on goal-driven requirements engineering is thorough and reliable, although it is thought primarily for the design phase of a product's life-cycle.

In the life-cycle of a product family, this presents little problem, as the evolution in requirements are addressed through different versions of the product; the requirements engineering process may then be repeated for each version of the product.

For the context of the nuclear industry, [5] shows the benefits of ontologies in modelling products and uses rule-based models to express business rules, which in the model are similar to requirements.

4   Specificities of a PLM Context in the Nuclear Industry

Modelling requirements for a nuclear plant in a PLM context presents specificities, among which some regarding the scale and complexity of the system, the length of the life-cycle, and the type of requirements considered.

The life-cycle of a nuclear plant, from the beginning of the requirements engineering phase to the end of dismantlement may well exceed a century. During this time-span, advances in the technology as well as experience in the field makes the requirements evolve, as well as the technical solutions available to satisfy them. While works exist regarding the evolution of requirements, they mostly focus on requirements that apply to software systems[4].

A nuclear plant is of large scale: the specifications elaborated through the requirements engineering process apply on billions of parts and systems. All those elements of the product are potentially interacting with each other in non- trivial ways. This makes the system too complex for manually going through the requirement engineering again. One of the characteristic examples is thermodynamic evolution of the reactor: the temperature and pressure inside the reactor can vary slowly in comparison to the speed at which a computer program is usually running.

The requirements on a nuclear plant include safety regulations that specify situations in which the plant has to return to a controlled, stable state when an accidental situation is to arise. This kind of requirements must be satis- fied in any configuration, regardless of the evolutions the requirements and of the maintenance on the plant, and through the evolutions of the plant itself. These requirements typically specify the time acceptable to return in a con- trolled state. As described above, the behaviour of the plant is not trivial, and complex behaviour and business rules may apply to the requirement to lead to the specifications.

To respond to the above-mentioned points, there is a need for a model al- lowing not only to define a coherent set of requirements, but also reference the specifications inside an as-complete-as-possible model of the plant, including what elements of said plant the specifications apply to. This model also must allow the engineers to make requirements evolve. This evolution can be in the form of new requirements being added over time, as well as changes to existing requirements.

5   Proposal of Modelling Approach

5.1   Generic Modelling of Requirements

Models based on ontologies have the expected benefits of completeness of infor- mation, due to the language expressivity, and of embedded intelligence thanks to the reasoning abilities associated with it [5]. There is also a need to model links between a requirement itself and several other elements of the requirements engineering process, namely the logical statements composing it, both premises and conclusions; the reference phrasing of the requirement, be it a legal doc- ument or a rule known by experience; the deontic nature of the requirement, whether an obligation or an interdiction[1]; the specifications they contribute to and information on their validity. These links can be modelled in the form of ob- ject properties, to allow for a diversity of relations between the elements, rather than using classes.

To allow for this, it is necessary that requirements, logical statements, deontic functions, business rules, specifications, etc. are modeled as individuals in several classes[2]. Those classes are not necessarily all disjoint (for example a business rule can also be a requirement), thus making use of the non-canonic representation of data in ontologies.

An example of such a model is given in Fig.1: A requirement is modeled as an individual. Its nature is defined by the link it has (is a) with a member of SDL function, in this case the interdiction function of FOSDL[6]. Its predicate are also identified with object properties (has premise _and has conclusion in this example) and are FOSDL object expressed in RIF[16]. It should contain a data property representing the origin and a verbatim of the reference document it is translated from, for verification.

---

[1] According to [12] and [7] a requirement might also be any function built from obli- gation (O), interdiction (F), necessity ($\Box$), possibility ($\Diamond$) and negation ($\neg$).

[2] The reader should remain aware a class in ontologies is representative of a concept, an open set of individuals, rather than a generator thereof[3].

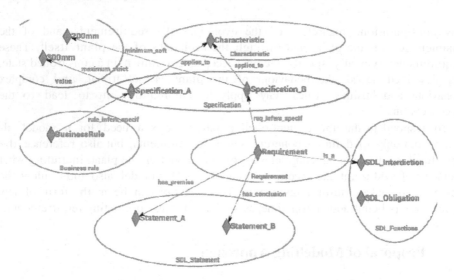

Fig. 1. Schematic representation of the object properties network around a requirement individual: individuals are represented by diamond-shaped symbols, classes by ellipse-shaped regions in the figure

The specifications are also represented as individuals, in their simplest form they link a Value individual to a Characteristic individual thanks to object properties. The choice to model the values themselves as individuals is intended to allow reasoning through the object properties themselves rather than to rely on the data properties, and to open a way for the logic refining of the individuals network, so that individuals can be treated as identical[3].[10]

The links from a Specification to a Value can, propagate the constraint to the characteristic because of the inferences the ontology-based model is capable of. Examples given in Fig.1 are inspired by goal driven requirements engi- neering and represent soft or strict constraints corresponding to soft or functional goals. The Requirement is also mapped to the specifications it infers (through the design phase), in the same way a business rule is mapped to another spec- ification (and may also pair with a requirement, or be composed of statements in the same fashion, links that are not represented on the Fig.1 for clarity). Lastly, the characteristic can be mapped itself to a measured value, completing the path from the formal requirements model, and the physical implementation of the system.

5.2   Case of a Safety Requirement: Physical Separation of Electrical Networks

For the safety of the plant, it is needed that the control system remain functional is case of an incident. This is achievable through a wide array of means, ranging from the protection of the plant's organs to the liability of elements under

---

[3] That is to say, they share the same identity, as 200mm and 20cm.

cir- cumstantial stress. In this part we will present a possible way to model part of the requirement network associated with the physical separation of redundant electrical networks. Let us consider the requirement : "In case of an incident, the plant remains functional".

As stated above, we will represent this requirement as an individual Req 1 in the Requirement class. The premise for this requirement is "in case of an incident" : this premise is modelled as another individual Statement 1 in the SDL statement class. Statement 1 contains in its data properties the men- tion of the source sentence: "In case of an incident" and its translation as a RIF expression, namely occurs(inc,ctxt),Incident(inc),Context(ctxt) with Incident a class to which all incidents belong, and Context the class of contexts for simulation or domain-restricted requirements.

A link (in the form of an object property) is established from Req 1 to Statement 1 so that has premise(Req 1,Statement 1).

In the same fashion, a Statement 2 individual is created in SDL statement. It represents "the plant remains functional" in the above-mentioned requirement, with a RIF rule in the form Context(c),Functional(sys),inContext(sys,c). This rule needs Context to be a class of contexts[4]; Functional is a unitary function (a class defined by axioms) qualifying the functional state of the sys- tem; finally inContext is an object property for evaluation or simulation set-up, describing whether a context applies to a physical individual. An object prop- erty is set so that has conclusion(Req 1,Statement 2). As it is mandatory, Req 1 is also connected with an object property is a to SDL Obligation, in class SDL Function. -

Next step is to describe business rules derived from this requirement. For instance consider the business rule "Redundant electric systems are to be sepa- rated physically". It is a business rule for it is a consequence of a requirement in a certain domain: it applies only to redundant electrical networks.

This business rule will be modelled as an individual BusRule 1, itself con- nected with object properties to SDL statement individuals, that represent it premise (Electric(A),Electric(B),redundantWith(A,B), translating "Re- dundant electric systems") and conclusion (physically separated(A,B), trans- lating "be separated physically").BusRule 1 is also linked with SDL Obligation by a is a property.

As the network is added to the model, more individuals are created : in this case exploring the physically separated object property make apparent the need to define criteria to set or not this property between two objects.

---

[4] In the scope of this work, a context is a subset of the worlds defined by some known circumstances [3, 7]

This approach being individual-oriented, we chose to define the object property through a set of rules, one of them given below.

Location(place1),Location(place2),
is in(A,place1),is in(B,place2),
DifferentIndividuals(A,B),physically separated(place1,place2)
→ physically separated(A,B)

This rule only states that "distinct elements located in physically separated places are physically separated themselves". Such rules reflect the experience and knowledge of the modellers, they are the interface from the requirements engineering to the knowledge management. Another rule can reflect the notion that "elements sufficiently far apart are considered physically separated"[5], with a rule in the form :

Element(A),Element(B),DifferentIndividuals(A,B)
distance(A,B)>FarApart
→ physically separated(A,B)

At the time being however, there is no direct way we know of to quan- tify a binary function (an object property), that is associate a value to a re- lation between individuals. It is not possible to directly use the expression distance(A,B)>FarApart. This is prevented only by the current implementa- tions of the model, that do not yet implement ternary functions; and as this can be worked around modelling the relation, it is not established yet if this solution is acceptable on large-scale models.

6   Conclusions and Perspectives

Using SDL and RIF definition for rules and requirements allows to model them as individuals in an ontology, and to leverage the reasoning abilities associated with the existing models. The simple pegging of requirements to specifications is not sufficient to check for the consistency of a set or requirements, or to verify and infer which requirements constrain each specification, and for which reasons. Doing so requires to introduce into the model more information, reflecting the business experience.

While the modelling of requirements into ontological models still need to be studied, it is a reasonable assumption that the ontological model would need to interact with a knowledge model, as well as a business rule model and a model of the physical system, for consistency check, and to allow for a sufficient mapping between informations that are all used in system engineering. Future works will have to investigate the interfaces between the different models.

---

[5] Any reader familiar with the field of nuclear security may object this rule does not exist. We are well aware of this, and this made-up rule merely serves as an illustration of the limits that may occur because of an ontological modelling. Similar rules do however exist regarding minimal distance between electrical cables, for instance.

Although the global work-flow comes from the requirements and leads to the specifications, a complex system and/or a vaguely formulated requirements imply using knowledge that belongs primarily to the designer : for a model to check or validate on a design selection, the knowledge used to make this choice must be incorporated to this model, in a form that allows for the users to incorporate it themselves, thus effectively making an ontological model the explicit representation of a shared conceptualization[9].

References

1. Cheng, B.H., Atlee, J.M.: Research directions in requirements engineering. In: 2007 Future of Software Engineering, pp. 285–303. IEEE Computer Society (2007)
2. Cholvy, L.: Checking regulation consistency by using sol-resolution. In: Proceedings of the 7th International Conference on Artificial Intelligence and Law, pp. 73–79. ACM (1999)
3. Corniere, A., Fortineau, V., Paviot, T., Lamouri, S.: A concept-based approach to Modeling shared ontology-based models for industrial applications. In: Proceedings of the 19th IFAC World Congress (2014)
4. Ernst, N., Borgida, A., Jureta, I.J., Mylopoulos, J.: An overview of requirements evolution. In: Evolving Software Systems, pp. 3–32. Springer (2014)
5. Fortineau, V., Paviot, T., Lamouri, S.: Improving the interoperability of industrial Information systems with description logic-based models-the state of the art. Computers in Industry 64, 363–375 (2013)
6. Garion,C.: Apports de la logique mathématique en ingénierie des exigences. Ph.D. thesis, Université de Toulouse (2002)
7. Garion, C., Roussel, S., Cholvy, L.: A modal logic for reasoning on consistency and Completeness of regulations (2009)
8. Greenspan, S., Mylopoulos, J., Borgida, A.: Onformal requirements modeling languages: Rml revisited. In: Proceedings of the 16th International Conference on Software Engineering, pp. 135–147. IEEE Computer Society Press (1994)
9. Gruber, T.: Towards principles for the design of ontologies used for knowledge sharing. International Journal of Human Computer Studies 43(5), 907–928 (1995)
10. Guarino, N., Welty, C.: An overview of OntoClean. In: Handbook on Ontologies, pp. 201–220 (2009)
11. Helming, J., Koegel, M., Schneider, F., Haeger, M., Kaminski, C., Bruegge, B., Berenbach, B.: Towards a unified requirements modeling language. In: 2010 Fifth International Workshop on Requirements Engineering Visualization (REV), pp. 53–57. IEEE (2010)
12. Jureta, I.J., Mylopoulos, J., Faulkner, S.: Revisiting the coreontology and problem in requirements engineering. In: 16th IEEE International Requirements Engineering, RE 2008, pp. 71–80. IEEE (2008)
13. Jureta, I.J., Mylopoulos, J., Faulkner, S.: Acoreontology for requirements. Applied Ontology 4(3), 169–244 (2009)
14. Masolo, C., Borgo, S., Gangemi, A., Guarino, N., Oltramari, A., Oltramari, R., Schneider, L., Istc-Cnr, L.P., Horrocks, I.: Wonderweb deliverable d17. The wonder- web library of foundational ontologies and the dolce ontology (2002)
15. OMG:Sysmlv1.3 (2012), http://www.omg.org/spec/SysML/1.3
16. W3C: Rifcoredialect (2013), http://www.w3.org/TR/rif-core/
17. Zave, P., Jackson, M.: Four dark corners of requirements engineering. ACM Transactions on Software Engineering and Methodology (TOSEM) 6(1), 1–30 (1997)

Toward Manufacturing System Composability Analysis: A Use Case Scenario

Boonserm (Serm) Kulvatunyou, Evan Wallace, Nenad Ivezic, and Yunsu Lee

Systems Integration Division, NIST, Gaithersburg, USA
{serm,ewallace,nivezic,yun-su.lee}@nist.gov

Abstract. Smart manufacturing system will be able to quickly adapt to new and changing requirements, implying that software and hardware components of the manufacturing system need to be easily recomposed. In addition, provision of software applications and components is trending toward distributed, heterogeneous, and cloud-based. However, engineers who need to compose a software system will have difficulty finding and using software components with the right functionality and compatibility without a standard to describe these software components. This paper identifies the need for a reference functional ontology to provide a common way to describe a software component functionality. Such an ontology would lead towards the needed standard to describe the software components. The objective of this paper is to discuss high-level requirements for such a functional ontology and provide an initial use case to illustrate how the functional ontology may enable composability analysis.

Keywords: computer integrated manufacturing, service-oriented manufacturing systems, industrial automation, smart manufacturing, functional ontology.

1 Introduction

Smart manufacturing (SM) systems are characterized by the ability to quickly adapt to new and changing requirements induced by disruptions and disturbances [1]. For this reason, SM systems are expected to be dynamically composed from network-connected devices and software components. This would allow SM systems to gather and analyze data from these devices and software components and adapt themselves to respond to disruptions and disturbances [2, 3].

The ability to dynamically compose software components is complicated by the proliferation of network-connected devices (also known as Internet of Things) and the increasingly available software in cloud marketplaces such as Oracle Marketplace, SAP HANA Marketplace, and Nimbis Marketplace[1]. With such marketplaces, virtually any individual can develop and provision software components. Such an open market environment will create heterogeneous, yet overlapping offerings of software

---

[1] https://cloud.oracle.com/marketplace;
http://marketplace.saphana.com/;
https://www.nimbisservices.com/marketplace/

B. Grabot et al. (Eds.): APMS 2014, Part II, IFIP AICT 439, pp. 658–666, 2014.

components in terms of their functionalities (the things components can do) and compatibility (the technical and pragmatic aspects of components that affect how they can work together). To effectively deal with such heterogeneity we propose to develop a reference functional ontology that leads to a standard that will facilitate common understanding of software component offerings. The objective of this paper is to outline requirements and methodology to develop such a reference functional ontology. Through a use case illustration, the paper demonstrates the application of the ontology to composability analyses and identifies future research direction.

Composability analysis supports the finding and evaluation of components that can be functionally and technically combined to perform a desired task. We envision that tools and methods for composability analysis will be developed to assist system and software engineers in composing SM systems. This analysis may also provide additional information, such as identification of additional components necessary for their interoperation.

For the purpose of clarity, we introduce a few working definitions of essential concepts that will be used in the rest of the paper. Components can be either software or hardware; however, for this initial investigation, this paper focuses only on software components. In this research, service orientation [5] is adopted as a predominant paradigm for manufacturing system composition. That is, software components expose their functionalities through services. For this reason, service is the focal point in the rest of the paper (rather than component).

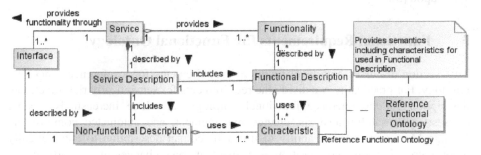

Fig. 1. A service-oriented concept diagram

Fig. 1 illustrates the concepts related to service that will be used in the rest of the paper. A service provides functionalities. Functionality is the ability to do things that is described by a functional description. Functional description (e.g., validate engineering change order) is typically included in the service description that also includes other technical details and constraints (e.g., message exchange pattern, communication and security protocols) about how to access the service through an interface. We label these technical details non-functional description. Functional and non-functional descriptions are described with a set of characteristics that are essentially a set of properties. In this paper, we stress the importance of the functional description part that is much less developed than the non-functional description part (although both should be formalized). Therefore a reference functional ontology should be developed that provides characteristics or properties for the functional description.

In the following sections, we briefly introduce the service-orientation. Then, high-level requirements for the ontology are provided in the form of competency questions. We outline the vision of how the ontology should be developed and maintained. Finally, an integration use case which illustrates the usage of a reference functional ontology is provided before giving the conclusion and describing future work.

2   Service Orientation

For software components to work together, the trend is to allow access to *functions* provided by these software components as services (hence a service can be viewed as a wrapper of a function or functions). This trend has accelerated recently with the arrival of cloud computing, which virtualizes computing and communication resources. That is, service consumers do not need to know how service providers offer their services – from where, by which, or by how many software components.

The service-oriented paradigm is essential to enable SM systems as it emphasizes visibility and semantics that enable (1) matching between needs and functionalities, and (2) composition of service functionalities to address those needs. The visibility and semantics are enabled by service descriptions and service contracts that capture the essential information the service consumers and providers need to be aware of and agree upon [5].

3   Functional Requirements for Functional Ontology

This section discusses high-level functional requirements for a reference functional ontology. For practicality, we divide the requirements for semantically rich functional description via the reference functional ontology into three increasingly-capable classes: composability analysis, change management, and automated composition. Change Management is the ability to use a functional description to automatically reconfigure an existing composition as a result of some changes in the participants. While some of the related works described earlier such as OWL-S aimed at automated composition, our goal is first set upon the composability analysis. For that specific goal, requirements for a reference functional ontology can be expressed with the following competency questions [4].

1. Does a provider's service functionality semantically match, at least partially, the functionality desired by the service consumer's goal?
2. Are the service's non-functional characteristics desired by the service consumer compatible with those of a provider's service, and if not what are the incompatibilities? (The non-functional characteristics include communication protocols, security constraints, pre-conditions, processing capacity, etc.)

4   Vision for Functional Ontology Development

Manufacturing is a large domain, even when considering only software functionalities and not hardware functionalities. In the ISA-95 manufacturing system control architecture [6], functionalities can range from process, sensor, equipment, cell, plant to enterprise levels. They can also vary by industries, types of processes, and products. Top-down, closed-effort ontology development has not prevailed; in the past decade, bottom-up, collaborative ontology development has garnered increased interest. This trend is notable from the following efforts. Linked Data (also known as Linked Open Data or LOD) [7] allows Web documents, Web data, and Web ontology to be linked, annotated, and queried in a structured way. FreeBase is a Web-based open platform that allows the publication of a Web ontology[2]. One of the most popular Web ontology development environments[3] has recently developed the Web version of the tool for collaborative ontology development.

Ontology development should be moving to include a significant bottom-up component [8]. Work in other industries have started to address this need, as reference models are developed to be tailored and/or extended for use by stakeholders [10].   In one of our past works [9], a framework is outlined for evolving a reference model for manufacturing capability information by applying structural canonicalization and semantic gap analysis methods using design patterns and inputs from proprietary models. Such a framework needs to be adapted for the reference functional ontology development.

5   Use Case Illustration of Composability Analysis

This section presents an integration use case as an initial illustration of the composability analysis idea using the envisioned functional ontology (the elements of the functional ontology are shown in italics throughout the tables in this section). The intention is to inspire further research rather than to provide a solution here. The use case sets the stage for gathering, analysis, and validation of requirements for the functional ontology.   Ultimately, we will be harvesting this and other use cases to identify the requirements.   In the paper, we focus on showing the use of the envisioned functional ontology.   The intended use of ontology terms are shown in the relationships and constraints supporting composability analysis (see tables in this section).   To enable ontology-based composability analysis, these relationships and constraints will be formalized as ontology axioms in future work, supported by an analysis of required representation and reasoning framework [11].

The industry use case is based on the need to streamline the engineering change management (ECM) process which may be composed as part of other larger processes such as a regular design update process and product fault monitoring process. It is also driven by the change in a company's applications landscape. Let's assume that a company initially only had a manufacturing application, namely MA, to manage

---

[2]   See http://www.freebase.org
[3]   See http://protegewiki.stanford.edu/wiki/WebProtege

product data for design and manufacturing. At this point, the ECM process is *stream-lined* within MA. Later on, the company purchased a new application to manage the whole product life cycle information, namely PLMA. PLMA expanded product data management functionality to track not only as-designed and as-manufactured product data but also as-maintained data. The company decided to use PLMA as the master application for product data management. Therefore, PLMA needs to be integrated with MA in order for the ECM process to be *streamlined* again.

In the first step of the integration, a high-level integration process is captured as part of the requirement documentation. Part of the process is illustrated through the UML sequence diagram in Fig. 2.

It should be noted that because this is an existing process, all the relevant functio-nalities and associated logic are known, i.e., there is no composition to create a new functionality in this case. Therefore, only the information necessary to invoke services with those functionalities on the MA side and the information necessary to inform PLMA of the result need to be identified (as opposed to the case when the integration involves building a new functionality wherein information necessary to achieve the new functionality is also necessary to be identified). It is determined that the Engi-neering Change Order (ECO) entity/object supports all the information necessary to both invoke the functionality on the MA and PLMA systems.

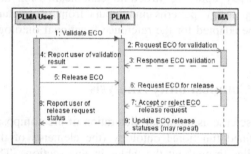

Fig. 2. UML sequence diagram of the integration requirement

Table 1. PLMA and MA native services

PLMA native service	MA native service
Export ECO outbound	Process ECO inbound
Import ECO inbound	Process ECO response out-bound

For a composability analysis, details of required services from each application are derived from the integration process requirement. Examples of service requirements are summarized in the last column on the right of Table 2 and Table 3[4] (the first col-umn indicates the characteristics of the service). The functional ontology should sup-port representation of this service requirement. It should be noted that only few cha-racteristics of the services are illustrated here. Additional characteristics will need to be modeled such as supported transmission protocol and other essential functional

---

[4] Note that only application to application interactions are accounted for. Also, we assume the following mapping from Fig 2 terminology to the last column of Table 2 and Table 3 terminology: Release → Create and Update → Notify. This mapping reflects presumed different terminologies used in integration and service requirements identification stages.

characteristics. Essential characteristics are artifacts that are expected to evolve over time as demanded by the users of services and the technological evolution.

Table 1 illustrates PLMA's and MA's native services. These are existing services on the two applications that need to be adapted to the service requirements. In a (service-oriented) smart manufacturing system environment, the service descriptions of these native services should be registered in a commonly accessible registry using the reference functional ontology to describe their functionalities. This is illustrated in the second column of Table 2 and Table 3[5]. These tables contain a row for each of the

Table 2. Composability analysis of PLMA services

Service Characteristic	PLMA's native service registration	Δ	PLMA Required service
Service	Export ECO outbound ⊃ *Validate ECO request outbound*	√	*Validate ECO request outbound*
List Oper	Y	≥	N
MEP	*Request Only*	√	*Request Only*
Msg	plmaECO ⊃ (*Validate ECO ∪ Validate ECO Response ∪ Create ECO ∪ Create ECO Response ∪ Engineering Change Notice*)	≥	*Validate ECO*

Table 3. Composability analysis of MA services

Service Characteristics	MA's native service registration	Δ	MA Required service
Service	Process ECO inbound [@action = 'simulate'] = *Validate ECO request inbound*	√	*Validate ECO request inbound*
List Oper	Y	≥	N
MEP	*Request Only*	√	*Request Only*
Msg	maECO ⊃ (*Validate ECO ∪ Validate ECO Response ∪ Create ECO ∪ Create ECO Response ∪ Engineering Change Notice*)	≥	*Validate ECO*
Service	Process ECO response outbound [@action = 'notify'] = *Notify ECO outbound*	√	*Notify ECO outbound*
List Oper	Y	≥	N
MEP	*Async Request Response ∥ Request Only*	≥	*Request Only*
Msg	maECO ⊃ (*Validate ECO ∪ Validate ECO Response ∪ Create ECO ∪ Create ECO Response ∪ Engineering Change Notice*)	≥	*Create ECO*

---

[5] In this paper, we do not attempt to formalize any semantics of relationships between services and characteristics including the relationships in the Δ column.

services needed from the components in focus for the ECM process in our example. Below each service row are 3 more rows that describe characteristics of the interface provided by the component to support the service. The first of these rows indicates whether the service supports or requires list operations (List Oper). The second row indicates the kind of message exchange pattern (MEP) supported or needed. The final interface row describes the type of message (Msg) supported by the service.

The second column of each of these tables is used to describe native services provided by the components. The description in this column identifies the particular service variant used, the message used to carry information for the service; and then maps these to descriptions created from elements of a reference functional ontology. The elements of the ontology are italicized for clarity. A $\supset$ indicates that the native component element provides a superset of (i.e., subsumes) the content or functionality required. The fourth column contains a description of the required service as defined in the ECM process. The Δ (third) column shows the relationships between the description of the registered native service in column 2 and that of the required service for each characteristic (in column 4). Two symbols are used to indicate the relationship. A '$\sqrt{}$' indicates that the native service or interface element can satisfy the required service or interface element. A '$\geq$' indicates that the native component has greater capability than needed but can be made to match the element.

Taking the service registration in Table 2 as an example, the first two columns indicate that the Export ECO outbound native service functionally subsumes the Validate ECO request outbound service; it is a list operation (List Oper), it supports the Request Only MEP; and its message definition (Msg), plmaECO, subsumes several messages including Validate ECO, Validate ECO Response, Create ECO, etc. In the Δ column, the '$\sqrt{}$' relationship on the Service row indicates that the Export ECO outbound native service and the Validate ECO request outbound matches; the '$\geq$' in the List Oper row indicates that the native service is more capable than the required service; the '$\sqrt{}$' in the MEP row indicates that the native service matches with the required service and no adaptation is necessary; and the '$\geq$' in the Msg row indicates that the message definition of the native service is more capable than that of the required service.

With these relationships established, the composability can be assessed. Firstly, the relationships between the Services and between the MEPs indicate that the native service can be directly piped into the required service without adaptation. Secondly, the required service does not need the list operation capability which means that there is no chunking or de-chunking required (in the mediator component that connects the PLMA with the MA service). Lastly, the fact that plmaECO subsumes the Validate ECO indicates that there will be adaptation needed – data transformation.

With the native service registration described in terms of the reference ontology, we expect that the relationship can be automatically determined. Determination of the relationship of some service characteristics will be more involved than others. For example, evaluating the relationship between messages of two services will generally require detailed semantic mapping analysis or semantic distance measurements.

The composability analysis should also be automatable. The algorithm will be specific to each service characteristic because of the differences in their underlying semantics. To enable such automation, additional semantics associated with expressing the integration requirement (e.g., required services) will need to be modeled. For example, although the List Oper row of the last service in Table 3 has the same information as that in the service in Table 2, de-chunking in the mediator may be necessary in the former case, while it may not be necessary in the latter. This is because, in the former case, it may not be controllable at MA to send the notification for a single ECO at a time as this is an existing automated process, while in the latter case it may be the integration behavior that the design engineer will send a single ECO at a time for validation purposes.

6   Conclusion and Future Work

This paper proposes development of a reference functional ontology. The hypothesis is that the availability of such an ontology will allow for more efficient and effective manufacturing system composition. The ontology is expected to be evolving; and hence, new development mechanisms have to also be developed. The purpose of the reference functional ontology is to allow for expressive descriptions of service's functionalities. The reference functional ontology along with other reference ontologies for non-functional characteristics will enable composability analysis of services as illustrated in a use case scenario of engineering change management integration. The use case provides an initial substantiation of the composability analysis idea. In terms of future work, we plan to develop more use cases, especially those that involve lower level manufacturing control functions (in the ISA-95 layers) and those that involve hardware equipment. High-level concepts in the reference functional ontology are being developed; and encoding of ISA-95 and the SIMA reference activities into the ontology is also being experimented with. In order to precisely encode the ontology, we will formally define key concepts, such as composition, and develop measurement methods and metrics for the composability analysis.

Disclaimer
Any mention of commercial products is for information only; it does not imply recommendation or endorsement by NIST.

References

1. SMLC, Implementing 21st century smart manufacturing, Workshop summary (2011)
2. Pellet, J.: Lessons learned from chief executive's manufacturing summit. Chief Executive Magazine (July/August 2013)
3. Floerkemeier, C., Langheinrich, M., Fleisch, E., Mattern, F., Sarma, S.E. (eds.): IOT 2008. LNCS, vol. 4952. Springer, Heidelberg (2008)
4. Gruninger, M., Fox, M.: The role of competency questions in enterprise engineering. In: Proc. of the IFIP WG5.7, pp. 212–221 (1994)
5. OASIS Reference Model for Service Oriented Architecture 1.0

6. ANSI/ISA-95 (IEC 62264) Enterprise-Control System Integration - Part 1:2010, Part 2:2010, Part 3: 2013, Part 4:2012, Part 5:2013
7. Bizer, C., et al.: Linked Data—The Story So Far. International Journal on Semantic Web and Information Systems 5(3), 1–22 (2009)
8. Recommendations for implementing the strategic initiative INDUSTRIE 4.0. Securing the future of German manufacturing industry. Acatech, Germany (2013)
9. Lee, Y., Peng, Y.: A Framework for Developing Manufacturing Service Capability Information Model. In: Prabhu, V., Taisch, M., Kiritsis, D. (eds.) APMS 2013, Part I. IFIP AICT, vol. 414, pp. 325–333. Springer, Heidelberg (2013)
10. CISCO Systems, Inc. Introduction to eTOM – White Paper
11. Fiorentini, X., et al.: An Analysis of Description Logic Augmented with Domain Rules for the Development of Product Models. Journal of Computing and Information Science in Engineering 10(2) (2010)

Hospital Planning Environment Variables Applied in Practice: A Multiple Danish Case Study

Vivi Thuy Nguyen[1], Anita Friis Sommer[2], Kenn Steger-Jensen[1],
and Hans Henrik Hvolby[1]

[1] Department of Mechanical and Manufacturing Engineering, Aalborg University, Denmark
{vivi,kenn,hhh}@m-tech.aau.dk
[2] Department of Engineering, University of Cambridge, UK
afs35@cam.ac.uk

Abstract. The issue of hospital planning has taken a central position in increasing hospital performance. Applied hospital planning methods are found to be misaligned with hospital environments in existing research. Thus, it is relevant to increase the understanding of hospital environment variables in order to improve applied hospital planning methods. In this paper, we identify and describe the hospital environment and applied planning methods from an environment variables perspective through an in-depth case study of three Danish hospital environments and their corresponding adaptive planning frameworks. The results include suggestions for further research on improving the match between identified environment variables and the corresponding planning methods.

Keywords: Hospital environment variables, hospital planning, case study.

1 Introduction

During the previous decade, public healthcare expenditures in Western European countries have increased drastically, especially in secondary healthcare providers, i.e. hospitals. Due to this large share of total expenditures the issue of hospital planning and control has taken a central position in increasing hospital performance. Existing hospital planning frameworks have been inspired by manufacturing planning and control [1] [2] [3]. In hospital industry, the patient flow is important and is not the same as the material flow[4]. Hence, the planning and control of the two environments will be different. Thus, it is relevant to conduct empirical evaluations of hospital planning and control approaches in the relation to the planning environment of a hospital. This papers objective is to describe the current planning processes based on case studies with the purpose of identifying and understanding the hospitals planning environmental variables in relation to planning and control. From previous research, we have identified planning environmental variables for the hospital industry, which can be grouped into three category, namely: patient, resources, and process [4]. Thus, this paper will identify the hospital environment and applied planning methods from an environment variables perspective through an in-depth case study of three Danish hospital environments and their corresponding adaptive planning frameworks.

B. Grabot et al. (Eds.): APMS 2014, Part II, IFIP AICT 439, pp. 667–674, 2014.
© IFIP International Federation for Information Processing 2014

2   Method

An in-depth multiple case study approach has been conducted comprising a total of three case studies [1] from different departments in two Danish Hospitals:
1.   The department of Heart-Lung Surgery (case 1),
2.   The department of ear and throat cancer treatment (case 2),
3.   The emergency department (case 3).

Both hospitals are large hospitals with a bed capacity of 929 beds and 482 beds respectively. The cases were chosen from different hospital processes to identify the variety in the processes of the operations within similar applied planning frameworks, but within the same country and regional setting to avoid cultural environmental effects [5]. Data on environmental variables was derived primarily through interviews, conducted using a semi-structured interview guide. The environmental variables were identified through previous research study [4]. Furthermore, the applied planning framework was identified through a triangulation between results from the interview study, the formal planning framework of the case, and the requirements of the planning forecasting software applied in each case respectively. The total amount of interviews was 72 divided among the three cases, which is presented in Table 1.

Table 1. Overview of conducted interviews during the multiple case study

Interviewees/Case	Case 1	Case 2	Case 3
Patients	7	3	13
Lab staff		3	2
Nurses	7	2	4
Administration/secretary	5	3	2
Special Doctors	2	4	12
General Practitioner			2
Ambulance assistants			1

Each interview lasted approximately one hour and, in addition, a total of 10 1-hour observation studies were conducted to observe the hospital processes in practice. All interviews were recorded, whenever possible, and notes were made during each session, followed by development of extensive summaries of each interview. Afterwards, recordings were transcribed and compared to the notes, and then analyzed using pattern matching and grouping of variables in a conceptually ordered display according to the procedures outlined by Yin[5],[6], [7].

3   Hospital Environment Planning Variables

The 3 case descriptions are structured according to the identified hospital environmental variable groups, explaining firstly the patients, secondly the resources, and thirdly the hospital process. The variables will be described in relation to their involvement in applied planning methods.

3.1   Case 1 - Surgery

Case 1 mainly performs surgical interventions after the treatment therapy of *the patient* has been determined. The department collaborates with other departments of the Clinical Center of Heart and Lung in determining a pathway of diagnosis and treatment of patients with heart and lung problems. Whenever, surgical intervention is needed to heart or lungs, the patient becomes the department's responsibility. In order manage and plan facilities and resources to job task, the patients are categorized based on their medical profile, where weekly surgery plans are made for only elective patients. The department has seven medical profile groups; four medical groups with heart specialty and three medical groups with lung specialty. However, prioritizing patients in the sequence of surgeries, the medical urgency is classified into emergent, urgent, and elective patients. Table 2 presents the classification of the patients;

Table 2. Patient group variables in case 1

Patient groups		Medical profile complexity	Planning time frame	Patient volume
Heart	Emergent	High	Short	Low
patients	Urgent	High	Medium	Low
	Elective	High	Long	Medium
Lung	Emergent	High	Short	Low
patients	Urgent	High	Medium	Medium
	Elective	High	Long	Medium

The *hospital resources* are classified for execution purposes, except for doctors, who are classified in order to match patients' medical profile and patient urgency to the right competences in the planning activity. Doctors are classified as either clinical or research doctors, and according to level of experience. Operating theatre nurses are divided into assistance nurses, direct nurses, and a coordinator nurse. The coordination nurse along with doctors are responsible for coordinating and changing plans of the operations activity, informing the patient's condition for preparation and share and align the information with anesthesia staff and other staff from different parts of the hospital. All activities are coordinated through frequent meetings during the day due to regular changes and disruptions.

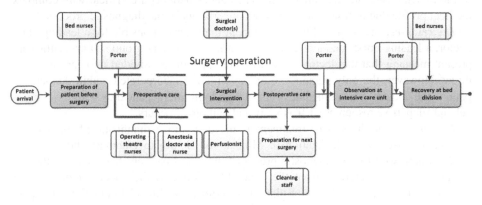

Fig. 1. Process flow in case 1

The *process* in the department mainly focus on the therapy phase, where there exist three entries for a patient to enter the department based on several gatekeepers or tiers in the hospital, which are Ambulatory of heart and lung, the Emergency Department, Cardiology, and Lung Medical department (in the clinical center). The elective patient can either come from the bed division or come from home before the surgery. A pre-operative process is organized to prepare the patient for the surgery by operating nurses, where the patient will be checked to make sure that their condition is as expected and medical supply will be prepared and checked before for the surgery. The surgical doctor, anesthesia doctor, and perfusionists will be involved during the surgical intervention until the end at postoperative care. After surgery the patient is transported to the intensive care unit for observation, thereafter the patient will return to the bed division for recovery. The process is depicted in Figure 1.

3.2   Case 2 – Diagnostic of Cancer

Case 2 is the Ear-, Nose- and Throat-department, treating ear and throat cancer particularly in the diagnostic phase. The department has classified *the patient* into three groups as depicted in Table 3.

Table 3. Patient group variables in case 2.

Patient groups	Medical profile complexity	Planning time frame	Patient volume
Emergency patient	High	Short	Low
Cancer patient	High	Short	Medium
Routine patients	Low	Long	High

Emergency patients are the most critical and are categorized as a highly complex medical profile. These patients are treated as fast as possible, whereas the volume of these patients are lowest, which is called a rush order in manufacturing terminology. The routine patients have a less critical medical profile, which gives the department a longer planning time frame. The volume of the routine patients is approximately 90% of the patients entering the department. The cancer patients are critical with complex medical profile due to time frame and high uncertainty in the diagnostic process.

The resources are managed by a department manager responsible for a leading chief doctor, a leading nurse, and a coordinator. Within the doctors group sub-specialties are present meaning that the doctors have different capabilities, divided into ear, nose and throat. However, the only planning resource, which is incorporated within the activity plan, is the doctors' work schedule, even though high interdependency with the personnel and supportive resources such as x-ray and pathology occurs.

The process of the cancer treatment is divided into a diagnostic phase and the treatment phase by the legislation of Minister of Health in Denmark, however the focus is narrowed to the diagnostic process flow The treatment begins when the department receives referrals from the general practitioner, the specialist doctors, or other departments, and a first consultation is required within 72 hours. Once the path coordinator books the first patient appointment, all the following consultations and therapy processes are booked in advance to make sure that they meet the service goal from legislation. Even though, forecasts are essential, they are based solely on subjective opinions and historical views of the calendar. Thus, in order to ensure available times, the path coordinator reserves time slots for patients in advance, approximately two months beforehand and then they reschedule continuously. During the first consultation, biopsies are taken in order to diagnose the type kind of cancer the patient might have. Based on the medical profile and examination, the doctors will design the treatment plan in the diagnostic phase for the patient. The biopsies are sent to the pathological department for analysis and they have a permitted analysis time of five days. Most patients have to get scanned, MRI, CT or PET-CT scanner, which have an analysis frame of no more than two days. As the pathological deadline is the longest, the patient must wait for this result and come back five days later for a second consultation to be informed of the results. If a complex biopsy is required at the first consultation, the patient has a slightly different flow. The patient is put in full anesthesia and transported to the operation theatre of the department, where the biopsy is taken. After wake-up, the patient is sent home with an appointment for the second consultation. A generic view of the process is presented in Figure 2.

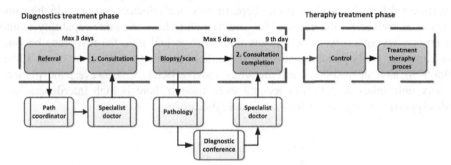

Fig. 2. Process flow in case 2

3.3   Case 3 - Emergency

Case 3 is the Emergency Department (ED) responsible for *accident and emergent patients*. The ED is a medical treatment facility specializing in acute care of patients without prior appointments, who come in either by their own means or by ambulance. Moreover, ED manages almost all hospital incoming patients and creates the opportunity to discharge patients more efficiently. The length of stay at the ED is maximum 48 hours, where other departments in the hospital need to take the patient into care afterwards otherwise a discharge will occur. This enhances the incentives to collaborate among departments of the hospital, integrate their plans with each other, and speeding the diagnostics process within the emergency department. In order to accommodate the variety of incoming patients the department has categorized the patients based on the triage-categorization as illustrated in Table 4. The triage-categorization is based on the planning time frame of medical urgency. If the patient is the triage color red then they are treated immediately in the trauma section. If the patient is orange or yellow and have to wait they are referred to the waiting section. The same is present with the green and blue triage colors. The department chief forecasts the volume of incoming patient types, which is used to estimate the peak of incoming patients every day and create an overlap between morning shift and day shift in order to accommodate the volume of patients.

Table 4. Patient group variables in case 3

Triage-Patient	Medical profile complexity	Planning time frame	Patient volume (% of total)
Red	High	Zero	1 %
Orange	High	15 min	10 %
Yellow	Medium	60 min	13 %
Green	Low	120 min	26 %
Blue	Low	N/A	50 %

The chief of the department, the nurse coordinator, and the administration manager manage the department's *resources*. Each of these is responsible for doctors, nurses and secretaries respectively. From the resource capability perspective, the emergency department differs from other special departments as all doctors can provide the same job task, as well as for the nurses. They are trained to have the same capability within the emergency specialty, which means that manage and plan the resources become less complex. Daily planning consists of frequent meetings with all involved stakeholders to allocate resources and facilities most efficiently. However, the planned activity only takes doctors into account even though there is high interdependency with supportive resources such as x-ray and laboratory.

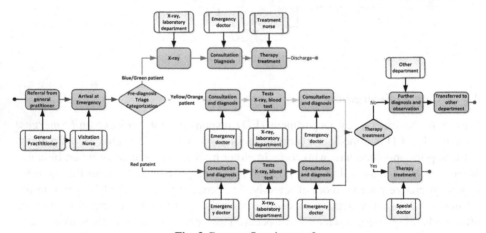

Fig. 3. Process flow in case 3

Figure 3 shows *the process*, which begins when patients are referred to the ED by practitioners in the office hours and by doctor from the emergency services outside office hours. The patient is then placed in a triage category (red, orange, yellow, green and blue) by a visitation nurse based on the information from practitioner's referral and examination of the patient. If, the ED can provide therapy treatment, the patient can go home afterwards. If, on the other hand, observation of the patient is necessary, the patient will be transferred to the emergency bed division. During the process the ED interacts with different supporting resources such as X-ray, laboratories, and other special departments. Therefore, a need for close collaboration and integration with plans with others unity is necessary to provide efficient health care service in the ED.

4   Discussion

The analysis indicates several challenges regarding planning and control of incoming patients and resources. The cases are different in patient requirement, resource availability, and process flow. It indicates that there does not exist a silver bullet approach for hospital planning and control. Thus, a more patient oriented approach such as differentiated planning and control is needed. The process flow of case 1 shows, the focus should be predicting the lead time, since this is the most critical element. Time is also critical in case 2. Hence, the process flow shows that it is important to be within the estimated lead time otherwise postponement will occur for other planned surgeries in line. The process in case 3 is very different from the other two cases, since it has the least linear process flow. Therefore, the focus here relies on short timeframe, patient predictability, and fast determination of resource requirement for incoming patients. Thus, Case 3 planning environment requires flexibility and agility in the planning in order to accommodate the different type of patients.

All three cases deal with the high complexity, high variability, and high uncertainty, especially within patient variables. The high uncertainty increases the risk of induced changes and disruptions in the process affecting other patients negatively [8], unless appropriate approaches of dealing with uncertainty occur. To accommodate for the uncertainty, all three cases use large time slots, slack time, and frequent meetings for both information sharing, coordination, and re-scheduling. Furthermore, all three cases use simple planning methods, which only include elective patients, even though historical data is stored for use in more reliable planning methods. Thus, we suggest that *'applied hospital planning can be significantly improved through incorporation of existing patient variables and historic data in hospital planning methods'*.

Resource constraints are one of the cornerstones in hospital planning [9]. Despite interdependencies between limited resources, none of the three cases' planning approaches acknowledge the diversity of involved resource types beyond doctors, which frequently stresses the system and involved staff with overload of job tasks. Thus, we propose that *'under- capacity of limited resource types is enhanced or even generated by lack of incorporation of relevant resources in hospital planning.'* Based on this proposition, we call for further research on incorporation of all necessary interdependent resource types into hospital planning methods.

Finally, the process variables are neglected in similar ways in planning at all three cases, predicting and planning only on simple process flows and without iterations due to emergent changes regarding patient conditions or interdependencies to support processes. To compensate there active planning approach, there occur several coordination meetings during the day. This approach, however, leads to frequently re-planning and re-scheduling which is time consuming for multiple resources. Thus, we propose that *'deterministic processes are unsuitable for adapted hospital planning due to the degree of emergent changes and continuous iterations related to dynamic patient variables.'* Thus, we recommend further research clarifying the appropriateness of process design and performance measures in different planning environments in hospitals.

5   Conclusion

The aim of this paper is to increase understanding of hospital environment variables in order to improve applied hospital planning methods. We have identified and described the hospital environment and applied planning methods from an environment variables perspective through an in-depth case study of three Danish hospital environments and their corresponding adaptive planning frameworks. It indicates that several challenges regarding planning and control of incoming patients and resource, where further suggestion might be in a direction of a more patient oriented approach such as differentiated planning and control. All three cases use simple planning methods, which only include elective patients, even though historical data is stored for use in more reliable planning methods. Thus, large time slots, slack time, and frequent meetings for information sharing, coordination, and re-scheduling are necessary in order to overcome the uncertainty of patient planning. The results include suggestions for further research on improving the match between identified environment variables and the corresponding planning methods and framework.

References

1. Roth, A.V., Van Dierdonck, R.: Hospital Resource Planning: Concepts, Feasibility, and Framework. Prod. Oper. Manag. 4, 2–29 (1995)
2. Vissers, J.M.H., Bertrand, J.W.M., De Vries, G.: A framework for production control in health care organizations. Prod. Plan. Control. 12, 591–604 (2001)
3. Hans, E.W., Houdenhoven, M.V., Hulshof, P.J.: A framework for health care planning and control, vol. 168, pp. 303–320. Springer, N. Y. (2011)
4. Nguyen, V.T., Sommer, A.F., Steger-Jensen, K., Hvolby, H.H.: The misalignment between hospital planning frameworks and their planning environment – A conceptual matching approach. In: Grabot, B., Vallespir, B., Gomes, S., Bouras, A., Kiritsis, D. (eds.) APMS 2014. IFIP AICT, vol. 439, pp. 675–682. Springer, Heidelberg (2014)
5. Arbnor, I., Bjerke, B.: Methodology for creating business knowledge. SAGE, Los Angeles (2009)
6. Yin, R.K.: Case study research: Design and methods. Sage (2009)
7. Auerbach, C.F., Silverstein, L.B.: Qualitative data: An introduction to coding and analysis. NYU Press (2003)
8. Adan, I.J.B.F., Vissers, J.M.H.: Patient mix optimisation in hospital admission planning: a case study. Int. J. Oper. Prod. Manag. 22, 445–461 (2002)
9. Blake, J.T., Carter, M.W.: A goal programming approach to strategic resource allocation in acute care hospitals. Eur. J. Oper. Res. 140, 541–561 (2002)

The Misalignment between Hospital Planning Frameworks and their Planning Environment – A Conceptual Matching Approach

Vivi Thuy Nguyen[1], Anita Friis Sommer[2],
Kenn Steger-Jensen[1], and Hans-Henrik Hvolby[1]

[1] Department of Mechanical and Manufacturing Engineering, Aalborg University, Denmark
`(vivi,kenn,hhh)@m-tech.aau.dk`
[2] Department of Engineering, University of Cambridge, UK
`afs35@cam.ac.uk`

Abstract. Scientifically developed hospital planning frameworks have emerged during the last decade to support and prescribe planning and control practice in hospitals. The three presented frameworks are generally based on manufacturing planning and control frameworks attuned for manufacturing environments. This is critical to the adaptability of the frameworks, since manufacturing environments are focused on optimization of repetitive production processes whereas hospital processes are characterised by complex problem-solving processes with a high degree of uncertainty. In this paper, we identify and describe the misalignment from an environment variables perspective through analysis and comparison of three prominent hospital planning frameworks and hospital planning variables derived from empirical studies in existing research.

Keywords: Hospital planning frameworks, hospital planning and control, planning and control frameworks, hospital environment, conceptual matching.

1 Introduction

Inspired from manufacturing industry, scholars from the field of operations management have proposed several frameworks for effective and efficient hospital planning. However, the planning environment of a hospital is different from the planning environment of a manufacturing company, and since research on hospital planning and control is a relatively new research area, little empirical evidence currently supports the applicability of planning and control frameworks in a hospital environment. Thus, the purpose of this paper is to conduct evaluations of adapted frameworks for hospital planning and control in relation to the planning environment of hospitals.

Hence, the main focus of this paper is the relation between the planning environment and the planning framework used for hospital planning in practice. Jonsson and Mattson [1] used a similar analysis between planning environment and planning methods in manufacturing environments both empirically and conceptually. However, this paper will only focus on the conceptual matching between planning frameworks and planning environment, where the reasoning is that the planning environment and

B. Grabot et al. (Eds.): APMS 2014, Part II, IFIP AICT 439, pp. 675–682, 2014.

planning framework must be aligned and match in order to derive value from the planning methods in practice. Based on this notion, the three dominant planning frameworks for hospitals are first presented followed by identification of hospital environment variables through existing research. Afterwards, the appropriateness of the planning frameworks in the hospital environment is conceptually explained.

2   Conceptual Frameworks for Hospital Planning and Control

During the last decade several hospital planning and control frameworks have been proposed, many of which are based on or heavily inspired by frameworks from production planning and control scholar, like Hax and Meal [2], Silver et al [3], and Vollman [4]. Through a broad literature review, three predominant frameworks have been found to highlight the variety between existing frameworks, and are also the most academically recognized; Roth & Van Dierdonck [5], Vissers et al.[6], and Hans et al. [7]. These frameworks have inspired researchers within the field to structure the scope of research studies such as literature reviews [5], adaption to different areas of health care [6] [7] , and further development of the frameworks [8]. An overview of the characteristics of the three frameworks is presented in Table 1.

Table 1. Characteristics of three dominant hospital planning frameworks

Author	Objective	Focus	Hierarchical Planning levels	Environment Assumptions
Roth and Dierdonck, 1995	Minimizing cost	Patient flows	3 levels (Aggregate admission planning, master admission planning, hospital resource planning, order releasing planning)	Predefined patient pattern, Superior capabilities for managing capacity an resources, procedure and treatment protocol standardized
Visser et al, 2001	Optimize resource utilization	One department	5 levels (strategic, patient volumes, resources, patient groups, patient)	Predictive, homogenous patient group, predictable treatment process, low variability on patient's condition
Hans et al, 2011	Efficient hospital decision making	Entire healthcare organization	4 levels (strategic, tactical, offline operational, online operational)	Elective and urgent patients only, integration of all managerial areas in health care delivery, operational integration focus

In 1995, Roth & Dierdonck introduced a framework called "Hospital Resource Planning" aimed specifically at healthcare cost reduction through improved hospital planning and control. The framework is based on the introduction of a classification system that identifies the health care services received by patients. The framework is directly inspired by the manufacturing system approach, with materials requirement planning as the backbone. The framework considers both the resource capacity planning and material planning of hospitals and introduces a classification system as the bill of resources to classify products or services hospitals provides including calculating prices of services [9]. The study is an exploratory study based on longitudinal data from two hospitals, one 300-bed community hospital and one 1,100-bed teaching hospital. Hence, they acknowledge that the traditional MRP logic has shortcomings. Thus, the key assumptions of the framework are that:

1. Hospitals have superior capabilities for managing capacity and resources.
2. Procedure and treatment protocols are standardized, and variation in patient flow decreases over time.
3. All necessary processes are well defined.

Based on the requirements, the framework will fit a hospital environment with repetitive processes and variables similar to a mass-production environment with mature planning and control processes.

The second framework was developed by Vissers et al. in 2001 [10]. The framework is based on existing literature at the time, partly inspired by De Vries et al.[11], which was limited to resources capacity planning and patient flow, including optimization of batching rules for resource utilization, frequency of service to a patient group and size, and composition patient batches. However, most of the literature within hospital planning and control takes point of departure of this paper in relation to their empirical studies such as within operating theatre [12] [13] [14]. The framework prescribes identification of planning horizons and different types of decisions that have to be taken in an organization, distinguished by five hierarchical levels including strategic planning, patient volumes planning, resource planning, single patient/patient groups planning. The key assumptions of the framework are that:

1. Hospitals are organized in independent business units.
2. The patient-group is homogeneous
3. One primary predictable and stable process flow of treatment for each patient group.

Thus, this framework is suitable for a predictable process after the treatment plan setup, including low variety in the treatment process, common requirements in quality and service, homogeneous in resource requirement and no requirements for flexibility within the patient-group.

Finally, Hans et al. [15] proposed a generic health care framework with the objective to structure the various planning and control functions in a health care system, which is the latest framework among these three The framework is based on hierarchical planning principles divided by planning horizons and is intended to be applicable to any type of health care delivery. Furthermore, Hans et al. [15] argue that traditional planning frameworks are often too simplistic as they are oriented towards one managerial area (in particular resource capacity planning or material planning) and neglect the reactive decision functions, which are important given the inherently stochastic nature of health care processes. The framework integrates the managerial areas of medical planning, resource capacity planning, materials planning, and financial planning. These are integrated due to the authors' assumption that collaboration and dialogue between all types of managers in healthcare planning is a core mechanism for optimized planning of the entire system. Related to the broad scope of the framework, the prerequisites of the framework are blurred. The framework can be applied at all health care levels from a supply chain of care providers down hospital departments, and thus from a contingent viewpoint, the framework must be tailored according to environment characteristics. Hence, the key assumptions of the framework are that:

1. Planning is an interdependent process between managerial hospital areas.
2. Patient groups are homogeneous across the healthcare system.
3. Two distinctive processes; reactive processes (offline (elective) patient), proactive processes (online (emergency) patient)

3 Hospital Environmental Variables

Jonsson and Mattsson [1] identify that environmental variables have significant impact on the sustainability of planning methods in manufacturing companies. Therefore, the hospital environmental variables must be identified. All three framework studied are addressing the environmental characteristic, which can be divided into three groups of patient, resource, and hospital process.

In health care, the **patient** is both a customer and involved in the health care production process [16]. Demand can be defined as the patients' need for health care services, which is partly predictable and partly random too which it is similar to the demand in the industry [17]. However, the differences between a traditional definition of a product and the patient as a product are that the patient's condition may even change during the time while waiting as well as during the process of treatment [12], which is causing the high variability and uncertainty in hospital planning and control. Patients are classified in the range of medical urgency categorization at hospitals, which is based severity of their condition in order to prioritize job task of patients; elective, semi-urgent, and emergency [18]. Looking from the planning point of view, it is frequently interrupted by both the unexpected arrival of critically emergency patients and by the changes of the patients' condition during the admission process [16]. In order to capture patients' needs for health care, it requires a flexibility and agility in operations from the hospital. There is a high variability of patients in hospitals, needing individual hospital health care services, and to some extent they can be grouped based on their medical profile [11]. However, patients also need an individual evaluation of the medical profile complexity in order to determine the process of treatment generating variation within a patient group [10]. Furthermore, patient volume needs to be considered especially in relation to limited resources [11] Hence, the patient variables are deduced to be patient medical profile complexity, medical urgency, patient variety, demand uncertainty, and patient volume.

The **resources** in a hospital environment refer to all resources involved in the hospital's planning and control processes. The main resource types include human resources (doctors, nurses, secretaries, porters, and planning personnel), medical equipment (operation packages and medicines), and facilities (beds and operating theatres) [19],[20]. Furthermore, the resource type is dependent on the profiles and experience of the particular resource. For human resources the profile includes, for instance, the nurse profile (operational or ward), and the doctors' clinical profile including their experience. For medical equipment the profile relates to the treatment area, and the experience is for instance the maturity of the medicine technology or treatment, which in some situations is short-lived down to a few hours lifetime from development. Apart from the main resource types, supporting resources are also essential to include as an environmental variable [21]. Supporting resources include all influencing resources that are not directly part of the hospital process in question including for instance hospital managers and expensive critical care resources. Thus, the hospital resource variables include; resource types, profile, experience, and supporting resources.

The **hospital processes** can be divided into operation processes and organizational support processes, and operational processes can be further divided into diagnostics process phase and therapy process phase [11]. The operation processes are driven by resources such as medical specialists, mainly in charge of the medical treatment, researching and teaching with the aim of providing and developing new medical methods of health care services to increase the inhabitants' health quality of life [22] [10]. The individual caregivers such as doctors and nurses are patient-centred in their work, where different knowledge and experience has an impact in planning and scheduling incoming patients on top of the degree of complexity of the process itself [23]. The organizational processes are often divided in groups of clinical specialties focusing on single procedures or patient groups in order provide most effective care for the patients. Building up around disciplines enhances the specialization of treatments of different patient group, where the clinical staff develops an in- depth knowledge and experience, resulting in a high quality, fully integrated, operational organization at its disposal [12]. Thus, the hospital processes are identified as the diagnostic and therapy processes, process task complexity, interdependency with other resources, and organization support processes. In Table 2, the hospital planning environment variables are presented within the category of patient, resources, and hospital processes based the study of this section.

Table 2. Overview of hospital planning environment variables

Hospital environmental variables		
Patient	**Resources**	**Hospital processes**
Patient medical profile	Resource types	Diagnostics and therapy phases
Medical urgency	Profile	Process task complexity
Patient variety	Experience	Interdependency with other resources
Demand uncertainty	Supporting resources	Organizational support processes
Patient volume		

4   Conceptual Matching

Overall, frameworks presented above are addressing the hospital environmental variables to some extent, as they all include aspects of patient variables, resources, and the hospital processes. However, the frameworks generally simplify the complexity of the system by only including the simplest variables, omitting, for instance, the condition of the patient, their medical profile, or the variety of patients [8]. In the three frameworks prioritization of patients is only briefly addressed through the by 'first in first out' principles, whereas the medical urgency is not being addressed. Hans et al [15] acknowledge the importance of medical urgency in the planning processes by including both elective patient and emergency patient processes. Even so, uncertainty of the medical profile and the patient's condition is missing along with the need for flexibility in the health care system generating robustness of the framework. On the other hand, Visser et al [10] acknowledge the need for high flexibility during the diagnostic process due to high degree of uncertainty, but then choose to limit the framework to the therapy process phase, where the process flow is more predictable. Thus, it indicates that hospital planning can be improved through inclusion of patient variety and medical profile variables in applied hospital planning frameworks.

The theoretical frameworks generally regard resources as a constraint in hospital planning and consider mainly the resource type variable. However, as the environment variables imply, this approach is not sufficient in planning environments with varying resource profiles, varying experience, and the influence of supporting resources. One consequence is the lack of precision in hospital planning practice in situations where these variables are not distributed evenly according to the applied planning model. Hence, it indicates based on the findings that hospital planning accuracy can be improved by inclusion of resource profiles, experience, supporting resources in the hospital planning model oriented around patients.

The planning frameworks in this paper are all hierarchical in nature, where the purpose is to improve coherent and efficient planning of operational hospital processes. However, the point of departure such as objectives and point of view differ. In Visser et al [10], one of the assumptions is that hospitals are organized in independent business units, whereas, Hans et al [15] emphasize the need to incorporate both multiple managerial areas to capture the complex relationships in health care and the reactive decision functions, which are important given the inherently stochastic nature of health care processes. Oppositely, Roth and Van Dierdonck [24] focus at the process flow but disregard the hospital organization. In a sense, the hospital can be categorized as a hybrid organization as introduced by Van Merode et al [12], where one part of the organization is of a mechanistic nature suited for rather deterministic processes and another is a more organic part, directed to non-routine, innovative tasks. Thus, suggest for further research that hospital planning include both deterministic and complex process models in accordance with phases, process task complexity, interdependency and influencing support processes'.

The mismatch identified between the theoretical frameworks and theoretically derived environment variables generates incentives for further investigation of how a more general hospital environment relates to applied frameworks in practice. Thus, based on the developed propositions we suggest the following research question for an empirical explorative study: *"What is the misalignment between hospital environmental variables and applied planning frameworks, and what are the effects on operational practice? "*

5   Conclusion

This paper contributes to existing research with a conceptual analysis of existing hospital planning and control frameworks, and a set of propositions for further research improving the match between planning frameworks and the hospital environment. Based on the study, it indicates that hospital planning frameworks need a more integrated holistic planning perspective. It is found that the hospital environmental variables can be grouped into three; patient, resource, and process. However, existing frameworks do not properly addresses these variables in the hospital planning environment, nor do they acknowledge the hybrid nature of hospital organization.

We propose that the existing frameworks are misaligned with several environment variables, and thus further research on alignment is recommended. This includes explorative in-depth studies on the empirical matching between hospital environments and applied planning frameworks.

References

1. Jonsson, P., Mattsson, S.-A.: The implications of fit between planning environments and manufacturing planning and control methods. Int. J. Oper. Prod. Manag. 23, 872–900 (2003)
2. Hax, A.C., Meal, H.C.: Hierarchical integration of production planning and scheduling. DTIC Document (1973)
3. Silver, E.A., Pyke, D.F., Peterson, R.: Inventory management and production planning and scheduling. Wiley, New York (1998)
4. Vollmann, T.: Manufacturing Planning and Control Systems for Supply Chain Management: The Definitive Guide for Professionals. McGraw-Hill Education (2005)
5. Hulshof, P.J.H., Kortbeek, N., Boucherie, R.J., Hans, E.W., Bakker, P.J.M.: Taxonomic classification of planning decisions in health care: a structured review of the state of the art in OR/MS. Health Syst. 1, 129 (2012)
6. Adan, I.J.B.F., Vissers, J.M.H.: Patient mix optimisation in hospital admission planning: a case study. Int. J. Oper. Prod. Manag. 22, 445–461 (2002)
7. Testi, A., Tanfani, E., Torre, G.: A three-phase approach for operating theatre schedules. Health Care Manag. Sci. 10, 163–172 (2007)
8. Brailsford, S., Vissers, J.: OR in healthcare: A European perspective. Eur. J. Oper. Res. 212, 223–234 (2011)
9. Forgione, D.A., Vermeer, T.E., Surysekar, K., Wrieden, J.A., Plante, C.C.: DRGs, Costs and Quality of CARE: An Agency Theory Perspective. Financ. Account. Manag. 21, 291–308 (2005)
10. Vissers, J.M.H., Bertrand, J.W.M., De Vries, G.: A framework for production control in health care organizations. Prod. Plan. Control. 12, 591–604 (2001)

11. De Vries, G., Bertrand, J.W.M., Vissers, J.M.H.: Design requirements for health care production control systems. Prod. Plan. Control. 10, 559–569 (1999)
12. Van Merode, G.G., Groothuis, S., Hasman, A.: Enterprise resource planning for hospitals. Int. J. Med. Inf. 73, 493–501 (2004)
13. Hans, E., Wullink, G., Van Houdenhoven, M., Kazemier, G.: Robust surgery loading. Eur. J. Oper. Res. 185, 1038–1050 (2008)
14. Guerriero, F., Guido, R.: Operational research in the management of the operating theatre: a survey. Health Care Manag. Sci. 14, 89–114 (2011)
15. Hans, E.W., Houdenhoven, M.V., Hulshof, P.J.: A framework for health care planning and control, vol. 168, pp. 303–320. Springer, N. Y. (2011)
16. Hall, R., Belson, D., Murali, P., Dessouky, M.: Modeling patient flows through the healthcare system. Patient Flow Reducing Delay Healthc. Deliv., 1–44 (2006)
17. Womack, J.P., Jones, D.T.: Lean thinking: banish waste and create wealth in your corporation. Simon and Schuster (2010)
18. Vos, L., Groothuis, S., van Merode, G.G.: Evaluating hospital design from an operations management perspective. Health Care Manag. Sci. 10, 357–364 (2007)
19. Blake, J.T., Carter, M.W.: A goal programming approach to strategic resource allocation in acute care hospitals. Eur. J. Oper. Res. 140, 541–561 (2002)
20. Harper, P.R.: A framework for operational modelling of hospital resources. Health Care Manag. Sci. 5, 165–173 (2002)
21. Carter, M.: Diagnosis: mismanagement of resources. MS TODAY 29, 26–33 (2002)
22. Kopach-Konrad, R., Lawley, M., Criswell, M., Hasan, I., Chakraborty, S., Pekny, J., Doebbeling, B.N.: Applying Systems Engineering Principles in Improving Health Care Delivery. J. Gen. Intern. Med. 22, 431–437 (2007)
23. Williams, S., Crouch, R.: Emergency department patient classification systems: A systematic review. Accid. Emerg. Nurs. 14, 160–170 (2006)
24. Roth, A.V., Van Dierdonck, R.: Hospital Resource Planning: Concepts, Feasibility, and Framework. Prod. Oper. Manag. 4, 2–29 (1995)

Understanding Customer Needs to Engineer Product-Service Systems

Fabiana Pirola[1], Giuditta Pezzotta[1], Daniela Andreini[2],
Chiara Galmozzi[3], Alice Savoia[3], and Roberto Pinto[1]

[1] CELS - Research Group on Industrial Engineering, Logistics and Service Operations,
Department of Engineering, University of Bergamo, Italy
{giuditta.pezzotta,fabiana.pirola}@unibg.it,
roberto.pinto@unibg.it
[2] Department of Management, Economics and Quantitative Methods,
University of Bergamo, Italy
daniela.andreini@unibg.it
[3] ABB S.p.A., Sesto San Giovanni (Milano), Italy

Abstract. Starting from the 90s, an increasing number of companies have been starting to move from a product-centric perspective towards Product-Service-System (PSS). In this context, suitable models, methods and tools to collect, engineer and embed in a single solution all the knowledge that meets or exceeds people's emotional needs and expectations are required. Despite that, only few authors have proposed methodologies that can be easily adopted by industrial companies to design and engineer a product-service solution starting from the customer needs. Thus, this paper focuses on the customer needs analysis and aims at proposing a methodology to support companies in identifying customer needs, representing the starting point to the engineering and/or reengineering of PSS offering and the related delivery processes. An industrial case study in ABB S.p.A. has been carried out in order to test the methodology.

Keywords: Product-Service System, Service engineering, customer needs, Persona model.

1   Introduction

Starting from the 90s [1], an increasing number of companies have been enlarging their offers starting to provide services in addition to their products moving from a product-centric perspective towards Product-Service-System (PSS). This change was spurred by "a continuous strive to create new sources of value for the company, by either reactively fulfilling explicit requirements or proactively providing new integrated product–service solutions to the customer" [2].

The design and development of product-service solutions, along with the management of its whole lifecycle, require the implementation of suitable models, methods and tools for collecting, engineering and embedding in a single solution all the knowledge that meets or exceeds people's emotional needs and expectations [2,3]. In this context,

B. Grabot et al. (Eds.): APMS 2014, Part II, IFIP AICT 439, pp. 683–690, 2014.

Service Engineering (SE) has emerged as a discipline calling for the design and the development of an integrated product-service offering adding value to customers [5]. In spite of the great success of the SE as a discipline in the academic context, only few authors have proposed methodologies and tools, which can be easily adopted by industrial companies during the design of a product-service solution [4, 6,7].

In order to fill this gap, the SErvice Engineering Methodology (SEEM) has been developed [8] with the aim to support companies during the (re)engineering of product-service offerings. As depicted in Fig.1, the SEEM is divided into two main areas: the customer area and the company area. The former deals with the analysis of customer needs and of the current product-service offering(s). The latter, starting from the customer needs identified in the "customer area", aims at defining, through the process prototyping and validation phases, the service features and the delivery process that allows for the best trade-off between customer needs satisfaction and company performance. Once the new service is validated, the service offering is updated.

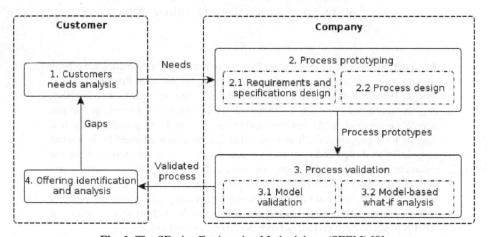

Fig. 1. The SErvice Engineering Methodology (SEEM) [8]

This paper focuses on the customer area of the SEEM and, in particular, on the "customer needs analysis" phase. In this area, the Persona Model (PM) is proposed as tool to collect and present information about customers [9]. This tool is based on *Personas*, fictional people describing the prototypical users of a product or service in terms of demographics and main values or needs. Thus, the objective of this paper is to propose a methodology to support companies in developing their customized customer needs list and therefore to build their *Personas*. These *Personas* are the company reference point when engineering and defining the service offering. In addition, an industrial case study in ABB S.p.A. has been carried out in order to test the methodology and to create the ABB Service *Personas*.

The reminder of the paper is structured as follows: section 2 presents a literature review on the persona model and on the main tools developed to gather customer values, section 3 introduces the proposed methodology, while section 4 presents the test and the implementation of the proposed methodology in ABB. Section 5 concludes the paper with final remarks and future development.

2   Persona Model and Customer Needs

Persona Model is a method useful for product and service development since it deals with the detailed design and representation of virtual users of the specific product or service [9, 10]. This tool is based on *Persona*, which provides fictitious, specific and concrete representations of target users, based on real inputs and formally structured. It is composed of a demographic part with data related to age, gender, educational background, occupation, career and so on, and a narrative part, containing the type of individual that the persona is, what he likes and dislikes, skills, attitudes and decision states. It also includes a third part related to persona's specific needs or values and personal goals in the context of the service (or product) being designed. Some imaginary data (usually a name and a picture) are added to the description in order to provide product and service designers with a vivid representation of target users and to make the persona more tangible and alive. A Persona represents a customer segment.

PM is used in both Business to Consumer (B2C) and Business to Business (B2B) contexts. The main difference is that in B2C the *Persona* is composed of a list of value while in B2B of a list of needs. Values represent what individual desire and influence their actions. Values are "ideals" which individuals respect and believe in. On the other hand, needs represent a "deficiency state", something required or wanted, for which the individual feels a necessity to be satisfied. This difference is justified by the fact that in industrial situations individuals do not have the goal to achieve their ideals (as in B2C context) since they are interested in the satisfaction of their needs.

Regarding customer values, a first investigation of the literature shows that many researchers have tried to understand them and they have proposed methods to measure them accurately. The value term is used variously to refer to interests, pleasures, likes, preferences, duties, moral obligations, desires, wants, goals, needs, aversions and attractions. More precisely, values can be defined as cognitive representations of universal human requirements as biological needs, social interactional requirements and social institutional demands on the individual [11]. There are different ways to list and measure these values, the main ones are hereafter listed: Values, Attitudes and Lifestyles System (VALS) [12]; Rokeach's Value Survey (RSV) [13]; Schwartz [14]; List Of Values (LOV) [15] and SERPVAL scale [16]

All the above-mentioned lists refer to the value and they are all focused on B2C customers. From this analysis, it emerges that in B2B a defined default list of needs is still missing, even if there are several studies related to B2B needs. Thus, the aim of this paper is to propose a methodology to gather and analyze industrial customer needs and build *industrial Personas*, as presented in the next section.

3   Methodology

In order to overcome the main gap presented in literature, the objective of this paper is to propose a methodology to support companies in developing their customized customer needs list and therefore to build their *Personas*. This methodology will then be adopted in the SErvice Engineering Methodology (SEEM). The methodology (Fig. 2) is structured as follows.

1. *Qualitative interviews.* They allow to collect insights about respondent views, experiences, beliefs and/or motivations and decision making process. Semi-structured interviews are adopted, therefore several key questions that help to identify interviewer's needs and decisional processes are defined. The flexibility of this approach allows the discovery or elaboration of information that may not have been previously thought from the research team. After the validation of the questionnaire, decision makers of customer companies are then interviewed face to face to identify their main needs and characteristics. The interviews, which are tape-recorded, are detailed in a report and then analyzed by the research team. The main output of this step is the creation of a list of specific needs derived from the interviews.

2. *Quantitative questionnaire.* The main customers' needs arisen from Step 1 are utilized for building a specific questionnaire. This survey is structured in order to apply the MaxDiff methodology [17] to score the needs and identify which are the most important ones for the B2B customers. Reliability of the questionnaire is verified using a pilot test. Company performance according to these needs, structured with a five point rating scale (Likert-type scale), and customer features are also asked. An appropriate sample that represents the customer population is selected. The questionnaire is submitted to the customer's decision makers in the service area. Aim of this analysis is to get a representative sample of the company target market.

3. *Analysis.* All respondents' data are collected and statistically analyzed through the MaxDiff analysis [17]. The MaxDiff uses a sophisticated estimation technique to produce scores for each respondent on each item, the Hierarchical Bayes estimation (HB). The output of the tool is an estimation of scores related to each of all the fourteen needs, namely the rescaled (probability) scores. These positive values reflect the likelihood of items being chosen within the questionnaire. After that a cluster analysis is also performed to segment customer and therefore to identify the *Personas.* Each *Persona* defines a fictitious customer who represents the cluster and its characteristics. The definition of the *Personas* is fundamental in order to propose and engineer services able to satisfy different customers with different needs.

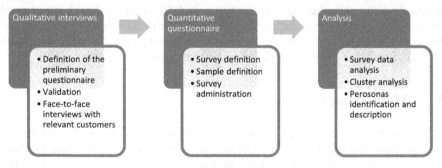

Fig. 2. Methodology

4   Case Study

ABB is one of the largest power and automation technology companies in the world. The company employs today 150.000 people all over the world and in 2013 had annual revenue of 42 billion of dollars.

The company operates in 5 divisions (Power Products, Power Systems, Discrete Automation and Motion, Low Voltage Products and Process Automation). This case study refers to the Italian Discrete Automation and Motion division, and in particular to Robotics, with the objective of creating *ABB Personas* based on the needs of their industrial partners (called "customer" or "partner"). Their partners are system integrators (who install ABB products after having customized them) and OEM (suppliers with a large scope of provision that use ABB components only in a small percentage of final outputs). They represent the ABB direct customers but not the final customers of their solutions. Specifically, market segmentation will be conducted: customers will be grouped in different clusters in order to produce different *ABB Personas*, providing a solid representation of target customers to be used during the definition of new services and update of the existing ones.

The implementation in the ABB context of the three above mentioned methodology steps in ABB is briefly described hereafter.

4.1   Qualitative Interviews

Following a series of meetings and workshops with ABB experts in service, marketing and robotics, a semi-structured questionnaire based on open questions has been built and then validated.

Starting from general company characteristics, decision makers of customer companies are called to give their opinions regarding service in general and their experience, service management inside their company and their main objectives. Furthermore, a question regarding how much the service could affect the eventual choice of a supplier is posed to respondents. Concluding, an evaluation of ABB service is asked.

Combining all the needs emerged from respondents, the list of needs has been generated (see table 1). This list has been then used to build the quantitative questionnaire.

4.2   Quantitative Questionnaire

After the definition of the customers' needs list and consulting the ABB Service and Marketing experts, a quantitative questionnaire has been designed. The questionnaire is structured in three main parts: the first section refers to the evaluation of customer's selection criteria when choosing a services supplier; the second section contains an evaluation of ABB performances and the last section is characterized by general questions about the company and its approach to service.

The questionnaire has been validated by an internal pilot test with two experts of the commercial area. Then, the survey has been conducted online and, in case of relevant partners, with face-to-face interviews. In total, 95 contacts (representative of 43 different direct customers) have been defined: among these, 40 respondents fully completed the survey, with a 43% response rate.

4.3   Analysis

Once all answers have been collected, the first step has been to perform the MaxDiff analysis [17]. Thanks to this analysis, the customers' needs have been ranked on a scale from highest to lowest for each respondent. Table 1 reports for each analyzed need the average score of the sample.

Table 1. MaxDiff average score of the sample

Needs	Rescaled Scores
The supplier is fast in issue resolution	16,95
The supplier has people with the right competences	13,25
The supplier is able to answer customer request at any time and all over the world	11,99
The supplier supports in reducing breakdown risks (or their impact) during warranty period	11,25
The supplier is able to deliver spare parts in 24h all over the world	9,33
The supplier is fair and cooperation is ruled by clear and transparent commercial terms	7,05
The supplier is transparent (gives visibility) in programming interventions and reporting activities	6,08
The supplier supports during engineering and commissioning period	5,79
The supplier supports in offering services to end customers after warranty period	5,65
The supplier has a low price	3,28
The supplier trains my people for service purposes	2,99
The supplier cooperates with us in service marketing and sales	2,87
Maintenance of products is done by the manufacturer	2,31
The supplier has a recognized reputation and strong brand	1,14

As emerged from the table, the needs receiving the highest scores are those ones related to the concepts of responsiveness and efficacy, customer assistance and availability of high-skilled personnel able to solve issues.

The least important need seems to be the reputation and the strong brand associated with the firm. This could be explained by the fact that when choosing a service provider the brand is not so relevant, while it is instead for the product (robot) itself.

Especially noteworthy is the score received by the need *"The supplier has a low price"*: it has received a low score, even if is not in the bottom part of the ranking.

Once defined the score for each need, the cluster analysis has been adopted in order to segment customers and generate the Personas. In particular, a two-stage sequence of analysis has been applied:

1. A hierarchical cluster analysis using Ward's method and applying squared Euclidean Distance has been chosen to determine the optimum number of clusters.

Ward's method uses an analysis of variance approach to evaluate the distances be-tween clusters. The Ward's method has been selected in this case because the ana-lyzed dataset do not include any outliers [18];
2. The hierarchical cluster analysis has been re-run with the selected number of clus-ters. This second step has allowed the allocation of each case to a particular cluster.

As result, the following three ABB Personas have been identified:

- *Persona 1,* representative of cluster 1, is a young technician with some years of experience, working in a big company (specifically, a system integrator). He needs spare parts in short time and requires fast issue resolution.
- *Persona 2,* representative of cluster 2, is the owner of a big company operating as a system integrator. He has a lot of experience in the field. He takes for granted common service needs and focuses on high-level needs: he is interested in a part-nership with ABB, asking for a strong partnership and cooperation with supplier.
- *Persona 3,* representative of cluster 3, is a mechanical engineer working in a small OEM company. He is a young man that requires constant support from ABB since he has not all the right competences.

5   Conclusions

This paper has provided a deep understanding of customers' needs, as required in the first phase of the SErvice Engineering Methodology (SEEM), highlighting the impor-tance of a customer-centred approach as the starting point in the service engineering process. To this purpose, the Persona Model is used to gather and represent the main product-service users, in terms of demographic features, personal characteristics and needs. Thanks to the literature review, different lists of values emerge related to the B2C contexts, while in the B2B industrial context a similar list of needs is missing. Thus, since in the B2B context each single case has to be considered as unique, a structured methodology to define a list of needs in the Persona Model have been pro-posed. In addition, to test the validity and applicability an industrial case study in ABB has been provided. This has allowed to generate the list of industrial customer needs and therefore to segment them in different clusters and identify three customer *Personas* on which the service offering should be engineered.

The main limitation of this work, however, is represented by the difficulty to gene-ralize the list of the industrial customers' needs, since they are strongly linked to the specific industrial reality. In order to have more robust results, it would be optimal to have a higher number of respondents. For this reason, future developments will be to improve the analysis considering much more respondents and add other variables useful for the description of the clusters.

Acknowledgement. The research leading to these results has received funding from ABB S.p.A Italy.

References

1. Vandermerwe, S., Rada, J.: Servitization of Business: Adding Value by Adding Services. Eur. Manage J. 6(4), 314–324 (1988)
2. Cavalieri, S., Pezzotta, G.: Product-Serice Systems Engineering: State of the art and research challenges. Comput. Ind. 63, 278–288 (2012)
3. Berry, L.L., Carbone, L.P., Haeckel, S.H.: Managing the Total Customer Experience. MIT Sloan Management Review, 85–90 (Spring 2002)
4. Cavalieri, S., Pezzotta, G., Shimomura, Y.: Product–service system engineering: From theory to industrial applications. Comput. Ind. 63, 275–277 (2012)
5. Bullinger, H.J., Fahnrich, K.P., Meiren, T.: Service engineering-methodical development of new service products. Int. J. Prod. Econ. 85(3), 275–287 (2003)
6. Rapaccini, M., Saccani, N., Pezzotta, G., Burger, T., Ganz, W.: Service development in product-service systems: a maturity model. Serv. Ind. J. 33(3-4), 300–319 (2013)
7. Shimomura, Y., Tomiyama, T.: Service modeling for service engineering. In: Arai, E., Fumihiko, K., Goossenaerts, J., Shirase, K. (eds.) Knowledge and Skill Chains in Engineering and Manufacturing. IFIP, vol. 168, pp. 31–38. Springer, Boston (2005)
8. Pezzotta, G., Pinto, R., Pirola, F., Ouertani, M.: Balancing Product-Service Provider's Performance and Customer's Value: the SErvice Engineering Methodology (SEEM). In: 6th CIRP Conference on Industrial Product-Service Systems (2014)
9. Pruitt, J., Adlin, T.: The Persona Lifecycle: Keeping People in Mind Throughout Product Design. Morgan Kaufmann (2006)
10. Shimomura, Y., Hosono, S., Hasegawa, M., Hara, T., Arai, T.: A Methodology of Persona-centric Service Design. In: 19th CIRP Design Conference - competitive Design, Cranfield, UK (2009)
11. Kamakura, W.A., Novak, T.P.: Value-System Segmentation: Exploring the Meaning of LOV. J. Consum. Res. 19(1), 119–132 (1992)
12. Vincent, T., Selvarani, D.: Personal Values Approach for a Better Understanding of Consumer Behaviour. Int. J. Innov. Res. Dev. 2(3), 509–517 (2013)
13. Vinson, D.E., Munson, J., Nakanishi, M.: An Investigation of the Rokeach Value Survey for Consumer Research Applications. Adv. Consum. Res. 4(1), 247–252 (1977)
14. Schwartz, S.H.: Universals in the content and structure of values: theoretical advances and empirical tests in 20 countries. In: Zanna, M.P. (ed.) Advances in Experimental Social Psychology, vol. 25, pp. 1–65. Elsevier (1992)
15. Kahle, L.R., Beatty, S.E., Homer, P.: Alternative Measurement Approaches to Consumer Values: The List of Values (LOV) and Values and Life Style (VALS). J. Consum. Res. 13(3), 405–409 (1986)
16. Lages, L.F., Fernandes, J.C.: The SERPVAL scale: a multi-item instrument for measuring service personal values. J. Bus. Res. 58, 1562–1572 (2005)
17. Almquist, E., Lee, J.: What Do Customers Really Want? Harvard Bus. Rev. 3 (2009)
18. Ward Jr., J.H.: Hierarchical grouping to optimize an objective function. J. Am. Stat. Assoc. 58(301), 236–244 (1963)

Service Performance Assessment:
A PI Toolset Methodology for VEs

Alessandra Carosi[1], Mohammadreza Heydari[1], Christian Zanetti[1],
Marco Taisch[1], and Yves Ducq[2]

[1] Politecnico di Milano, Piazza Leonardo Da Vinci 32, 20133, Milan, Italy
[2] Université Bordeaux, IMS, UMR 5218, F – 334400, Talence, France
{alessandra.carosi,mohammadreza.heydari,cristiano.zanetti,
marco.taisch}@polimi.it, yves.ducq@u-bordeaux.fr

Abstract. Nowadays service sector is becoming more and more relevant in building successful collaborative economies. In this environment Virtual Enterprises (VEs) are forcing a change in the way traditional manufacturing systems are managed. Therefore measuring service performances plays an important role in turning company strategic goals into reality. Performance Indicators (PIs) consist in a supporting tool to assess service efficiency and effectiveness. Consequently, determining the most significant activities which need to be controlled and measured through proper PIs becomes essential. Within this paper, a PI Toolset is going to be presented and tested through industrial use case. The PI Toolset has been developed to support VEs in selecting significant activities, to manage governance processes and to support the design and implementation of specific PIs related to the precise use case objectives. Finally, a lesson learnt approach has been adopted so to stress strengths and weaknesses of both proposed methodology and tools.

Keywords: Virtual enterprises, Performance measurement systems and Performance Indicators, Service governance support toolset, PI Toolset.

1 Introduction

Participating in collaborative networks has become a key factor for service and manufacturing enterprises that try to gain differentiated advantages in today's market competitiveness. Indeed enterprises cannot work in an autonomous way anymore as responsiveness, interoperability and collaboration become keywords of a successful business management in service industries [1-3]. During recent years, a large number of studies about collaborative networks have been developed to support enterprises survive in market increasingly turbulences [1 & 4-5]. Therefore, for both manufacturing and service enterprises collaboration became a key issue in addressing market demands through sharing competences and resources [4]. Collaboration can be defined as a common environment where companies are actively cooperating to reach common goals and objectives [2]. A Virtual Enterprise (VE) is an aggregation of enterprises that represent a temporary alliance through sharing tangible and intangible

B. Grabot et al. (Eds.): APMS 2014, Part II, IFIP AICT 439, pp. 691–698, 2014.
© IFIP International Federation for Information Processing 2014

assets such as information, knowledge, risk and profits [1] or [3 & 6]. A VE is created in order to perform a fast reaction and better respond to market demand and opportunities single enterprises would not be able to face individually. When the development of a new service is involved or if the temporary alliance of enterprises shifts from a product oriented approach to a service oriented one, literature refers to it as "Servitization[1]" process [7]. In order to be successful in the turbulent markets, VEs significantly need to deal with Performance Measurement Systems (PMS) and apply governance principles for managing the system. Hence PMS can support VE as a quantifying procedure in order to measure and monitor the effectiveness and efficiency of its past and current actions [8]. Nevertheless it can be stated that, although the advantages of VE are well known at the conceptual level, VE practical implementation is still far from the expectations [9]. At the same time several VE phases such as planning and creation as well as operation phase are still difficult to instantiate because they need to be properly adapted by advanced collaborative networks [1 & 10]. Some of the lacunas include the lack of common reference models and appropriate tools able to support these particular tasks. Therefore, in this paper a new methodology for VE governance and PI assessment has been developed so to support organizations and help decision makers to enhance VE services provided to support manufacturing products. In the next paragraphs, a literature review regarding PMS is proposed in order to present scientific open challenges and key issues evaluated while developing the PI Toolset. Several tools and methods have been developed by different authors and researchers in the last decades, each one with different advantages, disadvantages and measuring approaches such as ECOGRAI, PRISM, Balance Scorecard (BSC) and European Foundation for quality Management (EFQM) [11]. BSC model is based on the principle that a PMS should provide to decision makers at the strategic level relevant information to help managing several perspectives such as innovation and learning, customer relationship, internal processes and financial issues. On the other hand, EFQM model can be easily applied at any level of the enterprise and offers a comprehensive and coherent picture of an enterprise's health. With respect to their popularity several authors expressed some criticisms on using those models in collaborative strategies environment [1, 4 & 8]. Indeed there is an ample proof that both models are focused on single enterprise strategies and not in strategies based on collaboration [5]. ECOGRAI method has been developed to design and to implement performance indicator system to evaluate performances inside and among enterprises based on the strong principle that performance must support decisions. It can be used to evaluate the enterprise performance related to objectives in a global and detailed approach in a coherent way. Indeed ECOGRAI method clearly studies the decompositions of decision levels and focuses on the coherence of objectives. Furthermore, it is able to analyse enterprise systems in a very detailed view linking

---

[1] The transition from product to product+service or service is named Servitization process: "There is clear evidence that manufacturing firms are servitizing–either adding Services to or integrating services in their core products" (Davies et al 2006; Neely, 2009; Vandermerwe and Rada, 1988). Servitization levels vary from "tangible product" (lowest) to "product as a service" (highest level).

governance issues with the control of performances [1, 12]. Graph with Results and Activities Interrelated (GRAI) model consists in a governance modelling tool which can help the decision makers harmonizing their enterprise systems and defining clearly the decisions, objectives, and actions variables that need to be managed. GRAI model facilitates also the integration among decisional levels (i.e. Strategic, Tactical & Operational) and functions, but does not supply a reference PI list. Nevertheless, in order to define and to implement a PMS based on decision model, a model driven approach would be required . The chosen one is MDSEA and is developed in the frame of MSEE project. Model Driven Service Engineering Architecture (MDSEA) consists in a standard framework for activity modelling that takes into consideration three different abstraction levels, in order to separate business and technical preoccupations and specifications but to ensure their alignment: Business Service Modelling (BSM), Technical Independent Modelling (TIM) and Technical Specific Modelling (TSM). In particular BSM level presents three levels of decision decomposition: strategic, tactical and operational according to activity temporal period and horizon. In conclusion, similarly to PMS, a proper governance modelling and assessing methodology will help the decision makers harmonizing VE creation and measuring its progress towards the desired goals. Therefore, the scientific result of this research activity will lead to the creation of the PI Toolset methodology which focuses on managing service systems governance issues and its performance assessment. In particular, the second chapter of this paper presents PI Toolset features and components dividing its main composing elements into progressive paragraphs. Finally chapter three describes the toolset adoption results considering also further steps in scientific research.

2   PI Toolset

PI Toolset has been developed to support VEs managing and controlling their system activities. It is composed by a Service Governance Methodology, a PI method and a PI List that, when adopted together, create a coherent linkage between governance issues and PI assessment. A Performance Indicator (PI) is a quantified data which measures the efficiency of actions in the achievement of specific results. A methodology to drive PIs creation and selection has been developed so to turn it into a strategic tool. This methodology allows the development of a coherent list of service driven PIs able to monitor and regulate value exchange in enterprise networks. The PI Method has been created in order to generate specific PIs according to use case objectives which describe use case Governance processes mapped through Service Governance Framework methodology. Indeed, both PI Method and Service Governance Framework have been developed in order to create an integrated engineering approach on business management & assessment tools.

2.1   Service Governance Framework

Service Governance Framework methodology has been developed to support service modelling within a VE environment focusing on business goals definition. This conceptual framework has been developed on one hand in order to lay down the foundations for a governance model which can be then linked with coherent monitoring and controlling activities. On the other hand it is able to help the selection of highly exploitable PIs related to End User governance objectives. Therefore every Servitization process could be modelled through the proposed framework first of all defining clear functions and secondly defining the objectives at different decisional levels (i.e. Strategic, Tactical and Operational levels). Finally, the actions to achieve abovementioned objectives need to be specified. Service Governance Framework relies on a structure created merging, on one side, the GRAI method, and, on the other side, MDSEA model. In detail GRAI method has been selected for the linkage it creates among governance processes and the definition of precise objectives. While MDSEA model has been adopted as a standard reference in order to classify PIs into different level of decomposition; it means decomposition by level of abstraction (BSM, TIM and TSM) and decomposition by level of decision (Strategic, Tactical and Operational). At BSM we define the PIs, at TIM the formula to calculate the PI and at TSM the data and their origin required to execute the formula as well as the IT request and data base. In particular the framework focuses on BSM (Business Service Modelling) level used to elaborate high abstraction level model from users' point of view.

		Service Governance Framework							
		IDEATION	CONCEPT	REQUIREMENTS	DESIGN	IMPLEMENT	OPERATION	DELIVERY	DECOMMISSION
BSM	STRATREGIC								
	TACTICAL								
	OPERATIONAL								
TIM									
TSM									

Fig. 1. Service Governance Framework (conceptual schema)

2.2   PI Method

PI method has been created to design, implement and classify, at BSM level, specific PIs related to specific use case objectives. After the Servitization process is modelled through Service Governance, PI Method can be adopted to generate proper PIs. Similarly to Service Governance Framework, PI Method has been created merging GRAI and MDSEA models. In particular, GRAI approach has been adopted because of its good integration between the consistency with decisional process and the focus on results. Hence, this method focuses on why we need PIs (i.e. to make which decisions), instead of sorting out the best indicators directly [5]. In addition, also Value Reference Model (VRM) has been used as a supporting tool to define and prioritize which PIs are needed to manage business processes. Indeed VRM provides a wide description of standard processes, their inputs and outputs and also metrics and best practices. Therefore use cases could be supported by a wide sample of process categorization which can be used to select the business processes affecting use case strategy. MDSEA model has been used as a reference too, so to define at which level business processes affect Service Lifecycle Management (SLM). As described in Fig.2 PI Method provides a methodology to design and implement relevant PIs generated on the basis of the requirements identified within the Governance framework at the BSM level. Once the Service objectives have been defined, the identification of functions and affected business processes has been facilitated thanks to the support of VRM process classification. Finally PI can be defined: a PI List can be surfed in order to select proper PIs which are strictly linked with the already identified use case processes and objectives. A personalized PI List can be created so PIs can be exploited to monitor service activities.

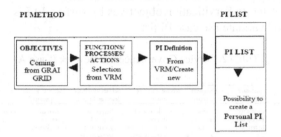

Fig. 2. PI Method (PI Method and PI List)

2.3   PI List

Coherently with Service Governance Framework and PI Method, the PI List structure has been created so to facilitate PIs selection and the linkage to defined objectives and functions. The list represents a supporting tool when assessing service performances and managing enterprise resources efficiency. In a similar way, also PI List has been created following MDSEA structure so to divide PIs into different levels of decomposition. On the other hand also VRM has been used as a reference so to adopt its categorization. Table 1 shows PI list structure: PIs are listed respecting VRM process categorization and are described reflecting also VRM processes features.

Table 1. PI List structure

MDSEA	VRM process Classification	PI field	Dimension	PI metrics	PI formula

3   Results

A first toolset adoption has been addressed on a real industrial pilot so to optimize the scientific results and maximize the efficiency of the proposed PI Toolset. This action has been conducted in order to test the method validity on the manufacturing world and to simplify the structuring approach on industrial partners. All the Scientific results have been obtained through testing the activities together with Case A industrial pilot. The company is one of the largest European manufacturing industries in white goods sector aiming at providing its consumers with new advanced services. Therefore the toolset has been enhanced and refined through the implementation of a real Servitization process conducted by an industrial use case. The results still need to be validated but this contribution can be considered as a first step towards the development of PI Toolset scientific methodology. The following List of Actions synthesizes the passages use case has been asked to face when adopting the method:

1. Identify use case Virtual Enterprise;
2. Design service processes and map the phases with service modelling tool;
3. Identify Servitization process objectives (Governance Framework methodology);
4. Adopt PI Method to select PIs (PI Method and PI list);
5. Identify PIs related to Servitization objectives by surfing PI List;
6. Personalize and validate use case PI list.

Table 2. Service Governance Framework (Case A)

	EI	F1	F2	F3	F4	F5	F6	II
	External Information	Customer decision	Customer ideation	Service -Product design	Service -Product Implementation	Service -Product planning	Service -Product delivery	Internal Information
STRATEGIC H= 2 Years P= 6 Month	Existing Services in competitive companies	Customer expectation in terms of services	Business plan for service proposition	Selection of design methodologies and partners	Selection of targeted goods and technologies	Annual service planning	Partner relationship organization	Business Strategy and Master planning
TACTICAL H = 1 Year P= 1 Month	Existing HW & SW Implementation technologies	Feedback on customer satisfaction	Assessment of existing services	Definition of PSS functions and design specifications	Action plan to modify production process	Planning of the specific service actions	General planning of service delivery	In- house Available technologies
OPERATIO-NAL H = 1 Month P = 1 Week	Advertising	Customers orders; Customers claims	Brainstorming meeting;	Detailed design planning	Implementation of modifications	Service scheduling; Feedback measurement	Short term delivery planning	Status of service production and service system

Table 3. Personalized PI List (Case A)

	F1	F2	F3	F4	F5	F6
)SEA	Customer relationship	Service ideation	Product-Service System design	Product-Service system development	Product-Service system planning	Product-Service system delivery
STRATEGIC H= 2 Years P= 6 Month	ROI for each product-service (like the minimum ROI range); Net margin expected	Capability to implement cross-selling (through a CRM system)	Total cost of product-service system design	Global implementation costs	Amount of product-service sales for the next two years	Cost of delivery channels
TACTICAL H = 1 year P= 1 Month	Service Exploitation	Amount of sales per month	Time to design the PSS	Time to market	Turnover	Number of new customers/contracts
OPERATIO-NAL H = 1 month P = 1 week	Time to start up the service, Customer satisfaction rate	Increase of of the new ideas	Delay/advance in design	Checking of timing and costing (deviation in%) of master plan	% of WMs with Carefree Washing Service produced in time	Product-service frequency

Table 2 shows the results related to the definition of Case A Service Governance Framework at the BSM level. In the horizontal axis (CC stands for Code-Category and NC for Name-Category) several functions have been identified following the SLM phases. Use case objectives have been defined at each stage: strategic, tactical and operational. While Table 3 presents the results obtained for Case A Personalized PI List definition. Service Objectives have been linked with VRM Process categorization in order to facilitate involved business process selection. Secondly the PI List has been analysed so to define which are the proper PIs to be linked with Case A objectives, business processes and decision variables. Finally, a personalized PI List could have created in order to be used and exploited for performance assessment.

3.1   Lesson Learnt

A lesson learned approach has been carried out in order to provide a roadmap for continuous improvement after validating the PI Toolset. PI Toolset implies a strong collaboration between scientific theoretical research and practical application. In order to maximize the methodology efficiency, pilots and researchers worked together both to develop and exploit methodologies and tools in a continuous "back and forward" process. Therefore scientific results optimization comes from both use case practical application and scientific-industrial collaboration. The final optimization of scientific results is presented synthesized in Table 4.

Table 4. Scientific results optimization

LESSON LEARNT	STRENGHT	WEAKNESS	TREATS & OPPORTUNITIES/ IMPROVED TASK
-Need for an easier method; -Need for clarification on the tool; -Need for practical examples; -Need to make the user independent; -Need for optimization of PI selection.	-Reiterative methodology; -Validation of proposal -Exploitation of results; -Reduce the time to identify PIs; Personalization of PIs.	-It takes time for the user to understand the language of the methodology; -It takes time to make the user adopt the methodology; -Abundance of PIs.	-Easy to use methodology; -Methodology optimization of PI selection; -One tool for each component of the method; -Ready to use ICT tool; -Practical tools application explanation; - Independence of the user in the use of the tool; -Avoiding PIs proliferation; -Personalization of PIs.

3.2   Further Steps

A further steps section investigates additional features which can be taken into account to improve the toolset in the future. Indeed, to generate additional positive results on Servitization managing tasks, some other scientific activities can be proposed to be integrated within the toolset for further development. PI toolset does not include them at the moment although they can be presented as scientific requirements to be considered for future integration. The list of additional features includes: PI calculation activity, visualization of performances, internal audit, trend analysis and feedback on performances. The implementation of above mentioned elements could allow VE partners managing better the whole Servitization process through the adoption of new strategic actions. PI Toolset could become a learning tool for enterprises offering an integrated vision on performance assessment and governance management able to increase organizations service maturity level. Finally, as additional further step, a new validation phase could be proposed through another industrial case adoption.

4   Conclusion

This paper defines a PI Toolset for VEs able to support organizations in managing their governance issues and identifying a proper performance assessment by selecting the activities to be measured through coherent PIs. PI Toolset can be adopted as a decisional supporting tool as it assists the selection of activities associated with use case objectives which need to be managed; secondly it helps linking those objectives and actions with PIs able to measure those tasks. Consequently it helps maximizing the evaluation of performances and optimizing the management of service governance. In conclusion PI Toolset is able to help VEs in identifying and understanding service system requirements, assess current and future service capabilities, identify significant PIs so to help taking correct decisions and finally avoid PIs proliferation.

Acknowledgements. This research has been partly funded by the European Union through the FoF-ICT Project named MSEE: Manufacturing SErvice Ecosystem (No. 284860).

References

1. Heydari, M., Taisch, C., Carosi, A.: Service performance monitoring and control Toolset. In: The 6th CIRP Conference on Industrial Product-Service Systems, Windsor, Canada (2014)
2. Camarinha-Matos, et al: Collaborative networked organizations, Concepts and practice in manufacturing enterprises. Computers Industrial Engineeringn 57 (2008, 2009)
3. Afsarmanesh, H., Camarinha-Matos, L.: A framework for management of VO breeding environment in Collaborative networks and their breeding environments. Springer (2005)
4. European Collaborative Networked Organizations Leadership IST IP506958 project (2007)
5. Ducq, Y., Vallespir, B.: Definition and aggregation of a performance measurement system in three Aeronautical workshops using the ECOGRAI Method. Production Planning and Control 16(2), 163–177 (2005)
6. Martinez, M.T., Fouletier, P., Park, K.H., Favrel, J.: Virtual enterprise organisation, evolution and control. Int. J. Production Economics 74, 225–238 (2001)
7. Thoben, K.D.: Extended Products: Evolving Traditional Product concepts. In: Engineering the Knowledge Economy through Co-operation, Bremen, pp. 429–439 (2001)
8. Neely, A., Adams, C., Kennerley, M.: The Performance Prism: The Scorecard for Measuring and Managing Business Success. Pearson Education, Harlow (2002)
9. Dignum, V., Dignum, F.: Towards an agent-based infrastructure to support VOs, Collaborative Business Ecosystems and VEs. Kluwer Academic Publishers, Boston (2002)
10. Camarinha-Matos, L., Afsarmanesh, H.: Elements of a base VE infrastructure ‖. Computers in Industry 5, 139–163 (2003)
11. Sveiby, K.: Methods for Measuring Intangible Assets. Sveiby Knowledge Associates (2007)
12. Ducq, Y., Chen, D., Doumeingts, G.: A contribution of system theory to sustainable enterprise interoperability science base. Computers in Industry 63, 844–857 (2012)

Programming Integrated Surgical Operations and Preventive Maintenance Activities

Michel Gourgand[1], Janvier Pensi[1,2], and Alain Tanguy[1]

[1] LIMOS CNRS UMR 6158-Université Blaise Pascal-Campus des Cézeaux,
63173 Aubière Cedex, France
{michel.gourgand,janvier.pensi,alain.tanguy}@isima.fr
[2] Faculty of Industrial Engineering, Douala University, Cameroon

Abstract. The operating theatre (OT) represents a significant component of the technical means centre. This facility is the largest cost and revenue centre. To be efficient, it needs an optimal operational pro- gramme, which takes into account maintenance activi- ties and not only surgical operations. To build such a programme, various methods have been used: mixed integer programming (MIP), three classic heuristics for Bin-Packing and a coupling of the first alterna- tive with a stochastic descent (SD). Then we compare the obtained results from generated data.

Keywords: Surgical unit, operating planning, MIP, heuristics.

1 Introduction

The renovation of the hospital centre: Laquintinie Hospital of Douala (LHD) in Cameroon has started for a few months with the aim to improve work conditions in the medical system environments. It was launched by the Cameroonian public authorities. Hospital team manager wants to reduce cost and to maximize the level of patient satisfaction. The OT was firstly chosen, to be optimized. Researchers having carried out works on the OT are unanimous: it is an important care provider, which generates large incomes and it is among the most important sources of expenditure. It is consuming between 10% and 15% of the hospital budget [1]. Hospital is generally organized in centres of responsibilities [2]. Each one is divided into functional units. Hospital is thus a complex structure, where various functions are provided by a multi-field corporation. Managing the OT is hard due to the conflicting priorities and the preferences of its stakeholders [3], but also due to highly stochastic OT activities, such as the breakdown of equipment in the operating rooms. The actual realization of the planning and scheduling cannot be perfectly predicted. To improve management of the OT, this randomness has, to be taken into account. The problems the OT are known for the greatest part, and researchers proposed tools of decision-making aid, based on modelling, simulation and optimization. In this paper, we propose a tool to help OT managers in LHD, to improve the realization of the directing programme of surgical operations (DPSO), which takes into account surgical operations but also preventive maintenance activities (MA).

B. Grabot et al. (Eds.): APMS 2014, Part II, IFIP AICT 439, pp. 699–706, 2014.

The paper is organized as follow: in the next section, we review the related litera-ture. The third section describes the problem to be handled. In the fourth section, we describe our model. The fifth section presents the generated data and the compared results, finally, we conclude and discuss extensions.

2   State of the Art

The aim of this literature research is to guide the OT managers in programming (planning and scheduling) this facility, by taking into account the impact of equip-ment breakdowns, on functioning and the benefice of the equipment maintenance. In the 60 last years, researchers focused on the OT management. Regarding planning and scheduling within the OT, [4] present a substantive state of the art survey. What the planning concerns, its resolution is quite not easy considering the number of con-straints, namely: the intervention duration, the emergencies, the material availability, etc. In this section, we focus on proposed models and methods to solve problems having stochastic aspects. In the related literature, we met the following approaches: mixed integer programming (MIP), heuristics, simulation and Markov theory.

MIP method has been applied in various OT studies, with the aim to optimize the management of this facility. Most of the studies are concerned with the optimization of costs. For instance, minimization of costs of overused or underused operating rooms [5], or with the maximization of the daily benefit [6]. Authors focus on the minimization of the allocated time slots of surgeons [7]. To build a stable and flexible operational programme, others [8] applied MIP method so as to maximize the use of operating rooms.

Heuristics are more and more used. To minimize the costs of the intervention hours, [9] designed a genetic algorithm coupled with a procedure implementing a taboo search. In [10], they used heuristics after they identified the problem as a two level Flow-Shop, they minimized the overtime costs in the recovery rooms.

The simulation approach has been used to investigate particular cases, taking ad-vantage of its main asset, i.e., the ability to model specific systems in details. In [11], a Monte Carlo simulation was coupled with a heuristics to maximize the room occu-pation rate and to minimize the overtime. Authors proposed a planning method to solve emergency problem [12], they combined a Monte Carlo simulation with MIP, to minimize overtime costs and the operation day costs.

Markov chains have been applied to health care management in various studies too. In [13], they proposed an analytical approach to evaluate the risks in the OT, to determine the number of operations which must be planned, in order to limit over- time.

Concerning the equipment maintenance, industrial managers are unanimous: the zero risk does not exit unfortunately, because human and material failures ever occur.

We focus works that proposed methods for solving maintenance activity problem and its impact to production activities. Several approaches have been developed to address MA problems. In [14], they used mathematical models solved with LINGO and MATLAB, to optimize integrated planning, taking into account preventive MA in production. In industrial systems, production programme could not be designed with- out regarding MA. This reality must be regarded too in health care systems. We have not found any papers solving together OT optimization and MA. In the present work, we proposed a model that combines the flows of planned surgical operations (SO) and preventive MA.

3   Problem to Be Handled

The research originates from collaboration with a Cameroonian hospital in the Douala area, from which we will receive real data that can be used to evaluate the reliability of our approach and illustrate its application. This hospital is composed of three surgical units: a gynaecologist-obstetrics unit, an emergencies unit and an OT, this OT is the object of our study. In this hospital, the OT is open five days a week (except for emergencies), for 8 hours a day. It can happen that the duration of an operation overflows closing time. The OT comprises six operating rooms (OR). Four rooms are dedicated to visceral surgery and urology, orthopaedic surgery, orthopaedic surgery and neurosurgery, and endoscopic surgery; the two other rooms are reserved for emergency cases. They are open 24 hours a day. But in this present work, we consider that all those as versatile rooms (able to accommodate any type of surgery). Each OR has his team consists of: 2 nurses, 1 instrumentalist, 1 anesthetist nurse, 1 team leader, 1 health care assistant, 1 anaesthetist doctor who supervises two OR. If the OR is not in service, the team is going to serve in other units. According to the operation, the team is supplemented by a surgeon and his assistant. The number of operations per OR and day does not exceed 4 (except for emergencies). After one operation, the staff has 30 minutes rest. The average time of decontamination is 25 minutes. To realize a daily scheduling in the OR, some criteria are applied: medical or clinical ones and availability of equipment.

4   Approach

In order to construct the DPSO model, some hypotheses are made: the open strategic planning and scheduling are used, DPSO is focusing only on the OR, the operation day is communicated to each patient, there is the possibility to postpone one planned operation, no criterion is considered to appointing patients, the equipment in the OR is only taken into account, emergencies are not regarded, the operation duration is estimated; health care units, induction and recovery rooms are well sized. We propose a tool to help OT managers in assessing the impact of equipment breakdown by planning DPSO. The aim is to help them, by guiding their decisions at an operational tactical level. We have to assign of MA and SO, it is a similar problem to that of Bin-Packing. It is a NP-hard problem. This problem is solved by three heuristics, a MIP model and the first heuristic variant coupled with a stochastic descent. We established first the algorithms First Fit (FT), Next Fit (NF) and Best Fit (BF). An MA can be planned at the opening time, either just before closing or in midday. So the day of medical use of a room can be cut in one or two periods. The approach is described as follows:

- Insert the MA on the weekly schedule: indicate the day, the room, the starting hour and the end hour of every MA
- For every day

  − Operating day planning: indicate the day, the room and the period 1 or 2;
  − Daily sequencing of the SO and the appointment of the surgeons: indicate the room and the time slot, postpone the SO in conflict the next day.

- Publishing of the weekly schedule and the untreated SO

The heuristics principle ones is to affect MA and SO respecting various constraints. We applied followings heuristic variants:

- Heuristics 1 (H1) affects SO in arrival order, according to the ascending order of the compatible rooms, days and period duration, without exceeding the maximum period use (First Fit Decreasing).
- Heuristics 2 (H2) proceeds initially by sorting SO in decreasing order of duration, then to their assignment (Next Fit Decreasing).
- Heuristics 3 (H3) proceeds by sorting SO in decreasing order of duration. Every day and before assignment, rooms are maintained sorted in ascending order of the remaining period duration. It assigns an SO to a compatible room period having the smallest availability duration (Best Fit).

4.1   Mathematical Formalization

Only one mathematical model is presented, because various mathematical formalizations of the Bin-Packing problem, in one dimension are similar.

Data, parameter and variable used in the model for the main problem are

NR	number of operating rooms
ND	number of days
NSO	number of surgical operations
NMA	number of maintenance activities
DC_c	duration of SO c (including decontamination)
DM_m	duration of MA m (including cleaning-up time)
Q	duration of the room opening (8 h)
c	index of surgical operations
r	index of operating rooms
d	index of working days of the horizon
m	index of maintenance activities
Z_{mrd}	1 if MA m is allocated the d day in room r; otherwise = 0
X_{crd}	1 if SO c is allocated the d day in room r; otherwise = 0

Constraints

Respect of the room opening duration

$$(\sum_{c=1}^{NSO} DC_c * X_{crd} + \sum_{m=1}^{NMA} DM_m * Z_{mrd}) \leq Q; r = 1 \dots NR, d = 1 \dots ND \qquad (1)$$

SO c is allocated in only one room and in only one day

$$\sum_{r=1}^{NR} \sum_{d=1}^{ND} X_{crd} \leq 1 ; c = 1 \dots NSO \qquad (2)$$

Parameter verifier

MA m is allocated in only one room and in only one day

$$\sum_{r=1}^{NR} \sum_{d}^{ND} Z_{mrd} ; m = 1 \dots NMA \qquad (3)$$

Integrity constraints

$$X_{crd}, \ Z_{mrd} \in \{0, 1\}; c = 1 \dots NSO, r = 1 \dots NR, d = 1 \dots ND, m = 1 \dots NMA \qquad (4)$$

Multi-objectives function

We have first to minimize the number of not allocated SO (*NNASO*), then the number of used room-day couples (*NURDC*) and finally, the minimum activity time (*MAT*)

$$NNASO = NSO - \sum_{c=1}^{NSO} \sum_{r=1}^{NR} \sum_{d=1}^{ND} X_{crd} \qquad (5)$$

A Boolean function

$$Y_{rd} = (\sum_{c=1}^{NSO} X_{crd} > 0) \in \{0, 1\}, r = 1 \dots NR, d = 1 \dots ND \qquad (6)$$

$$NURDC = \sum_{r=1}^{NR} \sum_{d=1}^{ND} Y_{rd} \qquad (7)$$

$$MAT = \min_{r,d}(\sum_{c=1}^{NSO} X_{crd} * DC_c + (1 - Y_{rd}) * 10) \qquad (8)$$

The following multi-criterion objective results from the three ones (*MCO*)

$$MCO = (NNASO * 100 + NURDC) * 10 + MAT \qquad (9)$$

5   Results

5.1   Generated Data

We illustrate the obtained results from generated data. It is composed of 15 preventive MA and 80 SO. Table 1 indicates following information: for the MA (number, type, start hour, end hour, room, day and the worker). Table 2 contains the data of SO: number, type and duration (Du). The decontamination time is 25 minutes. All durations are given in minutes.

Table 1. The MA data

MAnum	MAtype	Sh	Eh	Room	Day	Worker
1	2	0	45	1	1	X1
2	1	180	240	2	1	X2
3	4	450	480	3	1	X3
4	5	0	60	2	2	X4
5	7	240	300	4	2	X1
6	3	0	30	3	2	X2
7	6	90	140	4	3	X3
8	6	90	140	1	3	X1
9	3	0	30	3	3	X4
10	2	429	474	1	4	X3
11	1	0	60	2	4	X2
12	7	420	480	4	4	X1
13	5	120	180	2	5	X4
14	5	0	60	3	5	Y1
15	4	300	350	4	5	Y2

5.2   Mixed Integer Programming

Firstly, we generalized the mathematical model so as to deal with room-day-periods. Then we used two tools [15] (Gl and Gu) and [16] (Lp). Gl (Glpsol) and Gu (Gusek) used different solving options. Table 3 presents results with 60 seconds limited resolution duration. It indicates the number of allocated SO (Naso) and the room utilization duration (Rud). The first objective is studied using a MIP model solved with [15] and [16]. The multi-criterion objective is studied using a classic stochastic descent meta-heuristic coupled with a heuristic variant.

Table 2. The SO data

Sonum	Sotype	Du	Sonum	Sotype	Du	Sonum	Sotype	Du	Sonum	Sotype	Du
1	3	90	21	10	90	41	3	90	61	8	120
2	1	120	22	8	120	42	5	150	62	5	150
3	2	90	23	9	120	43	7	90	63	4	120
4	4	120	24	5	150	44	4	120	64	9	120
5	5	150	25	6	90	45	2	90	65	9	120
6	10	90	26	2	90	46	1	120	66	1	120
7	8	120	27	1	120	47	8	120	67	1	120
8	6	90	28	4	120	48	9	120	68	2	90
9	7	90	29	3	90	49	10	90	69	3	90
10	9	120	30	7	90	50	6	90	70	10	90
11	1	120	31	5	150	51	4	120	71	2	90
12	2	90	32	1	90	52	1	120	72	5	150
13	8	120	33	4	120	53	8	120	73	4	120
14	9	120	34	2	90	54	3	90	74	8	120
15	3	90	35	3	90	55	5	150	75	10	90
16	5	150	36	6	90	56	6	90	76	3	90
17	4	120	37	7	90	57	6	90	77	2	90
18	10	90	38	10	90	58	8	120	78	6	90
19	7	90	39	8	120	59	7	90	79	4	120
20	6	90	40	9	120	60	7	90	80	5	150

Table 3. MIP results

Horizon	Gl		Gu		Lp	
Day	Naso	Rud	Naso	Rud	Naso	Rud
1	21	2415	21	2505	21	2415
2	38	4550	42	5010	38	4580
3	57	7155	58	7390	55	7075
4	71	9335	74	9890	72	9570
5	80	10700	80	10700	80	10700

5.3   Heuristics Results

Table 4 presents obtained results with the three heuristics. It gives Naso, the number of used room-days (Nurd) and the number of room day periods Nrdp).

Table 4. Heuristics results

Horizon	H1			H2			H3			SD
Day	Naso	Nurd	Nrdp	Naso	Nurd	Nrdp	Naso	Nurd	Nrdp	Naso
1	15	6	7	17	6	7	17	6	7	21
2	32	12	14	35	12	14	34	12	14	40
3	49	18	20	51	18	20	51	18	20	57
4	70	24	26	72	24	27	68	24	26	75
5	80	27	30	80	27	31	80	29	33	80

H1 does not affect SO better than H3 and H2. H2 affects more and uses in less Nurd than H3. When all SO are allocated, horizon 5, H1 uses less Nurd and less Nrdp than the other heuristics. In MIP, the options used for Gu allocate more SO than Gl, Lp and the three heuristics. The meta-heuristic SD generates scheduling and optimizes the criteria. H1 evaluates them for the tested scheduling. SD gives the best results.

6   Conclusion and Extensions

We proposed a mathematical model for our problem and we implemented and applied exact methods and estimations on generated data. The obtained results are satisfying, especially the multi-criterion stochastic descent. Our tool of decision-making aid will be used in the hospital on real data. The prospects concern the surgical unit programming, the SO planning, the allocation of material resources and the management of the curative maintenance activities.

References

1. Macario, A., Vitez, T.S., Dunn, B., Mcdonald, T.: Where Are the Costs in Perioperative Care?: Analysis of Hospital Costs and Charges for Inpatient Surgical Care. Anesthesiology 83, 1138–1144 (1995)
2. Combes, C.: Un environnement de modélisation pour les systèmes hospitaliers. Thèse de Doctorat, Université Blaise Pascal, France (1994)
3. Glauberman, S., Mintzberg, H.: Managing the care of health and the cure of disease. Part I: Differentiation. Health Care Management Review 26, 56–69 (2001)
4. Cardoen, B., Demeulemeester, E.: Operating room Planning and scheduling: A literature review. European Journal of Operational Research 201, 921–932 (2010)
5. Jebali, A., Hadj Alouane, A., Ladet, P.: Operating rooms scheduling. International Journal of Production Economics 99, 52–62 (2006)
6. Marcon, E., Kharraja, S., Simonnet, G.: The operating theatre scheduling:an approach centred on the follow-up of the risk of no realization of the planning. In: Proceeding of the Industrial Engineering and Production Management, Canada, pp. 18–21 (2001a)
7. Hammami, S., Ladet, P., Atidel, B.H.A., Ruiz, A.: Une programmation opératoire robuste. Logistiqueet Management 15, 95–111 (2007)
8. Agnetis, A., Coppi, A., Corsini, M., Dellino, M.C., Pranzo, M.: Longterm evaluation of operating theater planning policies. Operations Research for HealthCare 1, 95–104 (2012)
9. Fei, H., Duvivier, D., Meskens, N., Chu, C.: Ordonnancement journalier dans   unbloc opératoire danslecadred'unestratégie openscheduling. In: Gestionet Ingénieriedes Systèmes Hospitaliers (GISEH 2006), Luxembourg (2006)
10. Iser, J.H., Denton, B.T., King, R.E.: Heuristics for balancing operating room and post-anesthesia resources under uncertainty. In: Winter Simulation Conference, Miami, USA, pp. 1601–1608 (2008)
11. Hans, E., Wullink, G., Van Houdenhoven, M., Kazemier, G.: Robust surgery loading. European Journal of Operational Research 185, 1038–1050 (2008)
12. Lamiri, M., Xie, X., Dolgui, A., Grimaud, F.: Astochastic model for operating room planning with elective and emergency demand for surgery. European Journal of Operational Research 185, 1026–1037 (2008)
13. Tancrez, J.-S., Roland, B., Cordier, J.P., Riane, F.: Assessing the impact of stochasticity for operating theater sizing. Decision Support Systems 55, 616–628 (2013)
14. Fitouhi, M.C.: Optimisation de la planification intégrée de la maintenance préventive et de la production des systèmes multi-états. Thèse de Doctorat, Université Laval, Québec (2011)
15. Glpk (2014), http://www.gnu.org/software/glpk/
16. Lpsolve (2014), http://lpsolve.sourceforge.net/5.5/

Author Index

710   Author Index

Printed in the United States
By Bookmasters